Bible Commentary
by
E. M. Zerr

Volume IV
Jeremiah—Malachi

© **Truth Publications, Inc. 2018.** All rights reserved. No part of this book may be reproduced in any form without written permission from the publisher. Printed in the United States of America.

ISBN 10: 1-58427-184-1

ISBN 13: 978-1-58427-184-0

Truth Publications, Inc.
CEI Bookstore
220 S. Marion St., Athens, AL 35611
855-492-6657
sales@truthpublications.com
www.truthbooks.com

Foreword: The E.M. Zerr Bible Commentaries

Cecil Willis
Reprinted From *Truth Magazine* XX:26 (June 24, 1976), pp. 3-5

The Cogdill Foundation, which publishes *Truth Magazine*, has obtained exclusive publication rights to the six volume *Bible Commentary* written by Brother E.M. Zerr. . . .

Information About E.M. Zerr

Brother Zerr was quite well-known among a group of very conservative brethren, but he may not have been known among brethren in general. Hence, a little information concerning him is here given. Edward Michael Zerr was born October 15, 1877 in Strassburg, Illinois, but his family soon thereafter moved to Missouri. He was the second of six children born to Lawrence and Mary (Manning) Zerr. Brother Zerr's father was reared as a Catholic, but after he married Mary Manning, he obeyed the gospel. At the age of seventeen, young Edward was immersed into Christ in Grand River, near Bosworth, Missouri.

In June, 1897 young Brother E.M. Zerr received a letter from A. L. Gepford asking him to go to Green Valley, Illinois, and to preach in his stead. His first sermon was entitled, "My Responsibility as a Preacher of the Gospel, and Your Responsibility as Hearers." In the years between delivery of this first sermon on July 3, 1897, and the delivery of his last sermon on October 25, 1959, Brother Zerr preached about 8,000 sermons, from California to Connecticut, and from Washington to Arizona. It is noteworthy that his last sermon was built around Matt. 13:44, and was entitled "Full Surrender." Brother Zerr preached the gospel for a little over 60 years.

Among the brethren with whom Brother Zerr was most frequently associated, it was then common to have protracted periods of concentrated Bible studies, commonly referred to as "Bible Readings." Young Brother Zerr attended a three month "Bible Reading" conducted by the well-known teacher, A.M. Morris, in 1899. During this study which was conducted at

Hillsboro, Henry County, Indiana, Brother Zerr stayed in the home of a farmer named John Hill. After leaving the John and Matilda Hill farm, "E.M." began correspondence with their daughter, Carrie. The following year, while attending a "Bible Reading" conducted by Daniel Sommer in Indianapolis, "E.M." and Carrie were married, on September 27, 1900. The newlyweds took up residence in New Castle, Indiana, where their four children were born, one of whom died in infancy.

In 1911, Brother A.W. Harvey arranged for Brother Zerr to conduct a "Bible Reading" which continued for several months at Palmyra, Indiana. These "Bible Readings" usually consisted of two two-hour sessions daily. Young Brother Zerr's special ability as a teacher was soon recognized, and he continued to conduct such studies among churches of Christ for 48 years. Edward M. Zerr died February 22, 1960, having been in a coma for four months following an automobile accident at Martinsville, Indiana. His body was laid to rest in the little country cemetery at Hillsboro, Indiana, near the church building in which he had attended his first "Bible Reading."

Brother Zerr's Writings

In addition to his oral teaching and preaching, Brother Zerr was a prolific writer. He was a regular contributor to several religious periodicals. Brother Zerr also composed the music and lyrics of several religious songs. Two of these, "The True Riches," and "I Come to Thee," may be found in the widely used song book, *Sacred Selections.*

One of the books written by Brother Zerr is entitled *Historical Quotations*, and consists of the gleanings from 40,000 pages of ancient history and other critical sources which he read over a period of twenty years. These quotations are intended to explain and to confirm the prophetic and other technical statements of the Bible. Another book, a 434 page hard-cover binding, consists of a study course containing 16,000 Bible questions. This book, *New Testament Questions*, has at least 50 questions on each chapter of the New Testament. A smaller book, *Bible Reading Notes,* consists of some of the copious notes which Brother Zerr made in connection with the "Bible Readings" which he conducted. But the crowning success of his efforts was the writing of his six volume commentary on the whole Bible.

These six volumes were published between 1947 and 1955. Brother Zerr has the unique distinction, so far as is known to this writer, of being the only member of the church to write a commentary on the entire Bible. Many other brethren have written excellent and valuable commentaries on various books of the Bible, but no other brother has written on the entire Bible.

Foreword v

The writing of this commentary consumed more than seven years of full-time labor. In order that he might devote himself without interruption to this herculean effort, Brother Zerr was supported by the Newcastle church during this seven year period. It is unfortunate, in this writer's judgment, that other competent men have not been entirely freed of other duties that they might give themselves to such mammoth writing assignments. Through *Bible Commentary*, Brother E.M. Zerr, though dead since 1960, will continue to do what he liked best to do—conduct "Bible Readings" for many years to come. The current printing is the fifth printing of the Old Testament section (four volumes) of the commentary, and the sixth printing of the New Testament section (two volumes).

Many Christians spend but little money on available helps in Bible study. Some own perhaps only a *Cruden's Concordance*, a Bible dictionary of some kind, and then *Johnson's Notes*. It would be interesting to know how many copies of B.W. Johnson's *The People's New Testament Commentary With Notes* have been sold. If I were to hazard a guess, it would be that at least 1,000,000 copies of this superficial commentary have been sold. *Johnson's Notes* contains the printing of the entire New Testament text in both King James Version and the English Revised Version (the predecessor to the American Standard Version), and his comments, all contained in two volumes. In fact, a single volume edition also is available. Thus one is buying two copies of the New Testament, and B. W. Johnson's *Notes*, in one or two volumes. So necessarily, *Johnson's Notes* are very brief.

If brethren somehow could be made acquainted with Brother Zerr's *Bible Commentary*, it is possible that it could be as widely used as has been *Johnson's Notes*, first published in 1889. Brother Zerr printed very little of the Bible text in his commentary. He assumed you would have your own Bible nearby. To have printed in the commentary the entire Bible would have required at least three other volumes. While it would have been helpful to have the Bible text printed by the comments, this unnecessary luxury would have been very expensive, since we all have copies of the Scriptures already. Furthermore, Brother Zerr intended that one be compelled to use his Bible, in order that his commentary never supplant the Sacred text.

A Word of Caution

I am sure that Brother Zerr, were he yet living, would advise me to remind you that his *Bible Commentary* is only that of a man, though a studious man he was. In fact, in the "Preface" to this set of books, just such a word of warning is sounded by Brother Zerr. The only book which we recommend without reservation is the Bible! But Bible commentaries, when viewed merely as the results of many years of study by scholarly men, can be very helpful to one.

Brother Zerr spent his life-time working among those brethren who have stood opposed to "located preachers" and to "Bible Colleges." However, he has not "featured" these distinctive views in his *Bible Commentary*. If one did not know of these positions held by Brother Zerr, he might not even detect the references to them in the commentary. However, I want to call such references to your attention. Along with the opposition to "located preachers," Brother Zerr also held a position commonly referred to as "Evangelistic Oversight." This position declares that until a congregation has qualified elders appointed, each congregation should be under the oversight of some evangelist. With these positions, this writer cannot agree. References to these positions will be found in his comments on Acts 20:28; Eph. 3:10; 3:21; 4:11; 1 Tim. 5:21; 2 Tim. 4:5, and perhaps in a few other places that do not now come to memory. Brother Zerr also took the position that a woman should never cut or even trim her hair. His comments on this position will be found at 1 Cor. 11:1-16.

But aside from a very few such positions with which many of us would disagree, Brother Zerr's *Bible Commentary* can be very helpful. Some restoration period writers of widely used commentaries held some rather bizarre positions regarding the millennium. Brethren scruple not to use *Barnes' Notes*, in spite of his repeated injection of Calvinism, and *Clark's Commentary*, in spite of his Methodist teaching.

Brother Zerr's *Bible Commentary* is far superior to *Johnson's Notes*. Though there are some extraordinarily good volumes in the well-known Gospel Advocate commentaries, there also are some notoriously weak volumes in this widely used set. Viewed from the point of consistent quality, Brother Zerr's *Bible Commentary* is superior to the Gospel Advocate set. Some brethren whom I consider to be superior exegetes of the Word have highly recommended Zerr's *Bible Commentary* and have praised the splendid and incisive way in which he has handled even those "hard to be understood" sections of God's Word.

Our recommendation regarding E.M. Zerr's six volume commentary can be paraphrased from the words of a well-known television commercial: "Try it; you'll like it!"

Bible Commentary

JEREMIAH 1

General remarks. Jeremiah lived and wrote about a hundred years after Isaiah. The captivity of the ten tribes under the Assyrians had taken place over a century before, and that of the two tribes by the Babylonians was soon to occur. About all of the prophetic books contain some history although the books as a whole are classed among the books of prophecy. It will be necessary for us to be careful not to confound the parts that are intended as actual history with those that are predictions and yet may seem to be historical in their form of speech. Jeremiah is often called the "weeping prophet" because of his emotional and sympathetic interest in the misfortune of others. He was also a true patriot and had a deep love for his country. This accounts for his many sentimental passages, and his repetitions of the same phrase with the apparent purpose of impressing his readers with the seriousness of his grief. He belonged to the priestly line, but it is not clear whether he was directly descended from Abiathar or Zadok. The genuineness and authenticity of his writings is beyond question, for he was quoted with approval in Matt. 2: 17 and 27: 9, there spelled Jeremy. This prophet wrote about the captivity, also he made predictions concerning the Gospel age of religion. In addition to writing prophecy and history, he, like Isaiah and the other prophets, wrote many severe passages of rebuke against the sinful nation, particularly its leaders, for which he was persecuted most shamefully by them. Many of the matters pertaining to Jeremiah will appear as the study of the book proceeds and will be commented upon in the order of their appearance.

Verse 1. *Land of Benjamin* refers to the district that was allotted to that tribe when Joshua divided the land among the 12 tribes (Josh. 18: 11-28). *Anathoth* was a city in this district of Benjamin but was not far from Jerusalem. It was the site of the homes and landed estates of the priests of the common order.

Verse 2. The date when Jeremiah began to write by *the word of the Lord* was the 13th year of Josiah, king of Judah. Josiah began to reign B.C. 639, which would make it B.C. 626 when Jeremiah was inspired by the Lord and began his writing. This was 20 years before the Babylonian captivity began. He continued his writing about the same number of years after it began. We shall see near the close of the book that the date of the termination of his writings is somewhat obscure on account of the difficulties thrown around him by his enemies.

Verse 3. The preceding verse states the time when Jeremiah began to write, this one gives the date when he completed his work on the book that bears his name. The books of the Bible were thus not composed all at any one "sitting," but many of them were written just as the Lord would have something more he wished the writer to record. For instance, we have just seen that Jeremiah began to write in the 13th year of Josiah and concluded his writing in the 11th year of Zedekiah. But the work was not continuous through that period for this verse also tells us he wrote some in the days of Jehoiakim, another king of Judah who followed Josiah. It is interesting to note that the close of Jeremiah's writing came at the same time the city was taken into hands by the Babylonians and the people taken off into captivity. That fact doubtless will account for the termination of his writings; not that he personally was taken out of the land. But there will be more information on this subject before the end of the book.

Verse 4. Having given the important dates of the book of the prophet, this verse comes to some of the particulars regarding his "call" to the work of a writing prophet. Not all of the prophets in the Bible were writing prophets but many of them did their work orally only, while others both wrote and spoke in the name of the Lord, hence the distinction "writing prophet" just stated. In the beginning of this verse the pronoun *me* is used which, when connected with the statement in the first verse, shows definitely that Jeremiah is the author of the book. It is significant that Jeremiah began to write after *the word of the Lord* came to him which settles the question of his inspiration. It also agrees with the statement made in *General remarks* where the endorsement of the New Testament is cited.

Verse 5. God sees into the future with as much certainty as he does in the present. But he does not always determine what that future shall be; he never interferes with the personal responsibility of any as regards matters of right and wrong. Yet he does frequently decree certain facts that pertain to his great work, and one of such instances is that of Jeremiah. Before he was even conceived by his mother God *knew* him. The lexicon definition of the original Hebrew for this word *knew* includes, "To ascertain by seeing" and "designation." So God not only saw the fact of Jeremiah's conception and birth, but also designated (predetermined) that it should take place. Before he was born God *sanctified* him for the work of a prophet. That word is from QADASH which Strong defines, "A primitive root; to be (causatively make, pronounce or observe as) clean (ceremonially or morally)." Since the word is here used in regard to Jeremiah as a prophet, the part of the definition that applies is "ceremonially." Foreseeing that Jeremiah was going to be born by divine decree, and that he would be personally a righteous man, God decided to have him for one of his prophets. *Nations* is from GOI which has been rendered in the A.V. by Gentile 30 times, heathen 142, nation 373 and people 111. Jeremiah was a Jew and his work was primarily on behalf of his own people. However, the Jewish nation had more or less dealings with other nations, hence the prophets of God wrote about them and made predictions either of blessings or punishments against them depending on the circumstances. Not only did they write about them, but many of their predictions referred to the coming of Christ which was to be of interest to the whole world.

Verse 6. *Then* is an adverb of time and refers to the occasion when *the word of the Lord came* first to Jeremiah. The exact date of his birth is not available; Funk and Wagnalls Bible Dictionary says he was perhaps twenty when he received his prophetic call. At any rate his own statement in this verse indicates he was young at the time; we also have the information of the lexicon. The word *child* is from NAHAR and Strong defines it, "A boy (as active), from the age of infancy to adolescence." Jeremiah seemed to underestimate his qualification as a prophet due to his tender years. He certainly overlooked the truth that inspiration does not need to rely on natural talents for its work since the power comes from Him who made all things.

Verse 7. *Say not I am a child* does not mean to dispute the fact of Jeremiah's age, but the thought is that he was not to consider that as an obstacle in the way of the work before him. There is nothing too hard for the Lord, and he who caused the dumb beast to speak (Num. 22: 28-30) can surely enable the weakest of man to do so. *I shall send thee* and *whatsoever I command* gives the explanation of how Jeremiah was to be able to speak regardless of his youthful age. But the ability to speak is not all there is of importance in this passage. *Thou shalt speak* indicates that Jeremiah will not be at liberty to say just what he might personally wish to say, but he must say what the Lord directs him to say. The same restriction is placed on the teachers in the kingdom of Christ. (2 Tim. 4: 2; 1 Pe. 4: 11.)

Verse 8. The word for *faces* is sometimes rendered "countenances" and that is the idea in this place. Jeremiah was destined to go up against people who would not like his teaching and who would give him many threatening looks. The Lord is assuring him of his support and that he need have no fear because of the threats of enemies.

Verse 9. The Lord sometimes resorts to literal actions, both by himself and through his servants, in bringing about certain results. This doubtless is for the effect of making a strong impression. In Jeremiah's case his inspiration was indicated by the hand of the Lord being brought into contact with his mouth. The action would especially denote his inspiration when speaking to the people.

Verse 10. It is evident that Jeremiah did not actually contact the institutions of the world to pull them down, hence the words are used in some indirect sense. A similar statement was made by Ezekiel (ch. 43: 3), and the marginal reading at that place is, "When I came to prophesy that the city should be destroyed." The same kind of rendering should be made in our verse. It means Jeremiah will be instructed to prophesy to the nations and kingdoms that God is going to cause the threatened calamities, or else bring the favorable events according to the circumstances of the case.

Jeremiah 1: 11-17

Verses 11, 12. The word *almond* is SHAQED and Strong's definition is, "The almond (tree or nut; as being the earliest in bloom)." *Hasten* is from SHAQAD which Strong defines, "A primitive root; to be alert, i.e. sleepless; hence to be on the lookout (whether for good or ill)." Here is an unusual coincidence of words. The two in italics have no similarity of meaning in the English, yet the originals are almost identical in meaning. The circumstance gives us one of the methods the Lord takes in his use of words that get their meaning from the characteristics of the objects bearing the names of said words. The almond is one of the earliest of trees to show up in the spring blooming season. Because of this fact the Lord chose the word in his descriptive prediction because it was practically the same in meaning as another word in the Hebrew vocabulary that specifically does mean to hasten or be on the alert. And the underlying reason for this peculiar phrasing was the truth that the things being predicted were soon to be fulfilled; not be on the list of happenings that were many years in the future. As a visual circumstance for the impressions on the mind of the prophet, God caused him to see a *rod* or limb taken from the almond tree. The event that was soon to occur was the Babylonian invasion that was to result in the captivity of the nation. Jeremiah began to write in the year 627 B.C., and the invasion came in 606 B.C., only 21 years later. This short interval of time would justify the prediction made by the imagery of the almond tree.

Verse 13. Again the Lord causes the prophet to see an object in his vision. It is a *seething pot* and the context indicates according to the original that it is seething or boiling because it is being fanned by a brisk wind. *Toward the north* is rendered "from the face of the north" in the margin and the lexicon agrees with it, also the next verse so renders it in the text. This seething pot which contains a hot mixture that is being made more intense by the brisk blowing, represents the Babylonian army that was soon to come against Jerusalem and the country in general.

Verse 14. This verse expressly predicts that the evil is to break forth *out of the north*. The map shows that Babylon was east and not north of Jerusalem. But the picture represents the invasion as it will appear to the people of Palestine when they first see it. They will actually see that the Babylonian army is coming upon them from the north of the land of Palestine. This fact of history is explained by a lengthy note in connection with Isa. 14: 31 in the 3rd volume of this Commentary.

Verse 15. This is more along the same line as the preceding verses and is expressed in more direct language. The Lord told the prophet that he would call the people from the *north* as has been explained. At the time of the invasion there was to be but one government engaged in the movement, which would be the Babylonians. The terms *families* and *kingdoms* refer to the divisions of the army that were to operate in unison under the authority of the emperor. *Set every one his throne* or seat means these various units would fix their proper places in the siege against Jerusalem which was the capital of the Jewish nation. Of course at the same time the necessary attention would be given to the other cities of Judah to see that nothing is done to hinder the siege. The fulfillment of this invasion and siege is recorded in 2 Ki. 24 and 25 for the Biblical account. The historical fulfillment was quoted with the comments on Isa. 3: 1 in the 3rd volume of this Commentary.

Verse 16. *Cities of Judah* in the preceding verse is the antecedent of *them* and *their* in this. *Their wickedness* refers to the idolatrous practices that the people of Judah (the 2-tribe kingdom) had been following for so long. It has always been true that "no man can serve two masters." When the Jews took to serving idols it was after they had forsaken the true God. *Other gods* and *works of their own hands* refers to the different kinds of idolatrous worship. They worshiped the sun and moon and other things in the creation, and also formed idols by hand out of wood and stone and metal. Part of the idolatrous worship (even as was true of that rendered to God) consisted of animal sacrifices burned on altars erected for that purpose. In other cases it consisted of burning of incense to the gods. The latter is the form that is charged against the people in this instance.

Verse 17. *Gird up thy loins* is a figurative expression for the prophet to "Get hold of himself" or brace himself to meet the test. He is to meet the corrupt people and rebuke them for their sins, and it will arouse their anger and bring forth many threats if not actual physical violence. The Lord bids him not to be dismayed at their *faces* which means their threatening countenances. The prophet is also placed under a threat from the Lord in case he shrinks from the struggle which is decreed he shall have. To *confound* means "to prostrate" or "break down" according to the lexicon definition of the original word. Should Jeremiah flinch before those unworthy people then he will get some of the wrath of God poured out upon him.

Verse 18. The pronoun *thee* stands for Jeremiah and the passage is a figurative assurance to him that he will be able to withstand the attacks of the enemy. As a *defenced city, iron pillar* and *brasen walls* would provide a condition of security in literal things, so Jeremiah was to be just that secure against the would-be thrusts of those wicked Jews. The itemizing of *kings, princes, priests* and *people* would indicate that the prophet was to be set against all classes in the nation, for all had departed from the Lord. However, while all classes as a whole had departed from the Lord, we will bear in mind that a few exceptions existed among them such as our prophet Jeremiah and other men like him in character.

Verse 19. *They* refers to the kings and other persons mentioned in the preceding verse. The prophet was not only warned to prepare for opposition, but he is now plainly told that it will come from these sources. Again the assurance is given him that his enemies will not prevail. The reason for that assurance is also stated, that it is because the Lord is with him. (See Rom. 8: 31.)

JEREMIAH 2

Verse 1. The prophet frequently will tell us the source of his information, that it is the word of the Lord.

Verse 2. *Cry* means "to call out" and *in the ears* means to speak so that they will hear. Jerusalem was not the only place where the guilt of idolatry existed, but it was the capital of the nation and hence was of special importance. Being the capital it was where the kings resided and reigned. Also, the temple was there and hence the priests were concerned personally with the religious activities on behalf of the nation. In view of these facts the guilt of idolatry was especially laid at their feet. As an aggrieved husband would remind a cool hearted wife of her original affection, so God reminds Israel of the time when she gave him the *kindness* of her warm devotions. *Espousals* (note the plural form) is from KELUWLAH and Strong's definition is, "bridehood," hence it is not restricted to the period of engagement, but applies to the early days and years of marriage. It would especially apply to the honeymoon. During that period a bride is usually kindly disposed toward her husband and manifests a warm affection for him. In this passage the honeymoon is used in an illustration that applies to the journey *in the wilderness*. However, this bride was not as true during the honeymoon as fleshly brides usually are, for many times even in course of that period she became dissatisfied and complained to her husband of her lot. And after all, the illustration holds good even in this respect, for we have heard of instances where couples became involved in marriage difficulties that began as early as the days of the honeymoon and finally ended in divorce. But this husband was more lenient and patient and always heard the complaints of his bride. He sometimes gave her very earnest rebukes, but proceeded to supply the things that would make her more comfortable and happy.

Verse 3. *Israel was holiness* is rather a ceremonial term, meaning the nation had been accepted as a peculiar possession of the Lord. Firstfruits means she was regarded as the choice of products, even as a young husband will think his bride is the most desirable person in the world. Should anyone attempt to molest this bride he would be due some serious trouble. *Offend* is defined in the lexicon "to be guilty," and the person who would make any improper advances toward this bride would be deemed guilty and would be avenged by the husband.

Verse 4. *Jacob* and *Israel* refer to the same people, the former (whose name was changed to Israel, Gen. 32: 28) being an ancestor of the latter. This people is now called upon to hear the word of the Lord as delivered by the inspired prophet.

Verse 5. Sometimes a wife will listen to the counsel of her parents who are objecting to the husband even after years of married life. If those objections are made on a true basis it is well for them to interfere, but they

Jeremiah 2: 6-10

should be sure that such is the case before trying to dissolve the marriage. This husband demands to know what are the objections which have led to the coldness of the wife. That coldness had arrived to the extent that the wife was going off after others who offered her some of their possessions; she had gone *after vanity*.

Verse 6. A true wife will take pleasure in recounting the many acts of kindness and tender regard that her husband showed her in their honeymoon and the early years of their married life. But this wife of the Lord had ceased even to talk about those days, much less to be held in her devotion to her husband in the later years. Those acts of devotion were not mere displays of sentiment with little or no substantial value as is sometimes the case with fleshly husbands. Sometimes a honeymoon will have to be taken against the wishes of other members of the family, and there have been instances where actual danger to life had to be encountered in order to remain together. Under conditions like those a loving husband will not evade any danger necessary to protect his bride. That was the case with the Lord and his bride, for they had to travel together through a country that was filled with pits and deserts and where the shadow of death hovered over them. But through it all the husband remained steadfast and helpful and had a constant care for his bride.

Verse 7. This bride was brought safely through the honeymoon until she was conducted to the place that was to be her home. And what a great home it was that her loving husband had provided for her! An entire tract large enough to accommodate a country, and thriving with luscious fruits and everything one could reasonably desire. With such provisions it would be expected that a bride would be contented and happy, and satisfied with nothing short of wholehearted devotion to such a wonderful companion. Sad to say, this bride not only became coldhearted toward her husband who had provided her with such a wonderful home, but she began at once to corrupt this good dowry with wild plants and weeds of idolatry.

Verse 8. One person cannot perform the duties of another in the service of the Lord, yet the degree of responsibility is not always the same with different men. God always charged the leading men in the nation more severely than he did the common people. Hence this verse names several classes of persons who were chiefly guilty in the coldness against the Lord. The priests were the ones who had charge of the altars and the services pertaining thereto. They that *handle* means they who wield or execute or teach the law. *Pastors* is from RAAH and Strong's definition is, "a primitive root; to tend a flock, i.e. pasture it; intransitively to graze (literally or figuratively); generally to rule." The original has been rendered by various words in the Old Testament, but the book of Jeremiah is the only one that has *pastor*. The term refers to the men in the Jewish nation whose special work was to give instruction to the people. The prophets were of two classes as regards their work. One class may be designated "writing prophets," among whom were Isaiah and Jeremiah and others. However, these men were not restricted to writing, but God used them also to make oral predictions to the people. They also served to admonish and chastise the men and women of the nation for their many sins. The other class of prophets did all of their work orally and among such were Elijah and Elisha and others whose names and work appear along in the Bible. All of the men mentioned above had become indifferent toward the true God, but these prophets had not stopped at their coldness. They were *prophesying by Baal* which means they did their work in the name of this heathen god and pretended to believe that he would bring their predictions to pass.

Verse 9. The prophet seems to have dropped the illustration of bride and wife and now takes a direct form of language. In spite of all the unfaithfulness of the people, the Lord pleads with them and even promises to do so from generation to generation.

Verse 10. The Lord purposes to shame his people by referring them to others who have far less advantages as nations and yet have been more faithful to their gods. *Chittim* is rendered Cyprus (an island in the eastern Mediterranean) by many works of reference including Strong's lexicon. *Kedar* is a tribe of Arabians who were an unsettled kind of people. Such people as are referred to in these two places would ordinarily not be expected to display unusual qualities, yet a contrast is going to be made between

Jeremiah 2: 11-19

them and the people who had been favored by the Lord.

Verse 11. The question asked has the negative answer implied. These inferior nations had been true to their idol gods although in truth such objects were no gods. But God's people had forsaken the true God and replaced him (in their hearts) with *that which doth not profit*. We would condemn a man if he deserted a friend of some standing, even though the one for whom he deserted the first one offered greater favors than had been provided by the other. It would be regarded rather in the nature of a bribe. But the people of God had done worse than that. They had turned their backs upon a true friend and gone after one who could give them nothing.

Verse 12. All intelligent beings are meant by the expression *ye heavens*, and they are told to be astonished at the horrible thing that has been done. To *be afraid* does not mean that the false gods can do anything effectively against the works of the true God. The expression really means that the situation is appalling and dark.

Verse 13. One evil is enough to bring the condemnation of the Lord, but these people of his had committed *two evils*. One was to forsake the true fountain of living water. Had they stopped with that evil it would have been bad enough. But they did not pause in their unfaithfulness of leaving the true fountain. They pretended to provide themselves a better supply of water by hewing out their own cisterns which proved to be broken and unable to hold any water. In all ages of the world men have committed the same kind of folly that is described in this verse by the illustration of cisterns. They have become dissatisfied with the Lord's plan of salvation and implied that He did not know just what man needed. Then they have proceeded to invent ways of their own for the benefit of sinful man. The inconsistency of such conduct is so evident that it is today a matter also at which to be appalled. If an infinite God did not know what was best for his own created beings, it is extremely foolish for those very creatures to think they can better the situation with their innovations.

Verse 14. This verse is a prediction in question form of the calamity that was to come upon Israel in a few years. The passage means to humiliate the people by speaking as if they were no better off than a servant or slave. *Spoiled* is rendered "become a spoil" in the margin which is correct. In a few years the Babylonian army will come against the capital and *spoil* or dispossess its people of their goods. The fulfillment of this prediction is recorded in 2 Ki. 24: 13.

Verse 15. Lions roaring and storming out of their thickets against a civilization is used to illustrate the invasion of the Babylonian army. *Cities are burned* took place in course of the siege and attack recounted in 2 Ki. 24 and 25. Most of the accounts of that campaign pertain to Jerusalem because it was the capital city. But the phrase *the mighty of the land* in 2 Ki. 24: 15 indicates that a general attack was made in the country; it was then the cities were burned.

Verse 16. Babylon was the country where the people of Israel were to be taken into captivity as a whole, but other places were permitted to make inroads and accomplish some gains. *Noph* (or Memphis) and *Tahapanes* were cities in Egypt and they are mentioned as having a share in the victories accomplished by their king Pharoah. The record of this event is in 2 Ki. 23: 33-35.

Verse 17. This is a severe but just rebuke of the nation and lays the blame for the misfortunes of the people of Israel at their own door. They had been warned even as long ago as the days of Moses (Deut. 28) that such experiences would come upon them if they went after false gods.

Verse 18. *What hast thou* means to ask them what right they had to go to those heathen places to partake of what they had. They did not always literally go to those places, but in their hearts they turned in that direction, and in a few instances they made literal application to those heathen localities for favors. *Sihor* is another name for the Nile in Egypt, and *the river* means the Euphrates in Babylonia. The last place is called Assyria because at the time Jeremiah wrote, the land through which the great river flows was still in the possession of Assyria, though it was destined to be brought under control by the Babylonians by the time the Jews were to be taken to begin their long-predicted captivity of 70 years.

Verse 19. Sin often works its own rebuke on the principle that "whatsoever a man soweth that shall he also reap" (Gal. 6: 8). This is especially true in moral questions if the Lord takes an active part in the case as he was to do with these people of Israel. *It is an evil thing and bitter* means their conduct toward God was evil as it pertained to Him, and it would be bitter for them when they realized the punishment it brought them. This bitterness is predicted in terms of deep sadness in Psa. 137. *My fear is not in thee* refers to their lack of reverence for God and his law. For the fulfillment of the prediction in the first part of the verse, see the long note that shows their complete recovery from idolatry. It is given with the comments on Isa. 1: 25 in the 3rd volume of this Commentary.

Verse 20. The weakness of inconstancy was nowhere more evident than in the conduct of Israel through the long history of the nation. Time after time in the journey through the wilderness the people did wrong, felt sorry and promised to do better, then fell back into sin again. After reaching the promised land and being established in it as a nation of the Lord, the same old tendency to forget God showed up from time to time. The most outstanding sin was idolatry, and the evident explanation is that it was the most prevalent iniquity in sight. Man is inclined to be affected most by that which is nearest him. All of the nations near Israel were idolaters and produced a strong influence over the people of God. *Trees* in themselves are not evil things but are among the noble objects of God's creation. But the heathen nations had connected their idol worship so generally with the groves that the mere sight of even one *green* (living) tree suggested the erecting of an idol. If no means were available for making the idol, the devoted idolater would fall down before the tree and offer his worship. This practice led God to make laws regarding the planting of groves, especially near any altar of the true services. *Playing the harlot* is using the corruption in the moral world to illustrate unfaithfulness in the religious. The comparison is logical and not just a strict notion of God as his enemies might think. If a married person has intimate relations with some one besides the lawful partner, it is recognized by everyone as being wrong and receives the name of adultery. On the same principle, if a person who professes to be married or joined to the true God should have intimate religious relations with some other god, it is like the unfaithfulness of the married partner. That is why God associated jealousy with the sin of idolatry in his law on the tables of the ten commandments (Ex. 20: 5).

Verse 21. Various things in the natural world are used to illustrate those in the religious or spiritual realm. In this verse the object chosen is a vine, and that doubtless is because it was one of the most familiar things in Palestine. The nation of Israel is compared to a *noble vine*. These words are not separate terms in the original but together come from *soreqah* which Strong defines, "a vine stock (properly one yielding purple grapes, the richest variety)." The fundamental meaning of *strange* is something foreign or from the outside. In this verse the Lord has a plant doing that which nature alone would not do. Any vine might degenerate and become fruitless or fail to produce as good a crop as it should. But this "thoroughbred" vine had changed its breed into the kind that grew in the territory outside of the vineyard. The literal explanation is that Israel had reached out and absorbed the substance of the idolatrous territory surrounding the Lord's vineyard, and was producing wild fruit in the form of false religion.

Verse 22. *Nitre* is defined in the lexicon as "potash" which corresponds to lye. If both lye and soap are used on a surface without getting it clean, it is certainly very much defiled and the uncleanness would be deep seated. *Marked* is from KATHAM which Strong defines, "a primitive root; properly to carve or engrave, i.e. (by implication) to inscribe indelibly." It means the uncleanness is deeper than the surface and is engraved into the body of the object, hence mere cleansing articles such as lye or soap would have no effect on it. The application is to the iniquity of the nation of Israel, and means that nothing the people can do for themselves will remove the mark. This is another passage that might seem to conflict with others where the Lord exhorted his people to reform and make themselves "clean" and he would receive them. The apparent difficulty is explained by observing the difference between the nation as a whole, and certain individuals in it. There is a long note on this subject with the comments on 2 Ki. 22: 17 in Vol. 2 of this Commentary.

Verse 23. Sometimes a person will deny an accusation when the evidence of his guilt is displayed in full sight. Israel denied the guilt of idolatry but the Lord pointed to signs of guilt that were unmistakable. *Baal* was one of the heathen gods that was also worshiped by the people of Israel. For more information on this word see the comments at Judges 2: 11-13 in volume 1 of this Commentary. *Way* is from a word that Strong defines, "A course of life or mode of action," and the Lord is pointing an accusing finger to the actions of Israel in the *valley.* This word is from GAY which Strong defines, "A gorge (from its lofty sides; hence narrow, but not a gully or winter torrent)." From this definition it may be seen the word refers to a dry depression in the earth that can be used for human activities. The conduct to which this verse refers is that of idolatrous sacrifices which the Israelites offered in this place. Incidentally, the name of one particular valley is the source of the word GEHENNA, one of the words translated "hell" in the New Testament. It will be well to give the reader some information from the lexicons on this interesting but much-perverted word. "The name Geenna . . . the narrow valley skirting Jerusalem on the south, running down from the west into the valley of Jehoshaphat, under Mount Zion. Here the ancient Israelites established the idolatrous worship of Moloch, to whom they burned infants in sacrifice; 2 Ki. 23: 10; Jer. 7: 31, 32; 32: 35; compare Jer. 2: 23 [our present verse]; 19: 6, 13." Robinson's Greek Lexicon. "Gehenna, properly the valley of Hinnom, south of Jerusalem, once celebrated for the horrid worship of Moloch, and afterwards polluted with every species of filth, as well as the carcasses of animals, and dead bodies of malefactors; to consume which, in order to avert the pestilence such a mass of corruption would occasion, constant fires were kept burning; hence, hell, the fires of Tartarus. the place of punishment in Hades. Matt. 5: 22, 29, 30."—Greenfield. With such practices as here described, and they being conducted so near the very capital of the nation, it was foolish for the people of Israel to deny their guilt of idolatry. *Traversing* means to travel or move back and forth, going over the same spots again and again. Comparing Israel to a *dromedary* (a young camel) is to indicate the greater activities in the practice of idolatry since a younger animal would be likely to be more energetic. In the beginning of this paragraph the reference was to Baalim, while the above quotations from the lexicon refer to Moloch. That is the name of another heathen god, but the various false gods were so much alike, and the services offered to them had so many principles in common, that a person guilty of devotion to one was justly charged with devotion to the other.

Verse 24. In the preceding verse Israel (I use the word with its general meaning) is compared to a young camel. In this the comparison is to a wild ass spending her days in the wilderness. She has been in such surroundings so much that she is used to the experiences. *Sniffeth up the wind at her pleasure* denotes an independent attitude toward the things that will g i v e her pleasure regardless of whether they are things worth while or not. *Who can turn her* is in question form, but it means no one can turn her from her determination to have her own way. Any male wishing her association might as well not bother to find her out there in the wilderness. *In her month* (meaning the mating time) she will show up prompted by her own desires at which time the male companion will easily have access to her. Likewise, Israel is interested only in her own pleasure and *in her occasion* (at her opportunity) she submits to mating with another wild (strange or outside) creature, the false god, with whom she will unite in intimate association.

Verse 25. The comparison to a wild ass continues, representing her as being without the benefits that could be provided for her, though on account of her own stubbornness. The owner bids her not go longer with unshod feet or with a thirsty throat, for he has been willing all the time to supply these needs. She replies *"there is no hope";* as much as to say, "there is no use to talk to me for I am in love with creatures on the outside and will still go after them." This peculiar illustration literally means to predict that Israel will persist in her idolatry until she has learned her lesson and then she will be ashamed.

Verse 26, Yes, just as a thief is ashamed when he has been caught, so Israel was destined to regret her idolatry and will express her grief in humiliating terms, even including the kings and other leading men in the confessions of shame.

Verse 27. The thing of which the people of Israel will be ashamed is their silly devotion to dumb idols described in this verse. The first two clauses are not intended to be direct quotations from the people, for they never actually said those things; the thought is their conduct logically said them. Certainly no being but one's creator would have the right to such devotion as they were giving to idols that were made of a stock (a tree) or a stone. Thus their service to such objects implied that they had been produced by them. *Have turned their back unto me* is a direct charge from the Lord against his people, and that was what justified the implied statements in the beginning of the verse. For all of this they were being punished or would be in a little while, and for it all they were to be heartily ashamed. The last clause is on that subject and the form of their expression of grief is well described in Psa. 137. The same is historically described in Ezk. 37: 11 about the dry bones.

Verse 28. The prophet resumes his chastising remarks against Israel in this verse and on to the end of the chapter. If the gods are worthy of devotion in time of peace, they ought to be able to help their devoted worshipers in time of trouble, and the prophet calls upon his people to apply to them for help. No excuse could be made on the ground that these gods were not available, either because they were busy or were too far away. No, they had them in every city and hence were in close contact with the people. *Judah* is named in this verse whereas *Israel* is mentioned in the chapter in the same connection. But at the present stage of the history the two names may properly be used interchangeably. Israel as a distinctive name of the 10-tribe kingdom has been in exile from the native land for over a hundred years. The 2-tribe kingdom known as Judah is still in Palestine. But both of these kingdoms were composed of the people of Israel, hence either term is proper and will continue to be, for the 12 tribes will not be divided again during and after the captivity.

Verse 29. *Wherefore will ye plead* is the Lord's way of telling the people they have no ground on which to make a plea for favor. *Ye all* would include the various classes in the nation. It is true the leaders were more to be blamed for the corruptions, but Ch. 5: 31 says the people loved to have it so. The principles of the Bible are that if a person takes pleasure (is satisfied or pleased with) in the actions of another it makes him a partaker of the same (Rom. 1: 32).

Verse 30. *Smitten your children* does not refer to the personal offspring of any individuals. The second word refers to them as a nation and the third means the citizens of the nation. The phrase is a reference to past chastisements that God had imposed upon the nation but which had not caused it to repent. Even the prophets who dared rebuke the people for their sins were not spared from the murderous sword.

Verse 31. A *wilderness* is a place without the products of life and the question asked of Israel is a reminder that God had supplied all of her needs. For that reason she had no right to say *we are lords*. That phrase means they had no right to claim a dominion of their own; that was what they had been claiming.

Verse 32. This is another use of the marriage relation for an illustration. A fleshly bride will long remember her wedding formal and will take pleasure in looking at it and showing it to others. And if she is sincere, the mere sight of it will recall the man who stood beside her at the happy event. But this spiritual wife of the Lord had forgotten her husband *days without number*.

Verse 33. *Trimmest* is rendered "dresseth" in Ex. 30: 7 about trimming the lamps. The thought is this wife was making herself attractive so as to interest another lover. She was not content to gratify herself with unrighteous practices, but induced others to do the same if she saw they were already inclined to evil.

Verse 34. *Skirts* is used figuratively, meaning Israel's g a r m e n t s were stained with the blood of innocent persons. *Secret* is not in the original as a separate word but is a part of the same word for *search*. It is MACHTERETH which Strong defines, "a burglary; figuratively unexpected examination." The thought is that God did not have to make any "lie test" kind of examination or try to "catch" the guilty people when they were not expecting it. *Upon all these* means the Lord saw the evidences of their guilt plainly displayed.

Verse 35. In spite of the many evidences of her guilt, Israel was so bold as to deny it and then ask God to take her word for it and be favorable toward her. But this false plea of innocence was to be an extra reason for the anger of the Lord. It is bad enough to commit sin, but it makes the degree of that sin greater when the guilty one denies it in the face of plain evidences.

Verse 36. *Gaddest* is from AZAL and Strong's definition is, "A primitive root; to go away, hence to disappear." *Way* is from a word that means "a course of life or mode of actions." We know the general opinion of a wife who is seldom in her home, for she may be suspected of seeking indulgences that she cannot have in her home. (See Titus 2: 5.) The wife of the Lord was frequently "gone from home" in search of someone with whom to enjoy unlawful pleasures and to receive from him some favor. Among the ones she thus flirted with were Egypt and Assyria. The Lord warns her that she will be ashamed of such paramours.

Verse 37. *Him* refers to the unlawful lover with whom the unfaithful wife had been intimate. *Hands upon thine head* is a gesture of shame for some humiliating event that has taken place, like the action of Tamar in 2 Sam. 13: 19. The difference between the cases, however, is that Tamar was not to blame; but the shame was there and it was indicated by placing her hand upon her head. Israel was at fault in this unlawful intimacy, but she was destined to realize it and would feel the shame as much as did the innocent Tamar.

JEREMIAH 3

Verse 1. *They say* is rendered "saying" in the margin, and the American Standard Version and Moffatt also translate it thus, making it a continuation of the preceding chapter. The words from *if* through *polluted* are a quotation of what the unfaithful wife was saying in her awakening of shameful realization of her unworthy conduct. She is represented as admitting that if a fleshly wife is untrue to her husband he will not live with her again, because to do so would pollute the land. But in spite of such a well-established principle the Lord is willing to take back his unworthy wife. In so doing He shows himself to be more lenient than a wronged fleshly husband. This case is even worse than an ordinary one in that the wife has been intimate with *many lovers*.

Verse 2. The comparison between idolatry and adultery is a familiar one and it is continued in this verse. When any particular subject or fact is selected for the purpose of illustration, the terms used will generally be those that are literally true of the illustration, even though the writer means the subject being illustrated. Thus the Lord calls attention of his unfaithful wife to the many *high places* (spots where idols were erected) where she has committed spiritual adultery. An Arabian wanders in territories where there are not many people, and if a woman desires the unrighteous experience there she will sit down and wait for a chance passer-by, so eager is she for the corrupt act.

Verse 3. The prediction was made in the preceding chapter that Israel would come to be ashamed of her harlotry. This verse is not a prediction but is a charge as to her condition of mind at the time of the writing. The withholding of rain and other natural blessings had been threatened many years before. (See Lev. 26: 19, 20.)

Verse 4. The comparison is changed in this verse to the relation of father and offspring. Israel is admonished to remember who it was that guided her all her life. All the good things she has ever enjoyed were provided by this kind Parent. But Israel has been acting the part of a child that was overindulged, and seems to think there will be no limit to the patience of her Father.

Verse 5. These questions are asked by this Father in a way that implies a negative answer. Israel had *spoken evil things* as she had opportunity, and the divine patience was about exhausted.

Verse 6. The books of the Bible were not written at any continuous period, but different parts of them were composed whenever the Lord was desiring something to be put in writing. I wish the student would now read again my comments on ch. 1: 3. The present verse starts one of the passages referred to above. *Me* refers to Jeremiah since he is the writer of this book, and he is telling us some things the Lord said to him in the days of Josiah. It was in the reign of this king that Jeremiah began his great book, but the verse of this paragraph and several that follow contain a severe complaint against Judah. The significant thought in these verses is the condemnation of this kingdom based on the contrast between it and the 10-tribe kingdom of Israel. But the contrast will not be appreciated unless we know how bad was the kingdom with which Judah is to be compared. Israel (the 10-tribe kingdom) had been in exile over a hundred years as a punishment for her idolatry. But the Lord recounts to the prophet the great and many instances of the sins of that nation. *Every mountain* and

Jeremiah 3: 7-13

every green tree had been used by that backsliding people as a place for the practice of idolatry, here called harlotry. For this sin Israel had been given over to the Assyrians, and Judah as well as the world knew about that fact of history.

Verse 7. Israel as the 10-tribe kingdom is the subject of this verse and refers to the many admonishments that God gave it but all in vain. All of this was known to Judah (the 2-tribe kingdom) and it should have been a lesson to it.

Verse 8. In verse 4 the relation of father and offspring was used for an illustration. In keeping with that the two kingdoms of the people of God, Israel and Judah, are spoken of as sisters in a few of the verses. The former sister persisted so long in her spiritual adultery that her husband finally put her away with a bill of divorce. Even this severe chastisement did not influence the other sister for good, but instead she went and committed the same unfaithfulness for which the other had been divorced.

Verse 9. The sister, Israel, is being spoken of yet and the extent of her sins is described. *Lightness* is from QOL which Strong defines, "From an unused root meaning to call aloud; a voice or sound." In the King James translation it has been rendered by aloud, bleating, crackling, cry, fame, claim and proclamation. The thought of the writer is that Israel was so bold and unreserved in her spiritual adultery that the land became disgraced. *Stones* and *stocks* (trees) were materials with which the spiritual adultery was committed.

Verse 10. An extreme case of bad conduct that becomes known all over the land will generally cause others to be admonished, but this did not prove so with Judah when she saw how awful was the corruption of her sister. Judah is called *treacherous* because the word means to cover or act secretly. So the Lord charges her with ignoring the example of her sister and with being insincere (*feignedly*) in her service to Him.

Verse 11. This verse must be understood on the principle that men are held responsible according to the opportunity they have, and part of the opportunity consists of their knowledge of right and wrong. Judah had the information direct from God that idolatry was wrong and would bring the wrath of God on the guilty. Israel had that direct information also, but she did not have that knowledge confirmed by the actual experiences of others whose career was everywhere recognized. Judah did have that advantage by observing the history of Israel. This increased her responsibility greatly and caused God to make the statement of this verse. In the actual performances of idolatry Judah did not go as far as Israel, and also in actual good qualities there was more to be said in favor of Judah than of her sister. Judah had at least a few kings who were free from the guilt of idolatry, but Israel did not have a king who was not an idolater. However, in view of the above considerations Judah was far more guilty in the Lord's sight than Israel.

Verse 12. At the time of this writing, Israel (the 10-tribe kingdom) was in exile in the land of Assyria. The prophet is instructed to *go and proclaim* some words to that people. This was done evidently to provoke Judah to jealousy, for we know the Lord sometimes uses such methods to accomplish his purposes. (See Rom. 11: 14.) However, while the immediate purpose was to provoke such reaction from Judah, the predictions that will be made throughout the remainder of the chapter will have special reference to Judah. Mention is made of the *north* which might seem confusing in view of the actual direction of Assyria from Palestine, but this circumstance is explained in connection with the comments on Isa. 14: 31 in Vol. 3 of this Commentary. There is no deception in this passage, for what will be true of Judah will also be true of Israel when the time comes for the end of the captivity. At that time the 12 tribes will have been in practically the same territory, and all will share in the favors that appear to be promised especially to Judah.

Verse 13. God calls upon his people to acknowledge their guilt and thus show a proper spirit regarding their great unfaithfulness toward Him. The ten tribes are already in exile at the time this is being written and the two tribes are very near the time of their captivity. Moreover, nothing can be done to prevent the awful event, yet it is always best to acknowledge a sin and thus become more worthy of the favor when the time comes to be released from an unpleasant situation. In the governments of men a prisoner will be required to "serve time" for his misdeeds, yet often when the term of his sentence is being regulated he may

Jeremiah 3: 14-21

be given more consideration if he has been a "model prisoner."

Verse 14. In verse 8 the people of God are said to be divorced from him while here it is said that God is *married* to them. The word is from BAWAL and Strong's first definition is, "A primitive root; to be master." Being their master the Lord will be able to do by and with them as he sees fit, hence he makes the prediction that he will come to their rescue at the proper time. *One of a city and two of a family* is the familiar prediction of the "remnant" that was to be saved from the captivity. See 2 Sam. 24: 9 and Ezra 2: 1, 64 and note the decrease in their number. It will be seen that the proportion is practically that which is indicated in the italicized words.

Verse 15. See the comments at ch. 2: 8 for the meaning of *pastors*. The prediction in this verse was fulfilled according to Neh. 8: 7, 8.

Verse 16. Many things written by the prophets had a twofold bearing, applying in some sense to both fleshly and spiritual Israel and this verse is one of them. When God's people get back into their own land they will be so happy over their escape from the Babylonian captivity they will cease to repine for the ark of the Lord which then will have been lost. All this was true of the Jews as may be seen in the books of Ezra and Nehemiah. But the "telescope" (see illustration offered in "General Remarks" at Isa. ch. 1) is here extended and the prophet sees into the time of the reign of Christ. The ark represents the Jewish Dispensation which will be replaced by that under Christ. When that time comes spiritual Israel will not be calling for the ark (containing the 10 commandments issued at Sinai), but all attention will be centered in the law of Christ that will be issued at Jerusalem. *Neither shall they remember it* does not teach that Christians should literally forget all about the Old Testament law, for Rom. 15: 4 and 1 Cor. 10: 11 teach that they are expected to remember its history. The meaning is that the people under Christ will not be longing to go back to the old law for guidance, for to do so will cause them to lose the favor of God. (See Gal. 5: 4.)

Verse 17. When spiritual Israel comes into being the people of God will regard Jerusalem (not Sinai) as the place from which their law was given. *All nations* is a prediction that the Gentiles as well as the Jews will be included in the new system of salvation. This is what Peter taught by "all flesh" in Acts 2: 17 and "every nation" in Acts 10: 35.

Verse 18. *Those days* refers to the time of return from the captivity. When *Judah* and *Israel* are named in one connection it means the 2-tribe and 10-tribe kingdoms. When the return from exile takes place both of these kingdoms will have been there in the same territory that was ruled by the Babylonians, and will all be released as one people. This prediction refutes the notion so long held by some that the ten tribes were lost while in captivity. The inspired prophet saw all twelve tribes returning to their native land *together*. For the explanation of *the north* see the comments on Isa. 14: 31 in Vol. 3 of this Commentary.

Verse 19. *How shall I put thee among the children* is the same as asking on what basis the Lord can receive back the wayward nation as his people, when it has been so unmindful of the goodness bestowed upon it. We can give the answer in the light of other passages; it is because of the divine compassion. Yes, these unworthy people will again look upon God as their father and will not again commit the national idolatry.

Verse 20. God did not wish his people to forget the reason they were to be so bitterly chastised. Even in the midst of passages predicting their return to divine favor, they were often reminded of their shortcomings. Various things and relations in human life are used as illustrations. In one verse it will be the relation of parent and offspring, then perhaps of husband and wife. The latter is used in this verse although the word *husband* is rendered "friend" in the margin, which is also the definition in the lexicon of Strong. But there is no conflict in the rendering, for a husband should be considered the best earthly friend a woman can have. This wife (the house of Israel) had been unfaithful to her husband and had tried to do so secretly, which is the meaning of doing it *treacherously*.

Verse 21. *A voice* means the voice of the people of Israel in their idolatrous worship, calling on the gods to hear them. *High places* means the hills and other spots where altars were erected for the services of heathen gods. *Perverted their way* denotes the corruptions that Israel had injected into the way of life. When men go after things that are contrary to the right way it is evident that they *have forgotten the Lord their God* which is here charged against Israel.

Verse 22. In some of the passages containing admonitions to reform, the dates are applicable to the conditions in force before the captivity. In such cases the subject should be considered in the light of the comments at 2 Ki. 22: 17 in Vol. 2 of this Commentary. But the present verse is a prediction of conditions that are to be true at the conclusion of the captivity, for Israel is represented as saying *we come unto thee*. This predicts the actual state of mind of that people after they have had the chastisement of the captivity. They will then have repented of their backsliding, which includes their complete cure from idolatry. The historical confirmation of this prediction is quoted in connection with Isa. 1: 25, vol. 3 of this Commentary.

Verse 23. The people are again reminded of the uselessness of idolatry. *The hills* is a reference to the "high places" where idol gods had altars erected for their worship. The long period of the captivity caused the Jews to reflect upon their experiences in the home land with reference to the idol worship. After many centuries of this devotion to idols they were finally brought to national humiliation, and this verse is an acknowledgement of their failure. They also confess their belief in the Lord God as the only true source of salvation.

Verse 24. The Jews became ashamed of their past conduct and the humiliating situation to which it brought them. The fruit of their labors had been taken over by the enemy and they were reduced to a low estate.

Verse 25. This is more along the same line of the state in which Israel was to find herself as a punishment for her iniquity. I believe I should again remind the reader that although the form of language is in the past or present tense it is generally a prediction. The Jews came to realize their sins and acknowledged them which is the prediction in this verse.

JEREMIAH 4

Verse 1. Jeremiah began to write in the days of Josiah and God had told that righteous reformer that nothing he could do would prevent the captivity Hence we should understand the exhortations of this and several verses that follow in the light of advice to individuals to reform their lives. The reader is requested to see the note in connection with 2 Ki. 22: 17 in Vol. 2 of this Commentary.

Verse 2. *Thou shalt swear the Lord liveth* is a contrast with the practice of swearing by the name of the false gods as the idolaters were doing. Under the Jewish Dispensation the people of God were permitted to make oaths but Christians are forbidden to do so (Matt. 5: 33-37; Jas. 5: 12). If the Jews professed to swear by the Lord it would not avail them anything unless they were doing so in truth and justice and with a righteous motive. *Nations shall bless themselves* means that if the people (one definition of *nations*) will base their oaths on the Lord they will be blessed and glorified.

Verse 3. *Men of Judah and Jerusalem* is said because that city was the capital of the kingdom of the two tribes, the ten having been in exile more than a century. The verse is still an exhortation on the principle of the note referred to in verse 1. *Break* means to cultivate and *fallow ground* means ground that is ploughed and gleaming with richness. The clause denotes the wisdom of using the good soil for their seed and not waste it by sowing it among thorns. Of course it is figurative and means they should sow their lives to the true God and not to idols. (See Gal. 6: 7, 8.)

Verse 4. When *circumcise* is used figuratively it means to cut off the deeds of unrighteousness and be consecrated to God. *Lest my fury come* does not mean the national captivity might be prevented, but God's wrath against individual sinners is based upon the phrase from the standpoint of their personal conduct. If we consider the captivity then *lest my fury come* means for the individuals to reform before that fury comes. All who did so fared better even though they had to share in the national disgrace of the captivity. Here is another place where the reader should see the note and comments at 2 Ki. 2: 17 in Vol. 2 of this Commentary.

Verse 5. *Blow ye the trumpet* is a call for a general reformation in the conduct of life. A trumpet was an instrument that was used when any important event was at hand that pertained to all the people. (See Ex. 19: 13; Lev. 25: 9.)

Verse 6. Zion was the principal spot in Jerusalem where the Law of God was recorded. The Jews are here admonished to recognize that lawful standard and not continue to serve

Jeremiah 4: 7-14

false gods. The evil from *the north* is explained at Isa. 14: 31.

Verse 7. *The lion is come up from his thicket* is a figurative prediction of the roaring army of Babylon coming up to invade the land of Palestine. There is an interesting explanation of this statement in secular history which is as follows: "The propriety of this will appear, when it is known that in ancient times the river Jordan was particularly infested with lions, which concealed themselves among the thick reeds upon its banks. Let us then imagine one of these monarchs of the desert asleep among the thickets upon the banks of the river. Let us further suppose him to be suddenly awakened by the roaring, or dislodged by the overflowing of the rapid, tumultuous torrent, and in his fury rushing into the upland country; and we shall perceive the admirable propriety and force of the prophet's allusion. 'After having descended,' says Maundrell, 'the outermost bank of Jordan, you go about a furlong upon a level strand before you come to the immediate bank of the river. This *second* bank is so beset with bushes and trees, such as tamarisks, willows, oleanders, etc., that you can see no water till you have made your way through them. In this thicket anciently, and the same is reported of it at this day, several sorts of wild beasts were wont to harbor themselves; whose being washed out of the covert by the overflowing river gave occasion to that allusion, he shall come up like a lion from the swelling of Jordan.'" Horne, Introduction, vol. 1, p. 368, and note. This overflowing of Jordan took place at the season of harvest according to Josh. 3: 15. *Gentiles* is used in the general sense of nations, for the Babylonian Empire had subdued all other important nations in its grasp for power. The verse is a prediction of the invasion of the Babylonian army which was followed by the destruction of Jerusalem and other cities of Palestine. The Biblical fulfillment of this prediction is shown in 2 Ki. 24: 10-16.

Verse 8. *Gird you with sackcloth* is a prediction of the sadness and humiliation that was to come upon the nation as a result of the invasion and captivity. *Anger is not turned back* means the captivity was inevitable in spite of all the reformative work of Hezekiah and Josiah.

Verse 9. *Heart shall perish* refers to the disheartened state of mind that would be experienced by the king and citizens in Jerusalem when they saw the Babylonian forces.

Verse 10. *Greatly deceived this people* will confuse us if we do not carefully consider the subject in the light of other passages. We know that God never causes a good man to become a bad one, nor does he directly mislead a worthy person who sincerely wishes to go in the right way. But if a man persists in going in the wrong path or shows a determination to follow false teachers, the Lord will deliver him over to his own ways that he may learn "the hard way" a lesson he is not willing to learn directly from the true source. (See Ps. 81: 11, 12; Ezk. 20: 25, 39; Rom. 1: 24, 28; 2 Thess. 2: 11, 12.) The false prophets of Israel had promised peace to that disobedient people (ch. 6: 13, 14) in spite of the warnings of God that trouble was in store for them. Since they preferred the words of their false prophets to those of the Lord, he just let them take their own unwise course. In this way it was true that the Lord indirectly deceived the people by suffering their false prophets to lead them into a false sense of security.

Verse 11. *At that time* refers to the time of the sword mentioned in the preceding verse. The march of the Babylonian army from the wilderness is compared to a wind, but it is not for the purpose of fanning or threshing grain in a desired sense. Instead, it is a *dry wind* which means a hot blast that will have a withering effect.

Verse 12. This blowing of the high wind will be according to the sentence of God, that his unfaithful people might learn a lesson by the chastisement.

Verse 13. *He shall come up* refers to the king of Babylon who will come up against Jerusalem by means of his army. In a previous verse this army is compared to a withering blast and in this it is called a whirlwind which means a storm or tempest. The lexicon definition of the original is "a hurricane," which indicates it will sweep everything before it. That was true of the Babylonian invasion as may be seen in the history of 2 Ki. 24 and 25.

Verse 14. *Wash thine heart . . . mayest be saved* may be considered from two viewpoints. In its immediate application it is an exhortation to individual reformation of life, explained in the note on 2 Ki. 22: 17 in Vol. 2 of this Commentary. In another application it is a prediction of the cleansing effect of the impending captivity on the nation as a whole. The evidence is that Israel was completely cured of idolatry after the period of the captivity. (See Isa. 1: 25 in Vol. 3 of this Commentary.)

Verse 15. *Dan* was one of the ten tribes and *Ephraim* was often used to mean all the ten that formed the kingdom of Israel. That kingdom had been in exile more than a century when Jeremiah wrote this verse. *A voice declareth* is a figurative way of telling Judah to take a warning from the fate of her sister kingdom.

Verse 16. *Mention to the nations* means for the prophet to make a prediction that may be heard by the peoples of the world. He was to predict that *watchers* (besiegers) were to come from a far country (from Babylon) who would denounce the cities of Judah. These movements preceded the taking of Jerusalem and the carrying away of its people into captivity.

Verse 17. A man set to keep guard over a field will watch that nothing therein shall escape. Likewise the Babylonian army was predicted to besiege Jerusalem to see that the people might not flee from it. The Lord was to suffer this calamity to come upon the city because *she hath been rebellious.*

Verse 18. *Way* means a course of life as a whole and *doings* refers to the individual acts in that way. The language is present tense in form but is a prediction of things soon to happen to Judah. She is told that all of her *bitter* and heartfelt experiences will have been brought on by her own conduct.

Verse 19. Jeremiah took an intense personal interest in the experiences of his countrymen which he indicated by the use of the word *bowels*. That word is from an original which Strong defines, "A primitive root; to fondle; by implication to love, especially to compassionate." The inspired writers of both the Old and New Testaments used words as they were understood by the people for whom they were writing, and did not stop to inquire whether such was based on some erroneous theory; such was the case with the word in question here. In his Greek-English lexicon, Thayer says this of the word for bowels: "In the Greek poets the bowels were regarded as the seat of the more violent passions, such as anger and love; but by the Hebrews as the seat of the tenderer affections, especially kindness, benevolence, compassion." In other words, the ancients thought the intestines were the seat of the mind and emotions, while we consider the brain in that light. By adding the word *heart* to his statement the prophet means to emphasize the intensity of his feelings, because the word means the center or most important part of anything. *Thou hast heard;* the prophet addresses himself and as an inspired man he can hear the war cry and alarming sounding of the trumpets of the Babylonian army coming to besiege his beloved city.

Verse 20. The prediction of the Babylonian invasion continues and the repetition of *destruction* is for emphasis. *Land is spoiled* is a reference to the loss of various items of property, and *tents* and *curtains* are terms for the dwelling to be demolished.

Verse 21. All scripture is inspired of God and when anything is said it is from that source. But Jeremiah is so impressed personally with the condition of his people that he speaks for the Lord in the first person much of the time. The *standard* and *trumpet* refer to the war signals of the Babylonian army.

Verse 22. *Foolish* and *sottish* have the same meaning which refers to the lack of judgment shown in the conduct of the people. Not that they are lacking in natural intelligence, for it is expressly said that they are *wise*, but they are using the wisdom for evil purposes instead of that for which the Lord gave it to them.

Verse 23. Figures of speech are based on literal truths, and when a writer selects any particular subject for his illustration he continues his discussion with the various terms of that subject. In this and several verses the prophet uses the realm of natural creation to illustrate the political and national institutions of the Lord's people. As in the beginning there was darkness, so the prophet sees his beloved country darkened by the inroads of the enemy.

Verse 24. An earthquake would cause the mountains to shake, so likewise the Babylonian invasion will cause the cities and homes of Judah to be shaken.

Verse 25. At the start of the physical creation there were no men or other living creatures. And in the picture of conditions that the invading army would bring the prophet sees the country's loss of men. (See the fulfillment in 2 Ki. 24: 14.)

Verse 26. The figures of speech are

discontinued and the prophet sees the country actually in a ruined condition. *At the presence of the Lord* means the Babylonian forces are coming against the land at the decree of the Lord to punish its people.

Verse 27. *Whole land shall be desolate* is a summing up of the conditions and it is literal. *Not make a full end* is the oft-repeated promise that God would not let the enemy completely destroy his people although they will be greatly reduced. The amount of this remnant after the captivity is stated in Ezra 2: 64.

Verse 28. About the same time that Jeremiah was writing his predictions, the historian was also writing about the great reformative efforts of Josiah. In spite of that good work the nation had to go into captivity (2 Ki. 23: 26, 27).

Verse 29. The complete subjugation of the land of Judah is the prediction made in this verse. The Biblical fulfillment is recorded in 2 Ki. 24 and 25. The historical fulfillment is cited in Isa. 3: 1 in vol. 3 of this Commentary.

Verses 30, 31. There was no remedy for the undone conditions of the people of God short of the captivity. Josiah and other good men worked diligently to reform the character and conduct of the people, and doubtless won many individuals over to a better way of life. All such were to receive the blessings of God even in the midst of their misfortunes. But all of these individual cases of improvement were insufficient to head off the national calamity. This paragraph describes the state of discouragement that would overcome the people when they see the distressful condition upon them. This terrible situation had been predicted in doleful terms by David in Psa. 137 hundreds of years before. Now as Jeremiah writes the time is near for the awful event to take place which will begin with the captivity in the land of Babylon.

JEREMIAH 5

Verse 1. When God was threatening to destroy Sodom (Gen. 18: 26) he promised Abraham he would spare the city provided certain conditions could be found. He knew those conditions did not exist and hence was determined to go ahead with his plan for the destruction of the wicked place. Likewise the Lord puts the case of Jerusalem (capital of Judah) on a proviso, which is that a man can be found that executes judgment or administers justice. It is true that some individual, unofficial men were there who were righteous, but the city in its official conduct was corrupt. The last word of the verse is a pronoun and refers to Jerusalem, meaning that if the city could produce the characters described the Lord would pardon *it*, the city.

Verse 2. Mere professions of respect for God do not count for anything. The people of Judah were outwardly very liberal with their compliments even as they appeared to be very active in the sacrificial services. But God knows the heart and he declares the professions of his people are false.

Verse 3. This verse specifies the false professions referred to in the preceding verse. Every statement is the truth but it was not made with sincerity.

Verse 4. The prophet incidentally tells us what constitutes a poor and foolish man; it is one who knows not the way and judgment of God. And that does not mean one who is thus ignorant because of circumstances beyond his control. The Lord has offered full information on these subjects in his law and all have the privilege of learning it for it has been composed in language adapted to man's understanding.

Verse 5. According to Strong the original for *great* means "great in any sense." It is like the teaching of Jesus in Matt. 5: 19, that keeping the commandments of the Lord constitutes true greatness. The leaders in the kingdom could have been great men in this good sense had they been obedient to the law of God. They were disobedient and hence incurred the wrath of God. On the other hand, there were some of the common people who were respectful toward the divine statutes. *Get me unto* means the Lord would look with favor upon the humble folks. This great truth is a divinely established principle and is taught in Isa. 66: 2. The pronoun *these* refers to the disbodient leaders described in the first of this paragraph. But in thus classifying the leaders we should not restrict the subject to them personally. They were chiefly to blame, but since the people generally "loved to have it so" (v. 31), almost the entire nation would come under the same condemnation.

Verse 6. Some figurative language is again used and the wild animals named refer to the Babylonians. The *forest* means the territory in the region of the Euphrates River. God was going to suffer these enemies to come against his people *because their transgressions are many.*

Verse 7. *Thee* means the nation of Judah and the *children* are the individual citizens of the kingdom. The captivity could not be avoided because nothing else was able to purify them from their love of idolatry, and until they are thus purified the Lord would not pardon them. Idolatry is again compared to adultery because in both evils a companion proves untrue to the one who is the rightful partner. *When I had fed them* is significant and portrays the ingratitude that is often shown by a fleshly wife. She will make full use of the home and support her husband provides for her, then turn her attention to the unlawful admirer to whom she is under no obligation either morally or socially. *Troops* has no word in the original, but the clause means the people of Judah assembled in the houses (temples) of harlots or the false gods.

Verse 8. Idolatry is illustrated by different figures. Sometimes it is a human being betraying his true love companion by an unlawful affair with a stranger. In this verse the comparison is drawn from the conduct of a horse that is full of vim from a plentiful supply of feed, then seeks to give vent to that energy by spending it on the creature that the owner intends to mate with another.

Verse 9. Strong's definition of the original for *visit* is, "A primitive root; to visit (with friendly or hostile intent)." It is used in the latter sense because God was determined to show his disapproval of his people by delivering them into captivity. In treating the nation thus the Lord would obtain vengeance against it, and it would be righteous vengeance because that authority belongs to Him. (Rom. 12: 19.)

Verse 10. God's feeling of compassion never ceases, and usually it will be expressed even in the midst of severe threatenings. It is predicted that the walls of the people were to be mounted and destroyed, *but make not a full end.* This is a reference to the "remnant" that has been mentioned frequently and fulfilled in Ezra 2: 64.

Verse 11. *Israel* often means the whole nation of the Jews or any part of it; however, when used in connection with Judah it means the ten tribes. *Dealt very treacherously* means they have been deceitful and acted as if they believed they could mislead the Lord into accepting their professions of devotion. Israel has been in exile more than a century and Judah is soon to suffer a like experience. Both kingdoms were guilty of the same iniquity which was the worshiping of idols.

Verse 12. To *belie* one means to accuse him of falsehood, and the houses of the Jews had acted as if the Lord did not mean what he said. *Not he* was a short way of saying that if evil should come it would not be the Lord who brought it. And since the Lord would not bring evil upon his people (as they thought) they need not fear that any will come; such was the false reasoning of the nation.

Verse 13. *Prophets shall become wind* denotes that the unrighteous prophets will be proved to have been false in promising peace to the nation, and all people will see that they were not speaking by the word of God.

Verse 14. The singular pronouns *ye* and *thy* refer to Jeremiah who was a true prophet and spoke *this word* which came from the Lord. *Fire* and *wood* are used figuratively and refer to the severe predictions which the prophet was inspired to make. His fiery threatenings were to be against *this people* who had been so unfaithful to God. This suggested the figure of *wood* because the unrighteous people will be as fuel for the burning wrath of God.

Verse 15. The figures are dropped and the prediction is made of a literal fact to be enacted. *House of Israel* is used in its general sense although it is Judah who is specifically meant. The *nation* that was to be brought upon Israel was that of the Babylonians, and it would be *from far* since that kingdom was located beyond the Euphrates River. This nation did not use the language of the Jews hence it would be strange to the people who were to be the victims of this *mighty* and *ancient* nation.

Verse 16. A quiver is a case for carrying arrows, a common weapon in ancient ties. *Open sepulchre* is figurative and means the Babylonians will be so successful in their war activities that the narrow case may be compared to a tomb for the dead.

Verse 17. This verse is almost literal in that it predicts what was done by the Babylonians in taking possession of the property in Palestine. The last chapter of 2 Kings gives a history of the final invasion wherein the country was taken over.

Verse 18. *Not make a full end* is a prediction referring to the remnant that was to be spared from the captivity or from its destructive effect. Ezra 2:64 states the number as 42,000 whereas the previous population was about three million.

Verse 19. A spirit of inquiry will naturally arise as to why the Lord would thus deal with his people. The answer is given by reminding them of their unfaithfulness in going after *strange* or foreign gods. *Shall ye serve strangers* predicts that during the captivity the Jews were not permitted to practice the service required by their law. One thing that was to be accomplished by that period of chastisement was the cure of idolatry. Being compelled to continue in idolatrous worship would help serve that end in that they would thus realize the folly of such a system.

Verse 20. The Lord directs the prophet to declare this prediction in a public manner. *Jacob* and *Judah* refer to the same people but from different standpoints. The first was the common ancestor of all the tribes, the second was that portion of them that made up the kingdom of Judah.

Verse 21. There is no one as blind as a man who will not see, nor as deaf as one who will not hear. The ignorance of the people was not due to any lack of intelligence but it was because they failed to use that faculty in connection with the word of the Lord. The prophet Isaiah (ch. 1:3) explains their ignorance by saying it was because they "doth not consider." The sad experiences in Babylonian captivity was intended to open their eyes to see the truth of all the divine warnings.

Verse 22. The foolish people are asked to consider the might of God as it is demonstrated before their own eyes. The boundless sea even is limited by His power so that it cannot pass beyond the decreed limits. Certainly a Being so great deserves the most respectful attention of mortal man who is powerless before those wild billows. They were unwilling to show proper regard while their way seemed prosperous in the homeland, therefore the captivity was decreed to force that impression on them.

Verse 23. *Revolting* and *rebellious* are about the same except as to the degree of their unfavorable attitude. The latter refers especially to the state of mind and the former means the act of leaving due to that attitude. The people had not gone away literally but had done so in conduct, hence the Lord decided to send them out of the land bodily and as a nation into the territory of another.

Verse 24. Ingratitude is one of the most outstanding shortcomings of man. The people of Israel were enjoying the blessings of God in their seasons and harvests yet they failed to remember it. Instead, they were using part of those very blessings in service to false gods that could give them nothing.

Verse 25. The leaders had such a power over the people that most of the good things of life were appropriated to themselves and the common people were defrauded.

Verse 26. The *wicked men* were leaders so frequently mentioned who took advantage of the people. The *snares* and *traps* were the deceptive means they used to make them think they were being favored.

Verse 27. A *cage full of birds* is a figure to describe the completeness of the oppression suffered at the hands of these wicked leaders. *Waxen rich* gives the key to the deceptive procedure of these evil men. The love of money is not a corruption that was restricted to the days of Paul but was prominent in those of ancient Israel.

Verse 28. *Overpass the deeds of the wicked* is rendered "overpass in deeds of wickedness" in the American Standard Version. The phrase is intended to state the degree of wicked zeal shown by these covetous leaders. *Judge not the cause* means they were not concerned to see that justice was done for the poor and unfortunate people.

Verse 29. To *visit* means to bring some form of vengeance on the nation, which was to come in the way of the Babylonian captivity.

Verse 30. This verse is a general description of conditions that existed at the time Jeremiah was writing; the situation will be itemized in the next verse.

Verse 31. The citizens of the nation are put in three classes, the *prophets*, *priests* and *people*. The duty of the first is to teach the law of the Lord, that of the second to *bear rule* or execute that teaching, and the third to be regulated in their conduct by the leadership of the others. But the principle of responsibility is never confined to any one person or group of persons. This verse is very fundamental in its portrayal of God's requirement of his servants. The degree of responsibility is not always the same, but no one can bear that which belongs to another. (See Gal. 6: 5.) The leaders (prophets and priests) were chiefly to blame for the evils of the nation and hence are usually condemned in especially severe language. But the common people also were at fault because they agreed to the corrupt leadership. A man does not have to take active part in a sinful practice to share in its guilt. This verse and the one in Rom. 1: 32 reveals the truth of God's law on the subject. If a man is merely favorable towards the wicked teaching and practices of another it makes him a partaker of those evils.

JEREMIAH 6

Verse 1. The kingdom of Judah was composed of the tribes of Judah and Benjamin. The latter was one of the least and had its possession adjoining the former on the north. It is not commonly mentioned separately by the writers but does receive special notice in this verse. *Gather yourselves to flee* is a form of prediction that the people of that part of the kingdom were going to be taken away from their homes and from Jerusalem their capital city. *Blow the trumpet* is an allusion to the ancient practice of notifying the public that some move of importance was about to be made. *Set up sign of fire* was another practice for the same purpose (Judges 20: 38). The towns named were in the territory of Judah, but being near Jerusalem they were significantly mentioned in connection with the exile from the capital. Out of the *north* is explained by the historical quotation at Isa. 14: 31, Vol. 3 of this Commentary.

Verse 2. *Daughter of Zion* is a figurative reference to Jerusalem and the expression occurs some 18 times in the books of Isaiah and Jeremiah. In the present passage the city is further compared to one who is beautiful and likely to attract strangers.

Verse 3. The comparison is continued in order to account for the literal prediction that is to be made soon. This *daughter* is so attractive that the shepherds will bring their flocks to be near her so they can attend to their duties at the same time they are paying attention to her.

Verse 4. The language is becoming more literal in that it predicts war against *her* (Jerusalem). *Prepare ye* is the divine order for the shepherds (the Babylonians) to come against the city. The figurative terms of the verse are *noon* and *evening*. The shepherds are represented as bewailing the shortness of time they have left. The meaning is that the siege by the Babylonians is near at hand.

Verse 5. The "day of grace" was gone and the "night" had come when the invasion and siege would begin. The figure was literally true for when Jeremiah began to write there were only about 20 years until the first attack from the Babylonians was to take place, and much of that time was past when this passage was written.

Verse 6. An inspired prediction is often made in the form of a command for the thing to be done. In fact, the Lord did decree that the Babylonian army should come against his beloved city although it did not realize that it was carrying out such an edict. A *mount* is a military position prepared for conducting a siege. Such a position needed to be supported by a rampart and that called for the trees, hence the prediction *hew ye down trees. She is wholly oppression* refers to the injustices that Jerusalem (through her leaders) had committed against the people, and for which the siege and captivity was to be a punishment.

Verse 7. The Lord tells us the meaning with which he uses the word *fountain* by the other word *continually* in the same connection. It is bad enough for one to do wrong once or just occasionally, yet it might be through forgetfulness and the common weaknesses of the flesh. No such explanation can be offered for one who does wrong *continually* for he is bound to be doing so deliberately and by his own choice. Thus the very appropriate illustration of a *fountain* is used in reference to the conduct of Jerusalem. A jet would discharge the water occasionally while a fountain is *continually* flowing. The *grief* and *wounds* means the injustices imposed on the common people by the leaders who took advantage of their authority or position as teachers.

Verse 8. *Let my soul depart* and *lest I make thee desolate* would ordinarily mean for Jerusalem to *be instructed* in order to prevent those misfortunes. We know it cannot have such a bearing here on the nation as a whole, for the teaching all along is that nothing can be done to avoid the captivity. So if the phrases are applied to the whole nation the meaning is to be prepared in mind for the *instruction* that the captivity will give.

If the application is made to individuals the explanation may be seen in the long note offered in comments on 2 Ki. 22: 17, Vol. 2 of this Commentary.

Verse 9. The vine industry is again used as an illustration. After a man has gathered the main crop of grapes he will go back over the vines to see if he has overlooked a cluster here and there and he will probably find one. But in the case of the nation of Judah it has become so corrupt that a gleaner will not be able to find a man (among the leaders) who is true to the Lord.

Verse 10. *To whom shall I speak* is a continuation of the thought in the preceding verse. The leaders have gone so far away in their iniquity that they would not listen if the Lord would speak a warning word to them. *Ear is uncircumcised* means they are unconsecrated to the Lord. Logically such an ear *cannot hearken* to the words of God The further reason for their attitude is given in the words *have no delight in it.* If a man finds no delight in a thing he certainly will not consecrate or devote himself to it. That is why David pronounces the blessing on the man whose "delight" is in the law of the Lord (Psa. 1: 2).

Vers 11. Every word in the Bible is the word of the Lord and as such it may be in the form of the first person grammatically in some passages. In others the writer will assume the first person in his speech and that will place the Lord in the third person. In this verse the prophet expresses his personal interest in the situation. *Weary with holding in* indicates the intensity of feeling the writer has and serves as a warning against the corrupt people regarding the fate soon to come upon them; when it does there will be no sparing of any classes of society.

Verse 12. This has direct reference to the Babylonian invasion into and capture of Judah whose fulfillment is recorded in 2 Ki. 24: 14-16.

Verse 13. The main reason why the Lord caused the captivity is stated in this verse. The same statement was made and commented upon in ch. 5: 31.

Verse 14. The pronoun *they* refers to the *prophet* and *priest* in the preceding verse. *Healed the hurt slightly* is a figure of speech drawn from the act of relieving a wound or disease. A mother may soothe a child's hurting by some reassuring words that the place "is not very bad and will soon be all right," even though the case may be serious and soon is destined to overcome the child. Thus the false prophets and other leaders calmed the corrupt people into believing that nothing much was wrong and that the present appearances of danger would soon be gone. The greatest harm from such teaching was from its evil effects upon the people. While they believed it they would not be inclined to repent of their sinful practices nor listen to God.

Verse 15. *They* still has special reference to the prophets and priests who were encouraging the people in their idolatrous practices. *Were not ashamed* means they were stubborn and bold in their false teaching and did not seem to regret the evil influence they were having on the common people. *Fall among them that fall* denotes that no special favors will be shown to them when the siege and capture takes place. Their position as *prophet* and *priest* will be ignored and they will have to go along with *them that fall* which means the citizens in general.

Verse 16. *Old paths* being plural refers to the two items that are mentioned separately in Isa. 35: 8. The comments and definitions of the original words are given at that place which is in the third volume of this Commentary. When these unfaithful men were exhorted to follow in the pathway of righteousness they not only refused to do so, but defiantly declared that they would not.

Verse 17. Many ancient cities were walled for protection and on the walls were towers. These were called watchtowers in which were stationed men whose duty was to be on the lookout for any enemy that might be approaching. Being in that position they would be able to see farther from the city than the citizens on the streets and they were to sound an alarm when any danger appeared. The *watchmen* referred to in this verse were the faithful and inspired prophets who were able to see into the future and behold an enemy when the people were not able to see him. But they not only refused to heed the warning given by these *watchmen* but boldly declared they would not.

Verse 18. The English word *nations* generally conveys the idea of organized governments as units of society, and yet at the time Jeremiah was writing God had only one nation in Palestine. But the warning announcement to be made was intended as information for the nations of the world.

Verse 19. *Hear, O earth* is similar to *hear, ye nations* in the preceding verse and is to have the same comments. *Fruit of their thoughts* reminds us of Paul's statement that "Whatsoever a man soweth that shall he also reap" (Gal. 6: 6). These people of God had turned their thoughts to idols and were following idolatrous practices. They were thus to reap the fruit of such a sowing which was to be the captivity in a strange land. The prediction was made by the inspired prophet and recorded, giving an opportunity for all nations of the earth finally to know about it.

Verse 20. At the same time that the people of Judah were devoting themselves to the service of idols they were professing belief in the true God and were offering incense and animal sacrifices to Him. But it has always been true that "No man can serve two masters." After they became so corrupt in their general way of life, the ritualistic acts they performed that even were a part of the divine law became objectionable to God. (See the long note on this subject with the comments at Isa. 1: 10 in Vol. 3 of this Commentary.)

Verse 21. The central meaning of a *stumblingblock* is something that will cause one to fall; it does not always mean to fall in sin. If a man were headed toward a precipice a thousand feet deep and only a few yards ahead it would be a favor to stop him by any means possible. If he would not hearken to the warning shouts of a friend, then it would be a favor to trip him and cast him down. It would be better to cause him to suffer a comparatively short fall of his body's length than to go on and plunge down the chasm that would completely crush him. So it would be better for Judah to fall nationally into Babylon than to be allowed to remain in the home land and fall into total spiritual ruin toward which the national corruption of idolatry was heading the people at the time the prophet was writing.

Verse 22. We know this is the meaning the prophet puts into his use of *stumblingblocks*, for this verse which follows immediately begins with the word *thus* which is a word of comparison. He then makes a literal prediction of what that obstacle was to be; it was the invasion of some people from the *north*. (See the explanation of that last word in a note at Isa. 14: 31 in Vol. 3 of this Commentary.)

Verse 23. This entire verse is a prediction of the Babylonian siege, with a description of the kind of people who compose that army. *Lay hold on bow and spear* refers to some of the weapons that will be used against the men of Jerusalem and Judah. The bow was used to shoot arrows and the spear was a larger dart that was cast by hand. The Babylonians are described as being cruel and merciless and secular history bears out the description.

Verse 24. *We have heard* was true both prophetically and historically. The fame of the Babylonians was so great that all had heard of it, and the prophet could hear it with his inspired ears. *Hands wax feeble* refers to the state of fear and disappointment that the people of Jerusalem will feel at sight of the Babylonian army.

Verse 25. The people of Jerusalem were advised not to try fleeing from the king of Babylon, for it would be in vain. It was the will of God for him to take over the sinful city and to undertake escaping from him would be like fleeing from God. The last king in Jerusalem with his army ignored this advice and fled out of the city, but he was taken and his army was dispersed (2 Ki. 25: 4-5).

Verse 26. *Daughter of my people* is a phrase of close relationship that is found frequently in the prophetic writings to designate the nation of the Jews. Sackcloth and ashes were used in ancient times in conditions of great anxiety or grief or humiliation. This passage is a prediction of the sorrow that was about to come on Jerusalem and her people because of the iniquities practiced by them through the years. *The spoiler* refers to the Babylonians with their army that would soon come against God's people and take their possessions away.

Verse 27. We here have the pronoun *thee* and the antecedent is Jeremiah, for the things said of this person were true of the prophet only. The word *tower* is from BACHOWN and Strong's definition is, "An assayer [tester] of metals." *Fortress* is from an original that means "defender," and Jeremiah was to test his people as to their faithfulness and defend them as the circumstances might suggest and justify.

Verse 28. The Lord gave Jeremiah "advance information" on what the test would prove; that the people were grievous revolters. *Walking with slanders* means they were associating with falsifiers and talebearers. *Brass and iron* are inferior metals (if compared with silver and gold) and are mentioned to illustrate the inferior quality of character that the people of Judah displayed. *Corrupters* is from SHACH-ATH and Strong defines it, "A primitive root; to decay, i.e. (causatively) ruin (literally or figuratively)." The leaders in Judah not only practiced sin personally but influenced others to do the same. That is the thought in ch. 5:31 which declares that "the people love to have it so."

Verse 29. An illustration is drawn from the work of a smelter or refiner of metal. In that process a hot flame is produced by a bellows or other means and the heat is supposed to melt the mass taken from the mine. The better part of it will run out and leave the dross or coarse part so that the two can be separated. The Lord represents his people as being so completely evil that when the mass is melted there is still no separation between the ingredients for they are all as dross. *Bellows are burned* means that a fire is made to glow with intense heat, yet nothing is accomplished because of the condition of corruption in the materials.

Verse 30. This verse continues the illustration of the refiner except that a change is made in the kind of ore to be refined. The result, however, is the same as it was with the lead ore. After the heat has done its work the metal will prove to be *reprobate* which means worthless. If a refiner should have such an experience with a quantity of silver ore he would just abandon the whole mass. A spectator would conclude that the smelter was dissatisfied with the whole mass since he had gone away and left it. That explains the verse of this paragraph as it shows the men saying the silver is worthless and rejected by the Lord.

JEREMIAH 7

Verse 1. This verse tells of one of the times when the Lord called upon his prophet to "take dictation" again. (See the remarks on this thought at ch. 1:3.)

Verse 2. *Gate* is from a word that is defined, "An opening, i.e. door or gate," in Strong's lexicon. Since the passage concerns the temple in Jerusalem the word should take the former of the two in the definition. The temple was the place where the national worship took place, hence the priests and other leading men of Judah would frequently be met at that place. It was very appropriate, therefore, that the prophet be instructed to take up his position there to declare the important message.

Verse 3. We do not believe there are any contradictions in the Bible, and what seems to be such may be made clear by considering all of the facts and truths involved. In this verse the people were exhorted to correct their ways and they would be permitted to dwell in the land. In other passages they were plainly told that nothing they could do would avert the captivity. The main key to this question is a distinction between the kingdom as a whole and certain individuals in it. Another thought to consider at such a place as the present verse, is that the statement means that had they made the amends suggested at the proper time they could have saved themselves from the shame and distress of the captivity. For a more extended explanation of this subject see the note and comments at 2 Ki. 22:17 in Vol. 2 of this Commentary.

Verse 4. The *lying words* against which the people were warned were those of the false leaders who had been calming the citizens by false assurance of peace. (See ch. 6:14.) These corrupt priests would profess to be interested in the *temple of the Lord* but they were not sincere. Though they entered the temple at times to officiate in the services appointed for that place, their heart's real interest centered in the vain worship of false gods.

Verse 5. *Thoroughly amend your ways* indicates the reformation that might have avoided their downfall had they produced it at the proper time.

Verse 6. The reformation that was mentioned in general terms in the preceding verse is given specific notice in this. It requires that justice be shown all unfortunate classes of citizens, and that they discontinue the worship of false gods.

Verse 7. *Cause you to dwell* is explained at verse 3. *For ever and ever* literally means "to the end of the age." The term *for ever* always means "age lasting" or "agelong," regardless of whether the age being considered is a short or long or endless one. Had Israel been true to God her national sun would not have gone down till the end of the Jewish age or dispensation. But the sin of the nation in following after idolatrous practices brought upon it the calamity of the captivity which put out the light of national life. That misfortune occurred in 606 B.C. and hence that many centuries before the Jewish age or dispensation came to its divinely-appointed end.

Verses 8-10. This completes the line of thought pertaining to the inconsistency of the people of Judah. After committing all the abominations mentioned in the preceding verse, they had the boldness to come into the temple of the true God for worship. They were not coming for the purpose of making atonement for their many iniquities, for that would have been very appropriate. Instead, they even declared they were *delivered to do these* things which means they were justified in doing them.

Verse 11. *Is this house* seems to be another question but it really is a direct accusation against a very corrupt nation. God charged that his house, called by his name, had become a den of robbers. *In your eyes* denotes that all of the evils named were being committed under the eyes of these very people.

Verse 12. *Shiloh* was the first location of the tabernacle after the Israelites were ready to pitch their camp in the land of Canaan. (See Josh. 18: 1.) The people whose headquarters were at that place committed sin in those days and received the chastisement of God for it. This verse refers to that history for the purpose of warning the ones living in the days of Jeremiah not to make the same mistake their fathers made and thus incur the same kind of misfortune at the hand of the Lord.

Verse 13. This verse accuses the generation in the days of Jeremiah with being guilty of the same sins as was that in the days of Shiloh. And all of it was in spite of the many admonitions from the Lord.

Verse 14. Because the men of the present days are as guilty as were those at Shiloh, God will punish them as he did the others.

Verse 15. This verse is a direct prediction of the captivity of Judah. *Ephraim* was frequently named to represent the kingdom of Israel (Isa. 7: 9). That kingdom had been taken into captivity more than a century before the time of Jeremiah and it was for the same abomination of which Judah was guilty. Now the Lord warns Judah of what is soon to be done for her.

Verse 16. There is no use to pray for something that is impossible or that has been positively denied by the Lord. He had already decreed that Judah should be sent out of the land into captivity, hence it would be vain to pray for any favors that would interfere with that decree. However, this does not mean that no prayers or other efforts should be made for any individuals in that nation. (See the note at 2 Ki. 22: 17 in Vol. 2 of this Commentary.)

Verse 17. The Lord addresses the prophet, calling his attention to the evil practices of Judah. They were so bold as to do these things in the streets of Jerusalem which was the capital of their country.

Verse 18. All the members of the families participated in the abominable worship of idol gods. In the service of sacrifices it was necessary to have fire and that made it necessary also to obtain wood. This called for the services of the children who would not be able for more responsible activity. The fathers were more developed in years and experience and so they could build the fire. In the service of altar performances both animals and vegetable objects were offered. The latter was in the form of cakes which brought forth the work of the women. *Queen of heaven* pertains to idolatry or the worship of the planets. It has special reference to the moon as the feminine associate of the masculine sun. The planets were worshiped as deities by the heathen and God's people took up the practice. Smith's Bible Dictionary says the following on the subject: "Queen of heaven, Jer. 7: 18; 45: 17, 18, 19, 25, is the moon, worshiped as Ashtaroth or Astarte, to whom the Hebrew women offered cakes in the streets of Jerusalem." *Drink offering* means the offering of something that could have been useful for drink. When it was so used it was either poured out on the ground before some idol or poured over the larger sacrifice on an altar, and it was done as a religious performance to the god. A motive for the idolatrous practice is indicated by the words *that they may provoke me to anger*. The word *provoke* is not in the original as a separate word but is taken from the same one as *anger*. The Hebrew word is KAAC, which Strong defines, "A primitive root; to trouble; by implication to grieve, rage, be indignant." Moffatt renders the word as "spite," and the context justifies the thought. The people thought they would "spite" the Lord by their worship of idols.

Verse 19. Many times a man's acts intended as an injury to another will rebound against himself. The Lord declared that in committing idolatry they were spiting themselves. It was like a patient who would swallow poison in order to spite the physician who had prescribed wholesome medicine. The people of Judah were told that their foolish conduct would result in their own confusion which referred to the shame or humiliation that the Babylonian captivity would bring upon them.

Verse 20. The preceding verse does not mean that God would not be angered by the vain worship to false gods for he was; but that anger was to react against the guilty nation and its country. The things threatened referred to the general work of desolation the Babylonian army was to produce upon its invasion of Palestine. *Shall not be quenched* is a prediction that nothing the people could do would cause the Lord to hold off the threatened captivity.

Verse 21. This verse means the same as if it said: "Get all of your sacrifices together and consume them upon yourselves, for I will have nothing to do with them." Many things the people of Judah were doing had been commanded by the Lord, but they became objectionable to him when they were performed as a mixture with so much abomination of idolatry. This thought is discussed at length in the note and comments on Isa. 1: 10 in Vol. 3 of this Commentary.

Verse 22. The rites and ceremonies of the Mosaic system were not mentioned to the Israelites when they first were told to flee from Egypt; the Lord was not ready for that form of service yet.

Verse 23. Outward or physical acts are the visible signs of the faith that is supposed to be in the heart of the performer. A man's service to God (in whatever dispensation he lives) begins with faith in Him. (Heb. 11: 6.) If that faith exists and will become active, then the man possessing it will prove it by performing what the Lord commands, whether that consist of animal sacrifices, burning of incense, baptism in water, or prayer and song, or any other act commanded through inspired teaching. So this verse holds out the idea that had the Israelites been true to the faith they professed they would never have stooped to the abominable worship of idols.

Verse 24. *Inclined not their ear* indicates not only failure to observe the commands of the Lord, but it shows they were not even interested to the extent of listening to see what was expected of them. *Walked in the counsels* means they followed the opinions of their own hearts regardless of the divine law. The popular theory of man is that the inventions he has produced in religion indicates progress forward, but the people are told here that the evil productions of man are a backsliding instead of a move in the right direction.

Verse 25. The record of unfaithfulness in the nation goes back to the beginning of its existence, for it had its start when Moses led them out from Egyptian bondage. Through all of the centuries God was patient and watchful over his people. The *prophets* whom He sent to his people were the inspired men in general, not only those who made predictions. It was the duty of these men to admonish and instruct the people and try to influence them into the proper way of life.

Verse 26. For comments on *hearkened* and *inclined* see those on verse 24. *Hardened their neck* is a figure of speech and refers to the stubbornness of the people.

Verse 27. Jeremiah was told to speak to the people and yet he was warned that his words would not be received. This apparent contradiction has been explained a number of times. The reader will find the original note on the subject with comments at 2 Ki. 22: 17 in Vol. 2 of this Commentary.

Verse 28. After offering the law of God to the people it will be fair to chide them for their rejection of it. This conclusion is true even though the prophet had been told beforehand that such would be the outcome. Again I request the reader to see the note referred to in the preceding verse as to the apparent contradiction.

Verse 29. Jerusalem has been referred to in the figure of a woman and the comparisons would hence be made from that viewpoint. A woman's hair is one of her main adornments (1 Cor. 11: 15) and the absence of it, especially if it has been removed by or because of an enemy, would indicate a situation of shame. (See Isa. 50: 6.) That is why Jerusalem was told to cut off the hair and throw it away; it was a token of the humiliation that the Lord was going to impose on the unfaithful city.

Verse 30. Sometimes Judah and at others Jerusalem is named in the passages, and that is because the latter was the capital of the former. In the phrase, *children of Judah*, the last word means the kingdom and the first is the citizens. They not only committed idolatry but introduced its tokens into the temple that had been honored by being called by the name of the Lord.

Verse 31. *Tophet* was a spot in the famous valley of Hinnom near Jerusalem. This place had been used as a disposal plant for the waste materials of the city and for that reason there were fires kept continually burning. The idolatrous worshipers were using the place for their abominable practices until Josiah defiled it in his great reformative work (2 Ki. 23: 10). The people of Judah went so far as to use their children as sacrifices to the false gods that were represented in this valley.

Verse 32. *No more be called Tophet* does not mean the name will be forgotten, but the place will not be referred to merely as one that was known by such a name. But the great work of the Lord in destroying the enemies of righteousness who assembled in that place will be so outstanding that it will be remembered and mentioned because of such a great *slaughter*.

Verse 33. The idolaters who were slain and cast down in this place will not receive any honorable burial. When the fowls and beasts come to devour the decaying bodies the Lord will see that no one will be allowed to fray (oppose) them away from their gruesome feast.

Verse 34. This verse is a literal prediction of the carrying away of Judah into the Babylonian captivity. After that was done the natural result was that *the land shall be desolate*. The Biblical fulfillment of this prediction is in 2 Ki. 24 and 25.

JEREMIAH 8

Verse 1. *That time* means the time of the Babylonian invasion referred to in the close of the preceding chapter. It was known that kings and other men of importance had their personal belongings buried with their bodies. The looting of these tombs would hence have the motive of material gain as well as that of showing dishonor toward the persons whose land the victorious Babylonians will have taken over.

Verse 2. The pronouns in this verse have three antecedents implied and I shall express the passage as follows: "And *they* (the Babylonians) shall spread *them* (the bones) before the sun . . . whom *they* (kings and other idolaters) have loved, etc." The dishonor will be further shown after having dragged the bones from the tombs, by refusing to reinter them even after having secured the valuables that had been buried with them. *Shall be for dung* is used figuratively here and in many other passages in the Bible. Dung is and has been regarded as a valuable substance, both as fuel and fertilizer. Its use in a bad sense, therefore, is due to its being the refuse of other articles or bodies of living beings, and to the further fact that it is scattered out and made to disappear from view.

Verse 3. There are some things worse than death such as physical or mental torture. The Babylonians were a harsh people (ch. 6: 23) and their cruel treatment of the people of Judah would cause them to wish for death.

Verse 4. The Lord bids Jeremiah remind his people of their persistence in wrong doing. It is reasonably expected that though a man falls he will rise again, at least on behalf of his own interests. The men of Judah were "challenged" to make amends for their evil record and return to the right way of living.

Verse 5. This verse is another which seems to exhort the people to reform so as to avert the calamity of the captivity, and this in spite of the decree that nothing could be done about it. The explanation lies in the distinction between the nation as a whole and certain individuals in it. (See the note at 2 Ki. 22: 17 in Vol. 2 of this Commentary regarding this apparent contradiction.)

Verse 6. This is another comment on the persistence of the people in rejecting the Lord's counsels and warning of the dangers ahead.

Verse 7. In the beginning of the book of Isaiah the ignorance of God's people was emphasized by reference to some dumb beasts (ch. 1: 3). In our verse the same thing is done by referring to some smaller dumb creatures. *Stork knoweth her appointed times* might be misunderstood because of a popular notion connecting this bird with the birth of children. Smith's Bible Dictionary says the following about this creature: "It was believed that the young [of the stork] repaid the care of their parents by attaching themselves to them for life, and tending them in old age. That the parental attachment of the stork is very strong has been proved on many occasions. Few migratory [wandering] birds are more punctual to the time of their appearance than the white stork." The word *appointed* is from MOWADAH, which Strong defines, "Properly an appointment, i.e., a fixed time or season." The idea is that although the stork is a roving sort of bird, yet because it is permanently committed to the care of its parents, it does not forget when it is time to return to the home nest to see after the welfare of the parents. The illustration is that this dumb creature is more thoughtful and aware of its obligation to its parents than Judah was of the Lord.

Verse 8. *The law of the Lord is with us* means they assumed that they could be a law unto themselves; that the writing of the scribes was worthless and not binding.

Verse 9. *The wise men* refers to these corrupt leaders who considered themselves wise enough not to need the word of the Lord. Such self-assumed wise men were destined to be brought to shame for their rejection of the word of the Lord.

Verse 10. This verse specifies the particular classes among the people of Judah whom God was condemning. The *prophets* and *priests* thought they were above being dependent on the word of the Lord. Their motive in turning away from the divine law was their desire to increase their own gains by false dealing with the common people.

Verse 11. This verse takes the same comments as ch. 6:14 which the reader is requested to read again very carefully.

Verse 12. Sin is always to be condemned but it is worse when done brazenly and when the doers of it show no regret. *Fall among them that fall* means the leaders will fall when the people in general are taken captive out of the land; their position as leaders will not save them from the downfall.

Verse 13. *No grapes* and *no figs* might suggest that not even a remnant will be left after the great calamity is over that is being predicted. Yet the promise has already been made that a remnant would be saved and we are sure the Bible does not contradict itself. The matter will be clear if we observe that God is here talking about the wicked leaders who have brought the nation into such an evil state by their corrupt teaching. It was true that all such characters were expelled; not a "grape" or "fig" survived when the flood of God's wrath was poured out upon the nation.

Verse 14. *Why do we sit still* is the language of the people. They have been informed by the prophet that nothing they can do will stop the enemy from invading the land. Therefore they seek to bestir themselves to "make the best of it" by entering into fenced (walled) cities and there *be silent*; that is, make no active resistance but await, as calmly as the bitterness of their situation will permit, the attack of the foe. They now seem to realize that their bitter state is because of their sins.

Verse 15. *We looked for peace* was because they listened to the false prophets who cried "Peace, peace; when there is no peace" (ch. 6:14). Now they are aware of the false nature of the assurances because instead of peace they are having *trouble*.

Verse 16. *Was heard* is prophecy and means the snorting will be heard. Dan was a city at the northern boundary of Palestine, and the language means the horses drawing the war chariots of the Babylonians will cause their snorting to be heard as they enter the country. *Are come* and *have devoured* is still in the future, being predictions of the calamity soon to come upon the nation. *The city* means Jerusalem which was the capital of the kingdom of Judah.

Verse 17. The pronoun *I* means the Lord who is going to use the Babylonian army to chastise the unfaithful people. This army is represented by the figures of poisonous reptiles in order to make use of the additional figure of not being *charmed*, as was believed that serpents could sometimes be. The literal meaning of the prediction is that nothing can be done to persuade the Babylonians to lift the siege.

Verse 18. The words of the prophet may always be regarded as those of the Lord also, but sometimes the prophet expresses the passages as his personal view as well as that of God. Such is the case in this verse and so on to the end of the chapter.

Verse 19. *Daughter of my people* is an affectionate way of referring to the citizens of Judah. Their cry is *because of them that dwell in a far country* which means the Babylonians who were about to come against the city of Jerusalem. The Lord is in Zion, the capital of the kingdom, and yet the nation has a king on the throne. This leaves them without any pretext for needing the assistance of man-made gods.

Verse 20. But it is too late now to expect further leniency from God. He has pleaded and instructed and warned them for many years but all of the offered instruction has been rejected. In just a few more years the nation will be overthrown and given into the hands of a foreign power. All these facts and truths bring the guilty people to make the noted statement of this verse. I say noted because it has long been a favorite quotation in the mouths of public speakers when exhorting sinners to make preparation to meet God before it is too late. Such an exhortation is proper and it is proper also to refer to such instances as the one before us as a lesson. Further than that the verse has nothing to do with individual responsibility to God today. It was written as a picture of Judah at the time of her national downfall which was near. The figures of the passage very impressively illustrate the long continued neglect of the nation to correct itself before the Lord made his decree to reject it. The *harvest* and *summer* means the period of Judah's reign in Jerusalem, during which time she could have developed a national character of religious devotion to God that would have been a sure protection against all enemies. But now it is too late; all of the time for such a work is gone and the nation is *not saved* but must suffer national death in Babylon.

Verse 21. Jeremiah is again "taking it to heart" about the sad prospect of his countrymen. *I am black* is figurative and means he is in mourning for his people.

Verse 22. Gilead was an extensive region just east of the Jordan and opposite the northern part of Palestine. Gilead was specially noted for its balm from "balm of Gilead" trees, which was worth twice its weight in silver. Funk and Wagnalls Bible Dictionary says of this balm that it was "used for the treatment of wounds." Jeremiah uses the word figuratively and in a plaintive strain asks if there is no physician in Gilead who could heal his people.

JEREMIAH 9

Verse 1. The "weeping prophet" again expresses himself on behalf of his people because of the misfortunes soon to come upon them. The reference to *waters* and *fountains* is figurative and indicates the intensity of his grief.

Verse 2. The deep grief of Jeremiah was not the kind that caused him to excuse the sins of the people. It was not mere sentiment or a fellow feeling for them in the suffering he knew they were destined to undergo, although he doubtless had that kind of grief also. But the chief motive for his sorrow was his disapproval of their sinful course. He was so disgusted with them that he wished he could get away out of their presence. So earnest was this feeling that he would have been willing to stay in a public lodging house in the wilderness in order to get away out of their sight. Overindulgent parents sometimes allow their personal feeling to cause them to excuse or try to explain away the mistakes of their children. Such was not the case with Jeremiah for he used strong language in describing and condemning the conduct of the people of Judah. *Bend their tongues* is a figure of speech based on the use of a bow. If one were eager to shoot an arrow to some distant point he would bend or pull back the bow in order to send the arrow on its mission of destruction. In like manner the people (especially the leaders) were so eager to use their tongues for sending lies that the illustration is drawn from the act of pulling back a bow in preparation for the discharge of a deadly weapon. *Valiant* means strong and the prophet describes the inconsistency of his people by the illustration just mentioned. Continuing the figure of a bow he shows them exerting themselves enough to pull back the instrument when an arrow of falsehood was to be discharged, but they would not use enough strength to bend it to send forth a truth. *From evil to evil* means they would go from one sinful practice to another; they were so devoted to the abominable way of life which they had adopted under the system of idolatry. *Know* is used in the sense of "recognition," and the phrase *know not me* means the people of Judah were interested in the false gods of the heathen but refused to recognize the true God.

Verses 3, 4. The corruption of the people was so general that no confidence could be had in anyone, hence the warning advice of this verse. The motive for the state of iniquity was twofold; fleshly indulgence (v. 2) and desire for material gain (ch. 8: 10). It seems that such a disposition of selfishness has been characteristic of the

Jews all through ancient times. (See Matt. 10: 21.) *Walk with slanders* indicates an association with those who lie against others in order to get some advantage of them.

Verse 5. Mutual mistrust and false dealing is still the subject of the prophet. The people not only dealt in falsehood but cultivated it for it is said they *taught their tongue to speak lies*. *Weary themselves to commit iniquity* means they were so persistent in their work of wickedness that they became tired over it.

Verse 6. The various terms used in these verses are for the purpose of describing the depth of Judah's iniquity. *Deceit* denotes fraud in their dealing with each other. Their practice of this wickedness was so constant that the Lord called it their habitation. Good and evil never dwell together, hence the Lord accused the people of ignoring him so they could give their attention to the fraudulent practices.

Verse 7. *Melt* is from a word that means to refine such as the work of a smelter of ore. It was a prediction of the captivity that was near at hand which was destined to refine them by curing them of idolatry. *For how shall I do* means "for thus shall I do," because nothing short of the captivity would refine them.

Verse 8. An arrow is sharp, swift in flight, and strikes one before he is aware of its existence. In many instances the arrow was pointed with a deadly poison so that the victim not only suffered from the mechanical wound, but would have to take the effect of the poison into his body. Such an instrument was referred to as an illustration of the falsifying tongues of these people.

Verse 9. *Visit* means to inflict some punishment of a severe character and the Lord declared that he would do so to *such a nation* as Judah had come to be. In making this *visit* the Lord declared he would be avenging his soul on the sinful nation. There would be nothing wrong in that because Paul has declared that vengeance belongs to God (Rom 12: 19), and He always does the right thing with that which is his own.

Verse 10. This passage refers to the wasted condition in which the land was to be left after the Babylonian invasion. *Burned up* was not literal but the territory was so ruined that all inducement for occupying it was removed.

Verse 11. The preceding verse has to do with the country in general while this one is concerned with Jerusalem especially because it was the capital of Judah. *Heaps* is from a word that is defined "ruins" in the lexicon, and it is a prediction of the disorder that will be wrought in the city by the enemy. The desolated condition in which the cities were to be left is the reason for mentioning the wild creatures that would live there. The Biblical account of the fulfillment is in 2 Ki. 24: 10-16.

Verse 12. This verse is in the form of a question which implies that inspiration was necessary to enable a man to see what was coming on the nation. The people in general and even its leaders such as the priests and regular prophets (teachers) did not realize what was to be the fate of the country. The Lord therefore sent the spirit of divine foresight unto Jeremiah and other prophets like him that the predictions might be made. One purpose for making the predictions was that certain worthy individuals might be induced by the warning to repent of their part in the iniquity of the country. Should they do so they would be spared much personal humiliation even though they have to take their share of the national misfortunes. (See the note at 2 Ki. 22: 17 in Vol. 2 of this Commentary.

Verse 13. The Lord always has a reason for what he does though he does not reveal it to man in every case. In the present one, however, the reason is stated and has been many times. It was because of their rejection of Gods law that he was determined to expel his people out of their own land and cause them to languish many years in a foreign country.

Verse 14. It is wrong to disobey the word of the Lord even once, but it is much worse to *walk after* such a life, and that is what the people of Judah did. *Imagination* is rendered "stubbornness" in the margin and the lexicon defines the original word as "obstinancy," and both renderings truly describe the spirit and conduct of the people of Judah. The specific thing which their stubbornness led them to do was to worship the idolatrous gods of Baalim. They accepted the instructions and followed the example of their fleshly ancestors instead of obeying their spiritual Father.

Verse 15. *Wormwood* and *gall* are used figuratively to represent the awful experiences the people of Judah were to have in Babylon. Of the first word Smith's Bible Dictionary says the following: "The word occurs frequently in the Bible, and generally in a metaphorical [figurative] sense. In Jer. 9: 15; 23: 15; Lam. 3: 15, 19, wormwood is symbolical of bitter calamity and sorrow; unrighteous judges are said to 'turn judgment to wormwood.' Amos 5: 7. The Orientals [people of the East] typified sorrow, cruelties and calamities of any kind by plants of a poisonous or bitter nature." *Gall* is from ROWSH, which Strong defines, "A poisonous plant, probably the poppy (from its conspicuous head); generally poison (even of serpents)." In the King James version the word has been rendered by gall, hemlock, poison and venom. The sorrowful existence which the people of God went through while in captivity was certainly very bitter and might well be likened to poison for it just about killed their morale. (See Psa. 137 and Ezek. 37: 11 for a description of their suffering.)

Verse 16. Some of the bitterness predicted in the preceding verse came upon the people while yet in their home land. This verse has more direct bearing on the captivity in Babylon which was accomplished in part by the use of the sword.

Verse 17. Josephus mentions "hired mourners" who were employed in ancient times by unfortunate people who thought their circumstances were unusually distressing. It was in allusion to this practice that Jeremiah mentioned the *mourning women*, though he uses it figuratively and in prediction of the sad state of affairs soon to come upon the nation. *Cunning* is from CHAKAM, which Strong defines, "wise, (i.e., intelligent, skillful or artful)." The idea is that the condition awaiting the nation will be so pitiable that it will require a wise person to describe it fully.

Verse 18. *Make haste* means to be prompt in forming a wailing for the people for the captivity is but a few years in the future. The reference to *tears* and the *eyes* is just another figurative prediction of the distress about to come.

Verse 19. *Voice of wailing is heard* is present tense but is a prediction of things to come though not very far off. *Have forsaken* and *have cast* is past or present tense but refers to the exile soon to happen to the kingdom of Judah.

Verse 20. *Yet* is used in the sense of "also, furthermore," etc., meaning a call to attention of these "mourning women." They made a profession of their mourning exercises, but they were admonished to hear the word of the Lord and then make their mourning a genuine expression of grief. They were also told to pass the sorrowful word on to their daughters and neighbors.

Verses 21. 22. *Windows* is used figuratively to indicate the activity of death at invading the homes. It will not wait for an open door to admit the black monster but will come through the perforations (which was the kind of windows they had in ancient times) of these openings to the houses.

Verse 23. All human accomplishments and talents are failures when the might of the Lord is turned against them. The most influential men in the kingdom of Judah had been dominating the common people for many years and they had led them into sin. Now they themselves were destined to feel the wrath of God whose law they had broken.

Verse 24. The man who trusts in God and respects his laws may be considered very ordinary in the opinion of human beings, yet even his weakness will prove too much for the unrighteous oppressor if he puts his reliance in divine support.

Verse 25. God often used heathen nations as instruments with which to punish his own people. But he likewise chastised those heathen groups because of their cruelty upon the unfortunate nation, and because of the personal satisfaction they took from the service. Hence the prediction in this verse threatens vengeance upon the various nations whom God had been using and intended yet to use. The terms *circumcised* and *uncircumcised* are used to classify all of the peoples to be involved in the chastisement of the Lord; the first of the terms refers to the Jews.

Verse 26. This verse groups all of the people together that were involved regardless of race or nationality because all of them were uncircumcised in one sense or another. The foreign nations were uncircumcised physically and the people of Israel were uncircumcised (unconsecrated) spiritually.

JEREMIAH 10

Verse 1. *House of Israel* was used in the general sense although the kingdom of Judah was specifically meant. The kingdom of Israel (the 10 tribes) had been in exile more than a century.

Verse 2. Idolatry was the greatest corruption of Israel and for which the nation was destined to be driven out of the home land. Idol worship was of three kinds that might well be termed as natural, artificial and imaginative. The first was the worship of the planets, the beasts, the trees and the rivers. The second was that of images made by hand out of wood, stone and metal. The third was some invisible god such as Baal and Ashtaroth. This verse deals with the first because *signs* is the same word as that in Gen. 1: 14 where we know it means the sun and other heavenly bodies. God is admonishing his people not to be in dread of these planets for to do so would make them as foolish as the heathen.

Verses 3-5. These verses should form a bracket and the subject is the weakness of idolatry. *Customs* refers to the practices of the idolaters which are so foolish and inconsistent. The most ordinary intelligence would enable a man to conclude that a god worthy of being worshiped should be greater and stronger than the worshiper. But in the case of these manmade idols (number 2 of the forms of idols noted in the preceding verse) the entire object to be worshiped is the work of the worshiper. It is true that a man might make an instrument that could perform some mechanical feat which he could not do with his bare hands. In such a case, however, the praise for the instrument would be given to the one who made it. But the matter of this form of idolatry is just the opposite to that. After the god has been taken out of the forest, shaped into the desired form, decorated to taste and placed in the desired location, it is as helpless as a standing tree. If the worshiper wishes the god to occupy some other place he must carry it to that location since it is unable to move an inch. It is strange that any human being could be so foolish as to engage in such a practice, especially for the Jews to do so when they had so much information about the true God. But it proves the truth of an old saying that "There is only one step from the sublime to the ridiculous."

Verse 6. Having described the emptiness of idolatry the prophet turns his speech into praise for the God of the Hebrews. There is no one like unto Him, for he is the one who created the materials from which the idolaters obtained the images they worship.

Verse 7. Not only are the dumb things of creation such as the trees the work of the Lord, but He is greater in might than the greatest and wiser than the wisest among all the nations of the world. *To thee doth it appertain* means that fear or reverence is due to be given to the Lord because he truly is the *King of nations*.

Verse 8. *They* refers to the wise men of the nations mentioned in the preceding verse. *Altogether* denotes that all of these "wise" idolaters are in one class and that they are *brutish* (stupid) and foolish.

Verse 9. This verse is similar to the bracket of verses 3-5 in that it portrays the weakness of idolatry. Every material advantage is given the idol gods. The silver brought from Tarshish and the gold from Uphaz were among the best in fineness, and from these metals the images were formed. After the idol forms were made they were decorated with blue and scarlet fabrics which were among the most beautiful materials. And yet with all of this arrangement the most that can be said of them is that *they are the work of cunning men*.

Verse 10. The attractive appearance which the idolaters gave to their image did not make it able to show even any signs of life, much less enable it to do anything. On the other hand the Lord of Israel is the *living God*. He not only is a king but an *everlasting* king. Instead of being made out of earthly materials as was the idol god, the earth is altogether within the power of this living God. The heathen nations merely offer foolish and ineffective service to their material god, while they tremble at the wrath of the God whom Jeremiah worshiped.

Verse 11. *Thus shall ye say unto them* is the instruction of the Lord, telling Jeremiah what he should say to the people of his nation. They are to be told that their idol gods will cease to be and hence it will be seen all idols are powerless.

Verse 12. *He* refers to the Lord who was named in verse 10. Three important qualifications are possessed by Him and were used in the formation of the universe; *power, wisdom* and *discretion*. The first made it possible for him to do the work, the second furnished him with the general information as to how it should be done, and the third suggested the most useful or practical plan of the whole arrangement.

Verse 13. This verse is simply a statement of God's control over the ele-

Jeremiah 10: 14-22

ments in the universe. Moisture goes up from the earth and is condensed into rain and produces even such quantities of it that a *multitude of waters* results. (Gen. 7.)

Verse 14. In view of God's power over the whole earth, the men who pretend to worship the images which they make out of a mere speck of this great universe are *brutish* (stupid). When the wooden or metal image is put to the test the maker and worshiper of it will be *confounded* or confused. He will learn to his sorrow that these breathless images can accomplish nothing for him and that all expectations offered to him by the idolatrous prophets were *falsehood*.

Verse 15. *They are vanity* means that idols are useless and can accomplish nothing. *Work of errors* denotes the whole system of idolatry is a mistake. *Time of their visitation* signifies that when the gods of the heathen are put to the test they will be proved a failure, and they who worshiped them will be put to shame.

Verse 16. The original for *portion* is defined "allotment" in the lexicon and refers to the favors that Jacob or the people descended from him will enjoy. *He* is a pronoun for God who is *the former of all things* and who can bestow actual blessings on his people. *Hosts* is from TSEBAAH and Strong defines it, "A mass of persons (or figuratively things), especially regularly organized for war (an army)." *Name* is from SHEM, which Strong defines as follows: "A primitive word . . . through the idea of definite and conspicuous position. An appellation [name], as a mark or memorial of individuality; by implication honor, authority, character." A *name* that signifies all these important characteristics is certainly one that is properly given to Him who made and rules the universe.

Verse 17. *Gather up thy wares* is like telling a person to get his personal belongings together and be ready to leave. It is a prediction that the inhabitants of the *fortress* which is Jerusalem will soon have to leave.

Verse 18. The same prediction is continued but in more direct terms. To *sling* out means to expell with force and *at this once* signifies that the hour of departure is at hand. That was literally true for Jeremiah began to write less than 20 years before the Babylonian captivity started. *Distress* is from a Hebrew word that is defined "to cramp" in the lexicon, and is used with reference to the Babylonian captivity for the people of God certainly were cramped when they were huddled in that country. *Find* is from MATES and Strong defines it, "to come forth, i.e., appear or exist; transitively to attain, i.e., find or acquire." The gist of the clause is that Judah was to be shut up in Babylon in order to *find* by experience what it means to disregard the law of the Lord.

Verse 19. The prophet speaks in the first person but is really concerned about the *hurt* of the nation. The hurt refers to the downfall that his people are soon to suffer from the enemy. *I must bear it* corresponds with the decree that nothing could be done by any man to avoid the captivity.

Verse 20. *Tabernacle* and *cords* are used figuratively because the nation had not used that structure since the days of Solomon. The clause means the temple was about to be demolished and 2 Ki. 25: 9, 10 records the fulfillment of that prediction. *My children* has reference to the citizens of Jerusalem who were taken by the Babylonians and 2 Ki. 24: 14 shows its fulfillment. *Tent* and *curtains* are used in the same sense as *tabernacle* and *cords* in the beginning of the verse.

Verse 21. *Pastors* is from a word that means rulers and feeders, and applies especially to the priests to whom was given the twofold duty of ruling, and feeding spiritual knowledge. (See ch. 5: 31 and Mal. 2: 7.) But these pastors who were expected to acquire and teach knowledge had become *brutish* which is defined "stupid" in the lexicon. A pastor or shepherd who becomes uninformed or stupid will not be aware of approaching danger and as a result his flock may be scattered from him. Such was soon to be the lot of these pastors in Judah, for the Babylonians were going to take possession of the flock (citizens of Jerusalem) and drive it away to a strange fold beyond the Euphrates River.

Verse 22. *Bruit* is now an obsolete word in the English language. In this verse it is from SHEMUWAH and Strong defines it, "Something heard, i.e., an announcement." It represents the prophet as hearing a sound or rumor that is not favorable for his people, for it is the sound of the army of Babylon that soon will be marching down upon the country. The sound is coming from the *north*, which is explained by the note and comments at Isa. 14: 31 in Vol. 3 of this Commentary. Making the cities *a den of dragons* refers to the unthinkable condition they will be in after the captivity.

Verse 23. The prophet is much impressed at the helplessness of man, especially as it pertains to questions of proper living. Had his fellow countrymen realized that truth and acted accordingly the war clouds now approaching would never have arisen.

Verse 24. Jeremiah personally was righteous but the prayer he utters is on behalf of the people of Judah. And the prayer is a kind of prediction that the nation is to be *corrected* in a foreign land *but with judgment*. *Not in thine anger* is not absolute for other passages tell us that God's anger was kindled against his people which caused him to decree the captivity upon them. The idea is that a limit would be observed in the treatment administered so that a remnant would be saved and the nation would not be *brought to nothing*.

Verse 25. Jeremiah personally doubtless felt incensed against the heathen nation that was soon coming against his beloved country, but the passage is also a prediction of the vengeance that God would take on the very instrument that he had chosen by which to chastise his disobedient people, because of the cruelty with which they did their service and because of the satisfaction they got from the sufferings of Judah.

JEREMIAH 11

Verse 1. The Lord is going to make another revelation to Jeremiah which is to become a part of his book. Not necessarily new subject matter but a special reference to a subject that was delivered from the Lord before this time.

Verse 2. *Hear* is addressed to Jeremiah and he is having his attention called to an important document which the Lord calls a *covenant*. A few lines later in the chapter it may be seen that the document referred to is the so-called ceremonial law given by Moses. We therefore have the information that the commandments on the tables of stone did not constitute the *covenant* exclusively. *Men of Judah* and *inhabitants of Jerusalem* were the same except as to the extent of territory included. Jerusalem was the capital of the kingdom of Judah.

Verse 3. The second half of this verse is almost identical with Deut. 27: 26 which is directly connected with the "ceremonial law" and which is called a *covenant* in the preceding verse in our chapter.

Verse 4. No written law had been given the Israelites previous to their release from Egyptian bondage. *The day* therefore refers to the period in their history when they were able to leave Egypt and receive a law by which they could be governed as a separate people. During the 430 years of their sojourn they were merely a race with no national standing. When the chains of slavery were broken off of them they were in a position to be ruled by whatever law would be placed over them by the One who had given them their freedom. Hence they were told that if they would obey their great Liberator they could become a *people* which was used in the sense of nation and not a race only.

Verse 5. The Lord is still speaking to Jeremiah and repeating to him the words he said to the Jewish fathers in the day they were led out of Egypt. God told that generation that he had sworn to their fathers (Abraham, Isaac and Jacob) to give unto their descendants a good land for a possession. But that promise was made on condition that they obey the divine law, and it was on that basis that He would bless the people of Jeremiah's day. This was the message the prophet was directed to tell his people that they might learn a lesson from the history of their forefathers. Jeremiah now writes in the first person to tell the reader of this communication from God and to let it be known that he favored and accepted it. He expresses his endorsement by the three words *so be it* according to the King James translation. It is interesting to know that these words are from the Hebrew word AMEN and Strong defines it, "Sure; abstractly faithfulness; adverbially, truly." In the King James translation the word has been rendered amen 27 times, truth 2, so be it 1.

Verse 6. Having received the favorable response from the prophet, the Lord told him to go to the people of Judah (the kingdom) and Jerusalem (the capital) and proclaim the words of the covenant to them. Not only was he to let the people *hear* them, but he was to exhort them to *do them*.

Verse 7. Through all the history of the nation from its escape from Egypt to the present time, God had never ceased to admonish and insist on obedience to his law. Their corrupt walk, therefore, was not due to any lack of information; it was due to their disregard for it. (See this thought in Isa. 1: 3.)

Verse 8. The people not only fell short of obeying the law, but they were not even *inclined* nor willing to show a favorable attitude toward it. *Imagination* is from a Hebrew word that Strong defines as "obstinacy." It is the same thought that is elsewhere expressed by the word "stiff-necked." *Bring upon them the words of this covenant* means that part of the covenant that threatened the disobedient ones with severe punishment for their rebellion. (See this part of the covenant in Deut. 27.)

Verse 9. It is bad enough for one man to commit sin independently of any others, but it is worse when he forms an alliance with other persons for the purpose of doing wrong. This principle is recognized by the laws of civilized nations and penalties for such misdeeds are severer than for other kinds. Even the daughters of Zelophehad understood it and gained a point with the Lord and Moses on the basis of it. (See Num. 27: 3.) The men of Judah had conspired together for wrong and God's wrath was kindled against them which is here being threatened through the prophet's words.

Verse 10. The motive for the conspiracy was to take up the sinful practice of the forefathers. While on the subject the Lord included his charge against his people in general. *House of Israel* means the 10 tribes and the *house of Judah* is the 2-tribe kingdom now in authority in Jerusalem at the time Jeremiah wrote. The former has been in exile already for more than a century and the latter is due to be taken very soon.

Verse 11. The *evil* which the Lord said he would bring on his people was the Babylonian captivity and it was only a few years in the future when this was written. *Not be able to escape* means his people cannot escape being taken into captivity; not that they never would be released from it, for they were.

Verse 12. *Then* is an adverb of time referring to the conditions that will come in Palestine as a result of the captivity. The people having turned away from God and gone to idols, He will turn away from them and bid them go for help to those dumb things. When that takes place they will realize as never before just how useless are the false gods.

Verse 13. Baal was one of the masculine gods in the class of invisible ones that was explained at ch. 10: 2. The people had become so devoted to idolatry that they had some one of the gods represented in every city. They were not satisfied at having a god in each city, but increased the iniquity by desecrating the capital city of Jerusalem in a special manner. They used every street as a place to erect an altar for the purpose of sacrificing to their god.

Verse 14. *Pray not thou for this people* seems to be a severe way for them to be treated, but it refers to the nation as a whole, not to every individual in it. (See the note at 2 Ki. 22: 17 in Vol 2 of this Commentary.)

Verse 15. *Lewdness* and *flesh* are literal terms and primarily are involved in fleshly immorality. They are used to apply to spiritual fornication which the people of Judah were committing in going after false gods. The question is, what business does such a people have in the house of the true God? The people not only practiced this great evil but took satisfaction from each instance of the abominable service.

Verse 16. The olive was one of the most important trees grown in Palestine, both because of the use made of the wood and for the fruit. The oil extracted from the olive berry was used for medicine, food and light. Hence the Lord likened his people to a green (living) olive tree and would have received their services as the most desirable fruit had they been true to their illustration. But since they were not the Lord caused a tumult (by the Babylonian army) to come against the tree and burn it to the extent that the *branches were broken off*. Note that the entire tree was not destroyed, which agrees with other predictions that the captivity was not to make a complete destruction of the nation.

Verse 17. Although *the house of Israel* (the 10 tribes) had been in exile many years before Jeremiah's time, it is frequently mentioned along with *the house of Judah*. The reason for it is that the Israelite race as a whole became corrupt by the same evil which was idolatry. The significant thought in this verse is that in committing this evil it was *against themselves*. When man commits sin he injures himself more than anyone else. He cuts himself off from the Lord and all of the benefits that would come from Him upon faithful service as commanded.

Verse 18. Every word in the Bible is inspired but the writers sometimes compose their passages in the first person and at other times they use another form. At times it will seem as if God is speaking directly and we almost forget that a prophet is speaking or writing the words all the time. After the language runs along in that line for a while, the writer will change his form and refer to himself in his relation to God or to the people. We have one of these instances in this verse. The prophet even brings in the Lord and acknowledges that *thou showed me their* (Israel's) *doings*.

Verse 19. Jeremiah became the target for the shafts of persecution from the wicked people of the nation. By glancing ahead to verse 21 we can see that the foregoing statement is correct. This came immediately after the statement that God had revealed to him (Jeremiah) a knowledge of the wickedness of the people. That caused them to hate him and to persecute him almost to the extent of death. People have a dread of any man whom they know to have "inside" information about their corrupt practices and they will conspire against him. But Jeremiah did not know this for a time, hence he went along from day to day not realizing the danger he was in. It is compared to the situation of an ox or a lamb that goes on toward the place of slaughter not realizing the danger ahead. The illustration of the olive tree is now transferred from the nation to the prophet, and the destruction which his enemies would bring on him was more complete than the Lord threatened to impose on the nation as an olive tree. He would break off the branches only while the prophet's enemies would destroy both the tree and its fruit. Not only that, but they would wipe out all sign that such a tree had existed so that it would be forgotten.

Verse 20. In his distress Jeremiah appealed to the Lord because he believed that he could thus receive righteous judgment. There is not much difference between *reins* and *heart*, but when used as distinct terms the first means the intellect and the second means the motives for applying it. Since God makes righteous tests of these matters the prophet longed for him to bring vengence upon these personal enemies.

Verse 21. Anathoth was a city near Jerusalem and was known as the unofficial headquarters of the priests. The other citizens of that place did not like the teaching of Jeremiah and even threatened his life. This is the thing referred to in verse 19 but of which the prophet was unaware for a time. But their dangerous attitude toward him finally became so outspoken that he heard of it, and then made the plea to God which we have just read and to which an answer of assurance was given.

Verse 22. In answer to the prayer of Jeremiah the Lord promised him protection. Not only was he to be shielded from death but his would-be destroyers were to be destroyed. Their men of military age were to die in battle and the remaining members of their families were to die by famine.

Verse 23. The vengeance to be brought upon the men of Anathoth was to be so complete that nothing would be left by which their names would be remembered.

JEREMIAH 12

Verse 1. The prophet does not question the judgment of God in deciding on the prayer he makes, only he desires to discuss the matter with Him. *Wherefore* means "why is it" or "how does it come" that the way of the wicked prospers? Jeremiah seems confused that treacherous men are happy whereas they have no right to happiness.

Verse 2. *Thou has planted them* means the good things possessed by these treacherous dealers were all received from the Lord. It is on the principle of impartiality which God maintains toward both good and bad men. (See Matt. 5: 45.) *Near in their mouth and far from their reins*. The last word is from a Hebrew original whose central definition is "the mind." The clause means the people would say favorable things about God but their mind or heart would not be in it. Jesus made the same accusation against some pretenders in his day. (See Matt. 15: 8.)

Verse 3. Jeremiah does not class himself with the unrighteous men of his day. He believes his faith has been tried and that it has stood the test. *Pull them out*, etc., is a prediction that God would *pull them out* which means to separate these evil men (chiefly the leaders) from the rest of the flock

Jeremiah 12: 4-13

(the congregation) and reserve them for the *day of slaughter* which means the captivity.

Verse 4. Jeremiah laments the sad condition of the land in his day and makes a personal complaint of it to God. Many of the terms used in the verse are figurative but truly represent the deplorable conditions. To a good man like the prophet it might seem as if matters had come to the limit of confusion and that it could not get any worse. But the Lord will soon show him that it could be worse, which will be the thought in the next verse, figuratively expressed.

Verse 5. The terms used in this verse are figurative also and are for the sole purpose of comparison. The literal subject under consideration is the condition of distress which Jeremiah's personal enemies were inflicting upon him. The former is compared to a race with footmen, the latter with running against horses. And then, comparatively speaking, the prophet was living in a land where peace still existed (since no foreign enemy had as yet intruded), while soon the same land will be shaken by the foreign invasion referred to by the *swelling of Jordan*. That phrase is based on an event in the seasonal history of Palestine. There is an interesting quotation from history on this subject in connection with comments on ch. 4: 7. To save space I shall request the reader to see that place for the history quoted.

Verse 6. The Lord explains what he had been talking about by referring to the mistreatment that Jeremiah was suffering from his own countrymen.

Verse 7. This verse through the 13th should be marked as a bracket and labeled "the captivity," then consider the comments on the several verses in their order. The captivity had not yet taken place but the Lord had actually forsaken his people and abandoned them to the enemy. It only remained for Babylon to carry out the program by coming against Jerusalem, and that great event was about due when this prediction was being written.

Verse 8. *Heritage* means possession and the term is applied to the Jewish nation as something that belonged to the Lord. *A lion in a forest* would be unrestricted and free to exert violence against any creature that came within his sight. God likened his people to this wild creature because they were wildly reproaching Him for his condemnation of their abominable lives.

Verse 9. A *speckled bird* would attract other birds and she would be regarded as a bird of prey. God compared his people to such a creature and predicted such an event would happen to them. The other birds refers to Babylon and her allies who were soon to attack Judah. *Come ye*, etc., is a prediction in the form of an invitation for the creatures or *beasts of the field* (nations allied with Babylon) to come and *devour* (take possession of) the kingdom of Judah.

Verse 10. The *pastors* were the men in Judah whose duty it was to feed the people with knowledge. But they had become corrupt and taken advantage of the people in their greed for gain and in their desire for sinful gratification. This situation was part of the reason for the Lord's determination to abandon his people to the enemy.

Verse 11. The spiritual condition at the time Jeremiah was writing was desolate, but the physical result of the invasion and captivity was the thing to come next and this is a prediction of that. The language is present or past tense in form but it is a prediction in meaning. *No man layeth it to heart* indicates the indifference which the people in general and the leaders in particular manifested in the matter.

Verse 12. *The spoilers* refers to the Babylonians who were coming against the land and capital city of Jerusalem. 2 Ki. 24: 13 and 25: 11-16 shows the fulfillment of this spoiling. *Sword of the Lord* means the sword of the Babylonians since that army was performing in this action according to His decree.

Verse 13. The first clause might seem to contradict Gal. 6: 7 which declares that "whatsoever a man soweth that shall he also reap." But it will not when all the factors in the context are considered. Instead of its being a contradiction, it is similar to the case in Matt. 13: 26, 27 where tares came up after a man had sowed wheat. Verse 25 tells that another person sowed the bad seed from the one who had sowed the good. It is the same in our passage that the Lord will be the one who will sow the seed for thorns in the place where the people had sowed wheat. But it will be just to prevent the people from reaping a good crop in order to punish them for their unfaithfulness to Him. He will cause the disappointment by sowing the *thorns* consisting of the devastating work of the Babylonian army. *Put themselves to pain* is as if it said they had taken the pains or trouble to put in a good crop but would not be allowed to reap from it. *They shall be ashamed* is rendered "ye" in the margin and the connection agrees with it. Logically the people who have engaged in the unlawful business are the ones who will be ashamed when the anger of the Lord is poured out upon them.

Verse 14. God has made use of various agencies to accomplish his purposes. He has not always used those whom we would consider righteous persons from a moral or religious standpoint, but they would be such as best served the Lord's purpose. He used the heathen nations to chastise his people for their idolatry; the Assyrians to punish the 10 tribes and the Babylonians to chastise the 2 tribes. But in all of such cases he never tolerated any personal satisfaction the heathen instrument of his plans took from their experience. After the Lord's people had been dealt with according to plan, then the heathen in turn would have to feel the hand of God. Such is the meaning of this verse, for it speaks of the heathen as *mine evil neighbors*, referring to the nations beyond the Euphrates River. *I will pluck them* is general and applies to all of the tribes in captivity. *Pluck out the house of Judah* is specific and doubtless is named because that kingdom was still in control in Jerusalem at this writing but was destined to be overthrown in a few years.

Verse 15. This verse is a prediction of the return from captivity of the Jews and their reestablishment in the home land. The Biblical account of the fulfillment of this prediction is given in the books of Ezra and Nehemiah. The historical account of it was quoted at Isa. 14: 1 in Vol. 3 of this Commentary.

Verse 16. The promises and conditions stated in this verse were to be in force after the return from captivity. *They* and *my people* are named in a way that might lead us to think it has reference to different races. Such is not the case, but *they* means the individual man (referred to as *every man* in the preceding verse), while *my people* means the nation as a whole. However, the conditions on which the individual men might dwell in the land also applied to the nation as a whole. This combined responsibility must be borne in mind as we approach the next verse.

Verse 17. Idolatry was the chief corruption of the nation and for which it had to go into captivity. It was cured of that evil and never had a "relapse" of it. But there were other matters of conduct required by the law and Israel is warned not to disregard them after their return from captivity. Should the nation again prove unfaithful it will not be "let off" with a "prison term" of captivity, then be restored to its place as a nation. Instead, it will be *utterly plucked up* and *destroyed*. This threatening warning might well be regarded as a prophecy, for the nation was indeed overthrown by the Romans in 70 A.D. and has never regained its original place and extent among the nations of the world. There is much that may be said on this subject, both by way of comments and by citation to secular history, both ancient and present-day. But this is not the most advisable place to go into it in full; I shall reserve that for comments on several passages in the book of Daniel.

JEREMIAH 13

Verse 1. On various occasions the Lord has required his prophets to go through what I have termed some "acting." This subject was introduced at 1 Ki. 20: 35 in Vol. 2 of this Commentary; one of those instances is the present verse. Linen was a material commonly used for the making of clothing hence the instruction to get a *linen girdle*. It was to be worn next to the body but was not to be removed at any time for cleansing in water.

Verse 2. The prophet obeyed the instructions and it is important that what he did was *according to the word of the Lord*. Inspired prophets were subject to divine regulation notwithstanding their special qualification.

Verse 3. It has been stated previously (ch. 1: 3) that the books of the Bible were not composed all at one time. That is, the writer did not begin a book and then continue uninterruptedly until the document was complete. When the Lord had something more for the writer to put down in writing or for him to do he would call upon him for that purpose. Hence this verse is simply one of those times when God is giving further instructions to his servant the prophet.

Verse 4. It is significant that Jeremiah was to hide the girdle near the River Euphrates, for that was the territory in which the people of Judah were to be in captivity.

Jeremiah 13: 5-16

Verse 5. When the prophet carried out the command his present duty was fulfilled. He was not yet told what it was all about. The motive of the prophet in hiding the girdle is expressed by the words *the Lord commanded me*. That should be all the reason necessary for anyone to serve the Lord; that it is commanded.

Verse 6. Further instructions are given the prophet and he is still not informed as to the meaning of his performance. After hiding the girdle he had returned to his former place for now he is told to *go to Euphrates* to get the girdle.

Verse 7. There is no logical explanation for the state of the girdle nor for the lesson the Lord means to teach by it. That still remains to be brought out after the importance of the subject has been emphasized by the "acting" of the prophet. All that Jeremiah saw was that the girdle was ruined when he found it.

Verse 8. This verse shows that up to the present time the prophet did not know the significance of the program. He was acting by faith in the Lord and the spirit of obedience that faith should produce in God's servants. So now it was necessary to give him some additional information which is to be understood as a prediction.

Verse 9. The meaning of the performance with the girdle is to be given by the Lord beginning with this verse. *Pride* is from a Hebrew word that is defined "arrogance or majesty." Judah (especially the leaders) had a feeling of importance that caused her to resist the teachings of the Lord. The first word in the definition is another word for "stubbornness," and the people of Judah (likewise of Israel) certainly had manifested much of that spirit in all of their history. But the Lord was determined to mar that pride through the captivity in the region of the Euphrates River.

Verse 10. *Imagination* is practically the same as stubbornness and also like the original for *pride* in the preceding verse. The stubbornness of Israel was manifested by the determination to serve the false gods. The Lord proposed to render his people to be like the girdle in its condition which was to be *marred*.

Verse 11. The application of the illustration is beginning to be more apparent. As a girdle would be worn near the body so the Lord attached Israel (as a whole) close to him. This girdle of the people was composed of living and intelligent material and should have partaken of the characteristics of the wearer. Such an article of wearing apparel would be so intimately connected with a man's body that it would come to seem like a part of himself. That was why the Lord chose a girdle in this instance to illustrate his people. He had attached them so intimately near him that they should have partaken of the holy principle. However, such an effect could have come only through hearing the words of Him who put on the girdle, *but they would not hear*.

Verse 12. Such terms as wine and grapes and wine press are used figuratively in the Bible to denote wrath or vengeance or extreme confusion as if drunk. Jeremiah was instructed to tell the people that every bottle was to be filled with wine. The Lord expected them to think (or at least pretend to think) that it meant literal wine and that they were being promised a bountiful harvest from the vineyards.

Verse 13. Then the prophet was to tell them plainly that it was not meant to be taken literally. That it meant they were to be overcome with drunkenness or confusion by the deluge of God's wrath because of their unfaithfulness. This state of drunkenness on the wine of divine wrath was to affect the nation as a whole. However, the kings, priests and prophets are named particularly since they were chiefly responsible for the state of iniquity.

Verse 14. This verse predicts the state of general confusion that will arise after Jerusalem has been shut up by the Babylonian siege. Even the members of families will turn against each other with the result that many will be destroyed. This was to be a part of God's plan for bringing vengeance on his unfaithful people. We may read of other instances in the history of the Jews where the nearest blood relatives became deadly enemies against each other. (See Matt. 10: 21.)

Verse 15. The simple declaration that *the Lord hath spoken* is the only reason given here for paying attention to what is being spoken. *Be not proud* is equivalent to saying "be not stubborn." Pride is manifested in many ways by human beings and one of them is to be too self-willed to obey the commands of another even though the one giving the commands is supremely above all others.

Verse 16. The things threatened are figurative and refer to the calamity about to come on the nation. The captivity was bound to come regardless of all efforts at reformation, but individuals who heeded such admonitions as these had the assurance of God's blessings on them even while in the captivity.

Verse 17. *Shall weep in secret places* denotes the regret that God will have (all to himself) over the sad plight of his people when it becomes necessary to punish them for their rebellious conduct. God does not weep for the fate awaiting his country.

Verse 18. The invasion into and capture of Judah would be a personal blow to the king and his family. That is why he is exhorted to humble himself, and if he did he would be spared the personal humiliation the nation as a whole was destined to suffer.

Verse 19. This is a direct prediction of the captivity soon to come upon the kingdom of Judah. *Cities of the south* is said on the same basis that caused Babylon to be referred to as coming from the "north." This subject is explained historically in connection with Isa. 14: 31 in Vol. 3 of this Commentary.

Verse 20. This historical note referred to in the preceding verse will explain the *north* of this verse. *Where is the flock* is a prediction in question form. It means that the flock of God (the people of Judah) will be taken over by this army that is to come from the *north*, which is the Babylonian army.

Verse 21. *What wilt thou say* means, what defence or answer can you offer when you see the condition about to be described? The pronoun *he* refers to God who is going to punish *thee* (the people of Judah) by the hand of the Babylonians. *For thou hast taught them* (the Babylonians); not literally, but by their devotion to the same kind of gods the Babylonians worshiped, these heathen people were encouraged to take the reins over the people of God (and this by His decree). The result will be that the people of Judah will be thrown into the terrors of national sorrow compared with the tremors or pains of a woman approaching childbirth.

Verse 22. Judah might wonder why all this disgrace was brought upon her and will inquire about it. The answer is indicated by the latter part of this verse. All through the Bible idolatry is likened to adultery and the various factors connected with such a life. A harlot could be punished by having her body exposed contrary to her desire and at a time when she did not wish to engage in her accustomed loose occupation. Such is the meaning of the threat to remove her skirts and expose her body to public scorn. This figurative prediction was to be fulfilled when Judah was taken into Babylon and there forcibly committed to a life of spiritual adultery (idolatry) with the nation that had practiced that iniquity from its beginning.

Verse 23. The unchangeable coloring on the surface of these living creatures is used to compare the fixed character of the nation of God's people as a whole. Take note it does not say that the coloring cannot be changed, but that the creatures cannot change it themselves; some outside power must do it if it is changed. Likewise the kingdom of Judah had become so settled in its iniquity that only by some outside force could it be changed. That force is God and he is going to bring about the change by sending his nation into Babylonian captivity.

Verse 24. They were to be *scattered* by being exiled into the land of the Babylonians. Such terms as *stubble* and *wind* are used to compare the lightness of the character of the kingdom of Judah as it pertained to the matter of faithfulness.

Verse 25. *Lot* and *portion* and *measures* are used as if the passage said, "This is what you are going to get from me." This is followed by the reason for the treatment to be imposed upon the people; it was because they had forgotten the Lord. That fact alone would have been bad enough had they merely sat down and done nothing except to dismiss God from their minds. But they replaced their acceptance of God's truth with the *falsehoods* of the corrupt prophets and priests.

Verse 26. *Discover thy skirts* is explained at verse 22 which see. The addition of *upon thy face* is to visualize the completeness with which the nakedness of this spiritual adulteress would be exposed.

Verse 27. *Neighings* is from MATSHALAH, which Strong defines as follows: "A whinnying (through impatience for battle or lust)." The mildest form of evil desire should be condemned, but this unfaithful wife was so eager for the sinful indulgence that she manifested her impatience for it by whining for her desired partner in lust. The same thought of increased extent in sin is expressed by the words *lewdness of thy whoredoms.* The first is from ZAMMAH and Strong defines it, "A plan, especially a bad one." To commit adultery on the occasion of the temptation that comes up unexpectedly would be bad enough, but this unfaithful wife planned to commit the act. A corrupt woman would accept her evil partner anywhere in the open areas, whether it be in the *fields* or on the *hills.* Likewise the people of Judah committed idolatry in the various spots where they could find or build an altar to their false gods. The questions in the end of the verse are for the information of the reader especially. It is an implied reminder of the thing that has often been predicted as to the cure from their idolatry. That prediction is to the effect that the nation had to be sent into captivity to be cured of the great national iniquity.

JEREMIAH 14

Verse 1. The Lord was ready for the prophet to add some more to his book, and this time the subject was the dearth that was soon to come on the land. Such a form of punishment had been threatened many years before (Deut. 11: 17; 2 Chron. 7: 13). The people became guilty of the very sin for which that kind of punishment was predicted.

Verse 2. The gates were the places through which the citizens passed to and fro in the activities of their public life, also when the products of the ground were to be offered for use. But the dearth was to stop such activities and plunge the inhabitants into gloom. *They are black unto the ground* means the people will give up in despair and sit down on the ground clothed in mourning garments.

Verse 3. The country was even so short of water that the natural places of the precious liquid *(the water),* and the *pits* (man-made cisterns) were dry. When the children or servants were sent to such spots for water they returned with their vessels empty. This threw them into a state of confusion because they realized that the condition was from the Lord.

Verse 4. *Chapt* is from CHATHATH and Strong defines it, "A primitive root; properly to prostrate; hence to break down, either (literally) by violence, or (figuratively) by confusion and fear." The physical earth cannot have the efforts described in the definition, therefore it means the farmers had such feelings. So depressing was the situation that they covered their heads which was a custom practiced by people in ancient times under conditions of great distress.

Verse 5. The *hind* or deer *calved* which means she gave birth to her young in the field. Then she was forced to forsake the calf, being unable to nurse it because of the lack of pasture brought on through the withholding of rain.

Verse 6. *Stand in the high places* denotes that these beasts were forced to the higher spots to get more air and even there they panted, *snuffed up the wind,* in their "shortness of breath." *Eyes did fail.* Hunger caused the eyes of these wild asses to become dulled so that they gazed into space.

Verse 7. The awful condition was to bring the people to a sense of shame and acknowledgement of their guilt. *Do thou it* is the prayer of the people for the Lord to do something for them. Not that the punishment was not just for they admitted their guilt. But they appealed to God that he would have mercy *for his name's sake.*

Verse 8. This verse is a pitiful plea to God as the only hope for *Israel* (used in its general meaning) to find relief. *Be as a stranger in the land.* A stranger is one who is only temporarily in a place and then soon gone. In the midst of the conditions brought on by the dearth, the people felt as if God had forsaken them and that he had been with them for a short time only, then left the land as a *wayfaring man* or a temporary sojourner would do.

Verse 9. It appeared to the people of Judah that the Lord was so *astonied* (astonished) at their conduct that he was like a man in a helpless daze. Yet their better judgment told them such was not the case and that He was really still present even though apparently they were being forsaken. With that understanding in their mind they made another pathetic plea that the Lord *leave us not.*

Verse 10. In answer to the plea and complaint of his people, the Lord reminded them of their evil conduct. They had not been "overtaken in a fault," but loved to wander or stray instead of directing their feet in the way which God had pointed out to them. Because of all this he decreed to *visit their sins* which had reference first to the dearth about to come and next to the captivity a little later.

Verse 11. *For their good* is said in the sense of the favor they desired, which was that they might be spared the punishment that had been threatened to come upon them. There was no use for Jeremiah to pray for such a favor upon the nation for it was bound to be punished according to the prediction previously made. Let the reader now see the note at 2 Ki. 22: 17 in Vol. 2 of this Commentary.

Verse 12. Fasting was encouraged and burnt offerings were commanded under the law, yet now the Lord told Jeremiah that he would not accept these services. For an explanation of this remarkable decision of the Lord, see the note and comments at Isa. 1: 10 in Vol. 3 of this Commentary. *Sword, famine* and *pestilence*. These three things are grouped together in various places as a prediction of calamities to come upon the unfaithful nation. The fulfillment of the three may be seen by considering the history found in the Bible. In 2 Ki. 24: 2 is the history of the sword, and in 2 Ki. 25: 3 is the famine. And famine was generally followed by pestilence, so we see the fulfillment of the threefold prediction in at least one instance.

Verse 13. By *prophets* Jeremiah means the false prophets referred to in ch. 5: 31 and 8: 10, 11, who had tried to calm the people with their assurance of peace. Jeremiah was not denying the words of God, yet he seemed to be worried that there were prophets who would give such promises of peace when there had been so much prophecy to the contrary. What doubtless added to Jeremiah's confusion was the fact that these men prophesied in the name of God.

Verse 14. The Lord explained to Jeremiah that these men forged His name to their lying prophecies. People will often swallow a false doctrine if the speaker of it uses the name of the Lord in connection with it. But God had never even asked the men to go forth as prophets, much less authorized them to give the people any assurances of peace. *Vision* and *divination* are practically the same and mean some supernatural insight into the future. *Nought* is from a word that Strong defines "good for nothing," and the original for *deceit* is defined "fraud." The two words just defined form a very significant thought. It would be possible for a thing to be useless without doing any particular harm actively. But the teaching of these false prophets not only was of no good purpose; it was fraudulent which means it acted in a way to defraud the people of some of their rights.

Verse 15. Not only will these false prophets be exposed for their corrupt teaching, but they will perish by the very instrument they said would never come.

Verse 16. The false prophets will not be the only ones who will feel the wrath of God, but the people to whom the false teaching was given will likewise suffer. The justice of such dealing is explained by ch. 5: 31 which says "the people love to have it so." It is the same principle of responsibility that Jesus taught (Matt 15: 14) that "if the blind lead the blind, both shall fall into the ditch." Paul taught the same idea in Rom. 1: 32 regarding those who are pleased with the wrong doing of others.

Verse 17. God does not personally weep, and when such language is used that would indicate such an act, it is the prophet Jeremiah who is doing it. It was also true that Jeremiah was personally affected by the misfortunes of his people. He therefore was to tell them how he felt about their situation and that the Lord was supporting him in that attitude. *Virgin daughter* is an affectionate and figurative term often used to designate the people of God.

Verse 18. The pronoun *I* refers to Jeremiah in his mournful viewing of the sad state of his people that was soon to come upon them in fact, and was even then being foreshadowed by the mental confusion of many persons. The *prophet* and *priest* whom he mentions are the false prophet and unfaithful priest referred to in ch. 5: 31 and 8: 10. *Go about* is from the Hebrew word CACHAR which Strong defines, "A primitive root; to travel round (especially as a pedlar) intensively to palpitate." These corrupt leaders were dealing in the abominable business of idolatry, and Jeremiah slips in a prediction that they would soon be taken to a strange land, *a land that they know not*, and there they will be compelled to continue their sinful traffic.

Verse 19. In this verse Jeremiah is expressing the sad meditations of his people over their undone condition to be brought upon them soon. *Judah* and *Zion* are both named because the former is the kingdom and the latter is its capital. *We looked for peace* was their mistake because no one but the false prophets had assured them of such a favor (ch. 6: 13, 14; 8: 11).

Verse 20. This acknowledgement or sin was doubtless sincere, but it came too late to save the nation from the captivity. It is noteworthy that they recognized their sin to have been against the Lord. This confession if followed by a consistent reformation in conduct, would win for them individually the favor of God even though they would have to take their share of the national downfall at the hand of Babylon.

Verse 21. This fervent plea for mercy was not made on the basis of their merit, but for the sake of the Lord's name. *Break not thy covenant* refers to the many promises of God to save them for His possession and never to forsake them entirely.

Verse 22. *Vanities of the Gentiles* (heathen) refers to the false gods whom they had been serving. This clause is in question form but it is really an acknowledgement that no power is possessed by these gods; not one of them could even cause it to rain. The same admission is intended by *can heavens give showers* but with a still more significant reason in their implied confession. Reference to *heavens* has in mind the planets which the heathen worshiped. These false gods are right in the vicinity from where the showers come, yet with such direct contact as an advantage they are powerless to produce results. No, these objects of worship did not make any of the things in the material creation, neither can they show any control over them. Acknowledgement is made that *our God* made them all and a promise is made to *wait upon* Him which means to rely and serve him.

JEREMIAH 15

Verse 1. In the preceding chapter Jeremiah expressed his feelings for the sad fate overhanging his beloved nation. It is true the wording of it sounds as if the people were doing the pleading for themselves, and doubtless there were many of them who had made such complaints as we may read in the passages. However, the prophet actually was making his personal intercession on behalf of his countrymen. He may have thought the Lord would change his verdict in view of this faithful service he had always rendered, and because he was a recognized prophet; his importance would surely count for something in the case. God did not wish Jeremiah to think there was anything lacking in his life that was causing the divine decree to be so strongly reaffirmed. As evidence of this, the Lord named Moses and Samuel and said that even they would not be able to change the degree. Moses was the first national lawgiver and Samuel was the first national prophet (Acts 3: 24; 13: 20). Surely Jeremiah could not expect to have more weight with the Lord than those great men. No, the time and condition had come when intercession was not in order. We should be careful not to form a wrong conclusion on this critical occasion. It was not on account of God's lack of mercy that he declared nothing could stop the invasion and captivity. He is a God of infinite knowledge and was able to see that the captivity was the only thing that would cure the people of the sin of idolatry. Knowing this awful truth it would have been an unmerciful thing to prevent such an experience from occurring just because a period of exile seemed to be a severe treatment. It would have been like refraining from performing some necessary surgery because the treatment would be painful. Therefore the Lord in actual kindness though with apparent harshness gave Jeremiah to understand that His decision was "final" and that the people must be let go out of his sight which meant out of his favor as a nation in their own land.

Verse 2. The preceding verse closed with the order for the people to be driven from the sight of the Lord. It would be natural for them to ask for some particulars as to their faith or the experiences about to be forced upon them; this verse is a reply to that inquiry. In a siege there will be various "chances" appearing before the besieged, and those chances may not seem the same to all of the besieged people. To some of them it will look as if death in any manner might as well be awaited. To others it might seem that a hand to hand fight with the sword could be preferred. Others might calmly be resigned to starvation as the siege is prolonged. While another group would decide that unresisting submission to the enemy would be the less painful way out. It is as if the Lord said: "These various ways are bound to come upon you, either one or the other on the various ones among you, so take your choice." In ch. 21: 9 is a more direct statement on this phase of the subject, explaining how the various items of this group of "chances" might be carried out. I insist that the reader see that verse in connection with the present passage.

Verse 3. Suppose that when the people are told to take their choice of these "chances" some would choose death; how will that be accomplished? This verse is an answer to that inquiry. The various means of death had been threatened or predicted previously by the great man Moses (Lev. 26: 16-22; Deut. 28: 26).

Verse 4. After the siege with all these terrible effects has accomplished its purpose, the nation as a whole will be taken away *into all kingdoms*. Babylonia was the only universal government among the heathen at that time. However, *kingdoms* comes from a word that includes in its meaning a territory or land, and the various lands of the heathen people were at that time under the control of the Babylonians. God had a grievance against Judah that covered the entire period of her rule, but it was aggravated by the very wicked deeds of Manasseh the kingdom in Jerusalem.

Verse 5. *Who shall have pity* is a declaration in question form that the Lord will not have pity on Jerusalem, but she must go through the punishment that has been threatened. *Who shall ask*, etc., is a form of speech to indicate that Jerusalem will be abandoned to her fate with nobody to save her from the doom awaiting her.

Verse 6. Having forsaken the Lord and gone after strange gods, Jerusalem shall in turn be forsaken by Him. This may seem like "returning evil for evil," but it was to be the only remedy possible. (See the comments on verse 1.) *Repenting* is used in the sense of being longsuffering and easy with his people and giving them one opportunity after another to make amends for their sins but all to no good result. Now He is tired of it and is going to deal with them in a stern manner.

Verse 7. *Fan them with a fan* literally means to scatter them as one would scatter the chaff with a winnowing shovel. It is a prediction that the people will be dispersed by the enemy. God was going to suffer his people to be imposed upon by the Babylonians because they had refused to return to the right manner of life.

Verse 8. *Widows are increased* is a prediction that more married men would be slain by the enemy thus leaving more widows in the land. *Have brought* is past tense in form but is a prediction that God will bring a foreign nation upon his people, and that even mothers with young children will not be spared. *Spoiler at noonday.* The last word should be considered in the light of the word *suddenly* later on in the verse. An army generally puts forth its greatest exertions when the heat of the day is past. But this ravager is going to be so intent on ruining the country that he will not wait but will attack without warning.

Verse 9. The pronoun *she* stands for the nation or kingdom of Judah. *Sun is gone down* is figurative and refers to the national daylight that ceased to shine. *While it was yet day* is also figurative and means that Judah's national sun was to go down prematurely. It will be like the natural sun going down when the timepiece said it was noon time. Not only will Judah lose control of her capital city of Jerusalem, thus suffering a national sunset, but many of her citizens will be destroyed by the enemy. (See the fulfillment of this in 2 Ki. 24 and 25.)

Verse 10. Again Jeremiah shows his personal attitude in the distressing situation and "takes it to heart" that his country is to be so oppressed. But it is also true that he personally had to suffer at the hand of his countrymen who did not like his plain teaching. He seems to regret that he had been born at such a time of strife. *Have neither lent on usury* is an allusion to the grasping leaders of this nation who had imposed upon the poor of the land to increase their own possessions unlawfully. Jeremiah had never done such a wrong to his people, yet he was being persecuted as if he were such a guilty man.

Verse 11. The Lord frequently follows his threatening of punishment with a prediction of a more favorable nature. This verse jumps over the period of the captivity to the time of the return to Palestine. There will then be a remnant of the nation that survived the destructive effects of the exile (Ezra 2: 64). When these remaining Jews go back to rebuild their city they will be *entreated* (treated) well. This favorable prediction was fulfilled in Ezra 1: 1-4.

Verse 12. Favorable and unfavorable predictions alternate in rapid succession through several verses. Through verse 10 the prediction of the captivity with its many painful experiences was made. Then verse 11 came in with an easement by predicting the kind treatment that Judah was to receive at the hand of the heathen. Now the prophet must resume the gloomy picture of the fate of this countrymen. The first *iron* refers to Babylon that was to come from the north. The verse is in question form but the meaning is that Judah is not a strong enough piece of iron to break the greater and stronger piece to roll down from the *north*. For the explanation of this word see the historical quotation at Isa. 14: 31 in Vol. 3 of this Commentary.

Verse 13. This verse refers to a particular feature of the calamity to come upon the nation and that was the loss of their personal property. The fulfillment of it is recorded in 2 Ki. 24: 13. *Without price* means that the Babylonians will take this property but will not pay for it.

Verse 14. After being stripped of their valuables, the people of Judah will be taken away into captivity. *Land thou knowest not* means that the land to which they were to be taken was one they had never seen and of which they knew nothing by personal contact. This *fire* is figurative and means the anger of the Lord over the unfaithfulness of his people and their corrupt practices with the idolaters.

Verse 15. This verse through the 18th should be marked into a bracket and given the title "Jeremiah's complaint." The prophet has taken a deep personal interest in the whole matter of his country's undone condition. He has been persecuted by the wicked citizens, especially the leaders, and this bracket expresses his personal plea for God's favor. He protests that his sufferings have been thrust upon him because of his faithfulness to the Lord and the divine law. We shall soon learn that God did not reject the claims of the prophet nor deny the requests that he made.

Verse 16. *Words were found . . . did eat them* is Jeremiah's way of saying he had desired the word of the Lord and when they were offered to him he consumed them as food. These professions of the prophet as to his interest in the divine law were true. He gives a logical reason for his attitude toward the Holy Word, that he was wearing the name of its Author. Surely, then, if one calls himself by the name of such an important Being, he should be interested in all of the instruction that would come from such a source for his benefit.

Verse 17. *Sat not . . . nor rejoiced* is a significant remark. A person may be guilty of a wrong without being active in it. Paul taught that God will judge those who are pleased with the evil conduct of others (Rom. 1: 32). Jeremiah would rather sit alone, be without any company, than be associated with evildoers.

Verse 18. *Pain* and *wound* refers to the sorrow and humiliation that the prophet had to suffer on account of his wicked countrymen. He was in a perpetual strain because they would not give him any relief from their persecution. It was in that sense that he declared his *wound* (bitter persecution) to be incurable. The word *liar* seems very harsh to us and we know that Jeremiah did not use it as an accusation against the Lord. However, certain characters may be used for comparison at some points without extending the likeness to all the points in general. The comparison in the mind of Jeremiah was in the fact that a liar would disappoint anyone who would rely upon him. *Wilt thou be*, etc., is merely Jeremiah's way of beseeching the Lord to have mercy upon him and not let him be disappointed. We are sure this was the point the prophet was making because of the comparison at the end of the verse. *Waters* need not be thought of as anything objectionable unless they failed to continue, and in that case they would be the cause of disappointment as would the words of a liar.

Verse 19. The applications of this verse are somewhat complicated and we should study them carefully. Jeremiah has not been charged with any unfaithfulness, therefore the exhortation *if thou return* could not mean him personally. Yet the phrase is in the second person grammatically because the prophet not only had made earnest pleas for personal favors, but had spoken anxiously on behalf of his beloved countrymen. So we are logically required to interpret the passage in a way to include these truths; I would word it as follows: "If thou (as a representative of the nation) return (repent), then will I bring thee again and thou shalt stand before me (shalt be reinstated in my favor)." The same view should be taken of the words immediately following through the word *mouth*. But this exhortation to reformation with promise of favor again reminds us of the apparent contradiction of which mention has been made a number of times. That subject is explained by the note offered at 2 Ki. 22: 17 in Vol. 2 of this Commentary. The last clause of the verse changes the implications in its wording. Here the pronoun *thee* means Jeremiah personally because he was righteous and a true example of living for the people to imitate and a true teacher to heed.

Thus the Lord notifies him that *them*, the people, should return unto him in the sense of heeding his teaching. But he must not let his personal interest in and love for his people influence him to *return unto them* or fall in with them in their evil ways.

Verses 20, 21. *Fenced brasen wall* is a figure meaning a situation of strong protection. The paragraph is an assurance to Jeremiah that God would not "let him down." His unrighteous countrymen would persecute him and if possible would kill him. But God promises not to let his enemies succeed in their designs to destroy him. We shall see the whole subject demonstrated near the close of the book. There seems to be a popular notion in the minds of mankind that if one does not like the sound of some unpleasant truth, he can prevent the predicted outcome of it by destroying the man who utters the unwelcomed truth. That was the principle that caused the Jews to kill the Saviour of the world and that also killed millions of His followers.

JEREMIAH 16

Verse 1. This verse announces that the Lord has another inspired installment to give the prophet for his book.

Verse 2. *This place* means Anathoth, the city near Jerusalem where many of the prophets resided. The Lord was looking after the social or family welfare of Jeremiah and hence told him not to start his married life in that place.

Verse 3. This verse is on the same subject as the preceding, and goes into more details as to who would be affected were the prophet to start a family in the surroundings that existed there at that time.

Verse 4. Misfortunes were to be brought upon the people of Judah in general because of the iniquity of idolatry that had been committed for many years. The community of Anathoth, however, had especially incurred the displeasure of the Lord because of the wicked persecution that had been imposed upon Jeremiah in their hatred for his teaching. (See ch. 11: 21-23.) The experiences described in this verse might be extended to Jeremiah's family were he to produce one in that community.

Verse 5. The natural temperament of the prophet would prompt him to sympathize with these evil people of Anathoth, notwithstanding they deserved all of the punishment threatened against them. Yet he was forbidden by the Lord to give way to this sentiment of pity. There is something significant in the reason assigned by the Lord why Jeremiah should not manifest any pity for these evil persons. It is expressed in the words *for I have taken away*, etc. In other words, Jeremiah should not be any more lenient or sympathetic toward evildoers than the Lord is. Today we may hear it said that even though a man may turn from the right way and take up with some new doctrine, yet we should not forget the good he has done. But the Bible teaches that God will forget it if the man ceases to be true to the former life of faithfulness. (See Ezk. 18: 24.)

Verse 6. The strange conduct mentioned in this verse referred to the performances that people practiced in ancient times on occasions of grief and anxiety. The reference to that subject as it is here was a prediction that not only would the people of that community be punished severely, but God would see to it that they would not even have the satisfaction of the sympathy of their friends.

Verse 7. This verse is on the same subject as the preceding one, giving a few more details of the bitter experiences that were in store for the wicked citizens of Anathoth who had been so keen in their persecution of Jeremiah.

Verse 8. Some of the people of Anathoth will be disposed to ignore all of the warnings uttered in their ears and will go on in their selfish enjoyments as long as they can. The prophet was to stay away from them even at the times of such mirth because they were unworthy of his company.

Verse 9. Jeremiah began to write near the end of the kingdom of Judah and many of the things predicted were about due when this chapter was written; such is the significance of the words *in your eyes and in your days*. The Lord would not wish to shut off all mirth while his righteous prophet was enjoying it, hence the instructions of the preceding verse.

Verse 10. It is a trait of human nature to profess innocence even when one's guilt is evident. But the denial is not always made directly; it is often done in a surprised attitude as if the subject were new. The Lord knew these people would take that turn when Jeremiah informed them of the message and prediction. He wished the prophet to be prepared for their action and hence the present verse.

Verse 11. This verse recounts the background of the nation's corruption. The *fathers* refers to the earlier citizens of the kingdom. They were not the first ones of the Jews who took up the sins of the heathen, for the book of Judges is full of that subject, and that was before there was any kingdom of Judah. But at the time when Jeremiah was writing it was the national fate that was being predicted, so the term *fathers* need not go back any farther than the history of the kingdom.

Verse 12. The question arises as to why this generation should be penalized for the sins of their fathers. They were not, but it was because they had *done worse than their fathers*. Then why mention the sins of their fathers if it was to be for their own conduct they would receive the punishment? It was because they had the example of their fathers with all of its results to teach them the danger of such a life. The Lord always expects his servants to profit by the example, either good or bad, that is left for their observation. Paul very aptly teaches this in 1 Cor. 10: 11.

Verse 13. This verse is one of the direct predictions of the captivity. *Land that ye know not* was said because none of these people had ever been in the land of Babylon. *Serve other gods* was literally fulfilled because the nation as a whole was not suffered to cease its idolatrous practices even after being taken into Babylon. See the note on this subject at 2 Ki. 22: 17 in Vol. 2 of this Commentary.

Verse 14. It is a usual thing in literature or oral conversation to identify certain facts by their relation to historical dates. For instance, for many years people could be heard to say that such and such an event happened before the Civil War. Later the saying was changed and it would be dated by the World War. Likewise it was a long-standing saying to identify the Lord by his connection with the deliverance of Israel from Egyptian bondage. This was because it was the most important event that had taken place with the descendants of Abraham since their origin. This verse announces that a change will be made in the practice and another event will be referred to.

Verse 15. This verse gives the event for the change indicated in the preceding verse. The release of the people of God from the Babylonian captivity was to be such an important event that it would amount to an epoch in their history. Because of that importance it is here predicted that informed persons will identify the Lord by his connection with the event. Of course in making such a prediction it includes that of the return at the end of the captivity. The Biblical account of its fulfillment may be seen in the books of Ezra and Nehemiah. The historical account was cited in connection with comments on Isa. 14: 1 in Vol. 3 of this Commentary. Reference to the *north* is explained at Isa. 14: 31 in the same volume referred to above.

Verse 16. The unchronological style of the prophetical books of the Bible has been mentioned a number of times, and the matter should be kept in mind to avoid confusion in the studies. The preceding verse predicts the return of the Jews from the Babylonian captivity. Those conditions of national corruption were so extreme that the Lord decreed the capture and enslavement of his people by a foreign foe or foes which is the subject of this verse. The capture of the people is predicted in figurative language, the *fishers* and *hunters* referring to the Babylonian Empire and its able military men. The illustration is very appropriate because a practical fisherman or hunter does not merely wish for a place to fish or hunt, but he will search for such a spot. Likewise the army of Babylon was to make a "clean sweep" of the affair and see that none of the people of Judah would be missed by the dragnet. (See 2 Ki. 24; 10-16; 25: 4-12.)

Verse 17. *Mine eyes are upon* means the Lord was seeing everything his people were doing, not that he was looking with approval as the expression sometimes means.

Verse 18. The original word for *first* is defined in the lexicon as referring to "place" or "rank" as well as to time. The thought is that God regarded the punishing of his unfaithful people as of primary importance. *Carcases* is from NEBELAH and Strong says its figurative meaning is "an idol." The verse charges the people with idolatry that is so extensive that the whole land had become filled with the *detestable things*.

Verse 19. The prophet is speaking of and for the people by making an acknowledgment and prediction. The acknowledgment is to the effect that the nation had depended upon falsehoods which we understand were offered chiefly by the unfaithful priests and prophets. The prediction is to be twofold in its fulfillment. The first was when the *Gentiles* (heathen nations) came to look with favor upon the Jews after they had returned to their own land, entirely cured of their idolatry (books of Ezra and Nehemiah). The second is also predicted in Isa. 2: 2, 3, and the fulfillment may be read in Acts 2: 41; 4: 4; 5: 14; 12: 24.

Verse 20. This verse is an accusation that Judah had adopted some gods to worship that did not amount to anything.

Verse 21. *This once* means that once for all the people of Judah will be convinced that one Being only has the right to be called *Lord* (ruler). The verse also agrees with the truth that God's people never again practiced idolatry after the captivity. See the historical confirmation of this at Isa. 1: 25 in Vol. 3 of this Commentary. The Jewish nation has done many unwise things and it did the wickedest of deeds in killing the Messiah, but it never backslid into idolatry and to this very day they as a people are strict believers in the idea of only one true God.

JEREMIAH 17

Verse 1. The writing instruments are used figuratively to illustrate the permanency of the record. It is another form of declaring that nothing in the power or plans of man could erase the guilt of the national sin. God only is able to alter the situation, which he is going to do by means of the captivity. *Horns of your altars* is a reference to the altars erected for the worship of the false gods. *Graven upon the heart* is literal in the sense that the love of idolatry was imbedded in their minds.

Verse 2. The present generation *(their children)* followed in the footsteps of the fathers and erected their idols and altars everywhere.

Verse 3. *Mountain* refers to Jerusalem and the *field* is the land of Judah of which Jerusalem was the capital. The verse is another prediction of the invasion by the Babylonians and their taking of the goods of the land. (See 2 Ki. 24: 13; 25: 13-17.)

Verse 4. *Discontinue from thine heritage* denotes that Judah was to lose her possession of the land that she had inherited from the forefathers. God had given this land to the fathers and their descendants on condition that they continue faithful.

Instead of remembering with gratitude the God who created them as a nation, the people of Judah went off after strange gods and served them. Now as a punishment God decreed to send them into a strange land, one that had always worshiped these false gods, and there they should serve these foreign enemies and continue their idolatrous practices. *Anger burn for ever.* The primary meaning of the last two words is "age lasting." In principle it means to the end of the particular age or epoch of which a declaration is being made. Its application here is that God's anger was so hot because of the unfaithfulness of his people that he would not cease to burn until he had brought that epoch to a close by the captivity.

Verse 5. The great sin of Judah was the worship of idols while this verse indicates that devotions to men was the trouble. There is no conflict of thought on the subject, for it was Judah's faith in her unfaithful teachers that led her into idolatry. (See ch. 5: 31.) All of this goes along with the general history of mankind on the subject of leadership. It has been divinely declared and humanly demonstrated that when men turn from God and listen to men they always get into trouble. Jesus taught this truth in many of his conversations but I will cite only two of them now, and they are in Matt. 15: 9 and verse 14 of that same chapter.

Verse 6. *Heath* is from ARAR, which Strong defines, "A juniper tree (from its nudity of situation)." Smith's Bible Dictionary says it "was some species of juniper, probably the savin, a dwarf stunted juniper which grows in the most sterile parts of the desert." Funk and Wagnalls Standard Bible Dictionary says the following: "There is no heath in Palestine or in the deserts near by. The plant referred to in Jer. 17: 6, 48: 6 is thought to be a variety of juniper, with small scale-like leaves close to the stem, and consequently called ARAR ('naked')." From all this data we may gather two distinct characteristics of the heath in the desert; nakedness and isolation. That makes the illustration especially appropriate, for Judah was destined to experience both. She was stripped of her authority and made bare of her belongings which answers to the characteristic of nudity. And she was exiled into a strange land with nothing but heathen religious atmosphere around

Jeremiah 17: 7-15

her which corresponds with the description of a desert or a state of isolation. The same thought is pictured in Isa. 1: 8 where God's people are likened to a lodge in a garden of cucumbers.

Verse 7. *Blessed* means happy and the declaration is not merely a decree of the Lord. The logic of it was already apparent in the experiences of that generation. The people of Judah had deserted the Lord for the sake of unfaithful prophets and priests and the result was the unhappy state they were in.

Verse 8. The first clause is the same in thought as Psa. 1: 3, and the comparison implies that as a tree demands constant moisture, so the happiness of man requires a never failing source of strength. The Lord will never fail to be that source to those who put their trust in Him. All of this is opposite of the result of trusting in false gods or deceptive leaders which the nation had been doing for years.

Verse 9. *Heart* is from LEB and in the King James Version it has been rendered by consent 1 time, heart 494, midst 12, mind 11, understanding 20, wisdom 6. Strong defines the word, "The heart; also used (figuratively) very widely for the feelings, the will and even the intellect; likewise for the center of anything." *Is deceitful* does not mean that the intellect of man is necessarily evil, for that would amount to the false doctrine of "inherited sin." But since the mind is invisible to the public it makes it possible for a wicked man to deceive others.

Verse 10. The Lord only can read the mind of man and he will expose that of an unrighteous one in due season. The leaders in Judah had misled the people for many years, but the reckoning was about to come through the exile under the Babylonians.

Verse 11. This is a very confusing translation and clouds the very thought the Lord wished to convey through the prophet. If a bird would be found that would sit on eggs and yet not hatch them, it would be no illustration of man taking possession of riches that another had produced. *Sitteth* is from DAGAR and Strong defines it "A primitive root; to brood over eggs or young." *Hatcheth* is from YALAD and the part of Strong's definition that applies here is, "A primitive root; to bear young; causatively, to beget." This makes the language intelligible and gives us a clear illustration. A partridge takes possession of young birds which had not been produced either by her laying the eggs or by hatching the ones from which the young had come. Such a circumstance does compare with a man taking to himself the goods that have been produced by another. The leaders in Judah had done that very thing (Isa. 58: 3-7; 3: 13-15; 5: 23), and the Lord was going to bring his judgment against them.

Verse 12. From this through verse 18 should be marked as a bracket and given the title, "Prayer and complaint of Jeremiah." We should constantly keep in mind that an inspired prophet is speaking for and of the people, as well as being considered a spokesman for God. Another thing that plays an important part in this book is Jeremiah's personal interest and sympathy for the people. Hence, when he is writing as if he were making a personal plea for mercy or sympathy, he may be expressing the sentiments of the people as a whole, or at least what he considers should be their sentiments, at the same time wording it in the way he naturally would have done from his personal feelings even had he not been inspired. This verse is a recognition of the greatness of the headquarters that the Lord had provided for his people. Had they always taken that view of the subject and acted accordingly, they would never have gone off after strange gods.

Verse 13. This verse continues the acknowledgement of God's authority and importance. *Shall be written* means that all who forsake God will make a record of shame that will be known by the people of the earth.

Verse 14. The general principles revealed in this verse could be affirmed at any time and from any standpoint. The "healing" that had been done by the false leaders (ch. 6: 13, 14) was a deception, and that which the Lord performs is true. Individuals of the country who proved worthy were promised restored health (forgiveness of sins) upon repentance. The nation also was promised a cure by the only treatment that would answer the needs of the case which was the Babylonian captivity.

Verse 15. This verse has reference to the persecutions imposed on Jeremiah by his unworthy countrymen. They did not like his teaching because it condemned their wicked lives. As a screen for their unruly attitude they pretended not to recognize the word of God in the mouth of the prophet and hypocritically asked, *where is the word of the Lord?*

Verse 16. Jeremiah insists before God that he was not guilty of their insinuations, but declares he had been a faithful *pastor* (spiritual feeder) of the people. *Not desired the woeful day* indicates he was not responsible for the day of woe about to come upon the country. He earnestly professes that what he had spoken to the people was the right teaching according to the will of the Lord.

Verse 17. Jeremiah believed the Lord would protect him from the terror of his enemies. His hope was in God and this verse is a prayer based upon that hope.

Verse 18. This verse continues the prophet's prayer for help against his persecuting townsmen. The closing words of the verse seem to be a selfish and cruel wish against the enemies of Jeremiah and we might wonder why such a good man would express such feelings. Again we should remember that he is an inspired prophet and many of the things which sound like his harsh wishes are really predictions that such things are to occur and that by the divine decree.

Verse 19. The most important cities were walled as a protection against enemies, and hence persons entering or passing from them would need to go through the gates. That would make an advantage for one who wished to meet the citizens with some kind of a message, and the prophet was told to go to the gate for that purpose.

Verse 20. The people in general were to be addressed, but the kings were referred to especially because a military situation was about to take place and the diplomatic exchanges would be made through them. Judah was the country or kingdom and Jerusalem was the capital hence the mention of the two. The word of the Lord was to be delivered to these inhabitants through the prophets, and they were to listen to its utterance.

Verse 21. The national corruption of the Jews was the worship of idols. When man takes up a religion that is contrary to that of the Lord he is sure to neglect some of the duties that belong to the service of God. Hence when the Jews took up the practice of idolatry they began to neglect their duties to God, and one of them was that of observing the rest which they were commanded to give the land. They continued their disregard for that ordinance until they had defrauded the land out of 70 such years of rest. That was why the Lord decreed that they should be in captivity for that many years so that the land could "catch up" on its years of rest. It would not be surprising if a nation violated such an ordinance that involved whole years of rest, that other ordinances would likewise be treated with lightness such as regards secular interests. All the above considerations will explain this and the next verse. The present one referred especially to imports into the city on the sabbath.

Verse 22. This verse would have special reference to going out with one's possessions for the purpose of trading with others. The prophet was to instruct the people not to deal in such transactions but to give the Sabbath its deserved rest.

Verse 23. This verse describes the record of the Jewish people for most of the years of their residence in Palestine, and it shows the reaction they displayed against the teaching of Jeremiah concerning their unrighteous conduct.

Verse 24. We have clearly understood that at the time Jeremiah was writing this the Babylonian captivity was about due. No only so, but the Lord had decreed many times that nothing that any man could do would save the nation from the captivity. Yet several verses seem to hold out the promise that it could be done by the repentance of the people. The apparent contradiction can be explained from two different standpoints. These verses show what could have prevented the national downfall which would have been the conduct described in this and the verses through the end of the chapter. In that view of the case it will help clarify the subject to make the words *if ye diligently hearken* read as if they said, "if ye had hearkened." Another phase of the explanation is to distinguish between the nation as a whole and certain individuals in it. See the note for an explanation of this matter at 2 Ki. 22: 17 in Vol. 2 of this Commentary. Among the things they would have done to retain the Lord's favor was the observance of the sabbath law both as to the land and the weekly activities.

Verse 25. Had Judah been true to God from the beginning the throne in Jerusalem would have continued to have kings sitting upon it who would have been respected, and whose rulership would have been attended by men of dignity. *City shall remain forever.* The last two words mean "age lasting." Had the nation been faithful its capital would have remained to the end of the age, or even as long as the earth lasted.

Verse 26. The political life of the nation would have been continued, also the religious activities that centered in Jerusalem would have been undisturbed as long as that religious age (or dispensation) continued to be in force. And even after the practice named ceased to be recognized by the Lord as of religious use (Rom. 10: 44), they could have continued as part of the national customs.

Verse 27. *If ye will not hearken* is to be understood as if it said, "since ye did not hearken." As a penalty for this violation of the law of God they were to have their city destroyed by fire and themselves be sent away into captivity. *Shall not be quenched* was fulfilled both literally and figuratively. The capital was actually destroyed by fire (2 Ki. 25: 9, 10), and the fire of God's anger was not quenched until the captivity was accomplished.

JEREMIAH 18

Verse 1. Here is another revelation from the Lord to become a part of Jeremiah's book. The verses from this through 10 should be grouped as a bracket and the general subject is "responsibility," showing especially that God's dealings with man are based upon his conduct, and not on some arbitrary decree that was formed before man was created. The several verses of the bracket will be commented upon in their order.

Verse 2. Jeremiah does not know what lesson the Lord has in store for him because nothing had ever been said before about a potter. He was to get the message while seeing the potter at work, and thus he would receive inspiration through both eyes and ears in the same connection.

Verse 3. *The wheels* is a part of a potter's machine and may be likened to the turntable of a phonograph. A lump of clay is placed on this platform which is revolving. The potter works this clay by pressing it between the fingers of both hands until it is of the shape and thickness desired. As the platform is revolving, the potter needs to work at one spot in the circle only, the circular motion having the effect of making the shape and thickness of the vessel uniform throughout its entire circuit.

Verse 4. Some kinds of vessels would be more difficult to make due to the particular fineness of their shape, and this because of the more important use that is intended to be made of them. Because of these facts the better vessels would require clay of better quality. The potter thought the lump would be good enough to form into one of the better vessels and was trying to do so. But the clay would not stand up to the requirements and fell apart in the workman's hands, so he had to be content with making it into a coarser kind.

Verse 5. Having let the prophet watch this procedure, God was ready to tell him the lesson he was to draw from the circumstance.

Verse 6. This illustration of the potter and clay has been greatly misused by some religious teachers. It has been made to teach that man (the clay) is helpless in the hands of the potter (the Lord). That his future state and usefulness is altogether in the hands of God, and whether he turns out to be a desirable character or the other kind, is subject to the divine decree and man has nothing to do in the matter. But such a theory is contrary to the evident facts of the performance the prophet saw. It is true this verse says man is as clay in the potter's hands and also that He can do with him as the potter did the clay. But the theory ignores the fact that he first tried to make a better vessel out of the clay, and did not decide to make the lesser one until the clay failed to meet the requirements of the better. But according to the doctrine of "predestination," the potter had decided to make this particular lump of clay into a coarse vessel before he even tried to make the other. The theory even requires that the clay had been destined for this less desirable use before it was dug out of the ground, for the predestinarians teach that God decreed "from all eternity" who should be saved and who lost. This would be before the man was born and before he had been tried and given a chance to be made into the better vessel.

Verse 7. *At what instant* is used in the sense that "in every instance that I speak," etc. The speaking means the threatening or predictions that may be uttered against a nation because of its sinful practices.

Verse 8. This verse states the principle on which God deals with nations and individuals, but "circumstances alter cases" in this as well as in other matters. Judah had been practicing idolatry for many years and was still guilty at the time Jeremiah was writing. Some great reformers such as Hezekiah and Josiah saw the evil and tried to correct it. There were also other unofficial men who were righteous and would have removed the abomination had they been able. But the iniquity was so general and had become so deep-seated that it was too late for even the good work of these reformers to get it corrected. On this account the Lord said that he would carry out his decree for the captivity as the only means of saving the nation. The reader should see the explanatory note in connection with the comments on 2 Ki. 22: 17 in Vol. 2 of this COMMENTARY.

Verse 9. *At what instant* has the same sense as in verse 7. God often made favorable promises and predictions concerning nations as well as individuals, but they were made subject to certain conditions or restrictions.

Verse 10. *I will repent*, both here and in verse 8, means the Lord will change his mind concerning what he had said he would do for the nation. The fundamental meaning of repentance is "change," whether done by man or the Lord. When man repents he changes his will, and when God repents he wills a change—a change in his plans—due to the changed conditions surrounding the nation or persons involved.

Verse 11. The preceding verses of the chapter describe a special communication between God and Jeremiah in which some very important principles of divine dealing were set out before the prophet. This verse instructs him to deliver the message to the people. Jerusalem was the capital of Judah and hence they are named together frequently as in this passage. *Frame evil* is used in the sense of something unpleasant but not in the sense of wrong as the word *evil* usually means. *Return ye* is another instance of exhortation for reformation of life and calls for the distinction between the nation as a whole and certain individuals in it.

Verse 12. *There is no hope* was the way the people had of saying it was useless for the Lord to admonish them for they were determined to do as they pleased. Not only at the time of Jeremiah did they show that kind of a spirit, but it had been that way all through their history. That was why God decreed to use the only means that would bring them into a right mind regarding Him, which was to be the captivity.

Verse 13. *Virgin of Israel* is a figurative way of designating the people of God because they were supposed to be pure in their religious conduct. However, they were not and God is going to shame them by comparing them to the nations that did not have half the advantages that the Lord's people had.

Verse 14. Those advantages are compared with the pure snow on the mountains of Lebanon and the crystal waters that come from it. No man would reject such blessings for the sake of some polluted stream in another place.

Verse 15. Yet God's people had done that which was as bad or worse than such foolish conduct as described in the preceding verse. They had forsaken the true God and turned to *vanity* (false gods) and offered service to them. The result of such perversion was a stumbling from the pathway of truth and staggering along in a way not *cast up* or improved properly for traveling upon.

Verse 16. *To make their land desolate* does not mean these people committed idolatry for that purpose. But it is the Lord's decision that their course of conduct would cause him to thrust the land into such a condition. The country was to be so ruined that all who saw it would *wag their heads* which means to toss the head in scorn.

Verse 17. *East wind* is referred to a number of times in the Bible as something especially unpleasant or destructive. Smith's Bible Dictionary says the following on the subject: "The east wind crosses the sandy wastes of Arabia Deserta before reaching Palestine, and was hence termed 'the wind of the wilderness.' Job 1: 19; Jer. 13: 24. It blows with violence, and is hence supposed to be used generally for any violent wind. Job 27: 21; 38: 24; Ps. 48: 7; Isa. 27: 8; Ezk. 27: 26." Funk and Wagnalls Standard Bible Dictionary says of it: "The hot, dry wind from the desert, that fills the air with dust and is exceedingly unpleasant for man and often fatal to young vegetation. It blows generally in the spring. It is frequently referred to in the Old Testament." The figurative east wind was to consist of the Babylonian army that was to invade the country with such devastating results. *Shew them the back* means that when the enemy came against the people it would be useless for them to appeal to God, for he would turn his back upon them.

Verse 18. Physical persecution has long been a weapon of men who do not like the teaching that condemns their sinful practices. That kind of persecution was imposed on Jeremiah at times, but in the present instance they proposed attacking him with their tongues by devising some slander against him. Their grievance was his charge that the priests and other teachers such as the wise men and prophets were failing in their duty of delivering counsel according to the law. They agreed among themselves to deny Jeremiah's accusation and to maintain that the prophets would continue to deliver the proper teaching contrary to Jeremiah's predictions.

Verse 19. The attitude of the people worried Jeremiah so that he came to the Lord with a prayer for help.

Verse 20. The prophet did not complain of any physical persecution in this case, but that they had digged a pit for his *soul*. This was a reference to the persecution the enemies had devised of slandering him concerning his teaching. In doing so Jeremiah charged that they were recompensing to him *evil* for the *good* he had done in proclaiming to them the word of the Lord.

Verse 21. This verse is another of the passages that seem to show a cruel spirit in Jeremiah. But we should keep in mind that he was a true prophet of God and that such a wish as was here expressed was really an inspired prediction that such experiences were destined to come upon that wicked generation. Jeremiah was naturally a tender-hearted man and personally would not be inclined to be harsh. Yet he was always a faithful prophet and was always obedient when called upon to make severe predictions in spite of his personal feelings of pity.

Verse 22. This prediction was to be literally fulfilled when the *troop* (the Babylonian army) came against the city of Jerusalem. When the people observed the siege that was set up against them they would cry out in dismay.

Verse 23. Again let the reader consider the remarks on verse 21 as he observes the severe language of this. *Forgive not their iniquity* is the same decree in another form that has been discussed frequently in this work. The nation as a whole had gone too far in its corruption to be let off with anything less than the captivity. It was expressed as a personal prayer of Jeremiah but was really a prediction made through him, and it was to be fulfilled by the siege and captivity about to take place.

JEREMIAH 19

Verse 1. In various instances God has caused his inspired men to go through a performance that may be called "acting." The exact reason for it has not been told us, but I have offered comments and given reference to various cases in 1 Ki. 20: 35, Vol. 2 of this COMMENTARY. One of those instances of acting is in the present verse with others in the chapter. An earthenware bottle was chosen because when it is broken it cannot be repaired as might a vessel made of skins of animals. *The ancients* means the older persons among the people and the prophets. These were to represent the nation in the performance that was to be carried out in their sight.

Verse 2. The scene of the acting was to be *the valley of the son of Hinnom*, a place near the city of Jerusalem. This spot was chosen because it was the place where some of the most abominable practices of idolatry had been committed by the people.

Verse 3. When Jeremiah and his selected group reached the place he was to make the speech to them that follows. *I will bring evil upon this place, the which whosoever heareth, his ears shall tingle.* The last word is from an original that literally means to vibrate or rattle. However, the word is used figuratively and means the report of what is about to happen to this place of idolatry will overwhelm with astonishment all who hear about it.

Verse 4. *Estranged this place* has reference to the misuse that was made of it. The place had formerly been used as disposal plant or incinerator for the waste materials of Jerusalem. Such a use was right and could truly be regarded as a service pleasing to the Lord since he requires that man be cleanly and careful about that which pertains to health. But in using it for the practices of idolatry they *estranged* or took it away from the service that

God had sanctioned. *Filled with blood of innocents* was literally true for among the fearful practices of idolatry was that of burning their children as sacrifices. (See Lev. 18: 21; 2 Ki. 16: 3; 17: 31.)

Verse 5. The mere fact of having an altar on a high place would not be sinful for such a practice was done by the servants of God and without any rebuke for it (Gen. 12: 8; Judges 6: 25; 1 Sam. 7: 10; 13: 9; 1 Chr. 21: 26; 1 Ki. 18: 30). But God knew what his people would meet with when they got to the promised land, so he had it put into the law of Moses that such places for worship should not be arranged by them. Furthermore, they were to destroy all such places that had been erected by the heathen before them. Baal was one of the heathen gods of the imaginary class, and the Jews became worshipers of him even to the sacrificing of their children. The last lines of this verse simply means that such foolish practices were never a subject in the mind of God even in the least favorable sense.

Verse 6. *Tophet* was a spot in the famous valley of Hinnom near Jerusalem. This place had been used as a disposal plant for the waste materials of the city and for that reason there were fires kept burning continually. The idolatrous worshipers got to using the place for their abominable practices until Josiah defiled it in his great reformative work (2 Ki. 23: 10). The people of Judah went so far as to use their children as sacrifices to the false gods that were represented in the valley. *No more be called Tophet* does not mean the name will be forgotten, but the place will not be referred to merely as one that was known by such a name. But the great work of the Lord in destroying the enemies of righteousness who assembled in that place will be so outstanding it will be remembered because of such a great *slaughter*.

Verse 7. The priests and false prophets of Judah had given forth much *counsel* or instruction to the people that promised them peace and safety from their enemies. God said he would *make void that counsel* which means he would overthrow all their plans. The destruction of life and desecration of human bodies was to be caused by the Lord through the hand of the Babylonians.

Verse 8. Jerusalem was to be made so desolate and ruined that its sight would cause people to *hiss* or express scorn over it. Such a calamity was brought upon it and the record of it may be seen in 2 Ki. 25: 9-17.

Verse 9. It is hard to think that even a siege could produce such a state as predicted here, in which parents actually made food of their children's bodies. But such a thing had taken place before (2 Ki. 6: 29), and it should be accepted as an inspired prediction that the horrible deed would happen again.

Verse 10. Having made this speech reported in the hearing of his group, Jeremiah was to break the bottle in their sight. They would know that an earthen vessel thus shattered could not be repaired (at least by man) and thus that it was not to be used again; that its former status was over for good.

Verse 11. The prophet was then to interpret the whole performance to his group. The Lord further instructed Jeremiah to see that *they* (the men with him) would bury the pieces right there in the valley where so much of the idolatry had been committed.

Verse 12. Jeremiah was to give them further interpretation by predicting that Jerusalem would be treated in the same manner as was Tophet.

Verse 13. *Tophet* was not the only place where idolatrous worship was practiced. The houses had flat roofs and the people went up there for their services because of the convenience. Also, since they wished to offer devotions to the *host of heaven* (the planets) they would have unobstructed view of these false gods, hence their houses were to receive the same fate as Tophet. A *drink offering* was the offering of something that would have been used for drink by man and hence an article of value.

Verse 14. The preceding program was carried out in the valley of Hinnom near Jerusalem, and in the presence of the group of men that had been especially chosen to represent the nation. Jeremiah then came back into the city to speak to the people in general. He did this speaking in the *court of the Lord's house* because that was the part of the building where the common citizen was permitted to enter.

Verse 15. At the place designated in the preceding verse the prophet repeated the prediction he had uttered in the valley. *Hardened their necks* is a figure of speech, meaning they became stubborn and refused to listen to the words of the Lord. This characteristic was prominent all through the history of that nation.

JEREMIAH 20

Verse 1. All material buildings require the services of someone or more to oversee them, who might be classed as a janitor of the higher class. Having such a work it is clear as to how this chief overseer, Pashur, overheard the remarks of Jeremiah.

Verse 2. A familiar argument (?) of men who cannot answer an unpleasant exposure of their sins in old times was a resort to physical violence. Pashur having a sort of public office took undue advantage of it and persecuted Jeremiah. He first smote him then put him into the *stocks*. This was an instrument of torture used in ancient times, made in various ways and used for the purpose of revenge in many instances. Smith's Bible Dictionary describes them as follows: "Stocks. (An instrument of punishment consisting of two beams, the upper one being movable, with two small openings between them, large enough for the ankles of the prisoner.—Ed.) The term 'stocks' is applied in the Authorized Version to two different articles, one of which answers rather to our pillory, inasmuch as the body was placed in a bent position, by the confinement of the neck and arms as well as the legs, while the other answers to our 'stocks,' the feet alone being confined in it. The prophet Jeremiah was confined in the first sort, Jer. 20: 2, which appears to have been a common mode of punishment in his day, Jer. 29:26, as the prisons contained a chamber for the special purpose, termed 'the house of the pillory.' 2 Chron. 16: 10 (Authorized Version "prison-house"). The stocks, properly so called, are noticed in Job 13: 27; 33: 11; Acts 16: 24. The term used in Prov. 7: 22 (Authorized Version "stocks") more properly means a fetter." The prophet was kept in this state of torture until the next day.

Verse 3. Human nature might have prompted Jeremiah to manifest some personal resentment over the way he was treated by Pashur. However, he only delivered to him the message which the Lord had authorized concerning this wicked man. The long name to be applied to him is defined "affright from around" in the lexicon. Many proper nouns in the Bible have significant meanings and one such was used here.

Verse 4. *Terror to thyself* is something like a popular saying that a man "is afraid of himself," or that he "is afraid of his shadow." That would be an awful state of mind to come to Pashur, and just as his nerves would be in a tension, his friends and fellow citizens would be seized and taken away into the Babylonian captivity.

Verse 5. *Deliver all the strength* refers to the chief citizens of the place and 2 Ki. 24: 14-16 shows the fulfillment of the prediction. *All the treasures* means the moveable belongings and that was fulfilled in 2 Ki. 24: 13.

Verse 6. Since Pashur was a member of the nation it would be supposed that he would be taken into captivity along with the others. On account of his personal mistreatment of Jeremiah, however, he was singled out in the prediction. Another thing that made his case special was the decree that he was to die and be buried in Babylon, which was not to happen to all of the nation. Not only should he meet with that special fate, but also his friends who had endorsed him by giving a listening ear to his false prophecies. This gives us the lesson that the Lord regards a willing hearer of error in the same light as he does the speaker of it. Paul taught the same principle in 2 Tim. 4: 3, 4 concerning the false teachers of his day.

Verse 7. The word *deceived* has been rendered also by "allure" and "entice," and means that Jeremiah had simply followed the instructions of the Lord. That required him to make the unpleasant predictions against Pashur and other evil characters, and as a result he was being held in derision daily among the citizens.

Verse 8. That derision took the form of *violence and spoil*, such as his confinement in the stocks of which we have read in the beginning of the chapter.

Verse 9. The first clause of this verse indicates that Jeremiah was almost intimidated against speaking the unwelcome word of the Lord because of the pressure of persecution that was present. But his conscience, which he describes as a *burning fire*, would not let him hold back the truth, so he determined to speak it to people regardless of the persecution that might follow.

Verse 10. This verse refers to the spying and whispering conversations that were going on around the prophet.

The *defaming* means they were plotting for some sort of scandal they could start against the man who had cried out against their corrupt practices. They were all watching for his *halting* or hoping he would make some kind of slip in his life. They agreed with each other that if anyone saw the least mistep he was to tell it to the others and they also would *report it*, which means they would give the scandal further circulation. Jeremiah would not especially object to the mere fact of being watched, for he did not intend to do anything wrong anyway. But he knew that such spies as he had to deal with would not stop at any scheme within their means to trump up some false charge against him.

Verse 11. Jeremiah's dread of the enemy did not weaken his faith in the Lord and he felt confident that with His support he could overcome all opposition. One word in the definition for the original of *terrible* is "powerful," and it is used in that sense here. The word sometimes means "fearful" and it would have that meaning in this verse as it applies to the enemies of the prophet.

Verse 12. The kind of vengeance that a righteous man like Jeremiah would desire would be just and proper. *Triest the righteous* means that God suffers his righteous servants to be tested by the hardships of this life. *Reins* and *heart* ordinarily have the same meaning, but when used distinctly as in this case, the first means the intellect that rules one's conduct and the second denotes the motive that prompts it.

Verse 13. Jeremiah could personally express these sentiments because he appreciated the many favors that the Lord had given him. But he likewise wished his brethren to see the propriety of giving God all praise for their blessings.

Verses 14-18. *Cursed* is used in the sense of being unprofitable. It is an extremely strong statement of humility to show how vain the life of the prophet would have been when mentioned in the light of human strength alone. Jeremiah just got through rejoicing in the support that God had given him, which shows he believed the Lord considered him to be worth preserving. The passage therefore means to express the great appreciation the prophet had for the goodness of God, that he would preserve and care for an unworthy creature like him. Job made almost the same statements, and I have commented on the passage verse by verse. I ask the reader to see Job 3: 1-7 in Vol. 2 of this COMMENTARY.

JEREMIAH 21

Verse 1. The *Pashur* named here is not the same one who put Jeremiah in the stocks, although he was just as wicked a man. The events connected with the first man took place in the reign of Jehoiakim, while this one was in the reign of Zedekiah, the last king of Judah. At the time of this verse the army of Babylon was at the gates of Jerusalem engaging in the siege. Zedekiah wanted some information as to the prospects and sent this Pashur to Jeremiah to obtain it.

Verse 2. The inquiry that Zedekiah sent Pashur to make really amounted to a prayer for help against the king of Babylon. The spelling Nebuchadrezzar is for the same man whose name is spelled Nebuchadnezzar elsewhere.

Verse 3. Jeremiah recognized the request of Zedekiah, for he was still the king of God's people, and directed Pashur to give the answer to him.

Verse 4. When God makes use of a man or army or any other means to accomplish a certain purpose, then to oppose that means is equivalent to opposing Him. This is true even if the thing to be accomplished would have been wrong under other circumstances. For instance, the revolt of the ten tribes was a thing wrong in itself, but the time had come and the circumstances were such that God knew the king in Jerusalem deserved such a misfortune. Therefore when he sought to interfere with the movement he was rebuked by the Lord. (See 1 Ki. 11: 26-35; 12: 21-24.) Likewise when the kingdom of Judah became so corrupt with idolatry, the Lord decreed to punish it by bringing the Babylonians against the city and taking the people into captivity. Because of all this it was the same as opposing God for Judah to oppose the Babylonians, and the more submissive anyone was to them the easier it would be for him in the outcome. (See the comments at ch. 15: 2.) This is why Jeremiah sent word to Zedekiah that his weapons of defence would fail and the enemy would finally enter Jerusalem. *Babylon* was the empire whose capital was the city of that name, and the *Chaldeans* were a special group of people who were the most influential among the others. Politically the two names were used interchangeably in the time of the captivity.

Verse 5. This verse does not mean that God would have a literal army fighting as allies of the Babylonians, but he would see that their movements would succeed.

Verse 6. The success of the siege and the destruction that accompanied it were decreed by the Lord and hence would be carried out in spite of resistence from Judah.

Verse 7. *Afterward* means at the end of the siege and when the city has been taken. There will be many in it who survived the ravages of the ordeal, among whom will be King Zedekiah. God knew that this king would refuse the advice of the prophet to submit to the king of Babylon and would try to escape by fleeing. This verse is especially directed against him and his army (2 Ki. 25: 4-7).

Verse 8. The siege and captivity was inevitable, but the personal experiences of the besieged would depend upon their attitude at the time. The two kinds of experiences were generally listed under the headings of *life* and *death,* and it was left to them to decide which it would be.

Verse 9. This verse goes into more details as to the terms *life* and *death* mentioned in the preceding verse. The prediction of *sword, famine* and *pestilence* is commented upon at ch. 14: 12 which the reader should see.

Verse 10. *Evil* and *good* are not used in the moral sense but in that of being unfavorable and favorable. *Set my face* is a figurative way of saying the Lord had made up his mind and it would not be changed. *Burn it with fire* was literally done by the Babylonians as recorded in 2 Ki. 25: 9.

Verse 11. The *house* of this verse is the same as the "house of David" in the next verse which means the kingdom that descended from David.

Verse 12. This verse is worded in the form of a command as if the Lord expected the king and his people to put the order into effect at that time. It should be understood in the sense of saying these things were what they should have been doing in the past years. Actually it was too late for them to do much in the carrying out of the order for the enemy was then at the gates. *Lest my fury go out* should therefore be considered as if it said, "because of your failure to do these things mentioned my fury will go out."

Verse 13. We are sure the last comments are correct for this verse comes directly to that form of speech and the Lord says *I am against thee. Inhabitant of the valley* means the inhabitant of Jerusalem, the last word being a figurative reference to the city. (See Isa. 22: 1, 5.) *Rock of the plain* refers to the expanse of territory of which Jerusalem was the capital. The people of the city and country had boasted that no power could succeed against them hence they had turned deaf ears to the warnings that God had given them for years by the mouth of his prophets.

Verse 14. This verse is a mingling of literal and figurative language. The houses were literally burned and many of the inhabitants were slain. We have no direct history of material destruction of the forests, but they did boast of their great wooded territories. Moreover, they used trees from the forest in their service of idolatry and the captivity was to put an end to that practice.

JEREMIAH 22

Verse 1. A reference to ch. 21: 1 will tell us that Zedekiah was the king to whom the prophet was to deliver this special message.

Verse 2. The *throne of David* always meant the throne in Jerusalem because the one in Samaria was never occupied by a descendant of David. And the one in Jerusalem was attributed to that great servant of God because he received it first after it was taken from the tribe of Benjamin in the days of Saul. The crown remained in the tribe of Judah ever after as long as the people had a kingdom.

Verse 3. The conduct described in this verse is what should have been the practice all along. Instead, the strong had been permitted to overcome the weak and the rich were suffered to defraud the poor through bribery and other means.

Verse 4. We have here a passage similar to ch. 17: 24, 25 and it calls for like comments. We know it had been decidedly announced that nothing could be done to prevent the captivity and national downfall. Therefore the passage must mean that had they performed such transactions in time they would have obtained the favors described.

Verse 5. *If ye will not* should be taken to mean "since ye did not." As a punishment for it the house in Jerusalem was to become desolate.

Verse 6. A man often discards a possession because it had never been valued highly anyway. But that was not the case with Judah for God compared her to *Gilead* and *Lebanon*, two very desirable districts in Palestine. Notwithstanding this estimate of the land of Judah, God determined to cast it off for its sins against Him and to cause its cities to become depopulated.

Verse 7. God did not directly perform the acts of punishment here described but strengthened the heathen nations that came against Palestine to do so.

Verse 8. The devastation of Jerusalem was to be so evident that the passers-by would notice it and make remarks. The heathen nations did not know the Lord as the people of Judah did, yet they knew that Jerusalem had for centuries been known as a city possessed by a being called the *Lord*. Their questioning one with another was concerning the reason why the possessor of such a city would suffer it to fall into this state of desolation.

Verse 9. It was more or less common knowledge that the Jews were restricted against the worship of strange gods, and that penalties were to be imposed upon them if they practiced it. Therefore it would be understood that the conditions of ruin that met the eye came as a fulfillment of the warnings.

Verse 10. *Weep ye not for the dead.* People sometimes show sympathy for the wrong person and overlook another whose fate is actually more to be regretted. Such was the case when Jesus was being led away to crucifixion. The women were weeping for him when they should have been weeping for themselves (Luke 23: 27-29). The dead man in this verse was Josiah, the righteous king of Judah. When he died under such unfortunate circumstances (2 Ki. 23: 29; 2 Chr. 35: 22, 23) it caused a great lamentation. The words *weep ye not* do not mean that it would be improper to lament his passing for Jeremiah himself did so (2 Chr. 35: 25). The thought is that another person was to have a misfortune befall him that would be more lamentable, which was to be exiled into a foreign land without friends to accompany him.

Verse 11. The person referred to in the preceding verse was the son of Josiah. That son was not dead at the time Jeremiah was writing this prediction, but inspiration told him of the circumstances under which he would die. He is here called Shallum but was elsewhere called Jehoahaz. The Bible does not give us the reason for the extra name but it was not unusual for people to have more than one name. This man succeeded his father Josiah on the throne but was allowed to retain it only three months. He was forceably removed from it by the Egyptian king Pharoah-nechoh and taken to Egypt from which he never returned (2 Ki. 23: 33).

Verse 12. It is a sad experience not to be allowed even to see one's native land again after being banished from it. So this Shallum was destined to die in this far-away land without even being permitted to see his native land again (2 Ki. 23: 34). No wonder Jeremiah bade his people to mourn for him who suffered such a disgrace, rather than for his father who died without seeing the misfortune coming upon his son.

Verse 13. This has reference to the leaders who had enriched their own possessions at the expense of the common and poor people. They used their position unfairly because of their official standing and forced the others to serve them without wages.

Verse 14. These selfish men even boasted of the fine houses they had built, using the labor of the under classes in an overbearing way.

Verse 15. *Shalt thou reign* is a question the Lord asked these selfish leaders in his nation. Houses built of cedar usually indicated places to be used either as palaces of kings or the mansions for their residences. There would not have been so much wrong in their owning these good houses had they obtained them in a just way and also were occupying them in connection with a righteous life. As proof of this truth they were reminded of the case of their righteous ancestors who enjoyed the good things of life and at the same time received the favor of the Lord. But the reason for it was stated in connection with the subject; they practiced judgment and justice.

Verse 16. Further details are given as to why the forefathers fared so well. They judged the cause of the poor and needy, which means they gave consideration to the claims of the unfortunate classes of the citizens.

Verse 17. But the present generation was given to selfishness, even at the expense of the righteous poor of the land. If these covetous desires called for the slaying of innocent men the horrible plots were carried out.

Verse 18. The remarks of the preceding verses could truthfully have been made of the leaders generally, but the

Jeremiah 22: 19-28

Lord now comes to particulars and names a certain man. Jehoiakim was a son of Josiah and obtained the throne through the power of the Egyptian king who had deported his brother Jehoahaz, otherwise called Shallum. But Jehoiakim was a wicked ruler and practiced the injustices described in the preceding verses. Because of the oppression he forced upon the people they were actually relieved when he died, for they did not make any lamentations over it.

Verse 19. Honorable burial has always been regarded as an indication of the respect with which a person had been held, therefore the lack of it would indicate the opposite. Jehoiakim was to have his body dragged out of the city and buried with no more respect than would have been given to a dumb beast.

Verse 20. Lebanon was one of the favorite districts of Palestine from which the people sometimes got trees to form into idols. Bashan was a city in the heathen territory where much of the idolatrous practice was learned. *Thy lovers are destroyed* is an allusion to idolatry because that iniquity was compared with unfaithfulness in the marriage relation. The spots just named were connected with that corruption but were destined to be cleared of it by the captivity. The language of this verse is in the present tense as to grammatical form but is a prediction in thought.

Verse 21. *In thy prosperity* means the Lord gave his people full warning during the time when all things were going well with the nation. Had they heeded the instruction at that time they could have avoided the humiliation of the captivity.

Verse 22. As a wind will sweep things before it because of their lightness, so these *pastors* (unfaithful teachers) were to be swept away by the ("east") wind of the Babylonian army. When that takes place all the guilty ones will *go into captivity*. *Be ashamed and confounded* refers to the humiliation and confusion that was to result when the nation has been taken into Babylonian captivity.

Verse 23. *Inhabitant of Lebanon* is not literally restricted to the people who lived in that territory for it was not very near to Jerusalem the condemned city. It is mentioned in this connection because of the pride the people had in that spot and also because of the idolatrous practices that were connected with it. *Gracious* is from CHANAN and the part of Strong's definition that applies here is, "to implore (i. e., move to favor by petition)." The thought is that when these guilty people see the enemy at their gates they will plead for God to be gracious unto them.

Verse 24. The last three kings who sat on the throne of Judah were wicked men and all have been given attention by the prophet. They have not always been mentioned in the order of their reign for Zedekiah has been named already and he was the last one. The one who reigned last before him is the one named in this verse. This man had three names or at least that many forms of spelling it. To avoid confusion I will state them which are, Coniah, Jeconiah and Jehoiachin. This man was not allowed to reign but three months when he was taken off by the king of Babylon. However, he submitted to the invader according to the advice of ch. 15: 2; 21: 9, and was taken unharmed to Babylon. *Though . . . were the signet upon my right hand* means that even the most valuable possession of the Lord would be discarded if it became corrupt. This man had to suffer the humiliation of captivity, also be destined to some other personal misfortunes, yet some exceptions were made in his case as we shall see later.

Verse 25. *Seek thy life* does not mean necessarily that he would be slain, but that his life would be taken over by another. Nebuchadrezzar was king of Babylon and the Chaldeans were a special group who were outstanding citizens of the country.

Verse 26. The *other country* was Babylon and mention was made of his not being born there to emphasize the fact of its being a foreign land. *There shall ye die*. In 2 Ki. 25: 30 it is stated that certain treatments were accorded Coniah in Babylon "all the days of his life." That would mean he lived his entire life in Babylon after being taken there which fulfills the prediction in the present verse. The Biblical account of the capture of this man and his relatives is given in 2 Ki. 24: 10-16.

Verse 27. Exile in a foreign land is sad enough, but Coniah and his family were notified that they never would be permitted to return to their native land.

Verse 28. The general context shows this verse is a declaration of the Lord and not merely a question as the form of sentence construction would indicate. Therefore the words should be arranged to make them read, *this man Coniah is a despised broken idol*, etc. This does not add a single word to the passage but truly translates the original. We are not told just what particular evils Coniah had committed but they certainly were bad to have brought upon him and his family this shameful treatment.

Verse 29. The word for *earth* is also defined "land" by Strong. The verse means an emphatic call for all the people of the land to hear the word of the Lord.

Verse 30. *Childless* does not require that he never did have any children, for verse 28 says his *seed* was cast out into a strange land, and one word in the lexicon definition of *seed* is "posterity." The rest of this verse also indicates that he had seed but that no one of them would be allowed to succeed his father on the throne as was the usual procedure. Instead, the king of Babylon made his brother king of Judah who was called Zedekiah. (See 2 Ki. 24: 17; 1 Chr. 3: 15; 2 Chr. 36: 10).

JEREMIAH 23

Verse 1. The original word for *pastor* was defined at ch. 2: 8 which the reader should see. The outstanding thought is one who feeds, figuratively or literally. The priests were expected to give spiritual food or knowledge to the people (Lev. 10: 8-11; Deut. 17: 9-11; Mal. 2: 7), and the prophets were to give any special messages that the Lord regarded necessary at times. But these leading men became negligent of their duties and misused their position for their personal advantage. The Lord accuses them of scattering the sheep and threatens woe upon them.

Verse 2. *Have scattered my flock* is a figure of speech that is appropriate in connection with a shepherd which is the illustration chosen in the case. *Have driven them away* had not yet been done literally except that the people were actually alienated from God by the evil practices of these pastors. *Have not visited them* is another term appropriate to the illustration of a pastor or shepherd. A shepherd is supposed to go and look after his flock to see if any of the sheep are in need. These shepherds had about lost all care for the flock and were bestowing the provisions on themselves that the chief Shepherd had placed in their hands for His flock (Ezk. 34: 8). For this great neglect of duty the Lord decreed severe punishment upon them.

Verse 3. This verse is a prediction of the return from Babylonian captivity. The original word for *countries* also means "lands." The Babylonian Empire was considered one institution but embraced practically all the lands in the civilized world, and the Lord's people were scattered over many of these lands. *Folds* is another term that is appropriate in the list connected with a *flock*. It literally means that God's people who survive the effects of the captivity (the "remnant") will be returned to their native land in Palestine. The Biblical account of the fulfillment is in the books of Ezra and Nehemiah. The historical account of it was cited with the comments on Isa. 14: 1 in Vol. 3 of this COMMENTARY.

Verse 4. The imagery or line of illustrations of a shepherd and his flock is still used. The *shepherds* of this prediction were such teachers as Ezra and Nehemiah and the good feeding of those men is recorded in Neh. 8: 1-9.

Verse 5. Jeremiah used the same practice as that of Isaiah (though not nearly as frequently) of passing from affairs of ancient Israel to those of spiritual Israel under Christ. David was the first king of ancient Israel from the tribe of Judah, hence it was fitting that he be named in connection with the spiritual King (Jesus) who also was from the tribe of Judah (Heb. 7: 14). *Branch* means something that has sprouted from another plant and is properly applied to Christ as he was a lineal descendant from David.

Verse 6. *Judah* and *Israel* being mentioned together indicates that all 12 tribes of the nation would be in existence when Christ came to the earth. But they were to *be saved* as followers of Christ and not as Jews. At the time of this writing, however, the Jews were the people who were in the front line of attention from the Lord, hence it was logical to mention them in this specific manner.

Verses 7, 8. These verses are identical with ch. 16: 14, 15 and the reader is referred to that place for the comments.

Verse 9. Jeremiah is expressing his own feeling in this verse although the remarks also truly represent the attitude of the Lord. An inspired prophet is always speaking for the Lord even when the language sounds as if he were expressing only his own sentiments. However, Jeremiah was so unusually concerned about the affairs of his people that he would put himself into his speech at the same time he was speaking by inspiration. *The prophets* refers to the false ones who have been the object of much complaint from Jeremiah all along. *Because of the Lord* denotes that Jeremiah's disturbed condition of mind and body is caused by the disregard the prophets have for the words of the Lord.

Verse 10. Doubtless there were many men in Judah who were adulterers in the physical sense, but the charge has special reference to idolatry, which was always classed as adultery. *Swearing* is from a word that also means a curse, and here refers to the curse that the unfaithful prophets have brought on the land. The evil conditions named are somewhat prophetic and refer especially to what is destined to come upon the land as a chastisement from God.

Verse 11. The *prophet* and *priest* are the unfaithful ones who have been mentioned in so many places because of their false teaching to the people. (See ch. 5: 31.) They are called *profane* and the reason for the charge is the fact that they were practicing their wickedness in the Lord's house. Profanity consists in making a common or temporal use of a sacred thing, which these leaders were certainly doing.

Verse 12. *Slippery* is from a word that is defined "treacherous" in the lexicon, and the thought is the Lord would deprive these false teachers of any certain guidance. They have been so indifferent about His instruction for many years anyway, so now they were destined to face the future in great uncertainty.

Verse 13. This verse makes reference to the 10-tribe kingdom although it had been in exile for a century when this passage was written. When distinguished from Judah, that kingdom was called *Israel* and its capital was *Samaria*. That kingdom also had false prophets and God mentions them in this connection because he was threatening the false prophets of Judah with a punishment similar to that imposed on the others. *Prophesied in Baal* means they issued their declarations in the name of Baal.

Verse 14. Jerusalem was the capital of Judah and many of the prophets resided there or at least were near enough that much of their activity was done in that city. Adultery is continuously compared to idolatry in the Bible because both corruptions constitute unfaithfulness of one partner in a unity to the other. However, we have evidence that when these unrighteous leaders are accused of adultery it refers to the physical kind, for sometimes it is said they commit adultery with their neighbors' wives (ch. 29: 23), which would have no meaning were the writer merely considering spiritual evil. *Strengthen hands of evildoers* was done by not admonishing them of their deeds, which resulted in their continuance in sin through the encouragement given. *They are . . . as Sodom . . . as Gomorrah* means the Lord regarded these false leaders with the same disfavor as he did those ancient wicked people.

Verse 15. *Wormwood* and *gall* are used figuratively because of the meaning of bitterness that is indicated by the words. For the technical comments on the words see those offered at ch. 9: 15. *Profaneness* is defined in the lexicon as "impiety," which means a lack of true devotion.

Verse 16. This verse is directed to the people of Judah and they are admonished not to listen to these false prophets. *Vision of their own heart* means the prophecies they issued were the fruit of their own mind and not the inspiration of the Lord.

Verse 17. The main subject of these false prophecies was *peace*. They pacified the people by assuring them that no trouble was in store for them. Such false prophecies were not only a denial of the word of God, but also encouraged the people not to make any improvement in their lives.

Verse 18. This verse might properly be called a challenging question that the Lord asked concerning the false prophets. *Stood in the counsel of the Lord* would mean to have taken their stand according to the instructions which the Lord would give. These false leaders had not done so and the verse calls upon them just to name one among them who had done so, and of course they could not point to a prophet of that unfaithful group who could say he had relied upon the Lord for his instructions.

Verse 19. *Whirlwind* is a figure of speech to illustrate the storm of God's wrath against these evildoers. It was to fall in a special manner on the heads of these men who were foremost in the corrupt practices.

Verse 20. The key to the significance of this verse is in the words *not return until*. The passage is a prediction of the captivity that was to cure the nation of idolatry. When that is accomplished then the Lord's anger will *return* to himself because it will be satisfied with the results. *Latter days ye shall consider* is a specific prediction that when the captivity will have run its course, the people will take a serious view of the whole situation and will be done for good with idolatry.

Verse 21. These false prophets were acting solely as their own minds dictated and thus were on their own responsibility with no regard for the Lord.

Verse 22. Had these men been desirous of giving the proper advice to the people they would have been used by the Lord. The result of such teaching would have been to turn them from their evil way into the ways of righteousness.

Verse 23. *At hand* and *afar off* are the contrasting terms of this verse and represent the attitude the false teachers maintained toward God. In other words, they seemed to think that if God were near them they would need to "watch their step," but since he was afar off it would not matter so much. The thought offered for their pondering is that God is not so far away that he does not know what they are doing, and will bring upon them the chastisement their conduct deserves.

Verse 24. The first clause of this verse justifies the comments on the preceding one. Adam learned to his shame that man cannot hide from God because He is everywhere. On this important subject it will be well to read Psa. 139: 7-12.

Verse 25. Since God is everywhere at the same time he also sees and hears all that is done and said. When these false leaders were deceiving the people with the supposed importance of dreams, the Lord heard and knew all about it. It is true that one form of inspired revelations was that of dreams and these lying prophets took advantage of the common feeling of respect for dreams. But like many other things that God sometimes uses, these dreams were also relied upon by the unfaithful prophets.

Verse 26. This verse is the same in thought as verse 16.

Verse 27. This verse gives the motive these false prophets had for offering their deceitful dreams to the people. Jesus said that no man could serve two masters and these false prophets seemed to realize that truth. On that theory they knew the people would not become interested in Baal as long as they had the proper regard for God, hence their efforts to turn them away from Him.

Verse 28. There is nothing wrong in having a dream nor even in relating it to others, provided one does not make any false claims for it. But when a man has the ordinary experience of a dream and then pretends it to have been an inspired one he becomes a false teacher. These remarks are the explanation of this verse. If a man has a dream *let him tell a dream* (tell it as a dream only) and not pretend it to be a revelation from God. If a man really has the word of God he will be able to prove it and should be faithful in revealing it to others. The inspired writer compares a dream to *chaff* in contrast with inspired words which are *wheat*.

Verse 29. The word of the Lord is compared to *fire* because it consumes the waste materials, and to a *hammer* because it can crush the stubborness of wicked men.

Verse 30. *Stealing my words* if considered alone would not be true because no one can take anything from God by force. The explanation is in the words *from his neighbor*. By deceiving his neighbor through false dreams and prophecies he prevents him from hearing the words of God, and in this manner he steals the words from the people.

Verse 31. If the reader will underscore the pronouns *their* and *he*, the meaning of the verse will be seen. These false prophets would say what they wanted to then claim that God said it which amounted to a forgery of God's name.

Verse 32. *Prophesy false dreams* means to make false prophecies on the basis of their dreams. The chief grievance against them was that it caused the people to go astray. The original word for *lightness* is defined in the lexicon as "frivolity." God never sent out such men to prophesy to the people hence their speeches were not doing any good.

Verse 33. *Burden* means a statement or saying or message. If the people should ask these false prophets what message they had from the Lord they would be compelled to ask, *what burden?* That means they would have none to deliver, for the Lord had forsaken these false prophets and would not entrust them with any inspired messages.

Verse 34. The three classes, prophet, priest and people, had composed an informal alliance against the Lord. The first two would express false teaching and the people took pleasure in it (ch. 5: 31), and now they were all claiming these false prophecies to be a burden or message from the Lord; but God said he would punish all guilty ones.

Verse 35. Instead of affirming that such is a message from the Lord, they should only be inquirers asking truly what the message of the Lord is.

Verse 36. The people had perverted the words of the Lord and hence were unworthy of being speakers of the burden or message of the Lord. So the truth of the matter was that God's judgments would finally be poured out upon the whole nation.

Verse 37. It would always be a proper inquiry to ask a prophet what the Lord had to say, but not proper to assume that these false prophets could discover for themselves what the Lord would have them say.

Verse 38. The charge the Lord had was that these false teachers would assert that certain words were from the Lord when they were not. The Lord had even forbidden them to claim their messages were from the Lord. By considering the general context of this run of verses we may understand that the unauthorized *burden* or message these false prophets were circulating was the promise of peace assuring them that nothing was going to happen to mar their peace (ch. 6: 14).

Verse 39. In reply to the false assurances of peace preached by these unfaithful leaders, the Lord again announced the surety of the captivity.

Verse 40. The captivity was not to last for ever, for the return from it was predicted many times, but the shame of it was destined to be remembered by future generations. This has been verified by the history of the Jews down to our own times.

JEREMIAH 24

Verse 1. We have previously had some occasions of prophets who were "acting" as a means of emphasizing a subject under consideration. In this chapter we have a case where the Lord does some of it, or at least makes a literal use of the matter he wishes to impress upon Jeremiah. The case is one where some baskets were set before the temple because both represented coming events to which that institution was related. The date of the vision of the baskets is given which is just after the king of Babylon had taken Jeconiah (Jehoiachin) from his throne in Jerusalem and carried him to Babylon; that event is recorded in 2 Ki. 10-16.

Verse 2. This verse only describes the character of the figs in the basket. The good ones are said to be so because they are ripe or mature and useful, which means the others are the opposite and hence not useful.

Verse 3. We know the Lord did not ask this question for information, but for the purpose of impressing the scene on the mind of Jeremiah. The mere act of repeating a statement or describing a situation will often fasten it firmly on the memory.

Verse 4. Having fixed the scene vividly on the mind of the prophet, the Lord is going to tell him its meaning.

Verse 5. The nation as a whole was doomed to fall into the hands of the invader and be taken out of the land. But certain parts of it would be treated in a special manner through the Lord's decrees. Most of the people were to be taken unharmed to the country of Babylon proper and finally have a remnant returned to their native land of Palestine. This portion of the nation was illustrated by the good figs.

Verse 6. *Good* is used in the sense of something pleasant or favorable and not as the opposite of wrong. The good was to consist of their return to their native land, and being rebuilt as a nation with Jerusalem as its capital. *Not pluck them up* was an assurance that the nation would not again be taken into captivity as before.

Verse 7. This wholehearted return in devotion to God was fulfilled and it is recorded in the books of Ezra and Nehemiah.

Verse 8. As stated before, a part of the nation was to fare less favorably than others and that part was represented by the bad figs. This had specific reference to Zedekiah and his relatives, he being the last king to sit on the throne in Jerusalem. He ignored the admonitions of the prophet to submit peaceably to the king of Babylon. He thought he could outwit the invaders and thus thwart the inspired predictions of the prophet. He tried to escape but was overtaken, and he and his relatives were treated with great disgrace by the king of Babylon. The history of this may be seen in 2 Ki. 25: 4-7.

Verse 9. Some of the scattered people of Zedekiah's kingdom were taken off to Egypt or other places in the earth many of whom were never accounted for afterward. A glimpse of this misfortune can be seen in Jeremiah 43.

Verse 10. For comments on the three items, *sword, famine* and *pestilence*, see those in connection with ch. 14: 12.

JEREMIAH 25

Verse 1. This verse gives some clear information on important dates. We notice that the fourth year of Jehoiakim corresponds with the first year of the king of Babylon. (See 2 Ki. 24: 1.) Again we are reminded that the Bible is not strictly chronological in its record of events. This verse leaves the time of the capture of Zedekiah who was the last king of Judah, and takes us back to the time when the king of Babylon made his first hostile invasion into Palestine. That date should be remembered as the beginning proper of the historic 70-year captivity. This is treated at length in the comments on 2 Ki. 24: 1 in Vol. 2 of this Commentary.

Verse 2. *The which* means *the word* referred to in verse 1. Since the inspired revelations were given to the prophets in "installments," we can understand why the same date may be given for various "words" from the Lord.

Verse 3. The actual date of the present "word" is the 23rd year of Josiah according to the calculation of this verse. In this instance the prophet goes back to the time when he had first begun to write and gives a brief review of his work of admonition for the people and of their indifference to his words.

Verse 4. There were other prophets in the service of the Lord who were not classed as writing prophets but who delivered their messages orally. Many of these had tried to admonish the nation but their words also had been ignored.

Verse 5. *They said* means these lesser prophets who did not write their exhortations. They admonished the people to return to the faithful service for the Lord in order to retain His protection from the enemy.

Verse 6. The chief corruption of the nation was the worship of idols which are called false gods. Had they been true to the God of Heaven they would always have received the divine blessings. *Do you no hurt* means that God would not have decreed to punish the nation as he now is threatening.

Verse 7. All of these admonitions were refused and the people continued to serve their man-made gods to the disrespect of the true God.

Verse 8. *Because ye have not* is a key to many of the passages in this book that may not be worded as clearly as this. Frequently the language will seem to offer the promise of continued favor from God on the condition *if ye will* do so and so, when we know that according to the general context all hope for averting the national downfall was past. With the above key we may understand all such indirect passages to mean the people must go into punishment because they had not done as commanded.

Verse 9. This verse is a prediction of the invasion by the Babylonian army. The *north* is explained by the historical note at Isa. 14:31 in volume 3 of this Commentary. Nebuchadrezzar is called *my servant* because he was to carry out the plan of the Lord regarding the invasion, and not with reference to his personal life.

Verse 10. Grain for bread was ground by millstones, but the country was to be so desolate and shorn of its crops that the millstones would not be needed. Hence the stopping of such sounds would be caused by the condition of famine.

Verse 11. This predicts the total length of the Babylonian captivity which was to be 70 years. It began with the fourth year of Jehoiakim and ended with the overthrow of Babylon by the Persians in 536 B.C.

Verse 12. Babylon was to be punished for her wicked attitude towards God's people. He used various heathen men and nations to carry out his plans, but never would permit them to take any personal satisfaction out of it. *Babylon* was the name of the kingdom and the *Chaldeans* were a special group of citizens in that kingdom. The historical fulfillment of this overthrow of Babylon is quoted with the comments on Isa. 13: 1 in volume 3 of this Commentary.

Verse 13. *That is written in this book* could mean either that Jeremiah's predictions against Bablyon had been composed at the date of this chapter, or that the declaration was

Jeremiah 25: 14-28

made in prospect of the completed book. In either case the important thought is that God would back up the predictions of the righteous prophet and bring the deserved punishment upon the wicked nations.

Verse 14. *Serve themselves of them* denotes that many nations will take advantage of the ones that have mistreated God's people. As one specific instance we might cite the Medes and Persians who *served themselves* (helped themselves) to the property of the Babylonians on the night of Belshazzar's feast (Dan. 5: 30, 31).

Verse 15. The prophet now comes to the front and does the speaking for the Lord, whereas he has been wording his writing as if God was doing the speaking direct. Wine and all items connected with the industry are used figuratively in the Bible to represent wrath and vengeance. In keeping with this usage of figures the prophet is told to take charge of the cup of wrath that is in the hand of God and cause the nations to drink from it. This is a figurative way of telling the prophet to pass the Lord's threats of vengeance on to the nations.

Verse 16. This verse describes the confusion that will be caused among the nations over the chastisement that the Lord will inflict upon them.

Verse 17. Again the figurative cup is used to indicate that Jeremiah obeyed the order of the Lord and delivered to the nations his predictions against them.

Verse 18. This cup of God's wrath contained enough to serve all who were deserving of it. So the first drink was taken by Judah with her capital of Jerusalem. That drink was to be realized when the Babylonians took possession of the city and led the people away into captivity.

Verse 19. Another nation that was to drink from the cup of God's wrath was the Egyptian. God had a grievance of long standing against it, for he never forgot the 4-century enslavement by that country of his people in the time of Moses. And down to the time of this writing it had and was still unfriendly toward them.

Verse 20. The cup of God's wrath must have been large and well filled in view of all the nations that needed to drink from it. The exact time or circumstance when they took this drink may not be known at present, but I shall try to identify them. *Uz* was the land south and east of Palestine and is familiar to Bible readers because of its connection with Job (ch. 1: 3). The *Philistines* were a people located along the eastern shore of the Mediterranean Sea and on the western side of Palestine. The other names in this verse were towns in the country of the Philistines.

Verse 21. The land of *Edom* was occupied by the descendants of Esau. The *Moabites* and *Ammonites* were descended from Lot, and these three countries were just east of the Jordan located in a north and south line of territory.

Verse 22. *Tyre* and *Zidon* lay near the sea on the northwest border of Palestine. *Isles beyond the sea* is worded in the margin, "region by the seaside," and the lexicon agrees with it.

Verse 23. The towns named were trading centers for Tyre and located near her.

Verse 24. *Arabia* was the vast extent of territory east of Palestine. It was referred to as a desert but various tribes occupied it from time to time and occasionally made journeys into other countries.

Verse 25. *Zimri* was an unimportant person whose ancestry is uncertain. *Elam* later became known as Persia and the two formed the Medo-Persian Empire which is well known to all students of history.

Verse 26. The *north* is a general reference to the various peoples who lived north and east of Palestine, and who generally appeared from the north when coming into the land. Among all these peoples one is especially named for obvious reasons and that is *Sheshach*. According to Strong, Moffatt and Smith's Bible Dictionary this is a symbolic name for Babylon. It is interesting that in this group of verses mentioning the heathen people who were to drink of the cup of God's wrath, the list begins with Egypt and ends with Babylon. That agrees with the history because Egypt was the first nation to enslave Israel as a people and Babylon was the last.

Verse 27. This verse is an emphatic summing up of the experiences to be had by those who were destined to drink of the cup of God's wrath.

Verse 28. Sometimes a child or other patient refuses to drink of a cup prepared for his condition. In such a case it is necessary for the parent or nurse to use force and compel him to drink. On the same principle it might be these heathen nations would not be willing to drink of this cup, hence the prophet was told to see that they *shall certainly drink.*

Verse 29. The preceding verse dealt with the enforced drinking from the cup of the wrath of God. The nations were notified that they would be compelled to drink of the cup which means they would have to feel the sting of divine chastisement. This verse continues the subject and a reasoning is given for the decree. God reminds them that even his own city was to be chastised, and so they could not reasonably expect to escape. This circumstance offers a useful comment on 1 Pe. 4: 17, 18 where it is said that judgment was to begin at the house of God. If such a group must feel the strictness of God's discipline then surely the ungodly and sinners will not escape.

Verse 30. The Lord is continuing his instructions to the prophet and urging him to prophesy to the nations. He is to warn them of the vigor with which God was going to express himself from his throne. *Shout as they that tread the grapes* is just an illustration of the intensity of God's voice drawn from a custom connected with wine making. Smith's Bible Dictionary gives a description of that activity and among other things it says: "The 'treading' was effected by one or more men, according to the size of the vat. They encouraged one another by shouts."

Verse 31. The original word for *controversy* is defined as "contest" by Strong. The meaning of the clause is that the nations have opposed the Lord which virtually amounts to a challenge from them to show His power as against that of the gods of their service. God has accepted the challenge and all who are acquainted with the ability of God will have no doubt as to the outcome.

Verse 32. The figures of speech in this verse refer to the general disturbances that will arise between the nations. One of the means that God has frequently used to defeat his enemies was to set them against each other. The effect is often like a whirlwind coming through the country.

Verse 33. *The slain of the Lord* means those who will be slain by each other through the effect of the Lord's plan concerning them.

Verse 34. The *shepherds* were the priests and prophets who were supposed to feed the flock of God with spiritual food. (See Lev. 10: 11; Deut. 17: 9 and Mal. 2: 7.) But these shepherds had fed themselves instead of the flock. *Days of your slaughter* refers to the time when they were doomed to be cut off in their iniquity. *Your dispersions are accomplished* is a prediction that the unfaithful are soon to be captured and taken into exile in a foreign land.

Verse 35. The whole nation was destined to suffer when the captivity came but the *shepherds* (leaders) were condemned more severely.

Verse 36. These terms are rather figurative, and all have reference to the leaders of the nation, such as the prophets and priests. They had been living for themselves and enjoying the pasture instead of leading the flock into it; now that pasture is to be taken from them.

Verse 37. *Peaceable habitation* refers to the condition of security that these pastors made themselves believe they possessed. Those "habitations" were going to be destroyed by the ravages of the Babylonian invasion.

Verse 38. A *covert* is a hiding place such as the den of a lion. The beast is secure in his covert in ordinary circumstances, but when a flood from the overthrow of the river reaches the den he will forsake it. The Lord was going to bring the flood of the invading army over the land and the unfaithful shepherds would be driven from their situation of false security.

JEREMIAH 26

Verse 1. According to 2 Ki. 24: 1 and Dan. 1: 1 the Babylonian captivity proper began just after the third year of Jehoiakim king in Judah. The present verse is dated at the first year of this reign and hence on the very eve of the captivity.

Verse 2. The Lord's house was the headquarters of the nation both religiously and politically. That would make it the most appropriate place in which to utter the important messages of divine instruction and warning. At this place the prophet would have opportunity to speak to *all the cities of Judah* because their people had to come here to perform their worship and other duties.

Verse 3. *If so be* again brings up the apparent difficulty in the language concerning the fate of the country. This and many other passages sound as if the people were still given the chance to reform with the promise of averting the captivity, yet it had been declared that nothing could be done to prevent it. But the matter will be clear if we observe the distinction between the nation as a whole and certain worthy individuals in it. Had the nation always done the things that are now being mentioned in connection with the proviso *IF*, then it as a whole would never have been doomed to the captivity. Since that was not done, the Lord decreed that the captivity was necessary to refine the nation as a whole, but that the better individuals could be given special consideration on condition of their personal reformation of life, hence the many exhortations of which we may read. It will be well for the reader to see the note at 2 Ki. 22: 17 in volume 2 of this Commentary.

Verse 4. The words *if ye will not hearken* should be understood in the sense of "since ye did not hearken."

Verse 5. A word that is offered through a servant of the Lord is just as binding as that delivered directly by Him. *Rising up early* is a figure to indicate the promptness and eagerness with which the true prophets delivered their inspired mesages.

Verse 6. *Shiloh* was the headquarters for the ark at the time of its capture by the enemy (1 Sam. 4: 11). That was a great misfortune for Israel and one from which they never fully recovered, for the ark never again was replaced in the tabernacle. The circumstance is referred to as an illustration of the disaster soon to come upon Jerusalem the capital of Judah. *Curse* is from a word that means "to make light of," and that was done to Jerusalem by the nations after the city was demolished by Babylon.

Verse 7. The three divisions of the nation were represented at the hearing when Jeremiah uttered the predictions against them. Responsibility for the national corruption was placed on the three classes though not to the same extent. The relative degree of responsibility may be seen in ch. 5: 31.

Verse 8. It has always been a trait of man to dislike even the truth if it condemns his conduct, but the foolish thing about it is that he will blame it onto the one who delivers the unwelcome truth. What is still more unreasonable is his notion that he can avoid the fulfilment of unpleasant predictions by destroying the one who has spoken them. It would be as logical to think of escaping the effects of a cancer by slaying the doctor who discovered the disease. So the three classes of the people of Judah threatened Jeremiah with death because of his predictions.

Verse 9. There was a general protest against Jeremiah over his prophesying against the city, among the ones who had assembled in the house of the Lord.

Verse 10. The report of the protest reached the ears of the *princes*. The original for that word is defined, "A head person (of any rank or class)." It is used to refer to the important attaches of the palace of personal residence of the king. Upon learning of the commotion in the house of the Lord these princes came up and sat down at one of the entries.

Verse 11. Note the priests and prophets pronounced a death sentence upon Jeremiah merely because he had prophesied against the city, not that it was a false prophecy. They were incensed at the mere thought of being criticized by Jeremiah.

Verse 12. Their tirade against Jeremiah did not intimidate him, but he declared that his prophecy against the place was by the order of the Lord.

Verse 13. This verse is another instance that calls for the distinction between the nation as a whole and certain good individuals in it. See the long note at 2 Ki. 22: 17 in volume 2 of this Commentary.

Verse 14. Jeremiah had done his duty and his conscience was clear. He would not use any resistance against them no matter what they saw fit to do unto him.

Verse 15. As a solmen warning, however, he affirmed that his death at their hands would bring the guilt of innocent blood upon them. This warning might not prevent them from putting him to death, but it would clear him of all responsibility for the act. Should he not protest his innocence, his very silence might be interpreted as an indication of guilt of some kind.

Verse 16. The princes and people then took a more favorable view of the case. They declared that the prophet was not worthy of death; not merely because of what he had said, but because it was said in the name of the Lord. Whether favorable or unfavorable, when a man delivers the word of the Lord it should be respected.

Verse 17. These *elders* were not officials but were men who were influential because of their advanced years and extended experience.

Verse 18. The elders took up the case in behalf of Jeremiah and supported their position by citing a case in the history of their nation. They referred to Micah who prophesied against Jerusalem in the days of Hezekiah the king. That prophecy may be read in the book that bears his name (ch. 3: 12).

Verse 19. It was asked if the king of Judah acted as these men demanded to be done to Jeremiah. They made their own answer which was a negative one. Instead of doing violence to Micah, Hezekiah repented and went to the Lord in a plea for mercy and the prayer was heard and God showed him great compassion.

Verse 20. Another case in point was cited that took place in the days of Jehoiakim. Urijah prophesied *according to* which means he prophesied in a similar way as did Jeremiah against the place.

Verse 21. Jehoiakim was angered by the words of Urijah and threatened to kill him, but he fled to Egypt and thus escaped death for the time being.

Verse 22. In his wickedness Jehoiakim determined to have his way against Urijah. He got up a group of men headed by Elnathan and sent them into Egypt after Urijah.

Verse 23. These men forced the prophet to come with them back to Jehoiakim in Jerusalem. That wicked king slew the prophet and showed his contempt for him by putting him in the graves of the *common people* which means where the public in general was buried. This was intended as an insult to Urijah's position as a prophet, because they had tombs set apart for their especial use (Matt. 23: 29). By denying Urijah honorable burial in the tombs of the prophets Jehoiakim thereby deposed him from the honorable class of the prophets of God.

Verse 24. All of the facts connected with the case of Jehoiakim are not stated here, but they were doubtless known by the persons dealing with Jeremiah, that the wicked king of Judah had to suffer for his treatment of Urijah. In view of the cases that had just been cited in the preceding verse (16-23), Ahikam, a righteous man, spoke up in behalf of Jeremiah. *Nevertheless* is a somewhat difficult rendering of the original word which Strong defines, "a particle of affirmation, surely." The thought of the verse is that the writer is affirming that Ahikam took Jeremiah's part and defended him against being put to death.

JEREMIAH 27

Verse 1. Jehoiakim's original name was Eliakim but it was changed to this other name by the king of Egypt who had taken a hand in the affairs of Jerusalem (2 Ki. 23: 31-35). Jehoahaz was the natural successor of his father Josiah, but he was displeasing to God who suffered the king of Egypt to take this temporary control and place his brother Jehoiakim (Eliakim) on the throne. It was in the first year of his reign that Jeremiah received the message from God that is in this chapter. It was about the time when the king of Babylon was coming up to Jerusalem to form a sort of alliance with the king of Judah. God knew that could not be permanent and that Nebuchadnezzar, king of Babylon, would take control over Judah and other lesser kingdoms near. It was God's will that all nations be subject to the king of Babylan that he might form the first of the four world empires later spoken of by Daniel (ch. 2: 36-40; 5: 17-19). It was best therefore for the nations to submit peaceably to Babylon and the present message from God to Jeremiah was on that subject.

Verse 2. Here is another case where the prophet was to do some of the "acting" that has been mentioned a number of times. Governments have frequently been illustrated by a yoke (Matt. 11: 29; 1 Tim. 6: 1). That is because a yoke must be used by two if it is of the desired force, and a government must also be a co-operative proposition if it accomplishes the expected purpose. "A government derives its just power from the consent of the governed" is as true in this instance as all others. That does not mean that people cannot be controlled against their will for we know they can and have been so controlled. But the most satisfactory situation will exist when the governor and the governed co-operate. That is why the prophet was to bear the present message to the nations being represented soon at the court of Zedekiah. A *bond* was the same as a halter signifying the creature was under control, and a *yoke* indicated that he would be required to do service. Jeremiah was first to put them on his own neck which was his part of the acting and to denote that certain restraints and services would be imposed on human beings.

Verse 3. The first three places named were just east of the Jordan and the next two were on the west side of Palestine. These representatives of the governments came to counsel with Zedekiah about resisting the power of the king of Babylon. They were all weaker than Judah and thought that together they could throw off the yoke of the distant ruler.

Verse 4. These ambassadors of the governments were to be shown the bonds and yokes that Jeremiah had worn for a little while on his neck. This sight was supposed to impress them with the importance of the situation, and they were to take a message back to their masters in their home communities.

Verse 5. The message was to begin by a statement as to who made everything, that it was the God of Israel. Very logically, then, the maker of anything would have the right and power to give it to whomsoever he saw fit.

Verse 6. In the exercising of this right the Lord had given the things into the hand of Nebuchadnezzar king of Babylon. *My servant* does not refer to his personal life for he was a heathen and had many grievous faults. It refers to the service he was called upon to render to God in his great plan of the nations.

Verse 7. This short verse contains a very important prediction that will extend through a period of 70 years. *Son and son's son* indicates that the rule given to Nebuchadnezzar was to continue for some generations after him. *Until the very time of his land come* means the rule of Nebuchadnezzar would continue through his successors until the time when his land, too, was to be ruled by another power. *Then many nations . . . shall serve themselves* (help themselves) to the land of Babylon. The history of the ages shows the fulfillment of this prediction, for the Babylonian Empire lasted 70 years and was taken over by the Medes and Persians. The Biblical account of this is in the books of Ezra and Nehemiah, and the historical account may be seen with the comments on Isa. 13: 1 in volume 3 of this Commentary.

Verse 8. Since this rule of the king of Babylon was to be by the decree of God it would be folly for any other nation to resist it. The best thing for them would be to accept the yoke of his government (symbolized by the literal yoke that Jeremiah showed them) and submit peaceably. To resist Nebuchadnezzar in this case would be the same as resisting God which no king could do and succeed. Such a nation was destined to be punished with the threefold rod of *sword, famine,* and *pestilence.* The manner in which this kind of chastisement was accomplished is described at ch. 14: 12.

Verse 9. The *prophets, dreamers, enchanters* and *sorcerers* were persons in the ancient nations who claimed to have supernatural knowledge of the fates overhanging cities and kingdoms. They were frauds but possessed a strange influence over their people. They had been advising them to resist the power of Nebuchadnezzar and assuring them that they would be able to throw off his yoke.

Verse 10. *Prophesy a lie . . . to remove you.* This does not mean their purpose in prophesying the lie was to remove them, but the Lord means their false promises of security will result in that. The reason is that the people will believe these lying prophecies and refuse to submit willingly to the king of Babylon. Then they will be taken over by that king who will remove them out of their own land. The king of Babylon will be able to accomplish this because the Lord declared it so when he said *I should drive you out.*

Verse 11. The nations that accept the Babylonian yoke without resistance will be compelled to be under the rule of Babylon, but will be permitted to live in their own communities and serve as tillers of the ground.

Verse 12. Jeremiah gave the same advice to Zedekiah that he had given to the ambassadors of the heathen groups. Zedekiah was still on the throne of Judah in Jerusalem but was destined to be the last king that nation was ever to have because of its resistance to God's will. Had the king of Judah accepted the counsel of Jeremiah he would still have been subject to Babylon, but he would have been permitted to serve out his days in Palestine as a vassal king of Nebuchadnezzar. It also would have saved the lives of his people instead of having them destroyed by the invader.

Verse 13. Even though the nation as a whole was doomed to go into captivity, Zedekiah and his family could have escaped personal hardship had they conducted themselves in the proper manner. Jeremiah pleaded with them to hearken to the word of the Lord which he was delivering unto them.

Verse 14. Jeremiah realized that his people were being misled by the false prophets and hence he warned them not to listen to their advice.

Verse 15. *That I might drive you out* is explained at verse 10. The false prophets and the people who listened to them were doomed to perish.

Verse 16. The priests were the ones who had charge of the service of the vessels in the house of the Lord. Many of these vessels had been taken away by the king of Babylon (2 Ki. 24:13). In keeping with the other false prophecies of consolation, these lying prophets assured the priests their instruments of service would soon be returned to them. Jeremiah exhorted them not to believe these promises for they were not authorized of God.

Verse 17. *Serve the king of Babylon* means for them to submit to his rule politically. That is as far as their service would have been required if they had submitted as the Lord demanded. But all who did not thus submit were also to serve the false gods of the Babylonians as a cure for their own idolatry (ch. 16:13).

Verse 18. Not all of the vessels of the Lord's house had been taken to Babylon at this time. Had the proper conduct been performed by the king of Judah and his leading people, many of the articles of service could have been retained at Jerusalem. The necessary number of priests could have been left in the city to continue the service, even though they would have been under the rule of the Babylonians. These false prophets had claimed to be speaking by the sanction of God. Now Jeremiah challenges them to act consistently and pray to that same God whom they profess to be serving and ask him to spare these vessels.

Verse 19. The articles named had been made by Solomon the third king of Israel in Jerusalem (1 Ki. 6 and 7); they had not yet been taken away by Nebuchadnezzar.

Verse 20. But he had taken the king who had preceded Zedekiah whose name is here spelled Jeconiah. He had also taken captive many of the chief men of the city.

Verse 21. The present message to Zedekiah and his leaders is that many of these articles were still left in the house and should have been destined to remain longer if the king had obeyed the word of the Lord.

Verse 22. But upon the evil conduct of the king, all these things were to be taken to Babylon and remain there until the Lord *visited them.* That means the day when God would overthrow Babylon and reclaim his people from captivity. At that time these vessels also were to be returned to Jerusalem and the fulfillment of this prediction is recorded in Ezra 1: 7-11.

JEREMIAH 28

Verse 1. The preceding chapters dealt with the false prophets generally while this one gives the history of a particular one. Hananiah was a false prophet but went into a more particular form of prophesying, even to the extent of doing some acting as other prophets had done. This man appeared in the house of the Lord and in the presence of Jeremiah and the priests and the people assembled there. Thus the setting would seem to give to this prophet an appearance of dignity.

Verse 2. Hananiah opened his prophecy by connecting it with the true God, the same One whom Jeremiah served. And, like the true prophets, he made his prophecy in the present tense in speaking of an event yet to come.

Verse 3. It gives a prediction the appearance of genuineness to go into particulars, so Hananiah stated the time when his would be fulfilled. Since it was to be only two years to wait it would naturally sound good to the people who were then stinging with the disgrace of subjugation to Nebuchadnezzar's forces. It would certainly be heartening to see the return of the holy vessels of service that had been taken to Babylon, hence this prophet promised that event to the priests.

Verse 4. Jeconiah had been taken to Babylon and it was declared that he would never leave that place (ch. 22: 24-30). Now this prophet Hananiah reversed this and predicted that the said captive would be returned to Jerusalem together with all the others who had been taken into that foreign land.

Verse 5. Jeremiah made his reply to Hananiah in the presence and hearing of the priests and people. What he had to say would be a matter of record having been witnessed by a number of persons and in a public place.

Verse 6. Jeremiah was entirely free from prejudice or envy of another prophet. He also was affectionately interested in the happiness of his people. If the Lord had changed his mind and had decreed to reverse the prediction which had been made, his faithful prophet was willing to say *amen* to it.

Verse 7. *Nevertheless* signifies that Jeremiah was not accepting the favorable prediction of Hananiah blindly and without expressing himself on the subject.

Verse 8. He reminded Hananiah that they were not the only men who had ever prophesied of unfavorable events to come upon the nations. The implication was that when the wars came it proved those men to be true prophets.

Verse 9. On the same principle of the preceding verse, if Hananiah has prophesied with authority, then the Lord will sustain it by bringing about the desirable events predicted. The whole circumstance may be likened to that of Elijah and the prophets of Baal (1 Ki. 18) in which a test was made to prove who was the true God. Jeremiah was willing for the outcome to prove whether he or Hananiah was a true prophet, and thus it amounted to a challenge to make such a test.

Verse 10. Hananiah virtually accepted the challenge by doing some "acting" in that he took the yoke from the neck of Jeremiah and broke it.

Verse 11. The yoke having been broken in the presence of the people, Hananiah spoke to them also and interpreted his action, that it meant the Babylonian yoke would be broken from the necks of all the nations then bearing it. This ended the issuing and accepting of the challenge for the time and Jeremiah went his way to await the action of the Lord regarding the proposed test.

Verse 12. After the preceding "challenge" had been made and apparently accepted, the Lord entered the case again and spoke to Jeremiah.

Verse 13. He was to contact Hananiah and deliver the latest message from the Lord. The pronoun *thou* occurs twice but has different antecedents. The first is Hananiah and the second is Jeremiah, for the Lord was still speaking to him. He was to say to Hananiah, *Thou hast broken the yokes of wood*. Then the Lord, speaking directly to Jeremiah said, *but thou shalt make for them yokes of iron*. The force of the language was that nothing would be gained by destroying the yokes of wood, for other and stronger ones would be made and fastened upon their necks.

Verse 14. The Lord here made his interpretation of the action and prediction. It left the matter where it was before Hananiah intruded with his false prophecies of peace. The several nations then under the power of Nebuchadnezzar were still to serve him and he was to have control of their personal property.

Verse 15. Having received this confirming message from God, Jeremiah knew that Hananiah was a false prophet and he accused him accordingly to his face.

Verse 16. Moreover, he pronounced a sentence of death upon him. He did not make his prediction in general terms as a false prophet might have done, but set the time which was to be yet that same year.

Verse 17. Hananiah died the 7th month of that year and the prediction of Jeremiah was made the 5th month (verse 1), thus bringing a prompt fulfillment of the sentence against this wicked man.

JEREMIAH 29

Verse 1. The Babylonian captivity as a whole began in 606 B.C. and ended in 536 B.C., 70 years in all. It began at the end of Jehoiakim's 3rd year and ended at the overthrow of Belshazzar on the night of his noted feast. However, the period had three stages in the beginning which are sometimes referred to as the 1st, 2nd and 3rd captivities for the purpose of fixing certain dates. Another manner of designating them is to do so under the name of the king who was reigning in Judah at the time of the one referred to. The three kings were Jehoiakim, Jeconiah (Jehoiachin) and Zedekiah, who were subdued by Nebuchadnezzar but allowed to sit for a time on the throne in Jerusalem. These facts must be kept in mind or confusion may result from some of

Jeremiah 29: 2-14

the statements regarding the Jews in their relation to the Babylonians.

Verse 2. The capture of Jeconiah and his family marked the "second" captivity and Jeremiah sent his letter to his brethren in Babylon after that event. The prophet was under the authority of the Babylonian Empire, but was not required to leave Palestine due to the respect the captain had for him (ch. 40: 1-6). Jeremiah wished his brethren in Babylon to be like a "model prisoner" while in captivity and sent the letter for that purpose which was for their own advantage.

Verse 3. The men named were the bearers of Jeremiah's letter to the Jews in Babylon. They went by the authority of Zedekiah, king of Judah, and hence their mission had the dignity of an official one.

Verse 4. The Jews in Babylon should have been impressed with the letter of Jeremiah since it was dictated by the Lord. Also by the fact that He was the one who had caused them to be taken into captivity. With the assurance that God always has an important purpose for everything he does, then profound attention should have been given to any message sent to them by His direction.

Verse 5. The general subject of the letter was for them to prepare for a long stay in Babylon. That they should plant gardens and eat of the products of the same. They should not only build houses, which could be merely an occupation for exercise, but they were told they would get to live in the houses.

Verse 6. It was predicted that the number of the Israelites would be generally reduced by the captivity (Isa. 1: 9; 10: 22), yet it also was indicated by these same predictions that a number would be left and the history shows that it was done (Ezra 2: 64). But in order for that to occur it was necessary for the people to continue their normal ways of family life as far as the conditions would permit. So the prophet told them to marry and produce families for the continuance of them as a people.

Verse 7. *Seek the peace of the city* meant for them to be orderly and respectful toward the city in which they might be located. If they were resentful under their bondage it would only add to their unpleasant situation. Also, if the said town where they were having their residence should have any difficulty with outside people, these Israelites would have to share in that trouble, hence they were to seek its peace.

Verse 8. Before the captivity ever began the false prophets kept telling the people there would be no war nor trouble. Their visions of peace proved to be false and yet in the face of that fact they had the boldness to claim that the captivity would soon be over. Jeremiah admonished his people not to be deceived by them.

Verse 9. Jeremiah plainly charged these prophets with lying, and that they were uttering their falsehood in the name of the Lord. A man might write a check when he knew he had no funds to make it good and that would be a sin. It would be still worse if he made out a check and signed the name of another man to it without his consent. That would be like the wicked action of these prophets, for they delivered their false predictions and then claimed to have the authority of the Lord for them.

Verse 10. The exact length of the captivity was predicted here as it had been done in ch. 25: 12. History shows it began B.C. 606 and ended B.C. 536. *I will visit you* is a prediction of the influence God would exert on the governments concerned, which would cause them to release the Jews so that they could return to their own land of Palestine. That history is in the books of Ezra and Nehemiah for the Biblical account, and the secular history may be seen in the comments on Isa. 14: 1, volume 3 of this Commentary.

Verse 11. *Thoughts* and *think* have the same meaning except as to grammatical form, the first being a noun and the other a verb. The clause means that God understood what he was planning concerning his people. The plots referred to in this place were in regard to the restoration of the people of God to their own country.

Verse 12. *Then* is an adverb of time and applies to the date when the captivity was to be terminated. It would then be according to God's will to pray for deliverance from captivity, hence such a prayer would be answered.

Verse 13. However, even when it is God's will that his people be released, their prayer for divine favor must be offered with sincere hearts.

Verse 14. *All the nations* refers to the various peoples that made up the

Babylonian Empire. In course of the 70-year period the Jews became more or less scattered among various districts, and this verse was a prediction that they would be called out from such places to return to Palestine.

Verse 15. The preceding verses were that part of Jeremiah's letter intended for the encouragement of the Jews who were better disposed toward the Lord. This verse starts the part directed toward the false prophets among them and the people who had been listening to them. Certain ones had been denying the predictions of Jeremiah about the extent of the captivity. They also denied that any more of the nation yet remaining in Jerusalem were to follow their brethren into Babylon.

Verse 16. The king referred to was Zedekiah who was the last man to occupy the throne in Jerusalem. It was called the throne of David because he was the first man of the tribe of Judah to sit on that throne.

Verse 17. The things threatened in this verse were to come on the Jews still left in Palestine and who had been listening to the false prophets.

Verse 18. *Persecute* does not have the ordinary meaning for God never treats anyone in that way regardless of his deserts. It comes from the Hebrew words and the meaning is to pursue or chase one with hostile intent. The means the Lord proposed to use in bringing about the punishment threatened against his people was the one frequently mentioned; sword, famine and pestilence. (See the comments on this subject at ch. 14: 12). The meaning of the *nations* is explained at verse 14.

Verse 19. God always gives man an opportunity to know what is right before punishing him for wrongdoing. He had sent his inspired prophets to the people to instruct and admonish them but they would not give heed. *Rising up early* is from SHAKAM and Strong defines it, "Literally to load up (on the back of a man or beast), i.e. to start early in the morning." The meaning here is that God was prompt in starting his prophets on their mission of admonition to his people.

Verse 20. The part of Jeremiah's letter starting with this verse is again directed toward the captives in Babylon to warn them concerning the false prophets.

Verse 21. The punctuation as the A.V. has this verse might be somewhat confusing in the use of the preposition "of." It will help clarify the thought by wording it as follows: "The God of Israel says thus of Ahab, etc." This Ahab and Zedekiah were false prophets in Babylon who deceived the captives by their lying predictions, and whose false assurances had a tendency to incite a spirit of rebellion against the king. The letter said that these false prophets would be delivered into the hand of the king of Babylon who would slay them in the sight of the captives.

Verse 22. The manner of death that Nebuchadrezzar inflicted on these false prophets was by roasting them in the fire. The publicity that was given to this terrible execution is indicated by the fact that "all the captivity" would talk about it.

Verse 23. If a man loses his respect for the truth of God he is likely to become corrupt in his personal conduct. These false prophets committed *villany* ("moral wickedness."—Strong) by violating their neighbors' wives. They sought to hide their abominable conduct by issuing false prophecies in the name of God.

Verse 24. Shemaiah was a false prophet in Babylon who sent rebellious letters to certain ones back in Jerusalem, and Jeremiah's letter was addressed to him in part.

Verses 25, 26. One of the letters of Shemaiah was sent to Zephaniah who was a priest in Jerusalem. We know that priests were expected to be teachers of the people as well as to be presiding at the sacrifices (Lev. 10: 11; Deut. 17: 9; Mal. 2: 7), but it is not clearly shown that they were to exercise the kind of work claimed by Shemaiah. But regardless of that question, it is certain they would not have had the right to persecute a good man as this false prophet demanded to have done.

Verse 27. Shemaiah did not like the message that Jeremiah had sent to the Jews in Babylon, and he complained to Zephaniah because he did not criticize the prophet.

Verse 28. Shemaiah correctly reported the contents of Jeremiah's letter although he did not like it because of his own falsifying prophecies to the captives.

Verse 29. There is no evidence that Zephaniah attempted to reprove Jeremiah, but he did let him hear what Shemaiah wrote against him. It is also reasonable to conclude that Zephaniah went to the Lord about the situation.

Verse 30. After the exchange of communications between Shemaiah and the priest Zephaniah, the Lord gave Jeremiah another message to send to Babylon.

Verse 31. The message was to be in regard to the false prophecies of Shemaiah that he had uttered among the captives; the Lord accused him plainly of lying.

Verse 32. Shemaiah was already in Babylon as a captive, hence some additional punishment was to be inflicted upon him. His family was to become extinct and he also was to die before the return of his brethren to their native land.

JEREMIAH 30

Verse 1. This verse pertains to a direct word from the Lord to Jeremiah concerning instructions about to be given him.

Verse 2. The Lord had spoken many predictions directly to the mind of Jeremiah, and he in turn had repeated them orally in the ears of the people. But now he was to write them down which would get them in permanent form.

Verse 3. This verse predicts the return of all the people of God to their own country. *Israel* and *Judah* means the 10 tribes and the 2 tribes. Israel had been taken captive by the Assyrians before the Babylonian Empire was established; but the territory that had been controlled by the Assyrians was taken over by the Babylonians, who found the people of the 10 tribes scattered among the cities. Then when the Babylonians brought the 2 tribes from Jerusalem it practically got the entire nation of the Jews together, hence the return after the captivity would logically include the 12 tribes.

Verse 4. This verse is an introduction to the predictions that Jeremiah was to write in a book.

Verse 5. *Have heard a voice* means the Lord heard the mournful complaints of his people in Babylonian captivity and had compassion on them.

Verse 6. The pains of a woman approaching childbirth are used to illustrate the depressed state of mind suffered by the people of God in captivity.

Verse 7. The miseries of *Jacob* (the founder of the race of Israel) is still the subject of this verse as far as the word *trouble*. The subject is then changed and the remainder of the verse begins another prediction of the return.

Verse 8. *That day* refers to the time when the 70-year captivity would be over, and *his yoke* means the bondage under the Babylonian king. *Strangers* refers to the same people signified by the yoke, who had been *serving themselves* or helping themselves to the services of the people of God.

Verse 9. When the captivity is ended *they*, the people of God, will no longer give their services to Babylon, but will give them to the Lord their God. *David shall be their king* is a leap of over 500 years, from the close of the captivity to the beginning of the kingdom of Christ in Acts 2. This is not the first nor will it be the last instance where the prophets pass from fleshly to spiritual Israel in their predictions. The new or spiritual Israel is frequently spoken of as that of David. It is fitting that it should be so done, for David was the first man of the tribe of Judah to sit on the throne of fleshly Israel, and the reign never left that tribe as long as the nation had a kingdom. And through respect for the righteousness of David, the Lord promised him with an oath that when the time arrived for the reign of spiritual Israel, its king would be a lineal descendant of this great man and hence One of the tribe of Judah. This was carried out according to Heb. 7: 14. Some of the passages that connect the reign of Christ with David are Psa. 89: 3; Isa 55: 3; Ezk. 34: 23; 37: 24; Luke 1: 69; Acts 2: 30; 13: 23.

Verse 10. After making a brief but pointed reference to the time of Christ, a prophet will usually resume his original line of writing concerning fleshly Israel. This verse, therefore, continues the prediction that the fleshly people of God will be released from the captivity and be permitted to return to their own country.

Verse 11. Some of the predictions pertain to the release from captivity in general. This verse concerns a special condition that will exist at the end of that experience and that is about the remnant that was to be saved from the ravages of that period. The nation numbered some millions when it went into the captivity but was reduced to a much smaller number according to Ezra 2: 64. However, this reduction had a favorable significance for the severity of the captivity might have completely snuffed out the nation had it not been for the care and oversight of God.

Verse 12. We have observed that the events in the history of the Jews are not always recorded or predicted in chronological order. This verse and the three that follow pertain to the fate which God had decreed against his people. *Bruise is incurable* is a figurative statement that Judah had sinned so grievously that nothing that man could do would cure the condition.

Verse 13. *None to plead* could not mean that no one was willing to speak on behalf of Judah, for both Hezekiah and Josiah had tried to bring the nation to repentance with a view to securing the favor of the Lord. The key to the statement is in the words *hast no healing medicine.* Human plans could not work the cure necessary for the reinstatement of the nation in the favor of God.

Verse 14. Since human means could not cure the diseased condition (which was idolatry) the Lord only could heal the nation of it. This healing was to consist of a severe treatment, even *the chastisement of a cruel one,* which means the enslavement of the people in the land of Babylon.

Verse 15. *Why criest thou* has the effect of telling the people there was no use to make their complaint with the expectation of avoiding the captivity. God was punishing them by the hand of this cruel agency (the Babylonians) in order to bring about their cure from the terrible disorder of idolatry.

Verse 16. God would never suffer the nations whom he used to chastise his own people to take personal satisfaction out of their service for Him. After they have accomplished the purpose for which God brought them into action, they were made to suffer for their motives of cruelty toward the unfortunate people; hence this verse predicts the overthrow of Babylon. It was to be done through another world power but God would be the planner of the whole event. The Biblical account of the fall of Babylon is in Dan. 5. The historical account of it is cited with the comments on Isa. 13: 1 in volume 3 of this Commentary.

Verse 17. The Lord continued using the figures of speech pertaining to disease and its cure. The treatment of some diseases is sometimes so severe that it causes wounds temporarily, and then those wounds have to be healed. So the disease of idolatry was so deep-seated that the nation needed to have its national dignity wounded by the captivity in a foreign land. The people of that land looked upon these national wounds and belittled the unfortunate victims of their cruelty. The Lord promised to heal those wounds, which was to be accomplished by the release from captivity and the return to their own land. The predictions of that glorious event is the subject of the next five verses which might be marked by a bracket.

Verse 18. *Bring again the captivity* means God will reverse the captivity, etc.

Verse 19. At the end of the captivity the number of the Jews was to be greatly reduced, but this verse promises that the Lord will multiply them so that national glory may be again enjoyed.

Verse 20. This verse repeats much that has been promised, extending the prosperity to their descendants. It was to be accomplished after having punished their former oppressor, and it also promises to punish any who would attempt to oppress them after their return to Palestine.

Verse 21. *Nobles shall be of themselves* means the nation will not be dependent upon others for its outstanding men, for they will produce them of themselves. The same kind of prospect was held out before them with regard to their rulers. The principle on which these favors will be granted is a heart *engaged* or disposed to approach unto the Lord to learn and do his will.

Verse 22. In one sense the Jews never ceased to be God's people, but he had cast them off from being his people as a nation.

Verses 23, 24. This paragraph is a prediction of the overthrow of Babylon and takes the same comments and historical note as verse 16.

JEREMIAH 31

Verse 1. The first 14 verses should form a bracket and the general subject is the return of the Jews from captivity. Some special details of that event will be noticed in various places hence the verses will be commented upon in their order. *At the same time* refers to the event predicted in the last of the preceding chapter.

Verse 2. The language is in the past

tense as to grammatical form, but it is a prediction of events at and after the overthrow of Babylon. *Wilderness* is a figurative reference to the desolating captivity in a foreign land. *People left* are the ones elsewhere referred to as the remnant that survived the ravages of the long exile.

Verse 3. *Appeared unto me* represents Israel as speaking and acknowledging the mercy of the Lord. That mercy was extended to the people because the Lord loved them notwithstanding their many acts of unfaithfulness toward Him.

Verse 4. *I will build thee* is a prediction of the restoration of the people to their native land and the rebuilding of their national institutions. The mention of *tabrets* and *dances* is a prediction of the joy that was to come to Israel upon their return to the home country after 70 years of enforced absence.

Verse 5. Not only were their homes to be restored, but their agricultural pursuits were to be resumed. Samaria was the part of Palestine that had been occupied by the 10 tribes. This prediction indicates that they will be returned to their former homes as well as would the 2 tribes; no "lost 10 tribes" taught here.

Verse 6. The tribe of Ephraim included the capital of the kingdom of Israel and their people did not go to Zion (or Jerusalem) for worship because they had revolted from the kingdom of Judah. This verse predicts that after the return from captivity they all will go to the original headquarters in order to meet with the Lord. It indicates that Israel will be a united kingdom after the return from captivity.

Verse 7. *Say, O Lord, save thy people* is the prophetic style of language. It is a prediction that the Lord would come to the rescue of his people while there was still a remnant of them surviving the captivity.

Verse 8. For the significance of *north* see the historical note given in connection with Isa. 14: 31 in volume 3 of this Commentary. *Coasts* means the various regions in the vast Babylonian Empire where the Jews had been scattered. *Blind* and *lame* and other people with different handicaps will all be enabled to come to Jerusalem when God is ready to restore his people to their own country.

Verse 9. *Weeping* was fulfilled in Ezra 3: 12 when the older men observed the reduced appearance of the temple as compared with the original one. This view of the case is made clear by Hag. 2: 3. *Supplications* is rendered "favors" in the margin, and the context as well as the lexicon agrees with it. The meaning is that their supplications or desires were granted as to the favors of rebuilding the house. (See Ezra 1: 1-4.) *Ephraim* once meant the 10 tribes separate from the other tribes, but after the captivity all the tribes were to be together. Hence *Israel* (as a whole) and *Ephraim* are referred to in the same relation to God. *Firstborn* is used in a complimentary sense meaning "chief," also as the first nation to be formed by the Lord to be his own peculiar (or purchased) people.

Verse 10. *O ye nations* predicts that the great event of the return of Israel and re-establishment in Palestine will become generally known. The first definition of the original for *isles* is "A habitable spot," and it is used here in about the same sense as *nations*. God's love and care for his people is assured which will be evident to the peoples of the earth. The flock will be brought together again.

Verse 11. *Jacob* is used to include the nation of the Jews because that patriarch was the father of the tribes forming the nation. Babylon was the hand that was stronger than Jacob, but that was because the Lord willed it to be so as a chastisement.

Verse 12. *Height* is from MAROWM and is defined "elation," and *Zion* has reference to Jerusalem as the capital of the nation. The clause means the Jews will come to Jerusalem after the captivity and will be so elated over the situation that they will sing together. *Flow* is from NAHAR, which Strong defines as follows: "A primitive root; to sparkle, i.e. (figuratively) be cheerful; hence (from the sheen [luster] of a running stream) to flow, i.e. (figuratively) assemble." The phrase *flow together* is a beautiful prediction and pictures the Jewish nation or its people assembling at Jerusalem through *the goodness of the Lord*. Their happy state of mind is likened to the luster on the bosom of a calmly-flowing stream. The mention of *wheat, wine, oil* and the possession of *flocks* is to indicate the return of prosperity after they have regained possession of their land. *Not sorrow any more* means especially that they will not again be taken bodily into captivity.

Jeremiah 31: 13-23

Verse 13. Dancing was engaged in by various age groups in ancient times, but the indications are that the practice was an expression of joy. The women and men danced separately, for the motive of happiness did not even suggest the familiar association of the sexes at such a time. This verse predicts their engaging in the dance as an evidence of the joy and lightness of heart the people would have after being made free from their bondage in the land of Babylon.

Verse 14. *Satiate* means to quench and *soul* means the vitality or life of a creature. The clause means God would make the priests feel satisfied with their lot after coming back to their former work with the nation of the Lord.

Verse 15. The prophet has been writing about the past sorrows of God's people and their joy that came afterward. Following the prophets' practice, Jeremiah regards this as an opportunity to speak of another event in the future in which a condition of great distress was to be turned into a cause of joy. That event was the coming slaughter of the infants by Herod (Matt. 2: 16-18) in his attempt to destroy Jesus. That crime was overruled by the Lord for the good of humanity, just as the captivity of the Jews was to be reversed and replaced by a condition of rejoicing. The reference to Rahel (Rachel) is figurative and doubtless is in recognition of her sorrowful life, ending at her death in childbirth at Ramah, near Jerusalem.

Verse 16. Having extended the "telescope" (See illustration at Isa. 1: 1) to get a glimpse of an event many years in the future, the prophet resumes his prediction of the return of Israel from Babylonian captivity. *Refrain from weeping* predicts the happiness that is to follow the return to their own land. *Land of the enemy* refers to the Babylon country.

Verse 17. *In thine end* refers to the end of the Babylonian captivity.

Verse 18. *Ephraim* stands for the 10 tribes when used in this way because the capital of that kingdom was in the possession of that tribe. That kingdom had been removed from their land a century before this writing of Jeremiah, and the prophet is predicting their release from the exile which was to occur at the same time with the 2 tribes. *Turn me and I shall be turned* refers to the cure from idolatry that was accomplished by the captivity. The historical note that shows the fulfillment of this prediction was quoted at Isa. 1: 25 in volume 3 of this Commentary.

Verse 19. This is still considering the 10 tribes in exile, and shows them as brought to repentance by their punishment. *Smote upon my thigh* is simply a gesture of shame for the sins that were committed in the days *of my youth* which means that the 10 tribes committed idolatry from the beginning of their separate existence as a nation. The first thing their king did after pulling off from the capital at Jerusalem was to set up the golden calves to be worshiped as gods (1 Ki. 12: 28-30), and the nation practiced idolatry as long as it lasted as a kingdom.

Verse 20. The first clause of this verse sounds as if it questioned the matter, but actually it is a declaration that Ephraim (the 10 tribes) was the dear child of God. For that reason the Lord loved him in spite of his sins and wished to save him.

Verse 21. The 10 tribes had been in exile more than a century when Jeremiah wrote and they really were beyond the opportunity of erecting *waymarks* or monuments to mark their way back. The language is figurative and prophetic, meaning that God could conduct them on their return home as definitely as if they had set up such marks.

Verse 22. At verse 15 we observe the prophet extending his vision to the time of Christ for a few sentences, then resuming his line concerning ancient Israel; he is doing the same thing in this verse. He speaks in reassuring terms to his dejected people by promising that a very important event was to happen in their home land, which was that *a woman shall compass a man*. This evidently referred to the virgin conception and birth of Christ. It might be asked if this clause could not be said of all conceptions. There is a special fact in the case of Mary and Christ. *Man* is from GEBER and Strong defines it, "A valiant man or warrior." This gives to the word a peculiar meaning that could apply especially to Christ. According to John 8: 58 Jesus existed before he was conceived by Mary, and also according to Luke 10; 18 he was a powerful being before he left Heaven. Hence we can understand that when Mary received him into her body she really did *compass a man*, "a valiant man" as the lexicon has it.

Verse 23. This verse resumes the

good fortune of Israel after the return from captivity. *The Lord bless thee* is a prediction that the nation will be blessed by being restored to its native land.

Verse 24. The agricultural pursuits will be resumed without being even threatened successfully by a foreign enemy.

Verse 25. *I have* is past tense in form but is future in meaning. To *satiate* means to satisfy fully which was to take place after the return from captivity.

Verse 26. *Upon this* means that on account of the good fortune to be given the people they will be able to enjoy refreshing hours of rest.

Verse 27. *Sow . . . with man . . . with beast* means the land will again increase its population and they will be permitted to have their needed beasts of service. *Israel* and *Judah* are mentioned because after the captivity the 12 tribes were all to return to Palestine and live together as one nation.

Verse 28. When God saw fit to overthrow his nation he did so according to his wisdom. Likewise when the time comes to reverse its sad state He will accomplish that.

Verses 29, 30. The language is figurative and teaches individual responsibility. The people had to suffer the captivity largely because of the sins of the leaders; that will not occur again.

Verse 31. This and the three verses that follow should form a bracket which contains a very important prediction. The passage is cited almost verbatim in Heb. 8: 8-12. *Israel* and *Judah* are both named because those were the names that included the 12 tribes. However, in the fulfillment both Jews and Gentiles will have a part.

Verse 32. *The day* is a reference to that period in general, for the covenant was actually delivered at Sinai which was about two months after the exodus from Egypt. The *new covenant* was to be different from the Sinaite covenant, and some of the differences will be described in the following verses.

Verse 33. One of the differences between the two covenants is indicated by the words *write it in their hearts*. Under the Jewish covenant a boy baby was circumcised when 8 days old which made him a full member of the group. But the new covenant has to be entered by accepting it in the heart or mind.

Verse 34. *Not teach . . . his brother.* Circumcision made an 8-day-old boy a full brother to all other members of the covenant. Yet that boy could not know anything about the Lord, and when he became old enough he had to be made acquainted with Him by his "brother" in the Jewish covenant. Under the new covenant a person must be old enough to know the Lord before he can become a member. See the comments on this subject at 1 Sam. 3: 7 in volume 2 of this Commentary.

Verse 35. The greatness of God as shown in the created universe is the subject of this verse. *Ordinances* is defined by Strong, "An enactment; hence an appointment (of time, quantity, labor or usage)." It means that God made the moon and stars for light (not to be inhabited). *Divideth* is from a word that means to manage or control and refers to God's power over the sea.

Verses 36, 37. The surety of God's predictions is illustrated by these conditions in the universe. No one doubts the permanence of the planets, neither should he doubt the surety of His predictions. Man's ability to measure (comprehend) the heaven above is no more unlikely than God's failure to carry out his promises to Israel.

Verse 38. *The city* refers to Jerusalem and the *tower of Hanameel* was an important part of the wall; it was near the place where the work of rebuilding was to start. The fulfillment of this prediction is recorded in Neh. 3: 1.

Verse 39. *Gareb* and *Goath* were spots near Jerusalem. The *measuring line* or extension of the city's occupation was to reach unto these spots.

Verse 40. *Valley* is from EMEQ which Strong defines, "A vale (i.e. broad depression)"; this has special reference to the Valley of Hinnom near Jerusalem. This place and the fields nearby had been the scene of much destruction in former times. After the return from captivity that whole territory was to be brought into peaceful control by the people of the Lord.

JEREMIAH 32

Verse 1. The attention of the reader has frequently been called to the unchronological character of parts of the Bible. This is particularly true of the prophetic books. On this point I shall quote from Smith's Bible Dictionary as follows: "Apparently the prophets kept written records of their predictions, and collected into larger volumes such as were intended for permanent use." As the different parts of the prophetic writings were not written at the same time, it can be understood that in collecting them into one book they might not always be compiled in just the same order as they were written. Thus the present chapter through chapter 36 should be read or at least dated after chapter 37, for that chapter closes with the same subject that begins the present one. With this explanation settled, let us now consider the passages in their order and as they occur in the common version before us. We are in the tenth year of Zedekiah's reign and he has just one more year to sit on the throne. The army of Babylon is at the gates of Jerusalem and conducting a distressing siege against that city that is about to end in defeat for the besieged.

Verse 2. The siege had started in the ninth year of Zedekiah's reign (2 Ki. 25: 1), and at the present time (tenth year) Jeremiah was a prisoner in the *court of the prison*. This was an open space occupied by the guard where the prophet was kept for the present. But though he was a prisoner his friends could visit him since the area was more or less unrestricted as to the public.

Verse 3. From ancient times it has been a notion of mankind that the effect of unwelcome truth could be avoided by suppressing the one who uttered it. Zedekiah was angry at the predictions of Jeremiah and had him imprisoned.

Verses 4, 5. These verses state the unpleasant predictions of Jeremiah. A part of this prophecy has been charged with being a contradiction of another (Ezk. 12: 13) which says that Zedekiah should not see Babylon although he would be taken there. The explanation is very simple and needs only a brief bit of history (2 Ki. 25: 6, 7).

Verse 6. This verse through 14 should be marked as a bracket and labeled "A literal transaction or some more 'acting' to indicate the surety of the return to Palestine."

Verse 7. The offer to buy a piece of real estate was a test for Jeremiah to show his confidence in his own predictions. There had not been any indication that he had any doubts but the performance was for the benefit of others. A piece of land would not be worth anything to a man who could not use it. The Lord told Jeremiah that his cousin was coming for this purpose, and thus he would know that the circumstance was by the Lord's arrangement.

Verse 8. *Right of inheritance* means he was in line as an heir; that if the land was going to be sold he was the one to "have the first chance." *Then I knew* means that by the act of his cousin in offering him the land just as the Lord said he would, Jeremiah knew the whole proposition was from Him.

Verses 9, 10. The *evidences* were the equivalent of our notarizing a document. It shows that according to the transaction Jeremiah favored the idea of personal ownership of property with individual title to the same.

Verse 11. *Law* and *custom* means it was not only customary but lawful to perform the transference of real estate from one individual to another.

Verse 12. *In the sight* was to have the force of a record as for a deed to the property. This was not only to make the sale legal, but for its effect on the public as to Jeremiah's faith in his own predictions.

Verses 13, 14. Baruch was acting as secretary for Jeremiah and was charged with the care of the document concerning the transaction. *Sealed* and *open* means the parts of the deal that were written and those that were merely beheld with the eyes and heard with the ears as audible agreements.

Verse 15. This verse is the prophet's interpretation of the whole transaction just enacted in the presence of the people. If Jeremiah was willing to invest money in land that was then in control of a foreigner, he surely believed that such a condition would be removed so that he could make his own use of that land.

Verse 16. Having performed the demonstration of his faith, Jeremiah offered a prayer to his God.

Verse 17. *Nothing too hard for thee* means that God can do anything if it is a matter of power or knowledge. There are some things God cannot do because they are wrong, but He has the power and knowledge to do anything that is right.

Verse 18. Recompensest . . . iniquity . . . fathers . . . children. This may seem to teach that children are punished for the sins of their fathers which we know is not the way God deals with man. The statement is from Ex. 20: 5 where the fuller wording adds the proviso "of them that hate me." The passage means that God will punish the sinful children with the same penalty he used on their sinful fathers.

Verse 19. *Counsel* means advice and *work* is the practice of it; God is great in both. *Eyes open upon* means that God sees everything that is done.

Verse 20. *Set signs* refers to the miracles which God did in Egypt on behalf of Israel which they had not forgotten *unto this day*. These facts gave God a name that was respected by the nations of the earth.

Verse 21. After the above-mentioned signs in Egypt (which means the 10 plagues), God delivered his people by the miraculous crossing through the Red Sea.

Verse 22. *This land* means the land of Palestine where Israel had been living for centuries. It was necessary for the Lord to perform many more miracles in order to give them the land that had been promised to the fathers.

Verse 23. This verse is an acknowledgement of the sins of the nation. It also accounts for the sad condition into which it was plunged.

Verse 24. *Mounts* is rendered "engines of shot" (machines for hurling large stones) in the margin and the original seems to be used in that sense in some places. However, Strong defines the original, "A military mound, i.e. rampart of besiegers," and Moffatt renders the word "siege-mounds." The word evidently was used in both senses since those engines would be planted on the ramparts for the purpose of battering down the wall. At the time when Jeremiah was writing this the Chaldeans (or Babylonians) were at the walls of Jerusalem and conducting a siege. That would result in the three evils, *sword, famine* and *pestilence*, explained at ch. 14: 12.

Verse 25. The prophet makes it a matter of personal interest because he has always been sympathetic towards the woes of his people. In reminding the Lord of the recent business transaction he is not necessarily expressing any doubt, but is making a plea for further instruction from God.

Verses 26, 27. The requested information came, in which Jeremiah was also reminded of the greatness of the One who was doing all this. It was repeated that nothing was *too hard* for the Lord, therefore he could suffer the siege and captivity to occur, and then return the people so that they could use the land that was purchased. With this assurance the immediate situation with its outcome was described again to Jeremiah.

Verse 28. The siege was in progress when this verse was spoken by the Lord but the city had not yet been taken.

Verse 29. The *Chaldeans* were a special group who were in the lead in the Babylonian Empire, hence the two words are used interchangeably. This verse was fulfilled as here predicted and the account of it is in 2 Ki. 25: 9.

Verse 30. When *Israel* and *Judah* are named separately but in the same sentence it means the 10-tribe and the 2-tribe kingdoms. Both groups had sinned against God by the *works of their hands* which means their manmade gods.

Verse 31. *This city* means Jerusalem which was the capital of the nation and was where the temple was located. *Day that they built it* means the day they repaired and arranged it as their capital city.

Verse 32. This verse includes the Jews of all the tribes, and all ranks of men in the tribes. All of them had been guilty of idolatry although the leaders were charged with being the ones who set the example and the others followed them.

Verse 33. *Turned the back* denotes they had deserted the Lord and had faced themselves toward their idols. It was not for lack of information, either, for God had been prompt, *rising up early*, in teaching them the good and the right way.

Verse 34. It was not enough to build altars for idol worship in the groves, but they brought their false gods into the Lord's temple.

Verse 35. These horrible human sacrifices are commented upon at 2 Ki. 16: 3 in volume 2 of this Commentary. *Baal* and *Molech* were invisible gods of the idolaters.

Verse 36. *Ye say* refers to Jeremiah's complaint that Jerusalem was about to fall into the hands of the king of Babylon. The Lord does not deny it but is going to authorize the prophet to make another prediction of the return from the captivity.

Verse 37. During the 70-year captivity the civilized world was all practically under the control of Babylon. The various parts of that empire included many lands, here called *countries*. Naturally, then, the Jews would get dispersed among these regions and the Lord would need to gather them out of all such places.

Verse 38. The word *people* is from the Hebrew word *am* and occurs over 1800 times in the Old Testament. Strong defines it, "A people (as a congregated unit); specifically a tribe (as those of Israel); hence (collectively) troops or attendants; figuratively a flock." Israel never ceased to be God's people in the sense of race or nationality, but during the captivity they were not a collected group.

Verse 39. *One heart* refers to the unity of mind the Jews were to have when they return from captivity.

Verse 40. *Everlasting* means agelasting, and God promised to protect them as a collected group throughout that dispensation.

Verse 41. *Plant them* means God would establish them in that land as a strong nation. That was done after the captivity and as long as they were faithful they continued to be a strong force in the world.

Verse 42. *Like as* means only to make comparison of the certainty of God's predictions. His threat of the punishment was fulfilled. so likewise his promises would be fulfilled in their appointed time.

Verse 43. A demonstration of the prediction that *fields shall be bought* was enacted by Jeremiah in verses 6-14. By that transaction the prophet showed his confidence in the predictions which the Lord inspired him to make.

Verse 44. Private ownership of property has been endorsed all through the Bible. Not only so, but some form of title with legal or public security of it has been practiced. See Gen. 23: 17-20; 33: 19.) Hence the prediction is made here that the transference of property would be *subscribed* and *witnessed* and *sealed*.

JEREMIAH 33

Verse 1. See the comments on ch. 32: 1, 2 as to this imprisonment. The following message from the Lord was to be the second one Jeremiah received while in prison.

Verse 2. The pronoun *it* refers to the earth that contains the fields spoken of in the preceding chapter. The point in the discussion is the fact that God made the earth, therefore He has the power to give it to whomsoever he will.

Verse 3. This verse invites the prophet to call upon the Lord for information concerning things hitherto unrevealed.

Verse 4. *Houses of this city* and *of the kings* means the families in those places. They thought to retain possession of the houses but had failed; they had been thrown down by the *mounts*. For explanation of this word see the comments at ch. 32: 24.

Verse 5. *They* refers to the people of the houses mentioned in the preceding verse. They thought they could resist the Chaldeans (or Babylonians) but they failed. As a result their cities were filled with dead bodies which God had caused to be slain.

Verse 6. This verse through 14 is a bracket on the return from the captivity with a few special predictions in connection with that event. The only difference between *health* and *cure* is that the first is the result of using the second. It has general reference to the national soundness in their native land.

Verse 7. *Judah* and *Israel* are again named separately but in the same sentence. It is a prediction that the 12 tribes were all to be returned to Palestine.

Verse 8. *Cleanse them from all their iniquities* refers to the cure from idolatry. The historical note that shows the fulfillment of this prediction was quoted at Isa. 1: 25 in volume 3 of this Commentary.

Verse 9. The restoration of Israel to national greatness made an impression on the other nations. This can be seen by a careful reading of the books of Ezra and Nehemiah. *Fear* and *tremble* means the nations will have respect for the Jewish nation.

Verse 10. This verse describes the condition of Jerusalem at the time Jeremiah was writing. The people had complained of it and God was giving them a prediction that it was to be changed.

Verse 11. This is a prediction of the general condition of goodness that was to exist after the return from captivity. The various relations of society and family life were to be restored.

Verse 12. This verse predicts the return of industrial and agricultural pursuits. *Flocks to lie down* indicates two blessings; sufficiency, and peace while using it under the protection of the God of Israel.

Verse 13. Not only was the capital city of Jerusalem to be restored, but the smaller cities of the whole land were to be repossessed. *Him that telleth them* means the shepherds will be able to enumerate their flocks and retain their number in peace.

Verse 14. The bracket concludes very much as it began, with a prediction of the general prosperity that was to follow the captivity.

Verse 15. The *"telescope"* (See illustration at Isa. 1: 1) is again extended and the prophet sees farther into the future. This verse through 22 is a bracket and the subject is the kingdom of Christ. *Branch* is a reference to Christ because the word means a sprout or shoot from a former plant. That would mean David who was the illustrious ancestor of Christ through two family lines of descendants.

Verse 16. *Judah* and *Jerusalem* were to be saved spiritually by the benefits of the church that was to be set up by the descendants of David.

Verse 17. *Never want a man* is a prediction that David's great Descendant would occupy the throne continuously. He was not to be succeeded by other kings as were the ones in fleshly Israel.

Verse 18. *Levites* is used figuratively because they furnished the priests under the Mosaic system. Under Christ all of God's people will be regarded as priests (1 Pe. 2: 5, 9; Rev. 1: 6; 5: 10). The other terms of the verse also are figurative, referring to the services in the kingdom of Christ.

Verse 19, 20. The Lord rather interrupts the passage to make a comparison of the surety of his promises. They are as sure as the established law that regulates the day and night.

Verses 21-23. The subject of *David* and his Son is explained at verse 15, and that of *priests* is commented upon at verse 18. *Ministers* means servants and applies to all who are citizens in the kingdom of Christ since they are all servants.

Verse 24. The *two families* refers to the 10-tribe and the 2-tribe kingdoms. The first had gone into exile under the Assyrians more than a century before, and the second was already in the beginning of their 70-year captivity.

Verse 25. The condition of the universe and the movements of the planets had been regular for centuries. Their surety is used to compare that of the predictions of their Creator as to other things about His people.

Verse 26. The predictions related to the fleshly descendants of David through Jacob. They were destined to suffer the full 70-year period of captivity, but the Lord assured them that he would *cause their captivity to return.*

JEREMIAH 34

Verse 1. To avoid confusion the reader should frequently consult the information as to the "three" captivities, or rather the three divisions or stages of the main period. Each of these divisions is sometimes referred to as a captivity and certain predictions or other statements are made on the basis of such a date. A fuller statement was made at 2 Ki. 24: 1 in volume 2 of this Commentary. At the time of our present verse the third of the captivities was about due and Zedekiah, the last king of Judah, was still on the throne in Jerusalem.

Verse 2. Zedekiah was still resisting the siege and thought he could avoid capture by the king of Babylon; Jeremiah was instructed to go to him with a message.

Verse 3. This verse has been thought to contradict another prediction, but it is explained at ch. 32: 4 which the reader should see for the sake of the information.

Verse 4. *Not die by the sword* means he would not die in war or other physical contest. He was taken, blind, from Riblah to Babylon where he lived the rest of his life.

Verse 5. Incense and sweet odors were burned at the burial of people, especially men of distinction. Although he was to spend the rest of his days in Babylon, he was to be honored at his death by this custom.

Verse 6, 7. Jeremiah faithfully delivered the message to Zedekiah, king of Judah. At the time the city of Jerusalem was in a state of siege, and other cities of Judah, Lachish and Azekah, having walls of defense about them, were still holding out in resistance against the king of Babylon.

Verse 8. Zedekiah promised to obey the law of Moses regarding the releasing of servants, and had secured an agreement from the princes to release them. But they broke their agreement and then the Lord gave Jeremiah a message as mentioned in the first part of this verse.

Verse 9. The law of release referred to is in Lev. 25: 39-46. This was in consideration for the hard times that might be thrust upon them.

Verse 10. The princes and others who had servants at first agreed to let them go free. The servants enjoyed a short period of freedom as required by the law.

Verse 11. The greed of mankind for property is great, as well as the desire to be dominant. The princes broke their word as well as the law and forced their servants to resume their burdens of servitude.

Verses 12, 13. It was at this point the Lord gave Jeremiah the message referred to in the first part of verse 8. *Word of the Lord . . . from the Lord* is not an empty repetition. Many of the speeches were offered to the people in ancient times that were claimed to be the word of the Lord. Those speeches, however, were not *from the Lord* and therefore were not His word. For comments on *the day* see ch. 31: 32.

Verse 14. Many of the regulations under the Mosaic system were related to the idea of the unit "seven." They had the seventh day of the week as a holy day, the seventh-year rest for the land, and the seventh-year release for the servants. The last was the ordinance involved in the truce breaking charged against the princes.

Verse 15. When this agreement was made the masters of the servants were in the house of the Lord. That did not make the covenant any more binding as far as their moral obligation was concerned, but it amounted to an acknowledgment that the Lord was concerned in the transaction. Hence their breaking the contract not only violated a moral law but it constituted trucebreaking against the Lord.

Verse 16. In breaking their covenant concerning the servants the princes were accused of polluting the name of the Lord. That was because they had made that agreement in the house that was called by His name.

Verse 17. *I proclaim a liberty for you* means the Lord was going to punish these trucebreakers who were His servants by releasing them from their present servitude. In other words, their present Master was going to turn them over to another master who would treat them very cruelly. He was to punish them with the sword and other harsh measures, then remove them from their own country.

Verse 18. Verse 15 states this covenant was made in the house of the Lord. That would be in connection with the altar services, and important ceremonies were often made in connection with an animal sacrifice. In preparing a beast for the altar they sometimes cut it into two parts and *passed between the parts*. They could do this literally or with some motion of the hand, indicating they offered the sacrifice as an evidence of good faith in the transaction.

Verse 19. Judah was the kingdom and Jerusalem was its capital. The kingdom was represented by the princes or leading men in the presentation of the sacrifice.

Verse 20. Since the kingdom was represented in the transaction, including the making and breaking of the agreement, it was to be given the threatened punishment.

Verse 21, 22. A special punishment was to be imposed upon Zedekiah which was that he was to be taken from his throne and delivered into the hands of the king of Babylon. *Are gone up from you* refers to the action of the Babylonian army when Zedekiah fled from Jerusalem. This army pursued the king and overtook him near Jericho. Turning him over into the hands of Nebuchadnezzar at Riblah, a temporary judgment seat, the army returned to finish the overthrow of Jerusalem. The history of this may be seen in 2 Ki. 25: 4-10.

JEREMIAH 35

Verse 1. Again the book drops back several years and stops at the reign of Jehoiakim. A glance at verse 11 will tell us this writing was in the days when Nebuchadnezzar had come against the land of Judah.

Verse 2. The value of a good example will be the subject of a number of verses. There was a family called the Rechabites dwelling in Jerusalem at the time of this story. Jeremiah was told to bring them into the house of the Lord and offer them wine.

Verse 3. This verse names the members of the family of Rechabites who were brought in and offered wine.

Verse 4. The particular room where these people were brought was in charge of one who was a *man of God*, hence the Rechabites would know that no evil was intended as far as the association was concerned.

Verse 5. In this room the prophet offered to entertain his guests with wine. It should be remembered that what was offered these people was not wrong in itself in those days, for wine was generally used by the best of people. The wrong in this case will be revealed in the rest of the story.

Verse 6. The Rechabites refused to drink the wine. They did not object because they thought it was wrong in itself, but because their father had forbidden it.

Verse 7. Their father further commanded them not to build houses to live in but to dwell in tents. They also were not to follow agricultural pursuits. We know such activities are not wrong in themselves, therefore the conclusion is that the wrong would have been in disregarding the commandments of their father.

Verses 8, 9. The only reason given by these people for their conduct was that they *obeyed the voice of their father*. That is the principle of obedience that should be the motive of all who are under authority. We may not understand why God has given certain commands, but if we respect His authority we will obey his orders.

Verse 10. By dwelling in tents these people would be in better condition to move if circumstances required it. They could do so and remain together, thus retaining their tribal unity as seemed to be the desire of their father.

Verse 11. This verse explains why the Rechabites were living at Jerusalem at this time. They had been living in other parts of Palestine, and, while friendly toward the full-blooded Israelites, and favorable to the doctrine of only one true God, they maintained a tribal independence.

Verse 12. After this experience with the Rechabites, the Lord was ready to draw a lesson for the use of Jeremiah with his people.

Verse 13. He was first to go to the men of Judah and call for their attention to the instructions which he was about to give.

Verse 14. The obedience of the Rechabites to their father's commands was contrasted with the disobedience of the men of Judah to the words of God. The contrast will stand out all the more when it is considered that it was the words of an earthly father in one case, and those of the God of Heaven in the other.

Verse 15. This passage is another where the apparent disagreement appears which has been mentioned a number of times. The explanation lies chiefly in distinguishing between the nation as a whole and certain individuals in it. See the note at 2 Ki. 22: 17 in volume 2 of this COMMENTARY.

Verse 16. The contrast between the obedience of the Rechabites and the disobedience of the men of Judah was made the basis for the next message from the prophet.

Verse 17. The message consisted of the same prediction that had been made before. Judah and Jerusalem were to be punished because of their disobedience of God's words.

Verses 18, 19. Stress is laid by Jeremiah on the fact of obedience on the part of the Rechabites. The reward promised for this good conduct was to be an honor for their father. *Not want a man* means that the family would be perpetuated. That was just what their father hoped to accomplish by his instructions to the family, for he said (verse 7) *that ye may live many days in the Land.*

JEREMIAH 36

Verse 1. The preceding chapter gave a general statement as to the date of the writing, but this gives the year which is the fourth of the reign of Jehoiakim. According to 2 Ki. 24: 1 that was the first year of the great 70-year captivity.

Verse 2. The difference between a *roll* and a *book* is in the fact that after a roll has been written upon it is called a book. The clause means as if it said: "Take a roll and make a book out of the things I have said to you by word of mouth." The subject matter of the book was to cover the whole time since the days of Josiah. It would be impossible for a man to write all of that from memory unless he had the inspiration of God to guide him, such as the Spirit did for the apostles (John 14: 12).

Verse 3. The key to this passage is in the words *may return every man*. It agrees with the distinction that has been made between the nation as a whole and the individuals in it. Even most of them refused to heed the admonitions of the Lord, but at least they were given the opportunity with the promise of personal consideration even though they would have to go along with the nation into captivity.

Verse 4. Baruch was a faithful attendant upon Jeremiah and acted as his secretary. He wrote the words on the roll as the prophet dictated them.

Verse 5. *Shut up* does not mean he

was in prison, for ch. 37: 4 shows he had not yet been imprisoned. One part of Strong's definition of the original is "to hold back." Jeremiah was hindered in some way from entering the temple where the book was to be read because of the opportunity of meeting the greater number of people.

Verse 6. Baruch was to select a day when some fast would be proclaimed because he would then have opportunity of meeting the people coming there to worship.

Verse 7. *It may be* should be considered in the light of the comments, ch. 35: 15.

Verse 8. *According . . . the prophet commanded him* is a significant statement. The inspired prophets represented the authority of God and to disregard their commands was the same as disobeying Him.

Verse 9. This verse gives the date when Baruch had the opportunity of reading the book. He was to wait until a fast was proclaimed so as to meet the people in the temple. The work of writing it was begun in the fourth year of the reign of Jehoiakim and it was in the fifth year that the fast was proclaimed.

Verse 10. The places named here were parts of the house of God where the people could assemble to hear the reading of the book. Baruch read in such a manner that *all the people* could hear.

Verse 11. Michaiah's grandfather was a scribe and he doubtless knew something of the importance of an inspired document.

Verse 12. Having heard as the book was read to the masses of the people in the temple, Michaiah went down to the king's palace where he found a group of special persons who were connected with the king's service.

Verse 13. *Declared all the words* means he declared about the words, for the book was still in the hands of Baruch who had written it.

Verse 14. The interest of these men was so aroused that they desired to hear from the book direct. They sent Jehudi to request Baruch to come with the book.

Verse 15. Having come to the group in the king's palace, Baruch was requested to read the book to them which he did.

Verse 16. *Afraid* is defined by Strong, "to be startled." This was caused by the unpleasant predictions the book contained against them, and they thought the king should be informed about it.

Verse 17. See my comments at verse 2 as to writing so much from memory. These men thought the same about Baruch and asked him how he did it.

Verse 18. The explanation was a simple one and would not require the work of the memory. Baruch was not an inspired man but had served Jeremiah as his secretary and was accustomed to "taking dictation."

Verse 19. No doubt the men understood the temperament of the king and thought it would not be safe for Baruch and Jeremiah to show themselves.

Verse 20. Jehudi and the princes laid the roll aside in a safe place, but they went to the king and related the circumstances to him.

Verse 21. The report stirred up the interest of the king and he ordered Jehudi to get the roll out of its place in the scribe's room. The king then had the roll read in the hearing of himself and the princes attendant upon him.

Verse 22. The *winterhouse* was the winter apartment of the king's house; the mention of it was to explain the presence of the fire.

Verse 23. After Jehudi had read a few leaves, the king would cut that much from the main roll and cast them into the fire, continuing until the entire roll was burned.

Verse 24. The message of the roll did not produce the desired effect. Neither the king nor his princes showed any signs of regret for their unrighteous lives.

Verse 25. *Nevertheless* means that notwithstanding the pleas of these good men, the king destroyed the roll by burning.

Verse 26. This verse justifies the advice that was given Baruch and Jeremiah in verse 19. That verse merely told the men to hide from the sight of other men. This verse tells us the further particular that God helped them to find a safe hiding place from the wrath of the king.

Verses 27, 28. Men can destroy the material copy of God's word, but that does not do away with the truth taught therein. In this case the material copy of the word will be replaced with the same authority as was the first one.

Verse 29. Jeremiah was not a witness to the burning of the roll, but the king was to be informed that the prophet knew about it.

Verse 30. *Have none to sit upon the throne* ignores the 3-month reign of his son Jehoiachin. Such a short and uneventful reign was not considered worth noticing. The prediction concerning the dead body of Jehoiakim was made before and comments were made there at ch. 22: 19.

Verse 31. These predictions had been made by word of mouth from God to Jeremiah and they were written in the book which Jehoiakim destroyed. This verse was to remind him of them and to warn him that his burning the former roll would not let him escape the punishment threatened for his iniquities.

Verse 32. Some additional words were written in the second roll, hence the king made his case worse by his wicked act of burning the roll.

JEREMIAH 37

Verse 1. The last date we had was the fifth year of Jehoiakim (ch. 36: 9). That king reigned 11 years (2 Ki. 23: 36), and we are now in the first year of Zedekiah; hence a period of 6 or 7 years has passed since the preceding chapter. Coniah (or Jehoiachin) is mentioned here, but he reigned only 3 months so we may overlook him in making practical estimates of dates.

Verse 2. Zedekiah, like his predecessor, refused to hearken to the words of God which were spoken by the prophet Jeremiah.

Verse 3. Notwithstanding his rebellious attitude Zedekiah had the boldness to send men to Jeremiah to ask for his prayers.

Verse 4. This verse is explanatory on the subject of Jeremiah's freedom. Some previous passages had spoken of his imprisonment, but the parts of Jeremiah's book are not always chronological as to dates. This verse is necessary, therefore, to clarify the situation of the prophet.

Verse 5. The Egyptians were not favorably disposed toward the Babylonians, and when the latter had come up against Jerusalem, the Egyptians came up and offered to help the Jews to resist the siege. Seeing this, the Babylonians withdrew from Jerusalem for the time in order to meet the Egyptians; I shall quote some history on this event: "Now when Zedekiah had preserved the league of mutual assistance that he had made with the Babylonians eight years, he brake it, and revolted to the Egyptians, in hopes, by their assistance, of overcoming the Babylonians. When the king of Babylon knew this, he made war against him. He laid his country waste, and took his fortified towns, and came to the city of Jerusalem itself to besiege it. But when the king of Egypt heard what circumstances Zedekiah was in, he took a great army with him, and came into Judea, as if he would raise the siege; upon which the king of Babylon departed from Jerusalem, and met the Egyptians, and joined battle with them, and beat them; and when he had put them to flight, he pursued them, and drove them out of all Syria [Palestine]. Now as soon as the king of Babylon was departed from Jerusalem, the false prophet deceived Zedekiah, and said, that the king of Babylon would not any more make war against him or his people, nor remove them out of their own country into Babylon; and that those men in captivity would return, with all those vessels of the temple, of which the king of Babylon had despoiled that temple." Josephus, Antiquities, Book 10, Chapter 3, Section 3. I trust the reader will take careful note of this historical quotation as it explains many of the verses just now before us.

Verse 6. The prophet Jeremiah is often mentioned by name to distinguish him from false prophets. At the present time there were some of them trying to mislead the king of Judah into a false feeling of security.

Verse 7. There is no evidence that the prophet prayed for any special favor for Zedekiah as he evidently expected, but he did look to the Lord for information. God told him to inform the king of Judah that the army of Pharaoh, which was at that moment approaching the city of Jerusalem, would return to their own land and hence would be of no help for Zedekiah.

Verse 8. After the Chaldeans (or Babylonians) had driven Pharaoh back to his own land as per the preceding verse, they were to return to the siege about Jerusalem. (See the quotation from Josephus at verse 5.) This verse is a prediction of the destruction of Jerusalem which would complete the captivity. The fulfillment of this is recorded in 2 Ki. 25: 8-10.

Verse 9. *Deceive not yourselves* was said in allusion to the false prophets mentioned in verse 6. False assurances of peace are dangerous because they act as a hindrance to necessary reformation of life.

Verse 10. Wounded men do not literally rise up and perform military duty except by a miracle. The passage was so worded to mean that no apparent obstacle could prevent the Lord from carrying out his plans. The Chaldeans were bound to succeed now because God willed it to be so.

Verse 11. This refers to the time when the Babylonians withdrew from the siege of Jerusalem to meet the Egyptians, mentioned in verse 5 and illustrated with a quotation from Josephus.

Verse 12. The withdrawal of the Babylonian army gave Jeremiah an opportunity to get out of Jerusalem. The land of Benjamin was near the capital city and was a part of the kingdom of Judah, hence he was still within his own country.

Verse 13. Jeremiah's movement was misinterpreted by a guardsman and he was accused of trying to desert his country in favor of the enemy. This was not only a false accusation, but was foolish since the Benjamites were his fellow citizens.

Verse 14. Of course Jeremiah denied the accusation in strong terms, asserting that it was a falsehood. Nevertheless the guard ignored the denial and brought the prophet to the princes.

Verse 15. For some reason the house of a scribe named Jonathan was being used as a prison at this time. The prophet was given unjust and cruel treatment and shut up in this prison.

Verse 16. *Dungeon* is from BOWR and is defined by Strong, "A pit hole (especially one used as a cistern or prison)." The word therefore does not necessarily mean a place of darkness but only a place dug out for various uses. The original for *cabins* really means "a vault or cell," and here means the departments dug in the pit.

Verse 17. We do not know whether the king had anything to do directly with putting Jeremiah into the prison. However, he certainly knew about it for when he wished to obtain some information he had him brought out. He was given the *word from the Lord* which was practically what he had been told before, that he was to be delivered into the hand of the king of Babylon.

Verse 18. Now we know that the king had something to do with the imprisonment of Jeremiah, for in his protest he charged him with the words *ye have put me in prison.*

Verse 19. Jeremiah further shamed him for listening to his false prophets who had contradicted the predictions of the inspired prophet.

Verse 20. Jeremiah did not retract anything he had predicted; he did not even request to have his imprisonment entirely set aside. He only requested for himself that he not be returned to the cells lest he die.

Verse 21. Jeremiah's request was granted and he was placed in the *court* which was the yard around the prison and which was enclosed with a fence or other barrier. (See the comments at ch. 32: 2.) He was also favored by the king's command that he be given daily rations of bread as long as the supply lasted.

JEREMIAH 38

Verse 1. *Prince* is from SAR and Strong defines it, "A head person (of any rank or class)." In the King James translation it has been rendered by captain, chief, general, governor, keeper, lord, master, ruler. Generally speaking the word would apply to any leading or outstanding man whether official or unofficial. The men named in this verse are called princes in verse 4.

Verses 2, 3. These men were displeased with the predictions that Jeremiah had made against Jerusalem which they repeated in these verses. They gave a correct report but seemed to blame the prophet for the truth contained in them when he was only faithfully delivering to them the word of the Lord.

Verse 4. It is an old story that men have thought they could avoid the fulfillment of undesirable truths by removing the man who speaks them. These princes made a plea to the king to have Jeremiah put to death.

Verse 5. By giving these men unrestricted authority in their dealing with Jeremiah the king became a party to whatever they did.

Verse 6. Their motive might have been to let Jeremiah die of starvation and exposure without directly putting him to death. We have reason to suspect them of this for they had called for his death (verse 4). This *dungeon* has the same original as the word in the preceding chapter. We there saw the word could mean a cistern or a pit dug for other purposes. In this place it might have been dug for use as a cistern but it was almost empty except the mire in the bottom. Jeremiah sank down in the mire and was thus a **prisoner in a double sense.**

Verses 7, 8. Many persons of rank employed eunuchs as chamberlains instead of chambermaids. These servants had their duties in the houses, but the king was not in there at this time, having taken a seat at one of the important gates of the city to act as judge of affairs. So this eunuch, hearing of Jeremiah's plight, left his work and went out to the king to inform him of the prophet's situation.

Verse 9. The eunuch made no reference to the merits of the case against Jeremiah; he may have had no opinion on that subject. The plea the eunuch made was from the standpoint of humanity, that Jeremiah was being treated in an evil way in that he was exposed to the danger of a cruel death.

Verse 10. It would not require thirty men to pull Jeremiah out of the pit, but the eunuch would need protection against the princes. They had caused the prophet to be placed in the pit and might try to prevent his release.

Verse 11. *Cast clouts* and *rotten rags* mean practically the same. The latter means old garments and the former includes old rags in general. *Treasury* is from an original that means a storage place in general, and is used here to refer to some closet where were placed articles "not good enough to keep but too good to throw away."

Verse 12. *Armholes* is a strange translation and it comes from two Hebrew words: ATSTSIYL, which Strong defines "a joint of the hand (i. e., knuckle), and YAD defined, "a hand (the open one)." Jeremiah was to put the rags in the palms of his hands to keep the cords from cutting them in the strain of pulling him out of the mire into which he had sunk; he did as he was directed.

Verse 13. Jeremiah was not released after being taken out of the mire, but was returned to the court of the prison where he remained until the city was taken.

Verse 14. Zedekiah was selfish and wished to confer with the prophet in his own interests. He arranged a meeting at one of the important entries to the temple. He wanted to commit the prophet to a promise of confidence before asking some question.

Verse 15. Jeremiah was suspicious of the king which he had reason to be from his previous experiences. His statements indicated the suspicion, for he exacted a promise from the king before giving any information.

Verse 16. The king did not make any promises as to his compliance with the word of the Lord, but he did assure Jeremiah of his life. *That made us this soul* was a logical statement. The One who made the *soul* (from NEPHESH, defined "a breathing creature") would certainly know what that creature was saying and thinking. The oath, therefore, was supposed to be made in all solemnity.

Verses 17, 18. Jeremiah did not change his predictions from what he had made before. He admonished the king to surrender to the king of Babylon. We should note that no promise was made of ending the captivity even though the king should surrender peacefully. His personal welfare and that of the city could have been taken care of even while the captivity of the nation continued.

Verse 19. Zedekiah seemed to be in a state of nervous agitation. He was afraid of the Jews who had already been taken by the Chaldeans lest they be peeved because they had been taken while the king was still comparatively free. He feared they might cause him to be turned over into the hand of the enemy and that would make him an object of reproach.

Verse 20. Jeremiah assured the king that what he feared would not come upon him; if he would surrender peacefully all would be well with him personally.

Verse 21. *Refuse to go forth* is a key phrase in this situation. There was to be no avoiding the falling into the hands of the Babylonians. The question was whether it would be done through the unresisting surrender of the king, or that he would be taken by force and be treated as a captive of war would be.

Verse 22. If the king chooses to be taken by force, then the women who were still left in his house would be taken also by the king of Babylon. If that happens these women will reproach Zedekiah and say he had even been betrayed by *his friends* (meaning the false prophets who had deceived him). *Feet are sunk in the mire* is used figuratively, meaning he would find himself in deep trouble. The figure is an allusion to the persecution of Jeremiah whose feet were literally put in the mire.

Verse 23. Jeremiah concluded his speech with the summing up of what would happen if the king refused to surrender. He and his family would be taken, also the city of Jerusalem would be burned. That would be unfortunate, since the city might be spared notwithstanding the captivity of the nation by the Babylonians.

Verse 24. The king requested Jeremiah to observe secrecy as to the subject matter of their conference. We do not know what were the motives for this request, further than his wish to avoid trouble with the princes.

Verse 25. Zedekiah surely knew the character of his leading men to be questionable, at best, and that they might not stop short of murder were their plans hindered. Moreover, he did not want any serious harm to come to Jeremiah which he feared would be done if his conversation with the princes did not please them.

Verse 26. Jeremiah had made such a request of the king (ch. 37: 20) as was mentioned in this verse. Moreover, such a subject would be sufficient reason for the conversation between the king and the prophet.

Verse 27. Sure enough, the princes came and asked Jeremiah the question the king expected and the prophet gave them the answer as directed. It had the desired effect for they ceased their conversation with Jeremiah. *Matter not perceived* means they did not know all of the conversation that had taken place between Jeremiah and the king; only that part just stated.

Verse 28. Jeremiah's request was granted and he remained in the court (or yard surrounding the prison) of the prison until the end of the siege.

JEREMIAH 39

Verse 1. This verse is according to 2 Ki. 25: 1-3 which is the original history of the event. The city of Jerusalem was thrown into a state of siege which is one of the most effective military measures for taking a fortified place.

Verse 2. The city endured the inconvenience and suffering of the siege for about three years when it was finally taken. *Broken up* is from BAQU, which Strong defines, "A primitive root; to cleave; generally to rend, break, rip or open." The phrase denotes that a breach was made in the walls of the city which would let the Babylonian army enter. That would mean the capturing of the city as the people were not in any condition, either in body or mind, for putting up any resistance, having undergone the ravages of famine for several years.

Verse 3. The men named were important military leaders of the Babylonian Empire who took possession of the city. *Middle gate* signifies the central or most important gate of the city. The chief transactions between cities in ancient times were done at the gates since that would be the spot for direct contact with the people coming and going. The passages showing the importance of the city gates are too numerous to mention all, but the reader will do well to note the following. Gen. 19: 1; 22: 17; Deut. 25: 7; 2 Sam. 19: 8; Job 29: 7.

Verse 4. This verse through 8 should be marked as a bracket because of the important events recorded in connection with each other, and their connection with other passages in the Bible. I will suggest that the reader see also 2 Ki. 25: 4-7. The king thought he could make his escape if he selected the darkness for the purpose. Only a short time before this (Ezk. 12: 12) another prophet had predicted that the king would flee by night or "twilight."

Verse 5. Zedekiah did not get very far until the Babylonians overtook him in the plains of Jericho. He was seized and taken for a hearing before Nebuchadnezzar who was stationed at Riblah. This was a place on the way from the Babylonian country to Palestine and Egypt. The occasion for Zedekiah's being brought to this place will be understood better by a quotation from Smith's Bible Dictionary. "Riblah in the land of Hamath, a place on the great road between Palestine and Babylonia, at which the kings of Babylonia were accustomed to remain while directing the operations of their armies in Palestine and Phoenicia. Here Nebuchadnezzar waited while the sieges of Jerusalem and of Tyre were being conducted by his lieutenants."

Verses 6, 7. I have included these two verses in one paragraph because they pertain to an apparent difficulty or disagreement between certain statements in different places. In some passages it will be predicted that Zedekiah was to see the king of Babylon, also that he was to be taken to the city of Babylon and yet was never to see it. All is clear when we understand that he saw the king at Riblah and where he then had his eyes plucked out, after which he was taken to Babylon where he died. It would be well for the reader to make a group of the following passages. 2 Ki. 25: 6, 7; Jer. 32: 4, 5; 34: 3; 39: 6, 7; Ezk. 12: 13.

Verse 8. Having overtaken Zedekiah and turned him over to Nebuchadnezzar at Riblah, the Chaldeans completed their reduction of the buildings in Jerusalem. They destroyed the temple (2 Ki. 25: 9) and the king's house which means the palace.

Verse 9. There were still some people left in Jerusalem who had not been taken in the previous attacks. These were taken as captives to Babylon by the captain of the guard or commander-in-chief.

Verse 10. We are not told why the captain of the guard extended this favor to the poor, but we do know that certain personal favors were given to members of the Jewish nation. For instance, we shall learn that Jeremiah did not have to go to Babylon after the fall of the city. These *poor* of the nation had been the victims of the greedy leaders (Isa. 3: 15; 10: 2; 58: 3), and it was just for them now to have some enjoyment in the use of the lands that had been wrongfully taken from them.

Verse 11. Nebuzar-adan was captain of the guard or commander-in-chief for Nebuchadnezzar, and he managed the military affairs under the direction of the king. He was thus following the orders of his superior in what he did with the captives.

Verse 12. He was commanded to treat Jeremiah with special kindness, even permitting him to be granted any of his wishes. Of course we will understand that all these favors would have to be in harmony with his status as a prisoner of the Babylonians.

Verse 13. What Jeremiah's present wishes were we are not told but they can be surmised by what was done for him since it was of a desirable nature. The men named in this verse were officers in the Babylonian army but were under Nebuzar-adan.

Verse 14. The men named were sent to take Jeremiah out of the court of the prison where he had been held for a long time. He was put into the hands of Gedaliah who had been appointed as governor over the Jews (verse 10) after the siege of Jerusalem had been accomplished.

Verse 15. As an explanation of this kind treatment, the prophet goes back and tells us of a word that God spoke to him while he was still shut up in the court of the prison.

Verse 16. Ebed-melech was the eunuch who was friendly toward Jeremiah and procured his deliverance from the mire (ch. 38: 7-13). He was honored with a personal message from the prophet in which the predictions against the place were repeated.

Verse 17. In recognition of his trust in the Lord and his friendly services for Jeremiah, the eunuch was promised protection from his personal enemies.

Verse 18. Ebed-melech was assured that he would not die by the sword when the city fell. Thus we have another instance of personal favor bestowed for a righteous life even amidst the trials of the calamity that was to come upon the nation.

JEREMIAH 40

Verse 1. History and prophecy are blended together in the closing chapters of this book, and the events are not always chronological, either in the order of their occurrences or the dates. The principal thing for us to learn is what happened and to whom. The preceding chapter tells us of the special favor that was extended to Jeremiah on orders from the king of Babylon. It meant that he was to be taken out of the court of the prison and to be committed to the care of Gedaliah who had the oversight of the Jews at Mizpeh and other places. After telling us about that favor the writer proceeds to a later fact and says, *so he dwelt among the people*. However, this was not immediately carried out upon the fall of Jerusalem. In the general disturbance of that event Jeremiah was put in chains and taken to Ramah for the time where Nebuzar-adan had his headquarters. Then when this chief captain was ready to go to Babylon with the prisoners who were destined for that place, he first arranged to carry out the orders given him concerning Jeremiah; that is where this chapter begins. *The word that came to Jeremiah* refers to some message God gave the prophet after being released by Nebuzar-adan.

Verse 2. We know that God sometimes spoke to heathen persons when they were involved in some of the affairs of His people (Dan. 4: 14; Ezra 1: 2). Here the chief captain repeated to Jeremiah what the prophet had himself previously declared.

Verse 3. Nebuzar-adan was talking to Jeremiah but the pronouns applied to Judah as a whole of which nation the prophet was a member though innocent of any charge. So the words *ye* and *you* were said in reference to the guilty nation.

Verse 4. Nebuzar-adan was then ready to complete his charge concerning Jeremiah. He thus removed the chains that had been fastened upon him in the excitement of the fall of Jerusalem. He told him to take his choice between going with him to Babylon or remaining in the land of Palestine.

Verse 5. *Was not yet gone back* means this conversation was at Ramah before the captain left for his other activities. It repeats the same offer made in verse 4, and the context shows Jeremiah chose not to go with Nebuzar-adan, who then rewarded him with provisions and dismissed him.

Verse 6. Having been released at Ramah, Jeremiah went to Mizpah and dwelt among the people who had been committed to the care of Gedaliah. This is the fact that is mentioned ahead of time, in ch. 39: 14.

Verse 7. *Captains of the forces* means the war officers who had been serving Judah at the time of the Babylonian invasion. When Jerusalem fell these men ceased their operations, and they learned that Gedaliah had been made governor over the Jews who were left in the land by the commander-in-chief of the Babylonians.

Verse 8. The men referred to in the preceding verse are named in this. They came to Mizpah where Gedaliah was to have his headquarters. Ishmael seemed to be a leader among the group but we shall learn that he was an ambitious, jealous, wicked man.

Verse 9. Gedaliah was disposed to be a trustworthy captive of Babylon who would show the proper respect for the king who had conquered his country. He gave faithful advice to his fellow Jews and assured them it would be better for them to submit to the Babylonians peacefully whose prisoners they virtually were already.

Verse 10. Gedaliah expected to be kept busy with his appointment at Mizpah, not only in overseeing the poor Jews who were left in his care, but in his attentions to the members of the Chaldean nation who would resort to him there. But as for these officers who had formerly led the Jewish forces, they were advised to go out and gather of the fruits of the land (as per ch. 39: 10) and reside in the cities which they had succeeded in holding in the conflict.

Verse 11. The report of Gedaliah's appointment was learned by the Jews in the more distant districts, such as *Moab* and *Edom* which were east of the Jordan.

Verse 12. The Jews mentioned before had been driven into those countries by the invasion of the Babylonian forces into Palestine. Upon hearing the favorable news of Gedaliah's appointment they came gladly to him at Mizpah.

Verse 13. Johanan was mentioned in verse 8 but the writer then turned his attention to Ishmael because of his apparent outstanding importance. Now Johanan claims attention as bearer of a message to Gedaliah.

Verse 14. The Ammonites had long been enemies of the Jews though they were distantly related to the Abrahamic blood line. The king of these people heard of the honorable position of Gedaliah and conspired with Ishmael to have the good man killed. For that purpose Ishmael, whose personal ambition fitted him for the hateful work, was sent to Mizpah where Gedaliah was situated according to the appointment of the king of Babylon through his commander-in-chief. Johanan learned of this dark plot and gave Gedaliah the warning but he would not believe it.

Verse 15. Johanan was so confident in his view of the situation that he offered to prevent the plot by slaying Ishmael. That would have been a just act since all who plot to overthrow a lawful ruler by force have forfeited their right to live.

Verse 16. Gedaliah not only refused to authorize Johanan for the patriotic act of service which he offered to do, but charged him with making a false accusation. We shall learn how sadly true was the warning of this faithful man.

JEREMIAH 41

Verse 1. The coming of these men had been referred to in the preceding chapter as part of a general statement; this verse begins the direct account of the sad affair. Gedaliah showed that he had not been impressed by the warning of Johanan for he entertained Ishmael and his associates royally. *Eat bread together* was a positive mark of intimate friendship in Biblical times. (See 1 Cor. 5: 11.)

Verse 2. Ishmael and his group violated almost every rule of proper conduct that we can think of. They disregarded the law of gratitude; they took advantage of Gedaliah's confidence; they violated the laws of both God and man against murder, and that, too, by killing a man who was in a position of authority. Not only so, but they killed a man who not only had not sought his office, but who was appointed thereto on account of his evident worthiness, seeing it was done by a man who had it in his power to have humiliated him to the utmost had he been so minded.

Verse 3. Ishmael was so mad against Gedaliah that he slew all the Jews who were helpless and who had been entrusted to Gedaliah's care. He evidently wished to have no witnesses who might escape and be in the way of his further wicked plots.

Verse 4. This verse verifies the remark on the preceding one, for it says concerning the slaying of Gedaliah that *no man knew it.*

Verse 5. These men did not have animal sacrifices for the house of God and the articles of service had been removed. But the place where they had stood was considered, especially by these men who came from the region of the 10 tribes. They could burn incense even without the temple and its furniture. *Beards shaven* was a custom in ancient times on occasions of grief or humility. These Jews had much cause for those feelings, having lost their country and temple.

Verse 6. On their way toward Jerusalem these people passed near Mizpah and Ishmael went out to meet them. He thought it might not be suitable to his plans for them to be living but rather since "dead men tell nothing," it would be to his advantage and interest to get them out of the way. But to do so he must use some kind of deception, and he did so by pretending to sympathize with them and offering them some assistance. He invited them to come with him to Gedaliah who would be supposed to offer them some consolation.

Verse 7. These trusting people followed the wicked Ishmael into the city for they were not aware that Gedaliah and others had been slain. No sooner had they reached the city, the place where Ishmael had started his "reign of terror," than he slew these sorrowing worshipers almost to the last man, and disposed of their bodies in a disrespectful manner by casting them into a pit as if disposing of waste matter.

Verse 8. There were ten men who had survived the attacks of Ishmael. They bribed him to spare them on the ground that they possessed valuable fields and products. Should Ishmael slay them there would be no one to show him where to find these valuable products. On this ground Ishmael was himself misled and he spared their lives.

Verse 9. *Because of Gedaliah* indicates that Ishmael feared these men would have been friendly toward Gedaliah. He had reason to think thus since they had followed him into the city in order to *come to Gedaliah.* So his hatred for the governor was extended to these men also and hence their death was decreed. The purpose of identifying this pit as the one that Asa made was to give some idea of its size. Asa made it as a part of his preparation in his war with Baasha. It was a cistern and its use was that for water (pit meaning cistern) while engaged in the war and it would necessarily be large. That is the point being made here for it says Ismael *filled it* with the dead bodies.

Verse 10. After the aforesaid slaughter of the captives, Ishmael kidnapped the daughters of Zedekiah whom the king of Babylon had sent to Mizpah for safekeeping with some others, and started with them to go into the land of the Ammonites.

Verse 11. About this time Johanan got the news of what Ishmael had done, including the kidnaping of the king's daughters and other refugees.

Verse 12. He took his captains and pursued after Ishmael. They overtook him near a large pool at Gibeon which was a spot on the way to the land of the Ammonites.

Verse 13. When Johanan and his forces came in sight of the persons whom Ishmael had kidnaped *then they were glad.* They knew that it meant their rescue for Johanan was a good man and was the one who had warned Gedaliah of Ishmael.

Verse 14. Encouraged by the sight of these friends, these victims of Ishmael turned from him and joined Johanan and his group.

Verse 15. We do not know how much of a conflict took place at this time. However, Ishmael escaped with eight men and fled to the land of the Ammonites, the place to which he had started from Mizpah.

Verse 16. This sad experience made Johanan fearful in a general feeling of terror. Such a feeling sometimes causes a man to act with poor judgment. After his encounter with Ishmael at the pool near Gibeon, he gathered his captains with all the Jews he had recovered there, and joined them with the others who had escaped the sword in the terrible slaughter by Ishmael at Mizpah.

Verse 17. Johanan decided on fleeing to Egypt to get away from the Chaldeans. They paused in their flight at a spot held by an Israelite named Chimham which was near Bethlehem. This was a friendly region and Johanan considered it a safe place to rest while making his further plans for the journey into Egypt.

Verse 18. The Chaldeans (or Babylonians) had appointed Gedaliah as governor at Mizpah, and his murder might be regarded as an act of war against them. Since Ishmael was a Jew, the Chaldeans might develop a new feeling against the others. At least this was the panicky fear that possessed Johanan, so he planned to flee.

JEREMIAH 42

Verse 1. *Came near* indicates a more personal contact, sufficiently near to make a verbal request of Jeremiah. He doubtless was in the group as one of the persons whom Johanan had carried off from Mizpah, having escaped the sword of Ishmael.

Verse 2. Having paused at the habitation of Chimham, the group headed by Johanan made this personal approach unto the prophet to make an urgent request.

Verse 3. They professed to desire divine guidance in their way and in all their general conduct. To obtain such assistance they asked Jeremiah to pray God for them, he being a faithful prophet and servant of the Lord. Such a request would be praiseworthy were it coming from the heart; we shall see whether it was or not.

Verse 4. Jeremiah agreed to make the requested prayer for them. He also assured them that whatever the Lord revealed to him he would deliver to them faithfully.

Verse 5. The people even called upon the Lord to witness their promise to do whatever He should require of them.

Verse 6. They went into even more detail and specified their promise to obey whether *good* or *evil* were imposed upon them. These words are not used in the sense of right and wrong for God never brings anything wrong upon man. The words mean whether the things required would be pleasant or unpleasant.

Verse 7. The Lord used a waiting time of ten days before giving to Jeremiah the message in answer to his prayer on behalf of the people.

Verse 8. Jeremiah wished to present his message to the entire group of petitioners that no one might be left with any excuse. Hence it was said he called them *from the least even to the greatest.*

Verse 9. The identity of the source of the message was carefully attended to. It was the God of Israel, and the very one to whom they asked Jeremiah to go with his supplication on their behalf.

Verse 10. The message advised them to be submissive and *abide in this land.* This phrase meant for them not to go to Egypt but to remain where they were. They had not been required to go to Babylon although they were "prisoners of war" in reality, but had been given the privilege of remaining in their home land.

Verse 11. They were assured that no harm would result to them from their captor (the king of Babylon) if they would obey the word of the Lord.

Verse 12. The particular ones to whom this message was given were yet in their own land, but the promise applied to their nation as a whole. The return of the nation from Babylon would mean a blessing to these individuals also.

Verse 13. *But if ye say.* This phrase, considered in the light of the context shows that the people rejected the advice of God through the prophet, and declared their determination of going to Egypt. This and the following verse is their rebellious assertion against the admonition of the prophet.

Verse 14. They professed to believe that by going into Egypt they would escape the ravages of war. They probably based this hope on the few instances of apparent friendship that Egypt had shown to them recently.

Verse 15. From here to the close of the chapter the prophet describes the evils that will come upon them if they reject the advice of the Lord. *Remnant of Judah* means the ones who had been permitted to remain in Palestine when the others were carried off to Babylon.

Verse 16. There is no use to try to run away from God, and by going to Egypt against the admonition of the prophet they would be casting defiance against the Lord.

Verse 17. For the significance of *sword, famine* and *pestilence* see the comments at ch. 14: 12. The punishment was to be complete for all who attempted to make Egypt a hiding place from the Babylonians.

Verse 18. The ruin the Lord brought on Jerusalem was in punishment for the sins of the nation. Now that which was to be imposed on these who would not accept the punishment of Jerusalem submissively would also be great. An *execration* means something worthy of being cursed.

Verse 19. This verse sums up the warning that God gave to his people. *Remnant of Judah* means the small number of the kingdom of Judah who had survived the overthrow of Jerusalem, and had been given permission to remain in Palestine.

Verse 20. To *dissemble* means to act deceitfully or hypocritically. The prophet accuses the people of having acted in that way when they asked him to pray to God for them. They evidently thought their profession of trust in God would win for them some escape from the divine wrath, for when the answer of God was unfavorable they broke their word and declared they would go into Egypt as they had originally said.

Verse 21. In rejecting the warning of the prophet, the people were accused of disobeying the voice of the Lord God.

Verse 22. A final warning was given that they would perish in the very land whither they had fled for safety.

JEREMIAH 43

Verse 1. When Jeremiah spoke *all the words of the Lord* he fulfilled the promise he made to these people as recorded in chapter 42: 4.

Verse 2. We regret to see the change that seemed to come over Johanan. In the previous chapters he was devoted to the interests of Jeremiah and the other refugees and opposed the wicked plots of Ishmael. Now he is against Jeremiah and siding with the others who rebelled against the admonition of the Lord. He even accused Jeremiah of falsehood and denied his inspiration. These men were said to be *proud* which shows that pride is not always exhibited by some showy condition. In the present case it was demonstrated by a rebellious spirit. Paul gives a similar picture of it in 1 Timothy 6: 3, 4 where he accuses a false teacher of being proud.

Verse 3. Baruch was Jeremiah's secretary (ch. 32: 12-14) and was a good man. There was no ground for saying that he had influenced Jeremiah in the wrong direction. But some pretext had to be used for opposing the prophet since he had previously supported him in his teaching. If a good man could be influenced at all in the wrong direction, it would probably be possible to be done by the words of a friend; hence the mention of Baruch who was a trusted servant of Jeremiah.

Verse 4. Some people do not appreciate a good thing when they have it. These captives of Babylon had been given the privilege of remaining in their own home land, but now they ignored that favor and planned to flee out of the country. Such an action was as bad in principle as that of a "trusty" who abuses his parole by fleeing.

Verse 5. This revolt was headed by Johanan and included the scattered citizens of Judah from various territories.

Verse 6. All of these persons were herded into a band of escapees to be taken to Egypt. We have no direct information as to the attitude of these individuals, but we do know that Jeremiah and his faithful secretary Baruch were not willing to go. Hence we may justly say that they were kidnaped by Johanan.

Verse 7. This verse concludes the sad story of this rebellious action. The significant part of the whole affair was in the fact that it was in disobedience against the word of the Lord. Tahpanhes was the place where they settled which is in the northeast part of Egypt.

Verse 8. In ancient times the Lord frequently used one heathen nation to chastise another. This verse starts a bracket in which the prophet predicts a conflict between Egypt and Babylon and the victory will be on the side of Babylon. Following my practice where important information can be gained from secular history, I shall here make a quotation as follows: "The king of Babylon, taking advantage therefore of the intestine divisions which the rebellion of Amasis had occasioned in that kingdom, marched thither at the head of his army. He subdued Egypt from Migdol or Magdol, a town on the frontiers [borders] of the kingdom, as far as Syene, in the opposite extremity where it borders on Ethiopia. He made a horrible devastation wherever he came; killed a great number of the inhabitants, and made such dreadful havoc in the country, that the damage could not be repaired in *forty years*. Nebuchadnezzar, having loaded his army with spoils, and *conquered the whole kingdom*, came to an accommodation [agreement] with Amasis; and leaving him as his viceroy [representative] there, returned to Babylon [emphasis mine, E. M. Z.]." Rollin's Ancient History, Volume 1, page 232. This history is corroborated in Britannica, v. 7, p. 743, article Egypt; Josephus, Antiquities, Book 10, Chapter 10, Section 3.

Verse 9. It is related that Pharaoh was repairing his palace at the time of this prediction. The stones referred to were like those being used for the repair work of the self-satisfied Egyptian king.

Verse 10. The significance of the "acting" was just where the king of Egypt was feeling secure in his power, the king of Babylon would some day set up his throne. *My servant* is said of Nebuchadnezzar because the Lord was going to use his services in punishing the king of Egypt.

Verse 11. Famine, pestilence and sword were often threatened as a punishment from God in ancient times. That is practically what is meant in this verse. When an attack was made some might surrender without putting up any fight; they would be punished with *captivity*. Others would resist but would be finally slain by the sword. Still others would neither try to fight nor be submissive to capture willingly. All such would be hemmed in by a siege and finally meet *death* from the pestilence that usually resulted from a famine caused by a siege.

Verse 12. The Egyptians, like Babylonians, were worshipers of false gods and had houses erected for their services. These houses were destined to be set on fire by the Babylonians who are the antecedent of the pronoun *he*. It is a very easy thing for a shepherd to put on his garment when he wishes to go out about his business in control of his flock. The fact is used figuratively to illustrate the success of the king of Babylon in appropriating to himself the spoils of Egypt.

Verse 13. A general prediction was made against the gods of Egypt in the preceding verse. This specifies a place called Beth-shemesh which was considered as a holy city by the Egyptians because of the houses therein erected to the gods.

JEREMIAH 44

Verse 1. The closing verses of the preceding chapter were a prediction against Egypt, doubtless because the country harbored the fugitives of Judah who fled there contrary to the wishes of the Lord. This chapter is directed against the Jews who had thought to avoid the wrath of God by fleeing to this heathen land.

Verse 2. *Evil* is used in the sense of something unpleasant or in the nature of a severe punishment, not in any sense of moral wrong. The complete destruction of Jerusalem was cited as an evidence of what the Lord could and would do to those who resisted the divine admonitions and thus incurred His wrath.

Verse 3. Idolatry was the outstanding sin of Judah and it caused them to commit many other iniquities. Gods which they *knew not* means the gods that were foreign to them and which were thus called *strange* (from the outside) gods.

Verse 4. The transgressions of Judah were not from any lack of instruction. *Rising early* is a figurative expression, referring to the urgency with which God sent his admonitions to his people.

Verse 5. To hearken means to heed what is said and to incline the ear means to be a willing listener. The people of Judah refused to do either although the Lord earnestly admonished them about it.

Verse 6. God's fury would be in evidence in the streets of the cities by the destruction that the enemy was permitted to make in them.

Verse 7. *Against your souls* means against their own best interests. When men oppose the will of the Lord they become their own worst enemies. However, the interests of the *soul* in this case did not necessarily mean the spiritual matters, but those that were vitally concerned with their population and national life. Note that mention was made of their citizens and descendants, that all were to be destroyed.

Verse 8. It is remarkable to note how slow man is to learn a lesson from his own experiences. The citizens of Judah as a whole had been taken to Babylon in punishment for their idolatry. These few who were in Egypt had been given the special exemption of remaining in their home land though at the same time they were virtual captives. Now here they are in another country through desertion and are taking up the very practices their fellows did for which they had been taken into captivity.

Verse 9. The Lord asks these runaway Jews if they had forgotten the record of their fathers. It is in question form but really is a reproach upon them for not having profited by the end of the nation.

Verse 10. The Jews who were at that time in Babylon were as forgetful as these in Egypt and had not become humble through their severe punishment.

Verse 11. Coming back to the Jews in Egypt, the Lord warned them that he would set his face against them for *evil*. The last word means something very unpleasant as a punishment for their sins, not anything wrong morally.

Verse 12. The sum of the terrible things threatened in this verse is the most total extinction of the ones who sought residence in Egypt. They were to be consumed by the threefold curse previously mentioned, that of the sword, famine and pestilence. An *execration* means something considered worthy of being cursed.

Verses 13, 14. The threefold punishment is again threatened, and the comparison is made to that which was imposed upon Jerusalem. The significance of the passage is that the stragglers in Egypt were as guilty as the ones who had been taken into Babylon. Of course all rules may have some exceptions and the threat that the ones who had fled to Egypt would be destroyed meant that as a group that would occur. Yet a few individuals were to be suffered to escape as indicated in verse 28. Doubtless it was in some way through them that the world outside of Egypt received the writings which Jeremiah produced after being taken to that country.

Verse 15. A man is not responsible for what he cannot prevent or know, but if he can know it and does not oppose it, he is as guilty as those doing an evil thing. The men were aware of the idolatrous practices of their women and were hence in partnership with them in sin.

Verse 16. The men not only knew of the sins of their wives but spoke in defence of it. The words *we will not hearken unto thee* constituted a deliberate rebellion against the words of the inspired prophet.

Verse 17. According to Smith's Bible Dictionary the *queen of heaven* "is the moon, worshiped as Ashtaroth or Astarte, to whom the Hebrew women offered cakes in the streets of Jerusalem." We should understand that the women were speaking also in this rebellious conversation (verse 15). They were the ones who made the cakes to be burned in this idolatrous practice, hence were prominent in the defence of this iniquity.

Verse 18. These idolaters were vain enough to attribute their prosperity to the false gods which they worshiped. As long as the Lord is willing to tolerate an evil generation at all, he will continue to bestow the blessings of nature. (See Matt. 5: 45.) These corrupt people were so foolish as to give their false gods the credit for the blessings that came from the true God.

Verse 19. The question form of this verse is really an assertion on the part of the women referred to in verse 15. *Without our men* means they had the consent of their husbands in the practice of idolatry, and that made the men equally guilty with the women. Such a principle was taught in the law of Moses (Numbers 30: 6-9).

Verse 20. When Jeremiah replied to these people he spoke *to the men* and *to the women*. That indicated that he regarded both sexes as guilty of the corrupt practices.

Verse 21. *Did not the Lord remember them* signified that God was aware of all the corrupt practices of the people of Judah and would not forget it. He declared (Ex. 20: 5) that he was a jealous God, and when his people disrespected him by burning incense to false gods his wrath was kindled against them.

Verse 22. *Could no longer bear* means the longsuffering of the Lord finally was exhausted. The result was the desolation of the land and the deportation of its people.

Verse 23. It should be noted that the burning of incense in religious service was considered the most exclusive form of devotion. That was why it was what distinguished the rights of the priests from all others. (See 2 Chron. 26: 16-18.)

Verse 24. The *people* and the *women* are mentioned separately because the latter made the cakes to be used and the former accepted them to be offered to the idol gods.

Verse 25. *Mouths* and *hands* are both named very appropriately because it is not only words but also deeds that show a man's standing and by which he is to be judged. However, if the words are uttered first, the deeds cannot be thought to be prompted by some sudden impulse. It would show that the deeds were the result of a deliberate plot. This principle is recognized by the governments of the land today. In determining the degree of guilt of an accused man, if his previously-uttered words on the subject can be proved, they are given much consideration by the courts.

Verse 26. This prediction was against the Jews who had fled to Egypt, because of their twofold transgression. First, they had sinned in fleeing to that land, and second, by taking up the idolatrous practices of the people around them. God had determined they should not be allowed to engage in professed praise to Him in that land.

Verse 27. *Watch over them for evil* denotes the severe chastisement that the Lord would bring upon them. To prevent them from any success in their unrighteous plots, the Lord was going to *watch over them* or be always on the alert. As a result, the group as a whole was destined to be destroyed by the threefold calamity often mentioned.

Verse 28. These exceptions were commented upon at verse 14. *Shall know whose words shall stand* is the phrase that indicates these persons were destined to deliver the writings of Jeremiah to the world outside of Egypt.

Verses 29, 30. As a visible evidence that God could and would perform these threats against the people of Judah in Egypt, He would deliver Pharaoh-hophra (the then-ruling king of the country) into the hand of his enemies. For the historical fulfillment of this prediction see the quotation at chapter 48: 8.

JEREMIAH 45

Verse 1. In the compiling of the parts of Jeremiah's writing not much attention was paid to chronology. This chapter should be read just after chapter 36. Baruch was a good man and served as secretary to Jeremiah. After writing at the dictation of the prophet, he was addressed personally by him.

Verse 2. Jeremiah did not speak merely as a personal friend to Baruch although he was that, but passed on to him the words that came from *the God of Israel.*

Verse 3. Baruch was worried over the predictions he had been instructed to write at the mouth of the prophet. He seemed to take it as a personal misfortune that was to come upon him and that he would be the chief sufferer therefrom.

Verse 4. God instructed Jeremiah to hold Baruch's attention to the calamity to be brought upon the general work He had in the nation. The whole land was to be brought down in chastisement for its corruptions. That would be a far greater matter for grief than the interests of just one man.

Verse 5. Baruch was mildly rebuked for his personal worry in view of the greater misfortune to be imposed upon the land. However, he was given some assurance as a comfort that his life was to be spared to reward him for his righteous conduct.

JEREMIAH 46

Verse 1. After the digression of the preceding chapter, Jeremiah resumed his writings against various nations. *Gentiles* is from GOI and is defined by Strong as follows: "A foreign nation; hence a Gentile." In the King James version the word has been rendered Gentiles 30 times (always plural), heathen 143, nation 366, people 5. The verse means that the prophet was going to make some predictions against the heathen people of various classes and in the many places.

Verse 2. The prediction against Egypt was made and the historical comments cited in chapter 43: 8-13.

Verses 3, 4. A *buckler* is a small protector and a *shield* is a large one. A *helmet* is a piece for the protection of the head. To *furbish the spears* means to polish them. *Brigantines* were the coats of mail to be worn as a general protection for the body. The entire passage was a notice to Egypt to get ready for war because the Lord was going to bring the Babylonians against the people of that country.

Verse 5. *Wherefore* in the Bible usually means "why?" or "how?" and sometimes it means "therefore," which is its meaning in the present passage. The prediction had just been made that Egypt was to be drawn into war. God knows the future as well as the past and thus he could say *I have seen them* (the Egyptians) *dismayed,* etc.

Verse 6. *Let not . . . flee away* is a prediction in the style of the language used by the prophets, and means the people of Egypt will not succeed in their attempts to escape capture by the Babylonians. *Fall toward the north* denotes they will be overcome by the nation whose capital is on the Euphrates River. As to the reason for referring to the "north" see the note at Isaiah 14: 31 volume 3 of this COMMENTARY.

Verse 7. *Who is this*, etc., is a challenging question to Egypt. That country relied on its great River Nile for the life of its people as well it might. But it often filled its kings with an undue sense of importance as to their power.

Verse 8. Not only did the Nile furnish Egypt with the necessities of physical life, but the people worshiped it as their chief god and believed that through it they could *cover the earth* and take possession of the cities. That is why the prediction shows the nation in a mood of defiance against the Babylonians.

Verse 9. Many of the passages along here are in the nature of a challenge to Egypt. It is as if the Lord said to her: "Just come on and do your best if you think you can defeat My plans." In that spirit God bids Egypt to come on with her horses and let the (war) chariots rage. She is even challenged to attach to herself all the allies she wishes, such as the *Ethiopians* and *Libyans* and others.

Verse 10. *This* is a pronoun referring to *the day of the Lord God of hosts*, and that day was to be when He brought the Babylonians against the land of Egypt. *Sword shall devour* means the sword of the Babylonians will slay the people of Egypt. *Made drunk* does not mean intoxication in the ordinary sense of that word for blood will not do that. It means the same as to be satisfied or filled and gorged. The passage means the Babylonians will shed an abundance of blood when the Egyptians resist them. *Sacrifice in the north country*. The land of Egypt will not literally be taken to Babylon, but it will be sacrificed to the Lord's will and the service will be executed by a people from the *north* whose capital is on the Euphrates. (See verse 6 on the word *north*.)

Verse 11. A part of Strong's definition of the original for *virgin* is "figuratively, a city or state," and it is so used with reference to Egypt. Smith's Bible Dictionary says this of *Gilead*. "A mountainous region bounded on the west by the Jordan, on the north by Bashan, on the east by the Arabian plateau, and on the south by Moab and Ammon . . . Gilead was specially noted for its balm collected from 'balm of Gilead' trees, and worth twice its weight in silver." Because of the healing qualities believed to be possessed by this balm it was often used or referred to (both literally and figuratively) as a source of cure or relief. This verse means to tell the Egyptians that it will not do them any good to go up after the balm of Gilead. There is to be no cure for them against the predicted affliction, therefore it will be *in vain* for them to seek for any.

Verse 12. *Nations have heard* is a prediction that the nations will learn of the defeat of Egypt when it takes place. *Mighty man stumbled against the mighty* denotes that all the strong men of Egypt, together with their allies on whom they will rely, shall be overthrown together by the Babylonians.

Verse 13. This verse repeats the prediction previously made against Egypt, and names the particular man of Babylon (Nebuchadnezzar) who was to be the ruler there at the time. For the historical fulfillment of that prediction see at chapter 43: 8-13.

Verse 14. *Migdol, Noph* (modern Memphis), and Tahpanhes were principal cities in Egypt. They were singled out by the prediction and were warned to *stand fast and prepare*. This meant for them to get ready for war waged against them by Nebuchadnezzar.

Verse 15. *Why are? . . . because* means the utter defeat of their men of war will be due to the driving force of the Lord.

Verse 16. This is similar to verse 12, referring to internal troubles of Egypt.

Verse 17. This is a prediction of the boasting the Egyptians would do regarding their defeat by the enemy. The last clause of the verse is the statement of the Lord, and means that the time will have been passed when Egypt could defend herself when the Babylonians are brought up against the country.

Verse 18. *Tabor* was a high mountain and *Carmel* was a prominent range in the land of Palestine. Their impressive existence is used as an illustration of the surety and force of the king of Babylon when he comes against Egypt.

Verse 19. *Furnish thyself* means for Egypt to prepare for the worst; that the country was destined to be overcome by the enemy. *Noph* was another name for Memphis, one of the great cities of Egypt that was to be laid in desolation when the country was invaded by Nebuchadnezzar and his powerful army.

Verse 20. The Egyptians paid special attention and devotion to the cattle kind (as witness the golden calf of Israel just recently from that country), and hence her attitude of self-importance and fitness is compared to a *fair heifer*. But the Lord threatens her with destruction from the *north* which denotes from Babylon.

Verse 21. The leading men of Egypt felt independent and the country relied on them. *They are turned back* is a prediction that these men will fail the country when the king of Babylon comes against the land.

Verse 22. The pronoun *thereof* refers to *the time of their visitation* mentioned in the preceding verse. It was to take place against Egypt. *The voice ... like a serpent* means the voice of the men of Egypt when the Babylonian forces come against the men. Moffatt's version renders this, "She can but draw back hissing like a snake before her foes." When a strong force threatens to overcome a snake all it can do is to hiss at its attacking foe. That is what the great men of Egypt will do before the army of Babylon because *they* (the Babylonians) *shall march with an army*.

Verse 23. The Babylonians will cut down the forests of Egypt at the time of the invasion. *Though it cannot be searched* means the forest was supposed to be too great to be destroyed, yet God would enable the Babylonians to cut it down. *They* means the men of the invading army will be like a swarm of grasshoppers and they will cut down the trees as grasshoppers would consume a field of grass.

Verse 24. *Daughter* means the country of Egypt was to be *confounded* or confused and defeated. For the significance of the *north* see the note at Isaiah 14: 31, volume 3.

Verse 25. *No* was another important city of Egypt whose modern name is Thebes. It was among the cities that were to feel the hand of Babylon under the Lord's plan.

Verse 26. The desolation of Egypt was not to be permanent but *afterward shall it be inhabited*. This was set forth in the history quoted at chapter 43: 8-13.

Verse 27. Before proceeding to the predictions against other heathen nations, the Lord gave a brief piece of consolation for his own people who were at that time in captivity. They were promised that they would return out of the land of their captivity and rest securely again in their own land.

Verse 28. God's people as well as the heathen were to be punished for their sins against Him. However, there was to be a difference in the severity and results of the punishment. The heathen nations were to be put down permanently while God's nation was to survive the chastisement. The fulfillment of this promise may be seen in the books of Ezra and Nehemiah.

JEREMIAH 47

Verse 1. Again I will remind the reader that chronological order was not always observed in compiling the several parts of a prophet's writings. Historically we last knew of Jeremiah when he was being taken by force to Egypt, and little is known of what became of him after that. But his writings seem to have been available and were finally put together by the friends of Truth in the form now with us and known as the book of Jeremiah. Hence we shall read yet many of his prophecies that he wrote before the time he was taken captive. Many of those were against heathen nations that had mistreated the people of God, or had otherwise displeased Him by their practices. The present chapter was written against the Philistines and it was dated at a time prior to the fall of Gaza which was a prominent city of the Philistines. That date is mentioned in order to explain that a prediction was made against the Philistines and that its fulfillment was to be brought about through the Egyptian king.

Verse 2. *Waters* and *flood* in figurative language refers to great times of trouble. The application here is to the calamities that were to overthrow the land of the Philistines.

Verse 3. The reference to the *horses* and *chariots*, etc., is in view of the army that was destined to be brought against the Philistine land. *Fathers not look back to their children*. So great will the consternation be that parents will not be concerned for the safety of their children but will think of themselves only.

Verse 4. *Tyrus* and *Zidon* were cities of Phoenicia, a country lying near that of the Philistines. It was natural that they would have a fellow feeling for each other in times of distress, but the prophet warned them that such an alliance would not avail.

Verse 5. *Gaza* and *Ashkelon* were cities of the Philistines, and baldness was a figurative prediction that they would be made bare by the ravages of war. *Cut thyself* refers to the self-imposed motions of grief over the misfortunes of the country.

Verse 6. This verse represents the Philistines in a pleading mood asking the Lord to put up the sword; such is the meaning of *how long . . . ere thou be quiet?*

Verse 7. This verse is the answer of the Lord to the pleading of the Philistines. They are told that *it*, the sword, cannot be quiet because the Lord had given it a charge, which was against Ashkelon, one of the cities of the Philistines.

JEREMIAH 48

Verse 1. This entire chapter is against the land of Moab which was situated on the east side of the Dead Sea. Its people were descended from one of the sons of Lot (Gen. 19:37) and were hence related by blood to the line coming down from Abraham. For this reason the Lord would not permit his people to deal with them as they did with other nations with whom they came in contact (Deut. 2:9). Yet the relations between the two peoples were somewhat strained and in the main the Moabites were considered as enemies to the Israelites and were marked for some severe judgments from the Lord. The places named were cities of the Moabites that were destined to feel God's wrath.

Verse 2. *Heshbon* was another city in the land of Moab that was to be punished. *They have devised evil against it* means the forces whom God would see fit to use as his instruments when the time came for the punishment predicted.

Verse 3. *Voice of crying* means the bewailing that was to be heard in the city of Horonaim which was one of the special ones among the Moabites.

Verse 4. *Moab* is named and includes the land and the people. *Little* has a various definition in the lexicon, but the general meaning is to be small or helpless against the attacking foe, and that was to make the people of the land *cry* out so as to be heard.

Verse 5. *Luhith* and *Horonaim* were cities of Moab and their citizens were destined to be heard crying because of the destruction of their cities.

Verse 6. *Flee, save yourselves* is a prediction of the distressful condition that was to come upon the land of Moab. *Heath* means a tract of waste land, and the land of Moab was to become such a place for a time.

Verse 7. The feeling of security which the Moabites had was to be shattered and their helplessness was to become evident. *Chemosh* was one of the invisible gods of the land of Moab, the chief one that they worshiped. Idolaters relied on their gods for protection and help, but the prediction was against all their expectations.

Verse 8. *The spoiler* means one who would strip the country of its goods, and in this case it was to be the Babylonians. *City* and *valley* are named together to indicate the completeness of the desolation as it would affect the land.

Verse 9. There would be no use to try fleeing from the punishment that God designed against Moab. The language intends to picture the people in a state of panic and desire to escape the chastisement confronting them.

Verse 10. God had decreed the punishment of Moab at the hands of another country, and the work to be done by it (Babylon) would be the work of God. If the swordsman of Babylon should be negligent in using the sword against the victims of God's wrath, the divine curse will be upon him.

Verse 11. This verse is an interesting figurative description of the past state of the self-satisfied peace of Moab. The figure is drawn from the subject of wine and its various conditions. *Lees* are the settlings that fall to the bottom of a vessel in which the raw juice of the grape has been placed. After a time these settle and leave the pure wine undisturbed and clear on the top. To pour this wine from one vessel to another would disturb it which would represent the disturbed condition of the land of Moab when it is upset by the Babylonians. The land had not *gone into captivity* which means it had been left alone as a quantity of wine undisturbed with the *lees* at the bottom of the vessel. In such a condition the taste of the pure wine would remain in the vessel, not having been mixed with the dregs through being shaken up or poured out.

Verse 12. This condition of peace

was to be disturbed and the *wanderers* (the Babylonians) were to come and *break the bottles* (figuratively speaking) and destroy the peace of the land on which the people had been resting in their false security.

Verse 13. *Bethel* was one of the places where the 10-tribe kingdom of Israel set up the golden calves for idolatrous worship (1 Ki. 12:29). That did not save Israel from the shame of captivity (2 Ki. 17), neither was the idol god *Chemosh* going to save Moab in the day of its humiliation.

Verse 14. The Moabites boasted of their men in the war forces and virtually defied any nation to oppose them.

Verse 15. *Moab is spoiled* is present tense as to grammatical form but is prophetic in thought. When God says a certain thing will be done it is as certain as a thing that *is* done at the time it is predicted.

Verse 16. This verse is still a prediction in the present tense, but it is a little more definite as to time and says the fulfillment is soon to come.

Verse 17. The downfall of Moab was to be so evident and humiliating that the surrounding nations would lament over it. They are predicted as being so affected because the men of Moab had been regarded as great and strong and it would be a matter of astonishment to see them meet such great defeat.

Verse 18. *Daughter* is a figurative name for a country and *Dibon* was one of the cities of that country. The Moabites were proud and independent and had exalted themselves over the glory of this city. *Come down from thy glory* is a prediction that the Moabites would be taken down from that self-constructed pinnacle of glory and be made to *sit in thirst* which means they would be brought to want.

Verse 19. The countries of the ancient world counted much on their cities, and for that reason many of the military conflicts were directed towards those centers. *Aroer* was a city of Moab and its inhabitants were warned of the destruction to come upon the city. *Espy* means to look on and see the people fleeing from the city. They were then to ask the meaning of the excitement and would wonder *what is done?*

Verse 20. This gives the answer to the inquiry, which is that *Moab is confounded* or confused because it is broken by the invasion of the Babylonians. *Arnon* was a stream on whose banks the city of Aroer was located, and the stream is represented as lamenting the hard fate of the country through which it flowed.

Vere 21. The towns named in this verse were not very important and little is known of them. But the Moabites counted much on their many towns or cities, and the Lord wished them to get some idea of the greatness of His wrath by overthrowing them.

Verses 22-24. The cities named in this paragraph were to receive punishment similar to those previously named, hence they are grouped into the one unit.

Verse 25. When *horn* is used figuratively it is defined "power" in the lexicon. The power of Moab as a nation was to be taken from her by the Babylonians.

Verse 26. We should understand these terms are being used figuratively. A drinking man sometimes boasts of his ability to "handle" as much liquor as he chooses. God represents Moab in that frame of mind and predicts that he will be forced to swallow more than he can manage. He was to become repulsively sick from drink and then forced to wallow in the discharges of his besotted stomach.

Verse 27. Moab had made light of Israel and compared him to a man caught among thieves. It was true that Israel had met with misfortune as a chastisement from God for his sins, but the Lord would not tolerate having Moab *skip with joy* over it.

Verse 28. The burden of the oppression that was to come against the people of Moab would be directed chiefly against the cities. That is why the citizens of such spots were told (which was a form of prediction) to leave them and dwell among the rocks.

Verse 29. Pride is not always manifested by a display of outward glory. The original word is also rendered "arrogancy," which means an overbearing attitude. Moab had certainly shown that disposition against Israel, a noted instance being that in the affair of Balak and Balaam (Num. 22-24).

Verse 30. The same spirit described as *pride* in the preceding verse is here called wrath. In that attitude Moab threatened to destroy Israel (even as he tried in the days of Balak), but God knew all about it and decreed the failure of the plot. *Shall not effect it* means Moab would not be able to bring the effect against Israel that he conspired to do.

Verse 31. *Will I howl* is a form of prediction, meaning that Moab would howl for the miseries that the Lord would bring against the land. *Kir-heres* was one name of a place in the land of Moab that was destined to feel the sting of God's wrath.

Verse 32. Much of this verse is figurative but it has the same thought as the other predictions against the land. *Weep with the weeping* means that Sibmah will weep in the same manner as did Jazer, a city that had been taken by invaders (Num. 21: 32). *Plants* refers to the people who *are gone* (will go, according to prophetic style) *over the sea*. This clause is an indirect reference to the cities tributary to Babylon.

Verse 33. Grape cultivation was one of the principal industries of the lands of the Bible. For that reason an interference with that business would be considered a serious thing for the country; such a misfortune was to befall the land of Moab.

Verse 34. *Nimrim* was a stream in the region of Moab, and the other names were towns and places that depended on the waters for sustenance, but that was to be cut off by the curse the Lord intended bringing on the country. According to verse 11 Moab had never suffered much as a nation, even as a *heifer of three years old* had never known the hardships of work. The circumstance is used to illustrate the unaccustomed misfortune to be brought against the land.

Verse 35. The idolatrous practices of Moab were destined to be stopped by the Lord. This would be accomplished by the dearth that would come which would cut short the production of animals and other items commonly used in sacrifices.

Verse 36. The distressful situation of Moab is described figuratively in this passage. The prophet (speaking for the Lord) expresses a pitiable attitude toward the sad fate decreed to come upon the land. The figure is based upon an instrument called a pipe. The appropriateness of such a comparison will be apparent in the following quotation from Smith's Bible Dictionary: "The sound of the pipe was apparently a soft wailing note, which made it appropriate to be used in mourning and at funerals." This explains to us the reason for the language in Matthew 9: 23.

Verse 37. In ancient times a strange custom prevailed in cases of great distress or anxiety. People would mutilate their bodies and disarrange their hair and beards in the manner described in this verse.

Verse 38. Houses had flat roofs in the eastern countries so that people used them as places of prayer and other activities. (See Acts 10: 9.) Moab was destined to engage in mourning programs on the tops of their houses as well as in the streets, when the threatened punishment came upon the country.

Verse 39. *They shall howl* means that others shall express themselves at the shameful condition that was to come on the land of Moab. The significance of it is in the fact of the situation's being so evident that others would realize it and make remarks.

Verse 40. *He shall fly* denotes that the Lord will come down upon Moab with his punishment, even as an eagle would swoop over a land.

Verse 41. Kerioth was a town of Moab and it was to suffer the same fate as her sisters. When a woman is in the pangs of childbirth her entire nervous system is in a state of terror (John 16: 21). That circumstance is used to illustrate the state of mind that will overcome the men of Moab when they see the trouble in their gates.

Verse 42. The destruction of Moab was to be understood in a comparative sense and not in a total one as will be seen in the last verse of this chapter.

Verse 43. A *pit* indicates a place into which one might fall, and a *snare* means an instrument in which one would be caught. Both terms are used to indicate the downward plunge that the people of Moab would take in the hour of their adversity.

Verse 44. The varied experiences of escaping from one difficulty only to run into another describes the things that were destined to come upon the land of Moab. *Year of their visitation* means the year when God would visit Moab with his punishments.

Verse 45. *Heshbon* was a prominent city of Moab and the people thought they would find shelter in the shadow thereof. They fled there *because of the force* of the enemy that the Lord had chosen by whom to chastise the Moabites. But the *fire* of God's wrath had already shot forth even in the region of Heshbon so that it would not avail anything to flee thither for the purpose of finding refuge.

Verse 46. The *people of Chemosh* means the Moabites who relied on this god for protection. Instead of help from this false god his worshipers were to perish.

Verse 47. Moab never did go bodily into national captivity as we understand that term regarding the captivity of Israel. It rather indicated a state of domination under some other people in which its national progress was checked. The original for *captivity* is defined by Strong, "a former state of prosperity." Thus the prediction in the phrase *bring again the captivity* means that after having suffered punishment according to God's purpose, He would restore to the land of Moab its previous state of national prosperity and the liberty of enjoyment therein.

JEREMIAH 49

Verse 1. Several noted heathen nations will be considered in this chapter because the Lord had complaints against all of them. The first one is the *Ammonites* who were descended, like the Moabites, from Lot. More than once we have seen that God has used various foreign nations to chastise his own people, yet when those nations took improper joy from the misfortunes of Israel the Lord turned against them. In 2 Kings 24: 2, 3 is an account of the punishment of the kingdom of Judah, and the Ammonites were included in the forces God used for the purpose. Previously Israel (the 10-tribe kingdom) had been taken out of their possessions and Judah would logically have been the rightful inheritor of the territory left by Israel. But Judah incurred the wrath of God and forfeited the right to it and hence He brought the nations mentioned (including the Ammonites) against the country. However, that did not justify the Ammonites in acting as if Israel had no rightful inheritor of his estate. In seizing, therefore, upon the territory of Gad (a part of the 10-tribe dominions), the Ammonites brought upon themselves the predictions here recorded.

Verse 2. *Rabbath* was a city of the Ammonites and was destined to suffer the ravages of war. The last clause means that the people who had possessed the territory of Israel would be brought under by Israel.

Verse 3. This *Ai* is not the one so well known in Israelite history, but was one near Heshbon and belonging to the Ammonites. It was doomed along with other Ammonite cities to feel the weight of God's wrath. *King go into captivity* means a condition in which the leading men of the nation would be temporarily subdued, not that the nation as a body would be taken into another country.

Verse 4. *Daughter* is a figurative name of a city or country, and it is here applied to the Ammonites. They are called *backsliding* because they had slipped in their national conduct and had brought upon themselves the displeasure of the Lord. *Flowing valley* means the resources of their prosperity in which they gloried. They boasted that their wealth would provide them security against any who might *come to them.*

Verse 5. In spite of their material strength the Ammonites were destined to be thrown into a panic of fear. This would be similar to the predictions against Moab in chapter 48: 41. (See the comments at that place.) Under the confusion of this panicky state they would be scattered by the adversaries about them.

Verse 6. The unfortunate condition of the Ammonites was not to be permanent. *Bring again the captivity* has the same meaning as a like statement about Moab. (See the comments on it at chapter 48: 47.)

Verse 7. *Edom* was another name for Esau (Gen. 36: 1) and the Edomites were the descendants of that man. Esau was a full brother to Jacob (they being twins) and hence these people were closer of kin to the Israelites than were the Ammonites. The Edomites were always regarded as enemies of the descendants of Jacob and many predictions were made against them. *Teman* was a prominent district of the Edomites and was hence singled out in the declarations of the prophet. The question form of language is used in this verse, but the thought is that the area of Teman was destined to decline in wisdom.

Verse 8. *Dedan* refers to some other locality in the land of Edom. The prediction of misfortune that was to come on it was expressed in the form of a warning for its citizens to flee from the place. *Dwell deep* is a figurative exhortation to the inhabitants of the place to "prepare for the worst," or to make the best they can of a situation of distress when it is brought upon them.

Verse 9. The thought in this verse is that what was coming on the people of the land would be more desolating than the work of a grape harvester. He would at least leave enough fruit to justify going over the vineyard to glean. Or a thief would stop when he had secured enough for his appetite, then leave the rest to the owner.

Verse 10. But God threatened to make a more complete desolation than the invaders mentioned in the preceding verse. *Have made* is past tense in form but future in thought. *Esau* (or Edom) was to be exposed as a nation to the gaze of others, and the prediction is compared to the exposure of a man's body to his shame before the eyes of the public. *Seed is spoiled.* One word in Strong's definition of the original for *seed* is "posterity," and for that of *spoiled* is "to ravage." The phrase means that the Edomites were to lose their strong men in the conflicts with their foes.

Verse 11. This verse sounds like a favorable prediction in that the widows and orphans were to be cared for by the Lord. It virtually is a prediction of a misfortune since the very need for such special care indicates some form of disaster for the land.

Verse 12. *They whose judgment was not to drink of the cup.* The Jews were God's people and it might have been expected they would not have to drink the cup (figuratively speaking) of affliction on account of their nearness to the Lord. Yet He did not spare them in their sins notwithstanding their high relationship. Surely, then, a foreign nation should not hope to escape the wrath of God whom they had displeased.

Verse 13. *Bozrah* was one of the prominent cities of Edom, yet it and *the cities thereof* (meaning its suburbs) were to be made desolate.

Verse 14. The changing back and forth between the first and third persons in the language need not confuse us. It should be understood that God is the source of all the statements, and the prophet is the one who is delivering them to man. Hence we here have Jeremiah expressly confirming the declaration in the preceding sentence and telling us he has heard a *rumor from the Lord.* The first word is from SHEMUWAH, which Strong defines, "Something heard, i. e., an announcement." That announcement was a prediction that the heathen (nations) would gather force against Edom.

Verse 15. Edom was a heathen nation as well as were those destined to come against her. We should remember that the word has a national as well as religious use. The prediction means that Edom was to be looked down upon by other nations like her.

Verse 16. God had predicted (Gen. 27: 40) that Edom was to be a ruffian sort of people and would assume a hostile attitude toward others. This very condition was abused and they had come to feel so independent they "feared not God nor regarded Man." But the Lord declared their self-exaltation would not place them beyond the reach of Him.

Verse 17. Not only was Edom to be humiliated from its position of pride and haughtiness, but the country was to become desolate to the extent that passers-by would look with scorn and belittle it.

Verse 18. The land of Edom was to become desolate to begin with, but its desolation was to be as permanent as was that of Sodom and Gomorrah.

Verse 19. For the significance of the comparison to the enraged lion see the comments at chapter 4: 7. The second half of the verse refers to the power of the Lord over the Edomites. That was to be executed by bringing against them some invading force such as the Babylonian army.

Verse 20. The Edomites are considered as an unfortunate people being attacked by a hostile band of shepherds. The prediction is that even the weakest of those shepherds will be able to overcome the Edomites. Their power will be to chase them away even as a roaring lion would frighten a shepherd away from his flock.

Verse 21. This verse is figurative and means the downfall of Edom will be great.

Verse 22. The pronoun *he* refers to the Babylonian king who was to come against Edom. In this passage the comparison is to an eagle because of its ability to overspread the territory attacked. *Bozra* is singled out because it was one of the chief cities of the Edomites. For the explanation of comparison to a woman's pangs, see the comments at chapter 4: 31; 6: 24; 13: 21; 22: 23; 30: 6; 48: 41.

Verse 23. *Damascus* was the chief city of Syria hence the present prediction is against that country. The other places named also were cities of Syria and were destined to share in the hardships of the people. A troubled sea in which there would be a tossing about is used to compare the unsettled condition that was destined to come upon the cities of Syria according to the decree of the Lord.

Verse 24. Specific attention is given to *Damascus* because it was the metropolis of the country. But this mighty city was warned that it would be *waxed feeble* and would attempt to escape from the doom settling upon it.

Verse 25. *City of praise* refers to the admiration that the world would manifest about her. *Not left* indicates that when God brings his punishments upon the land of Syria He will not leave out Damascus.

Verse 26. It is a special blow to a country to have its military men overthrown. Not only were these men to be overthrown, belonging to Damascus, but her *young men* who should supply the future recruits were to be slain in the streets.

Verse 27. Ben-hadad was the name of three great kings of Syria. The destruction of the *palaces* therefore would mean a thrust at the very vitals of the kingdom.

Verse 28. *Kedar* is defined by Strong, "A son of Ishmael; also (collectively) bedawin [the Arabs] (as his descendants or representatives)." *Hazor* is identified by Strong as a city of Arabia, hence this verse is a prediction against the Arabians. They were to be attacked by the king of Babylon and overthrown.

Verse 29. The Arabians were a wandering people and had their dwelling in tents. This was likewise in keeping with their chief occupation of tending flocks. This is why it is predicted that the Babylonians were to *take to themselves* the *tents* and *curtains* of these people. The *camels* are mentioned because they were one of the usual means of travel over the deserts when the Arabs journeyed.

Verse 30. *Flee, get you far off* is the prophet's way of predicting that the inhabitants of the town of Hazor would wish to escape the hand of the Babylonians. This attack by Nebuchadnezzar was to be through the Lord, but the mighty ruler was to go about it according to his own *counsel* or advice also.

Verse 31. *Arise* is a prediction in the form of an order from God for the King of Babylon to make the attack on the Arabians. *Wealthy* is from SHE-LEVAH, which Strong defines, "Tranquil; (in a bad sense) careless; abstractly, security." They seemed to have the feeling that no danger could overhang them. *Neither gates nor bars, dwell alone.* This refers to their manner of life, dwelling in tents away from civilization in general.

Verse 32. This verse is a summing up of the material losses the Arabs were to suffer when the Babylonians overran their territory.

Verse 33. Wild creatures were to dwell in the city of Hazor and it was to be a perpetual desolation. To avoid confusion I shall explain that the Arabians were roving in their habits of life as described in the preceding verses. However, they had certain centralized places that existed as cities, and the form of government which they maintained was centered in them. These cities served as a background for the tribes who chose not to reside permanently in any certain place, but who wandered through the world at times in search of trade. We have an instance of such a business in the event of Joseph's sale as recorded in Genesis 37th chapter.

Verse 34. *Elam* was the name of a number of men but came to designate a country. It lay east of Persia proper but was finally referred to in various reference works under the same heading as Persia. This prophecy was made about 600 years B. C. while the overthrow of the Persian Empire as the second of the "four world empires" was not until 300 years later; it would seem, therefore, that the present prediction did not refer to that great event. We are sure this is correct for the last verse of this chapter shows the punishment was temporary, while the one 300 years later was to be permanent according to Daniel 2: 44. The prediction now before us was evidently concerning some earlier misconduct of this district and the chastisement was to be for a time only.

Verse 35. *Break the bow* is a reference to their defeat in war because one principal means of warfare in ancient times was the bow and arrow.

Verse 36. *Four winds* is figurative and means that the desolation to be wrought in Elam was to be general. The citizens of the country were to be scattered in every direction. That is indicated by the figure just used since it is equivalent to referring to the four points of the compass.

Verse 37. To be dismayed means to be confused and frightened at the sight of such powerful foes. The condition was to be brought about because of the Lord's *fierce anger* at their evil conduct. These people had shown too much interest in the opposition that other heathen kings had manifested against God's people. *Consumed* could not mean they were to be literally destroyed for the last verse says they were to survive. It means, therefore, that for the time being they would cease to be a people.

Verse 38. *Set my throne* means the Lord would overthrow the power of Elam and take charge of the country Himself and see that matters were run as he saw fit.

Verse 39. For the meaning of *bring again the captivity* see the comments at chapter 48: 47. This indicates the threatened punishment was to be temporary on Elam.

JEREMIAH 50

Verse 1. Various heathen powers are being threatened in the remaining chapters of this book and a large portion of the predictions will be against Babylon or Chaldea. It was the first of the "four world empires" so well noted in prophecy and history. God was using this empire to chastise his own people, but he never tolerated the hostile attitude of any nation toward His people, even though said people deserved the punishment.

Verse 2. God was especially displeased with the heathen nations because they worshiped false gods and pretended to rely so much upon them. *Bel* was a short form for Baal which was a god of the Babylonians. *Merodach* was a title used in connection with the same god otherwise known as Bel or Baal. *Is confounded* is a prophecy that when the day of the Babylonian doom arrives her idol will avail her nothing.

Verse 3. The Babylonian Empire was overthrown by the Medo-Persian Empire, and that empire is referred to in history under a variety of terms. Sometimes it is the one here shown which was the full and proper title; at other times it is referred to as the Medes and Persians; in still others either one of the names may be used to designate the whole empire. However, care must be taken not to apply this use of the single name in every instance, for in a few cases one of them is used as a distinction from the other. The reader will be informed when such use of either word is to be observed. The present verse is a prediction of the overthrow of Babylon and the power that was to accomplish that fact was the Medo-Persian (here called the Medes) and it was geographically north of the Babylonian territory. For the historical fulfillment of this decisive action see the quotation at Isaiah 13: 1 in volume 3 of this COMMENTARY. The downfall of Babylon takes up many verses of this chapter, and the reader will do well to have his copy of the historical statement ready for reference.

Verse 4. Many times the events of prophecy and fulfillment are not inserted in chronological order. In the present instance, however, the literal order has been observed. The release of the Jews from captivity in Babylon (which is the subject of this and the following verse) took place at the same time that Babylon was conquered. When the Medes and Persians took possession of Babylon, they gave the Jews permission to return to their own land. *Israel* and *Judah* are named distinctly because the former which was the 10-tribe kingdom, and the latter which was the 2-tribe kingdom had been in captivity. The former had been taken into the territory while the Assyrians had control of it, and the latter was taken into virtually the same area after the Babylonians gained possession. We might wonder why the Jews would be weeping at such a time, but it will not seem strange if we realize the mingled feelings of joy and penitence that must have possessed them at that time. They had been captives in a strange land where they were not permitted to serve the Lord. Now they are headed toward their own beloved country where they will have the lawful opportunity to *seek the Lord their God*. No wonder, then, that their emotions would be stirred so that they would be caused to weep. The historical fulfillment of the return of the Jews from captivity is quoted at Isaiah 14: 1, in volume 3 of this COMMENTARY. The Biblical account of it is in the books of Ezra and Nehemiah.

Verse 5. *They shall ask the way* was fulfilled in Ezra 8: 21-23. The *perpetual covenant* was the agreement which the Jews made to bring about all necessary reforms in their social lives, and to worship the true God only.

Verse 6. This verse is a glance back over the past experiences of the nation of the Jews. The language is formed from the occupation of a shepherd and his sheep. The leaders were the shepherds and the people were the flock. Those leaders had misled and neglected the people in the same way that an unfaithful shepherd would treat his flock. The result of such neglect would be that it would be caused to wander from one mountain to another until the sheep would lose sight of its fold or *restingplace*.

Verse 7. *Found them have devoured them* refers to the rough treatment the Jews received from the heathen nations whom God suffered to come against the sheep of His pasture. *We offend not* represents those nations as denying there was anything wrong in what they were doing to the Jews. They felt justified in it because that nation (the Jews) had *sinned against the Lord* and deserved what they were getting.

Verse 8. This verse comes back to the subject of the return of the Jews from Babylonian captivity. The passage is a prediction of the return stated in the form of an order for them to leave the land of their bondage. *He goats before the flocks*. A he goat being strong and rugged would be able to brave the wilderness and lead the way for the more timid sheep. In Ezra 1: 5 we see this prediction fulfilled when the *chief of the fathers* rose up because their *spirit God raised to go build the house of the Lord*.

Verse 9. Before the Jews could *go forth* out of the land of the Chaldeans (or Babylonians), that nation must first be overcome by another. That was to be done by *an assembly of great nations*, which refers to the Medes and Persians. That force was to come against the empire that had been holding the Jews in captivity for 70 years.

Verse 10. *Chaldea* here is the same as Babylonia and was destined to fall. *Shall be spoiled* means that the invading nation would take possession of the property of Babylon.

Verse 11. *Because ye were glad*. God would never tolerate a boasting attitude from those whom He had used to punish his own people. After they had served the Lord's purpose, they in turn were destined to be chastised. That was why the Medo-Persian Empire was raised up by the Lord as the conqueror of Babylon.

Verse 12. A mother's disappointment over an unworthy child is used to compare the humiliation that was destined to come upon Babylon. *Shall be* is in italics but is justified by the context, so that the clause should read "she shall be the hindmost of the nations"; it means that Babylon was to become the deserted nation. *Wilderness* and *desert* was a prediction that the city of Babylon would become such a spot as per the historical quotation referred to in verse 3.

Verse 13. In reading the historical quotation cited in verse 3 in connection with the several passages predicting the overthrow of Babylon, care should be taken to distinguish between the Babylonian Empire as a whole and its capital as a city. The former was to be taken over by another power but left intact for the possession of the victorious one, but the latter as a city was to be destroyed and never rebuilt. All predictions as to a desert and an uninhabited spot apply to the city only.

Verse 14. This verse is a prediction in the form of an order for the *North country* (referred to in verse 9) to come against Babylon. The overthrow of Babylon by Persia was not as a favor for the conquering power, but as a punishment upon Babylon because she *had sinned against the Lord*.

Verse 15. It is a general custom for the successful one in any kind of a contest to applaud even with a "yell" of triumph. That sort of performance was to take place against Babylon as predicted by the words *shout against her*. *Hath given her hand* means that Babylon would give way to the forces attacking her. *Vengeance of the Lord*. When any person or group carries out an action that results in vengeance against another, such action is regarded as the vengeance of God if He has called for such action. (This is the teaching of Paul in Romans 12: 19 and 2 Corinthians 7: 11.)

Verse 16. The Babylonian Empire (like all world-powers) was made up of various groups of people. In the time of her subjection she was to be rendered helpless as to occupations and other resources. The morale of the people was to be so lowered they would shrink into their individual refuges among their own lands.

Verse 17. *Israel* is used of the nation as a whole and the verse is a historical statement. Ten tribes were taken away by Assyria (2 Kings 17) and two tribes were taken by the king of Babylon (2 Kings 24 and 25). *Sheep* refers to the flock to which the nation is compared, and it was to be scattered over the wilds of the heathen fields.

Verse 18. Assyria was the first to oppress God's people and she was punished by being overthrown under the Chaldean yoke. Later the king of

Babylon was chastised by the invasion of the Medo-Persian Empire.

Verse 19. The event predicted at the close of the preceding verse was followed immediately by the release of God's people who were then in captivity in Babylon. They not only were to be released from the yoke of Babylon but were to be given possession of the cities and other important spots in their native land.

Verse 20. *Iniquity of Israel . . . sought for . . . not be found* is a prediction that Israel would be cured of the chief national evil of idolatry. For the historical fulfillment of this prediction see the quotation at Isaiah 1: 25, volume 3 of this COMMENTARY.

Verse 21. From this verse through 32 constitutes a bracket of predictions against Babylon or Chaldea. (See note at verse 3.) *Merathaim* and *Pekod* were cities of that country and the Persians were called upon to go up against them. When this nation brings utter destruction upon the cities of Babylon it will be *according to all that I* (the Lord) *commanded thee.*

Verse 22. *Sound of battle* was a statement both of present fact and a prediction of facts in the near future. The invasion by Persia into Babylon had not occurred in literal fact when the prophet began to write, but the gathering of the military forces of that eastern empire was going on under men destined to overthrow the Babylonians.

Verse 23. A *hammer* is a heavy instrument by which objects may be beaten and crushed. The Babylonian Empire had been just that kind of an instrument against the other nations of the world. Now that great hammer was to be broken and its holder (the city of Babylon) was to become a desolation.

Verse 24. The pronoun *I* means the Lord who had *laid a snare* for the capital city. *Wast not aware* was a prediction of the suddenness and surprise with which the Persians would take possession of Babylon. (See Daniel 5 for the fulfillment.)

Verse 25. An *armory* is a place for storing weapons of war. To open this place or speak of opening it is a figurative expression, referring to the use the Lord makes of one heathen nation when such services are needed to chastise another. The particular *armory* that was to be used in the present case was that against the Babylonians or Chaldeans. The motive for the opening of this place of weapons was God's indignation at the cruelty of Babylon against Israel.

Verse 26. This is a prediction made in the form of an order from headquarters, and it pertains to the overthrow of the city of Babylon by the Persians. The complete destruction of the capital city was predicted as well as the defeat of the men of war.

Verse 27. *Bullocks* (or bulls) is used figuratively in the Bible where the connection shows it means warriors or other strong men (Psa. 22: 12). Hence the strong men of Babylon were to be sacrificed to the vengeance of God and the Persians were to preside at the service. *Time of their visitation* means the visiting upon them of the punishment decreed by the Lord.

Verse 28. This verse is still a part of the bracket concerning Babylon, but is a slight diversion to note the escape of Israel from the doomed city. With inspired ears the prophet could hear his people announcing their release according to God.

Verse 29. *Archers* were the men who used the bow and arrow, a prominent weapon of warfare in ancient times. This is a prediction that such forces would be called together against the wicked city of Babylon. God always hates pride, especially when it is connected with cruelty, and the Babylonians were just such people in their doings.

Verse 30. This verse is literal and predicts the attack and overthrow of the men in the city of Babylon. The event took place on the night of Belshazzar's feast.

Verse 31. One way that pride is manifested is in being stubborn or rebellious against admonition. The prophet Daniel (ch. 5: 22, 23) charged this fatal conduct against the king of Babylon who had called for him on that noted occasion of the Chaldean downfall, while interpreting the writing on the wall.

Verse 32. The capital city of the Chaldeans was destined to be destroyed and never to be rebuilt. The country in general would remain in good condition in the possession of the conquerors, but the capital was to be in Susa or Shusan.

Verses 33, 34. The long passage of predictions against Babylon is broken into with these two verses to insert one on the return of the Jews to their own land. *Israel* and *Judah* are mentioned distinctively because both of the divisions of the nation of the Jews had been held in bondage in virtually the same territory. That is why it is said that they were *oppressed together*.

Verse 35. The prophet resumes his writings against the Babylonian Empire, also called the Chaldeans. The sword was another of the weapons commonly used in ancient warfare, and it is predicted that the men of Babylon were doomed to feel its edge. Not only were the military men to suffer from it, but the leading men in civilian life also were to be cut down by the sword.

Verse 36. *Liars* is from BEDIYL, which Strong defines, "A brag or lie; also a liar." The passage refers to the false prophets among the Jews who boasted that no country could harm them, thus lulling the common people into a false assurance of peace. But the sword of the Lord in the hands of the Persians was coming against them and they were going to *dote*, which means they would be made to feel and act foolishly and manifest the greatest of confusion.

Verse 37. This is more along the same line as the preceding verses. These leading men depended on their soldiers to protect the country against invasion but to no avail. The sword of the invading army was to overcome these men of war and they were to *become as women*. This comparison was made in view of the fact that women were not armed nor otherwise provided for military service.

Verse 38. *Drought* when used literally refers to a lack of moisture and that was actually brought about in this case. The Persians diverted the stream of the Euphrates River so they could march into the city of Babylon. The reader should again consult the historical note referred to in verse 3. This great event made a logical occasion for the predictions of the following two verses on the desolation of Babylon.

Verse 39. The historical note just cited will show the fulfillment of this prediction to have been literally true. The city of Babylon became an uninhabited spot, and only these doleful creatures of desert life could live there.

Verse 40. This verse emphasizes the preceding one by comparing Babylon to the city of Sodom in its complete desolation. The site of that wicked city and its neighbors became the Dead Sea because of the extent of territory involved, but the condition was the same as that of Babylon in that no human being could live there.

Verse 41. This verse predicts the attack from the Medo-Persian Empire whose territory lay north and east of Babylon. This twofold empire was to continue many years and be ruled by a succession of kings, many of whom were powerful.

Verse 42. A *bow* was used to shoot an arrow and a *lance* was thrust by hand; these two forms of weapons were used by the Persians. The rough practices of these people are predicted in this verse. The history of their long combined reign is too full of incidences and details to relate in this place.

Verse 43. This verse has specific reference to Belshazzar and his plight when he saw the handwriting on the wall (see Daniel 5: 6).

Verse 44. For comments and historical information on the lion's actions see chapter 4: 7. In the present case the lion is the Medo-Persian Empire. *Who shall appoint me a time* implies that no one will be able to plead any defence when the Lord brings the year of his vengeance upon Babylon.

Verse 45. *Counsel* means the advice and decision of the Lord concerning Babylon. *Land of the Chaldeans* means the same as the Babylonian territory. *Least of the flock* means that Persia will very easily conquer *their habitation* which refers to Babylon.

Verse 46. *Earth is moved* is a figure of speech and refers to the revolutionary effect upon the world of the report of the downfall of the Babylonian Empire.

JEREMIAH 51

Verse 1. This long chapter is a continuation of Jeremiah's predictions against Babylon. Much of the language is figurative even as the prophetic style often is. *Wind* is very destructive when it comes in great volumes, and the onrushing of the Persians was to be like such a wind. *Rise up against me.* Since the Lord was the power that was bringing the Persian army against the land of Babylon, those who opposed them were opposing Him.

Verse 2. *Fanners* is from a word that means a foreigner, and *fan* is from ZARAH, which Strong defines, "To toss about; by implication to diffuse, winnow." The statement means that Babylon was to be treated as chaff and the Persians were to be the workers who would use the fan. Since the empire of Babylon was become as chaff, when the fan has done its work it will leave the land empty.

Verse 3. The literal meaning of this verse is for the Persians to oppose the Babylonians. *Him that bendeth* means the Babylonian who bends the bow to shoot an arrow. The Persian archer (a user of a bow) is told to bend his bow to shoot an arrow at the other man. A *brigandine* is a coat of mail or metal armor. The Babylonian wore one and *lifted* himself up; that is, he stood up and trusted in the protection of his armor. The Persian soldier is told (in prediction) to stand against the other soldier who trusted in his armor.

Verse 4. This is a more direct prediction that the Chaldeans were to be slain in their own land. The streets of their cities were to be strewn with dead bodies.

Verse 5. These misfortunes were to come upon the Babylonians on behalf of *Israel* and *Judah* who had been held in captivity by these heathen. And all this was to be done in spite of the sins of God's people committed while they were in their own land. But the Lord would not tolerate the attitude of the Babylonians toward even an unrighteous nation when it was the peculiar possession of Him.

Verse 6. God's people were to flee out of the land of Babylon and this verse is a prediction of the return to their own land. The Biblical account of the fulfillment of the prediction is in the books of Ezra and Nehemiah. The historical account of it was quoted at Isaiah 14:1 in volume 3 of this COMMENTARY.

Verse 7. When *cup* is used figuratively it denotes an instrument containing the wine of wrath or other unpleasant lot to be experienced by someone. When God is said to be using the cup it is a signal that He is imposing upon some person some deserved chastisement. In the instance at hand Babylon is the cup and God has used it against certain nations to punish them for their wrongs. But Babylon took too much joy out of the distress that was brought onto the nations by drinking from this "cup" served to them, so now the Lord is going to bring her to suffer humiliation.

Verse 8. Babylon *is* fallen is present tense in form but future in thought. *Suddenly* refers to the surprise attack described in Daniel 5.

Verse 9. The gist of this verse is that Babylon was a self-willed nation and would never have accepted any instructions that might have prevented her downfall. She was to receive the chastisement that was due her wicked stubbornness. *Judgment reacheth unto heaven* (or to the skies) is a figurative expression, meaning the doom of Babylon was to be great.

Verse 10. The pronoun *our* refers to the Medes and Persians who were the instrument in God's hands for the punishment of Babylon. The verse means that in attacking the nation these people will be doing the right thing.

Verse 11. This is the same thought as the preceding verse. Mention of only the Medes is merely a common manner of the Old Testament writers in referring to the Medo-Persian Empire. God was back of this kingdom in its movements upon Babylon.

Verse 12. The *standard* is the flag or ensign of a nation or army. The passage is a prediction that the Medes would raise their flag in triumph upon the walls of Babylon. Having taken possession of the city, they would place a guard to be on the lookout for any who might attempt to wrest their victory from them. The watchers on the walls would not be enough protection, but others would be stationed at spots in hiding to detect any attempt of the enemy to surprise the conquerors in some attack.

Verse 13. *Waters* refers to the River Euphrates that flowed through the city of Babylon. It is a mighty stream and was the pride of the Chaldean capital. *Measure of thy coveteousness* denotes that the sad end about to come upon the city will be appropriate in view of her grasping disposition.

Verse 14. The men with whom the city was to be filled were the Medes and Persians. (See Daniel 5.) *Lift up a shout* refers to the cry of victory that a successful army makes when it has taken possession of the enemy position.

Verse 15. *He is the Lord of hosts* mentioned in the preceding verse. The earth was made by His power and certainly he can overcome even the strongest of the governments of men. This will be accomplished soon by the hand of the Medo-Persian Empire.

Verse 16. The thought in this verse is on God's control over the rain and other elements of the universe. Since the entire workings of the universe are subject to the divine power, then surely such a comparatively small thing as a human monarchy cannot resist that power successfully.

Verse 17. To be *brutish* means to be more like a dumb brute than a human being. When a man makes a graven image to worship he manifests a mind that is foolish and one that is to be compared to that of a beast.

Verse 18. *They* means the graven images which the heathen nations formed to worship. Such gods are *vanity* or vain. *Time of their visitation* means the time when they are put to the test. When that time comes the weakness of these idols will be manifested in that all who have relied upon them will perish.

Verse 19. *Portion of Jacob* means that which Jacob received from the Lord, which was the favor of divine help not to be compared with the advantages of the heathen. *He* means the Lord as the source "from whom all blessings flow."

Verse 20. *Battle axe* is from MAPPETS, which Strong defines, "A smiter, i. e., a war club." For the sake of Israel who came from Jacob, the Lord will use the Medes (and Persians) as a war club to hammer the nations that have mistreated His people.

Verse 21. *Horse and rider* were used in battle, and those of the enemy nations were to be broken or brought to defeat in war.

Verse 22. All ages and ranks and sexes of the hostile nations were to be brought under. None will be able to endure when God sends his forces as his agencies to carry out his vengeance against those who disrespect Him.

Verse 23. The reference to *shepherds* and *husbandmen* indicates that all agricultural pursuits will be stopped. *Captains* and *rulers* pertain to the governmental departments of a nation, and these also were to be overthrown in God's wrath.

Verse 24. This verse comes into more direct reference to the specific event which the prophet has been describing. *Babylon* and *Chaldea* are the same as to the present situation, and *Zion* stands for the nation of God which had been mistreated by the mentioned people of the heathen nations.

Verse 25. *Mountain* in symbolic language means a government, and in this place it means the government of Babylon. God was against this "mountain" because of the destruction that it had wrought in the earth. If a rocky mountain should be burnt into lava it would roll down and be flattened out and cease to exist as a mountain. Hence this mountain of Babylon is threatened with being dissolved by the fire of God's anger and be brought to nothing as a kingdom.

Verse 26. *They* (the Medes and Persians) will not use the building materials of Babylon for their own benefit for that will not be the purpose of their attack. However, they will destroy the city and make it desolate for ever.

Verse 27. The world empires such as Medo-Persia comprised the units of government in many localities. Some of such units are mentioned in this verse and they will be among the forces that Persia will bring against the capital of the Babylonians. *Set up a standard in the land* means the flag of the invading army will be planted in the conquered country.

Verse 28. This is virtually the same in thought as the preceding verse, and it means the Medes will gather with their accumulated forces and come against Babylon.

Verse 29. *The land of Babylon* has special application to the site of the capital city and perhaps the nearby territory. The country in general remained to be inhabited by the citizens whom it pleased the Persians to permit.

Verse 30. The war had been going on in the country at large before the city of Babylon was attacked. But all the while the active soldiers were in the field in defence of their country, the princes of the land, and especially those in the capital city were shrinking from their military duty. While this cowardly attitude was being maintained their houses were being burned by the invading forces.

Verse 31. Before reading this and the following verse it is very important to read the historical note or quotation made at Isaiah 13: 78 in volume 3 of this COMMENTARY. A *post* is a runner whose business it is to spread news or reports of great interest, and this verse is a prediction of the events that took place on the memorable night of Belshazzar's feast and death. City taken at one end. While the king was absorbed in his drinking feast, the Persians were making their way into the city at one end, the place where the Euphrates River entered beneath the walls. (See note again.)

Verse 32. *Passages are stopped.* The Euphrates River flowed through the city of Babylon and at every street coming down to it there were means provided for crossing over. After the Persians got within the city through the lowered river, they took possession of all these crossings. *Reeds* is from AGAM, which Strong defines, "A marsh; hence a rush (as growing in swamps); hence a stockade of reeds." A stockade is a sort of fortification made of stout posts and these heavy reeds on the banks of the river were so used. After the stream had been lowered in the way described in the historical note, the Persians set fire to these reeds. This would produce an alarming appearance which accounts for the prediction that *the men of war are affrighted*.

Verse 33. A threshing-floor is a place where grain is beaten and then the chaff is blown away. Babylon has already been compared to chaff (verse 2) and hence the prediction is repeated that the city was destined to be threshed.

Verse 34. The Lord speaks of the mistreatment of his people as if it had been done to Him. Jesus taught the same principle in Matthew 25: 45. The king of Babylon named in this verse was the one in power when the "three captivities" took place and hence he is the one named in the complaint.

Verse 35. The complaint that God expressed in the preceding verse on behalf of his people is made in this verse by the people themselves. *Zion* and *Jerusalem* are mentioned because the former was the most important district of the latter.

Verse 36. The invasion of Babylon by means of the Euphrates River is predicted by the phrase *dry up her sea*. Strong says the original for *sea* is sometimes defined as "a large river." By the ingenuity of Cyrus (the Persian commander) the river was rendered powerless as a defence for Babylon.

Verse 37. This verse is a repetition of the prediction that Babylon was to be completely destroyed and never to be inhabited nor rebuilt.

Verses 38-40. I have purposely combined these verses into one paragraph because of the direct relation of all the items to each other. The passage is a prediction of the scenes in Babylon on that last night of Belshazzar. The student will do well to read again very carefully the fifth chapter of Daniel. Then read again the historical quotation given at Isaiah 13: 1 in volume 3 of this COMMENTARY.

Verse 41. Strong's lexicon says *Sheshach* is a symbolic name of Babylon. The taking of such a great city was so unusual an event that it caused universal surprise. *Praise . . . surprised*. Those who had direct information on the noted event gave forth such great *praise* or laudation that the nations were astonished.

Verse 42. In figurative language such terms as floods and waters are often used to indicate great distress. The same thing is meant in the verse by *the sea*, referring to the army of the Persians that was to overflow the city of Babylon.

Verse 43. Doubtless many of the cities besides the capital were destroyed and the inhabitants slain in the general wars the Babylonians had to suffer. However, the permanent state of desolation as to inhabitants applied to Babylon only.

Verse 44. *Bel* was another form for Baal which was one of the heathen gods worshiped by the nations of the ancient world. They pretended to rely on the protection these idols could give them and God was determined to expose the vanity of such gods. On the night of the capture of Babylon the king and his lords "praised the gods of gold, and of silver, of brass, of wood, and of stone "(Daniel 5: 4). But these gods could do nothing to help Belshazzar; could not even furnish him a man who was able to explain the writing on the wall.

Verse 45. This verse is a prediction in the form of an order. God's people were to be released after Babylon was captured by the Persians, and they were to be given the privilege of returning to their own land.

Verse 46. *Lest your heart faint* means that God's people were told about the revolution that was to come upon the land wherein they were being held as captives, so that when they began to hear disquieting rumors about it they would not be faint. Moffatt renders this, "Never be daunted or dismayed by rumors that you hear."

Verse 47. One of the main objections that God had against the heathen nations was their worship of idols. By humiliating those nations that relied on such things, the weakness of false gods was demonstrated.

Verse 48. *Sing for Babylon* means that all intelligent creatures will feel jubilant over the downfall of the hated city. *Spoilers from the north* refers to the Medes who were located north of Babylon. They were to come down upon the city and take from her the

Jeremiah 51: 49-58

personal belongings in which she took so much pride.

Verse 49. A glance at verse 45 shows that Israel is being addressed still, and is being consoled over the downfall of the nation that had opposed them while in captivity. The original for *earth* is defined in the lexicon also as "the land." The passage means that as Babylon had caused the people of Israel to be slain, so the people all over the land of Babylon should be slain and made to fall.

Verse 50. *Escaped the sword* would refer to the same ones who are elsewhere considered the "remnant" that was to survive the ravages of the captivity. (See Isaiah 1: 9; 10: 21; 37: 31; Ezra 2: 64.) This group is notified through the prediction to leave the land of their captivity and return to Jerusalem their own capital city.

Verse 51. This verse expresses the sentiments of the people of Israel over their misfortunes. *Strangers* or people from the outside had invaded the holy places of God.

Verse 52. This sad state of mind is being comforted by the promise that divine judgment was to be poured out upon the oppressor nation. The heathens relied on their *graven images* and other false gods for support. The downfall of this government, therefore, would be a defeat for these idols.

Verse 53. *Mount up to heaven* is a figure of speech meaning the highest attainment possible for a human government. Babylon doubtless did reach such heights as a world power (see Daniel 2: 36-37), but this verse predicts her final downfall.

Verse 54. The *cry* that is predicted refers to the wail of distress that the people of Babylon were to utter at her shameful overthrow.

Verse 55. *Waves* and *waters* are figures of speech that mean the floods of distress and ruin that would come upon the land of Babylon. All of this was to be brought about through the service of the Persians, but it would be by the decree of the Lord.

Verse 56. This verse is more along the same line as the preceding verses. A *spoiler* is one who takes possession of the things in the hands of another. The Medo-Persian Empire was decreed by the Lord to come as a spoiler against Babylon. To *requite* means to impose upon one some chastisement for his unrighteous deeds.

Verse 57. This verse has specific application to the scenes that took place in Babylon on the night of Belshazzar's drunken feast. (See Daniel 5.)

Verse 58. *The broad walls of Babylon.* The walls of Babylon were one of the "Seven Wonders of the World," and they are referred to in this verse. In view of the importance of the subject I shall copy a description of these walls out of authentic historians. The reader should take careful interest in this quotation for it will not be again produced in full in this COMMENTARY. "First, the walls were very prodigious [of vast dimensions]: for they were in thickness eighty-seven feet, and in compass four hundred and eighty furlongs, which make sixty of our miles. This is Herodotus's account of them, who was himself in Babylon, and is the most ancient author that hath written of this matter. And although there are others that differ from him herein, yet the most that agree in any measure of those walls give us the same, or very near the same, that he doth . . . These walls were drawn round the city in the form of an exact square, each side of which was one hundred and twenty furlongs, or fifteen miles in length, and all built of large bricks, cemented together with bitumen, a glutinous slime arising out of the earth in that country, which binds in building much stronger and firmer than lime, and soon grows much harder than the brick or stones themselves which it cements together. These walls were surrounded on the outside with a vast ditch filled with water, after the manner of scarp [a steep wall] or counterscarp, and the earth, which was dug out of it, made the bricks, wherewith the walls were built; and therefore, from the vast height and breadth of the walls may be inferred the greatness of the ditch. In every side of this great square were twenty-five gates, that is, a hundred in all, which were all made of solid brass; and hence it is, that when God promised Cyrus [the Persian commander] the conquest of Babylon, he tells him, 'that he would break in pieces before him the gates of brass' (Iaiah 45: 2). Between every two of these gates were three towers, and four more at the four corners of this great square, and three between each of these corners and the next gate on either side; and every one of these towers was ten feet higher than the walls. But this is to be understood only of those parts of the wall where there was need of towers; for some parts of them lying against morasses always full of water, where they could not be approached by an enemy, they had there no need of any towers at all for their defence; and therefore in them there were none built; for the whole number of them amounted to no more than two hundred and fifty; whereas, had the same uniform order been observed in their disposition all round, there must have been many more. From the twenty-five gates on each side of this great square, went twenty-five streets in straight lines to the gates, which were directly over against them in the other side opposite to it. So that the whole number of the streets was fifty, each fifteen miles long, whereof twenty-five went one way, and twenty-five the other, directly crossing each other at right angles."—Prideaux's Connexion, 570 B. C.

The magnitude of the feat of Cyrus in taking Babylon may the better be realized after we ponder this description of the walls and gates. *The people shall labor in vain* means the labor the people had put on this vast structure will prove to have been in vain, for it was all destined to be lost in destruction that the Persians would bring to the city.

Verse 59. Jeremiah wrote a special copy of his predictions to be used as herein directed. We know it was a special copy, for it was to be destroyed, while we still have the major writing of the prophet. This was done in the fourth year of the reign of Zedekiah which was only seven years before the destruction of Jerusalem by Nebuchadnezzar. *Went with Zedekiah* means he went on behalf of the king since Zedekiah never went to Babylon until after his reign came to an end. *Quiet prince* is properly translated according to the lexicon of Strong. The point is that Seraiah was a chamberlain who was not active in any of the disturbances of the city and would be the most dependable kind of man for such a delicate mission.

Verse 60. The purpose of taking this special document with him was to console the Jews who were in captivity in Babylon. He was to read it (to himself) after he got there which doubtless was in order to have it fresh in his memory to relate orally to his people, for he was to destroy it as soon as he had read it.

Verse 61. Jeremiah instructed Seraiah to read the document after he had seen the situation at Babylon.

Verse 62. As a "check" on the correctness of his reading and his understanding of the words, Seraiah was to "repeat back" to the Lord what the prophecy contained. Since this was directly addressed to the Lord, we would understand that the people would not yet have learned about the message.

Verse 63. From now on the actions of Seraiah were in the presence and hearing of the Jews. He had told them of the contents of the message, that it predicted the downfall of Babylon. Furthermore, that the city would never be rebuilt but would be a perpetual desolation. In keeping with one of the practices where men of God "acted out" their predictions, Seraiah was to fasten a stone to the book and cast it into the River Euphrates. Of course it would not be expected that the book would rise to the surface with the weight tied to it. By that same token the city of Babylon, which boasted so much of its great river, was to be caused to sink, never to rise again. And it is significant that Babylon's ruin will be accomplished by means of this very stream into which the weighted book was thrown.

Verse 64. After explaining the meaning of his actions to his people, Seraiah was to cast the book into the river. He was then to add the words orally, *and they shall be weary*. That means that when Babylon is attacked her citizens shall tire of defending her and will surrender. *Thus far are the words of Jeremiah*. This concludes the book of Jeremiah, hence the next chapter was added by some man of God, taking it from the history already in existence, either as a separate document, or from the records of the kings that were kept in the royal accounts.

JEREMIAH 52

General remarks: From verse 1 through verse 27 this chapter is a duplicate of the history in 2 Kings 24: 18 to 25: 21. Since those verses have been commented upon in their proper place I shall not take up the space to repeat them here; they are in volume 2 of this COMMENTARY and the reader is requested to see that place.

Verses 28-30. This paragraph gives some historical details that are left out of the book of 2 Kings. We know the third stage of the great captivity took place at the end of Zedekiah's 11-year reign. At that time the king of Babylon took most of the citizens away with him, yet he left some remaining in Palestine. (See 2 Kings 25: 12, 13, 22.) Some of these who were left in the land became restless and escaped into the land of Egypt. (Jeremiah 42 and 43.) Of others who were still remaining, the king of Babylon finally brought into his realm those mentioned in this paragraph.

Verse 31. *Captivity of Jehoiachin.* The taking of this king off the throne in Jerusalem marked the "2nd captivity" (2 Kings 24: 10-16), and the things about to be related here are dated from that event. In the meantime Nebuchadnezzar had died and his son Evil-merodach came to the throne. Frequently a new ruler will celebrate his first year in office by some special act and favor. *Brought him forth out of prison.* Although Jehoiachin had been permitted to live after being deposed, he was made a prisoner in the land of Babylon until Evil-merodach released him.

Verse 32. *Set his throne* does not mean that he was permitted to act as king. It means he was treated with more courtesy and distinction than other kings in captivity.

Verse 33. *Prison garments* were replaced by those worn by free men in civilian life. Since eating with another meant so much in ancient times, this dining with the king of Babylon meant much for Jehoiachin.

Verse 34. Jehoiachin not only dined with the king, but was given a daily serving out of the provisions that had been prepared for the Babylonian king. We are not given the information as to the cause of this special friendship between this captive and his master, a favor he enjoyed to the end of his life.

LAMENTATIONS 1

Verse 1. This book consists chiefly of the lamentations of Jeremiah over the sad condition of Jerusalem and the people for whom it was the capital. The book was written after the destruction of the city and thus after the "3rd captivity." In view of this fact all of the statements regarding that event should be regarded as history. Other remarks will occur in course of the book that are mournful predictions of future sorrows in store for his beloved people. Some statements will be made concerning the future of Babylon, and still others will come of a favorable character pertaining to the return of Israel from captivity. *City sit solitary* refers to the desolated and isolated situation of Jerusalem. This very condition was predicted in Isaiah 1: 8. *Become tributary* means to become in subjection to another country.

Verse 2. Israel had doted on many nations but none of them stood by her now.

Verse 3. *Because* has no word in the original and if retained at all it should be understood in the light of the connection. The first clause should read, "Judah is gone into captivity to suffer affliction and servitude." *Overtook her between the straits* means her enemies found her in trouble and took advantage of it.

Verse 4. *Ways of Zion* means the roads leading to the city where the national feasts had been observed. They *mourned* (figuratively speaking) because no one was passing over them to attend the feasts. The rest of the verse is on the same subject.

Verse 5. *Her adversaries* means the Babylonians who had become *chief* or exalted above the people of Judah. But the prophet admits that such a sad state of affairs was just because it was from the Lord as a punishment for her many transgressions. *Her children* means the citizens of Judah who had gone into captivity.

Verse 6. The *beauty* referred to was the national and religious excellence of the city of Zion. The *hart* is of the deer family and is timid, especially when he is pursued in a wilderness in which he had become impoverished through the want of food. The princes or leaders are compared to this creature because they had been pursued by the enemies from a foreign land.

Verse 7. *J e r u s a l e m remembered* means the people who had lived in that city but had been taken into a strange land. (See verse 8.) After they got to Babylon they fulfilled the statement of this verse, which was also prophesied in Psalms 137.

Verse 8. Jeremiah again admits that his people had sinned grievously and for that reason she had gone into captivity. To *despise* means to belittle or look upon with contempt. Jerusalem had been so humiliated that her former admirers now considered her condition to be one of disgrace.

Verse 9. *Filthiness is in her skirts* is a figurative way of saying the guilt of Jerusalem is evident, referring to the religious corruptions of the nation as well as the personal iniquity of the leaders. *Remembereth not her last end* means that Jerusalem was unthoughtful as to the outcome of her course. *Came down wonderfully* refers to the completeness of the fall of the city. The prophet then expresses his personal sense of *affliction* at the downfall of his countrymen.

Verse 10. This verse has direct reference to the event of 2 Kings 24: 13.

Verse 11. The invasion of Babylon into Judah resulted in conditions of famine in various places. This caused the people to offer their cherished personal belongings for food *to relieve the soul*, that is, to restore their vitality. And again the prophet "takes it to heart" and considers the condition of distress among his people as his own personal sorrow.

Verse 12. Jeremiah's personal affliction refers to the sympathy he has for his beloved people, therefore the language of the verse is a reflection of patriotism.

Verse 13. We know that Jeremiah was a righteous man and was never the direct target of the Lord's shafts of anger. Hence, while he was personally affected by the situation, most of his remarks were made on behalf of the people.

Verse 14. Being a member of the nation of Judah, Jeremiah would have to share in the national disgrace. However, God never forsook him but bestowed upon him and other righteous individuals the personal favor that had been promised. It will be well here for the reader to see the note in connection with 2 Kings 22: 17.

Verse 15. *Mighty men* refers to the princes and others who were leaders in the nation who had been taken into captivity (2 Kings 25: 14-16). When Jeremiah says *me* he is impersonating the nation as a whole. The last part of the verse is a figurative description of the siege of Jerusalem and the downfall that followed.

Verse 16. This verse refers to the personal grief of Jeremiah over the distress of the people of Judah. He calls those people *my children* as an expression of the affection he has for his fellow countrymen.

Verse 17. The spreading forth of the hands is a gesture calling for help in distress. Zion (or Jerusalem) is represented as a woman in pain and sorrow but seeking in vain for assistance. This is because the Lord had forsaken his people and regarded them as unclean. The comparison to a woman in this condition was based on a law of Moses concerning such women (Lev. 15: 19-33). Of course we should understand that she was classed as unclean ceremonially and hence was required to submit to the ritualistic formula for cleansing. And the chief uncleanness of Judah was ceremonial or spiritual in that idolatry was the outstanding evil. And in keeping with the procedure under the law, Judah was put away from God for a period of national cleansing in the land of her captivity which did completely cleanse her of this iniquity.

Verse 18. The pronoun *I* is related to Jerusalem in the preceding verse. While Jeremiah is the framer of the language, he is speaking for the people who were guilty of the sins that have been the cause of God's wrath. The *virgins* and *young men* are especially named in the complaint about the captivity. They were not any more guilty of sin than the elders, but the growth of a nation depends on the reproduction of the species and the young persons are the ones upon whom the increase of citizens generally depends. For this reason it would be more regrettable for them to be taken.

Verse 19. *I* still refers to Jerusalem (as representative of the nation of Judah) and she is complaining of the unfaithfulness of her *lovers* which is a figurative reference to the idolatrous nations. In the Bible a comparison is made between spiritual and temporal love, and unfaithfulness in one is compared to that in the other. Judah had flirted with idolatrous nations and accepted them into her bosom (figuratively speaking), but now those nations had "jilted" her. They not only did that, but also took from her the necessities of life (had thrown the city into famine) which caused even the *priests* and *elders* to *give up the ghost* and die.

Verse 20. *Bowels* in the Bible means the affections when used figuratively. The sad experience that Judah was in was having a depressing effect on her affections and causing deep grief. But again the prophet makes her admit the rebellion that had provoked this punishment from God. Outside the city, *abroad*, the nation was suffering the effects of the sword, and in the capital the people were dying from famine.

Verse 21. The first half of this verse continues Judah's complaint of her enemies, and she even mentions the attitude of the enemies who had been the instrument in God's hand for the chastisement of His people. The rest of the verse is against that instrument because God never would tolerate any jubilant attitude from those whose services had been used for the punishment of the unfaithful nation.

Verse 22. The language truly represents the feeling of Judah against the Babylonians, but the remarks are worded by the prophet and are an inspired prediction of the vengeance of God upon that heathen people. That vengeance was destined to come upon them after the nation of the Jews has been put through the treatment necessary for the complete cure from her national corruption of idolatry.

LAMENTATIONS 2

Verse 1. This verse is a lamentation over the sad condition that was brought about through the righteous anger of the Lord. *Daughter of Zion* is an affectionate term for the people of the Lord who had their headquarters at Zion which was the principal district in Jerusalem. *Footstool* is an expression of humility which the prophet words on behalf of his people. *Remembered not* is used in the sense that the Lord did not spare his people when his anger was aroused to the extent of divine chastisement.

Verse 2. *Hath swallowed up* is a figurative reference to the overwhelming of the homes of the people. *Daughter of Judah* has the same meaning as *daughter of Zion* in the preceding verse. The Lord is said to have done these things, but we should understand that he accomplished it through the services of the Babylonians.

Verse 3. *Horn* in symbolic language is defined as "power" in Strong's lexicon. It means the power of Israel has been cut off, which was done when the kings in Jerusalem were taken from their throne. *Drawn back . . . from before the enemy* denotes that when the enemy approached against His people he withdrew his hand and left them to their fate. This was because they had sinned very grievously and caused His anger to burn like a *flaming fire*.

Verse 4. The Lord *bent his bow* by bringing the foreign army against the land of Judah. In the same way he *stood as an adversary* against the capital of the country.

Verse 5. All of these afflicting circumstances are attributed to the Lord which is correct. However, we should understand that He was dealing to his people the punishment due them for their abominable practices of idolatry.

Verse 6. *Tabernacle* is from a word that means a fence or barricade, and the idea is that God had withdrawn his protection from his people and suffered the enemy to invade the land. The *solemn feasts* had been caused to cease in that the assembling place (Jerusalem) had been taken over by the enemy. To *despise* means to belittle or humiliate any person or thing. God had shown this attitude toward his rulers in the capital city where the kings and priests had their place of operations.

Verse 7. *Cast off his altar* took place when the Babylonians were suffered to interfere with the altar service in the *sanctuary* which means the temple. The *palaces* also were destroyed which were the personal residences of the kings. The history of this event is recorded in 2 Kings 25: 9. *Noise* is from KOLE and Strong defines it, "To call aloud; a voice or sound." The word does not necessarily mean a boisterous use of the voice for such as that would not be done on the days of solemn feasts. The meaning is that the enemy raised their shouts of triumph in the very house where God's people had expressed their joyful feelings on the feast days.

Verse 8. *Destroy the wall* means to forsake his defence of his people and their city. Such is the meaning of the entire verse, figuratively expressed.

Verse 9. *Gates are sunk into the ground* is somewhat figurative, meaning they are a mass of ruins and are useless as a means of defense. *Law is no more* means there is no one in position to enforce the law. The *Gentiles* were the Babylonians among whom the people of Judah were scattered. *Prophets found no vision* indicates that God would not communicate any vision to them because they had made such an unlawful use of their position.

Verse 10. This verse is a vivid picture of the dejected state of the leading men of the nation who were at that time captives in the land of Babylon. *Keep silence* shows how completely they were depressed over the conditions, so much so that they were silenced. This very situation was predicted in the 137th Psalm.

Verse 11. The people of Israel were generally aware of the miserable condition and expressed their feelings in more ways than one. The greater portion of the several passages of this book are truly the sentiments of the people. However, while writing down their sentiments for the information of succeeding generations, Jeremiah is giving release for his own personal grief over the sorrowful plight of his beloved countrymen. *Fail with tears* means he had shed so many tears that his eyes were exhausted. *Bowels are troubled* denotes that his affections were stirred up over his concern for the nation. *Liver* is used figuratively and refers to the heavy load of worry that was agitating the prophet, caused by the fainting condition of the people, especially as it affected the children who were dependents.

Verse 12. *Where is corn and wine* was a literal plea the children were making with their mothers. Nothing could be any more pitiable than the sight of hungry children and the sound of their cry for food. These children were so undernourished that they became prostrated in the streets where they had been the victims of famine.

Verse 13. Jeremiah is without words to express fully his anxiety for his people or to say anything that would cause them to be consoled. *Thy breach* refers to the great gap that had been made in the defences and general provisions of security. *Who can heal it* indicates that nothing can be done for the present to head off the calamity facing the nation. It will be well for the reader to see the long note produced at 2 Kings 22: 17, volume 2 of this Commentary.

Verse 14. *Thy prophets* refers to the false prophets among the people who offered lying assurances of peace for them. (See Jer. 6: 14.) By thus delivering these flattering visions they prevented the people from feeling any fear of disaster, and consequently they did not make the reformation in their lives that might have *turned away their captivity* if they had started in time; now it was too late.

Verse 15. The central thought in this verse is the impression that was made on the nations of the world when they passed by and saw the situation. To *wag their head* was a gesture of mingled surprise and contempt over the downfall of such a wonderful nation that had so great a fame in the civilized world.

Verse 16. An outstanding characteristic of most nations is pride, hence the "face-saving" movements that we often hear of on the part of great national leaders. When a nation meets with some misfortune, especially one in the nature of a disgrace, it is natural that others will express themselves on the situation. Some may do so out of friendly sympathy, but usually it is prompted by a motive of exultation. It is always from this last named motive when coming from enemies as is the case at hand. Judah has been terribly defeated and the Babylonians rejoice over it, even boasting that it had been their intention of causing such a day to arrive. But they will some day learn by sad experience that the Lord had suffered them to accomplish this end only because His people needed some chastisement.

Verse 17. The first clause of this verse confirms the closing portion of the preceding paragraph. *Caused enemy to rejoice* means that God caused the situation that gave Babylon the occasion for her rejoicing. However, that was not the motive the Lord had in the affair, therefore the exulting nation will finally suffer for her attitude toward Judah. *Set up the horn* means the Lord had given Babylon the power to accomplish her work against the corrupt nation in Palestine.

Verse 18. The misfortunes which the Lord suffered to come on Zion caused her to cry unto Him. The *wall* means the defences of Zion which had been demolished, and they are personified as being able to weep for themselves over the sorrowful situation. *Apple . . . not cease*. The eye is used in weeping and the figure means for the apple (or forces) of the eye to use its strength in weeping for the distressful situation.

Verse 19. The unfortunate nation is bidden to make its complaint before the Lord day and night. The special motive for the prayer indicated in this verse is the distressing condition of the children who were starving.

Verse 20. This verse is still on the subject of the condition in a famine and indicates that the people were in the depths of want and despair. It was feared that if it got worse or continued longer, the women would be forced to eat their own babies. Such a tragedy had been done in the past (2 Ki. 6: 29), and it was predicted that it would be done again (Deut. 28: 53; Ezk. 5: 10). The word *and* after *fruit* is not in the original and is out of place in the translation for there is no call for a conjunction. The phrase that begins with *children* is merely explanatory of the one that ends with *fruit*. Also, *span long* is from TIPPUCH, which Strong defines with the single word "nursing." The clause should therefore read, "Shall women eat their nursing children?" The same mad hunger might induce some to slay the holy men who were engaged in the services of religious devotions.

Verse 21. The pain of destitution is still the subject of the prophet. So many of the homes had been burned that the occupants had to lie in the streets. The young men had been pushed to the front in the wars and had been slain by the enemy. *Thou hast slain* means God had brought the enemy army against the land of Judah to punish the people for their transgressions.

Verse 22. Jeremiah uses the first person in forming his sentences of address to God, but he is speaking on behalf of the nation whose people are so very near to the prophet. *Called as in a solemn day* refers to the call that God had made for the enemy to come into His service of punishing the disobedient nation. The *terrors round about* were those that the Babylonians had brought against Jerusalem. *Those that I have swaddled* is a figurative reference to the rising generations of the kingdom of Judah. They had become the victims of the enemy which means the Babylonian army.

LAMENTATIONS 3

Verse 1. It will be well for us to keep in mind both the personal experiences of Jeremiah and those of his countrymen. The prophet suffered some unpleasantness that his people did not because he "took it to heart" more than did they. Had they been as serious over the situation as he there would have been more genuine regret on their part over the state of affairs. Another thing that will assist us is the fact that Jeremiah had to feel the sting of divine chastisement on account of being a member of the nation and not as punishment for any personal wrongs of his. *Rod of his wrath* means the wrath of God against the sins of the people of Judah.

Verse 2. *Darkness* and *light* are figurative and are used in the sense of sunshine and gloom with reference to the conditions surrounding the case.

Verse 3. Jeremiah feels the weight of God's hand as it is extended against the doers of iniquity in the nation, particularly the princes or leaders among them.

Verse 4. No physical violence is meant here for the prophet was not suffering in that manner. Even when he was cast into the mire he was not harmed in this way. But the distress of his people bore down on him so that it gave him the feeling that is suggested in the expression "old before his time."

Verse 5. *Builded against me* means that God had reared up a wall of chastisement as to the nation in general, and surrounded the prophet with conditions like *gall* (bitterness), and *travail* which means weariness.

Verse 6. *Dark places* is said in the same figurative sense as *darkness* in verse 2, meaning the situation of gloom. This was true of Jeremiah personally and of the nation as a whole because of the official corruptions that had been practiced.

Verse 7. As to the prophet himself, there was no escape from the *hedge* of heaviness with which he was surrounded. The nation was literally taken captive and there was no way of escape. The *chain* was the shackle of anxiety which was so heavy and strong that resistance would be in vain.

Verse 8. Jeremiah had been told that his prayer on behalf of his countrymen would be in vain for they would not hear him (Jer. 7: 16).

Verse 9. Here is some more figurative language. *Hewn stone* indicates not only a strong substance for a barricade, but also is dressed so as to form a still firmer wall. Every way he would try to go the victim would be met with this wall of obstruction, making him turn here and there to look for escape; that would cause his ways to be crooked or uncertain.

Verse 10. The helplessness of one who is attacked by a wild beast that was unseen is compared to that of Jeremiah personally and of Judah as a whole.

Verse 11. This verse is virtually the same in meaning as verse 9.

Verse 12. This verse may be understood literally and figuratively. The Babylonian army had attacked the city with material weapons which included the bow and arrow, and that would constitute the application. The arrow has long been named as a symbol of persecution and other distress (Deut. 32: 42; Job 6: 4; Psa. 38: 2; Jer. 9: 8), hence the figurative sense is true here as it pertains to the prophet.

Verse 13. This is a repetition of the preceding verse in the sense of its main thought. A *quiver* is a case for holding arrows.

Verse 14. Yes, even as righteous a man as Jeremiah could not escape persecution from his own people. They falsified against him and even mistreated him by thrusting him into the mire (Jer. 37: 13, 14; 38: 6). To be *a derision* means to be treated sneeringly, and that was done to the prophet by his own countrymen as may be seen in the passages cited above.

Verse 15. *Wormwood* is an herb that has a bitter juice, and it is used in symbolic language to illustrate any bitter or unpleasant experience. The prophet regards himself as having to taste it through the chastisement which the Lord had brought upon the nation of which he was a member.

Verse 16. If a man were to attempt grinding gravel with his teeth he would get into serious trouble. The idea is used to compare the hard lot that Jeremiah and his people had been undergoing from the enemy. There was an old custom of using *ashes* literally in times of anxiety and distress. From this custom was brought the word into use figuratively under the like circumstances that called for the literal use.

Verse 17. *Soul* is from NEPHESH which Strong defines, "A breathing creature, i.e. animal or (abstractly) vitality; used very widely in a literal, accommodated or figurative sense (bodily or mental)." From this definition we understand the passage means that Jeremiah's entire being was denied peace. *Forgat* means to be removed and *prosperity* means the good things of life generally; these had been removed from the prophet through his connection with the nation.

Verse 18. *Perished from the Lord* recognizes the hand of God in all the distress of which the prophet is complaining. There is no criticism agaist the circumstance, for he elsewhere admits the justice of it because of the misconduct of the nation.

Verse 19. *Wormwood* is explained at verse 15; *gall* has the same meaning.

Verse 20. *Soul* means the whole human being as in verse 17. The afflictions had *humbled* him which is used in the sense of bearing him down with discouragement.

Verse 21. *Recalling* to his mind the purpose of these afflictions the prophet took hope in the outcome. He knew that God had brought them upon his countrymen for their own good, and that cheered him on to endure his own personal lot.

Verse 22. Had the nation been dealt with strictly as its iniquities deserved it would have meant its complete destruction. But the compassion of the Lord saved the people as a whole from being consumed.

Verse 23. This means the evidences of God's compassion appears anew every morning. *Thy faithfulness* denotes the Lord's constant attention to the welfare of Judah.

Verse 24. *Soul* is again used for the whole man, and Jeremiah has hope that the Lord will supply his every need, both temporal and spiritual. *Portion* is from a Hebrew word that is defined "an allotment" in Strong's lexicon.

Verse 25. To *wait for* the Lord means to rely upon him and seek to do his will. Upon all such *souls* God will bestow that which is *good*.

Verse 26. To *hope* and *quietly wait* are logically connected. If a man is restless and impatient regarding a desired blessing it indicates that his hope is weak. This very truth is taught by Paul in Romans 8: 24, 25.

Verse 27. *Yoke* is figurative and is used with reference to the burdens of adversity. If a man has that experience while he is young and strong, it will prepare him for the future when he will need the benefit of strength that experience gives.

Verse 28. *Sitteth alone and keepeth silence* means that when adversity comes he will not be overcome by it. Having accepted the *yoke* in his youth he is "prepared for the worst" or has himself "armed" for it in the sense of 1 Peter 4: 1.

Verse 29. This verse is one of the strongest kind of figures of speech. *Dust* refers to a condition of humility and distress, and putting the mouth in it means to "bite the dust" according to an old saying, yet stopping short of actual death. But the idea is that if a man learns the wholesome lessons the "hard way," he may have to right to hope for better times ahead.

Verse 30. The spirit of resignation to an unavoidable lot is the lesson here.

Verses 31, 32. This paragraph is a prediction of the return from captivity. Having said so much along the line of hope for better things to come, the prophet considers it an appropriate time to make some direct reference to those things.

Verse 33. *Not afflict willingly* denotes that God does not chastise his people just for the sake of causing them grief. The final good that might come from the afflictions is the sole object in view.

Verse 34. Many of the verses have a similar meaning which is to distinguish between different kinds of affliction. For instance, it is not God's desire to *crush* all the *prisoners* which refers to those in the prison of the captivity.

Verse 35. It is not God's purpose to deprive his people of any of their "rights," but only to punish them sufficiently to bring them to repentance.

Verse 36. *Cause* means a contest and *subvert* means to win the contest merely by force whether right or wrong. The Lord would not *approve* such an act on the part of man, so He would not do so against his people. It is true that the divine forces are infinitely greater than the human, but God does not use such force merely because he can, but it is becouse it is just and for the ultimate good of mankind.

Verse 37. The Jewish nation had many false prophets who threw the people into confusion very often. Those men were exposed by the failure of their predictions to be fulfilled. A noted example of such a character is described in Jeremiah 28.

Verse 38. *Evil and good.* The thought will be grasped if the conjunction is given the emphasis. God does not act inconsistently, so if his children deserve *evil* (meaning unpleasant experiences) for purposes of chastisement, they are not given the good or pleasant, for that would encourage them to go on in their evil course,

Verse 39. This verse is an indirect rebuke of any man who would murmur at the just punishment for his sins.

Verse 40. Instead of resenting the punishment, the wise thing to do is to find out what is wrong with us. Of course it will be expected that when we learn what it is, we will cease doing it and turn again to serve the Lord.

Verse 41. The point in this verse is that our prayers should be sincere. When we lift up our hands in prayer to God our hearts should be in it.

Verse 42. *Thou hast not pardoned* applies to the nation as a whole, and means that it must suffer the captivity until its end has been accomplished. See the note at 2 Kings 22: 17 in volume 2 of this Commentary.

Verse 43. *Persecute* is from a Hebrew word that means to pursue with hostile intent. The hostility might be justified which it was in the case of the Lord pursuing his disobedient people. His *anger* was in the form of righteous indignation. *Hast not pitied* is used in the sense that God did not spare his corrupt nation when it became so bad as to need chastisement.

Verse 44. We are sure this is another figure of speech. The literal truth is that their prayer for escaping the captivity was not heard, and it is represented by a cloud so dense that even sound could not penetrate it.

Verse 45. God has cast off his people as being unfit for His presence. They were turned over to the *people* which is from a word meaning nation; it here refers to the Babylonian nation.

Verse 46. It has always been a matter of reproach for a nation to be subdued. The nation of Judah had been brought under by the heathen and the others *opened their mouths* or looked staringly at them as if in derision.

Verse 47. Under the circumstances of enforced exile it was natural that Judah would be affected with fear, and the nation would realize it was in a *snare* or trap. That left their cities and country at home suffering the results of desolating ruin.

Verse 48. This strong figure has been used previously by the prophet, and is an expression of the deep personal feeling he had concerning his people. (See Jer. 9: 1.)

Verse 49. Jeremiah wished for a fountain of tears to shed on behalf of his people. That not being granted him, his eyes *trickled* or constantly shed the water that was induced by his profound grief.

Verse 50. The prophet did not look for any relief from his grief until the Lord *looked down*. This evidently means to look with pity and to remove the condition causing the tears. Such a time was to come after the nation was chastised enough.

Verse 51. Jeremiah was forced to weep so much that it was affecting his very heart or being. This was in sympathy for the citizens of Jerusalem.

Verse 52. *Without cause* means that the Babylonians did not have any personal reason for attacking Judah. They were only acting (unconsciously) as the agency of God for the punishment of Judah.

Verse 53. Jeremiah's personal sufferings would justify this language, for he had been cast into the mire. And it was also true of Judah in a more indirect sense, for the nation had its national life cut off by the captivity.

Verse 54. *Waters* of affliction is the meaning of this verse.

Verse 55. The prophet was personally cared for by the Lord because he was a righteous man. And the nation was also promised relief after suffering for a while.

Verse 56. This verse shows the answer to the prayer of the preceding verse.

Verse 57. God is not slack in his care for his own. When the righteous prophet appealed to Him he was heard promptly.

Verse 58. We should not forget the thought suggested frequently in the comments of this book of Jeremiah, that he writes in a way that much of his complaint and pleading may have a twofold bearing. It may apply to him personally, or it may mean the nation as a whole. Beginning with verse 55 and through the end of the chapter, the verses may appropriately form a bracket and be applied to the nation in captivity. In that view of the subject I suggest that the bracket be so marked and given the reference to the 137th Psalm.

Verse 59. This verse will give the reader a reason for the twofold application of these passages as a whole. The present verse could not apply to Jeremiah personally and hence refers to the nation. The people in Babylon will see their wrong and call upon the Lord to help them out of trouble.

Verse 60. The enemy took the wrong attitude toward the captives, and God was asked to consider it. The Babylonians had no national grievance against Judah and had no right to exercise any vengeance.

Verse 61. Even the reproaches that were uttered by the Babylonians were displeasing to God and he was determined to judge them for it.

Verse 62. This refers to the reproaches mentioned in the preceding verse.

Verse 63. *Sitting down* and *rising up* signifies the Babylonians took the situation lightly, and drew amusement from the pitiable state of Judah.

Verse 64. The Lord was always displeased when a heathen nation rejoiced over the misfortunes of His people. The Babylonians were serving a divine purpose by holding the Jews in captivity, but they were destined to feel the sting of God's vengeance.

Verse 65. This is a true picture of the attitude of the Jews with regard to the Babylonians. It is also a prediction of what God was going to do against them.

Verse 66. *Persecute* is from a Hebrew word that means to pursue with hostile intent. That is just what the Lord predicted he would do toward the Babylonians after they had served the end desired for the chastisement of the Jews.

LAMENTATIONS 4

Verse 1. The materials named in this verse have a somewhat figurative meaning. The passage denotes the loss by Jerusalem of her glory.

Verse 2. As clay is inferior to gold, so the *sons of Zion* (citizens of the capital city) had been demoted from the glory of free citizens to the state of captivity.

Verse 3. The state of destitution brought upon the Jews was so extreme that many of the natural emotions were quenched, and human mothers became colder toward their young than sea monsters were to theirs.

Verse 4. The famine is the subject being considered by the prophet. Having no nourishment due to the dry breasts of their mothers, the tongues of the babes stuck to the roofs of their mouths. When the other children cried for bread it was not given to them. Instead, the women even consumed their helpless babes as food for themselves. (See chapter 2: 20 and comments for this subject.)

Verse 5. The fallen state of the people is still the subject of the prophet expressed in figurative terms. Some had been accustomed to living on dainties and were not exposed to the rough side of life, but now they were wandering in the streets and were stunned with undernourishment. *Embrace dunghills* is a symbolic description of the condition expressed in the forepart of this verse.

Verse 6. *Punishment of iniquity* is all from the Hebrew word AVON and has been translated by the one word "iniquity" more than 200 times. It has been rendered also by "punishment" 6 times, and by our present phrase 4 times. It can thus be seen that the word might sometimes mean the results or consequences, likewise the retribution for the sin, as well as the sin itself. This verse means the punishment that Judah received for her sin was greater than was that put upon Sodom, not necessarily that the sin was greater. And yet, the people had committed idolatry for years, and that might be regarded as a more serious offence against God than sins of a moral nature such as that of Sodom. However, the Jews suffered national disgrace which reproached them for a century, while Sodom was destroyed in one day. Of the two instances of punishment that of the former might be considered the greater.

Verse 7. *Nazarite* is from a Hebrew word that Strong defines, "Separate; i.e. consecrated." The word in its primary use meant a special kind of vow but came to be used of all persons consecrated to the service of God, and it has that meaning in this verse. It describes in strong adjectives the former purity and glory of these persons while they were faithfully serving the Lord. It continued so while their lives were pleasing to Him, and he bestowed upon them more luster than the finest of gems.

Verse 8. After these consecrated men corrupted themselves with their abominable idolatries, the Lord deprived them of their glory. The figures of speech in this verse are a description of their state which contrasted from what it was before.

Verse 9. The ceremonial glory was taken from thsee men, and also they were exposed to the sword of the enemy. Of the two misfortunes, to perish with hunger was worse than to be slain outright with the sword.

Verse 10. See the comments at chapter 2: 20 for this verse.

Verse 11. This verse is both prophecy and history. The city of Jerusalem (or Zion) was then in the hands of the Babylonians, and the people were about all in the foreign land. But they were doomed to stay there until they served out the sentence of the 70-year captivity; and all this was because of the Lord's anger at their sins.

Verse 12. Jerusalem had been well known for centuries as the headquarters for a great nation. The histories of David and Solomon and their many important successors had raised the city to a high standing in the estimation of the world. In view of these facts the people of other countries were surprised to see the Jewish capital invaded and completely subdued as the Babylonians had done.

Verse 13. According to Jeremiah 5: 31; 6: 13, 14 these public men were chiefly responsible for the sins of the nation. If these wicked men were opposed by the righteous citizens they "won out" against them by causing them to be slain.

Verse 14. The word for *streets* is also rendered "abroad" in the common version. These corrupt men roved about with the guilt of blood upon them. (See Jeremiah 2: 34.) *Could not touch their garments*. The law of Moses (Numbers 19: 16) regarded one unclean who touched another person who had blood upon him.

Verse 15. *They* refers to men in general who observed the uncleanness of these murderers and bade them depart. When they were exiled among the heathen (the Babylonians) the remark was made by those learning of the situation that these Jews were no longer permitted to sojourn in their own land because of their uncleanness.

Verse 16. The men of the world (*they* of the preceding verse) are still talking and accounting for the dispersion of these wicked priests and prophets. They understood that the Lord's anger had caused it as a punishment. *They* now means these evil priests who disrespected the ones who were still righteous. (See 2 Chronicles 24: 18-21.)

Verse 17. The people of Judah are the ones talking now as if they were reminding themselves of some of their past mistakes. *Watched for a nation that could not save us.* While Judah was threatened by the presence of the Babylonians the Jews looked for help from Egypt (2 Kings 24: 7; Isaiah 30: 7; Jeremiah 37: 5-11); but the Egyptians could not save Judah from the captivity.

Verse 18. *They* means the Babylonians, and the people of Judah are still speaking. The presence of the invaders makes it difficult for the local citizens to be upon their own streets. *End is near.* The 70-year captivity began in the early days of the reign of Jehoiakim and the entire subjugation was accomplished in the 11th year of Zedekiah. (2 Kings 24: 1; 25: 2-7.) In course of this period Jeremiah did most of his writing, which explains why so much of it seems to be history and prophecy mixed.

Verse 19. This verse is a complaint of Judah about the treatment which they were receiving from their captors. They represent the attack as being so swift and general that there was no way of escape.

Verse 20. *Pits* means the pitfalls or snares the Babylonians used to capture the people of Judah whom they named *the anointed of the Lord. Breath . . . taken* denotes that the enemy was taking the breath of life from the unfortunate Jews.

Verse 21. The reader has been frequently reminded that God would not tolerate the attitude of the nations who rejoiced at the misfortunes of His people. This verse describes such an evil attitude on the part of the Edomites who had long been enemies of Israel. Edom is ironically told to do her rejoicing against the unfortunate nation while she had the opportunity. The *cup* (of affliction) was finally to come upon this nation as an expression of God's vengeance. *Drunken* and *naked* are terms borrowed from the literal results that often come from too much use of the cup of wine. It is applied to the staggering and shameful condition that was to come upon Edom.

Verse 22. In this one verse the prophet predicts the punishment of Edom and also the restoration of Israel. See verse 6 on *punishment of thine iniquity.*

LAMENTATIONS 5

Verse 1. The prophet is still lamenting the distressful conditions of his people in the siege. According to 2 Kings 25: 1-3 the siege lasted two years and threw the city of Jerusalem into the horrors of famine and pestilence. These forms of distress had been predicted as a warning more than once (Isaiah 14: 30; Jeremiah 14: 12); now the people cry unto the Lord for mercy.

Verse 2. Their property had been taken over by *strangers* which means those from the outside, and their houses were being occupied by *aliens* or foreigners.

Verse 3. These complaints were literal, for the men had been slain in the conflict.

Verse 4. In a siege all necessities of life are always rationed and often then they are not obtainable. Under such conditions the prices of the important items are increased by those taking advantage of the emergency.

Verse 5. *Neck* is from a word that Strong defines, "The back of the neck (as that on which burdens are bound)." The verse refers to the hardships imposed on them.

Verse 6. *Given the hand* denotes a gesture of submission, and the people of Judah had done this toward these foreign nations in their distress for the lack of food.

Verse 7. This generation is confessing the sins of the preceding one. *Borne their iniquities* means they were suffering the results of the iniquities of the fathers.

Verse 8. An instance of the subjugation to servants is recorded in Nehemiah 5: 15, and it shows the state of humiliation to which they were reduced.

Verse 9. After the city of Jerusalem had been overthrown by the siege it left the remaining inhabitants in a state of destitution. They had to brave the wilderness in search of food and it was at the risk of the sword in the hands of the Arabs.

Verse 10. The ravages of famine on the conditions of health can scarcely be imagined. It will cause a form of irritating heat that will be reflected from the skin. That is why the comparison is made to an oven.

Verse 11. It is an almost universal rule that where undue power is obtained, the commission of sex crimes takes place. The women of Judah were sacrificed to the lust of the Babylonian invaders.

Verse 12. Cruel tortures were inflicted upon the leading men, and no respect was paid to old age, the invaders being interested only in themselves.

Verse 13. *To grind* is from TECHOWN which Strong defines, "A hand mill; hence a millstone." This was what the young men had to work, and others had to carry such heavy loads of wood that they *fell* (staggered) under the load.

Verse 14. The gates of cities were the places of communication between them, and the elders or older men were the ones who occupied that position (Job 29: 7, 8). But that setup was absent, for the elders had been carried into captivity. Under these conditions the musicians would have no inclination to play.

Verse 15. This verse is somewhat general and refers to the same sadness of heart the other verses describe concerning their situation after the invasion.

Verse 16. This verse was true literally and figuratively. The king on the throne in Jerusalem was taken off to the land of Babylon. Also, the crown or glory of the nation had been removed by the humiliation of the exile.

Verse 17. The people of Judah had a prostrated feeling from both physical and mental causes. Their eyes had become dim through much weeping.

Verse 18. *Mountain* is sometimes used figuratively; it is so used here. Zion was the capital of Judah and it had been made so desolate that wild creatures ran over it.

Verse 19. The mourning people of Judah could not refrain from noting the great contrast between the throne of God and those of men. The changing from one generation to another does not affect the throne of God, for he is infinite and perpetual in power.

Verse 20. The disconsolate people of Judah are stinging under the thoughts of their fallen state. *Wherefore* is from MAH which Strong defines, "Properly in interrogation. What? how? why? when? Also an exclamation, what!" The Jews seemed to be astonished that their fortunes had fallen so low in view of the power of God. The term *for ever* is explained to mean *so long time*. Human experience tells one that a few years seem like many when he is in discomfort.

Verse 21. This verse may properly be regarded both as prophecy and present desire. The unfortunate citizens of Judah were then in a state of complete dejection; those especially who were in the land of Babylon. They did not have the heart to sing religious songs, but instead they hanged their harps on the willows of the streams and sat down on the banks to meditate. This was also prophesied hundreds of years before by David in the 137th Psalm.

Verse 22. The book and chapter closes with a repetition of the terrible state of mind possessed by the cast-off nation of God. The expressions represent the personal feelings of the righteous Jeremiah, a faithful prophet, and also those of the sinful nation who were suffering the just chastisement for their evil conduct.

EZEKIEL 1

General remarks. Before beginning my manuscript on this book, and especially the first chapter, I spent a considerable amount of time in study. I have consulted various commentaries and other works of reference such as histories and dictionaries. I was aware that most of the explanations that are offered as to the four creatures and their significance, insisted on recognizing the characteristics of the God of all creation, and this in opposition to the idea that they could signify any governments among men. However, there need be no difficulty on this point, for all of the glory and other greatness attributed to these powers of the world must be acknowledged as coming from God because He was concerned with the progress of them in view of the relations they had with His people. (See Daniel 2: 37; 4: 17, 32; 5: 18.)

Here is another thought that should be given consideration. Any explanation that is offered on a passage of the Bible should agree with the historical facts that may be learned from authentic sources. The interpretation that will be given on the meaning of the symbols shown in this chapter should be virtually true historically of the institutions that will be referred to. If this is true (and it is assured that it will be) then no violence can possibly be done the great subject at hand.

Verse 1. *Thirtieth year* refers to the age of Ezekiel when he began to write. Verse 3 says he was a priest and Numbers 4: 3 requires the priest to be at that age when he starts his term; not that he was acting as priest, for he was in Babylon at the time. The captives were scattered over different places in the land of the Chaldeans and Ezekiel was with the group that was by the river *Chebar*. This was a stream that flowed into the Euphrates some 200 miles north of Babylon. At this time and place the Lord began his communication with Ezekiel for the purpose of prophecy.

Verse 2. *Jehoiachin's captivity*. The Babylonian captivity was accomplished in three stages and the account is in 2 Kings 24 and 25. After the third year of Jehoiakim king of Judah, Nebuchadnezzar took possession of Jerusalem which marked the start of the 70-year epoch. Yet the king of Judah was permitted to occupy his throne as a vassal under the authority of the king of Babylon. After eight years of such a reign Jehoiakim died and his son Jehoiachin came to the throne. But he reigned only three months, and then the king of Babylon took him off the throne and carried him to the land of Babylon. At that time the greatest portion of the citizens of Judah were taken and among them was the prophet Ezekiel. Eleven years later the third and final stage of the captivity occurred. These three stages of the captivity are frequently referred to as the 1st, 2nd and 3rd captivities. Since Ezekiel was taken with the 2nd one, or at the time when Jehoiachin was taken, he dates his writing from that event. In other words, Ezekiel had been in Babylon five years when he began writing.

Verse 3. Ezekiel speaks of himself in the third person in this verse while most of his compositions are in the first person. The word *expressly* has none in the original and does not add anything to the thought. However, we may note that in the first verse the Lord communicated with the prophet in a vision and in this verse it is by word. The conclusion is that he was both to see and hear in his service as an inspired prophet. *Hand of the Lord* is a phrase often used in the Bible and it means here that the Lord took Ezekiel in hand; not only to control but also to assist him.

Verse 4. The Babylonian captivity as a whole had been going on for 13 years when Ezekiel began to write, but the complete subjugation of Judah was still six years in the future. Hence it was appropriate for the prophet to start his great book as if it were all still in the future. This accounts for the coming of the *whirlwind* from the *north*, since the Babylonians came into Palestine from that direction. (See the note on that with the comments in Isaiah 14: 31 in volume 3 of this Commentary.) A whirlwind is not only strong and swift but its circulating motion tends to draw articles toward its center. That is why the whirlwind was seen *infolding itself*. The second word is not in the original but the first is from LAQACH which Strong defines, "A primitive root; to take (in the widest variety of applications)." The simple meaning of the passage is that this combination of whirlwind and cloud was taking hold of the surrounding materials. The appropriateness of this illustration will appear as the chapter proceeds. There is some uncertainty in the works of reference about the word *amber*, but all agree that it is something that has a distinctive glow as of something highly polished. Again the figure will be seen to be appropriate as we get to the central subject of the chapter.

Verse 5. There existed in ancient times what are referred to as "The Four World Empires," and they figure largely in the prophecies and history of the Bible. The names of those empires (with some variations in some of them which will be noted as occasion suggests) are Babylonia, Medo-Persia, Greece and Rome. These empires are the *four living creatures* of this verse. They will be seen to have possessed various characteristics, but this verse names only one and it is that which is common to all of them which is the *likeness of a man*. This signifies intelligence which further means the four creatures were powers among mankind; made up of human beings.

Verse 6. The very title "world empires" would suggest the idea of a rule that is over the whole world; that is, that part which is civilized and subject to government control, hence the *four* faces and *four* wings, corresponding to the four points of the compass. The figure signifies an institution that can look in all directions with its faces and go in all directions with its wings. Using some poetic words, "I am monarch of all I survey."

Verse 7. The illustrations for the four empires will be drawn from the characteristics of dumb creatures in many instances. However, since the powers are human institutions, the selection and description of the various beasts will be made to conform as far as possible to the higher traits of human beings. The word for *feet* also is rendered "legs," and their being straight denotes they are more graceful in their outline and do not have abrupt, protruding parts as the feet of many animals do. *Sole* means the paw as a whole, and according to Moffatt's translation these paws were "rounded like the feet of calves." Such members would give to the creature a more firm bearing upon the surface over which it traveled.

Verse 8. The writer takes care to tell us that the characteristics he is describing apply to the *four* creatures individually and alike. The general likeness unto *man* in verse 5 denotes intelligence. In this verse the comparison is narrowed down to the *hands* of the man, and that indicates skill which certainly was necessary in accomplishing world-wide dominion.

Verse 9. In symbolic language an animal or other object may be represented as doing things that are above nature, such as trees talking in Judges 9: 8-15. And here we see a creature that can fly and look in four directions at once. This is to illustrate an empire that began at some locality and then spread out in all four directions until it became a world power. *Wings were joined* indicates the ability to fly in any and all directions at one time or as if in one concerted movement. *Turned not* is the same as the preceding thoughts. The creature would not need to turn about to change his direction since he has the equipment and ability for traveling in all directions at the same time.

Verse 10. Let the reader not forget that all figures and their explanations apply to each of the four empires. That does not mean that no differences existed between the four in their general history for there were many, In fact, no two of them were uniformly alike in their whole make-up and conduct. But as far as this chapter is concerned they are the same for all of them possessed the characteristics portrayed by these symbols and figures of speech. Neither do I wish to appear arbitrary in my selection of characteristics to be attributed to these empires. There are numerous terms in our language that could be used correctly because such vast institutions as we are considering would have many things in common with each other. I only claim that among such traits, the ones that will be named were true of each of the empires. In keeping with the foregoing explanations the following comments are offered on this and the following verses of the chapter. Please note the writer says *they four* had these marks which is the reason for my comments in the beginning of this paragraph. The face of a *man* indicates intelligence; a *lion* is fierce and bold; an *ox* is strong; and an *eagle* has the quality of fleetness and exaltation.

Verse 11. A creature with four wings as described here would be well equipped. The two that were *stretched upward* would enable him to travel, and he would also be protected by the two that *covered his body*.

Verse 12. *Straight forward* and *turned not* was explained at verse 9. The *spirit* that prompted the movements of these creatures will be explained later in the chapter.

Verse 13. This verse is a general description of the four creatures, and the central meaning is that they were lively and attractive which was true of the empires.

Verse 14. *Ran and returned* does not mean they went back to their starting place, for history does not bear out that idea. The word denotes a successful traveling over the civilized world. *Flash of lightning* is not used to indicate that it was only a flash and then soon over. The comparison is to the universal presence of the creatures. This comparison to the general and simultaneous appearance of lightning is used in Matthew 24: 27 and Revelation 1: 7.

Verse 15. The symbol now changes but it is the same subject. There is nothing strange in the idea of another object to have the same meaning as that of the one form just presented. Jesus spoke many parables to illustrate the one institution, so we should not be confused over the use of two representations by Ezekiel. Furthermore, there is no more difference between the two illustrations of Ezekiel than there was between the many parables spoken by Jesus. All symbols must be interpreted in a way that will agree with the literal facts connected with the subjects intended to be illustrated. Such a procedure will be followed in explaining the *wheel* that is introduced into this passage. Notice it was *by the living creatures*, which denotes that each was to work with the other in their movements. This weel had *four* faces which corresponds with the four faces of the creatures. *Face* is from PANEH and Strong defines it, "The face (as the part that turns); used in a great variety of applications (literal and figurative) also (prepositional prefix) as a preposition (before, etc.)." From this definition we would understand that by *face* is meant that part of the wheel that turns; that is, its forward and outer edge. But this wheel will be seen to have moved in four directions at once just as the creatures did, which would require that it have four faces in harmony with the four faces of the creatures. A simple wheel would have but two faces, hence we will need the information that will be given in the following verse.

Verse 16. It is evident the wheel that Ezekiel saw was no ordinary one, either in its construction or size. Instead, it was composed of two parts or wheels and one was nested inside the other. *Middle* is from TAVEK and the definition of Strong defines it, "From an unused root meaning to sever; a bisection, i.e. (by implication) the center." Let us suppose two large hoops so nearly the same size that one will just slip inside the other. Now give this last one a quarter turn which will present an object whose four sections will resemble the four quarters of a globe; turning the hoop so that its plane will stand at right angles with the plane of the other. This will give what Ezekiel saw; a *wheel* in the *middle* of a *wheel*. And with an object thus constructed it would be prepared to roll in any one of the four directions without turning, just as the creatures with their four faces could do.

Verse 17. This verse takes the same explanation as that for the four living creatures in verse 9, 12. Since the wheel was a companion symbol with the four creatures it would need to travel along with them.

Verse 18. The *rings* were the felloes or rims, located at that part which is called the face in verse 15. They were *high* or lofty which corresponds with that quality of the eagle in verse 10. *Dreadful* is from a word that is defined "reverence" in Strong's lexicon. The rims or felloes were full of *eyes* and that indicates intelligence as per verse 10. It was appropriate for these eyes to be in the rims of the wheel since that was the part that would be outmost in seeing where to go.

Verse 19. The wheel went whenever the living creatures went because both symbols represented the same thing which was the four empires. By the same token the creatures and the wheel were *lifted up* (made exalted and important) at the same time.

Verse 20. The central meaning of the word for *spirit* is "life" in the sense of consciousness. The *living creatures* would have such a spirit because they were beings that belonged to the animal kingdom. The wheels were normally inanimate objects and hence would not possess such a spirit. Yet in the use of them for symbolical purposes they represented the same things as did the *living creatures* which was the reason for saying *the spirit of the living creature was in the wheels.*

Verse 21. This verse is virtually the same as the preceding one, and the concluding clause of each is exactly the same. The co-operation of the creatures and the wheels signifies that they represent the same thing which is the four world empires noted at verse 5. As to the appropriateness of two different kinds of illustrations for the same thing, see the comments at verse 15.

Verse 22. The *firmament* means a vast expansion like the arch of the sky above the earth. *Terrible* means it was awe-inspiring, and had the appearance of a huge mass of rock crystal formed like a dome to cover the creatures.

Verse 23. Beneath this vast arch or dome of crystal could be seen the winged creatures. *Straight* is from the same word as in verse 7 and means they were graceful. *One toward the other* is equivalent to *joined one to another* in verse 9. Throughout this whole imagery the one idea that predominates is that of unity in purpose. The wings were for the purpose of protection as well as for exalted traveling. (Verse 11.)

Verse 24. This verse as a whole is a passage intended to show the greatness of the institutions symbolized by the living creatures and the wheels. *Great waters* is a figure and when used in a favorable sense indicates a multitude of people. Such would be a fitting symbol of these empires for they were regarded as including virtually all of the civilized world. *Voice of the Almighty* means the voice of God. This statement is not made on the strength of the word's being capitalized, for all punctuations have been done by man, and while often they are correct, they are of no authority. I have examined the uses of the original word and without a single exception the connection shows it to mean God. Furthermore, Strong defines the original word, "The Almighty" with capital A. This indicates that God was recognized in the four empires, and that also agrees with Daniel 2: 37; 4: 17, 32; 5: 18. *Voice of speech* indicates not only that there was consciousness but intelligence in the creatures which agrees with the fact that the creatures represented governments of and by men. When these creatures were not flying they let their wings down, which indicates they used them then only for defence purposes.

Verse 25. This *voice* was evidently the same as that mentioned in the preceding verse. The Almighty could be heard by the inspired prophet and the force of it would be to confirm the declarations indicated by the passages cited in the preceding verse.

Verse 26. This *throne* was the source from where the voice issued just mentioned. Precious stones are frequently used to compare both the beauty and value of things pertaining to God's arrangements. On this throne was the *likeness of a man* which denotes the Almighty, for Genesis 1: 26 and many other passages teach that man was made in the image of God. However, it is God and not his image that is meant in this place for we have already learned that He was connected with these world governments.

Verse 27. This verse is a highly figurative description of the Almighty. The meaning is that God is as intense as fire, as resplendent as amber, and that the entire Being was radiant with this indescribable glory.

Verse 28. Another figure is added to the picture of the Almighty. He is likened to the rainbow that spans the heavens, betokening the calm that follows a storm and shedding over the earth all of the primary colors. This vision so impressed Ezekiel that he was prostrated and fell dispirited to the ground on his face, where he lay until he heard a voice speaking unto him.

EZEKIEL 2

Verse 1. The voice which Ezekiel heard in the preceding chapter bade him stand upon his feet and it would speak to him. *Son of man*. We have no information in the Bible on why this term was used; especially why it was restricted as it was. It was used at least 92 times for Ezekiel and once for Daniel (Dan. 8: 17). They were the only writing prophets who spent any time in Babylon, but whether that had anything to do with affecting the forms of address I am not able to say.

Verse 2. *Spirit entered into me* means the spirit of encouragement not the Spirit of God. It is true, that Spirit was communicating with the prophet, but it was when He (the Spirit of God) spoke to Ezekiel that his spirit came back to him. This shows the passage to mean that when God spoke to the prophet it encouraged him to "take heart" so that he felt able to stand up. This is similar to the experiences that Daniel had in chapter 8: 17, 18 and 10: 9, 10.

Verse 3. To avoid confusion I shall again explain that Ezekiel was in Babylon, having been carried there with the bulk of the people of Judah at the overthrow of Jehoiachin. Hence many of the predictions of the captivity had been fulfilled, while others were still to come since the "3rd captivity" in the 11th year of Zedekiah was yet pending. Another thing, God wished the captivity to work certain reforms in the lives of His people, and hence they were to be offered many admonitions and warnings. The Lord did not wish Ezekiel to be discouraged if his admonitions were rejected in most instances and therefore he told him that the people to whom he was sending him were a *rebellious nation*.

Verse 4. The Lord continued his description of the nation to whom he sent Ezekiel as a prophet. They were *stiffhearted* which means they were stubborn. But Ezekiel was to tell them he was approaching them with the word of the Lord.

Verse 5. A man's standing before the Lord does not depend on his success as a speaker of the truth. If he says that which is in harmony with the divine law he will be blessed regardless of whether his teaching is accepted or not. This principle was made known to Ezekiel in this verse. God knew that Israel as a people would not give heed to the admonitions of the prophet but wished him to give them the truth anyhow. But one thing would be accomplished regardless of their attitude and that would be to show them there was a prophet among them.

Verse 6. *Briers, thorns* and *scorpions* are used figuratively, and refer to the bitter persecutions the prophet would have to face by reason of his unwelcome warnings. The Lord gave Ezekiel the encouragement that he need not be afraid of the people.

Verse 7. The prophet was again told to speak the words of the Lord to the people regardless of their attitude toward his teaching. Timothy was given a like instruction concerning the Gospel (2 Tim. 4: 2, 3.)

Verse 8. The particular *rebellion* meant is that of rejecting the word of the Lord. Ezekiel was about to be offered something and he was warned not to rebel against it and thus be like the rebellious nation. The last clause is figurative and refers to some kind of spiritual food.

Verse 9. *Roll of a book* means a piece of writing material was rolled up and was in the hand that appeared. In ancient times books were not bound as they are today, but were written on long strips of the material and then rolled up.

Verse 10. The hand unrolled the book before the prophet and he saw that it was written on both sides. This was unusual because the rule was for the sheets to be written on one side only as it is done today in "regulation" correspondence. Yet in cases of special importance where space is limited and where much is to be said it is permissible to write on both sides. In the present case there was an urgent need for much space for the subject pertained to lamentations and warnings over the wretched state of God's people.

EZEKIEL 3

Verse 1. See the comments at 1 Kings 20:35 in volume 2 of this Commentary on the subject of prophets performing or acting. In Revelation 10: 8-11 John does the same thing that Ezekiel does here. The physical act (made possible by the miraculous help of God) was to symbolize a spiritual circumstance. Since this roll contained the words of God, the eating of it would denote the eating of spiritual food and it would inspire the prophet to speak the truth of God to the *house of Israel*.

Verse 2. *Caused me to eat* was a miracle and it is explained in the preceding verse.

Verse 3. In the case of John (Rev. 10: 8-11) the eating of the book had a twofold effect on him, sweet and bitter, but nothing is said about the bitterness in that of Ezekiel, because the personal attitude of the prophet toward the words is the only feature of it that was to be considered in the act. In the case of John in Revelation that of both the speaker and the people were symbolized, hence the bitterness. It was agreeable with Ezekiel to carry the message to Israel because he was a faithful servant of God the same as John. *Belly* and *bowels* are used to denote the body as a whole, and when used figuratively it denotes that Ezekiel was to be completely possessed by the article. Since the act was a symbol of his being inspired of God it made a circumstance like that of the apostles who were *"filled* with the Holy Ghost" (Acts 2: 4).

Verse 4. The Lord's purpose in the preceding verses is made known in this one. Ezekiel was to approach the house of Israel and speak the words He gave him.

Verse 5. *Strange* means foreign and *hard* means difficult, and the people to whom Ezekiel was told to speak did not use that kind of language, but they naturally spoke the same tongue that the prophet used since they both were Jews.

Verse 6. Ezekiel was not even asked to speak to a number of peoples; only to the one, whose native tongue he could understand without any special help from God. There is no difficulty for an inspired man to speak to any number or kinds of nationalities; that is not the point. On the other hand, a foreign nation might have more pretext for not receiving the words because they would not understand the language; and yet even they would have been more willing to receive the warning than were the Jews who were of a rebellious disposition.

Verse 7. It should be noted that in the frequent statements on the stubbornness of those to whom the prophet was sent, the idea is held out that it is *the house of Israel* or *the people*. This does not prevent any individual in the group from taking a different attitude, and that is largely the explanation of why the Lord insisted on giving them the truth regardless of the general rebellion. There were usually some exceptional instances when certain individuals would accept the admonitions and be profited. The value of this small minority was great enough to justify the work of presenting the word of the Lord though it might bring persecution upon the bearer of the words. It is about time again for the reader to see the long note that was offered in connection with 2 Kings 22: 17 in volume 2 of this Commentary.

Verse 8. This verse means that God was to give Ezekiel the boldness necessary to face the threatening looks of the people who would dislike the warnings offered.

Verse 9. An adamant is one of the hardest of stones such as the diamond. It is harder than a flint rock and the term is used figuratively for the firmness that God promised to give Ezekiel in his dealing with the hard-faced people of Israel. See a similar assurance given to the prophet Jeremiah (Jer. 1: 18, 19).

Verse 10. God communicated with Jeremiah for the purpose of inspiration in the form of speaking as well as by giving him the sense of it in his mind.

Verse 11. *Them of the captivity* had direct reference to the people of Israel who were then in Babylon. Ezekiel could appear to them because he was in that land also. There were some of the Israelites still in Palestine because the "3rd captivity" had not yet taken place. And again the prophet was commanded to speak the word regardless of their attitude toward it. This instruction that was repeated so frequently was to the end that Ezekiel need not conclude that he had made a failure just because he could not bring his people to accept the teaching. This subject of the respective responsibility of the speaker and hearer will be treated more thoroughly in a bracket of verses yet in this chapter.

Verse 12. *Spirit took me up* denotes that the Spirit took charge of the prophet and conducted him to a more suitable place where he could speak to the people. At the same time he heard a strong voice giving his evidence of the presence of God.

Verse 13. These *creatures* and *wheels* are the same that were described in chapter one, applying to the four world empires that succeeded each other.

Verse 14. *Spirit lifted me up* has the same meaning as "spirit took me up" in verse 12. These sentiments which the prophet expressed were because of the unfortunate situation of his people. The bitterness would be increased by the knowledge that their own stubbornness had brought these misfortunes upon them, and he had to be the bearer of the unwelcome message from the Lord.

Verse 15. *Astonished* is from SHAMEM and Strong defines it, "To stun (or intransitively grow numb), i.e. devastate or (figuratively) stupefy (both usually in a passive sense)." The thought is that when Ezekiel saw his brethren and beheld their condition, he was so overcome that he had nothing to say for seven days. A like circumstance is recorded in Job 2: 13.

Verse 16. The special message from the Lord came to Ezekiel at the end of the seven days mentioned in the preceding verse. The Lord seems to have respected the feelings of his prophet and did not disturb him for a period.

Verse 17. The subject of the special message was then stated to Ezekiel. He was to be placed in a very important position of responsibility with reference to the house of Israel in that he was to act as a *watchman*. That word is from TSAPHAH, which Strong defines, "A primitive root; properly to lean forward, i.e. to peer into the distance; by implication to observe, await." This definition agrees with the actual work of a man who occupied the walls of ancient cities to watch for any danger that might threaten the city. If he saw an army or other hostile force approaching he was to announce it to the citizens and give them the opportunity to escape if possible or defend themselves otherwise.

Verse 18. From this verse through 21 the subject is the respective responsibilities of a watchman and those over whom he has been oppointed. The principles involved in this situation have been stated frequently and they have always been in force wherever man's conduct toward others was involved. If a watchman fails to warn a wicked man of his danger it will not shield him from the effects of his wickedness. Yet his own death will not atone for the negligence of the watchman; he must die also.

Verse 19. A watchman might not be able to induce a wicked man to turn from his sinful course and the guilty one would have to suffer. But if the watchman has done what he could to turn the unrighteous man from his great error, the entire blame will be placed on his head and not on that of the watchman.

Verse 20. God does not desire that any man shall sin nor does He actually tempt him with evil in order to induce him to go wrong (James 1: 13). But the Lord subjects his servants to tests of faith and such things are meant by *stumblingblocks*. If a servant of God yields to this test and does wrong because the watchman did not warn him, then both the backsliding servant and unfaithful watchman will have to die.

Verse 21. The principle regarding the responsibility of a teacher as set forth in this verse is the same as the Lord has always maintained. The success of a would-be reformer will have nothing to do with his personal reward. It might be possible for him to achieve what would appear as a success and yet he would be condemned because he did not operate according to the truth. On the other hand, a man could fail to accomplish the desired result even when offering the word of God faithfully, because the hearer would not accept the teaching. In such a case the hearer alone would be condemned while the teacher would be blessed. How wonderful it is, then, when the teachings offered is right and the hearer accepts and obeys it; both will be blessed.

Verse 22. The foregoing speech was made to the prophet while he was in the midst of his people near the river Chebar. Now the Lord wishes him to go away into a plain for further inspired communications. *Plain* is from BIQAH and Strong defines it, "Properly a split, i.e. a wide level valley between mountains." It would be a place secluded and thus a suitable one for a private conversation between the prophet and God.

Verse 23. Ezekiel obeyed the instructions given him and went forth into the secluded spot. After arriving there the Lord appeared in the form of a glorious halo that overcame the prophet and he fell prostrated to the earth.

Verse 24. *The spirit entered* denotes that the prophet was rallied from his prostrated frame of mind. After regaining his strength he was told to go to his own house. It was not the time for him to be abroad among the people, for the Lord was going to give him very much information upon his work with the nation.

Verse 25. These *bands* were not literal but were the hindrances that the rebellious Jews would put against the work of the prophet.

Verse 26. *Tongue cleave to roof of mouth* was not to be a physical obstruction in every case. It was virtually the same kind of restriction that was placed on Jeremiah (Jer. 7: 16, 27). No use to waste words on the stubborn people, but when the proper time comes the Lord will inform him of it.

Verse 27. Doubtless the Lord had in mind some future date when a shall number of the Jews would listen to instruction. When that time came He would open the mouth of the prophet, which means he would authrize him to speak. When that was done there would be some who would hear and profit thereby. But before such an event occurs the prophet was to be given a series of revelations, some of which would be in the form of personal acting; see the comments offered on that interesting subject at 1 Kings 20: 35 in volume 2 of this Commentary.

EZEKIEL 4

Verse 1. The chief sin of the Jewish nation and for which it went into captivity was idolatry. In order to impress its people with the seriousness of the offence, the prophet was required to do some of the "acting" mentioned in the preceding chapter. He was to dramatize the siege of Jerusalem which was the capital of the nation. In this drama he was to do some very unpleasant performances. The city of Jerusalem was to be represented by a tile or brick, on which a likeness of Jerusalem was portrayed.

Verse 2. The 70-year captivity had been going on for some time when Ezekiel began to write, but the city of Jerusalem had not yet been destroyed because the 3rd stage of the subjugation was still to be accomplished. That great event was to be preceded with a siege, and the prophet was to "act out" the same by going through the motions of it in some figurative way.

Verse 3. The city had a protecting wall around it which would have to be attacked before it could be taken. As a representation of this wall Ezekiel was to get *an iron pan* which could be placed on edge in the position of such a protecting structure. This pan was to be raised up between the tile and the prophet who was to act as a besieging army. *This shall be a sign* means that the Jews were to take this performance of Ezekiel as a sign of what was about to happen to their city.

Verse 4. *Lay* is used figuratively and means that Ezekiel would be going through this unpleasant experience to emphasize the iniquity of the house of Israel. Each day he lay on his side stood for a year in the sinful history of the nation. *Bear their iniquity* denotes that the prophet was to undergo this affliction as a sign of the greatness of Israel's sin.

Verse 5. The children of Israel were inclined toward idolatry from the beginning of their history as was shown at Mt. Sinai and afterward. But the specific length of time named in this verse should be dated from the enactment of national idolatry (1 Kings 12: 26) which was in 975 B.C. to 585 B.C., and that was about the date of Ezekiel's performance just described.

Verse 6. The prophet was to lie on his left side when the case of Israel (the 10 tribes) was being treated. After that he was to lie on his right side to indicate the house of Judah, and that was to continue 40 days. Various theories have been offered in the works of reference as to why there was only the smaller number for Judah; but I am not convinced that any of them is well founded. It is true that Judah was regarded as the greater offender from the standpoint of responsibility, for she had the example of Israel before her and should have profited by the lesson. But in actual years devoted to the abominable practice, Israel far exceeded Judah. It is not necessary to go into any speculation beyond the known facts of history.

Verse 7. *Set thy face* means that Ezekiel was to take his reclining position to indicate the siege of Jerusalem. *Arm uncovered* indicates that all hindrances were to be removed that might make a siege ineffective.

Verse 8. No literal bands would have been necessary, for Ezekiel was an obedient servant and ready always to do the Lord's bidding. Yet he was under an obligation that was as binding as if he had been tied with ropes. In thus acting his part he would be showing the firmness of the siege.

Verse 9. Ezekiel was directed to prepare certain articles of food. This would require him to be up and about the community more or less, which indicates that his position of lying on his side was not literally continuous, but only for the greater part of each day. Short intervals had to be used for the preparation of these articles of diet. The materials designated were such as a famine would produce, and that was one of the subjects the prophet was to portray in his acting.

Verse 10. The short rationing of meat described was another circumstance usually connected with a famine that is brought on by a siege.

Verse 11. Even drinking water is frequently very scarce in a siege. There was no actual shortage of that with Ezekiel, but he was made to ration it for himself as a further sign of the famine about to come on Jerusalem.

Verses 12-15. The history of mankind is one in which it is common to see one man enduring unpleasant experiences for the sake of another. This has been especially true of the prophets according to Jeremiah 13: 1-8; 27: 2, and the case of Ezekiel's lying so long upon his sides. Now in the present verse we have another instance of a very disagreeable task imposed on the prophet. Smith's Bible Dictionary states that dung was sometimes used as fuel in ancient times. However, it was usually for heating purposes only, which would not be so objectionable. But in the case at hand the prophet was told to prepare his food with this substance as fuel. The necessary handling of such material in connection with cooking a meal would be very unpleasant, especially if the original order had been retained here. But upon the complaint of Ezekiel the Lord permitted him to substitute the discharges from a beast which would be less repulsive though bad enough. This unusual performance was to be a sign to the children of Israel of the unpleasant experiences which they were destined to have among the heathen nations where they had been sent as captives.

Verse 16. To avoid confusion it is well to keep in mind the fact of "the three captivities," or the three stages in the subjugation of Jerusalem and the kingdom of Judah. For a more extended comment on this subject see 2 Kings 24: 1 in volume 2 of this Commentary. Two of these captivities had taken place when Ezekiel began to write. The third one was still to come but not very far in the future. The famine that is predicted in this verse occurred in that terrible event, and the Biblical account of it is given in 2 Kings 25: 3. The statements of this verse are literal and were fulfilled when Nebuchadnezzar threw Jerusalem into a siege.

Verse 17. No material facts are added in this verse except to describe the immediate effects of the famine. *Astonied* is from SHAMEM which Strong defines, "To stun (or intransitively grow numb)." The lack of food caused the people to grow numb and behold each other with a stunned countenance. All of this was to be brought upon them as a punishment *for their iniquity*.

EZEKIEL 5

Verse 1. The prophet was directed to do some more acting to which reference has been made frequently. The head is the most important part of the body, and the Lord selected that part of Ezekiel's person in the present drama. The weighing of the hairs was necessary in order to make the equal divisions that were called for.

Verse 2. The bulk of the hairs was to be divided into thirds, corresponding to the three points in verse 12. *Midst of the city* could not mean Jerusalem literally, because Ezekiel was in Babylon and there is no evidence that he ever left it. The phrase means he was to perform these things in the midst of the people of whose former kingdom the city of Jerusalem was the capital. (See verse 5.) The prophet was to go out among the people and burn one division of the hairs in their sight. He would hold a division in one hand and with the other he would hack or hew it to bits. The other third of the hairs was to be tossed out and let be scattered with the wind. Apparently these last hairs, representing actual living persons, were set free to go where they would. Yet that was not to be so, for even those who escaped the first two fates were doomed to be pursued with hostile intent, hence the Lord said he would do what Ezekiel could not humanly do; make a sword follow after the scattered hairs.

Verse 3. Before making the divisions described in the preceding verse, Ezekiel was to reserve a *few in number*. (This refers to the "remnant" recorded in Ezra 2: 64.) He was to bind them in his garment which would indicate an act to shield them from the ravages of the three events just described.

Verse 4. The "remnant," however, was not to escape entirely from tribulation, hence Ezekiel was directed to take some of the hairs he had placed in the folds of his garment and burn them. The Lord explained that a fire (figuratively) would come out against the house of Israel.

Verse 5. *This is Jerusalem* explains that what Ezekiel was directed to do was to be fulfilled upon Jerusalem as was stated at verse 2. *Set it in the midst of nations*. God bestowed great honors on Jerusalem by giving her such prominence among the nations.

Verse 6. Jerusalem did not literally commit more or greater idolatry than the nations of heathendom, for that would have been next to impossible. But when considered in the light of her opportunities and her professions, she had committed abomination *more than the countries about*. Specifically, she had substituted *wickedness* for the *judgments* of the Lord and refused to walk in the law of God.

Verse 7. *Multiplied* is from HAMON and the definition in Strong's lexicon is, "A noise, tumult, crowd; also disquietude, wealth." The thought is that Jerusalem made a greater ado than the surrouding nations as to her importance of wealth and strength. In spite of such claims, however, she did not show as consistent an attitude toward the law she professed to follow as did the heathen nations.

Verse 8. It may be observed that much of Ezekiel's writing seems to be directed more especially against Jerusalem than against the nation generally. That can be explained by the fact that most of the nation was already in exile and suffering their punishment, while Jerusalem as a city was still standing and facing the third and last stage of the captivity. Jerusalem was the capital city and was largely responsible for the state of corruption among the people through the power and example of the leaders, hence God declared, "I am against thee."

Verse 9. This means that the punishment the Lord intended to inflict on Jerusalem would be greater than had ever been put on her before.

Verse 10. This verse predicts some of the awful effects of a famine that was to be brought upon Jerusalem by the siege. It would seem impossible for parents to be starved to such an extent that they would eat the flesh of their own children. But hunger is a terrible motive, and this very deed has been committed (2 Kings 6: 25-29).

Verse 11. The defilement refers to the practice of idolatry which the people of Jerusalem had mixed with the worship prescribed by the Lord. *Will diminish thee* was a prediction of the overthrow of the city, both as to its power or authority and also materially in that it was destined to be taken and burned.

Verse 12. These three means of reducing the great capital city would fulfill the symbolic prediction that was made by the acting of the prophet in verse 2. The three items would logically result in the almost total destruction of the nation. *Pestilence* and *famine* are tied together as one because a serious scarcity of food generally breeds disease. Some of the citizens tried to resist the enemy by fighting but were defeated in battle. Some escaped immediate death on the battle field and fled into distant regions, but they could not run away from God and the sword caught up with them.

Verse 13. *I will be comforted* could not mean that God takes personal joy out of the suffering of his people. The thought is that the Lord will be satisfied with his work of reproving the nation through the severe chastisement.

Verse 14. National "pride" is not endorsed by the Lord at any time, for pride is always condemned wherever it exists. Yet it is a strong punishment upon any nation to humiliate it before the eyes of other nations, and that was to be one form of divine judgment upon Jerusalem and her people.

Verse 15. There was a twofold purpose in punishing the people of Israel in the sight of other nations. One was to bring Israel to repentance and the other was to serve as a warning to those heathen groups. The like object was in the divine mind in recording the facts of ancient times for the use of men in the days of the Christian Dispensation (1 Cor. 10: 11; Rom. 15: 4). Such is the meaning of this verse by including the word *instruction* which was to apply to the heathen observers.

Verse 16. When God sends his judgments on Israel, it should be a lesson to *them* (the heathen) and cause them to improve their national ways.

Verse 17. The items threatened are a repetition of what has previously been stated. An important declaration is connected with it, *I the Lord have spoken it.*

EZEKIEL 6

Verse 1. Ezekiel was an inspired prophet and spoke or wrote only the *word of the Lord* as it came unto him.

Verse 2. *The mountains of Israel* were material objects and could have no moral responsibilities. But the people made a specialty of erecting altars and idols on the "high places" and offering their abominable services thereon. Hence in the form of personification the Lord directed his prophet to write against these mountains. *Set thy face* is a figure of speech and means that Ezekiel was to focus his attention upon the object mentioned and then write as the Lord directed him.

Verse 3. The thought of the preceding verse is maintained in this, and the impersonation is extended to include other geographical parts of the land. None of them has any responsibility in the corruptions being condemned, but the impression of guilt should be greater before the mind of the guilty ones by such an all-out picture of the scene. The particular complaint is literally denoted by the words *high places*.

Verse 4. The altars and idols were literally destroyed as the nation went down in captivity. But that fact may well be regarded as a sign of the complete cure from idolatry that was brought about by the exile in the land of Babylon. See the historical note at Isaiah 1:25 in volume 3 of this Commentary.

Verse 5. These dead bodies being laid before the idols would not be as a sacrificial offering, but as a token of the uselessness of false gods. If such deities could not preserve the physical lives of their worshipers, they surely could not provide them any spiritual help.

Verse 6. The weakness of false gods was to be further shown in that they could not protect the homes and cities of the country. It is a poor head that cannot take the proper oversight of its own body, yet these images that were worshiped by the people of Israel were powerless to preserve even the altars erected to their worship.

Verse 7. The sight of slain men right in the midst of the multitude of idols would prove their frailty. The logical conclusion that such a situation should suggest is that *I am the Lord*, meaning the God of Israel is the true Lord.

Verse 8. The *remnant* promised is numbered in Ezra 2:64. The captivity in Babylon lasted 70 years and the ravages of that period reduced the population of Israel from some millions to this number.

Verse 9. *Shall remember me among the nations* was sadly fulfilled by the children of Israel after they got into the land of Babylon. Their dejected frame of mind is forcefully described by a prophecy of David in Psalms 137. *I am broken*. Strong defines the original for the last word, "A primitive root; to burst (literally or figuratively)." Of course it is used figuratively here and means the Lord was deeply disappointed over the conduct of his people. *Whorish heart* means their lusting after false gods, as religious unfaithfulness is commonly compared to moral corruption in the Bible. *Shall loathe themselves* refers to the complete cure from idolatry that was accomplished by the captivity. (See the notes at Isaiah 1:25.)

Verse 10. The main object the Lord had in view by the whole work of the captivity was to convince Israel that He is the only true God. *Do this evil* means something painful, not anything wrong morally.

Verse 11. Strong says the original for *smite* means to strike, literally or figuratively. Ezekiel was to do this "acting" with his hand and foot as a gesture of emphasis. It would be a sign of the Lord's determination to impose a punishment upon the disobedient nation. The three items named were commented upon at Jeremiah 14:12 and other places previously considered in this Commentary.

Verse 12. A pestilence, however, could occur from conditions other than famine, and the Lord threatened to bring it upon some of the people who would not be hemmed by the siege. The general thought is that no one can escape the chastisement that He determines against the unfaithful servants.

Verse 13. *Slain men among their idols* was to signify the weakness of the false gods the children of Israel had been worshiping. The presence of these dead bodies in the same area with the idols would be proof of the helplessness thereof. *Hills* and *mountains* are named because they were favorite spots on which the idols and their altars were built. *Trees* also were used as desirable places for the idolatrous service, and they selected a *green* or living tree, which Strong defines, "to be . . . figuratively prosperous." Something alive might suggest a source of good whereas a dead one would not. There is nothing about a dead tree that would suggest anything to be worshiped. *Sweet savor* refers to the incense that was burned in sacrifice to a god because of its fragrant odor.

Verse 14. Concerning *Diblath*, the Funk and Wagnalls Bible Dictionary says the following: "No such place is known and the true reading may be 'to Riblah' in the extreme north of the Lebanon region, making the whole expression mean: 'from south to north, i.e., from one end of the land to the other." The significance to us is that God threatened a widespread desolation over the land as a punishment for their idolatry.

EZEKIEL 7

Verse 1. *Moreover* occurs frequently in the Authorized Version but seldom has any word in the original; whenever it does, it means "a repetition or continuance." It is a writer's casual way of saying he has something more to say.

Verse 2. *Land* is from a word that means literally the soil, but the application is to the people who inhabit it. It is a common way of referring to a land or country when the writer really means the people. It is true that if physical damage should be brought upon the soil it would be a misfortune to the people who depend on it for a living. To threaten an end to the land means the end of its productiveness for the inhabitants. Such a fate awaited the land of Israel, for it was to be taken over by a foreign nation. *Four corners* is a figure of speech meaning the entire area.

Verse 3. The antecedent of *thee* is "land" in the preceding verse. The application of the judgments upon the land also is explained in that verse. *Recompense . . . thine abominations* means the land was to be treated according to the abominable practices that it had harbored or encouraged.

Verse 4. The immediate purpose of most of the judgments upon Israel was to convince them that *I am the Lord*. The reason this was the outstanding issue was the national sin of idolatry of which the people of God were guilty. If they are impressed with the fundamental fact that God is the only true One, the conclusion would be established that idolatry is wrong in every particular.

Verse 5. *Only* is from ECHAD which Strong defines, "Properly united, i.e. one; or (as an ordinal) first." *Evil* does not mean moral wrong, but some kind of adversity. The verse means that one great calamity was at hand, which we are to understand was the destruction of Jerusalem and the complete subjugation of Judah.

Verse 6. *It is come* signifies the same thought as the preceding verse does; that the final downfall of the nation was about due.

Verse 7. Usually the word *morning* when used figuratively means something favorable; that a new day has come. But in the present case it is an unfavorable term because it signifies that *the day of trouble* had dawned. *Sounding again* is from one word and is defined "a shout" in Strong's lexicon. The thought is that no shouts of joy will be heard on the mountains, for it is to be a time of trouble.

Verse 8. *Shortly pour out* was a literal prediction, referring to the destruction of Jerusalem at the 3rd and final stage of the captivity.

Verse 9. *Eye shall not . . . have pity* sounds harsh, but it refers to the just penalty about to be imposed upon Judah in the loss of her capital city. That which will make it just is the fact that it was called for by *their ways* of iniquity.

Verse 10. These terms are all used figuratively and denote the same thought as that in the preceding verse; namely, the final overthrow of Jerusalem.

Verse 11. *Rod* means a ruling influence, and violence had become the ruling element in the nation. This was chiefly because the ruling or leading classes of men had become violently corrupt in their practices.

Verses 12, 13. Transactions in real estate will not be important, whether a buyer thinks he has obtained a bargain or a seller imagines he had to sell at a sacrifice. The foreign nation will have charge of the land and no deals will be of any force.

Verse 14. When a movement was about to be made in ancient times a trumpet was sounded as a signal to all interested parties. (Jeremiah 6: 1.) The people in Jerusalem were theoretically ready to travel yet no one was disposed to face the foe. The wrath of God was very much in evidence by the presence of the invading army, or at least by indications that it would be present at any time.

Verse 15. *The sword* was that of the Babylonians that was to hem the city of Jerusalem by a siege. That would throw the inhabitants into the grip of famine which usually causes a pestilence because of undernourishment.

Verse 16. A number would be able to escape, both of those in the city and also of the ones scattered out over the open country. However, to escape the contact with the sword would not mean complete satisfaction.

They would be forced to flee for refuge to places of safety among the mountains. Their mournful state is likened to that of a dove whose characteristic cry is known to all. But the bewailing of the people of Judah was to be embittered by the knowledge that it was for their own sins.

Verse 17. This weakness would be the mental reaction from the distressful situation. It would be the sadness of defeatism and loss of morale.

Verse 18. This verse is another reminder of David's prediction in Psalms 137.

Verse 19. When the people of Judah find themselves captured by the army of Babylon, they will realize that all of their wealth will avail them nothing. It will be impossible to buy their freedom and hence they might as well cast their money to the ground. The thing that caused the downfall of the people was the worship of idols. Many of them were made of silver and gold, hence they need not count on purchasing their deliverance with this corrupting material.

Verse 20. God had given his people one of the most beautiful temples ever possessed by any nation. The *majesty* of the Lord was in evidence all through the structure and the whole setup was adapted to the worship of the true God. But the people corrupted the holy building with *the images of their abominations* which they used in their practices of idolatry. *Therefore . . . far from them.* This beautiful building that had been blessed with the glory of the Lord was to be taken from them.

Verse 21. The temple was to be given *into the hands of strangers* (the Babylonians), and they *shall pollute it* (2 Kings 25: 9).

Verse 22. God was to turn his face away from his unfaithful people and the holy temple that He had placed among them. *They* (the Babylonians) would be suffered to enter the place where only high priests ever entered and that on only one day a year.

Verse 23. *Make a chain* was a prediction of the enslavement of the people by a foreign nation. It would be as a punishment for the violence and other crimes committed in the land and city.

Verse 24. *Worst of the heathen.* The first word is defined in the lexicon as meaning bad either naturally or morally. Both phases of the meaning could properly be applied to the Babylonians, and they were the ones whom the Lord was bringing against his own people. *Make pomp to cease* refers to the proud leaders in Judah who were destined to be humiliated by the captivity.

Verse 25. When the Lord decrees a state of trouble for unfaithful servants, it is then too late to seek for peace or any opportunity of avoiding the chastisement.

Verse 26. In their time of trouble the people would gladly have received some instruction and consolation from the teachers. It will be too late then, for even the priests and prophets had been corrupt, and God will not honor them with any vision.

Verse 27. The king and priests and prophets, also the people in general will all be rejected by the Lord because they all have conspired against Him. (See Jeremiah 5: 31.) All of this was to come upon the people *according to their deserts.*

EZEKIEL 8

Verse 1. *Sixth year* is dated from the year that Jehoiachin was taken off his throne and taken to Babylon, at which time Ezekiel also was taken. According to chapter 1: 2, 3 Ezekiel began his writing after he had been in Babylon five years, hence the present chapter was written after he had been there six years. *Elders* comes from ZAQEN and Strong defines it with the single word "old." The *elders* among the Jews is a term that has an indefinite meaning. The original law of Moses makes no provision for them as an official or ruling class, but later they became a very influential group. Sometimes the word is used with reference to age and at other times it refers to the leaders or representative men. The context must determine the meaning of the word in each case. Ezekiel was about to be given an important communication from the Lord and he was sitting in the presence of these elders. Though they were in the land of captivity, they had not lost their "seniority" among the Jews. *Hand . . . fell upon me* means that God took charge of the prophet to display before him a vision concerning the people of Judah.

Verse 2. God never appears in person before fleshly man, but does the work through a spiritual representative. Such a personage was sent to

Ezekiel for the momentous occasion at hand. (See a similar incident in Revelation 1:14, 15.)

Verse 3. *Spirit lifted me up* and *in the visions* are important keys to the meaning of this verse. By them the reader will understand that Ezekiel never actually left Babylon at all, and this must be constantly kept in mind or great confusion will result. The prophet saw the things described in a vision right while he was bodily in Babylon, in the same manner in which John saw things in Heaven while he was bodily in the Isle of Patmos. *Image of jealousy* means an idol, and it is called by this name in the sense of Exodus 20:5, where God forbade the making of any image to worship because He was a jealous God.

Verse 4. God's glory would certainly be inside the gate of Jerusalem since that was the capital of the nation that belonged to Him. *In the plain* refers to the events described in chapter 3:22.

Verse 5. The idolatry of ancient times consisted of three principal forms, and all objects of false worship were under one or more of the three. One was the worship of manmade idols, another was the worship of invisible or imaginary beings, and the third was that of things in creation. The first were made of metals, wood and stone; the second consisted of such as Baal, Ashtoreth, Tammuz, etc., and the third included animals, rivers, living trees, and planets ("host of heaven"). Our present chapter exhibits the three forms, and this and the preceding two verses include the first form.

Verse 6. Ezekiel had never manifested any tendency toward idolatry, and the vision which the Lord was showing to him was not for his personal benefit. But he was expected to report the scenes to his fellow countrymen and write them for the information of mankind in following generations. (The same was true of John and the book of Revelation.) *That I should go far off* means that God was deserting the house which his people had polluted with their idols.

Verse 7. The three forms of idolatry described at verse 5 are not treated in the same order in this chapter, which is no important item. Their description is the main thing because no special preference was observed by the idolaters. Having pointed out the first one described, in verse 5, the third one will come next in the chapter beginning with the present verse. *Hole* is from CHOR which Strong defines, "A cavity, socket, den." This was a place in the wall through which one could see but not intended as an opening for entrance.

Verse 8. *Dig* is from CHATHAR and is defined by Strong, "A primitive root; to force a passage, as by burglary." When Ezekiel was brought to where he could see the hole or cavity mentioned in the preceding verse, he was told to force his way through the wall. When he did this he was brought into sight of a door.

Verse 9. The door proved to be an entrance to an apartment containing *abominations that they do here*, a detestable exhibition of the unlawful worship.

Verse 10. The aforesaid abominations consisted of pictures or drawings on the walls of the apartment. These portrayals were general and included living creatures which were worshiped, as well as the other idols of *the house of Israel*.

Verse 11. *Ancients* is from the same original word as "elders" in verse 1, and the reader is requested to see the comments at that place. There were 70 of these men including Jaazaniah, who was a prominent man, and these were engaged in burning incense to their idols.

Verse 12. Despite the foolish example of Adam and Eve (Genesis 3:8), and ignoring the clear declarations of David in Psalms 139:7-12, these corrupt elders thought they could find a material hiding place for their idolatrous practices. The Lord had indeed forsaken the place as far as any endorsement was concerned, but that did not mean such a place would escape the all-seeing eye of Him.

Verse 13. God wished Ezekiel to have a complete vision of the corrupt state of the people of Judah. In a few more years the temple was to be demolished by the Babylonians, and the prophet should be furnished with a detailed view of conditions that provoked the Lord to deliver his people up to such a fate.

Verse 14. This verse presents another form of idolatry to which reference was made in the comments on verse 5, that of invisible gods. Ezekiel was taken to another spot where he saw *women weeping for Tammuz.* Strong's definition of the last word is, "Of uncertain derivation; Tammuz, a Phoenician deity." A marginal comment is some Bibles says, "In a lewd and idolatrous manner, lamenting the death of Tammuz or Adonis, supposed to be Baalpeor." This comment is supported by various works of reference that I have consulted among which is Smith's Bible Dictionary, from which I shall make the following quotation: "Jerome identifies Tammuz with Adonis, of Grecian mythology, who was fabled to have lost his life while hunting, by a wound from the tusk of a wild boar. He was greatly beloved by the goddess Venus, who was inconsolable at his loss. . . A festival in honor of Adonis was celebrated at Byblus in Phoenicia and in most of the Grecian cities, and even by the Jews when they degenerated into idolatry. It took place in July, and was accompanied by obscene rites." Much of the information on this point is drawn from mythology but it is evident that the verse deals with the case of idolatry designated at the beginning of this paragraph.

Verse 15. The prophet is informed that he is yet to see another display of idolatry being practiced by the people of Judea.

Verse 16. This verse includes an item on sun worship, which is one of the three forms of idolatry mentioned in the comments on verse 5. The sun is an object of creation and is in the same class as the planets and other things of nature that were worshiped as gods first by the heathen, then by the Jews. *Backs toward the temple* was an insult to the Lord, for it was an attitude in which these men turned from the true God and gave their homage toward the east where they would see the sun.

Verse 17. Having given Ezekiel a full and detailed vision of the evil conditions in Judah, the Lord "puts it up to him" to form a conclusion on the subject. However, God states his own conclusion and affirms (in question form) that what Judah is doing is no *light thing*—it is not something to be regarded lightly. Certain trees were considered sacred by idolaters, and these corrupt men of Judah were showing their insolent contempt for the true God by exhibiting a desire to smell of such trees in connection with their worship of the sun.

Verse 18. This verse adds nothing new to the threats that God had previously made against his people. It is a summing up of the conclusions already formed and uttered with the emphasis that is implied in such a frequent repetition.

EZEKIEL 9

Verse 1. The reader should be cautioned against confusion over what is going on in these chapters. Beginning with chapter 8 and continuing through 11, Ezekiel was seeing things performed in a vision, as if he had been taken to Jerusalem where the events were supposed to be happening. In reality, the prophet has been in the land of Chaldea or Babylon all the time. (See chapter 11: 24.) So bear in mind as we are considering the various performances along in these passages that they are what Ezekiel was seeing in the vision. It is true, however, that many of the events and conditions that were shown the prophet in a vision in the land of Babylon, were actually existing in the land of Judea. With these explanatory remarks for the clarification of the matter, I shall proceed to comment on the verses. *Have charge over the city* means those whose duty it was to execute any decrees that may have been made concerning it. These men were ordered to come forward, armed for the task placed upon them.

Verse 2. Upon the order mentioned in the preceding verse, six armed men came forward. All of this indicated that they would be used to execute the decrees of God. Another man was in the company of these six and he was *clothed with linen* which indicated that he represented the priestly or ritualistic class of men. The brazen altar was used for the offering of bloody sacrifices, therefore it was appropriate that this group of seven men should take their position by the altar. The priests would make an account of the creatures to be considered with reference to the altar service, hence the inkhorn hanging at his side for convenient use.

Verse 3. *Glory of God . . . from the cherub* refers to the glory that was bestowed upon the ark in the beginning of the Jewish Dispensation. (See Exodus 25: 22; 2 Samuel 6: 2.) This glory moved to a position of communication with the man clothed with linen (representing the priesthood). Such a move indicated that the Lord was about to inspire the man with the inkhorn so that he could do some writing or marking.

Verse 4. Before any general destruction or calamity is brought upon mankind by the Lord he always makes provision to spare those who are worthy. We may recall the cases of Noah and the flood, Lot in Sodom, the Israelites in Egypt, and the plan of salvation as an escape from the perdition in the next world. In keeping with that principle, the Lord was making provisions to spare certain ones from a general slaughter which these six men would soon be told to execute. The ones to be spared were described as those *that sigh and cry for all the abominations* that were being done in Jerusalem. These men were not responsible for the corruptions that had crept into the religious and public life of the city, hence they were to be spared from the severe punishment about to be inflicted upon the majority. The reader should consult the long note offered in connection with 2 Kings 22:17. This exception was to be indicated by being marked upon their foreheads by the man with the inkhorn.

Verse 5. *The others* are the six men mentioned in verse 2. They were to follow the man with the inkhorn who was to be marking the ones exempted from the slaughter. The executioners were charged to smite the others without pity.

Verse 6. No age or sex was to be spared in the slaying by these six men. The only exception they were allowed to make was those who had the mark upon them. *Begin at my sanctuary.* This was because the greatest blame was laid upon the leaders and officials of the Lord's service. They were to be held most guilty because of their position. The thought is similar to that in 1 Peter 4:17, 18.

Verse 7. The house of the Lord had been defiled doctrinally by the abominable idolatry of these evil men, now it will be fitting to defile it physically by filling it with their dead bodies. So the men were again told to go forth and slay in the city.

Verse 8. As the men were performing their duty of slaying the inhabitants of the city, the prophet was left alone and he became prostrated by the scenes. Falling upon the ground he prayed earnestly and expressed anxiety over the terrible situation.

Verse 9. The Lord explained his great fury for the information of the prophet. Just at that time Israel (the 10 tribes) was in exile and had been for more than a century, yet her sins came up for remembrance now in connection with those of Judah, some of whose men were still in Jerusalem.

Verse 10. The people of Israel and Judah had shed blood in their evil practices of idolatry, but God was determined to shed their blood in the righteousness of His indignation over the false worship that was going on.

Verse 11. The men sent forth to execute the decree of God did their duty, and the man with the inkhorn came back with his report of the same.

EZEKIEL 10

Verse 1. The objects named in this verse are used figuratively and refer to the glory that is to be attributed to the Lord.

Verse 2. *He* is a pronoun standing for the Personage described in verse 1; the man to whom he spoke was the one with the inkhorn. We have previously learned (chapter 9:2) that this man repersented the priestly services of the house of God. The regular order of those services had been discontinued since the invasion of Judah by the Babylonians, but there were other things needed to be done and this man would be the appropriate one to do them. The *wheels* and *cherub* will be explained later in this chapter. *Coals of fire* is figurative and refers to the fiery wrath of God, because the literal fire in the Mosaic service was on the brazen altar and not in the *inner court* (verse 3). *Scatter them over the city* indicated that God's wrath was to be poured out over the place in general.

Verse 3. There is a popular saying, "Wherever there is smoke there is fire." The saying may well be reversed and, with a slight change in the wording, make it say, "Wherever there is fire there may be a cloud (of smoke)." Verse 2 reveals the fire of God's wrath and this verse speaks of the cloud that arose from that fire. It was so extensive that it *filled the inner court.*

Verse 4. The cloud of this verse was different from the preceding one. This was described as springing from the cherub (not the fire) and was *the glory of the Lord.* This cloud, also, filled the area of the court.

Verse 5. *Voice of the Almighty God* indicates that He had some connec-

Verse 6. Upon being commanded to get the fire, the man with the inkhorn entered the place containing the wheels.

Verse 7. The cherub participated in the activities by placing the fire in the hands of the man clothed with linen and who had the inkhorn. That indicated that the work of the man was approved by the institutions represented by the cherubs and wheels.

Verse 8. The appearance of a *man's hand* indicated the institutions in the imagery possessed the skill of human beings.

Verse 9. These wheels do not introduce any new subject matter as we shall learn in course of this chapter. *Color of a beryl stone* is merely a comparison to the brilliancy and many-sided faces for reflection of that stone.

Verse 10. These four wheels refer to the "four world empires" and the creatures of chapter 1: 5, and the wheel in the midst of a wheel is explained in verse 16 of that chapter. The following verses of this chapter will also deal with those empires, and many of the same symbols will be used that were used in the former chapter. There may be some variation in a part of them, but that is because more than one trait can be said of different creatures and things, and a writer may select one, now another, for his comparison, and all of them would be true. Let the reader please see the comments on verse 10 of the first chapter.

Verse 11. This apparently impossible movement refers to the universal spread of the world empires. A thing that would be physically impossible may be supposed in a symbol, if it will truly represent a possibility in some spiritual or other intelligent institution. If an object had a head on each of its four sides, then the body of that object could follow the head in any of the directions without turning about.

Verse 12. Naming the several parts of these creatures or institutions was for the purpose of emphasizing the completeness of the quality soon to be mentioned. *Full of eyes round about* indicates that quality to have been intelligence.

Verse 13. The key in this verse is in the words *O man*, and the meaning is that the wheels were called upon to give attention.

Verse 14. The description of each of the four creatures in this verse differs in only one item from the corresponding picture in chapter 1: 10. That has an ox while this has the cherub, but there is no difficulty involved, for both traits were possessed by these institutions being represented. Having the face of a *cherub* would indicate they were invested with something heavenly (1: 24; Daniel 4: 17), *man* indicates intelligence and also that the institutions included humanity, *lion* means boldness and *eagle* indicates exaltation and fleetness.

Verse 15. This verse settles the identity of the creature with that described in chapter 1, and represents the "four world empires" named in the first chapter.

Verse 16. The performances of the *cherubims* and *wheels* in this chapter are in the same line as those of the living creatures and wheels in chapter one. The figure is a representation of the four world empires. The co-operation between these objects is for the purpose of emphasis.

Verse 17. *They* and *these* are pronouns standing for the cherubims and wheels. The original word for *spirit* means life, and the clause means the cherubims and wheels had the same life as the living creatures that the prophet saw by the river Chebar.

Verse 18. *Departed* is not used in the sense of desertion, but the glory fixed itself upon the creatures.

Verse 19. The effect of the *glory* upon the cherubims is stated here. It caused them to *mount from the earth* or be exalted. Such a thought corresponds with the idea that God was interested in the four world empires. (See Daniel 4: 17.) *Every one stood* indicates an attitude of reverence for the demonstration.

Verse 20. This is virtually the same statement as verse 15.

Verse 21. This verse also is a repetition of previous statements, and the central thought in the *four faces* is the world-wide extent of the empires. *Hands of a man* indicates that the creatures were composed of human beings.

Verse 22. The concluding verse is a summing up of the imagery that has been considered throughout the first and present chapters of the book.

EZEKIEL 11

Verse 1. The vision was continued and Ezekiel saw the same men who were mentioned in chapter 8: 16, with one other named specifically. They were all leading men of Judah who were engaged in the worship of the sun which was one form of idolatry.

Verse 2. The men not only practiced that which was wrong, but planned and advised others in it and thus were guilty of conspiracy.

Verse 3. The main idea these evil men advocated was one of opposition to the warnings of the Lord. They were making light of the predictions that Jerusalem was to be overthrown, and expressed themselves by the figurative language of the last clause of the verse. It means as if they had said, "There is nothing in the threatening the prophet has given us. This city is all the caldron we will need to fear."

Verse 4. Ezekiel was told to prophesy against these evil men and their claims.

Verse 5. *Spirit . . . fell upon me* means the prophet was inspired to make his prediction against the men. The passage was introduced with the assertion that the Lord knew what was in their minds.

Verse 6. These evil men had been guilty of murder and caused men's dead bodies to be laid in the streets. But they had caused these deaths in their wicked contention against the others who wished to pay respect to the word of the Lord.

Verse 7. A caldron is a large kettle or boiler that is used for cooking the flesh of animals. The language was used figuratively and compared the city to the caldron and the citizens to the flesh to be boiled therein. The Lord admitted that these men had really made such use of the city and its unfortunate citizens, but denied that such a fact was the fulfillment of the divine predictions. It was warned that He would bring the citizens out of this "caldron" and thus disprove the rebellious declarations that Jerusalem was the only one they would need to fear.

Verse 8. Their fear of the sword of the enemy was used as an excuse for trying to hide behind the walls of Jerusalem. God warned them that the city would not save them from the sword for they were to be exposed to it through the divine decree.

Verse 9. The strongest walls that man can build would be no surety against the judgments of God. *Hands of strangers* means those outside of their own country, and in this case it referred to the Babylonians.

Verse 10. The judgments to be brought upon Israel would be started within their own *border*, which means they would be made to suffer even before leaving their land.

Verse 11. Jerusalem was only a city in the *border* or territory extending beyond the city. The experiences which these evil men said would be confined within the city were destined to include many outside of the city. In fact, the whole territory of Judah was to suffer. In that sense the Lord affirmed, *this city shall not be your caldron*. (See the comments on verse 3.)

Verse 12. Over and over the motive, *shall know that I am the Lord*, was stated to the people of Judah. That was especially fitting among a people who had been led off into the worship of strange and false gods.

Verse 13. A partial demonstration of the predictions Ezekiel had been hearing and which he delivered, was made by the sudden death of one of the leading men. The human side of the prophet showed itself by his complaint to the Lord of what looked to him like a threat of complete destruction of Israel.

Verse 14. This action or remark of the prophet brought another message from God.

Verse 15. The justice of what God was doing against the imhabitants of Jerusalem was indicated in this message to Ezekiel. They had assumed sole connection with the Lord and had virtually disfellowshiped all the other people of the country. For this reason they deserved the special judgments.

Verse 16. *Them* is a pronoun that stands for the people in general who had been imposd upon by the leaders in Jerusalem. At the very time Ezekiel was seeing this vision, he and the bulk of the nation were already in the land of Babylon, and that by the decree of the Lord. But He was not going to forsake them entirely while in the heathen land. *Sanctuary* means a place or means of security. Among those who had to go into captivity were many who were personally righteous and who were assured of the care of the Lord. It is appropriate the reader again see the note at 2 Kings 22: 17.

Verse 17. From this verse through 20 the subject is the return from captivity, with special mention of certain results to be accomplished by the exile. The same people for whom the Lord promised to be a "sanctuary" in the preceding verse were to be brought back to their own country. The great Babylonian Empire was composed of various countries of the civilized world, and the captives were scattered more of less over those sections. That is the reason for the prediction that the Lord would assemble them *out of the countries.*

Verse 18. *Take away all the detestable things* is a prediction of the complete cure from idolatry. For the historical fulfillment of this prediction see the quotation in connection with Isaiah 1: 25, volume three of this Commentary.

Verse 19. A complete change of heart is the meaning of this verse. We know that the human heart as to the body is literally flesh, therefore we must understand this language to be figurative. It means their heart (mind) had become hardened in sin and the captivity would humble them and make them become yielding to the law of God.

Verse 20. The difference between a *statute* and an *ordinance* as defined in the lexicon is so slight that we may well consider them in the same sense. A statute may be regarded as the more fixed and formal of the two, but when they come from God they both mean the rule of life which He expects his servants to follow. *Shall be my people.* These Israelites were always the Lord's as far as being a race or nationality according to blood, but now they are to become his people again in the sense of forming a nation or government, something they had not been for 70 years.

Verse 21. There were some of the Jews who would not give up their love of sin and they were destined to be given over to the ravages of the exile. That is why the period of the captivity was to reduce the nation to a remnant. (See Ezra 2: 64.)

Verse 22. These *cherubims* and *wheels* are the same that were mentioned in chapter 10: 14, 15, and they represent the four world empires. *The glory of the God of Israel was over them* because He is interested in the procedure of the governments of the world.

Verse 23. The story included in the vision was about finished, so the spirit of the Lord's glory departed and occupied an exalted place near the city.

Verse 24. Notice the passage says Ezekiel was brought *in a vision* into Chaldea (or Babylon). In reality or bodily he had been there all the time. This verse means that the vision was ended and Ezekiel was to act literally in communicating his message to the people or captives among whom he was then living.

Verse 25. *Them of the captivity* means the Jews who were literally in captivity along with the prophet who had been taken there at the 2nd stage of the captivity.

EZEKIEL 12

Verse 1. Instead of using a vision God spoke directly to the prophet.

Verse 2. Ezekiel and most of the Jews were in Babylon at the time he was doing his work as a prophet. At the same time there were still some left in Jerusalem, for that city had not yet been destroyed. That event was about due and would be the 3rd stage of the captivity. But in spite of the two events that had taken place, referred to as the 1st and 2nd captivities, as well as other evidences of God's truth, many of the Jews doubted that their capital would really be destroyed. Some of them in Babylon even professed to hope that they would soon return to Jerusalem which they would find unharmed. Eyes and ears which see and hear not, means they refused to use their own senses to perceive the truth.

Verse 3. The prophet was told to do some more "acting" which we have previously seen. (See at 1 Kings 20: 35.) In this case it was to emphasize the prediction that the people still left in Jerusalem would soon be *moved* out and taken to another place. *Stuff* means the outfit that one would use or need when going from one place to another. That is, the articles one would especially need were he going to spend some time in a strange locality. With these articles Ezekiel was to go through the motions of moving in the sight of the rebellious *house* or people.

Verse 4. *Day* and *even* are both named in a significant manner. He was to use the day in making the preparation, and when evening came he was to go out with the movements of one who had been banished from his native land.

Verse 5. The town where Ezekiel and other captives were living would be enclosed with a wall. He was to make an opening through that wall large enough for a man to pass through, then let the people see him leave by way of the opening.

Verse 6. Covering his face while going through this performance would indicate that the prophet was not seeing his own way in it, but was being directed by an unseen force. This would serve as a *sign* to the Israelites; the word is from MOPHETH which Strong defines, "A token or omen." By such an unusual performance of the prophet it was hoped to impress the people that something important was about to take place.

Verse 7. This verse merely records the carrying out of the orders which the prophet had received from the Lord.

Verse 8. The scenes described in the preceding verses produced some interest among the people as the night was passing, and in the morning the Lord spoke again.

Verse 9. God knew the people had asked the prophet for an explanation of his actions, and He was ready to furnish the answer.

Verse 10. *Burden* is a figure of speech and means an important prophecy or other message was about to be delivered. The *prince in Jerusalem* was Zedekiah, who was left on his throne there by the king of Babylon, but who was reigning only as a subject-king under Nebuchadnezzar. There were also some of the inhabitants of the city left in it and they were included in *the house of Israel that are among them*.

Verse 11. This verse connects the acting of the prophet with the event that was to be its fulfillment. Ezekiel was to tell his people that it was performed in their sight as a *sign*. (See the explanation of this word at verse 6.) *Them* and *they* are pronouns that stand for the persons mentioned in the close of the preceding verse. The prediction was that they were to go into captivity, meaning the "3rd captivity."

Verse 12. The apparent secrecy that Ezekiel maintained would prove to have foreshadowed some of the actions of Zedekiah. He had been warned to be submissive to the king of Babylon since the whole transaction of the captivity was of the Lord, but he thought he could elude the enemy and escape. *Dig through the wall* is what Ezekiel actually did as a sign, but it is used figuratively of Zedekiah. However, he did attempt to escape by means of the wall, and did it *in the twilight* or night. The fulfillment of this is recorded in 2 Kings 25: 4 and Jeremiah 39: 4.

Verse 13. This *net* referred to the forces of Babylon which the Lord was using in the overthrow of Jerusalem and its acting king. The apparent difficulty in the closing clause of this verse will be made clear by 2 Kings 25: 6, 7; Jeremiah 32: 4.

Verse 14. Some of the men of war in Jerusalem thought to elude capture by following Zedekiah in his flight. This verse predicts their failure, and the historical account of it is in 2 Kings 25: 4, 5.

Verse 15. Again we see the chief motive that was behind these great demonstrations against the unfaithful people of Israel from time to time was to make them *know that I am the Lord*.

Verse 16. These *few* were the "remnant" referred to frequently and the fulfillment is at Ezra 2: 64. See the note at Jeremiah 14: 12 regarding the *sword, famine* and *pestilence*, regarded as one form of judgment upon the evil nation.

Verse 17. *Moreover* means the same as furthermore. The Lord had something more to say to the prophet, and it was to be in connection with his next work.

Verse 18. This verse directed Ezekiel to do some more "acting." He was not in any personal want but was to deal with the conditions of famine that were to come upon the people still left in Jerusalem. The *carefulness* means he was to use the provisions sparingly as if they were being rationed out to him.

Verse 19. *People of the land* meant the Jews then in Babylon with the prophet, and *inhabitants of Jerusalem* were those still in the city but who were doomed to be soon removed. Ere that event took place they were to undergo the pangs of famine.

Verse 20. Some cities besides Jerusalem were still lingering on the verge of total destruction, and they, too, were soon to feel the final blows from Babylon.

Verses 21, 22. The Jews persisted in denying the warnings that had been so often uttered to them and which had been backed up by so much evidence of being from God. Just at the moment, most of the nation was in the land of Babylon, having been victims of the first or second stage of the captivity. And yet, when the prophet declared that all Jerusalem and its remaining inhabitants were to be overthrown, they either denied the truth of it altogether, or else were saying that it was not to be for a long time. If a threatened judgment upon man does not come as soon as he expects, then the seeming delay is interpreted to mean that the prediction is false. Solomon had such a condition in mind when he wrote Ecclesiastes 8: 11, and the same thought is set forth in 2 Peter 3: 4 regarding the end of the world.

Verse 23. *Proverb* is used in the sense of something that is repeated frequently as if it were taken for granted to be a truth. But the Lord declared that it would be caused to cease, for the *days are at hand* when the threatened event will occur. All of Ezekiel's writings thus far were done between the 2nd and 3rd stages of the captivities, and that period altogether was only eleven years. But most of that had passed at the time we are now studying, hence the final downfall of the capital city was truly *at hand.*

Verse 24. *Vain vision* and *flattering divination* refers to the false predictions and unauthorized assurances that the evil leaders had been giving to the people. The actual fall of the city would certainly put an end to that.

Verse 25. *In your days* denoted that the very people to whom these threats had been made would live to see their fulfillment and would personally suffer in them.

Verse 26. The frequent repetition of such language as this verse will keep us mindful that the prophet was being inspired by the Lord in all his utterances.

Verse 27. The attention of the prophet was called to the clamors of the people, relative to the far-off date of the affliction that has been made against them.

Verse 28. Ezekiel was assured that the fulfillment was not far off, and the reader may see the account of its fulfillment in 2 Kings 25: 1, 2.

EZEKIEL 13

Verse 1, 2. Ezekiel was himself a prophet in Israel, but he was to prophesy against the evil ones who were deceiving the people into a false feeling of security. *Out of their own hearts* means that these false prophets were not inspired of the Lord but were speaking their personal thoughts. They were to be called upon to cease issuing this unauthorized manner of statements and to hear the word of God.

Verse 3. *Having seen nothing* means they had not received any vision from the Lord, but were devising their own foolish predictions.

Verse 4. The fox is a destructive creature (See Song of Solomon, 2: 15) instead of a helpful one, and these false prophets were compared to them.

Verse 5. These prophets should have been concerned about the conflict threatening their city, even as a true husbandman would be, concerning the gaps he discovered in the hedge surrounding his vineyard. Instead, they not only were indifferent about the city's danger, but were even denying that there were any "gaps" to be closed.

Verse 6. The false prophets were not given any message from the Lord, but professed to have seen visions of the lot awaiting their city. *Seen vanity* means the things they professed were useless and *lying divination* denotes a deceptive form of speech. The sin of these false prophets was made worse by their claiming to have been inspired by the Lord. Such a claim would make Him contradict himself, for he had led Ezekiel to prophesy the near downfall of Jerusalem, and now these men claimed to have been inspired to say it was not coming soon if at all.

Verse 7. The central thought in this verse is to call attention to the inconsistency of the false prophets. That error is described by the comments in connection with the prophet's statements in the preceding verse.

Verse 8. *Seen lies* does not mean they had seen the lies of others, for that kind of action would have been to their credit. The passage denotes that the false prophets were lying as to what they professed to have seen.

Verse 9. *Divine lies.* The first word is from QACAM which Strong defines,

"A primitive root; properly to distribute, i.e. determine by lot or magical scroll; by implication to divine." It refers to some form of trickery by which these false prophets confused the people and caused them to believe the lies. *Not be in the assembly* denotes that such men would not be recognized in any of the affairs of the nation. And when the period of the captivity is over and the "remnant" comes back, these deceivers will not be among them, for they will have perished in the exile.

Verse 10. This verse is figurative and refers to the general attitude of confidence that was shown by the people in Jerusalem. That condition of "peace" was the *wall* and the *mortar* was the lies of the preceding verse. *Untempered* is from TAPHEL which Strong defines, "To smear; plaster (as gummy) or slime; (figurative) frivolity." A smeary or pasty material would not make a strong protection for a wall, hence it was a fitting comparison for the useless lies by which the false prophets had built up the "wall" of confidence in the minds of the people.

Verse 11. The purpose of daubing a wall was to form a coating to protect it from the effects of the weather. In keeping with the figurative description adopted in the preceding verse, the Lord declared that the weak mortar would be penetrated by the storm of *overflowing shower* and *hailstones* and *wind*. These figures had reference to the military storming of Jerusalem by the Babylonian army (2 Kings 25: 1-4).

Verse 12. A flimsy covering over a wall might look as well as the best, but when the wall collapses the deceptive nature of the plaster will be exposed.

Verse 13. This is a repetition of the thoughts in verse 11.

Verse 14. *Foundation* is defined in the lexicon as being figurative or literal, and its use here is the former. The chief motive for the great demonstration is again repeated; it is that all may be convinced *that I am the Lord*.

Verse 15. The verses are still on the subject of the downfall of Jerusalem that was due to occur soon, but it is also continued in figurative language; the untempered mortar meaning the false predictions, and *they that daubed it* the lying prophets.

Verse 16. This verse is the Lord's own interpretation of the figurative terms that were used in the preceding ones. A "calamity howler" is an undesirable person, yet he may not do as much harm as one who *sees visions of peace* when in reality a serious disaster is threatened. Such a character will lull the people into a false sense of security and hence they will not make the preparation necessary to meet it.

Verse 17. *Set thy face against* denotes that Ezekiel was to manifest his personal disapproval of the way the people were taking up with the delusions being preached.

Verse 18. All unusual or figurative language must be interpreted in the light of known facts. *Armholes* is rendered "elbows" in the margin and the lexicon agrees with it, for the original means a joint of the arm or hand. (See the comments at Jeremiah 38: 12.) *Kerchiefs* is rendered "veil" in the lexicon and refers to some kind of covering for the head that would enclose the wearer in a state of mystery. The thought of the verse is on the false peace that had been given the citizens of Jerusalem by the lying prophets. A pillow attached to the elbow would suggest a position of rest and ease while lying around, and that was a symbol of the state of contentment that was created in the minds of the victims. The women co-operated with the false prophets by making the pillows.

Verse 19. This whole verse is in the form of a question, but it is really an accusation of the Lord against the false prophets and other leaders. They were taking advantage of the trusting people for the sake of their own personal gain.

Verse 20. See the comments at verse 18 on the meaning of *pillows*. *Fly* is defined in the lexicon as denoting the rising of a bird, having been stirred up by some apparent cause of interest. But it was a case where the person making the appearance did so in order to get the fowl entangled in a net spread unseen to it. *I will tear them* means that the Lord was going to expose the deception that the false prophets had imposed upon the people and make its true nature manifest.

Verse 21. The *kerchiefs* or mystic veils were to be torn off, which also means the Lord would penetrate the shroud of deception that had been spread over the dupes.

Verse 22. In all situations there will be some righteous persons who try to resist the influence of false teachers. Such persons will anger the would-be deceiver and it will cause him to threaten some severe calamity to come upon them and it is in this way *make their heart sad*. But the wicked ones who deserve to be condemned will be encouraged by the false prophets to look for *peace*, and this will influence them to feel that nothing is wrong with their conduct and the result will be that they will not reform. (See the note at 2 Kings 22: 17, volume 2 of this Commentary.)

Verse 23. *Shall see no more vanity* means that an end was to be made of their vain (empty or false) predictions. *Divine* is a verb and the phrase means they would not be permitted to deliver any more *divinations* or false visions.

EZEKIEL 14

Verse 1. This action was done before and is explained at chapter 8: 1.

Verse 2. As these elders were sitting before Ezekiel, the Lord delivered another message which the prophet was to give over to the hearers. Whether any or all of them were guilty of the things to be charged or not, the information was timely.

Verse 3. These elders had come to the prophet on the pretence of wanting some information from God. The heart is the intelligent part of a man and from which the motives of his actions spring. (See Matthew 15: 19.) These men sitting before Ezekiel could not always have an idol present before them, but their heart was devoted to them and thus they had set *up their idols in their heart*. *Should I be enquired of by them* means that such men had no right to seek any communication from God.

Verse 4. God would not recognize such men in the usual manner, that is, through the established service of a prophet, with the expectation of obtaining any favor at his hands. Instead, He proposed to take charge of the case and handle the pretenders directly as they deserved as regarded such treatment that was coming to them.

Verse 5. Since these men had set up their idols in their heart, that would be the place for God to make his attack. Such is the meaning of *take the house of Israel in their own heart* which He declared would be done.

Verse 6. This verse should be considered in connection with verse 4. It all means that God would answer these pretended enquirers through the prophet to some extent, but the answer would not be as a recognition of the rights of the evil men, for they were not entitled to such notice. But instead of this, the prophet was told to admonish them to repent and give up their love of idols.

Verse 7. This verse explains in what sense the Lord would answer *by himself* as he announced in a preceding verse; it was to be by some direct judgment upon the wicked people of Israel. This was to be a practical rebuke to them because they thought they could by-pass Him and get their information through the prophet.

Verse 8. *Make him a sign* denotes that God would bring some humiliating punishment upon the man who had tried to ignore Him. This punishment would make him an example ("sign") to others and cause him to be the object of their sneers.

Verse 9. *I the Lord have deceived that prophet* applies to a case where a man has so persisted in his false teaching that God would suffer him to believe his own falsehood. The result of such a course would be his own undoing. Paul reveals a similar attitude of God toward the followers of the "man of sin" in 2 Thessalonians 2: 11.

Verses 10, 11. The most important thought in this verse is the joint responsibility of the false prophet and those who go to him for information. The passage declares that the punishment of the one will be *even as* that of him who *seeketh unto him*.

Verses 12, 13. This passage again gives an explanation of the Lord's statement to the prophet that he would answer the people *by himself*. He determined to punish the land by a shortage of the needs of life, this judgment to be considered to be against the country as a whole.

Verse 14. When general calamities are brought providentially on communities, the Lord provides special care for those who are personally innocent. But even they cannot extend the favor done because of their own virtues to those who are unrighteous; such is the teaching of this verse. It is another phase of the principle that responsibility is strictly individual as far as it pertains to moral conduct.

Verse 15. *Noisome* is from a Hebrew

word that means "evil or bad," and here it is applied to beasts that are fierce and destructive. God sometimes used such means to punish persons who were guilty of wrong. (See 1 Kings 13: 24; 2 Kings 2: 24.)

Verse 16. This verse is identical in thought with verse 14.

Verse 17. The Lord brought the sword upon the land by having a foreign army to make a hostile attack. This has been done on numerous occasions in the history of Israel, such as the Assyrians in 2 Kings 17 and the Babylonians in chapters 24 and 25 of the same book.

Verse 18. The same principle of individuality is taught here as in verse 14.

Verse 19. A prominent instance of using a pestilence as a punishment is recorded in 2 Samuel 24: 15.

Verse 20. Once more the thought in verse 14 is repeated here.

Verse 21. Famine, pestilence and the sword were frequently threatened as a punishment upon Israel. In this verse another instrument is named, the *noisome* (bad) beasts. This would be especially applicable where the land in general was to be penalized, since wild beasts would not have much access to the citizens of the city.

Verse 22. The *remnant* consisted of the number left after the ravages of the captivity had done their work, and the record of it is in Ezra 2: 64.

Verse 23. When all of the sad experiences have been suffered by the people of Israel, they will be able to look back over the history of their national conduct. When they do so and recall also the many warnings they were given but which were not heeded, they will realize that God did not punish them *without cause*.

EZEKIEL 15

Verses 1, 2. *Tree* is from an original that the lexicon defines as "wood" in general, hence the phrase means "the wood of the vine." The question form of the statement means to imply that a vine is inferior to the trees of the forest.

Verse 3. A vine at its best is not fit for any substantial use such as a piece of furniture for supporting the vessels of household living. In this sense it is less important than the regular trees, because they would furnish material that could be made into strong utility racks.

Verse 4. If the vine needs to be used at all, about the only thing that can be done with it is to use it as fuel. *Both ends* and *midst* is said to indicate how completely the vine would be affected were it cast into the fire.

Verse 5. If the vine in its original condition is not useful for any good purpose, it certainly would not be after being put through the fire.

Verse 6. The preceding illustration is used to compare the city of Jerusalem with her inhabitants; they are the vine and the heathen nations are trees of the forest.

Verse 7. The nations are compared to the forest trees when contrasted with Jerusalem. In the next section of the illustration, however, they will be used as the fire into which the vine (Jerusalem with her inhabitants) will be cast. *One fire and another fire* refers to the fire of the siege and also that which will overtake them *who go out*. (See 2 Kings 25: 3-7.)

Verse 8. The land was to be made desolate by having its populations removed away into the Babylonion captivity.

EZEKIEL 16

Verse 1. This is a very unusual and interesting chapter, in which the Lord supposed a situation pertaining to human relations to illustrate His relations with Judah, the 2-tribe kingdom. It is true that some of the items are out of the ordinary as to the general events in the field of romance, but we have previously seen that even figures of speech may be so managed as to cover the actual facts in the subject being illustrated. But the central thought that runs through the long parable is true to conditions and actions that either do or could exist in actual life. Let us keep in mind that the marriage relation with its various privileges and obligations is compared in the Bible to the union of mankind with God. By the same token, the corruptions of the marriage relation in temporal affairs are used to compare the abominations of idolatry that provoke the jealousy of God.

Verse 2. This verse is a solemn charge to Ezekiel; he was to cause Jerusalem to realize the greatness of her abominations and unfaithfulness.

Verse 3. Nations, like individuals, may rise from very humble circumstances to a position of dignity and favor. If that rise is caused solely by the unselfish favor of another nation or person, such advancement will be no just cause for the favored one to become proud or have a feeling of importance. Instead, such nation should show its appreciation by the most faithful devotion. This verse shows the insignificant and obscure origin of Jerusalem (or Judah). She was born in Canaan which was a country of much unworthiness before the Lord took it over and dignified it by His oversight. *Amorites* and *Hittites* were two of the inferior heathen peoples who inhabited the land of Canaan at the time God's people appeared. The terms *father* and *mother* are used figuratively to conform to the parable of family relations that has been adopted on the present occasion. We are supposed to think of a babe who is born of a very ordinary father and mother, in a land out of which no great personage would be expected to come. (For a like comparison see John 1: 46.)

Verse 4. This verse represents a possible though very unusual circumstance. It is the case where a babe arrives who was not wanted and of whom its parents are ashamed even though they have nothing of which to be so proud. They have such a feeling of contempt for the helpless creature that they do not give it the usual treatment of cleansing and surgical care usually accorded every newborn infant. They do not even furnish it with the swaddling band which was commonly used at such times, but which was a very meager article of clothing at best.

Verse 5. Not only did the parents of this unfortunate creature fail to administer to its needs, but none of the neighbors offered to lend a helping hand. Nor was that all; the infant was cast uncleansed and unclothed into the open field where it might have been the prey of wild beasts.

Verse 6. The man who was to represent God in this great parable was one whose affairs caused him to make various journeys through the country; on one of his trips he passed by the infant described in the preceding verses. He saw the miserable condition of the neglected creature and had compassion on it. *I said . . . live.* A story like this could not include all the details connected with the case. We are not told how the traveler could make his kindness effective but in some way he arranged that this baby girl could live in spite of the filthy and neglected condition. Having made the necessary preparation for the survival and growth of the babe, the traveler went on his way.

Verse 7. Through the arrangements referred to in the preceding verse, the girl baby experienced the things described in this which took place in the course of some years; such is the significance of *I have caused thee* that begins this verse. The developments indicated took place between the first and second journeys of the traveler through the community. *Multiply* is used because the parable really refers to the nation of Judah, although the imagery is that of a babe and her development into the adolescent age. *Excellent ornaments* means the attractiveness of a girl growing toward womanhood. Some of those ornaments are specified; female breasts, also long hair, which is one of the God-given ornaments of women (1 Corinthians 11: 15).

Verse 8. The baby girl has passed through childhood and adolescence and has reached *the time of love*, which means she has matured and become of marriageable age. Her benefactor then falls in love with her and offers to receive her as his wife. In ancient times there were no formal marriage ceremonies directly connected with the union of a male and female. Their fleshly relations made them one and entitled them to live together as husband and wife. By that token, the spreading of one's skirt over another signified the intimacy that was to start the couple on their journey in life as a united pair. Hence we have that action regarding the skirt mentioned in this verse and the phrase *thou becamest mine* is so used. (See Ruth 3: 9.)

Verse 9. In spite of the advancement that nature had made for this neglected girl, she had not become completely rid of the undesirable conditions that had been imposed upon her at the time of and after her birth. But after the man became so intimately interested in her, he gave her further attention to prepare her for the life with him as his life's companion in the marriage relation.

Verse 10. It would be proper for a man to take personal interest in and take part in the selection of clothing of his wife; he would wish her to have the most delicate robes even of such materials as silk and linen.

Verse 11. No ornaments of jewelry could be too good or costly for the woman whom a man loves, who has given herself to him and who has merged her being with his in the most intimate and sacred relation possible to the human body.

Verse 12. The *crown* was not used in the sense of authority, but as a token of the glory that he recognized it meant to him to have the love and association with such a creature. (See 1 Corinthians 11: 7.)

Verse 13. The husband continued his favors upon the woman he loved. The actual subject of the parable was indicated by the closing words, *thou didst prosper into a kingdom*. We know that a wife would not develop into a kingdom, so the idea is plain that God's relation with Judah was the subject of the illustration. But His love and favor toward that nation could not be described so as to overdraw the truth, even by the most extreme devotion that an ardent husband could lavish upon a wife whom he loved with his whole heart.

Verse 14. The terms and descriptions running through the chapter will be those directly applicable to a wife, yet the language will occasionally become so literal that we will know the prophet is considering the kingdom of Judah in her relations with God. This verse deals with such a thought when it says *renown among the heathen*. It is true that the kingdom which had Jerusalem for its capital became renowned in many parts of the earth. (See 1 Kings 4: 21; 10: 1, 6, 7.)

Verse 15. The husband continued his traveling to and fro and hence could not always be in the company of his wife. But if she were true to him she would not take advantage of his absence to receive the attentions of other men; that is where the wife of our story showed her disloyalty. She seemed to forget all of the tokens of love and unselfish service which her husband had shown to her in the first years of her life. It was evident that the favors thus lavished upon her had "spoiled" her and turned her head in the direction of unlawful lovers. She even admitted the men passing by to come in to her and commit fornication. Let the reader bear in mind that the idolatry of Judah is what the prophet was really considering, because that abomination is likened in the Bible to moral unfaithfulness.

Verse 16. This husband had given the fine clothing to his wife for her use as a virtuous woman but she abused the privilege. She changed them in such a way as to attract the attentions of evil men seeking lustful intimacy.

Verse 17. The wife was not satisfied with unlawful intimacy with strange men, but fashioned for herself some images of men that she might admire them in her private life. What added to the greatness of such abomination was the fact that she formed those images out of the precious metals that a loving husband had provided for her personal adornment as a wife.

Verse 18. She covered the unlawful images with the fine garments that her husband had given her to clothe her own body.

Verse 19. Let us keep in mind that the prophet is comparing the unfaithfulness of a wife to her true and loving husband with the faithlessness of Judah toward God. She took the dainty foods which her husband had provided for her use, and set them before these images of men that she had made from the precious metals, in a make-believe performance of religious sacrifice such as was done usually before other idols.

Verse 20. The lawful intimacy of this wife with her husband had produced sons and daughters for him. In her mad devotion to idolatry she sacrificed these sons and daughters. (That the people of the Lord actually did make human sacrifices, see the note at 2 Kings 16: 3 in volume 2 of this Commentary.) This unfaithful wife was asked if she regarded such whoredoms (spiritual fornication or idolatry) as a light matter.

Verse 21. If it were possible for a woman to be the sole producer of children, it would be bad enough for her to offer them in the fire as a sacrifice. But this woman had sacrificed *my children* said her husband.

Verse 22. Ingratitude is condemned very severely in the Bible (Judges 8: 34; 2 Chronicles 24: 22; Isaiah 51: 13; Jeremiah 2: 32; 23: 27; Romans 1: 21; 2 Timothy 2: 3). The corrupt interests this wife had acquired turned her into an ingrate of the worst kind, in view of the lowly and helpless condition from which her husband had raised her.

Verse 23. This wronged husband was deeply affected by the wickedness of his unfaithful wife. In the midst of the figurative parable the prophet injected a few words of direct significance from the Lord, to warn the unfaithful wife (Judah) that great woe was in store for her.

Verse 24. The word *place* occurs in the A.V. here and in a number of other verses but it has no original as a separate word. *Eminent place* is from one original word and literally means a higher spot of some kind. Idolatry is compared to moral evil, especially in the marriage relation, hence the conclusion is that this eminent place meant some provision for the entertainment of men in fornication.

Verse 25. *Head of the way* means the street corners, they being places to attract the eyes of the passers-by on the several thoroughfares. *Opened thy feet* refers to the voluntary position taken by a harlot in yielding her body for the act of adultery. *Beauty to be abhorred*. This wicked woman had made advances to *every one that passed by*, and that made her to be detested even by the men who practiced immorality. Men seeking the unrighteous indulgence will finally tire of a woman who goes too far in her brazen solicitations.

Verse 26. Since idolatry was compared to the sin of fornication, we would expect the comparison to be continued by naming some of the guilty partners. Those partners would be the idolatrous nations with whom Judah committed her spiritual lewdness, and a number of them will be cited; the Egyptians were the ones named here.

Verse 27. Some of the nations with which Judah committed spiritual fornication (idolatry) were suffered to torment her. The Philistines are named here in that connection, and an account of it may be read in 2 Chronicles 28: 18, 19. *Ashamed of thy lewd way* was true, for even the Philistines did not go to the extremes in adopting gods foreign to their own nation (See Jeremiah 2: 11) that Judah did.

Verse 28. *Unsatiable* means to be difficult if not impossible to be satisfied. Judah was not content with her own idols but looked elsewhere for gratification. In this inflamed desire for spiritual adultery she turned to the Assyrians.

Verse 29. This verse is somewhat of a summing up of the extensive corruptions of the nation. *Canaan unto Chaldea* takes in all the territory from the home land to that country where the bulk of the Jews were already in captivity, and to which the remaining ones in Jerusalem and its vicinity were soon to be taken.

Verse 30. *Imperious* means to be domineering or overbearing. An imperious woman of loose morals would be determined to procure the gratification of her lust by any means possible. The extent to which this wicked woman went for that purpose will be seen in some verses that follow.

Verse 31. *Eminent place* and *head of the way* is explained at verses 24, 25 which the reader should see. This unfaithful wife was worse than the ordinary public women. They engage in prostitution for the sake of money, but this wife *scorned hire*.

Verse 32. Ordinary harlotry is bad enough, where a professional woman practices it for the sake of money. But the woman of our parable was a married woman with a husband who was true to her and who loved her very deeply. Not only so, but he was one who possessed the strength of functioning to the fullest degree and who could and was willing to give her complete satisfaction in their intimate relations. Yet that did not satisfy her; instead, she turned her polluted gaze toward strange men.

Verse 33. The depth of this woman was shown in another manner, As a rule, men are willing to hire the professional harlot to contribute to their lust, while this corrupt wife even scorned taking money from the strange men. But she did not stop at such depravity; she actually offered them gifts to induce them to come and be intimate with her. Another thing that added to the blackness of her abominable life (if that were possible), was the fact that she hired those strange men with the gifts that had been furnished her by her faithful husband (verses 17-19).

Verse 34. The Lord summed up the special corruptions of this unfaithful wife in this verse. She was not in the class of regular harlots but was so bad that even other loose women would not associate with her. They practiced their trade for the money they made from it while this woman did it out of a strict desire for lustful gratification. In such a manner of trade the other women would have no part with her.

Verse 35. While most of the language will continue to be in terms adapted to the marriage relation, we should keep in mind that the idolatry of Judah is really the subject. That will account for the direct and literal expressions that will occasionally appear in the verses.

Verse 36. An instance of the thought offered in the preceding verse occurs in this. Here we have *whoredom* and *idols* mentioned in the same connection. though the first pertains ordinarily to the marriage relation and other things involving morals. and the second pertains literally to the corruptions that have been the basis of the parable all along. *Blood of thy children* is a literal reference to human sacrifices that idolaters made in ancient times. On this item see the information offered at 2 Kings 16: 3 in volume 2 of this Commentary.

Verse 37. *Taken pleasure* in the way of spiritual fornication, regardless of her personal feeling toward her lovers as to sentimental affection. *Hast loved.* An unfaithful wife might have an affectionate sentiment for some of her guilty partners as well as enjoy the immoral association with them. *Hast hated.* By the same token as that just indicated, an unfaithful wife might have immoral love (fornication) with a person whom she would hate or abhor sentimentally. It is true that the people of God had been taught to have that attitude toward the Ammonites and Moabites (Deuteronomy 23: 3, 4), while they were instructed not to feel that way toward the Edomites (verse 7). And yet God's people committed spiritual fornication (idolatry) with the gods of these nations. *Discover thy nakedness* is a figure of speech, meaning that these same strange nations would be allowed to see the humiliation of this unfaithful wife (Judah), even though they had been intimate with her frequently in their idolatrous cohabitations.

Verse 38. Judah was to be treated as an unfaithful wife. A jealous husband sometimes exhibits his feelings by physical violence upon the unworthy woman who had once professed to love him only. Likewise the Lord was going to bring the strangers (idolatrous nations) against Judah and some of her citizens would be slain (2 Kings 25: 7).

Verse 39. The first part of this verse was literally fulfilled when the Babylonians took and destroyed Jerusalem. The second part is in the figures that were used in verse 10 of this chapter. The glorious favors that God had bestowed upon Judah and Jerusalem were taken over by the army of Babylon.

Verse 40. This verse is a direct and literal reference to the siege and destruction of Jerusalem that was soon to be made by the Babylonians.

Verse 41. For the fulfillment of this see 2 Kings 25: 8-10. *Sight of many women.* Idolatry was compared to fornication and idolatrous nations to immoral women; hence this phrase refers to the heathen nations that would witness the downfall of Jerusalem.

Verse 42. *Jealousy shall depart* was looking forward to the time when Judah would no longer be a worshiper of idols, since such worship was the cause of the Lord's jealousy according to Exodus 20: 5.

Verse 43. *Days of thy youth* refers to the early years of the nation, described figuratively in verses 6-14, where Judah is represented as a young girl who had been deserted by her parents and then taken into the care of this wronged husband.

Verse 44. It is a common thing to hear such a comparison made as this. Some may do so merely as a coincidence, while others will think that depravity is inherited. Still others will regard the situation as one where the daughter was influenced by the character and practices of the mother.

Verse 45. See verse 3 for explanation of this parentage. If idolatrous nations were compared to immoral women, they would all be related to Judah who was in that class, hence *sisters* means the various heathen people around her.

Verse 46. One word in the definition for *elder* is "great." Samaria was indeed greater than Judah in that she had 10 tribes out of the 12. Also because the 10-tribe kingdom was the first of the two to make idolatry a national affair when she set up the idols at Dan and Bethel. (1 Kings 12: 29). Sodom would be *younger sister* (by contrast) on the same principle that Samaria was elder.

Verse 47. *Not walked after their ways* means that Judah did not stop at becoming as bad as Samaria and Sodom, but went on and became worse.

Verse 48. Sodom was considered less guilty than Judah on the principle of the responsibility due to the difference in opportunity. Jesus taught this identical lesson in Matthew 11: 23, 24.

Verse 49. The corruptions of Sodom were described in order to make the guilt of Judah appear still greater, since that had been already declared to be worse than the sins of Sodom.

Verse 50. The history of Sodom's destruction is in Genesis 19.

Verse 51. *Neither half of thy sins* is to be understood in the same light as the thoughts in vrese 48. Judah had many advantages for spiritual encouragement not least of which was her possession of Jerusalem and the temple service. Also, she had seen the years of service to idols which Samaria had experienced and should have observed how useless such a service is. In view of all this the Lord regarded Judah with greater condemnation and pointed the finger of shame at her.

Verse 52. *Sisters* means the other idolatrous nations who did not have the advantages for knowing better that Judah had. This fact is the explanation of the phrase *more righteous than thou.*

Verse 53. Much of this verse and others following is figurative or general in its application. *Sodom* was not actually ever restored, but God was promising to extend his mercy to those who had disobeyed the law that was binding upon them.

Verse 54. Judah had encouraged the inferior nations in their sinful course by the eaxmple she had set. However, while being more or less responsible for the abominable life manifested by the other nations, Judah professed to abhor them in their evil ways. When the time came that it would all be changed by the powerful hand of the Lord, Judah was to be humiliated over her own wicked conduct.

Verse 55. Judah as well as the other groups that had dishonored God was destined to be placed in a better condition, but the comparative improvement at that time will be measured by the extent of responsibility that each group had borne.

Verse 56. Judah had felt above Sodom in the years she was a powerful kingdom, although that wicked city was to be justified rather than Judah in view of the principle of responsibility that has been discussed in the preceding verses.

Verse 57. This verse continues the thought begun in the preceding one, and the attitude of Judah toward Syria and the Philistines is to be regarded in the same sense as Sodom because it is principles of action that are being considered.

Verse 58. *Hast borne* is past tense in grammatical form but is prophetic in thought. Judah was to bear the penalty of her *lewdness* (idolatry) at the hand of the Babylonians and by the decree of God.

Verse 59. *As thou hast done* denotes the reason for dealing out the punishment to Judah; that it will be what her conduct deserved.

Verse 60. After the chastisement has reformed the wayward wife, her husband will receive her to himself again. *Remember my covenant* is a reference to the days of their first love, when the husband pledged his constancy for the young wife. He had never broken that promise though she had betrayed his confidence.

Verse 61. This verse is a prediction of the cure from idolatry. See the note at Isaiah 1: 25 for the fulfillment of this prophecy. Judah was to be united with her former associates after the captivity. *Not by thy covenant* signifies that Judah had not made any agreement that would have entitled her to this reunion.

Verse 62. One meaning of *establish* is to confirm. God had covenanted with Judah to bring her back to her home land after the captivity had cured her of her iniquity. In so doing it would prove that He always makes his word good. The final fact that would be proved by this restoration would be that all might *know that I am the Lord.*

Verse 63. The human memory is very frail at times, especially when some obligation would place a heavy or difficult line of duty upon the individual. The long period of affliction imposed upon Judah by the captivity was to make such a deep impression upon the people that they would never forget it. Yea, they were to remember with shame how unfaithful they had been and be thereby held back from any complaints. It will be well for the reader to see Nehemiah 9th chapter in connection with this prediction of the penitent mind that would be manifested after the return from the captivity. By this state of mind and by their avoidance of idolatry from this time onward, the Lord was *pacified* toward his people as predicted in this verse.

EZEKIEL 17

Verses 1, 2. *Riddle* and *parable* are used for the same story. The distinction is slight, but the latter merely means a comparison, while the former indicates that the story will be somewhat puzzling. The parable has to do with the affairs of God's people in connection with the Babylonians and Egyptians. The Biblical history that corresponds with it is in 2 Kings 24 and 25.

Verse 3. The *great eagle* was Babylon, *Lebanon* was Jerusalem and the *cedar* was composed of the leading men or princes of the city. Of course all of these terms were used figuratively and will be referred to by their proper names before the chapter is finished. Since Babylon was represented under the figure of an eagle, in describing its greatness the use of corresponding figures would naturally be maintained. A flying creature that could soar from the region of the Euphrates and arrive so successfully at the distant point of Jerusalem, would require the kind of wings described.

Verse 4. This verse is a prediction of the captivity that was soon to be effected over the leading citizens of Jerusalem. *Land of traffic* was literally true of Babylon. Situated at the Euphrates and Tigris, and also not far from the gulf, she was in a position to deal with the merchants of the world.

Verse 5. When Nebuchadnezzar first made his attack upon Palestine he did not entirely destroy the capital and other cities. He took charge of the country and allowed the Jews still to have a king of their own peopel. He also permitted some of these chief men to occupy places of importance in Jerusalem, and the kingdom of Judah continued to reign in its own land. *Fruitful field* and *great waters* are figures of speech to indicate the favorable situation that the nation was allowed to enjoy even though the king of Babylon was over the whole realm.

Verse 6. This verse is a picture of the relative prosperity of Judah under the domination of the *great eagle* which represented Babylon. *Vine of low stature* means it prospered as a spreading vine, but was not permitted to raise its head to the equal of Babylon. *Turned toward him* means that Judah had to look to Babylon as a superior.

Verse 7. The *great eagle* was Pharaoh, king of Egypt, who would have come to the side of Judah had he been able; this fact is also revealed in 2 Kings 24: It may be seen also that Judah would have been eager to have the support of Egypt, which is the meaning of *branches toward him* in this verse.

Verse 8. This verse shows the prosperous state of Egypt and what that country could have done for Judah had the Lord not interfered.

Verse 9. The central idea in this verse is similar to the preceding one. In spite of the many natural resources of Pharaoh's kingdom, that monarch would not be able to save Judah from her overthrow when God decreed it to be otherwise.

Verse 10. Maintaining the figurative form of a vine for Egypt, the writer predicted that the plant would not *prosper*, which means it would not succeed in the plans for coming to the aid of Judah.

Verses 11, 12. The *king of Babylon* corresponds with *great eagle* of verse 3; *Jerusalem* is to identify *Lebanon* of that verse, and *princes* was called *the cedar*. The events pictured are recorded in the closing chapters of 2 Kings.

Verse 13. *King's seed* is indefinite and refers to the leading men in Jerusalem whom the king of Babylon pressed into service. However, among these leading men there was one (Zedekiah) who was appointed to sit as acting ruler in Jerusalem.

Verse 14. *Kingdom be base* denotes that the realm of Judah was to be subject to the rule of Babylon even though the acting king was suffered to remain in Jerusalem.

Verse 15. Zedekiah thought he could get help from Egypt against the king of Babylon. He sent *ambassadors into Egypt* according to this verse, and the same is recorded in Jeremiah 37: 7 as a bit of history included in that prophetic book.

Verse 16. *King dwelleth that made him king* refers to the king of Babylon, for in 2 Kings 24: 17 we have the record of that appointment. This verse predicts that Zedekiah was to die in the very land of him who had given him his appointment as king.

Verse 17. It was predicted that the

attempted alliance with Egypt would prove disappointing. When God decrees that his people are to receive some chastisement for their unfaithfulness, it is useless for them to think they can avoid it by calling for help from others, for numbers and other might count nothing against Him.

Verse 18. Zedekiah had made an agreement with the king of Babylon to serve him while remaining on the throne in Jerusalem. He broke that convenant by calling on Egypt for help, and such an act was against the will of God, for it was the divine will that Babylon be given possession of Jerusalem and her people.

Verse 19. The oath that Zedekiah made with Nebuchadnezzar was the same as if it had been made with the Lord, since He had decreed that the Babylonians were to conquer.

Verse 20. *Spread my net* refers to the pursuit and capture of Zedekiah when he sought to escape by fleeing in the night (2 Kings 25: 4-7).

Verse 21. Some of Zedekiah's men tried to escape with him, but they were captured and taken from their king. This event is recorded in 2 Kings 25: 5.

Verses 22-24. These verses should be grouped in a bracket and given a twofold interpretation. The first is a prediciton of the return of God's people from captivity. The second is a prediction of Christ as King and Redeemer over all earth spiritually.

EZEKIEL 18

Verses 1, 2. There was no basis for the saying about the fathers' eating sour grapes and setting the children's teeth on edge. But it was a convenient way of shifting personal responsibility to blame the wrong on inheritance from the fathers. Such a theory never was true, but the falsity of it had not been exposed as clearly as the Lord threatened to do next.

Verse 3. The Lord declared he was going to take away all occasion for such a saying. *As I live* means the thing predicted was to be as sure as the fact that the Lord was a living Being.

Verse 4. *All souls are mine* signifies that God would have no reason to punish one soul on behalf of another since one of His beloved servants would be as precious as the other. The force of the last clause will be realized if the pronoun is emphasized and made to read, *the soul that sinneth IT shall die;* that is, one soul will not have to die for the sins of another.

Verse 5. Justice is described in this verse as consisting of doing that which is lawful and right in one's conduct toward his fellow man.

Verse 6. *Eaten upon the mountains.* The connection indicates this means the eating in the feasts instituted in the idolatrous services. The idolaters often selected mountains or other "high places" as points for setting up their idols. The last clause of the verse would have been a violation of Leviticus 18: 19.

Verse 7. It was lawful to accept a pledge from another to secure an obligation, but it was wrong to retain it overnight (Exodus 22: 26).

Verse 8. The general meaning of this verse is to take advantage of the misfortunes of another and make a gain thereby.

Verse 9. The *statutes* and *judgments* of the Lord means the divine laws enacted for the conduct of His people. The man who does them has the promise that he will live, while the one who disregards all of such regulations will be the soul that sins and *IT* was condemned to die.

Verse 10. A man who begets a son who goes wrong will not have to answer for the sins of that son; provided, of course, he does what he can to instruct his son aright.

Verse 11. Many of the wrongs previously mentioned are repeated because of the importance of the subject. *Eaten upon the mountains* is a reference to the idolatrous feasts that were performed on the various "high places."

Verse 12. *Spoiled by violence* means to use force in taking from another his property. *Not restored the pledge* refers to the law which required a lender to return a pledge at the end of the day.

Verse 13. It was unlawful under the law of Moses to exact *usury* (interest) of a Jewish brother. Instead, if a loan was made to him, the lender could require a pledge in the form of some article of value, but even that must be returned at sundown.

Verse 14. A father was not made to answer for the sins of his son. By the same token, if a father was a doer of wrong deeds, it did not furnish the son any excuse for doing the like. The son should *consider* the bad example set by the father and profit by it instead of following in the same line of conduct.

Verse 15. This verse is the same in thought as verse 6.

Verse 16. To *oppress* in the sense that is condemned means to take undue advantage of another. One way in which that could be done was to retain a pledge beyond the legal hour which was stipulated by the law to be at sundown.

Verse 17. *Taken his hand from the poor* denotes he has refrained from oppressing the poor, such as charging him usury or interest on money loaned to him. If a son follows these righteous principles in life he will not be punished because of his father.

Verse 18. It was likewise true that the good deeds of a son would not benefit an unworthy father. The son would "live" in the favor of God, but the father would have to die on the ground of his own responsibility.

Verse 19. The first part of this verse is a protest from the people because of the old notion that a son should bear the blame for his father's evil deeds. The last part is God's reply, and it is a restatement of what has been already declared.

Verse 20. The first sentence is an identical repetition of the closing clause of verse 4. This verse as a whole is a summing up of the several verses on a most important subject, that of individual responsibility.

Verse 21. This verse introduces another phase of one's responsibility as regards his personal conduct, but it still leaves the individual item where it was. No man will need to die for the sins of another, it is only the *soul that sinneth* that shall die. Yet even such a person needs not die, notwithstanding his past sins. Repentance or reformation of life is always open to all men and if such a course will be adopted the sinner may be forgiven his evil conduct and live in the favor of God.

Verse 22. When God forgives a man the matter is dropped. There is a popular saying uttered in prayers where the petitioner asks God to forgive our sins "and remember them against us no more." Such a statement is an insult to the Almighty, for it implies that God will promise to forgive and yet might remember our sins against us after declaring they had been forgiven. It puts God on a level with hypocritical man who agrees to "bury the hatchet," but who leaves the handle in sight.

Verse 23. The primary object in all scriptural discipline is the possibility of reforming the sinner (1 Corinthians 5: 5; 2 Corinthians 7: 12; 2 Thessalonians 3: 14, 15; Hebrews 12: 6-11; 13: 17). God does not obtain any pleasure out of the punishment of his creatures (2 Peter 3: 9), but inflicts it solely for their good.

Verse 24. This verse is akin to verse 22 at one very important point. When a wicked man repents and is forgiven, none of his former sins are mentioned against him. Likewise, if a righteous man backslides and deserts his life of righteousness, he will be dealt with according to his sins just the same as if he had never been a righteous man. It is one of the weaknesses of mankind to overlook the evil doing of a person for the sake of his previous record. It will be heard say, "We know he is not doing just right now, but we still remember the good he has done." Such persons are pretending to have a better memory or know better how to deal with a sinner than does the Lord. He declares he will not consider the former good deeds of the backslider after he takes up a life of sin but that *he shall die* in his sins.

Verse 25. Any accusation made against the Lord would be false, but this one was especially foolish in view of the declarations just made about the dealing meted out toward man. It shows that He treated all persons in an impartial manner in that a man's past conduct, whether good or bad, was not used as a basis for the treatment of him at present. In spite of this, the people of Israel accused God of using ways that were *not equal*, which means that he was partial in his dealings.

Verse 26. The conclusion that is in this verse is that when a man dies *IN* his iniquities, they are to be regarded as the cause for the penalty of death imposed.

Verse 27. Much repetition may be observed in this chapter, but human beings are so forgetful they need to be reminded frequently of the same truth. It should be seen that throughout this long passage one principle is out in front, and that is that man's fate is largely in his own hands, he will be dealt with according to his deeds.

Verse 28. Repentance is not something a man does unthinkingly or on the spur of the moment, but it is *because he considereth*. It is true that repentance must start in the mind (2 Corinthians 7: 9, 10), but if it is sincere it will manifest itself by a life of reformation and turning from the ways of unrighteousness.

Verse 29. In spite of the fairness of this principle in God's dealings, his people charged him with unequal or partial treatment of them.

Verse 30. God determined to proceed in the manner decreed and judge each man *according to HIS ways*, and not in consideration of the conduct of others. The fairness of this principle is evident in that it gives each individual an opportunity to avoid personal disaster by turning from his sins.

Verse 31. Repentance is an active and practical something. A sinner must accomplish it himself by putting away the evil things of his life; no one can do it for him. The New Testament teaches the same principle in 2 Timothy 2: 19-21 and many other passages.

After man has purged his manner of life by sincere reformation, God will purge him from the guilt thereof by forgiveness.

Verse 32. The primary object of discipline is discussed at verse 23.

EZEKIEL 19

Verse 1. The prophet was told to make a lamentation for the princes of Israel, which means Judah in this case since the 10-tribe kingdom of Israel had been in exile more than a century at the time of this writing.

Verse 2. The lamentation was to be in the form of a parable, using the lion species of animal for the comparison. The *mother* was the nation of Judah that was considered a lioness *among lions* or other kingdoms. The princes or chief men of the nation of Judah would be referred to as *whelps* in the figurative language of the parable.

Verse 3. This verse singles out one of the whelps and the context indicates it means Jehoahaz. (See 2 Kings 23: 30.) The figurative form of speech is continued, hence the evil conduct of this king is described as that of *catching prey* which really means that this king *devoured men* as is literally stated.

Verse 4. The conduct of this evil king (whelp) attracted the attention of other nations and the statement that *he was taken in their pit* is recorded in 2 Kings 23: 33.

Verse 5. There is a space between this and the preceding verse that is not apparent in the language. After Jehoahaz was dethroned, his brother Jehoiakim was put in his place and reigned 11 years, and he was succeeded by his son Jehoiachin who reigned but 3 months. For some reason unknown to me, these two rulers are not considered distinctively in the parable. The things that will be said of the *whelp* of this verse were not all true of the mentioned kings, but they were true of the last king in Jerusalem and his name was Zedekiah. *Waited . . . hope was lost* indicates that the return of Jehoahaz was looked for by some but it was in vain. It had been decreed (Jeremiah 22: 30) that no descendant of Jehoiachin was to reign in Judah, hence the nation had to use another *whelp* who was Zedekiah.

Verse 6. The figures are still drawn from the life of a lion but the verse refers to the actual conduct of Zedekiah who was then on the throne in Jerusalem.

Verse 7. Zedekiah was not a very acceptable ruler in the eyes of his countrymen, and even some of the foreign nations began to look upon him with mistrust.

Verse 8. Finally *the nations* (meaning the units of the empire of Babylon) came against Zedekiah and laid siege to his capital which fell as a prey of war.

Verse 9. Zedekiah tried to evade capture and fled his capital by night, but he was taken by the army of Babylon who *spread their net over him* (2 Kings 25: 4, 5). *In chains* refers to the shackles which they placed upon the fallen king of Judah, after which they took him to Babylon (2 Kings 25: 7). Much of this chapter so far is literal history and it may be read in 2 Kings 24 and 25. But the last part about Zedekiah is prophecy for he had not yet been taken from his throne at this writing.

Verse 10. *Thy mother* means Judah as the producer of kings and princes such as have been considered. The verse is a figurative description of the prosperous state of Judah under the blessings of God. *In thy blood* refers to the early hours of her life when the special favor of God was bestowed upon her. (See chapter 16: 6, 22.)

Verse 11. Here are some more figures and they refer to the standing that Judah enjoyed as a nation among nations. This state of exaltation seems to have filled her with pride and a disregard for her obligation to the Lord.

Verse 12. The closing verses of the chapter pertain to the final overthrow of Jerusalem which was the capital of the kingdom of Judah, which event was to complete the 3rd stage of the great 70-year captivity. *Plucked up in fury* refers directly to the heat of the Babylonian attack. *East wind* suggests the blast of the Babylonian army since that force came from the east. *Fire consumed* is a literal prediction and its fulfillment is recorded in 2 Kings 25: 9.

Verse 13. The *wilderness* was the land of Babylon which would be *dry and thirsty* as far as any national favors were concerned.

Verse 14. *No strong rod to be a sceptre to rule.* When Zedekiah was taken from the throne of Judah, there never was a successor until the time of Christ, who was to have the right to reign, but as a spiritual ruler. (See chapter 21: 24-27.) Christ was produced through the tribe of Judah and was to be the last king of that people.

EZEKIEL 20

Verse 1. *Seventh year* is dated from the dethroning of Jehoiachin, at which time Ezekiel was taken into Babylon. This sitting of the *elders of Israel* is similar to the instance given in chapter 14: 1.

Verse 2. The Lord, being aware of the purpose of these elders, will tell the prophet how to address them.

Verse 3. The speech was to be about the same as was given at the former instance. These people were not worthy of the attention they could have received had their conduct been of the proper kind.

Verse 4. Ezekiel was told to refer them to the abominable conduct of their fathers. This would not have been held against them had they profited by the mistakes of their fathers and learned the lesson that such an example teaches.

Verse 5. With this verse the Lord begins an account of his dealings with Israel from the time they saw His signs and wonders in the land of Egypt.

Verse 6. The history starts with the time the people were preparing to leave the land where they had been for four centuries. *Lifted up mine hand* refers to the means the Lord used to procure the release of his people from the land of bondage. *Glory of all lands* denotes the general desirableness of the land of Canaan, but which God had reserved for his own people.

Verse 7. The Egyptians were idol worshipers and during a stay among them of several centuries the Israelites had taken up with the corrupt practices. As they were leaving that country the Lord admonished them to cut off the evil manner of life. *I am the Lord your God* should have been sufficient reason for their giving up the vain gods of the heathen from whom they had just been rescued.

Verse 8. The children of Israel did not obey the admonition to put away their idolatrous interests. They had not been made free from Egypt but a few weeks until they made the golden calf, suggested no doubt by their life in that country. Yea, even before getting out of that land they manifested an inclination to cling to their evil practices and the Lord's anger was provoked to the uttermost.

Verse 9. But He would not bring his chastisement upon them while in that land, for to do so would be a pollution in the midst of the heathen. Such is the meaning of what God *wrought for his name's sake* by showing the divine power in the midst of that nation that had been accustomed to devotions paid to idol gods.

Verse 10. After thus demonstrating his love for his people, God sent them forth out of that country to travel a while in the wilderness.

Verse 11. There is very little practical difference between *statutes* and *judgments*. The first refers especially to a fixed law to be enforced upon the subjects, the second considers the ability and right of the Lord to decide what is the proper conduct. In the application of them both to man the whole thought is that God knows best what is good for man and has arranged a code of rules for his conduct. The result of such a life will be that man will *live* in the sense of enjoying the favor and protection of God. The propriety of some of these laws may be evident to the human mind while others would have to be accepted upon faith in God's wisdom.

Verse 12. This language refers to the time the children of Israel were brought out of Egypt. Of that time it is said by the Lord, "I gave them my sabbaths." This means that the observance of the sabbath days had not been required of God's people. Moreover, Nehemiah 9: 14 indicates they had not even known about such a practice as keeping a sabbath day prior to the law of Moses. It was to be a *sign* between the Lord and his people. The word means something visible as an evidence of a relationship between the parties involved. By observing the sabbath days the children of Israel showed to the world that God was guiding them in their program of life.

Verse 13. This verse describes in a general way the spirit of lawlessness displayed by the children of Israel soon after they were released from Egypt. *Despised my judgments* means they belittled them and treated them as if they were unimportant. The extent of their error is denoted by the Lord's words that the very rules which the Israelites belittled were so important that a man might *live in them*.

Verse 14. *But I wrought* means the Lord worked out his plan in order that His name would not be disgraced in the minds of the heathen.

Verse 15. The men responsible for the conspiracy against the Lord were all caused to die in the wilderness, thus being unable to reach the land of promise.

Verse 16. When men rebel against the righteous commandments of the Lord it is generally due to some other interests. In this case the verse explains it by saying *their heart went after their idols*.

Verse 17. God chastised his people while in the wilderness and many thousands of them died. But the nation as a whole was not wiped out but succeeded in reaching the land promised to their fathers.

Verse 18. The children were not to be punished for the sins of their fathers unless they followed in the evil ways set before them, and even then it would be in punishment for their own conduct and not for that of the fathers. For this reason they were admonished *not to walk in the statutes* of their fathers nor serve their idols.

Verse 19. Being the Lord God of these people was cited as the reason they should walk in the statutes and judgments He had given them.

Verse 20. Sabbath as a sign is explained at verse 12.

Verse 21. This verse is a repetition of the charge of rebellion previously made against the children of Israel.

Verse 22. *Withdrew mine hand* means God refrained his hand from punishing his people as they deserved. This was done for the sake of His own name that it might not be polluted in the midst of the heathen.

Verse 23. *Lifted up mine hand* here is figurative and refers to the Lord's determination to punish his nation finally by scattering them among the heathen.

Verse 24. The children of Israel turned away from the law of God, then became devoted to idols.

Verse 25. It might puzzle us to read that God would give people a law that was not good. The key to the verse is the sense in which the word *gave* is used. The lexicon says the original has a wide range of meanings. One way in which a thing may be "given" is to step out of the way and let a person who is stubborn have his own way in order that he may be taught a lesson by his own experience. God has used such a plan more than once when his creatures persisted in walking according to their own rules which are designated *statutes* in this verse. (See Psalms 81: 12; Acts 7: 42; Romans 1: 24; 2 Thessalonians 2: 11.)

Verse 26. *I polluted them* denotes that God pronounced his people as a polluted group because of their idolatrous practices. They had stooped to the most abominable form of the heathen worship, that of offering human sacrifices.

Verse 27. The word translated *blasphemed* is defined "to revile" in the lexicon, and it has also been rendered "reproach" in other passages in the King James version. God regarded it as a reproach against Him for his own people to take up with idols.

Verse 28. This verse is a description of the idolatrous conditions the Israelites found in Palestine when they entered it. They had been warned against just such things and hence had no reason to be taken by surprise. However, they fell right in with the situation and participated in all the abominable practices of the heathen.

Verse 29. *Bamah* is a word of indefinite origin and occurs only in this place. It is used in a derisive manner with reference to the high places that were approached by idolatrous worshipers.

Verse 30. The question form of the language really was intended as an accusation of the things named. The generation of Ezekiel's day were accused of following in the footsteps of their sinful forefathers.

Verse 31. With all these pollutions clinging to these people they were in no position to come to God for information. They had already belittled the instruction that was offered them in their law, hence it would be inconsistent for them to approach the Lord as sincere inquirers.

Verse 32. They had determined in their own mind to be as the heathen who served false gods that were made of wood and stone. They were foolish enough to think they could succeed and continue as a nation while relying on such false gods. But this verse informs them that such a thing *shall not be at all.*

Verse 33. This verse through 37 is a prediction of the captivity. The *rule* to be had over them was to be accomplished through the Babylonians in whose land they were to dwell throughout the historic 70-year captivity.

Verse 34. The captivity was intended to act as a season of discipline for the rebellious people of God. While in that state they were destined to feel the fury of Him whom they had disobeyed.

Verse 35. *Wilderness of the people* is a figure of speech, based on the event when they were led out from Egyptian bondage into the wilderness. (See verse 10.) The present passage applies to the history connected with their exile in Babylon.

Verse 36. In this verse the Lord makes his own comparison between the time of Egypt and that of Babylon.

Verse 37. *Pass under the rod* is another figure of speech and the meaning is that God would take account of his people. The figure is drawn from the practice of a shepherd who caused his sheep to pass under his rod as he counted them. The ones thus enumerated were to be retained as heirs to the covenant that promised a restoration to the favor of God after the chastisement of the captivity had met its purpose.

Verse 38. The principal item in this purpose mentioned in the preceding verse was the cure of idolatry and that is the subject of this verse. *Purge out from among you the rebels* refers to those who would still be favorably disposed toward idolatry. They were to be weeded out from the other Jews and also be drawn away from the land of Babylon. However, they were not to be permitted to reenter the land of Israel since only those who were weaned from idols were to be thus rewarded. This helps to explain why only a remnant was permitted to return (Ezra 2:64).

Verse 39. This verse should be considered in connection with verse 25. It was a part of the treatment for idolatry that the nation be compelled to continue its corrupt practice even while in captivity.

Verse 40. This and some following verses predict the return from captivity. Mountain in symbolic language means a government. After the captivity the Lord's people were to return to their own land and restore the religious way of life that was directed by the law. *There . . . offerings.* While in Babylon the Lord would not accept any sacrifices from his people, but when they will have returned to their own country their offerings will be received.

Verse 41. By accepting and blessing the offerings of the Jews in Jerusalem, the heathen would have before them the evidence of the high standing of that people.

Verse 42. Another evidence of the favor of God will be the fact of the restoration of the Jews to the land from which they had been taken 70 years before.

Verse 43. The outstanding effort of the captivity was to rid the Jewish nation of the corruption of idolatry. (See the historical note on this subject in connection with comments on Isaiah 1:25, volume 3 of this Commentary.)

Verse 44. Israel did not receive the severe treatment her conduct deserved, which is the meaning of *not according to your wicked ways.* But the Lord wished to take care of his good name and hence held back part of his fury.

Verses 45, 46. The 10-tribe kingdom had been in exile for more than a century. It was known in history as the northern kingdom as it related to the kingdom of Judah. The latter was in the south part of Palestine, and as Ezekiel was writing its capital had not been destroyed, hence the present passage directed at Jerusalem as the south.

Verse 47. The imagery of a forest was selected for the present passage hence the destruction of the kingdom of Judah was spoken of as the burning of the trees.

Verse 48. *Shall not be quenched* means that God's decree to overthrow the kingdom of Judah was bound to go through.

Verse 49. Ezekiel expressed a fear that this form of speech would not be taken seriously by his people; that they might think he was speaking with no end in view.

EZEKIEL 21

Verse 1, 2. The words *set thy face toward Jerusalem* will be understood by remembering that Ezekiel was in Babylon all the time he was writing, having been taken there at the time of Jehoiachin's captivity. But the 3rd and final stage of the 70-year captivity had not taken place, hence Jerusalem was still standing and the last of its kings, Zedekiah, was yet on the throne as a subject king under the Babylonians. Because of all this, much of Ezekiel's writings was prophecy though its fulfillment was about due and the remaining Jews were being warned to be prepared.

Verse 3. This verse was directed against the *land of Israel* in general, though its principal application was to the city of Jerusalem which was the capital and which was yet standing as per the preceding paragraph. The *righteous* and *wicked* were to be cut off in that all classes regardless of personal character had to share in the national downfall. It is a proper time again to read the note offered in connection with 2 Kings 22: 17, volume 2 of this Commentary.

Verse 4. *All flesh* is to be understood in the light of *righteous* and *wicked* as explained in the preceding verse. *My sword* refers literally to the sword of the Babylonians, but is so designated because God was using that nation as his instrument for chastising his people.

Verse 5. *All flesh* and *my sword* are explained in the preceding verse.

Verse 6. *Breaking of thy loins* is figurative and means his entire being was to feel the bitterness of the conditions for which he was sighing.

Verse 7. The sighing described in the preceding verse was a form of "acting" which has been spoken of a number of times, and it was for the purpose of making an impression upon the people. When they inquired the reason for the demonstration the prophet was to tell them it was because of the *tidings*. Of course that referred to the news of what was to come yet upon the city and the people remaining in it.

Verse 8, 9. The same subject is indicated in this paragraph and it pertains to the sword of the Babylonians. To *furbish* means to polish the body of the blade and to *sharpen* would affect the edge. The idea is that God would use the sword of the Babylonians and that it would have been put in the best condition for use.

Verse 10. By furbishing the sword it would be caused to glitter, thus making an impressive appearance in the sight of the victims. One use of a *rod* was as a scepter in ruling, but the scepter in the hands of *my son* (meaning Zedekiah still on the throne) was to be of no avail when the sword of the Babylonians came against it.

Verse 11. *He hath given it to be furbished* means that God had decreed that the sword of the Babylonians was to be effective in its work against Judah.

Verse 12. *Cry and howl* was for the same reason as "sigh" in verse 6. The impending calamity about to come on Jerusalem will be great and bitter and the prophet was instructed to indicate it by his physical expressions. In ancient times many actions were done to indicate the feelings of a person, such as to *smite upon the thigh*.

Verse 13. *Sword contemn* (belittle) *the rod* means the sword of Babylon would overcome the authority of Zedekiah. See the comments on verse 10.

Verse 14. *Sword be doubled* is an emphatic way of describing the success of the sword of Babylon. It was destined to slay many of the *great men* in Jerusalem. *Entereth private chambers* indicates the thoroughness of the work of the Babylonian army.

Verse 15. *I have set the point of the sword against all their gates* denotes that God had given the sword of the Babylonians the mission of attacking Jerusalem and her walls. There was to be no escaping from the attack since God was back of it.

Verse 16. The Lord is still addressing himself to the prophet, and in some figurative way is going to describe his actions toward the people. *One way or other* is a figure and the meaning is that there will be no way of turning that will not see the dealing to be meted out under the decree of the Lord.

Verse 17. *Smite mine hands* has the same significance as "smite upon the thigh" in verse 12. God was very determined to carry out his fury on those who provoked it.

Verse 18, 19. *Two ways* represents the king of Babylon in his march out of Babylon and coming to a point where two directions appeared before him. He is undecided as to which course to take but the prophet is told to *choose it* for him. We have learned that God takes a hand in the affairs of the nation (Daniel 2: 21; 4: 17), thus He will decide the present question for the king of Babylon. That decision will be that the Babylonian forces will be directed to follow up both ways since the numerous forces of Nebuchadnezzar would enable him thus to act.

Verse 20. This verse designates the two *ways* mentioned in the preceding paragraph, and shows they were to lead against the *Ammonites* and *Judah.* For a detailed explanation of the part the Ammonites played in the plans of the Lord, see the comments on Jeremiah 49: 1.

Verse 21. This verse deals with the state of uncertainty in the mind of the king of Babylon which was discussed at verse 19. *Use divination* refers to the way the king was using to bring him to a decision as to which way to choose, when the Lord intervened and made the decision for him. *Looking in the liver* refers to an ancient superstition of consulting the internal organs of various creatures in arriving at decisions. Myers' Ancient History (page 344) says the following on this subject: "From Etruria was introduced the art of the haruspices, or soothsayers, which consisted in discovering the will of the gods by the appearance of the entrails of victims slain for the sacrifices."

Verse 22. On one hand the king of Babylon saw the indication that he should go against Jerusalem. He was to advance against the capital city of Judah with strong military equipment that could lay and execute a siege.

Verse 23. *Be unto them a false divination* means the people of Jerusalem will at least pretend not to take the matter seriously. They will console themselves with the idea that the king of Babylon has been misled by *false divination*. But the Lord will remind them of their evil conduct and thus assure them that the so-called *false divination* will prove to be true, and *that they* (people of Jerusalem) *may be taken*, the Lord will carry out the results indicated by the signs.

Verse 24. The false security the people of Jerusalem had imagined for themselves was to be exposed. Their iniquity was not forgotten by the Lord and for that cause they were to be *taken with the hand*, meaning the hand of the Lord was in the work of the Babylonians in this final stage of the captivity.

Verse 25. This *wicked prince* was Zedekiah who was still on the throne in Jerusalem, ruling under the authority of Babylon but that rule was soon to *have an end*.

Verse 26. A *diadem* is a band worn on the forehead of a ruler, and a *crown* is the article worn on the top of the head to signify his authority. Zedekiah was still wearing this crown at the present writing although his reign was about to close. *Take off the crown* was a prediction and an order. The prediction was that Zedekiah was soon to lose his crown and that it would be by the decree of the Lord. *Not be the same* means the crown will not continue in the same line it has been enjoying as to its temporal scope. *Exalt* and *abase* indicates a reversal of conditions regarding the government of God's people.

Verse 27. To *overturn* means to overthrow and the threefold use of the word indicates emphasis. The antecedent of *IT* is "crown" in the preceding verse and it is the thing God was about to overthrow. With the downfall of Zedekiah and Jerusalem the final stage of the 70-year captivity will be accomplished and Nebuchadnezzar will not leave any other man on the throne of Judah. Such is the significance of the words *shall be no more.* However, while the throne of Judah as a temporal kingdom was never again to be, yet something else was to take its place which is introduced by the word *until*. Following up with the subject thus introduced by the word *until* the Lord declared a person would come *whose right it is*, meaning it would be his right to have the throne, and when that person comes God *will give it him*. That great person is Christ and he is the same person predicted in Genesis 49:10. This last passage together with our present verse makes the important prediction that Zedekiah was to be the last king ever to reign over Judah until Christ (the Shiloh of Genesis 49:10) came, and then He would reign as a spiritual king.

Verse 28. The place of the Ammonites of the transactions of the Lord has been described, and the reader may see it in fuller detail at Jeremiah 49:1.

Verse 29. The gist of this verse is that there were false prophets among the Ammonites as well as in Judah. They gave their people false assurances of peace, and their predictions seemed plausible because Nebuchadnezzar was seen to direct his course toward Judah and that would seem to remove any threat to other places.

Verse 30. The question is asked of Ammon if he thought that God would withhold the sword just because the diviners had predicted it so. The question was then answered in the negative and the Ammonites were warned of judgment in their own land.

Verse 31. The threatening continues and the Ammonites are notified that their judgment will be like a fire. The judgment will be executed by the services of other heathen armies whom the Lord designates as *brutish men*.

Verse 32. The fire threatened is largely figurative and refers to the heat of God's wrath. That heat was to be poured out against the Ammonites in the form of destruction in battle, conducted by the forces acting as an agency of God.

EZEKIEL 22

Verses 1, 2. The prophet is again told to direct his writing against the *bloody city* which means Jerusalem which was still standing. He was to recall to her the many abominations of which she was guilty, both physical and spiritual.

Verse 3. The city of Jerusalem not only harbored many idols, but also shielded men who were guilty of bloodshed against the helpless citizens.

Verse 4. *Caused thy days to draw near* referred to the closeness of the final downfall of the city. *Made thee a reproach* is past tense in form and to some extent it was so, for the bulk of the men of Judah were already in Babylon. However, the last act of the great drama was yet to come when the city would be destroyed by the army of the Babylonians.

Verse 5. When a great city like Jerusalem is utterly destroyed it always causes much comment from the people of the countries. Some might make remarks that were prompted by sincere regret that so great a city should come to ruin. Others would speak in derision and exultation as over the downfall of a dreaded rival.

Verse 6. The princes or leading men in Israel (Judah) used their advantage of position and prestige to carry out their personal wicked designs. Such a course included the shedding of innocent blood of which they were frequently accused by the inspired prophets and other teachers.

Verse 7. *Set light* means to make light of or belittle, and these wicked leaders in Jerusalem lost almost all "natural affection." If a man would lose respect for his own parents it might be expected that he would have very little regard for others. Hence these wicked leaders used oppressive measures against the visitors to their city, and also took advantage of the fatherless and widows.

Verse 8. These men *despised* (belittled) the holy things pertaining to the services of the temple. They *profaned* the sabbaths by ignoring the observance due the sacred days and by using the time in carrying out their wicked devices for gain.

Verse 9. There are three unrighteous practices mentioned in this verse. One is the peddling of gossip that led to the shedding of innocent blood. Another is to *eat upon the mountains* which means to participate in idolatrous feasts, and the other pertains to practices of immorality.

Verse 10. Ordinary lewdness was not enough for these wicked men, but they invaded the sacred rights of their nearest relations. They were so vicious in their immoral indulgencies that they violated Leviticus 18:19.

Verse 11. This verse refers to the general and promiscuous practice of immorality. No rank of social or blood connection furnished any protection against the assaults of these abominable characters who were blind to all sense of decency.

Verse 12. It is bad enough to shed blood in anger or on the spur of the moment, but these men deliberately did so for the sake of bribes. Their greed for gain was so great that they violated the law against usury in order to obtain it. They also took advantage of the urgency of a man's condition to extort money from him.

Verse 13. *Have smitten mine hand* refers to the gesture that was used in ancient times to emphasize the intensity of God's feelings against wicked men.

Verse 14. *Can thine hands be strong* was the Lord's way of telling them they would not be able to resist the wrath that He would soon bring against them.

Verse 15. This verse has direct reference to the captivity. It was to be accomplished in the Babylonian Empire which is a singular word, but that great institution was composed of many *countries*, hence the mention of that subject in connection with the scattering among the heathen. *Consume thy filthiness* applies specifically to the cure of idolatry which the captivity was to accomplish.

Verse 16. *Inheritance* is from CHALAL which Strong defines, "To bore, i.e. (by implication) to wound, to dissolve; figuratively to profane a person." The verse means that Judah would be humiliated in the sight of the heathen by her corrupt conduct.

Verses 17, 18. *Dross* is the worthless material that is found in silver ore, and the article is used to illustrate the sunken value of Judah in the Lord's sight.

Verse 19. These evil men of Judah were destined to be put through the fire of God's chastisement, and they were to be seized upon while *in the midst of Jerusalem.*

Verse 20. Not that these people were to be left in Jerusalem, except until they would be subjected to the siege and made to feel the heat of God's wrath.

Verse 21. The comparison of these verses is drawn from the work of the smelter, where fire is used to separate the dross from the silver.

Verse 22. The men of Judah were to be subjected to the test in order to learn about the wrath of the Lord. The warnings that had been repeatedly given them by the Lord through the prophets had fallen on deaf ears, so a physical test of chastisement was necessary to bring them to their senses.

Verses 23, 24. *Land not cleansed* has reference to the many pollutions both physical and moral of which the land was guilty. *Nor rained upon.* In those times God sometimes punished the land by withholding the rain (1 Kings 8: 35; Deuteronomy 11: 17).

Verse 25. These were the false prophets who joined with other leading men in a conspiracy to defraud the people. They had practiced their wicked devices for personal gain even to the shedding of innocent blood.

Verse 26. These priests had some encouragement for their unlawful conduct in the false teaching of the prophets. Jeremiah 5: 31 shows a conspiracy between the evil priests and prophets. One of the surest indications of degeneracy is the confusing of clean and unclean things. Profane things might mean simply the things of a temporal nature and not necessarily wrong. But when the holy or sacred things are put on a basis with the profane or temporal, great corruption results.

Verse 27. *Ravening* is from TARAPH and Strong defines it, "To pluck off or pull to pieces." The idea is the princes were vicious in their activities against the helpless. The terrible nature of this situation is shown in the fact that all this violence against the victims was for the sake of temporal gain.

Verse 28. This comparison to untempered mortar in the case of false teaching was used in chapter 13: 9-11 and commented upon in that place. The false prophets claimed to have received some vision from the Lord, whereas He would not even make any use of such persons in such important matters as pertained to the welfare of the nation.

Verse 29. *The people of the land* would have reference to those citizens who had advantages over the others. *Oppression* is from a word that is defined "fraud" in the lexicon. They used deceitful means to get hold of the possessions of the *poor and needy.* They did not stop at defrauding their fellow citizens, but extended their fraudulent dealings to the *strangers* which means people who were visiting the country.

Verse 30. *Make up the hedge* is figurative and means to build up the weakened condition of the city. No man could be found who was able to remedy the condition.

Verse 31. *Have poured out* was both history and prophecy. Most of the national ruin had taken place but some of it was still in the future. *Own way have I recompensed* means the Lord imposed upon his unfaithful people the judgment that was due them in view of the way they had acted. The Lord is always compassionate toward the creatures of His care, but when they become impenitent and ungrateful for divine favors, they must expect to receive the punishment their sins deserve.

EZEKIEL 23

Verses 1, 2. This entire chapter is on the subject of spiritual adultery which always means idolatry in the Old Testament. The figures and other terms will be directly those pertaining to the unfaithfulness of women in the marriage relation, but I am anxious that the reader always bear in mind that the real subject is idolatry. After all, the comparison is wholly fitting. When a woman becomes the wife of a certain man she cannot share her affections, either mentally or bodily, with any other man without being guilty of adultery against her husband. Likewise, when a man or group of men profess to have become united with God in their religious life, they have no right to patronize any other god or participate in any strange religious activities. If they do so they are guilty of spiritual adultery. So let me once more caution the reader not to get lost to the real subject as he sees the detailed picture of immoral conduct presented in this chapter. The women are the kingdom of Israel and Judah.

Verse 3. *Committed whoredoms in Egypt.* The two separate kingdoms had not come into existence when the children of Israel were living in Egypt and did not for a number of years. But these people were infected with the disease while there and participated in the unrighteous conduct. Its effect upon them was indicated by their making the golden calf in less than three months after leaving the land. The expressions in this verse refer to the unlawful intimacies permitted by an unfaithful wife preparatory to the act of adultery.

Verse 4. We are given the names of the two women involved in the unholy case at hand. *Samaria* and *Jerusalem* are named because they were the capitals of the two kingdoms. *Aholah* is called the elder because the 10-tribe kingdom was formed first, it being the one that revolted from the lawful standard in Jerusalem.

Verse 5. *When she was mine.* Immorality is wrong in any woman, but it is worse when she commits it against a man to whom she has been united in the lawful relationship. The *Assyrians* are named because at the time the 10-tribe kingdom was practicing her unfaithfulness (idolatry) the territory under consideration was under the control of that empire.

Verse 6. *Aholah* was attracted by the fine appearance of the men in the strangers' camp. Many a wife has been lured away from her husband by the showy appearance of another man.

Verse 7. The prophet combines the spiritual with the literal corruption in this verse. He accuses Aholah of whoredom with the Assyrians, and immediately says it was *with all their idols she defiled herself.* (See the comments at verses 1, 2.)

Verse 8. *Neither left she* means she had never left off the abominable practices she had learned in Egypt. Thus this unfaithful wife did not stop at the unlawful intimacies with one man, but took in others and so multiplied her pollutions.

Verse 9. This verse refers to the captivity of the 10-tribe kingdom by the Assyrian Empire. The account of this is in 2 Kings 17th chapter.

Verse 10. Aholah had *doted* on the Assyrians which means she had encouraged them to make "advances" toward her. Following the encouragement they *discovered her nakedness* which means they "went all the way" and had unlawful intimacies with her. After satisfying their lust on her they took her children from her and also slew her with the sword. Literally this means the Assyrians slew the leading men in the 10-tribe kingdom and took the other citizens into exile. *She became famous* means she became a conspicuous person by reason of her notorious conduct. In the language of the world on such a subject she became known and was familiarly referred to as a "character" and was mentioned with a shrugging of the shoulders.

Verse 11. This verse does not mean that Aholibah (Judah) actually committed more idolatry than did her sister, for such was not the case. Every king of the 10-tribe kingdom without exception was an idolater and encouraged it among his subjects. But Judah had a number of faithful kings who tried to stem the tide of corruption. The contrast is made on the basis of the superior advantages that Judah had over Israel. With increased advantages or opportunities come greater responsibilities. Judah had the bad example of Israel and its results before her eyes and should have profited by it. Besides, she had possession of the temple and the lawful priesthood to strengthen her and that should have bound her closer to the Lord in a faithful life. But she seemed to overlook all these factors and committed the abomination of false worship. That is why it is said that she became *more corrupt.*

Verse 12. No doubt the people of Judah were interested in the gods of the Assyrians, but it was the Babylonians (or Chaldeans) that had to do with the chastisement of the unfaithful nation. However, at the time of which Ezekiel was writing the country called Babylon was under the control of Assyria and that is why it is said *she doted upon the Assyrians.* The attractions described are the same as were explained in verse 6.

Verse 13. *Took both one way* means Aholibah followed in the same way that was practiced by her sister Aholah.

Verse 14. *Increased her whoredoms* is explained at verse 11 in the light of the degree of responsibility. *Chaldeans* (or Babylonians) are mentioned because at the time Judah reached her crisis that empire was actually in power.

Verse 15. The attractiveness of men lured her away from devotion to her husband, in the same way that her sister had been enticed as per verse 6.

Verse 16. *Doted upon them* means she gave improper encouragement to them as her sister had done according to verse 5. She even became the aggressor and sent messengers to them with "suggestions."

Verse 17. Such an attitude would be sure to interest men already disposed toward such indulgencies. They accepted the invitation and came to her and committed adultery with her. In actual practice it means the heathen nations would be glad to join with the people of Palestine in idolatrous practices.

Verse 18. *Discovered her nakedness* means she voluntarily assumed the position necessary for the act of adultery. *Mind was alienated* has the same meaning that is contained in cases where a husband charges a man with "alienating the affections of his wife." Idols had alienated the mind of Judah away from the true love for God.

Verse 19. Some women will recall with shame their "youthful follies" and will try to make amends by a virtuous life in later years. But this wife recalled with pleasure those disgraceful years and sought to repeat them.

Verse 20. A *paramour* is an unlawful lover which is here applied to the false gods of heathendom. The terms about *flesh* and *issue* are used to picture a woman who is so lustful that the more beastlike a man is the more she would crave his advances.

Verse 21. This verse repeats the thoughts of earlier verses, referring to the unlawful intimacies permitted by a young wife to strange men.

Verse 22. Sometimes a corrupt woman will tire of her paramours and will "break" with them *(from whom thy mind is alienated).* But they cannot always be cast off so easily and will come back to cause trouble for the woman. Likewise, there came a time when Judah would fain have remained distinct from Babylon. But the Lord determined that she must continue her idolatrous practices with that heathen group, even doing so after being taken into their land for a period of exile.

Verse 23. This verse gives a list of the heathen peoples with whom Judah had committed idolatry (spiritual adultery) at one time or another. Most of them had been swallowed up by the great Babylonian Empire at the time of Judah's captivity.

Verse 24. This is a literal prediction of the siege that the Babylonians planted about Jerusalem. *Chariots* and *wagons* are vehicles used for conveyances of men and materials in military operations. *Wheels* is from a word that indicates something very impressive because of its size, and somewhat like a whirlwind in its encircling formation. The other articles named are those used by soldiers in a siege or other war activities.

Verse 25. When God's jealousy is mentioned we are reminded of Exodus 20: 5 where the subject is idolatry. That is the subject of this present chapter, described and condemned in the form of adultery. This verse predicts the severe treatment that Jerusalem is to receive from the Babylonians in the last stage of the 70-year captivity, including a bitter siege of more than two years.

Verse 26. In line with an unfaithful wife that plays the part of a harlot, she is represented as having attired herself with gaudy and attractive garments as a lure for men. This verse shows that she will be stripped of those garments by these men.

Verse 27. *Make thy lewdness to cease.* Since idolatry is the real subject of all these comparisons, this expression is a prediction of the cure from idolatry that will result by casting his wife (Judah) into the hands of her evil associates. This prediction was fulfilled according to the historical quotation given in connection with Isaiah 1: 25 in volume 3 of this Commentary.

Verse 28. *Whom thou hatest* is to be understood in the same sense as *mind is alienated* that was explained at verse 22.

Verse 29. Men will sometimes tire of the very woman who has catered to their lusts, then they will "turn on her" and mistreat her with a vengeance. Likewise, the very heathen with whom Judah had played the harlot (idolatry) were to be given possession of her and they were to hold her as a captive for 70 years.

Verse 30. All these calamites were to come upon Judah as a punishment for her unfaithfulness to her husband who was the Lord.

Verse 31. *Give her cup* means that Judah was to receive the same *cup* or punishment as Israel and that was to be captivity. This was just, since she had taken up the same walk of life as that followed by her sister Israel.

Verse 32. *Deep and large* and *it containeth much* is used by way of emphasizing the statements of the preceding verse. The emphasis is certainly appropriate, for the subjugation of an established kingdom and the transferring of its population into a foreign land would be a very great humiliation and cause much comment.

Verse 33. *Drunkenness* is figurative and means they would be overwhelmed with humiliation and sorrow, even as the sister (Israel) had been a century before.

Verse 34. The language is still figurative, using a cup as the basis of the figure. With that form of imagery in view, the emphasis is expressed by representing them as being so greedy that they crush the cup by their action. *Pluck off breasts* indicates a gesture of despair by snatching at their breasts. Such a movement was an ancient custom used in times of great sorrow or astonishment. (See Luke 18: 13; 23: 48.)

Verse 35. When God's servants turn to other persons or objects with their devotions it is because they have forgotten Him. Jesus taught this truth in Matthew 6: 24. *Bear thy lewdness* has a twofold bearing. One is that they would have to bear the punishment due their sins, and the other is they would have to continue their lewdness which was idolatry, for they actually did have to continue that in the captivity.

Verse 36. *Wilt thou judge* is in the form of a question, but it really is an order from the Lord to judge the two women. The prophet was to charge them with the abominations they had committed against Him.

Verse 37. This verse combines the figurative with the literal terms for the same abomination. It explains the adultery of these women (Aholah and Aholibah; Samaria and Jerusalem) to be the practice of idolatry. They carried the service to the extent of offering their own children in sacrifice to the idols.

Verse 38. These wicked women went so far as to bring their immoral practice into the house provided by their husband, which is the meaning of the phrase *defiled my sanctuary*, for that was the house provided to shelter the sacred furniture.

Verse 39. These women are still being regarded as unfaithful wives, though this verse drops the figures and states the literal facts. The people of God actually made sacrifices of their children, and also set up idols in the temple.

Verse 40. These unfaithful wives were worse than the usual cases, for they even sent messengers to strange men to solicit their intimacies. This item is commented upon more fully at verse 16. When the men answered the invitation with their presence they found the women adorned with the "make-up" of impure characters.

Verse 41. After decorating their bodies in a suggestive manner, the men found them occupying a *stately* bed, one that belonged properly to the use of persons of special honor, there to receive the embraces of these strange men. Near the bed was a table on which were the materials with which they could refresh themselves at intervals with their unlawful intimacies with these wives of another person.

Verse 42. So inordinate were Aholah and Aholibah that they accepted men of both high and low rank. In order to give themselves an appearance of dignity, these men adorned themselves with hand decorations, and for the appearance of royal standing they wore crowns on their heads.

Verse 43. Men who are intent on full gratification of their lusts do not generally care for a worn out and old woman. These wives of the Lord were old at that business, hence He asks if these men will be satisfied with them.

Verse 44. *A woman that playeth the harlot* is usually one who is attractive from the standpoint of youth and who has plenty of sex appeal. These women had so adorned themselves that they made so great and favorable an appearance as to lure the men on. Consequently they went in unto them and committed adultery.

Verse 45. These women were guilty of spiritual adultery (idolatry) and of literal bloodshed. Hence righteous men were to judge them according to their just deserts. This does not mean the men would be righteous as to their personal character, but in executing God's judgment against the women they would be doing right.

Verse 46. This verse is an explanation of the preceding one. God was to use a foreign group to bring the unfaithful kingdoms into judgment and take them into exile.

Verse 47. The things predicted here actually came to pass according to the historical account given in 2 Kings 25th chapter.

Verse 48. *Cause lewdness to cease* is a prediction in figurative form that God's people would be cured of idolatry by the captivity. See the historical fulfillment of it at Isaiah 1: 25, volume 3 of this Commentary.

Verse 49. The figurative and literal terms for the same thing are again used in this verse. *Lewdness* means the same as *idols* and the unfaithful people of the Lord were to *bear the sins*, which means they were to bear the punishment due their sins.

EZEKIEL 24

Verse 1. The specific date of this chapter is given which is the *ninth year* after Ezekiel was taken to Babylon. The exact day and month of that year are also given, and on that day the siege of Jerusalem began.

Verse 2. Ezekiel was in Babylon and hence would have no knowledge of the exact movements of Nebuchadnezzar without the message from the Lord as here stated. To clarify the memory of the reader I will again state that the third stage of the 70-year captivity had not occurred, but it was about due and was to be started with a siege.

Verse 3. In illustrating what was soon to take place the people were to be impressed by a parable. This was to be done through the use of some more "acting" as we have previously seen in the history of the prophets. Ezekiel ordered someone to put on a pot or large kettle and put water in it. Such an action would mean that some process was to be done for the purpose of boiling something, and that was in order to effect some kind of purifying. If the fleshy parts of animals are boiled the objectionable portion will come to the top in the form of *scum* which can then be removed.

Verse 4. The city of Jerusalem was illustrated by the pot, and the pieces put into it were men of the nation. They were to be "boiled" or tested in order to remove the *scum* (wickedness) from them. Things that are physically impossible or at least highly improbable, may be supposed to happen in a parable. Thus the city of Jerusalem was the boiling pot to begin with because it was in that city where the characters were that needed to be purified by boiling. However, the actual purifying effect was to take place in Babylon, and for that particular phase of the whole transaction we must transfer the boiling vessel from Jerusalem to Babylon. In all other respects, though, the descriptive remarks apply to Jerusalem and the citizens remaining therein and in connection with it because of the many impurities in their lives.

Verse 5. *Choice of the flock* means the leaders or head men of the city. The word *burn* is from an original that means also "to pile." *Bones* is defined in the lexicon as meaning the body. The language means the pieces were to be piled round in such a way that would cause them to get the effect of the fire.

Verse 6. *Bloody city, to the pot.* For the explanation of this phrase see the comments on verse 4. *Let no lot fall upon it.* That is, make no exceptions among the pieces (the men of Jerusalem), for all of them must be put to the test in order to have the "scum" (wickedness) boiled out of them; all must either be killed or taken into captivity in Babylon.

Verse 7. The law of Moses (Leviticus 17:13) required that the blood of animals killed lawfully should be poured upon the ground and covered with dust. This was evidently as an act of respect, on the same principle that a dead body is buried honorably, since the blood is the life (Genesis 9:4; Leviticus 17:11). But these murderous adulteresses were even defiant in their disrespect for the innocent blood they had shed. They did not give it the courtesy of being covered out of sight by being absorbed in the ground, but poured it on a rock where every drop would be visible as a glaring proclamation of their arrogance.

Verse 8. Since these wicked women thus exposed disrespectfully the blood of innocent victims, the Lord in fury decreed that their guilty blood should likewise be exposed to the public view by spreading it upon a rock.

Verse 9. The *bloody city* is Jerusalem and the parable of the boiling pot is again referred to. The fury of God was to be manifested by making the fire great.

Verse 10. The thought of the preceding verse is continued in this. *Spice it well*. This was to make it more desirable so the foe would be more greedy in devouring it.

Verse 11. Here a slight change is made in the use of the parable. The enemy is to devour the desirable pieces that have been boiled, leaving the scum in the kettle. Then the pot is to be put back on the fire that the *brass* (the material of which the vessel is made) may get hot again. It was then to burn the scum right into the pores of the metal and thus be consumed.

Verse 12. She (Judah) had wearied or overworked herself in her eagerness to speak lies. This refers to the false prophecies and other misleading teaching that her outstanding men had done which had lulled the people into a state of false security.

Verse 13. The filthy lewdness refers to her idolatry which was never to be purged out of her until it was done by the Lord in the land of captivity. *Because I have purged thee* is in the sense as if it said "for this cause (namely, thy lewdness) I will purge thee (of idolatry) in the boiling pot of national chastisement."

Verse 14. There are no new thoughts offered in this verse, but several declarations of the determination of the Lord to carry out his threats on his unfaithful wife.

Verses 15, 16. Here we have a case where the Lord does some "acting" in the place of the prophet. *Desire of thine eyes* means something that he would desire to look upon, which it will be seen means his wife. It was doubtless a severe blow and seems regrettable that such a thing was made necessary by the cruel unfaithfulness of these wicked women. But God made a greater sacrifice when he gave his own Son to die in order to accomplish a universal benefit. And so the death of Ezekiel's wife was so necessary in the estimation of God that the prophet was forbidden to make any visible or audible complaint.

Verse 17. *Make no mourning for the dead* did not mean he was not allowed to have any feeling of grief, but that he was to make no outcry over it. In that sense he was to be dumb; not that he could not speak if occasion required. The closing expressions of the verse means he was to conduct himself in a normal manner and not act like one in mourning. *Eat not the bread of men.* When death enters a home it is customary for neighbors to relieve the family of the burden and worry of household tasks by coming in and providing the meals. Ezekiel was restricted from accepting any such favors, because that would be an outward demonstration of mourning.

Verse 18. There are two mornings spoken of in this verse, one was on the day when God was to take away "the desire of his eyes," the other was the morning of the next day. In the first morning Ezekiel spoke to the people about what was to happen and in the evening of that day the "stroke" came which was the death of his wife. The next morning the prophet started his attitude of apparent indifference *as I was commanded*.

Verse 19. The conduct of Ezekiel was so unusual for one whose home was darkened by death, and especially by the death of one's companion. This caused the people to ask him for an explanation of *what these things are to us*.

Verse 20. The prophet replied by telling them it was according to the *word of the Lord*. He had to speak in order to give them such a reply, which shows that the dumbness that was attributed to him for a period of years was not a physical defect imposed upon him. He was to be *dumb* or silent as to making an audible complaint.

Verse 21. Ezekiel continued the explanation of his strange conduct upon the death of his wife. In doing so we are given a clue as to the purpose of both the death of the prophet's wife and of the conduct he was directed to maintain. It was a symbol of what was to befall the people of Judah and the attitude they were to manifest. They, like the prophet, were to lose something that was dear to them namely, their capital city with its citizens. *Profane my sanctuary* means the holy city and temple were to be given over into the hands of the heathen who would strip them of their belongings and put a stop to the sacred ceremonies.

Verse 22. The people of Judah, like the prophet, were not to make demonstrations of grief over their loss. This was to preclude their accepting any favors from others who might be disposed to offer them, such as food and the comforts of life.

Verse 23. *Tires* is from PEER which Strong defines, "An embellishment, i.e. fancy head-dress." It would not usually be worn in times of distress, but these people were commanded to wear them just the same as if nothing had happened. *Not mourn nor weep* had reference to the formal outward demonstrations in the sight of the general public. But they were permitted to *mourn one toward another*, which means they could have their grief if they (people of Judah) kept it among themselves.

Verse 24. *Ezekiel is unto you a sign*. This gives the key to the situation, that the misfortune of the prophet and his conduct concerning it, was to be an example of how the people of Judah were to act upon the misfortune of losing their city.

Verse 25. The preceding verse informed the people of Judah of the connection between them and Ezekiel, and this verse, addressed to the prophet, informs him when the "sign" is to be carried out. It is to be when the Lord takes from them *the desire of their eyes* which we understand to be their capital city of Jerusalem.

Verse 26. *He that escapeth* means one who escapes from Jerusalem at the time of its capture and destruction. Ezekiel will still be in Babylon when that misfortune occurs, just as he was at the time all this "acting" was being done. The one who escapes will go to Babylon and tell the prophet by word of mouth of the destruction of Jerusalem, which will have been revealed to him that same day by inspiration.

Verse 27. *In that day . . . be no more dumb* means that the restrictions which Ezekiel had been under, explained at verse 17, will be lifted and he will be permitted to express himself according to his feelings.

EZEKIEL 25

General remarks. The writing against the people of Judah is now interrupted and for several chapters the prophet will give God's judgments against some heathen nations. The next time he writes concerning Judah it will be chiefly of a reassuring tone. But before taking up that line it will be appropriate to publish the Lord's denunciations against these foreign peoples because they had been so hostile against His people. It will be well, therefore, to regard these chapters as an interval in the general book of Ezekiel, and the comments will be made as if the several chapters were an independent document. It will also be seen that the chapters in this interval are not always chronological as to dates. We will now study the chapters as they come.

Verses 1, 2. *Set thy face* is a figurative way of telling Ezekiel to prophesy against the Ammonites. These people were distantly related to Judah but had been hostile against them and were considered their enemies.

Verse 3. God has always been jealous of his own people and would tolerate no rejoicing when they met with any misfortune. This verse explains why Ezekiel was told to *set his face* against the Ammonites. They had said *aha* when the land of Israel was made desolate and when the temple was defiled by strangers. That is an expression of derision and indicates a feeling of rejoicing over the misfortunes of God's people.

Verse 4. *East* is defined in Smith's Bible Dictionary as referring to the lands lying immediately eastward of

Palestine namely, Arabia, Mesopotamia and Babylonia. The *men of the east*, therefore, means the people of those territories who were to come against the Ammonites, destroy their buildings and consume their products.

Verse 5. Rabbah was the chief city of the Ammonites, and it would be a reproach to have it reduced to a stabling place for the beasts of service. The people in general were destined to become a couchingplace or place for resting for the flocks.

Verse 6. The bodily acts described were condemned because they were done in a tone of rejoicing over Judah's experiences. *With all thy despite* means they had a feeling of contempt for God's people.

Verse 7. *I will stretch out mine hand* indicates that God would be the cause of the defeat coming upon the Ammonites. That people was a heathen nation, itself, but the word is used in the general sense and the prediction meant that another nation was to be used as an instrument of the Lord for the purpose of chastisement.

Verse 8. Moab and Seir were two countries bordering against each other and joined in their belittling of Judah, which was bound to bring down the wrath of God upon them.

Verse 9. *Open the side* means the Lord decreed a general attack upon these people, beginning with the frontier cities named in this verse.

Verse 10. Verse 4 threatened the Ammonites with invasion by the *men of the east* and the lands of Moab and Seir are here destined to meet the same fate.

Verse 11. The primary motive of all these instances of chastisement is stated, which was that people would *know that I am the Lord.*

Verse 12. The Edomites were indirectly referred to in verse 8 where Seir ("Edom was called *Mount Seir* and Idumea,"—Smith's Bible Dictionary) and Moab are included in the same prediction. In the present verse they are considered as a separate people.

Verse 13. When God decrees that one nation shall come against another, that is regarded as the work of His hand. *Teman* and *Dedan* were districts in the Edomite country located in opposite directions from each other. The last clause of the verse means that the slaying of their men would take place from one of these sections to the other.

Verse 14. Sometimes the Lord chastises one heathen nation by the services of another, but in the case of the Edomites it was to be accomplished *by the hand of my people Israel*. In performing this service they would be manifesting the vengeance of God. (See Romans 12: 19; 2 Corinthians 7: 11.)

Verse 15. The Philistines were a people who lived near the Mediterranean Sea. *With a despiteful heart* means to do something "for spite," and these people were charged with that in their dealings with God's people. *Old hatred.* According to the lexicon the first word may be defined either by "old" or "perpetual." The history shows that either definition may apply, for the hatred of the Philistines against the Israelites was continually manifested from the beginning of their residence in Palestine and that would make it old.

Verse 16. The *Cherethims* were lifeguards according to Smith's Bible Dictionary and the lexicon of Strong agrees with it. Doubtless they were employed by the Philistines to serve and support them against the people of God. The present prediction threatened to take this support from them as a punishment for their hateful conduct.

Verse 17. Again the chief purpose of God in his chastisements of evil nations is stated, and it is that *they shall know that I am the Lord.*

EZEKIEL 26

Verse 1. The chapters in the "interval" (see "General remarks" at the beginning of Chapter 25) are interspersed with dates, but they are not always chronological. All of them, however, are dated from the captivity of Jehoiachin at which time Ezekiel was taken to Babylon. The present chapter is the eleventh year since that event, and it happens to be the last year of the reign of Zedekiah. There is no particular connection between these dates and the predictions uttered against the various nations. All we know is that the Lord saw fit to give us some of the dates.

Verse 2. Phoenicia was a narrow tract of country north of Palestine and lying along the coast of the Mediterranean Sea. Its principal cities were Tyrus (or Tyre) and Sidon and especially the former. Because of its outstanding importance it has been referred to in the prophecies and histories, even when the writers may have been considering the country in general. There are several chapters devoted to this nation and city beginning with this verse. See chapter 25: 3 for the meaning of *aha*. *Gates of the people* is a figurative expression used because of the position of the city as a commercial center. *Turned unto me*. The first person is used because Tyrus is the speaker, gloating over her imagined supremacy in her traffic against Jerusalem.

Verse 3. *Therefore* expresses the conclusion of the Lord against Tyrus. He decrees that many nations were to come against this city, so many and so powerful that it is compared to the waves of the sea dashing up against the land.

Verse 4. In connection with this verse I shall make a quotation from Smith's Bible Dictionary, and I request the reader to note especially the words *walls, dust* and *rock* as he reads the quotation because they are important words in the verse of the present paragraph. "At that time [Alexander's attack in 332 B.C.] Tyre was situated on an island half a mile from the mainland; it was completely surrounded by prodigious [huge] walls, the loftiest portion of which on the side fronting the mainland reached a height of not less than 150 feet; and notwithstanding the persevering efforts of Alexander, he could not have succeeded in his attempt if the harbor of Tyre to the north had not been blockaded by the Cyprians and that to the south by the Phoenicians, thus affording an opportunity to Alexander for uniting the island to the mainland by an enormous mole. (The materials for this he obtained from the remains of old Tyre, scraping the very dust from her rocks into the sea, as prophesied by Ezekiel, Ezekiel 26: 3, 4, 12, 21, more than 250 years before.)"

Verse 5. *Spreading of nets* refers to the act of washing out their nets by fishermen and spreading them out to dry. Such a use of a place would indicate that the region was practically barren, its inhabitants having been either slain or deported. *Midst of the sea* has reference to the new city of Tyre that was built on an island half a mile out into the sea when the inhabitants of the city on the mainland realized they were losing the contest to Nebuchadnezzar. *Become a spoil to the nations* means the reduced condition of the city would expose her to the nations who would take advantage of her lot and take her possessions to themselves. In corroboration of the many statements in this verse and elsewhere about Tyre, I shall give a quotation from history. The emphasis will be mine, added for the purpose of directing the attention of the reader to words of special significance. "With Jerusalem subdued, Nebuchadnezzar pushed with all his force the siege of the Phoenician city of Tyre, whose investment [formation of a siege] had been commenced several years before. In striking language the prophet Ezekiel (29: 18) describes the length and hardness of the siege: 'every head was made bald, and every shoulder was peeled.' After thirteen years Nebuchadnezzar was apparently forced to raise the siege." Myers, Ancient History, page 72. "Nebuchadnezzar laid siege to the great merchant-city, Tyre, which was still rich and strong enough to hold out for thirteen years. Ezekiel says that Nebuchadnezzar and his host had no reward for their heavy service against Tyre, and the presumption is that the city capitulated [surrendered] on favorable terms." Britannica, Volume 18, page 808. "Accordingly, at the time we are speaking of, she (Tyre) was in a condition to resist, thirteen years together, a monarch to whose yoke all the rest of the East had submitted. It was not till after so many years that Nebuchadnezzar made himself master of Tyre. His troops suffered incredible hardships before it; so that, according to the prophet's expression, 'every head was made bald, and every shoulder was peeled.' Before the city was reduced to the last extremity, its inhabitants retired, with the *greatest part of their effects*, into a neighboring *ISLE*, half a mile from the shore, where they built a new city; the name and glory of which extinguished the remembrance of the old one, which from thenceforward became a *mere village*, retaining the name of ancient Tyre. Nebuchadnezzar and his army having undergone the utmost fatigues during so long and difficult a siege, and having *found nothing in the place to requite them* for the service they had rendered to Almighty God in executing his vengeance upon the city, God was pleased to promise by the mouth of Ezekiel that he would give them the spoils of Egypt for a recompence." Rollin's Ancient History, volume 1, page 472. "The Tyrians also offered submission, but refused to allow Alexander [The Great] to enter the city and sacrifice in the temple of Hercules. Alexander was determined to make an example of the first sign of opposition that did not proceed from Persian officials, and at once began the siege. It lasted *seven months*, and, though the king, with enormous toil, drove a mole [huge wall laid in the sea] from the mainland to the island, he made little progress till the Persians were mad enough to dismiss the fleet and give him command of the sea through his Cyprian and Phoenician allies. The town was at length forced in July, 332; 8,000 Tyrians were slain, 30,000 inhabitants sold as slaves, and only a few notables . . . were spared. Tyre thus *lost its political existence*, and the foundation of Alexandria presently changed the lines of trade and gave a blow perhaps still more fatal to the Phoenician cities." Britannica, volume 18, page 809. Myers' Ancient History, page 275. Josephus, Antiquities, 11-8-3.

Verse 6. The original for *daughters* has a very wide range of meanings, even including "cities" and "townships." Land or earth cannot be literally *slain by the sword*, so the evident bearing of the clause is that not only will Tyre be attacked and her citizens slain, but the ones living in the surrounding areas will be killed. The purpose is to make the people realize *that I am the Lord*.

Verse 7. This verse specifically predicts the attack by Nebuchadnezzar on the city of Tyre. For the historical fulfillment of this prediction, see the long quotation in connection with verses 4, 5. *From the north* is explained by the historical note offered in connection with Isaiah 14: 31 in volume 3 of this Commentary.

Verse 8. *Daughters in the field is* explained at verse 6. *Fort* and *mount* means the embankments raised against a city, and *buckler* means a pointed instrument for the purpose of bodily defense in close-up conflict.

Verse 9. *Engines of war* were large instruments for the hurling of stones with the intent of battering down the walls. The *towers* were the structures erected in the most important places and the *axes* were for the purpose of cutting them down.

Verse 10. The great number of horses in the cavalry of the Babylonians is indicated by the dust they could stir up. It was to be so dense that it would envelop the people of Tyre. The *noise* would not literally shake the walls. The idea is that they would shake at the time of the noise, and the physical cause would be horses and chariots and other instruments and men of the invading army.

Verse 11. These horses were both the ones that drew the war chariots and those that carried the cavalrymen. The men in both divisions of the service were to use the sword against the common citizens of the city, and likewise the *garrisons* or fortified groups of soldiers were to be slain.

Verse 12. The invaders were to take possession of the personal effects and also were to seize upon their commercial wares. They were also destined to wreck the houses, both the ones used for storage and the ones used as homes. *Dust in the midst of the water* is explained at verse 4.

Verse 13. In captivity the people of Judah would not feel like singing or playing on their instruments. This state of mind is well described in the 137th Psalm.

Verse 14. *The top of a rock* would be a bare spot with no earth or other substance for supporting life. It would be fit only for uses such as the spreading out of nets for drying. Such a circumstance is used to describe the desolate condition Judah would be in after the Babylonians conquered them.

Verse 15. The Lord's feeling against Tyrus was so intense that the city is named 14 times in course of the chapters in this "interval." *Isles* is from an original that Strong defines "a habitable spot," and it means the people of various areas will shake or be shocked at the downfall of Tyrus.

Verse 16. *Princes of the sea* refers to the merchants of Tyrus whose traffic was conducted on the sea. In Isaiah 23: 8 they are spoken of as such where the passage says "whose merchants are princes." *Thrones* and *robes* are figurative and so used in view of the control that the merchants of Tyrus had over the sea traffic. In the place of such gorgeous or showy garments they were to wear those of *trembling*. That will be caused by the attack of the nation that God will bring against them.

Verse 17. *They* refers to the people of the "isles" as explained in verse 15. The *lamentation* here signifies the same as "shake" in the other verse. The frequent reference to the sea in one form or another is due to the position of Tyrus geographically. The city was located on the shore of the mainland at first, then it was situated on the island half a mile out into the sea. Such a location gave her an advantage over others in regard to sea traffic. But the city was very boastful of her advantage and became overconfident of her power against other cities.

Verse 18. The word *isles* still means habitable spots wherever located, but in this verse it has both meanings. They were isles because they were surrounded by the water of the Mediterranean Sea, and they were inhabited spots, hence were "isles" in that sense and their people were concerned in the predictions being made.

Verse 19. *Great waters shall cover thee* is both literal and figurative. The enemy army would be so overwhelming that it would be like a flood. And by destroying the walls and other structures of the city, the waters of the sea would actually flow over it.

Verse 20. *Pit* means a state of obscurity or forgetfulness, and such a lot was decreed against Tyrus. *With the people of old times* means people of earlier times who had gone down in defeat under the attacks of hostile forces. *Set glory in the land of the living*. By putting an end to the greatness of Tyrus so her glory will be dead, God's own glory will shine in the lands where national life still shines.

Verse 21. Nothing new is contained in this verse; it is a summing up of the desolate condition to be brought by the Lord upon Tyrus.

EZEKIEL 27

Verses 1, 2. The first verses are almost identically alike in many of the chapters of this book, hence I have combined it with the second verse after a comment in one or two places. And it will be well to make occasional reference to its significance, notwithstanding the general grouping just stated. The thought should be observed that Ezekiel received his instructions from the Lord and so his writings are inspired. On the phrase *son of man* see the comments at chapter 2: 1. *Lamentation for Tyrus* does not signify the personal sentiments of the prophet, although he may have felt some of them because of his humane temperament. The thought is that he was to predict a lamentable condition to come upon that city.

Verse 3. *Entry of the sea.* Tyrus was on the shore of the Mediterranean Sea and that gave the city a great advantage in commerce. She could trade with foreign ports without any land transportation, then send her land conveyances inland with the wares obtained oversea and exchange them for manufactured products. This fact is meant by the phrase *merchant of the people*, and the situation filled her with pride and caused her to say boastfully, *I am of perfect beauty*.

Verse 4. *Borders* means boundaries and the main thought in the verse is that Tyrus had full use of the sea for her traffic. Her *builders* or workmen and men in the service of the city used the advantages of the sea to bring their beloved metropolis to the highest possible perfection.

Verse 5. Having the "range" of the sea at her command, that encouraged these builders to make vessels for that purpose. And here we can see another advantage in being situated on the seacoast. It was near the famous forests of the Lebanon district and hence in easy access to some of the best materials for shipbuilding.

Verse 6. The oak timber was another good material connected with the building and propelling of ships in the special item of oars, for those parts would require strength to resist the strain of pulling. Cedar and fir are not so strong, but that quality was not important for the body of a ship; it was lighter in weight and hence better adapted to a vessel that was to float on water. The *benches* refers to the decks which were made of ivory, and this is another indication of the city's luxurious condition.

Verse 7. No ordinary material was used for sails although it might have served the purpose very well. But this city with such a "high standard" in her ambitions obtained linen that was produced in Egypt, which was of especially high quality. Smith's Bible Dictionary has the following to say of this product. "Egypt was the great center of the linen trade. Some linen, made from the Egyptian *byssus*, a flax that grew on the banks of the Nile, was exceedingly soft and of dazzling whiteness." (See 1 Kings 10: 28). *Blue* and *purple* are colors but the expression has reference to the fabrics that were so colored. *Elishah* was a place supposed to have been inhabited by the descendants of a son of Javan who had that name (Genesis 10: 4). These fine goods and dies were obtained from this territory because they were of exceptional quality. *Covered* is from

MEKACCEH, and a part of Strong's definition is, "an awning from the sun."

Verse 8. Because of the prestige of Tyrus she could "have her pick" of men for service. The inhabitants of *Zidon* (another city of that nation) and *Arvad* (a small island near the Phoenician coast) were skilled well enough for the general service expected of mariners, but the more particular business of guiding the ships was left to the trained and skilful men of the city of Tyrus.

Verse 9. *Calkers* were those who looked after leaks in a vessel and also supplied any extra girders that might appear to be necessary for the support of the ship. The *ancients of Gebal* were men selected for this important work because their age and experience made them more reliable.

Verse 10. The significance of naming these places in the several verses is to show the extensive resources of man power which Tyrus possessed. These men referred to in this verse took personal interest in the security and also the attractiveness of the chief city of Phoenicia.

Verse 11. The men of *Arvad* are mentioned in verse 8 who were used in the service of handling the work on board the ships. The same place furnished other men to guard the walls of the city. *Towers* were structures erected in important spots for the purpose of defense. The men who would be assigned to such a post would need to be brave and able in repelling a foe. *Gammadims* is from the Hebrew word GAMMAD which Strong defines, "A warrior (as grasping weapons)." A shield is a protective armor and these warriors were provided with such articles so well that they had them to hang round on the walls, indicating the completeness of their equipment.

Verse 12. *Tarshish* was a town on the western coast of the Mediterranean Sea. This seaport produced the metals named in the verse, then transported them over the sea to Tyrus and exchanged them for the goods on sale in her markets.

Verse 13. *Javan, Tubal* and *Meshech* were originally the names of men. but at the time of our verse the names stand for the groups of descendants coming down from them. Those groups supplied Tyrus with slaves, and material or inanimate articles.

Verse 14. *Togarmah*, like the names in the preceding verse, was the name of a specific man, but who had a host of descendants who formed a group that retained the name of their ancestor. In conjunction with the statements of this verse, I shall cite the statement of Smith's Bible Dictionary. "His [Togarmah's] descendants became a people engaged in agriculture, breeding horses and Mules to be sold in Tyre."

Verse 15. *Men of Dedan* means the group of people who descended from that man, who traded in the markets of Tyrus. *Isles* is defined in the lexicon as "a habitable spot." A great many places or groups have been and still will be specified as those dealing in the markets of Tyrus. The prophet interrupts that line to make a general statement concerning the extensive commerce of the city in the words, *many isles were the merchandise of thine hand. Present* is used in the sense of a return payment for value received. *Horns* is said of the ivory because the shape of the elephant's tusk resembles a horn, and the article was evidently transported in its natural form.

Verse 16. This verse is along the same line as the others of the chapter. Syria brought the products of her country to the city of Tyrus and exchanged them for the manufactured wares of that great seaport.

Verse 17. Among the many peoples and countries who traded with Tyrus was that of God's nation. There is not much difference between *Judah* and *land of Israel;* the first is a division of the second. *Minnith* is a place east of the Jordan that produced wheat which was taken to the market in Tyrus. Other products of Palestine are named among the ones carried to the Phoenician city. *Pannag* is said to be of uncertain meaning, but the nearest suggestion is in Strong's lexicon where he says it is "probably pastry." The other products are called by their usual names.

Verse 18. *Damascus* was the chief city of Syria which was an important country on the east border of Phoenicia. *Helbon* was a city near Damascus and Smith's Bible Dictionary says it was "celebrated as producing the finest grapes in the country." This product as well as a fine quality of wool was taken to Tyrus and exchanged for her wares.

Verse 19. *Dan* was a son of Jacob and *Javan* was a descendant of Noah, but both words came to be names of towns. The people of those places traveled to and from between their communities and Tyrus to deal in the markets of that Phoenician city. *Bright iron* is rendered "wrought iron" in the Revised Version, which indicates it was iron that had been refined to some extent. *Cassia* was the bark of some kind of tree that had an aromatic odor. *Calamus* was a plant of the reed family and one of its uses was that of making paper for writing and other purposes.

Verse 20. *Dedan* has already been mentioned (verse 15) as one of the traders with Tyrus, but that verse is not very specific as to its products. The present verse tells us that the article it took to Tyrus was *precious clothes for chariots.* The last word has a very indefinite meaning in the lexicon, including men who ride in chariots and those who ride on horses as cavalrymen. The phrase means some fine covering for the bodies of these men.

Verse 21. *Arabia* was an open country and its people worked in the production of sheep and goats. It is not strange, therefore, that such things were taken by them to be offered in exchange for the wares of Tyrus.

Verse 22. *Sheba* and *Raamah,* like some other words, were originally names of certain men, but finally were applied to groups of people who descended from them. They were among the ones who traded in the market of Tyrus.

Verse 23. Some of the names in this verse were once those of men, but at the time of this writing all of them referred to towns or countries. *Were thy merchants* means they traded with Tyrus, exchanging with each other their respective products.

Verse 24. The gist of this verse is that the places mentioned in the preceding verse made cedar chests, filled them with fine clothes, bound them shut with cords, and then took them to Tyrus to exchange for her manufactured merchandise.

Verse 25. *Sing* is defined in the lexicon, "To turn, i.e. travel about (as a harlot or a merchant)." Considering the general subject, and the correct rendering of the original for *sing,* the clause means the ships of Tarshish "travel for thee because of thy market." The result is that Tyrus is replenished or made richer, and is able to make a glorious appearance in the midst of the sea. However, the various success of the merchandising of Tyrus filled her with pride and a feeling of independence which caused the Lord to decree her downfall.

Verse 26. Up to the present time the subject matter has been the prosperous state of Tyrus. The Lord was sorely displeased with the city and decreed to humble her by a series of defeats at the hands of other nations. But as a partial reason for the chastisement of this enemy of His people, he had the prophet present to her a long list of the resources from which she had obtained her wealth and other advantages. After presenting to the proud city this picture, He changes the subject and begins to portray to her some of the calamities that are to befall her. In some of the verses the terms and imagery are those that belong to the sea and the business and activities of it. In some there is a mixture of the two kinds of illustrations. The comparisons cannot always be meant literally, for no history shows Tyrus ever to have suffered the ruin at sea that is herein set forth. The selection of terms, however, is appropriate, since the whole history of the city is one of the sea and of the traffic by Tyrus thereon. Let the reader bear in mind that while the language will be that of a sea and a ship and the men managing it, the real subject usually is the "ship of state," and the sea is the world of business and politics, and the mariners are the men in high places in the city. Hence in the present verse the *rowers* (rulers) have brought the city into *great waters* (in contact with others nations). The *east wind* (nations from the east) *hath broken thee* (defeated the city) *in the midst of the sea* (in the power of the besiegers).

Verse 27. This is one of the verses with a mixture of literal and figurative terms. *Fall into the midst of the seas* is figurative and refers to the defeat of Tyrus at the hands of attacking nations. The *calkers* are the men supposed to manage the affairs of the city, while the other terms are literal.

Verse 28. This short verse is an interesting combination of the literal and figurative. *Suburbs* is from MIGRASH and Strong defines it, "A suburb (i.e. open country whither flocks are driven for pasture); hence area around a building, or the margin of the sea." The literal territory surrounding Tyrus was to be taken over by the enemy and that would cause the men of the city to cry out in despair. Such an event will be like a ship that has been attacked and defeated, which would cause the pilots to raise a wail that could be heard all around the shore of the sea.

Verse 29. This verse describes (figuratively) the utter dejection the men of Tyrus will manifest when their beloved city is overthrown by the enemy.

Verse 30. This describes in literal terms the actual behaviour the men of Tyrus will show at the defeat of their city. The use of *dust* and *ashes* and *sackcloth* was an ancient custom resorted to in times of great distress or anxiety.

Verse 31. This verse describes some more of the customs of old times to express grief. They actually shaved off the hair of the head to produce artificial baldness.

Verse 32. This verse is all literal, even the reference to the sea, since the city of Tyrus was finally situated on an island half a mile out into the sea.

Verse 33. This refers to the extensive trade that Tyrus once had with other cities. The business was conducted by vessels that *went forth out of the seas*.

Verse 34. The first part of this verse is figurative and refers to the "seas" of enemy nations. This circumstance will literally cause the downfall of the commercial success of Tyrus, which will mean the loss of her main support.

Verse 35. *Isles* means "habitable spots," and the people in those places will be overwhelmed at the downfall of so great a city as Tyrus. *They shall be troubled* will be natural, for if so powerful a city as Tyrus can be thus brought to ruin, what might be the fate of other cities less strong?

Verse 36. *Never shalt be any more* is comparative, for Tyrus does exist even at the present time (1949). But it never regained its independence or commercial power, and was always a subject under other nations.

EZEKIEL 28

Verses 1, 2. The *prince* of Tyrus refers to the king of the city (see verse 12) who was very boastful. His successful dealings with nations and cities over land and sea had filled him with pride. *I am a god* is a strong wording for the actual feelings of the king, meaning he regarded himself as a sort of superman. The prophet was directed to declare unto this proud king of Tyrus that he was only a human being.

Verse 3. This verse is what is known in literature and oral speech as irony, a form of expression in which the author says the very opposite of what he means. It is a very pointed kind of rebuke, and generally is employed where the person addressed is regarded as being unworthy of more serious consideration. Job used such a form of speech in his reply to the three friends. (See Job 12: 2.)

Verse 4. The king of Tyrus was not as wise as he thought, yet he was not unintelligent, for he had succeeded in attracting the commerce of other cities. He had dealt with them in such a manner as to make a considerable profit.

Verse 5. The fact of gaining riches would not have caused the king to be condemned, but it was his pride of heart over it that condemned him. This principle is taught in the New Testament (Mark 10: 24; 1 Timothy 6: 10, 17).

Verse 6. *Set thine heart . . . as God.* He had let his heart at least pretend to think he was equal with God, because of his success in the accumulation of riches.

Verse 7. *Strangers* means persons of another country, and the terrible kind of people of such a country as that would be the kind used in the matter. The wisdom of the king of Tyrus will not be any defense against the sword of the enemy.

Verse 8. *Pit* is from a word that means obscurity or forgetfulness. Many of the men of Tyrus were destined to die a literal death, but also the city was to die figuratively in that it would lose its greatness never to be fully regained. (See the comments on the last verse of the preceding chapter.)

Verse 9. The king of Tyrus was very boastful and tried to believe that no being was as good as he. The Lord represents him as being so vain that he would even maintain his superiority while in the presence of the force that had him in subjection.

Verse 10. Physical circumcision would mean nothing to a citizen of Phoenicia, hence there would be no point in threatening him with some treatment by an uncircumcised person. History shows that when God uses an uncircumcised man to execute His wrath upon an individual it is considered a deep disgrace (1 Samuel

Ezekiel 28: 11-24

31: 4). Hence the word—is directly connected with *strangers* in this threatening prediction against the king of Tyrus. Another thing, it would be logical to expect God to impose his severest punishments upon the uncircumcised person because that means an unconsecrated one.

Verse 11, 12. *Take up a lamentation* is explained at chapter 27: 2. *Sealest up the sum* is a strained rendering of the original. The first is from CHATHAM which Strong defines, "to close up," and the last is from TOKNIYTH which the same authority defines, "admeasurement," and that is from still another Hebrew word that means "a fixed quantity." The phrase has to do with the conduct of the king of Tyrus, and of his changed state of mind after he became evil affected by his many successes. The key to it is in the words *till iniquity was found in thee* in verse 15. He had manifested a degree of wisdom and God had favored him with many good things because his conduct was pleasing to Him. But when great power and riches came to him he became vain and discarded his good judgment and wisdom; he "sealed it up" or ended it.

Verse 13. A few verses will describe the high standing the king had while his heart was right. The reference to Eden and mention of precious stones and metal is largely figurative and said to explain the subject by comparison.

Verse 14. This verse, like the preceding one, is figurative, portraying the favor of God that was bestowed on the king of Tyrus while he was worthy of it. We have evidence elsewhere in the Bible that God takes an interest in the affairs of earthly governments and their rulers. (See Daniel 4: 17; 5: 18, 21, 26.) The terms of this verse are also comparative and the *mountain of God* means the government of Tyrus was given to this king by the God who "rules in the kingdoms of men" as stated in the passages cited in the preceding verse.

Verse 15. This verse is explained in the comments on verse 12.

Verse 16. *Merchandise . . . violence.* The connection between these words is in the fact that the prosperity of Tyrus filled her with pride and that in turn caused her to become wicked and violent. *Cast out of the mountain.* See verse 14 for comments on *mountain* and the relation of Tyrus to it. The favorable condition was to be reversed on account of the evil turn in the conduct of the city.

Verse 17. Briefly speaking, the pride of Tyrus over the successes caused the city to destroy her good character. *Lay thee before kings* is a prediction of the subjugation to be suffered by Tyrus at the hands of foreign kings, such as Nebuchadnezzar and Alexander and possibly some others of less note.

Verse 18. *Defiled thy sanctuaries.* By her corrupt conduct and state of mind, the once fair name and standing of Tyrus was defiled. It was brought about by the prosperous results of the vast traffic on the sea. *Fire from the midst of thee* denotes that Tyrus would be "burned" by the *fire* of her own iniquity.

Verse 19. *Shalt be a terror* is explained at chapter 27: 35, and *never shalt be any more* is commented upon in the last verse of that chapter.

Verses 20, 21. Zidon was another city of Phoenicia about 20 miles north of Tyrus. It is otherwise spelled Sidon and is often referred to in other parts of the Bible including the New Testament. It was inferior to Tyrus yet was an important city in ancient times. The Lord had the prophet to deliver some warnings against that place because it had oppressed His people.

Verse 22. The primary object of all demonstrations against the city was that *they shall know that I am the Lord.* We can realize the need for such a display of power because of the almost universal tendencies toward idolatry in those days.

Verse 23. *Pestilence* (disease) and *the sword* (warfare) were to be brought upon the city of Zidon. This was to be accomplished through the services of some other strange people whom God would use as his agency in the matter.

Verse 24. Pricking brier refers to the bitter opposition that the Zidonians had waged against God's people. Some of the early accounts of the persecutions brought by these people against the children of Israel are recorded in Judges 3: 3. It is true God sponsored that oppression of His people to chastise them, but the Lord never would tolerate the personal motive the heathens entertained against them though they were carrying out the divine plan when they oppressed His people.

Verse 25. We have two verses that predict the return of the Jews from the Babylonian captivity. For about four chapters the prophet has been making accusations and predictions against the heathen nations that had mistreated His people, and soon he will resume his writing along that line. But God has always been jealous for the nation that was called by His name, and has been careful to let the other nations know of the divine care that is always over the Israelites. Many of the heathen people knew of the exile in Babylon of those people, and some of them even rejoiced over it. But the Lord determined to take their rejoicing over the unfortunate people away from them. Hence while this prediction was written in the book that could be read by the people of Israel, the immediate use of it was for the information of the heathen against whom He had been and still will be addressing the warnings. That explains why the challenging words *in the sight of the heathen* are inserted amid the prediction.

Verse 26. *Shall dwell safely* does not guarantee that Israel would never have any difficulty with other nations for she did. But she had no trouble in taking possession of the native land after the rulers in power came to understand the situation. (See the books of Ezra and Nehemiah.) The temporary difficulties that were intimated a few lines above were removed and the people of God went forward with their work of reconstruction and reformation. They even obtained material help and legal support from the heathen in their grand program of restoration. That is the meaning of the last half of the present verse, and once more the divine purpose was to be accomplished which was to make the people *know that I am the Lord*.

EZEKIEL 29

Verse 1. The prophet drops back a year in his prophecies and writes this passage in the *tenth year* which means the tenth year after he was taken to Babylon. He resumes his predictions against the heathen nations because of their mistreatment of Israel.

Verse 2. The next nation to be predicted against is Egypt and the writing is directed against *Pharaoh*. That does not mean any particular man for all the kings of Egypt took that name during a certain period, in the same manner as that of the Caesars of Rome or the Edwards and Henrys of England.

Verse 3. The lexicon defines *dragon* as a sea monster, and of course it is not applied literally to Pharaoh. The River Nile was virtually the life and support of the country by its deposit of silt on the land. This was caused by the annual overflow of the stream bringing the deposit down from the mountains, and also the moisture needed for vegetation was supplied by the flooding of this stream over the farm land. So important was the river to the life of the country that the Egyptians came to rank it among the most beloved of their gods. This called for the figurative phrase *lieth in the midst of his rivers*. The king even went so far as to claim the river as his own, and to make other vain and absurd statements.

Verse 4. We understand this language to be figurative, but all figures of speech are based on some literal facts or at least something that would be literally possible. The literal fact in the present case is the attachment of the king of Egypt and his people to the Nile and the creatures living in it, even to the extent of regarding them as gods. Hence the imagery is that of a great monster (the king) living in the river and mingling with the fish of the stream. By the same token, also, the capture of the king is likened to the taking of a large water creature wihch would be done by putting hooks in his jaws. *Fish . . . stick unto thy scales.* If the fish of a stream should stick to the body of a monster living therein, they would have to share the same fate with him when he is drawn out of the water. Likewise, the people of Egypt who adhered to Pharaoh in his wicked plots, would have to share with him when he is caught by an invader.

Verse 5. A fish cannot live long out of water, and so maintaining the imagery of water and fish in the illustration of the king of Egypt, it is predicted that he will be drawn out of his beloved river and cast out into the open field. Of course if a fish is left in the field it will become the prey of beasts and fowl, just as the king of Egypt was destined to become the victim of some other person.

Verse 6. *Been a staff of reed to Israel.* The Israelites turned their attention to Egypt when threatened with danger (chapter 17: 15) and that displeased the Lord.

Verse 7. It was not according to the will of God for his people to lean upon Egypt for support. However, since that nation evidently encouraged them to do so, it was like breaking a promise for it to come short of the assistance intimated that it would give. This failure was one cause of the Lord's wrath against that nation and it called forth His predictions against it which are here being recorded.

Verse 8. *I will bring a sword* refers to the attacks that were to be made upon the country of Egypt. When God uses a certain man or nation or army to accomplish an end, or even when He only predicts that it is to occur, it is often spoken of as if He is the one who does it. In the present case we shall see that God will be the cause of the particular invasion into Egypt.

Verse 9. In a land where people "worship the creature (created thing) more than the Creator," it is very necessary that they be taught to *know* the true Lord.

Verse 10. *Rivers* being in the plural form is not accidental for it is used in that sense a number of times in this chapter. The original word is defined by Strong as follows: "Of Egyptian origin; a channel, e. g. a fosse [ditch], canal, shaft; specifically the Nile, as the one river of Egypt, including its collateral [contributory] trenches." When the Nile overflowed something had to be done to take care of the water or it would be wasted. Hence the people of the country made these artificial channels to carry the precious liquid to the various parts of the land, even to the providing of small ditches that would bring the water to the very plants. All of these channels are called *rivers* and hence the word is used in the plural. The reader should see the historical evidence on irrigation quoted at Deuteronomy 11: 10, 11, volume 1 of this Commentary. The prediction is that Egypt was to be made *utterly waste*, but we shall learn soon that a specified period was to be decreed for the desolation. The location of *Syene* and *border of Ethiopia* makes the prediction mean that Egypt would be laid waste from one end to the other.

Verse 11. The specified period of time referred to in the preceding verse is named in this one, and the prediction is that the desolation will last *forty years*.

Verse 12. Only an inspired prophet could make such a definite prediction as the present verse records. This prediction is corroborated by history and I shall give a quotation as follows: "The king of Babylon, taking advantage therefore of the intestine divisions which the rebellion of Amasis had occasioned in that kingdom, marched thither at the head of his army. He subdued Egypt from Migdol or Magdol, a town on the frontiers of the kingdom, as far as Syene, in the opposite extremity where it borders on Ethiopia. He made a horrible devastation wherever he came; killed a great number of the inhabitants, and made such dreadful havoc in the country, that the damage could not be repaired in forty years. Nebuchadnezzar, having loaded his army with spoils, and conquered the whole kingdom, came to on accommodation [settlement] with Amasis; and leaving him as his viceroy [representative] there, returned to Babylon." Rollin's Ancient History, volume 1, page 232.

Verse 13. The desolation brought upon Egypt, like the captivity upon the Jews, was for the purpose of chastisement and not intended to be permanent. Thus the prediction is made of its restoration to national and industrial life after a time.

Verse 14. While Egypt was to return to national life it was not to come back to the height that it originally enjoyed but was to be a *base* or low kingdom. Verse 12 states that the Egyptians were to be dispersed among various countries, which occasions the prediction of the present verse about being brought back to Pathros, which was a part of Egypt.

Verse 15. The debasement of Egypt was to be comparative, not that it would cease to have any greatness at all. This verse expresses it by the phrase *not exalt itself above the nations;* it was to be subject to the influence of other countries.

Verse 16. *No more the confidence of the house of Israel* means that God's people will be convinced they cannot rely on Egypt for support. While they had at times in the past looked to it, the Lord was displeased and such iniquity was remembered by Him.

Verse 17. There is a long jump in the chronology of the writing of Ezekiel just for a more specific date of certain explanations to the prophet. God had told him that Egypt was to be visited with invasion and desolation, but that prediction was in the

Ezekiel 29: 18—30: 10

future as regards its fulfillment. Now the Lord sees fit to explain some things at this date which was after the prophet has been in Babylon 27 years.

Verse 18. When God uses one nation to chastise another He does not forget that agency if it renders faithful service. The Lord had directed Ezekiel to predict the successful invasion of Nebuchadnezzar into Egypt, but had not told him the reason for selecting that king as the instrument for the punishment of that country. That explanation is given in this verse, that it was to repay him for his faithful service against Tyrus, at which he did not reap any gain. It is necessary for the reader to see the long note quoted at Chapter 26: 4, 5, noting especially the words *found nothing in the place to requite them*, which definitely agrees with the present statement. *Serve a great service* is further explained by the clause *every head was made bald, and every shoulder was peeled*. This refers to the labor and hardships suffered in preparing a siege and attacking the walls with the battering-ram. In carrying baskets of material for the forts (which were carried on the head) the hair would be worn off that part of the body. A battering-ram was a large piece of timber with some hard substance on the end. This piece of timber was often used by being borne on the shoulders of the men, and that would wear the skin from their shoulders.

Verse 19. As a reward for his hard and faithful service against Tyrus, the Lord predicts that Nebuchadnezzar will invade Egypt and reap much from the spoils of the country. Again let the reader see the note referred to in the preceding verse.

Verse 20. *Have given him* is in the sense of something already done though it is prophecy, or at least some features of it are. *They wrought for me* denotes that when the soldiers of Nebuchadnezzar were carrying on the siege against Tyrus, it was regarded as work being done for the Lord.

Verse 21. When *horn* is used figuratively it means power or influence. When the people of Israel see the fulfillment of the prophecies that were delivered by Ezekiel, they will respect his place as a prophet of God. That will cause them to listen to his words and in that sense he will be given *the opening of his mouth*. As a further result of the entire circumstance, they will be made to *know that I am the Lord*.

EZEKIEL 30

Verses 1, 2. The prophet is told to express lamentation or *howl* in view of what is to happen to Egypt. *Worth* has no word in the original as a separate term, but is included with the same one for *woe* and means the same as saying "Ah, alas!"

Verse 3. The events just predicted are to take place in the near future from the time Ezekiel is writing this. *Time of the heathen* means the time when the nations are to come together in the manner alluded to in the predictions just made by the prophet.

Verse 4. Two chapters are given to Egypt, this and the preceding one. Ethiopia is included because that country lies just south of Egypt and became an ally in times of trouble. That is why its people will be in *pain* or fear when they see the people of Egypt being slain by the invading Babylonians.

Verse 5. *Libya, Lydia* and *Chub* were parts of Africa that were allied with Egypt for common support. If would follow, then, that when the land of Egypt is attacked, these allies will have to suffer with it.

Verse 6. The remarks offered in the preceding verse are verified in this. It is expressly stated that *they also that uphold Egypt shall fall*. It is as bad in God's sight to endorse an evildoer as it is to be the actual doer of it (Romans 1: 32).

Verse 7. *Shall be in the midst*. None of the cities of Egypt were to be actually moved into the territory of others. The expression means these cities were to share the same fate as the other cities suffered; would be in the same condition.

Verse 8. The fire to be set in Egypt will be the destructive raids of the Babylonians. The *helper* or allies of Egypt were destined to be defeated, and the whole transaction will cause the people to *know that I am the Lord*.

Verse 9. *In that day* refers to the day when Egypt would be attacked by the Babylonians. The Lord will then send men in ships to terrify Ethiopia for having been an ally of Egypt in her evil attitude toward the interests of His people.

Verse 10. *Multitude to cease* is a prediction that Nebuchadnezzar will attack the spoils of the country as well as its citizens. It will be *by the hand* of the Babylonian king, but he will be acting as the agency of God.

Verse 11. *He and his people* means Nebuchadnezzar and his military forces. *Terrible of the nations* is said of the Babylonians who had the reputation of being a fierce people. The Lord is going to bring these forces against Egypt to throw the country into a state of desolation and national humiliation.

Verse 12. In some way the Lord will interfere with the irrigation system of the country which will result in assisting the Babylonians in their attack upon the land. The effect of this interference with the watering program will be to lay waste the land.

Verse 13. The general subject of this chapter is the fate of Egypt, and the several verses specify certain cities or parts of the country. The prophet also reveals God's wrath against the idolatry that the country had practiced for centuries. The Egyptians worshiped everything in nature, both living and nonliving, and also set up their idols made of stone and other materials. God decreed that the manmade idols should be destroyed. That would teach them the uselessness of such gods, and also would prove that it is vain to rely on the things in nature as a means of superhuman assistance. The modern name for *Noph* is Memphis, which was an important city even then.

Verse 14. *Pathros* was a division of the country, and *Zoan* and *No* (Thebes) were cities, and the Egyptians had their idolatrous worship practiced in all of these places. God's jealousy against all forms of idolatry is so intense He will not tolerate it.

Verse 15. *Strength* is from an original word that Strong defines, "A fortified place; figuratively a defence," and the city of *Sin* is so described. The prediction is that with such a city on which to rely, it nevertheless will prove a failure as help for the Egyptians when the Lord brings the invading army against it.

Verse 16. This *fire* is explained at verse 8 where it is shown to refer to the upheaval that will be raised by the Babylonians. When it is started the people of these cities will *have great pain* which means they will be terrified by the presence of the invading forces that will be laying waste their strongest cities.

Verse 17. The *captivity* is not a formal or national one such as the Israelites were then suffering in Babylon, but refers to the capture of the citizens by the army of Nebuchadnezzar. *Aven* and *Pi-beseth* were cities where many of the *young men* or heroes of the country resided. These "braves" were to be destroyed by the Babylonian sword.

Verse 18. Smith's Bible Dictionary says the following of *Tehaphnehes:* "It was an important town, being twice mentioned by Jeremiah with Noph or Memphis. Here stood a house of Pharaoh-hophra before which Jeremiah hid great stones. Jeremiah 43: 8-10." The prediction is that even as strong a place as this city will be *darkened* which means to be subdued. *Yokes* is used in the sense of power or control, and this will be overthrown when Nebuchadnezzar comes into the country. The city will have her pride brought down by the death of her chief men, and her daughters shall be scattered among the cities of the various other heathen countries.

Verse 19. Again the main purpose of the judgments to be brought against an offending nation is stated, which is to make the people *know that I am the Lord.*

Verse 20. Another date is given for the message that God was giving to Ezekiel. The *eleventh year* is dated from the time the prophet was taken to Babylon.

Verse 21. *Broken the arm* means to destroy the force of the king of Egypt. *Shall not be bound up* is modified by the words *to be healed* following immediately. The idea is that nothing can prevent the calamity that is declared to be coming upon Pharaoh. *Roller* means bandage and the statement means the same as the preceding one explained above.

Verse 22. The Lord is using the imagery of a swordsman in the present form of speech. A man is holding a sword in his hand with the intention of using it against the approaching foe. But the Lord will strike and break the swordsman's arm which will cause the sword to fall from the hand holding it and it will fall to the ground.

Verse 23. If the ability to use their weapons is taken from them, the Egyptians will be helpless and will be at the mercy of their attackers.

Verse 24. Not much new is added in

this verse, but a specific statement of what is to happen to the land of Egypt is made. *I will strengthen* denotes that God will cause the weapons of the king of Babylon to be successful when he attacks Pharaoh. That will fulfill the prediction that was made to Ezekiel in chapter 29: 18.

Verse 25. God will perform two and opposite acts as regards Nebuchadnezzar and Pharaoh. He will strengthen the arms of the former and weaken those of the latter. Either one of these would have indicated defeat for Pharaoh, and hence the two will make it doubly certain and guarantee the fulfillment of the prediction.

Verse 26. Being utterly disarmed, the Egyptians will have no recourse on which to rest. As a result they will be scattered out in various places where they will languish for the period indicated in chapter 29: 12, 13.

EZEKIEL 31

Verse 1. The present message is dated in the same year that the one against Tyrus has, and it means the *eleventh year* after Ezekiel was taken to Babylon.

Verse 2. *Speak unto Pharaoh.* I do not take this to mean that the prophet was to make a personal contact with the Egyptian king. Ezekiel was in Babylon when he wrote this which is several hundred miles from Egypt and personal communications would be difficult if not impossible except by some miraculous performance. Furthermore, a like expression is found regarding the Ammonites and Tyrus, and we would not suppose that separate documents were sent to those places. The phrase could better be understood in the sense of "speak (or write) concerning Pharaoh." The whole book of Ezekiel was to become a unit in the Bible and the instruction of prophecy and its fulfillment was to be for the benefit of the world. *Whom art thou like* is in question form, but the thought is that the Lord announces He is going to make a comparison.

Verse 3. Care should be taken not to lose our "bearing" through the most of this chapter. It will be stating some things that actually happened to the Assyrians, but the purpose is to liken the case to Pharaoh. The Assyrians were a proud and cruel people and boasted of their strength, yet they were brought down in spite of their greatness. The parable as a whole is concerning Assyria and Egypt, hence, while the verses are directly applied to the former, some of the illustrations will be drawn from the conditions in the land of Egypt, since that country is really the one the Lord is denouncing at present. The illustration of a *cedar* is used because of the nature of that tree. Strong defines the original, "A cedar tree (from the tenacity of its roots)." We shall see the appropriateness of the illustration as we proceed in our study of the chapter. The *top* in a kingdom is the king and the *thick boughs* refers to the citizens of the nation, especially the princes and other leading men. This describes the position that the king of Assyria had in the day of his power (and of course is true of Pharaoh at the time the prophet is writing this).

Verse 4. The king of Assyria had a strong background in the day of his greatness, growing with the roots in the waters. (See Psalms 1.) The reference to waters is made because Egypt (which is the actual subject of this parable) depended upon the Nile with its canals and smaller channels.

Verse 5. The exaltation of Assyria is still being used to illustrate the pride of Pharaoh. And since he is the one who is actually the object of God's fury, the terms are those connected with a body of water such as the Egyptians possessed.

Verse 6. As a large tree would support and shelter many fowls, so the Assyrian Empire included in its folds many people of the world. This fact caused the king of Assyria to be filled with pride, just as Pharaoh was puffed up over his gains by the support from the Nile in its resources for irrigation.

Verse 7. A tree that lacks moisture will not be *fair* (beautiful), while one that can daily drink from "earth's sweet flowing breast" will leaf out and put on growth of foliage and shoots for new life.

Verse 8. The king of Assyria is still being compared to a tree that excels all others. Carrying out this imagery it is said that the trees in the *garden of God* (garden of Eden) could not *hide* ("over-shadow"—Strong) him. This comparison is very appropriate, for the trees in that first garden are spoken of as very desirable (Genesis 2: 9). Other trees are mentioned also as being inferior to this one of Assyria.

Verse 9. *I have made him fair.* It

was the will of God that the king of Assyria (likewise the king of Egypt) should have great power (See Daniel 2: 37; 4: 17; 5: 18; Romans 13: 1) provided he would use it right. *Trees . . . envied him* will be understood to be figurative and is another way of stating the superiority of Assyria (and Egypt for whose sake the comparison is being made) over other kingdoms.

Verse 10. True greatness is not to be condemned, but it is wrong for a man to exalt himself, or to become proud over any greatness that he really possesses. The king of Assyria did this and provoked the Lord to wrath.

Verse 11. The king of Assyria (who was Saracus at this time) was a "heathen" as well as were others, but the original means "nations" also, and the prediction means he was delivered into the hands of other heathen. The *mighty one* was Nabopalassar, father of Nebuchadnezzar. At this place I believe it will be well to make a quotation from history. This will give information from a secular source that will help the reader. There will be items that are related to the present verse and also some others to follow, therefore I urge the reader to give close attention and thus be prepared to refer to it as occasion may suggest. "Saracus, who came to the throne towards the end of the seventh century B. C., was the last of the long line of Assyrian kings. For nearly or quite six centuries the *Ninevite* [capital of Assyria] kings had now lorded it over the East. There was scarcely a state in all Western Asia that during this time had not, in the language of the royal inscriptions, 'borne the heavy yoke of their lordship'; scarcely a people that had not suffered their cruel punishments, or tasted the bitterness of enforced exile. But now swift misfortunes were bearing down upon the oppressor from every quarter. Egypt revolted and tore Syria away from the empire; from the mountain defiles on the east issued the armies of the recent-grown empire of the Aryan Medes, led by the renowned Cyaxares; From the southern lowlands, anxious to aid in the overthrow of the hated oppressor, the Babylonians joined the Medes as allies, and together they laid close siege to Nineveh. The city was finally taken and sacked [plundered], and dominion passed away forever from the proud capital (606 B. C.)"—Myers Ancient History, page 66.

"Nabopolassar (625-605 B. C.) was the founder of what is known as the Chaldean Empire. At first a vassal king [subject or dependent king], when troubles and misfortunes began to thicken about the Assyrian court, he revolted and became independent."—Myers Ancient History, page 72.

Verse 12. This verse will be the better understood after a glance at the historical quotation just made in the preceding paragraph. *Strangers* in the Bible means people from the outside or of another nation. This was fulfilled by the various foreigners who invaded Assyria and undermined her.

Verse 13. *Fowls* and *beasts* are figurative terms and refer to the nations who attacked the land of Assyria. *Remain* is an allusion to the continual ruin that was the lot of Assyria after being invaded by the hostile peoples.

Verse 14. *To the end* means the purpose of this revolution was to humble the king and country of Assyria from their position of pride. *Trees* and *waters*, etc., are figures used because, while Assyria is the one immediately in the mind of the Lord, it is for a comparison to Egypt which did boast of her River Nile with its canals and ditches.

Verse 15. The imagery of trees and water is being maintained throughout this passage because the chief subject is against Pharaoh and his country. And it is true literally that they boasted of their power as a nation, and that power was due to this great stream frequently mentioned. The *grave* means the national ruin of the country, and the *mourning* is the general state of regret that such a powerful empire would be brought so low after having been a great governing force so many years.

Verse 16. *His fall* refers to the downfall of Assyria which caused the reactions that are described in figurative terms. The nations all wondered at such a remarkable revolution, and all of them had a feeling of relief because they had stood in awe of such a powerful and heartless empire. *Hell* is from SHEOL and *pit* is from BOWR. Both are used figuratively in this place and mean that Assyrian greatness was to be buried and forgotten.

Verse 17. *They* refers to the allies of Assyria as is indicated by the words *dwelt under his shadow*. The Bible teaches that if one person associates with another who is evil, or if he sympathizes with and approves of his conduct, he is held responsible and must share in his fate. (See Romans 1:32; 1 Corinthians 15:33.)

Verse 18. The key to the entire comparison of this chapter is in the words *this is Pharaoh.* All of the things said of the king of Assyria were actually true and were known to be so, although they had taken place several years previously. The Lord used that great upheaval in history to compare with the fate which He was soon to bring upon Egypt. The first phrase of the verse is in the form of a question but it is really an assertion as if it were worded "to whom thou art like." If the reader will connect this statement with the one underlined above, he will have the thought the prophet has been getting ready for in the wonderful parable or comparison. God had predicted most of the things that happened to Assyria and they came true, which ought to be a warning that His predictions against Pharaoh will likewise be fulfilled.

EZEKIEL 32

Verse 1. *Twelfth year* is dated from the time Ezekiel was taken to Babylon. This would correspond with the year following the death of Zedekiah who was the last king to sit on the temporal throne of Judah.

Verse 2. *Say unto him* [Pharaoh]. See the comments at chapter 31:2 for explanation of such an expression. *Take up a lamentation* denotes that the fate of Pharaoh is to be lamented. A lion on land or a monster in the water would be something to be feared, and the king of Egypt is likened to them. A troublesome creature in the waters would cause them to be defiled, and likewise the king of Egypt had caused a defilement among the nations.

Verse 3. This verse is a direct prophecy of the invasion into Egypt of the forces of Babylon. The Lord calls them His *net* because the actions of the army of Nebuchadnezzar will be by the divine decree.

Verse 4. This verse is the same in thought as chapter 29:5.

Verse 5. *Height* is from RAMUWTH which Strong defines, "A heap (of carcases)." The verse is a strong statement of the extent of the slaughter that will be made of the Egyptians by the Babylonians.

Verse 6. The terms are used figuratively and are based on the literal conditions and facts of the land of Egypt. The Nile furnished the main resource for agricultural assurance, and the king and his people were boastful of their fortunate lot. With this in view, the prediction threatened to reverse the conditions, and instead of the water of the river of which the king boasted *(wherein thou swimmest),* the land was to be moistened with the blood of the people. This is said with reference to the bloodshed that will be done by the Babylonians. The terms are strong as most figures of speech are, but the amount of bloodshed was really bound to be great.

Verse 7. The literal things predicted are the overthrow of Pharaoh and the slaying of his people. *Put thee out* is rendered "extinguish" in the margin of the Bible and the lexicon agrees with it. This national blackout is expressed in the figurative use of terms connected with the natural universe.

Verse 8. The figurative description continues to be used with reference to the general defeat of Pharaoh and his country. If the sun and other lights in the heavens above the earth should be put out the earth would be thrown into darkness. Likewise, when Pharaoh and his leading men are put down by the predicted invasion, the country will be thrown into political darkness.

Verse 9. The attack that Nebuchadnezzar will make upon Egypt will cause her people to be scattered among the various nations. The original word for *vex* has a stronger sense than this, and the lexicon says it means "to trouble; by implication to grieve, rage, be indignant." When people are driven from their native homes and virtually "wished" on strange communities, the circumstance will not be taken favorably.

Verse 10. *Amazed* is from SHAMEM and the first definition of Strong is, "to stun." The overthrow of an ancient and powerful kingdom such as Egypt will have this stunning effect on other nations. *Tremble . . . every man for his own life* will be a natural result, for when so great a revolution is brought before their eyes the question will arise whether a similar calamity may come upon them.

Verse 11. *The sword of the king of Babylon* will be what Pharaoh will see, but it will also be the Lord's sword since He will be using that king as an instrument to execute the divine decree against the nation deserving the chastisement.

Verse 12. *The mighty* means the army of Nebuchadnezzar because it is a very strong military force. *Spoil* is from a word that is defined "to ravage" in the lexicon. (See the comments and historical note at chapter 29: 12, 13.)

Verse 13. The streams of Egypt were held sacred by the people, hence anything that would lower their importance or use would be regarded as a reproach. *Trouble* occurs twice in this verse but they come from different originals. The first means "confusion or uproar"; the second is defined "to roil [stir up the dregs] water." A beast would only defile a stream of water, while a man could create an uproar or commotion even though he was near one of these bodies of water that he professed to worship. The meaning of the prediction is that neither of these activities will be done for a period because both man and beast will be removed by the invader.

Verse 14. *Deep* is from SHAQA and Strong's first definition is "to subside." If the men and beasts are removed from the land by a foreign army, the described condition of the water will cease and it will be allowed to become *deep* or settled. The movement of oil would be smooth and it is used to compare the condition of the streams after the men and beasts have been taken from the land.

Verse 15. The main purpose of the chastisement from God is again stated, that the people of the land may be taught *to know that I am the Lord*.

Verse 16. *Lamentation* is from QIYNAH which Strong defines, "A dirge (as accompanied by beating the breasts or an instrument)." These literal performances are used to illustrate the attitude of *the daughters of the nations* at the desolation of Egypt.

Verse 17. The following prediction was made in the same year as the one we have just considered but was a few days later. The prophet is always careful to let us know the source of his information; that it is *the word of the Lord.*

Verse 18. To *wail* means about the same as "to lament" in some previous verses. *Cast them down* is a way of saying "predict that they will be cast down." This form of speech is used in Jeremiah 1: 10 and Ezekiel 43: 3. When an inspired man predicts that a certain thing will happen, it is virtually the same as if he will be the doer of it, for the Lord will see that all such predictions are carried out. The lexicon defines the original word for *nether* as "lowermost," and *pit* is defined in the same lexicon, "a pit hole (especially one used as a cistern or prison)." The people of Egypt were doomed to be taken into custody by Nebuchadnezzar and in that sense they will be prisoners. In other words, the land of Egypt was destined to go down in shame and her greatness was to be forgotten as other countries before had suffered.

Verse 19. This verse means the same as if the Lord said reproachfully, "Whom do you think you are; the most beautiful of nations?" Then the inspired answer is given, that the nation should be laid or classed with the uncircumcised or unfit.

Verse 20. *They* refers to the Egyptians who were doomed to be slain even as others who were *slain by the sword.*

Verse 21. *Him* is a pronoun that stands for Egypt and the king. *Strong among the mighty* refers to the valiant powers that had already gone down to *hell,* which is used in the same sense as "pit" in verse 18, and refers to the state of forgetfulness into which many nations had fallen. When *uncircumcised* is used figuratively it means unconsecrated or unacceptable.

Verse 22. *Asshur* (or Assyria) *is there* means that she had gone down into this state of forgetfulness or desolation. (See chapter 31: 3, 11.)

Verse 23. The pronoun *whose* refers to "company" in the preceding verse who are said to have gone down with Asshur. *Set in the sides of the pit* is all figurative and refers to the desolated condition that had come upon various kings and nations. The phrase means that the "company" or citizens were about their king, and all of them near each other in this figurative grave or pit. *Caused terrors in the land of the living* is explained at verse 10 of this chapter.

Verse 24. *There is Elam* means that she is another country that had gone down into the pit of forgetfulness. This nation was located in the neighborhood of Assyria and Persia and it was at one time an important power. See verse 21 for the explanation of *uncircumcised*, and verse 18 for the meaning of *nether*.

Verse 25. *Bed* is from MISHKAB which Strong defines, "A bed (figuratively a bier); abstractly sleep." It here is used with reference to the same state of forgetfulness that had been predicted for other evil countries. *Graves round about him* denotes that the king of Elam and his people had gone down together into the "pit." *Though their terror . . . land of the living* signifies that the national death was preceded by a period of terror at the presence of the attacking forces.

Verse 26. *Meshech* and *Tubal* were some more of the heathen peoples who incurred the wrath of God. They had been doomed to the same ruin as other nations suffered.

Verse 27. *Not lie with the mighty* indicates an undignified burial. *Swords under their heads* refers to an ancient practice of burying distinguished warriors with their weapons. These people had been denied the honor of having their swords buried with them, but instead, *their iniquities* were "interred with their bones."

Verse 28. This is the same reference to a dishonorable grave. *The uncircumcised* means the unacceptable, who were destined to meet death by the invader's sword.

Verse 29. The Edomites were descendants of Esau and were always hostile against Israel. A more extended description of Edom's fate is in chapter 25: 12-14.

Verse 30. The *Zidonians* dwelt near the sea and were north of the people of Israel. The fate that happened to these foes was similar to that decreed against other heathen nations. *With their terror they are ashamed of their might* means that in spite of their terrible might they were brought down to shame.

Verse 31. *Pharaoh . . . shall be comforted.* The heathen nations were generally hostile against each other, and by that same token each would rejoice at another's defeat.

Verse 32. More than a chapter is devoted to the condemnation and predictions against Egypt. No additional fate is here made as a threat against that country. The brief statement of its doom is made to explain why the country will "be comforted" at the downfall of the Zidonians.

EZEKIEL 33

Verses 1, 2. For 8 chapters the prophet has been writing against various heathen nations that had mistreated God's people. Some of that writing is in the form of predictions of things to come upon them, and other parts are a summary of what had previously taken place, and written by way of warning to future generations. Ezekiel now resumes his writing to his own countrymen. The general trend of the passages will be favorable and intended to give encouragement to the people of Israel. However, the seriousness of responsibility on the part of a prophet and and teacher will be given attention. The subject will necessarily include some remarks concerning the responsibility of the people under the work of the teacher or prophet. The first lesson on the subject of responsibility is drawn from the work of a watchman in times of danger, especially the dangers of war. At such times a man is placed in one of the watchtowers and equipped with a trumpet to use as a signalling device.

Verse 3. The duty of this watchman is to be always on the alert and observe any approach of the enemy. When he sees such a danger he is to blow a warning signal with the trumpet to notify the citizens that danger is near.

Verse 4. The blowing of the trumpet moves the responsibility from the watchman to the citizen. If he ignores the signal of warning and is taken by the sword of the enemy he will have to take all of the blame for his death.

Verse 5. *His blood shall be upon him* means he will be responsible for his own downfall. No blood shall be shed by any other person in his behalf.

Verse 6. Here is a rule that does not "work both ways." If the watchman fails to sound the warning, his neglect of duty will not save the life of the citizen. Besides that, the watchman also will be required to answer for the death of the victim.

Verse 7. So far the Lord has been speaking to Ezekiel in general terms on the responsibility of a watchman, now He comes to particulars and tells the prophet that he is being made one. His duty is to watch over the *house of Israel*, and deliver to them the words of warning that he receives from God.

Verse 8. The relation of a watchman

to his people in times of literal war is being used to illustrate a subject far more important. The matter of a man's personal conduct and its consequences is the thing the Lord would have the prophet consider. He was to warn the wicked man that death would be his lot if he did not repent and turn from his wickeness. If Ezekiel fails to deliver the warning the wicked man will die even though he is not made aware of his danger. Besides that, the negligent prophet will he held responsible for the death of the wicked man.

Verse 9. If the watchman warns the wicked man and he does not profit by it, he will die *in* or because of his iniquity. However, the watchman will have done his duty and will not be held responsible for the death of the victim.

Verse 10. This verse is a complaint of the house of Israel. They seem to think that the Lord is asking that which is impossible for them. They are expected to *live* in the service of God and yet He causes them to waste away in their sins. Their conclusion is that God wishes them to die, but that will be denied in the next verse.

Verse 11. The Lord declares that He has no pleasure in the death of the wicked, but just the opposite is what is desired. That is why the wicked man is exhorted to turn from his evil way. *Why will ye die* is a challenge to the evil man to show a reason for his decision to die. No reason can be given, for nothing lies beyond death that will repay him for his unwise course. Neither can he make the excuse that it is unavoidable, for the Lord not only is giving him full warning of what is before him, but also has promised to help him in his efforts to avoid it.

Verse 12. The gist of this verse is that as a man terminates his life, so will be his lot ever afterwards. If he turns from a wicked course and does good the rest of his days, the Lord will not hold his former sins against him. On the same principle, if a righteous man backslides and ends his days in sin, his previous good deeds will not save him when the test comes to determine his lot.

Verse 13. The paragraph comprised in verses 3-9 looks especially to the phase of responsibility of a watchman toward the people under his charge. This verse introduces the special thought of God's attitude toward the promises of good or threats of evil that have been announced to man. The promises or warnings of the Lord are made on conditions, either expressed or implied. Hence the promise of life made to a good man is not so fixed that he cannot come short of that promise. If he becomes so confident over his former good deeds and record of them that he begins to do wrong, the promise of life will be revoked. This overthrows the doctrine titled "Once in grace always in grace," for man's favor with God depends on faithfulness to the end.

Verse 14. This verse indicates that a wicked man does not need to give up in despair just because the Lord has told him he must die; he is encouraged to turn from his sins. We should notice the wicked man has a two-sided duty to perform if he is to obtain mercy from God. Not only must he turn from active sin but also he must *do that which is right.* "Cease to do evil; learn to do well" (Isaiah 1: 16, 17.)

Verse 15. This verse teaches the same lesson as the preceding ones, but it goes into particulars and specifies certain things the wicked man must do in order to obtain divine mercy and be made reconciled to the Lord.

Verse 16. This verse teaches the same lesson as chapter 18: 21, 22. It refutes the theory that an unrighteous man cannot do anything for his own salvation; that if he is doomed "from all eternity" to perdition, nothing can be done to change it.

Verse 17. The word *equal* is from an original that is defined "to balance" or be consistent and impartial. See the comments at chapter 18: 25 for further explanation on this subject of God's manner of dealing with the children of men.

Verses 18, 19. This is explained at verses 13-16 and elsewhere.

Verse 20. As a specific denial of the accusation made by the people that God is unequal or unfair, He declares that Israel will be judged "every one after his ways," not according to some decree made before the man was born. Since a man's *ways* are his own doing, that places his fate within his hands whether good or evil.

Verses 21, 22. *Twelfth year of our captivity* means that dated from the taking of Jehoiachin to Babylon, at which time Ezekiel was taken. Eleven years after that event king Zedekiah was taken and Jerusalem was destroyed, completing the third and final stage of the great captivity. That means therefore, that the present verse is located at the next year after Jerusalem was destroyed, expressed by the words *the city is smitten*. This verbal news was brought to Ezekiel by one who escaped at the time Nebuchadnezzar closed in on the city and completed the overthrow of the great capital of Judah. The distance from Jerusalem to Babylon is great enough that nothing strange will be thought of its requiring until the next year for the messenger to reach the presence of the prophet. It had been prophesied (chapter 24: 26, 27) that one who escaped would bring just such a message and here it is. It had also been prophesied (same passage) that when that message was delivered to Ezekiel he would be *no more dumb*. See the comments at chapter 24: 17, 27 for explanation of dumbness. The man who escaped was not depended on to break the news to Ezekiel as the first information, for the Lord told him about it the evening before according to the present verse. But the coming of the man with the message was to be the signal when the prophet was to consider himself free from the restrictions he had been under since chapter 24: 15-18.

Verses 23, 24. The reasoning of the people is in the form of a complaint. They refer to Abraham having possessed the land of Palestine although he was but one man. But here is a large multitude that should possess it since they are heirs of Abraham, but instead they are inhabiting *wastes* (in Babylonian captivity) and not enjoying the land that was promised to Abraham's descendants.

Verse 25. The prophet was told to explain to the people why they were being denied the land of their inheritance. It does not mean they were doing all the things charged against them at the time Ezekiel was writing, for they were captives in a foreign land. They could not practice all these things there, except some of their idolatrous performances, and that was because the Lord willed it so to teach them a lesson. But the things listed are the ones they did while they did live in their home land. *Eat with the blood* violated Genesis 9: 4, Leviticus 3: 17, and they practiced that while back in their own country. *Idols . . . and shed blood* includes the guilt of bloodshed in general, but it especially applies to the slaying of their children to make sacrifices of them for their idols.

Verse 26. *Stand upon your sword* refers to their use of the sword to accomplish their abominable advantages over their weaker brethren. Not satisfied with this iniquity, they committed adultery with the wives of their neighbors.

Verse 27. The greater portion of the nation of Israel had been taken to Babylon when Ezekiel began his writing, and in that sense were suffering the *wastes* mentioned in this verse. But the third stage of the 70-year period had been accomplished only recently, and there were still a great many who were left straggling in the wastes or desolated spaces in Palestine. A few had escaped the immediate effects of the invasion and were hiding in forts and caves and other places in an effort to shelter themselves. But although they might elude the invaders, they were doomed to feel the hand of God through His judgments upon them which would cause them to perish.

Verse 28. This verse is a general prediction of the desolated condition the whole land of Palestine was destined to suffer during the great captivity.

Verse 29. The Lord was determined that his people should not forget Him. They had special need for that lesson since they had given so much of their time and devotion to the strange gods that were worshiped by the heathen around them.

Verse 30. The Jews who were in exile in Babylon were more curious than sincere in their pretended inquiry for information. They would come to the prophet as if they really longed for instruction (chapter 8: 1; 14: 1; 20: 1), but after receiving it they refused to abide by it.

Verse 31. The people not only failed to accept the words of the prophet but acted hypocritically about it. They pretended to admire Ezekiel for giving them the information, but in their heart they were interested in the things of personal interest.

Verse 32. *A very lovely song* is a figurative description of the opinion the people pretended to have of Ezekiel's words. Their motive for such a pretended attitude could not have been sincere since they refused to abide by the admonitions that he gave them. By taking this false interest in him they hoped to obtain some more information, but without the purpose of profiting by it. Because of this the Lord defeated their attempt to deceive the prophet by enlightening him on the subject.

Verse 33. A prediction becomes an evidence of the truth when it is fulfilled and not before. Hence this verse offers the conclusion and assurance to Ezekiel that he will finally be shown to have been a prophet of God.

EZEKIEL 34

Verses 1, 2. *Shepherd* is from RAAH, which Strong defines as follows: "A primitive root; to tend a flock, i.e. pasture it; intransitively to graze (literally or figuratively); generally to rule; by extension to associate with (as a friend)." The word has such a wide range of meaning that it will apply to the kings and prophets and priests in Israel because of their position of leadership among the people. In such a relationship they could and should have guided them aright, and have instructed them in the right ways of the world by feeding them on the proper spiritual food. But instead, they looked to their personal interests and made use of the advantages that were intended for all the congregation and thus "fed themselves instead of the flock."

Verse 3. The items in this verse are literal in their nature and in the use that is generally made of them just as the statement shows it. But the passage is used figuratively to illustrate the selfishness of the shepherds in their treatment of the flock that was depending upon them for guidance.

Verse 4. A good shepherd would look after the sheep and administer whatever services their condition might require. But instead of thus guarding and assisting them, these leaders had been harsh and overbearing. It was because of this general corrupt life led by these leaders that even the things they did that would otherwise have been acceptable were rejected by the Lord. On this subject the reader should see the long note quoted at Isaiah 1: 10 in volume 3 of this Commentary.

Verse 5. It is a duty of a shepherd to protect his flock against wolves and other wild beasts. These selfish shepherds of Israel neglected their obligation and allowed the people to be exposed to the beasts (idolatrous nations) around them.

Verse 6. Some of the terms in this verse are used with a mixture of the literal and figurative senses. A flock that is neglected will literally be scattered among the hills and it was thus figuratively with Israel. And since the real iniquity in the country was idolatry which was often practiced on the hills, that phase of the subject is literal and pertained to such "high places" in the worship of the false gods.

Verse 7. The Lord is directing the present message especially to these shepherds, and they are called upon to hear His word by the mouth of the prophet.

Verse 8. *As I live* is a phrase that occurs numerous times in the Bible, and means that the thing about to be stated is as sure and true as the existence of God. It is a form of oath along the line of Hebrews 6: 13. Under such an oath the Lord charged the selfish shepherds of Israel with partaking of the food intended for the flock.

Verse 9. This verse takes the same comments as verse 7.

Verse 10. *I am against the shepherds* denotes the Lord's disfavor for the conduct of the shepherds, not that He is to be regarded as their personal enemy. *Require my flock at their hand* means they will be held responsible for the sad state of the flock because of their part in causing the situation. *Cease from feeding the flock* refers in the first place to the removal of those shepherds from the position of importance that they have been occupying. In the second place, the Lord is approaching a prediction that will reach far beyond the days of these shepherds over fleshly Israel. Such a subject will be introduced in the latter half of this chapter. We have observed it to be a practice of God through the inspired prophets to pass directly from ancient to modern Israel. That is due partly to the fact that many of the experiences, both favorable and unfavorable, of both Israels are similar. A favorable experience of fleshly Israel will be predicted first and then we shall read of a most wonderful favor that will concern spiritual Israel.

Verse 11. From this verse through 16 the passage is a prediction of the return from the Babylonian captivity. The several verses will be commented upon in their order. *Search . . . seek them out*. The Babylonian Empire was composed of various countries, and in course of the 70-year period the Jews became scattered among many of them.

Verse 12. The Lord promises to gather his flock out of these different countries as a good shepherd would do for his sheep that had been scattered. *Cloudy and dark day* refers to the gloomy period of the captivity.

Verse 13. The terms of this verse are literal, the *people* and *countries* being those mentioned in the preceding verse. *Own land* means Palestine from which they had been exiled all the years of the great captivity. The geographical terms, *mountains, rivers* and *inhabited places* were parts of Palestine, and the Jews were to be restored to them that they might again enjoy them.

Verse 14. This verse combines the literal with the figurative sense in predicting the future of fleshly Israel. She will actually enjoy the land of Palestine for temporal purposes, and at the same time will be treated justly in spiritual matters.

Verse 15. God will not depend upon selfish shepherds to care for the nation but will take close supervision over it. *Cause them to lie down*. A sheep will not lie down as long as he is unsatisfied with nourishment, therefore the act of lying down indicates a gratified appetite in the midst of plenty. (See Psalms 23: 1-3.)

Verse 16. The gist of this verse is a promise to help those who need and deserve help. *Destroy the fat and strong* means the Lord will judge the selfish shepherds who had been feasting at the expense of the weaker sheep of the flock.

Verse 17. The rulers and other outstanding men were not the only members who took advantage of the weaker ones. Among the "common people" or unofficial members of the flock there were some who were selfish and defrauded the others hence the Lord declares He will make a distinction between different members of the flock. The *cattle* refers to the weaker members of the flock and the *he goats* the stronger.

Verse 18. The imagery for purposes of illustration is still that of a pasture and the creatures living therein. These selfish ones among the Israelite nation are compared to the strong he goats that eat the best of the pasture regardless of the needs of others. But they did not stop at that in their cruel selfishness. After satisfying their own greedy appetite with the best of the field, they trampled the remaining part with their feet. And after satisfying their thirst with the *deep* or pure water, they wade into the other watering places in order to defile them.

Verse 19. Hunger will drive one to eat that which would otherwise be regarded as extremely repulsive. (See Job 6: 7.) Hence the weaker members of the Lord's flock had to eat and drink of the food and water that had been made foul by the wicked and selfish members of the group, which caused God to decree a distinction between the two classes in the flock.

Verse 20. Beginning with this verse and running through verse 31 will be given the prediction mentioned in the comments on verse 10. Christ and his church under the New Testament rule is the subject of the passage as will become evident in our study of the verses. However, the imagery of shepherds and all that pertains to that occupation will still be referred to for illustrations. The injustices of unworthy characters among the Lord's professed servants are carried over for consideration, and He is going to see that such evils will be guarded against in the great institution to come.

Verse 21. An overbearing animal will push with its *side, shoulders* and *horns* in order to crowd out a weaker one. Thus the "he goats" had behaved in fleshly Israel, but the Lord was determined that such irregularities would not be permitted in the new service under the son of David. (See Matthew 23: 8-12; 20: 25-28.)

Verse 22. *Shall no more be a prey* has a twofold bearing. It promises that Israel shall not be taken away into heathen captivity again; also that the Lord's sheep will be cared for and prepared against the captivity of sin. (See 1 Corinthians 10: 13.)

Verse 23. David, according to the flesh, had been dead four centuries when Ezekiel wrote this prophecy, hence he would not be intended as the shepherd to be set over the Lord's people. The apostle Peter makes the same point in Acts 2: 25-34, explaining to his audience that such reference to David with regard to the kingdom always means Christ. This is because of the high position occupied by the great king and patriarch of the former ages. David was the first man of the tribe of Judah to sit as king in Jerusalem; and the one who was to reign over spiritual Israel beginning at Jerusalem had been foreordained of God to come from the same tribe and a descendant of David. Because of this, it became the practice of the prophets and other inspired men to speak of Christ directly as David, and to refer to His throne as the throne of his illustrious ancestor (Isaiah 9: 6, 7; Psalms 132: 11; Luke 1: 32; Acts 13: 23; Revelation 3: 7). This verse makes it very clear, therefore, that the prophet is predicting the setting up of the kingdom of Christ which great event started at Jerusalem and is recorded in Acts second chapter.

Verse 24. The comments in the preceding verse on *David* apply here. *Will be their God* has special significance as a contrast with the false gods that ancient Israel worshiped. The new kingdom that will be established under the son of David will have the recognition of God in its divine origin and reign. God has always offered to be the supreme One for any individual who would serve him.

Verse 25. *Covenant of peace* is the one that Paul writes about in Hebrews 8: 8-12, which he cited from Jeremiah 31: 31. *Evil beasts* is figurative and refers to the spiritual protection that the Lord will provide for the citizens of the new kingdom. *Sleep in the woods* (or forest) is a figure to indicate the safety that was to be enjoyed by the people of the kingdom of Christ.

Verse 26. Rainfall at the proper time was very important in Palestine and the fact is referred to figuratively. The promise is, not only that a shower will come down, but it will come *in his season* or just when it is needed. *There shall be showers of blessing.* This statement has been made a part of a familiar church song, but it is 19 centuries out of date. It is a part of the prediction of the New Testament institution and hence has been fulfilled many hundreds of years ago. It is unscriptural to speak of something that "shall be," when the scriptures teach that it has already been fulfilled and that the Lord has carried out his promise.

Verse 27. This verse was literally fulfilled when the Israelite nation was released from Babylonian captivity. But its more important fulfillment came when the kingdom of Christ, of which the present group of verses is a prediction, was established with Him as its king. The figures of speech refer to the spiritual benefits that were promised for the citizens of that kingdom.

Verse 28. This verse is more along the same line as the preceding ones. It does not promise that Christians will never have any troubles, but that they will feel secure in spite of all their persecutions.

Verse 29. I shall offer some critical definitions in this verse before making the comments. *Plant* is from MATTA which Strong defines "Something planted, i.e. the place (a garden or vineyard), or the thing (a plant, figuratively of men); by implication the act, planting." *Renown* is from SHEM which Strong defines, "An appelation [name], as a mark or memorial of individuality; by implication honor, authority, character." From these definitions we may conclude the common translation is correct. It will be well to note the language of Jesus in Matthew 15: 13 where the word "plant" is also properly rendered. The entire illustration means the church or kingdom of Christ which is compared to a plant and that the Lord was the one who would plant it. It further means that every plant (church or kingdom) that God did not plant or start shall be destroyed by Him.

Verse 30. The benefits that will come to the faithful members of Christ's kingdom will be such that no human source could supply. Hence they will *know that I the Lord their God am with them* and that the institution is of divine origin.

Verse 31. The flock is to be in the Lord's pasture and therefore they will be *men* and not literal cattle. For that reason they may expect to obtain benefits in that field that mere man could not provide; they would have to come from the Lord.

EZEKIEL 35

Verses 1, 2. For some time the prophet has been writing against the wicked men in the nation of the Jews, especially the leaders among them. Now a chapter is given to Edom or Seir and certain condemnations will be uttered against that nation because of its hatred for God's people. *Set thy face against* means for Ezekiel to turn his attention against the nation that had disrespected God's people.

Verse 3. *Mount Seir* is a geographical term and refers to a tract of land lying east of the Dead Sea. It is often mentioned by name of Edom because the Edomites occupied that land for many years.

Verse 4. The prophet was told to predict a desolation for that land. A brief condemnation was made against it in chapter 25: 12-14, but a more detailed prediction is made here before the interests of Palestine are to receive further attention.

Verse 5. Edom had cherished a hatred against Israel for a long time and had been constant *(perpetual)* in it. He had shown that hatred by shedding the blood of the children of Israel. What made the mistreatment of Israel worse was the fact that the heathen nation took advantage of them in times of calamity.

Verse 6. *Sith* is an old rendering of a word that means "since" or any other word with a similar bearing. The verse means that since or inasmuch as the Edomites seemed to welcome bloodshed, the Lord will impose upon them an abundant share of it.

Verse 7. *Cut off . . . passeth out . . . returneth* means the land will be made so desolate that it will put a stop to coming and going. There will be nothing to encourage any kind of traffic and hence it will cease to be done.

Verse 8. Of course this verse is a strong statement not to be taken literally. The meaning is that dead men will be seen in all the places named.

Verse 9. Since the hatred of Edom for God's people was *perpetual*, so the desolation of the country was to be permanent. The purpose of such a chastisement was to make the people of the land *know that I am the Lord.*

Verse 10. The *two nations* and *two countries* refers to Judah and Israel, into which the Jews were divided after the death of Solomon (1 Kings 12). Edom was vain enough to think he could possess the lands of those contries. *Whereas the Lord was there* is the expression or comment of the prophet. It is Ezekiel saying, "Edom thought he could take that land, which was impossible since the Lord was there."

Verse 11. God proposed to deal with the Edomites according to the anger which they had shown toward His people. His judgments against these enemies of the Israelites will be a demonstration of the divine power.

Verse 12. The things the Edomites had said about the land of Israel might all have been true, but their motive in saying them was displeasing to God. He never would tolerate a spirit of triumph against His people no matter how much they deserved the chastisement or misfortunes. And such an attitude would be doubly offensive if it was claimed that the loss or misfortunes were brought for the benefit of the foes.

Verse 13. *Boasted* means the Edomites had magnified their own importance. They did that when they made the claim expressed by the closing statement of the preceding verse. *I have heard them* is a significant fact. God is everywhere with his infinite knowledge and will bring to account all the thoughts and words of wicked men.

Verse 14. The whole earth was to rejoice at the desolation of Edom.

Verse 15. This verse repeats the thoughts of the preceding one. It should not be regarded in the sense of "returning evil for evil" or as an act of retaliation, but as a just punishment of Edom for his wicked attitude toward God's people. *Seir* and *Idumea* are names that applied to the land occupied by the Edomites, the second word being another form of Edom.

EZEKIEL 36

Verse 1. Mountains, rivers, etc., are inanimate objects and incapable of receiving any communication of an intellectual character. Notwithstanding, this chapter through verse 15 is addressed to them and it will be necessary to keep that in mind in order to understand the sentence construction. We will bear in mind, of course, that all the good things that are said to and about the land are for the sake of the people of Israel who are again to return from captivity to their own land.

Verse 2. The land of Palestine had been made desolate by the heathen nations, the Assyrians and Babylonians, and they were boasting about it as if it had been solely through their own superior strength that it was accomplished. *Aha* is an expression that implies a feeling of derision and triumph.

Verse 3. *They* [the heathen nations] *have made you* [mountains of Israel] *desolate.* The Lord's motive in giving the land into the hands of the heathen was to chastise Israel. The motive of the heathen was that they might take possession of it for their own personal profit. Such a motive was wrong and the Lord determined to repossess the land for His peple. *Infamy* means slander and the land of Palestine was so spoken of by the people of the world.

Verse 4. God was grieved and made furious because of the haughty spirit of the heathen, although He had used them as instruments in chastising the disobedient Israelites. He therefore delivered a favorable prediction to the *mountains, hills, rivers, valleys* and other parts of the desolated land.

Verse 5. This verse is a summing up of the complaints that God had against the people of Idumea (Edom) and the other heathen nations. *Appointed my land into their possession* means these heathen countries claimed the possessing of the land of Palestine was by their own appointment, whereas they were able to obtain it only because God willed it so. The evil attitude in the matter stirred up the *fire of God's jealousy* and He was determined to "take the side" of the oppressed land. The foregoing verses of this chapter may well be regarded as introductory to the special prophecy that God is about to make on behalf of the land of Palestine. They state the reasons for the predictions which will now follow.

Verse 6. For the sake of brevity we will consider the word *land* as including the mountains and rivers and all other geographical parts of the country. *Ye* (the land) *have borne the shame of the heathen* means the nations had desolated the land and that provoked the Lord to jealous fury.

Verse 7. When a nation is subdued it is held up to shame in the eyes of others. God had decreed that all the heathen who had desolated His land should be thus shamed.

Verse 8. The land of Palestine had not been damaged by the heathen, but it had been made to lie uncultivated. That was in order for it to enjoy its sabbaths. (See Leviticus 26: 34, 35, 43.) The most significant thought is in the words *to my people.* Even had the land produced anything in the 70-year captivity, the people of Israel could not have used it because they were exiles in a country far away.

Verse 9. This verse is virtually the same prediction as the preceding one.

Verse 10. Remember, the pronoun *you* stands for the land of Palestine. The *men* to be multiplied upon it will be those of the Israelites who will be permitted to return from captivity, to rebuild and inhabit the cities as before.

Verse 11. This verse continues the prediction that Israel will increase in population upon the land. *Settle . . . old estates.* The last word has no separate one in the original. The clause means that the people of Israel will settle on this land as they formerly did. Once more, the great object to be obtained is mentioned, *and ye shall know that I am the Lord.*

Verse 12. This verse is virtually all literal and contains its own explanation to a great extent. The Lord promises the land that His people will be permitted to walk upon it and possess it. *Bereave* is from SHAKOL, which Strong defines as follows: "A primitive root; properly to miscarry, i.e., suffer abortion; by analogy to bereave (literally or figuratively)." The statement represents the land to have previously cast out the people who were living in i.t That was entirely just, for they had mistreated it by defrauding it of its 7th-year rest for so long. It is as if the land said to the Jews: "You have overworked me until I have been cheated out of 70 years of rest; now you must leave me until I regain that many years." The prediction of the verse is that such a revolution will never occur again.

Verse 13. When misfortune comes upon a man he sometimes will blame it upon another person or thing, when perhaps he is to blame himself. And so it was that when Israel was cast out of her own land she was inclined to accuse it for the calamity. (A similar circumstance is found in Numbers 13: 32 with the 10 spies who returned to Moses.)

Verse 14. However the preceding accusation may be, it shall not occur again, for nothing like a national removal from the land will be done in the future.

Verse 15. The land of Palestine is still the thing to which the language is addressed. The same assurance is given that it will receive its rightful citizens again, thereby being freed from the shame under which it will have lain for 70 years.

Verses 16, 17. A few verses will consist of a direct message of God to Ezekiel in the nature of explanation and for his information. He recounts the events in the history of Israel while they were still in their own land. Their conduct was so corrupt that the

Lord likened it to the condition of an unclean woman.

Verse 18. This verse explains why the house of Israel is at the very time all in the land of Babylon, except the comparatively few stragglers yet to be rounded up and taken if there should be any such still in Palestine.

Verse 19. *Dispersed through the countries.* The Babylonian Empire was made up of many small countries and kingdoms, and the captives were scattered out among them by the Babylonians after they brought them from Palestine.

Verse 20. When the Israelites came into the region of the heathen they were made the subject of sneers by those foreign people. *They* [the heathen] *profaned my holy name* refers to the scoffing remarks that were made by these heathen folks among whom the Lord had made his people to come. They belittled the unfortunate people of Israel by remarking that they had been thrust out of the land although they were the Lord's people. But we have seen more than once that God would never tolerate any rejoicing over His people rega.dless of how much they deserved the chastisement. Because of all this He has pity for his people and has determined to bring them out of their captive condition after they have been put through the necessary trial. Very logically, then, the next subject that God will give the prophet to deliver to Israel is that of the return, which will take up all the rest of this chapter which we will study verse by verse as they come in order.

Verse 21. The house of Israel was reproached by being taken captive among the heathen, and also the *holy name* of God was profaned by the situation. Hence He was concerned from that double viewpoint and decreed to reverse the conditions in time.

Verse 22. The house of Israel will be receiving better treatment than it deserves when God comes to its rescue and puts an end to the captivity. But the holy name of the Lord is at stake and He must restore it to its proper position in the eyes of the world. *Ye have profaned* does not mean the Israelites purposely belitted God's name while in Babylon, for the opposite was the case. Psalm 137 shows the deep regard they had for everything that pertained to Him. But the mere fact that God's people had to be cast among the heathen because of their unfaithfulness was a reproach to His name.

Verse 23. *Sanctify* comes from QADASH and Strong defines it as follows: "A primitive root; to be (causatively make, pronounce or observe as) clean (ceremonially or morally)." According to the definition the word can apply to that which is already clean and holy, as well as to cause something to be so. That is why a writer may properly speak of sanctifying the Lord and his name. The great name of God had been profaned among the heathen and He purposed to clear it of all such a cloud, and prove to the whole world that the name of Jehovah is and always has been clean and holy. The condition that implied any question about the Lord's name was the enslavement of His people in a heathen land. They must be rescued from such impure surroundings and be separated from all the moral and religious taint clinging to them.

Verse 24. This identical prediction has been made a number of times (Deuteronomy 30: 3; Jeremiah 23: 3; Ezekiel 11: 17; 20: 41; 34: 13). It is a prophecy that was to be fulfilled when the Jews were released from their bondage in the various countries that made up the great Babylonian Empire.

Verse 25. This verse pertains to the same people and conditions referred to in the preceding one, not to anyone of our day. God's people had been corrupted by the false worship of the heathen among whom they had been living for 70 years. It was required of the Jews that if they came in contact with something that was sinful and unclean, they should be purified by the use of a solution called *water of separation* (Numbers 19). In allusion to that ceremony the Lord promises to cleanse his people from their pollutions obtained from contact with idolatrous nations. Since the prediction was to be fulfilled upon the whole Israelite nation living at the end of the captivity, and also since a full record of that great purifying event is in the books of Ezra and Nehemiah, we know the sprinkling of clean water on them was figurative. The result of their entire experience was to cleanse or cure them from idolatry. See the historical note on this subject at Isaiah 1: 25 in volume 3 of this Commentary.

Verse 26. A complete change of heart is the meaning of this verse. We know that the human heart as to the body is literally flesh, therefore we must understand this language to be figurative. It means their heart (mind) had become hardened in sin and the captivity was going to humble them and make them yield to the law of God.

Verse 27. The reformation that the captivity was destined to bring about in the lives of the people of Israel was to result in a better spirit or mind toward God. They were to have such an abhorrence for heathenism that the law of God will be their delight, thereby causing them to walk in its instructions.

Verse 28. The books of Ezra and Nehemiah give the history of the repossession of Palestine by the Jews. *Be my people* means they would be a group of people forming a nation, and that it would recognize the Lord as the true God instead of the heathen gods whom they formerly worshiped.

Verse 29. The leading thought in this verse is the promise of prosperity in the land. God had at certain times punished his people by bringing a famine on the land (Ruth 1: 1; 2 Samuel 21: 1; 1 Kings 18: 2; 2 Kings 6: 25; 8: 1). Sometimes it was brought about by bringing a hostile army in to lay siege to the cities, and at the other times the Lord caused it directly by withholding the rain in its season. The prediction is that the land will not again be so visited.

Verse 30. This is virtually the same thing promised in the preceding verse, with the added thought that a famine in a country encourages it to be reproached.

Verse 31. This verse makes another reference to the cure from idolatry that was to result from the 70-year captivity. (See the note cited in verse 25.)

Verse 32. This verse takes the same comments as verse 22.

Verse 33. The bearing of this verse is that Israel would not be permitted to reinhabit the cities of Palestine until they were cured of the chief evil of idolatry.

Verse 34. The land did *lie desolate* during the captivity because the Lord desired it to regain the rest supposed to be coming to it under the law of the sabbatical year.

Verse 35. *Eden* is derived from a word defined "pleasure" in the lexicon. It is used figuratively to describe a place that is "pleasant to the sight" (Genesis 2: 9). The thought is that the land of Palestine, so long in a state of desolation, was again to be put under cultivation.

Verse 36. The renewal of the land into a state of fruitful life was to be proof that God is able to do a thing after He has spoken it.

Verse 37. There was a time when God ignored his people when they made inquiries of him (chapter 14: 3; 20: 3, 31), but after their reformation they will be heard. The further assurance is given that when they make their petitions known they will be favored with an increase of population.

Verse 38. The flocks that would appear at Jerusalem at the time of the solemn feasts would be the best in quality, because no other kind was accepted for that service. This is a comparison to the condition of things after the return from Babylonian captivity and settlement in the home land.

EZEKIEL 37

Verse 1. Various imagery has been used in course of the prophetic writings to describe the predictions being made. Some of them are related to the departure from Palestine and others to the return. There were always some people who doubted the truth of these predictions and even proclaimed loudly that they would never come to pass. We have seen the exposure of the false prophets who made light of the idea that any foreign force could take Israel into captivity. Now at this writing the thing has occurred and the nation is actually languishing in a foreign land. But many of them seem to have forgotten all those predictions notwithstanding they are actually fulfilling them by their own situation. Now then, they are just as doubtful about the prophecies of the return and are sighing and bemoaning their fate and saying that they will never get out of their lost estate. Hence the Lord is going to do some "acting" with the co-operation of the prophet, and demonstrate that even a nation that is dead can be brought to life again. He is going to do so by putting life and flesh on some dead bones. *In the spirit* means that Ezekiel will see in a vision the things that are about to happen.

Verse 2. The prophet was shown a valley that was full of bones, and he says they were *very dry*. They were so represented because they stood for the nation of Israel that was to spend 70 years in the valley which was Babylon. In that length of time all the flesh and moisture would be decayed and gone from the bones.

Verse 3. *Can these bones live* was asked of Ezekiel to represent the state of mind the house of Israel had at that time. The answer *thou knowest* is the prophet's way of saying that things which seem impossible to man are possible with God.

Verse 4. *Prophesy upon these bones* means for him to direct his speech to and for the dry bones. In the preceding chapter the Lord directed a prophecy to the land of Israel, in this He addresses Israel herself who is in the form of dry bones. The purpose is to give encouragement to the Jews in exile who are represented by the dry bones, and who are told to *hear the word of the Lord*.

Verse 5. The language is addressed to the bones because they represent the children of Israel in Babylonian captivity, and are in a state of discouragement bordering almost on total despair. Hence the Lord tells these dry bones that their breath will enter into them which will restore them to a living condition.

Verse 6. The parts mentioned here had been removed by time and decay leaving only the dead, dry bones. Again the main point is that *I am the Lord*.

Verse 7. When the sinews and flesh of a body have decayed and dried up it will leave a mass of disconnected bones. These will be lying about in a state as if none of them was related to the others. Before the former life of the body can be restored, the bones must resume their attachment for each other in the proper position. Hence the prophet heard the sound caused by the rustling of these bones as the various members sought its "next of kin" in the anatomy of its own peculiar structure. Let us imagine a valley where the bones of several thousand bodies have been lying around for years, dried up and lifeless. Then let us picture a power that causes all these bones to begin moving toward their proper joints, and we will have some idea of why Ezekiel heard the *noise* and felt the *shaking* of these bones in their act of assembling.

Verse 8. But a group of dry bones that is even carefully assembled, each one forming the joint for which it was created, would immediately fall apart again were not something added to hold them together. Hence the prophet saw the flesh for the immediate union come upon the bones, and the skin around them for a general binding. So far the form of the body is complete, but as yet it is a dead body—flesh, skin and bones only, having nothing within to enable it to move.

Verse 9. *Wind, winds* and *breath* are all from RUWACH and Strong's definition follows: "Wind; by resemblance breath, i.e., a sensible (or even violent) exhalation; figuratively life, anger, unsubstantiality; by extension a region of the sky; by resemblance spirit, but only of a rational being (including its expression and functions)." We can understand the verse means that the breath of life was ordered to enter into these bodies which had just been formed in the preceding verses. When a word is added to give the expression *four winds*, it means the four quarters of the earth into which the people of God had been scattered. *Breathe* is the verb form and has virtually the same meaning as the words already defined. That is, the breath of life was told to enter the dead bodies that they might live.

Verse 10. *Prophesied* is used because the event ordered to be done was to be in the future. It was still half a century away and would be accomplished after the 70-year captivity has expired.

Verse 11. The Lord gives Ezekiel the interpretation of the foregoing symbols, leaving nothing to guesswork or uncertainty. The second half of this verse is a statement of facts being done at the very time the prophet is writing. That makes history out of the circumstance, and since history shows the fulfillment of a prophecy, I will suggest that the reader connect this with the famous prophecy of Psalm 137.

Verse 12. *I will open your graves* is figurative and refers to the national graves of which Isaiah wrote in chapter 22: 14 of his book. That passage is commented upon in the 3rd volume of this Commentary. Of course the fulfillment of this national resurrection means the return from Babylonian captivity, recorded in Ezra and Nehemiah.

Verse 13. *Ye shall know . . . when.* A prophecy does not become an evidence until it has been fulfilled, hence the Lord says that He will be known as the Lord when this great deliverance has taken place.

Verse 14. *Put my spirit in you* means the spirit of life for the nation will be given to Israel from God. But even the condition of life would not be completely satisfactory if one had no place to live. Hence this nation that is to be brought to life again is promised the privilege of returning to its own land.

Verses 15, 16. The preceding vision

Ezekiel 37: 17-24

was for the purpose of demonstrating the surety of the national resurrection and the possibility of the departure from the grave which was Babylon. Having given unusual but visible proof of that great event, the next subject is a description of the return with specific attention to certain features of the revolution. From this paragraph through verse 23 the passage should be labeled "the return," and the several verses will be commented upon in their order. While doing this, it should be remembered that many things that are said are true of both fleshly and spiritual Israel; the first application, however, will be to the former. In the introduction of the long bracket the prophet is directed to do some "acting" in sight of the people. He is to use a stick in his acting and it is to represent a certain portion of the children of Israel, then take another stick to be for the other part of them. The house of Israel had been divided into 2 kingdoms (1 Kings 12) and they were known as Judah and Israel when considered as separate kingdoms; they also had other designations at times. Ezekiel is to write *Judah* on one stick, and *Ephraim* (because the capital of the 10-tribe kingdom, Samaria, was in the territory possessed by that tribe) on the other.

Verse 17. There is an erroneous doctrine in the world pertaining to the so-called "lost 10 tribes." It is maintained that the 10 tribes who went into captivity under the Assyrians were lost and that only the 2 tribes, Judah and Benjamin, were able to return to Palestine. There is not the slightest foundation for such a notion. On the other hand there is much evidence of the existence of the 12 tribes, and the present verse with the context is a positive denial of the mentioned false notion. Here are 2 sticks that are expressly named for the 2 groups of Israel, the 2-tribe and the 10-tribe kingdoms. It is also stipulated that both sticks are to be joined in such a way as to form one stick. If this means that the 10 tribes were "lost" then also the 2 tribes were, which nobody believes. It is true that in the second or spiritual application there is to be but one tribe (that of Christ who was a descendant of Judah according to the flesh), but that is as true of the 2-tribe kingdom as it is of the other. More on this union of the 2 sticks further on in the chapter.

Verse 18. This verse shows that Ezekiel was to do his acting in the sight of the people. The fact of their asking for the meaning of the demonstration will indicate that everything was done "above board," that it was not an act of trickery but was all in plain sight. The thing that they could not understand was the purpose or meaning of the scene that they had so plainly witnessed.

Verse 19. This verse explains the actions of verse 17. The 2 sticks became one in the hands of Ezekiel, and the 2 groups of Israel were to be one *in mine hand* says the Lord. God knows the whereabouts of all things and persons, and He is able to bring all the 12 tribes together.

Verse 20. It is carefully directed that Israel shall see the performance of Ezekiel.

Verse 21. This verse is a general statement with a literal meaning. The Babylonian Empire was made up of numerous groups from the four quarters of the civilized world. The dominions that were once the Assyrian Empire now belonged to Babylon, and that would naturally embrace the remnants of the kingdom of Israel that had been taken by Assyria, recorded in 2 Kings 17. All of God's people scattered throughout the various localities of heathendom were to be given the privilege of returning to the home land in Palestine after the fall of Babylon and end of the 70-year captivity.

Verse 22. *Make them one nation . . . neither divided into two kingdoms.* The subject of the 2-tribe and 10-tribe kingdoms has not been changed in the message, hence we have a final evidence that the theory of the "lost 10 tribes" is false.

Verse 23. The most important result to be accomplished by the captivity was the cure from idolatry. The first clause of this verse repeats the prediction of that fact and the historical evidence is quoted at Isaiah 1: 25. See the comments at that place in volume 3 of this Commentary.

Verse 24. The comment has been made (verse 16) that some things in this chapter would apply to both fleshly and spiritual Israel. The remainder of the chapter is a prominent specimen of that truth. In a general sense this group of verses applies to fleshly Israel restored to the land of Palestine with Jerusalem as the capital. Because of this the reference is made to David since Jerusalem was his capital. Also because under his *one* capital all the 12 tribes were to be ruled after the return from Babylon. And it applies more significantly to spiritual Israel because David was the ancestor of Christ who was to be king and shepherd over all the flock of God.

Verse 25. The fleshly and spiritual sense of the prophecy are combined in one statement. Fleshly Israel did occupy the land of Palestine after the return from captivity. It is also true that under Christ the son of David the people of God occupy the spiritual land of the kingdom of Christ, the church.

Verse 26. This *covenant of peace* is the one Paul writes about in Hebrews 8: 8-12 and Jeremiah in chapter 31: 31. *Sanctuary . . . evermore* means the kingdom that was pictured to Nebuchadnezzar and was predicted to "stand forever," Daniel 2: 44.

Verse 27. *Tabernacle with them* indicates the close relationship that was to exist between God and his people. The church is not far off, across the sea, up in the skies, in Samaria or Jerusalem, but anywhere that has "two or three gathered together in [into]" the name of Christ, which means by His authority and according to His law.

Verse 28. The literal heathen were shown that God was with Israel when He brought them out of the captivity, as may be observed in the books of Ezra and Nehemiah. And today the world may behold an institution, the church, that has stood for 19 centuries.

EZEKIEL 38

Verses 1, 2. In this paragraph I shall endeavor to identify the persons and places that are mentioned, particularly Gog and Magog. On such a subject it is necessary to refer to authentic secular authors. The first quotation will be from Thayer's Greek Lexicon: "Gog, indeclinable proper name, Gog, king of the land of Magog, who it is said in Ezekiel 38 will come from the remote north, with innumerable hosts of his own nation as well as of allies, and will attack the people of Israel, reestablished after the exile; but by divine interposition he will be utterly destroyed." Funk and Wagnalls' New Standard Bible Dictionary says the following: "Gog, a name given to a race or people inhabiting some part of the 'northern' region. . . . In Ezekiel 38 and 39 God is associated with Meshech, etc., as Magog is in Genesis 10: 5, and probably both refer to the same people." Some other authors make reference to this matter but I believe this is sufficient for our purpose. These people were evidently some wild or uncivilized ruffians from a territory far from the land of Israel. After the people of God were brought back to Palestine following the captivity, these barbarous people invaded the land and thought to do it much harm, associating with them certain other heathen groups as allies. It is against these people that Ezekiel is now instructed to write a series of predictions.

Verse 3. When considered as an individual, Gog refers to the leader among these barbarous people, or perhaps a line of kings with that common title, such as the Pharaohs in Egypt or the Edwards in England. He is singled out here as the one to whom the prophet is to address his predictions.

Verse 4. This verse predicts the counterattack that God will make against this army from the northern territory. After having rescued His people from captivity and settled them in their own land, certainly a rude force like this rough and uncivil horde will not be permitted to interfere with the peace of the country.

Verses 5, 6. These verses are grouped into one paragraph because they contain many of the allies of Magog that will join in attacking the land of Israel.

Verse 7. This verse is a form of challenge to Magog to make the best preparation possible. It is suggested (by way of taunt) that all these foreign allies stand by each other in the attack upon Palestine if they want to be sure of success.

Verse 8. *After many days* refers specifically to the days of the Babylonian captivity, and *the latter years* means the same. *Land that is brought back* denotes the restoration of the land of Palestine to the possession of Israel. *Against the mountains of Israel* means the hostile attack of Magog upon Israel's land. *Which have been always waste* refers to the condition of Palestine during the captivity. *They shall dwell safely* is the assurance from God that Israel shall maintain the possession of the land in spite of the invasion of Magog and its allies.

Verse 9. *Thou* refers to Gog or Magog; one is the country and the other is its king. The verse repeats the prediction previously made that Palestine was going to be invaded by this barbarous company, likened to a *storm* and large *cloud*.

Verse 10. The movements of this band of heathen from the north will

Ezekiel 38: 11-22

not be from a sudden impulse, but will be the result of *things come into thy mind;* will be deliberate.

Verse 11. *Unwalled villages* means the unfortified towns in which the people of Israel will be living with a feeling of security. They will have reason to feel that way after the captivity because God has promised them the security. The people of Magog (or Gog, as I use the terms interchangeably) will imagine they can take advantage of this apparent defenseless condition of the Israelites.

Verse 12. This verse tells the subject of the deliberations which the people of Magog had as stated in the preceding one. The Israelites will have acquired cattle and goods after their return from Babylon and these invaders will plot to get them. That is, it is here predicted they will do so at the time following the return.

Verse 13. *Sheba, Dedan* and *Tarshish* were mercantile people and were heathenish as were the people of Magog. For that reason they would be sympathetic toward any movement attempted against the people of God. This verse represents them as inquiring of the people of Magog about their purpose in coming into the land of Israel. The language is in question form but the thought is that they hoped the invaders would take these things from the people of Israel. Being merchants themselves, they were envious of the prosperous condition of the Israelites and took delight in the prospect of seeing them spoiled. The *young lions* is figurative and means the princes and other leading men of these merchant nations.

Verse 14. *Therefore . . . prophesy* is the proper form of speech because the things that Ezekiel is to write are to take place many years in the future. *Shalt thou not know it* is another expression in question form, but the thought is that the good condition of Israel will be known by Gog. We know that such is the meaning, for the following verse proceeds with the activity the heathen country will manifest on account of that knowledge.

Verse 15. These hostile people will come equipped with a strong force, consisting of both horsemen and foot soldiers. They will also be accompanied with *many people* which means their allies, some of whom are named in verses 5 and 6.

Verse 16. *In the latter days* agrees with "prophecy" in verse 14, and means that the things predicted will be later than the period of Israel's exile. *I will bring thee against my land.* God never forces a good man to become a bad one, but He does sometimes use an evil person to carry out a divine purpose. In this sense these wild people of the northern country were to be used in the way described *that the heathen* (other peoples) might *know* the Lord. *Be sanctified in thee* means that the Lord's goodness will be made manifest to these other countries when they see how He deals with this wicked army. (See the definition of "sanctified" at chapter 36: 23.)

Verse 17. *Of whom I have spoken in old time.* At the time Ezekiel is writing this passage, no prediction had been made specifically against God, but similar writing had been done against other heathen nations. Moreover, the statement italicized will be in the past tense when the time of its fulfillment comes.

Verse 18. *Fury come up in my face* means God's fury will be manifest to those concerned. It will be made evident before their eyes by the things He does to the abominable invaders into the home land of Israel.

Verse 19. A good parent will chastise his child very severely when his conduct deserves it, but he will not tolerate any criticism (even though it is correct) from outside persons. Likewise the Lord will not endure the attacks or even sneers of the heathen directed against His people. *Shaking in the land of Israel.* Not that the people of Israel will be shaken, but the invaders will be thus treated who will then be trespassers in the land of Israel.

Verse 20. We know the predictions are still against Gog and the allies that will be with him when he comes to attack the land of Israel. Much of the language, therefore, must be taken figuratively. If the *fishes, fowls* and *beasts* were literally disturbed, and the *mountains* were demolished in the land of Palestine, then the people of Israel would suffer as well as Gog. The conclusion is therefore reasonable that it is all an ideal picture of the disturbances which God will cause Gog to encounter with reference to his own situation.

Verse 21. One means of bringing defeat to an unrighteous group is to cause its own members to attack each other. (See Judges 7: 22; Isaiah 19: 2.)

Verse 22. Such calamities as are described here could be poured out upon

Gog and his associates without disturbing the people of Israel or Palestine in general.

Verse 23. The most important point to be made in these divine demonstrations will be to make all men know the Lord and to distinguish Him from all false gods.

EZEKIEL 39

Verse 1. This verse takes the same comments as chapter 38: 1, 2. The repetition will serve as emphasis and indicate the intensity of God's feeling against Gog.

Verse 2. *Leave but sixth* part is rather of indefinite meaning according to the lexicon. But it is clear the prediction means that the army of Gog will be almost totally destroyed. *Will cause thee to come* has the same meaning as "bring thee against my land" in verse 16 of the preceding chapter, which see. *Upon the mountains of Israel* will be explained at verse 4.

Verse 3. The bow and arrow was one of the weapons of combat in ancient times. *Cause thine arrows to fall* is equivalent to saying they will be disarmed.

Verse 4. *Fall upon the mountains of Israel* might seem like something unfavorable was to happen to Israel. The context shows it to have been opposite to that in its meaning and that the damage will have come to one who falls. (See a similar use of language in Matthew 21: 44.) It is like the result when a man would get a fall and light upon some injurious substance. That sense is intended in our verse for the result of the fall is to give the bodies that fall as prey to ravenous birds and beasts. The fall so bruised the victims that they were fit for nothing but to be used as food by other creatures that live on flesh.

Verse 5. The flesh of a mangled body is useless except as food for flesh-eating creatures, therefore these carcases were to be cast out into the field for that purpose. This is the figurative picture of the circumstances, and its meaning is that the forces of Gog will be destroyed.

Verse 6. *Magog* is the country from where the above army of invasion came. Its people were *dwelling carelessly* which means they were feeling secure and were not thoughtful of any possible danger. *Isles* denotes "inhabited spots," and the meaning is that the various places within the domain of Magog will feel the force of God's wrath.

Verse 7. The Lord now turns his attention to His own people and the prophet will write some predictions concerning them. To clarify the matter so that the reader may find his "bearings" as to the date, remember that Ezekiel writes this after the whole nation has been brought to Babylon and the greater part of the 70-year captivity is in the future. This explains the clause *I will not let them pollute my holy name any more*. It is a prediction of the cure from idolatry which was effected by the captivity. As a prediction he could say *I will not let*, etc. The way the Lord would prevent it was by holding them in captivity until every trace of love for idols was burned out.

Verse 8. *It is come* is still prophecy and not history although the language sounds like it. The force of the statement is that an inspired prediction is as sure as if it had taken place. *This is the day* is as if the Lord said: "I have been predicting that an important day was coming for my people and this is a description of that day." Then some verses will follow that

Verse 9. The subject is still the successful resistance of Israel against the forces of God. That success is pictured as being so great that they will be able to make fuel out of the weapons that were intended to be used against them.

Verse 10. The language here is strong and somewhat figurative, but the actual success of Israel was intended by the Lord to be very unusual. It is so represented by saying that the material for fuel out of the weapons of the enemy will be so plentiful that it will not be necessary to go to the forest for any of it.

Verse 11. *Graves in Israel* is a prediction that great numbers of the army of God will be slain right in the country where they expected to slay its citizens. *Stop the noses of the passengers*. Noses has no word in the original, and the various translations I have consulted leave the phrase indefinite. It seems clear, however, that the number of those who had to be buried of the people of Gog was to be so great that the attention of travelers will be attracted.

Verse 12. As a further indication of the great number of the people of Gog to be slain, it will take the men of Israel 7 months to bury them. *Cleanse the land* is said from a sanitary standpoint, for if that many corpses were left on the surface it would cause much danger to health.

Verse 13. It was seen in the verse preceding this that very many men of Gog were to be slain, and that the task of burying them would be great also; for this reason most of the people would be needed in the work. *Be to them a renown.* God will glorify Himself by destroying these wicked invaders, and by co-operating with him in this disposal of the dead bodies the people will share in that glory. The New Testament teaches the same principle in Romans 8: 17; 2 Corinthians 1: 7; 2 Timothy 2: 11, 12.

Verse 14. There is no separate word in the original for *employment,* but *continual* is represented and means men who were in constant search for dead bodies to bury. *Bury with the passengers* means the people passing through the land would finally be invited to help in this great task of burying the dead. However, it was to be after the 7 months' work was over that the extra help was invited, and a part of the assistance they were to render was to search to see if any dead had been overlooked in the course of the burying period of 7 months.

Verse 15. *Passengers* means the men passing through who were invited to join in the search for any stray bodies that might have been overlooked. If they came across such bodies they were to set up some kind of a marker so that the others whose special work was to handle the corpses would see them and bury them out of sight. *Hamon-gog* is not strictly a geographical name, but is used to designate the place where so many of the people of Gog were buried. *Hamon* meaning "a crowd" according to Strong.

Verse 16. The word for *city* is an indefinite one and means any locality that is marked by some unusual sight. In this case the sight was that of such a great number of graves; the word *Hamonah* meaning the same as Hamon which is a multitude.

Verse 17. The dumb creatures are invited to a rich feast provided by the Lord, consisting of the flesh of men who had come into Palestine on behalf of Gog. The preceding verses will explain how such a feast was possible. The number of slain men was to be so great that it would require 7 months to bury them. In that length of time many of the bodies would be stripped of their flesh (see *bone* in verse 15), the result of the activities of these creatures that had been invited by the Lord to come and feast themselves. *Sacrifice* does not indicate a religious performance, but the word means a slaughtering of the men of Gog, and that will supply the meat for the beasts.

Verse 18. The *mighty* and *princes* were the great men in the army of Gog that were to furnish meat for the beasts. *Rams* and other animals named are figurative and the terms are used in allusion to the creatures that were used under the law to be served at the feasts prescribed by the Lord.

Verse 19. The words *fat* and *blood* refer literally to the parts of the bodies, but they are used somewhat figuratively. Under the law no one was permitted to eat fat nor blood, but they must be offered to God as a sacrifice. The idea is transferred to these creatures that have been invited to the feast. The words *my sacrifice* give us the explanation of the matter, for if it is the Lord's sacrifice then He can consistently make whatever use of those materials that is considered proper.

Verse 20. The line of thought continues in this verse. *My table* is used in the same sense as *my sacrifice* in the preceding verse. The Lord prepares a table supplied with the bodies of men and horses taken from the army of Gog. He then invites the dumb creatures to feast themselves upon these articles.

Verse 21. The slaughter of the men and horses of the army of Gog will be known to the other *heathen* or other nations. And especially, as there will be such a great number that it will take 7 months to bury the men, the witnesses will be impressed with the glory of the Lord who has wrought such an imposing scene.

Verse 22. Once more the main object of all divine demonstrations is stated, which is that they *shall know that I am the Lord.*

Verse 23. *The heathen shall know,* etc., has this logical meaning. The heathen (or nations in general) knew that Israel had been in exile with one of those strange nations for 70 years. They might have concluded it was because the Lord wanted to show his favor for the heathen world. But when they see the great destruction of the people of Gog (another heathen group), they will know the mentioned conclusion was wrong. They will then be able to form the correct conclusion namely, that *Israel went into captivity for their iniquity*, and not as a favor to the Babylonians.

Verse 24. It was *according to their* [Israel's] *uncleanness* that God hid his face from his people, and let them be held in captivity for 70 years.

Verse 25. As soon as God's wrath was satisfied against his people, His mercy and love for them came into action and the captivity was brought to a close. The terms *Jacob* and *whole house of Israel* are very significant. Let the reader refer to the comments in chapter 37: 15-22 regarding the so-called lost 10 tribes, and connect them with the italicized words in this verse. It will be clear to all that the *whole house of Israel* does not mean 2 tribes only.

Verse 26. Regardless of the form of language as to past, present or future tense, the reader should remember that Ezekiel is writing about half a century before the end of the captivity. The purpose of the predictions is to encourage the people of Israel who had fallen into a state of despondency. (See at the valley of dry bones and 137th Psalm.) But they are given to understand that they must *bear their shame* as a matter of chastisement before being released.

Verse 27. God promised to bring his people out of the enemies' lands.

Verse 28. *Have left none of them any more there.* It is true that even after the 70-year captivity was ended, many Jews remained in that country according to the books of Ezra and Nehemiah. But they were voluntary citizens of Persia and not captives.

Verse 29. *Neither will I hide my face any more from them.* There were numerous times afterward when God was displeased with his people and punished them very severely. But the nation as a whole was never taken in a body from their home land as it was in the Babylonian captivity.

EZEKIEL 40

General remarks. The last 9 chapters of Ezekiel form a group that has been considered to be among the most puzzling passages in the Old Testament. In matters of "doctrine" or conclusions as to the personal conduct of man in relation to God no uninspired writer should be regarded as an "authority." The use that may and should be made of such writers is to seek their assistance in learning the facts and truths that pertain to the meaning of language that is used by the inspired writers. This is especially important as it pertains to statements that depend for their meaning upon history, and on lexicon authority as to the meaning of foreign words. I have consulted some half dozen such works with regard to the chapters now before us. Some of them insist on attaching a great deal of spiritual significance to them as being a picture of things pertaining to Christ and his church, even reaching over into the eternal age. Doubtless there will be found to be some parts of the group that may properly be so interpreted, and when I am convinced that such is the case I shall make my comments accordingly.

There is one point on which all of the mentioned writers agree, and that is that the chapters as a whole are an ideal prediction of the reconstruction period after the 70-year captivity, particularly including the rebuilding of the temple. I believe they are correct in that matter and shall make my comments from that viewpoint.

In studying descriptive compositions that are admittedly ideal and figurative, we should be careful not to make a literal application of the various statements. In symbolic language it is permitted to picture conditions that would even be impossible if taken literally. (See the comments on the first chapter of this book.) This use of illustrative speech is done in parables, in which certain actions or circumstances may be supposed that never did or perhaps never could actually happen, in order to compare some spiritual or moral principle that could occur. One purpose in making these extremes and physically impossible descriptions of things is to give emphasis to the facts and truths they are really intended to represent. Doubtless there will be other observations come to mind as we proceed with the chapters before us that could properly have been included in this introduction. However, I shall very earnestly insist that the reader go over this general statement a number of times before entering into the study of the verses, taking special interest in its several remarks and considering the whole composition as a KEY to the chapters.

Verse 1. This verse establishes the date of the present prediction. To understand it we must again refer to the three divisions or stages by which the great 70-year captiivty was accomplished, for the people of Judah were not taken in Babylon all at the same time. (See comments on the 24th and 25 chapters of 2 Kings in volume 2 of this Commentary.) Ezekiel was taken at the second stage which was 11 years before the *city was smitten* at the early stage. It is a simple case of addition to see that an event that came 14 years after the third stage would be 25 years after the second, which the prophet terms *our captivity* because he was taken to Babylon at that time.

Verse 2. Ezekiel did not go bodily into the land of Israel, but went only *in the visions of God.* This is similar to the experience of John in Revelation 1: 10; 4: 1, 2, who never actually left the island of Patmos, but saw and heard things in a vision. The prophet was shown the things in a vision and he saw a very high mountain (mountain meaning kingdom in symbolic language) and near it was a city.

Verse 3. Brass is a mixture of two or more metals mostly copper, hence the rendering would properly be that word. It is capable of being brought to a high polish, hence is a fitting material to represent something that is attractive. This man had two measuring devices in his hand, a tape measure and a reed or rod. The first was for longer distances and the second for closer and specific dimensions. The mere existence of a measuring instrument of any kind indicates that something is to be "checked" by the standard in force. The man stood *in the gate* which indicated that he was to be admitted into the place with authority for measuring it.

Verse 4. The gist of this verse is that Ezekiel was to give his undivided attention to what was soon to be said and done before him. *Thou brought hither* means the prophet had been put into a vision right there in the land of Babylon. The revelations about to be made to him will be for the information and encouragement of the people of Israel who were in a state of dejection from their bondage in the strange land.

Verse 5. Ezekiel saw a house surrounded by a wall that was to be measured with the reed mentioned in verse 3. Cubits as measurements of length were of different standards in ancient times. Most of them were based on the human body, beginning at the elbow and extending toward the tip of the fingers, or else reaching only as far as the wrist. The reed which the prophet saw was made on the basis of the cubit that extended from the elbow to the wrist, plus a few inches more, namely, a handbreadth. The measuring reed in the hand of this "man" was equal to 6 of the cubits described. The building was measured with this reed and it was one reed wide and one reed high.

Verse 6. The man entered the building to do some measuring of various parts of it. The point I wish to notice is that each of the parts the man measured was of the same dimension which was *one reed.*

Verse 7. Again the unity of measurements was observed, that they were each *one reed.* There was a space of 5 cubits (a little less than one length of the reed) between the chambers or rooms, but each of the rooms themselves was *one reed.* Here is an instance where the thing described was mathematically impossible (consult the KEY), for the rooms in a building could not each be the same in size as the whole structure. But such a thing would be possible were the measurements being checked by a law of principles and not of material proportions. The point is that God does not have a "double standard" in his dealings with mankind.

Verse 8. The porch was the same in size as the several parts of the building. See the comments in the preceding verse on the subject of principles of standards.

Verse 9. There could be no logical or mechanical reason for varying from the rule of *one reed* in some parts of the structure to be measured. Neither can we always see any special application of the peculiar descriptions given. In all cases, however, when the reader is confronted with some apparent contradictions or other puzzling statements, he should consult the KEY at the beginning of this chapter.

Verse 10. In giving the measurements of different parts of the structure the idea of unity will be frequently noticed, which is the case in the present verse as we see the term *one measure* is used twice.

Verse 11. Even in the instance where the figures differ from some others, we may observe the fact that only one basic standard of measurement is used; that is always the "regulation" unit of *cubit* or a multiple of it, or else an integral part of it. Such a rule is like the Lord's plan today, which is to require His people to use one rule only in gauging their speech and conduct; that one rule is "the oracles of God" (1 Peter 4: 11). But this divine rule does not make the same amount of demand of each person, it is to be according to his ability. But whatever difference of talent there may be, each servant of God must be measured by the same rule which is indicated in Philippians 3: 16.

Verse 12. A reference to verse 5 shows that a measurement of 6 cubits is the same as one reed. In this verse the idea of unity in the principles of an authoritative standard is maintained. We have either the whole reed or a recognized portion of it which is a cubit.

Verse 13. We usually think of a *gate* as meaning an opening in a fence or other external protective wall. The lexicon, however, defines it merely as an opening whether a gate or door. In the measurements of this verse the distance from one chamber to another lacked one cubit of being 4 reeds, and the doors were lined up so as to be directly facing each other.

Verse 14. In this chapter the word *post* is always from the same original and is defined in the lexicon as any part that is constructed as a prop or support for some other portion of a structure; the posts of this verse were 10 reeds high.

Verse 15. *Face* is from a Hebrew word that Strong says has many applications. But one part of his definition is that it refers to something that turns, which probably is the reason it is used in connection with the *gate* of this structure. The distance between the entrance gate to the porch over the inner opening was 50 cubits or 8 reeds.

Verse 16. *Narrow* means somewhat closed in the way of a lattice, and a *window* was a place that was perforated. This may be understood by remembering that glass and other transparent substances for admission of light had not been devised in those times. It is reasonable to suppose that the kind of windows just described would not admit the amount of light that could be done with transparent glass. That is why they had to have them *round about*. The *palm trees* were some kind of ornaments either carved or painted upon the posts.

Verse 17. The word *court* occurs a number of times in the Old Testament and it is from CHATSER which Strong defines as follows: "A yard (as inclosed by a fence); also a hamlet (similarly surrounded with walls)." Hence in this verse Ezekiel was taken into the open space surrounding the building which was paved. On this pavement there were 30 chambers which Strong defines as "a room in a building (whether for storage, eating or lodging)." There would doubtless be frequent calls for just such a service.

Verse 18. The general pavement described in the preceding verse was on a level with the gates, and they were therefore conveniently related to the floors of the chambers. The *lower pavement* of this verse was by the sides of the gates and not directly connected with the chambers as to the height.

Verse 19. The *lower gate* was one that corresponded in elevation to the *lower* pavement of the preceding verse. The distance from this lower gate to the wall of the inner court was 100 cubits or more than 16 reeds.

Verse 20. These courts all were inclosed by some kind of wall and they were provided with gates. All of these gates were measured in order to be "checking" on them to see how they compared with the standard adopted of a cubit or multiple of it.

Verse 21. There were three little chambers on each side of the gate that is mentioned in the preceding verse. The *posts* were reinforcing parts added to strengthen the porch and arched covering over the pavement. This combination or unit was an oblong, being 50 by 25 cubits or about 75 by 37 feet.

Verse 22. *Their windows* means the windows of the preceding verse, and the *arches* were the porches or shaded covering over the windows. The dimensions of these parts were the same as those described in verse 16.

Verse 23. *Over against* means it was opposite to the other gates in a way that caused the three to face each other. There was a considerable space taken up with this unit of the great structure, for it was 100 cubits or about 150 feet.

Verse 24. The parts of the structure described in this verse were similar to those stated in verse 21, which is indicated by, *according to these measures.*

Verse 25. The windows were perforated or latticed places for the admission of light. *Like those windows* denotes that the windows of the building as a whole were made along the same line, which is in harmony with the principle of uniformity which the Lord generally maintains in His works.

Verse 26. This last gate seems to have been higher than the area immediately adjoining it, for it required 7 steps to reach it. The *palm trees* were ornamental items that were either carved or painted on the posts.

Verse 27. This side was similar to the others in that it had both an inner and outer gate; the gates were 100 cubits or 150 feet apart.

Verse 28. Ezekiel and the "man" are still at the south side and the prophet is witnessing the measuring of the gate from the viewpoint of the inner court. *According to these measures* means he used the same standard that he did in the other places.

Verse 29. *Little chambers* are still the smaller rooms or resting places that were situated in various convenient places connected with the building. The windows and arches (covered porches) were like the others in both form and dimensions.

Verse 30. Lest the reader's memory be dulled by the many repetitions and become confused by the different measurements, I shall again explain that these *arches* were parts that were in the nature of porches or porticoes. They served as a protection for the gates, as well as to add beauty to the architecture by conforming to the principles of symmetry and thus pleasing the eye when beholding it.

Verse 31. These arches or porches served as an overhead shield or protective covering for the parts where they were erected. One of them extended toward the outer court and the posts of it were ornamented with the likenesses of palm trees. The elevation of this porch was 8 steps above the adjoining area.

Verse 32. The prophet was taken from one side of these structures to the other. He has been on the north and south, now he is brought into the inner court toward the east. *According to these measures* means the same standard of measurements was used that was adopted at the beginning of the inspection.

Verse 33. The *little chambers* were the small resting places that were built round at the outer border of the pavement. They were all covered by arches or porches, reinforced by the posts. These porches were provided with windows or perforated spaces and the entire unit was built *according to these measures* or in harmony with the authoritative standard issued by the Lord which consisted of 6 cubits to a reed.

Verse 34. The present work of inspection was in the inner court according to verse 32, but the arches or porches were extended toward the outward court. Since these arches were a sort of shield for the walkways, we are not surprised to find them in so many places. These arches were supported by the posts which were ornamented with the same kind of engraving or painting that we have seen in the other places. This walkway was higher than the surrounding area so that it required 8 steps to reach it.

Verse 35. Again the "inspector" went to the north gate and applied the same standard of measuring tape that was used in other instances.

Verse 36. The measurements and other details observed here are the same as they were at the other gates generally speaking. There was a wonderful uniformity in all of the major parts of the great building.

Verse 37. *Utter* means the exterior and the thought is that the posts were provided for the porch to the extent of the outside area. There were two rows of the posts and all of them had the ornaments of palm trees, and it was necessary also to make 8 steps by which to reach the floor of this walkway.

Verse 38. *Washed the burnt offering.* The law of Moses required that animals intended for sacrifice on the altar must be washed (Leviticus 1: 9, 13; 9: 14).

Verse 39. The people of Israel were promised their release from captivity after the proper period of chastisement, at which time they were to return to Palestine and resume their worship of the true God. That would include the offering of animal sacrifices, and these tables were provided for the slaying of the victims.

Verse 40. A great many beasts would be slain to meet the services of the people and many places of the entries to the building, 8 tables in all.

Verse 41. The location of the tables was in groups of 4 tables each.

Verse 42. The tables were hewn out of solid stone and were one and a half cubits square by one cubit high. The stone being less porous than wood made them more sanitary. The instruments needed in preparing the animals were kept on the tables. *Burnt offering . . . sacrifice.* For practical purposes these words may generally be used interchangeably, but when a distinction is made one means something voluntarily brought to the service while the other is specifically required. However, the two are so interwoven in their application that I shall quote the definition from Strong for each. *Offering* is from QURBAN and defined, "Something brought near the altar, i.e., a sacrificial present." *Sacrifice* is from ZEBACH which is defined, "Properly a slaughter, i.e. the flesh of an animal; by implication a sacrifice (the victim or the act)."

Verse 43. *Within* means just inside the porch were hooks and they were used for convenience in handling the parts of the sacrifices.

Verse 44. These singers were the persons who conducted the services that had been started by David. This group was provided with some of the chambers or resting places on the inside of the court. These "booths" were located by the side of the north gate and they faced toward the south. Then another was at the side of the east gate, and it faced toward the north.

Verse 45. These chambers were used also by the priests and their work was classified, one group having charge of the temple.

Verse 46. The other chamber was for the priests who served at the altar. *Sons of Zadok* means those who descended from that line of the priesthood.

Verse 47. This court was different from the one mentioned before. It was 100 cubits square and contained the altar upon which were burned the various sacrifices.

Verse 48. *He brought me* means the "man" introduced in verse 3 who was conducting this inspection tour for the information of Ezekiel. *Porch of the house* means an entry to the main building. It had large posts or columns on each side, seven and a half feet in thickness, for strength and massiveness in appearance.

Verse 49. This entry was a magnificent structure. It was 30 feet long and about 17 feet wide. Its floor was higher than the adjoining area and was reached by steps. In addition to the reinforcing posts there were pillars on each side of the entrance.

EZEKIEL 41

Verse 1. The heading on the pages of most Bibles, also the statements in works of reference, give to this chapter as a whole the subject of the temple. I believe that to be correct and will make my comments accordingly. In writing on that subject, however, the prophet makes occasional references to the temple of Solomon and the tabernacle built by Moses. It will assist the reader if he can take the time to read the description of those buildings as given in Exodus, chapters 25-30 and 1 Kings 6. But the descriptions that are in the present chapter will be found much more complicated and indefinite than the ones referred to. (See the KEY again.) The *posts* in this temple correspond to the boards of the tabernacle that Moses made.

Verse 2. The door was 10 cubits or 15 feet wide. The sides of the door, which means the door jambs, were 5 cubits or seven and a half feet square. *Length thereof* means that of the room to which the mentioned door was the entrance.

Verse 3. The measurements of this verse are what he found on the inside part of the entrance structure.

Verse 4. The dimensions of this *most holy* place were the same as those in the temple of Solomon (1 Kings 6: 20).

Verse 5. The wall of this was 6 cubits or 9 feet thick, and all round the wall of the building there were chambers or rooms that were 4 cubits wide. These were similar to the chambers of which we read in the preceding chapter.

Verse 6. The chambers were three stories high and were attached to the wall but not built as a part of it. No doubt such an arrangement was had so that each chamber could be made steady but not weakened by being merged with the other material.

Verse 7. The three-storied groups of chambers were unique in their plan, for each one was wider than the one under it. In going from the ground floor or pavement to the top story, the stairway was on the inside so that it was necessary to ascend by way of the middle story. Such a plan might give the unit a top-heavy appearance, and that would explain why it was braced by being fastened to the side wall.

Verse 8. The side chambers were built upon a raised platform that was a reed thick. *Great* is not from a word that means size; it is one that signifies something as a connection. The thought is that this platform that was supporting the chambers was in addition to the main wall or foundation of the building.

Verse 9. Much of the arrangement of this whole architecture was done so as to please the eye. For instance, it would look somewhat abrupt to have the platform on which the chambers were resting to extend wide enough only to hold them, but instead, there was an extension so as to give a margin of 5 cubits.

Verse 10. The chambers were not crowded up against each other in a way that would suggest any shortage of room; there was a space of 20 cubits between them.

Verse 11. These chambers had each a door on the side and one on the north. They were entered from the platform which was described in verses 8 and 9. This would be another reason why the chambers should not be jammed up against each other.

Verse 12. At one end of the building we have been studying was another that may be regarded as an addition or annex; it was 105 feet wide. Its wall was 8 feet thick and the whole annex was 135 feet long.

Verse 13. This verse is a summary of certain portions of the general structure that Ezekiel has been observing. The main house was 150 feet long, and besides this, there was an extension in length of 150 feet.

Verse 14. *Separate place* is from one original and refers to some part of the building on the east side. *Face* is evidently used figuratively because it was the rule to "face" the east with important buildings.

Verse 15. *Against the separate place* means that part near the place noted in the preceding verse. Strong defines the original for *galleries* as "a ledge or offset in a building." These were extensions of some kind on the outside of the main building and served as a walkway or arcade, and they reached 100 cubits or 150 feet.

Verse 16. Transparent glass was not known in those times, hence the *narrow windows* or latticed loopholes were provided to serve these arcades. There were three stories to these arcades and all of them were ceiled with wood. This ceiling not only covered the top as is usually done, but the walls also were ceiled from the ground up as far as the windows, and some kind of covering was made for the windows.

Verse 17. The ceiling described in the preceding verse extended over the parts named in this. *By measure* denotes that the ceiling was measured to harmonize with the areas already described and checked by the adopted standard.

Verse 18. These *cherubims* and *palm trees* were for ornamentation, and for added attractiveness the two kinds of ornaments were placed so as to alternate with each other. The cherubims had each two faces which will be explained in the next verse.

Verse 19. We usually think of a person who is "two-faced" in an unfavorable light, but such is not always necessary, even when the faces are not alike. Things may differ without being contradictory, and hence they may co-operate with each other in a common interest. By having two faces the cherubims could see the palm trees from two viewpoints or with two kinds of interests. The palm tree was one of the most admired of all the plants that grew in Palestine. It is referred to in poetic speech as a symbol of peace, and it was literally used for food and other practical purposes. Since the tree therefore was useful for both man and beast, it was appropriate that the faces of the cherubims would be those of a man and a lion.

Verse 20. The wall of the temple from the ground to the height of the door had these ornamental engravings or pictures of lions and palm trees.

Verse 21. This verse means that the general appearance of the posts or supporting columns, and the face or front of the building, were uniform and were square or 4-sided.

Verse 22. The *altar of wood* was for the purpose of burning incense, hence did not require to be covered with metal. *Table before the Lord* is in allusion to the altar of incense that was in the tabernacle, and located against the vail covering the ark of testimony where the Lord was represented by the glorious light.

Verse 23. There were two apartments in the temple hence the need for two doors.

Verse 24. The doors were what are called "folding doors" today.

Verse 25. These doors had the same kind of ornamentation engraved on them as was on the walls. The *thick planks* were the kind used as stepping pieces or thresholds.

Verse 26. The *narrow windows* were the same kind of latticed or perforated spaces that we have observed, because there was no transparent material in use at that time. The *thick planks* is from a different original from that in the preceding verse, and means some boards suitable for a protective covering or projection over the windows.

EZEKIEL 42

Verse 1. The *utter* court means the outer one that was on the north side. The *separate place* was the one commented upon in chapter 41: 12. There was one of the chambers at this place and Ezekiel was taken into it.

Verse 2. The dimensions stated here identify the place as the one described in chapter 41: 13 and the reader may see the comments at that place.

Verse 3. The separate place referred to was *over against* or near the point of the 20 cubits connected with the inner court, also near the pavement provided for the outer court. At this location was a three-storied unit of galleries or projecting ledges.

Verse 4. Running along the rows of chambers there was a passage that was 10 cubits wide, and the doors of the chambers opened out upon this walk.

Verse 5. These upper chambers were *shorter* to harmonize with the decreasing width of the building near it.

Verse 6. Many of the units of the structure were in threes but the reason for it is not stated. This place *had not pillars* as other parts had. For this reason the writer states it was *straitened* or contracted more than either lower or middle story.

Verse 7. The outside of this unit of chambers was a wall 50 cubits long, corresponding with the extent of the chambers.

Verse 8. The two fifties of cubits agreed with the 100 cubits that were before the temple so that there would be no unevenness in the combination.

Verse 9. It should be remembered that we are now reading about the chambers assigned especially for the priests, hence there was an entry into them provided that went under the chambers from the outer court.

Verse 10. *In the thickness* denotes the width of the chambers, and they were *over against* which means they were near the *separate place*, a description of which has been given elsewhere.

Verse 11. The main thought in this verse is one of uniformity of design and appearance. The dimensions and *fashions* of the parts are said to have a *like appearance*.

Verse 12. The fact of observing things of different sides did not reveal any great difference in general design. Instead, the statement is made that the one was *according to* the other in most cases.

Verse 13. *Holy chambers* furnishes the key to the particular purpose of these parts of the great structure. They are regarded as *holy* because of what was to take place in them namely, the ritualistic services of the Mosaic religion.

Verse 14. When the priests enter these chambers to perform their holy work, they are required to lay aside their personal garments and put on the ones prescribed for the sacred service, and that service was *for the people* as stated here.

Verse 15. *Prospect* means the direction in which the gate faced, and the man measured the area around this gate.

Verse 16. *Reed* is used in a general sense and means that the place was measured with a rod, and according to Moffatt's version it was about 500 cubits.

Verse 17. The north side was evidently measured with the same length rod as the east and it revealed it to be the same dimension as the other.

Verse 18. The south side was the same as the preceding ones already measured.

Verse 19. This completed the four sides and the symmetry of the spot was maintained by keeping the four sides equal in extent.

Verse 20. The four sides that have been measured were supplied with a wall extending throughout their entire boundary. *Sanctuary* means the holy part and *profane* refers to the part that was not sacred because it was not specifically used by priests.

EZEKIEL 43

Verse 1. Ezekiel was not taken to this gate to see it measured this time. The building having been measured and hence officially "checked," it was ready for use and the prophet was brought here with this in view.

Verse 2. If there is any figurative significance in the *east* as being the direction from which *the glory of God* came, it is due to the fact that the sunlight comes from that point. This glory of God was destined to show itself in due time on behalf of His people, and it was to have its effect upon the great country that was holding the people of the Lord in subjection at the very time that Ezekiel was writing this.

Verse 3. *When I came to destroy the city* is correctly rendered in the margin, "When I came to prophesy that the city should be destroyed." (See the comments on a like passage in Jeremiah 1: 10.)

Verse 4. The glory of the Lord that came from the east entered even into the house that had been measured with the *reed*.

Verse 5. Ezekiel saw the glory of the Lord enter the house, and then he was transported into the inner court where he could behold the greatness of that glory, which was so great that it filled the house.

Verse 6. Ezekiel has reference to both the Lord and the man who has been doing the measuring. The latter stood by him and the Lord did the speaking.

Verse 7. This verse is a prediction that was to be fulfilled after the captivity had been completed. The land of Palestine with the temple in Jerusalem is that which is referred to in the forepart of the verse. The personal location of the throne of God is in Heaven, but also wherever His worship is instituted the throne of the Lord is represented. That holy place had been defiled by the idolatry (spiritual whoredom) of Judah, but that was to be ended permanently by the 70-year captivity. See the historical note on this subject at Isaiah 1: 25 in volume 3 of this Commentary. *Carcases* is from PEGER, which Strong defines, "A carcase (as limp), whether of man or beast; figuratively an idolatrous image." This indicates that the idolatrous people of Judah may have represented their corrupt devotions by buying some images of their gods in the high places where they had the altars erected.

Verse 8. The gist of this verse is that the people tried to mix the true with the false religion, and such a practice was always abominable in the sight of God. (Leviticus 10: 10; 11: 47.) *Have consumed them* means they had lost their national standing by being exiled from their own land.

Verse 9. This exhortation came at the time when the great 70-year captivity was fully started, but the greater part of it was in the future. Since the people heeded the admonition given them, the verse may properly be regarded both as a warning and a prediction which was fulfilled according to the note cited at verse 7.

Verse 10. *Be ashamed of their iniquities* is another passage that is both an admonition and a prediction. That they became ashamed of their record is indicated by the language in the 137th Psalm and Ezekiel 37: 11. This attitude is also very evident in the books of Ezra and Nehemiah which are a record of things after the captivity.

Verse 11. *If they be ashamed* is a very significant phrase. The law of the Lord never has much effect on the life of an unrighteous man as long as he is interested in his evil life. But if and when he becomes ashamed of that life, he will be willing to give his attention to something good. The people of Judah (or Israel) were destined to become ashamed of idolatry and willing to turn back to the true God. Their former temple with its services having been destroyed, it was necessary that a restitution or restoration be made which the Lord purposed to have done. As an encouraging prediction for these people, Ezekiel was told to show to them the pattern of the restored institutions. He not only was to write out a report of what had been revealed to him, but was to do so *in their sight*.

Verse 12. Some details will be added to the foregoing chapters on the reconstruction of the divine institutions and the laws to regulate them. Strong says the original for *mountain* is sometimes used figuratively. This verse means the whole territory where the house is to be rebuilt is to be regarded as holy.

Verse 13. The altar meant is the one to be used for animal sacrifices. *Cubit is a cubit and an hand breadth* is explained at chapter 40: 5.

Verse 14. *Settle* means "a border" or ledge projecting from the face of the altar that would relieve the broad plainness of the instrument and add to its attractiveness. There were two of these borders; the first one started two cubits from the bottom and it was a cubit wide. Then four cubits up from that border was the next one a cubit wide.

Verse 15. After the top ledge the altar extended 6 feet higher, and on the four corners of the altar there were horns, one on each corner.

Verse 16. The altar as measured here was 12 cubits or 18 feet square.

Verse 17. The altar was 12 cubits long and the *settle* or ledge was 14 cubits long, which means that the ledge was one cubit in its extension beyond the side of the altar. The ledge had a border about it that was half a cubit, probably something added to give it a finished appearance. At the bottom of this altar there was a flange or base all round the piece that was a cubit broad. The *stairs* means the approach to the altar, not steps as we usually think of the parts, for that was forbidden by the law of Moses (Exodus 20: 26) which was the basis for the present institution.

Verse 18. Having given the details of construction for the altar, the Lord announced to Ezekiel that he would be told about the proper services to be done on it.

Verse 19. Priests, Levites; that is to be understood from the fact that while all priests were Levites, not all Levites were priests. At the time of which the prophet was writing they were restricted to the line of Levites coming down from Zadok (1 Chronicles 24: 3). The kind of animals that might be offered was the same as the law of Moses had designated (Exodus 29: 10).

Verse 20. The carcass of a beast was to be burned on the altar, but the blood was to be used as a cleansing agent. It was to be put on the various parts of the piece of furniture in the services to *cleanse and purge it*.

Verse 21. *Appointed place* denotes that the sacrificial services could not be performed at just any place that might suit the worshiper. The law of Moses prescribed the procedure that would be accepted and no change would be received and blessed after they returned from the captivity and resumed their religious practices for the Lord.

Verse 22. The repetition of animal sacrifices was calculated to impress the worshiper with the necessity of being thorough. The beast to be used must be one that is without blemish the same as required by Moses.

Verse 23. Another repetition is required even after the altar had been cleansed. It signified that the fitness of the divine institutions is not all that is required, but the worshiper must also be present with the suitable preparation.

Verse 24. *Before the Lord* means to do it in the presence of the altar, for the Lord would not recognize the offering if done in another place. See the comments on "appointed place" in verse 21. *Salt* may be referred to from both a literal and figurative viewpoint. It is a literal preservative, and when considered figuratively it denotes permanence in the thing with which it is connected.

Verse 25. These stipulations were similar to the requirements made in the law of Moses. (See Exodus 29: 35; Leviticus 8: 33.) The first 5 chapters of Leviticus give the details of many of the principal sacrifices the Jews were required to offer, and other items are to be found in later chapters of that book.

Verse 26. *Seven* is a symbol of completeness and it or a multiple of it is very prominent throughout the Bible. The altar was to be purified first, then the people were required to prepare themselves by being sincerely consecrated.

Verse 27. The initial service of 7 days was not to be the end of their religious activities. After that *and so forward* the offerings were to be offered on the altar under the supervision of the priests.

EZEKIEL 44

Verse 1. Chapter 43: 5 tells of the "man" taking Ezekiel to the inner court, and the present verse shows that he was *brought back* towards the outside again where he found the gate shut.

Verse 2. Chapter 43: 4 gives us the reason the east gate was shut; and it is so stated here. The Lord is the One whose right it is to use that gate, and it was to be closed to the people in general.

Verse 3. This gate was for the special use of the prince which would mean whoever was a leading man or one in a leading position among the people of Israel.

Verse 4. Wherever one looked about the holy building he would see evidences of the glory of the Lord. *Fell upon my face* was an ancient custom when a person wished to manifest great respect for another and humility in himself. We need not suppose that one performed any violent action such as would cause an injury to the body. But the act was done in such a decided

Ezekiel 44: 5-23

manner as to leave no doubt about the genuine humility of the worshiper or any person who wished to give special recognition to another.

Verse 5. This verse is virtually the same as chapter 40: 4.

Verse 6. *Let it suffice you* means for them to realize that they had already committed enough abominations, and they should be content to change their ways.

Verse 7. When circumcision is used figuratively or spiritually, it means consecration and devotion to duty unto the Lord. The people of Israel had become so inconsistent in their practices that the Lord regarded them as uncircumcised.

Verse 8. According to chapter 40: 45 the priests were the lawful keepers of the holy place. But these men had put others in their place, men who were not qualified either officially or morally for the holy work.

Verse 9. Under no condition was a stranger (one outside the nation) to be permitted to participate in the offering of sacrifices. This was not only because they were uncircumcised in the flesh, but also were unfit with regard to their character.

Verse 10. The Levites were the ones who had been appointed by the Lord for the services about the altar. However, they had corrupted themselves by going after the worship of idols and hence became abominable to God. *Bear their iniquity* means they would suffer the consequences of their unrighteous life.

Verse 11. *Yet they shall be ministers*, etc. It was the Lord's decision that the tribe of Levi should have exclusive charge of the priesthood, and their unfaithfulness did not make it lawful for anyone outside to meddle in the altar services.

Verse 12. The outside people had no right to be substituted for the lawful priesthood that was vested in the tribe of Levi; yet the unfaithfulness of that group was destined to bring forth the judgment of the Lord. They mixed the true worship with that of idols and for that reason God said *I have lifted up mine hand against them.*

Verse 13. Just as Ezekiel was writing this verse, the Levites were in Babylon where they were destined to remain for nearly half a century longer. While in that country they will not be permitted to perform the services of the sanctuary. And even after the return from captivity, the individuals who were stained with idolatry will not be permitted to *come near unto me* saith the Lord; that will be reserved for others.

Verse 14. However, these demoted persons will be required to perform some service.

Verse 15. In all cases of iniquity there have been exceptions although they were generally in the minority. We may note the instance of Lot and his family, Noah and his family, and the ones predicted by Jesus to be in evidence at the day of judgment. Thus it was when the people of Judah went astray as a nation, there were some priests who *kept the charge of the sanctuary*, and they are now promised the honor of being near the Lord to minister unto Him.

Verse 16. The *table* is the altar described in chapter 41: 22.

Verse 17. These worthy persons of the sons of Zadok were to be admitted into the sanctuary for the purpose of performing the services belonging to the priesthood. The wearing of linen instead of wool would be in accordance with the law of Moses.

Verse 18. The 28th chapter of Exodus gives the instructions for making the garments of the priests. It may be noted that linen was used extensively, while no mention is made of any woolen material for any of the garments.

Verse 19. This verse corresponds with verses 13 and 14 in chapter 42.

Verse 20. *Neither shave . . . nor grow long* may seem to be a contradiction but it is not. The first refers to a practice of shaving the hair down to the skin in certain places about the head. It was a heathenish custom and God's people were forbidden to follow it (Leviticus 21: 1-5). The second part of the citation means they were not to neglect the hair altogether but were to *poll* it which means to trim it off so that it would not be regarded as long hair. (See 1 Corinthians 11: 14.)

Verse 21. The reason for this law is given in Leviticus 10: 9.

Verse 22. This verse likewise is on the same basis as the law of Moses. The restriction against marrying a widow was not applicable in the case of one who had been married to a priest before.

Verse 23. *Holy* and *profane* differ from each other in that the latter means only the thing is temporal or earthly and not religious. It does not mean necessarily that it is something wrong morally. The sons of Aaron failed to distinguish between fire that was obtained from some ordinary (profane) human source, and that which was on the altar which was holy because it came from God (Leviticus 9: 24).

Verse 24. The priests were to render decisions when a controversy arose between the people, but it was to be *according to my judgments.* They were not to make laws regarding the conduct of the people, for their authority consisted only in making the application of the law of the Lord.

Verse 25. The law of Moses regarded a dead person unclean, but this meant especially from a ceremonial standpoint. There were men outside the priesthood who could take care of the dead and the priests could remain clean and always be ready to perform their own particular office. But for their near relatives an exception was made because the nearness of the relationship would sometimes make it necessary to touch them.

Verse 26. When it was necessary for a priest to handle a dead body, he was not permitted to resume his official service until he had been cleansed, which required a period of 7 days including certain ceremonies.

Verse 27. The 19th chapter of Leviticus should be studied in connection with the present group of verses, because it gives the law of cleansing under the Mosaic system. When the priest has completed the term of days required for his cleansing, he is to begin his activities by offering a *sin offering.* (See Leviticus 4: 1-12 for the regulations on this subject.)

Verse 28. *Be unto them for an inheritance.* The Levites were not given possessions of estates as were the other tribes, because they were to be employed in the services around the house of God. *I am their inheritance* means that instead of having land from which to obtain a living, they would be cared for by the Lord through the provisions of that service which He required of them. (See 1 Corinthians 9: 13.)

Verse 29. This verse states some of the details of how the priests lived from their service to God. From the sacrifices which the people of Israel brought to the altar the priests took certain portions for their food.

Verse 30. *Oblations* is another name for offerings which the people were required to bring to the service. Before they could make use of the products of the soil and herds, they must take the best of the fruit and turn it over to the priests.

Verse 31. The priests were restricted according to this verse in regard to the eating of certain things. For that reason the people would know better than to bring such articles to the service since these men had to "live of the things of the altar."

EZEKIEL 45

Verse 1. The figures and descriptions are so out of proportion to what the literal meaning could be here, I shall insist that the reader again see the KEY at the beginning of chapter 40. The whole passage is still an ideal and figurative description of the restoration work that was to be done after the release from Babylonian captivity. But although that is the over-all subject with perhaps very little significance attached to the details of the description, I shall try to explain the meaning of them. This verse begins the redistribution of the land which is an allusion to the division that was made by Joshua after the entrance of the children of Israel into Palestine. Almost all important operations that the Israelites performed were started with a sacrifice of some kind which is the meaning of *oblation.* The first portion was to be allotted to the Lord and it is called *an holy portion. Reeds* has no word in the original, but Moffatt's translation renders the numbers of this verse as eight and a third by six and two-thirds miles. This tract was to be regarded as holy ground.

Verse 2. Within the plot of holy ground described in the preceding verse there was to be a space reserved for the *sanctuary* (holy place) that was 500 reeds square, and it was to have some "spare" space of 50 cubits or 75 feet all around.

Verse 3. This verse states the same dimensions as in the first verse and adds some particulars as to its use, that it was to be used as a holy place.

Verse 4. The priests were the ones who had charge of the holy things and they were to have their dwelling places within this territory.

Verse 5. The extra space extending beyond the plot described for the sanctuary but within that measured off in verses 1 and 3 was to be used for the priests in which they would have erected 20 chambers or rooms.

Verse 6. This verse designates a strip of land to lie alongside that which is assigned to the priests, and it was to be for the use of *the whole house of Israel,* something like an open campus or common grounds.

Verse 7. The measurements of this verse are virtually within the restrictions already indicated. The added thought is the use to be made of this strip which is for the *prince,* which means the man in a leading position before the people.

Verse 8. *Prince* is from NASIY and Strong defines it, "Properly an exalted one, i.e., a king or sheik." In the King James version of the Bible it has been translated by captain, chief, governor, prince, ruler and others. It may or may not designate an official, but among the Jews it was used for both. The use of it in our present passage means one who has some rule over the people. The Lord predicts that his people would not be oppressed by this class of head men after the return from the captivity.

Verse 9. At the time this scripture was being written the people of Judah (or Israel) were in captivity and the princes did not have the opportunity to oppress them. The warning admonition was to chastise the wicked head men for their past wrong doing and to command them about their conduct in the future.

Verse 10. The *ephah* and *bath* were measures of quantity in ancient times. The princes used fraudulent standards and thus imposed upon the people under them. God decreed and predicted that such transactions would not be repeated after the return.

Verse 11. The Lord not only commanded that just measurements should be used, but gave instructions about what would constitute such standards. Strong says that an *ephah* is "a measure in general." It seems that some of the units of capacity were allowed to vary at different times and places, and that would give rise to questions as to justice in dealing with the people. The Lord put such disputes at rest by setting the standard for weights and measures. He ordained that whether the *ephah* or *bath* be used in a transaction it should be the same capacity which was a tenth of a homer.

Verse 12. *Maneh* is a unit of indefinite capacity and was to be recognized according to the custom in force in any given community. A shekel was to consist of 20 gerahs, but as to the number of shekels required to make up a maneh, whether 20, 25 or 15, the prevailing practice must be observed by the princes in their dealing with the people.

Verse 13. An *oblation* means an offering for the service of the Lord. If it consisted of grain it must be measured according to the standard set in verse 11.

Verse 14. The oil in use was olive oil and it was valuable because of its many purposes. It furnished light, was used as food and was valuable for medical treatment. The offering of it was therefore the giving of a thing of value. A *cor* was "a deep round vessel" in which the olive oil was stored.

Verse 15. The animal sacrifices had been instituted under the Mosaic law and the regulations are written in the beginning chapters of Leviticus. In the present case the Lord was very lenient and required them to offer only one lamb out of each two hundred. However, the requirements were the same as formerly in that the animal must be one that was well fed, which is the idea in the phrase *out of the fat pastures of Israel.*

Verse 16. *All the people* means the foregoing offering was to be for the congregation in general; none were excused from the obligation.

Verse 17. The *prince* in this case would be the priest "on duty" at the time. The people were to bring their gifts to headquarters for the service, then the priest would officiate or preside in the services at the altar.

Verse 18. The first day of the month was a special holy time under the Mosaic law, and that was the date stipulated by the Lord for this service of consecration of the land after returning from the Babylonian captivity.

Verse 19. Putting blood upon the door posts of a house is a formal way of consecrating the house. It is also a signal of the importance attached to the inside of the house. This recalls the ceremonies that took place in Egypt on the night of the first passover when the first born of the families was to be slain (Exodus 12).

Verse 20. The word *simple* is from PETHAIY which Strong defines, "Silly (i.e., seducible)." It is used in this verse to denote one who does not use his mind about his conduct, not that he is really lacking in brain power. Such a person is not regarded with as much criticism as one who deliberately does wrong.

Verse 21. This feast is identical with that prescribed in the law of Moses. The details of that feast are recorded in Exodus 12 and Leviticus 23.

Verse 22. The *prince* would be the priest in active service in this case.

Verse 23. This 7-day feast is also described in Leviticus 23.

Verse 24. The word *meat* means "meal" and it is so rendered in the margins of some Bibles. The formula for this offering, which was wholly vegetable except the salt, may be found in Leviticus 2. It was to be added to the animal sacrifices named.

Verse 25. This feast of 7 days in the seventh month is called the feast of tabernacles in Leviticus 23: 34. It was instituted to commemorate the experience of the children of Israel who dwelt in tents or tabernacles during the 40 years they were going through the wilderness.

EZEKIEL 46

Verse 1. A gate could be shut and not be fastened, and there is nothing said about that subject. However, the fact of its being opened on the sabbath indicates that the Lord's business was going on.

Verse 2. Sometimes the *prince* may be also the priest since the word has a general meaning. But both names are used in this place which leaves the first to mean a ruler or other outstanding man among the Jews. He will be required to make offerings for the Lord's service and the priest will be the one to preside at the altar.

Verse 3. *The people* means the unofficial Jews of the nation, and they were all required to contribute to the Lord's work. These offerings were to be made at the entrance of the gate and not in their private homes. Not all sabbaths were the days of the new moons, but every new moon marked the day as a sabbath, according to Numbers 28: 11; 1 Samuel 20: 5, 18, 24, 27).

Verse 4. The details of the burnt offerings are given in Leviticus 1. All the animals for the sacrificial altar must be perfect and the best of the herd or flock.

Verse 5. The *meat* (meal) offering was offered in connection with the animal sacrifice. This vegetable offering was accompanied with a small amount of olive oil.

Verse 6. *The day of the new moon* was the beginning of the month and was a holy or sabbath day. Like other special days, it was celebrated by offering animal sacrifices.

Verse 7. *According as his hand shall attain* means that a man was required to give according to his ability. Whether many or few, all animals must be without blemish and be offered with a small amount of olive oil as in verse 5.

Verse 8. The Lord was particular about some apparently incidental matters. The prince was told by what gate he should enter and leave the building.

Verse 9. This "one way" requirement is another one of the unusual regulations imposed by the Lord. We are able at least to realize that much confusion would be avoided by not trying to reverse one's direction in the midst of so many coming and going.

Verse 10. The prince was to become one of the crowd generally speaking, but that was not to interfere with his own personal activities as stated in verse 1 and 2.

Verse 11. This small amount of grain (*meat offering*) was added to the animal.

Verse 12. The law made a distinction between freewill or voluntary offerings and those specifically required. (See Leviticus 22: 23; Numbers 15: 3.) But the distinction did not exempt the worshiper from all restrictions as may be seen in this verse.

Verse 13. This verse refers to the well known "daily sacrifice" that was a prominent ordinance in the law of Moses (Exodus 29: 38-42).

Verse 14. This *meat* offering means the same as in other places which was a small amount of meal or ground grain. *Perpetual ordinance* means it was to be a continuous practice as long as the nation had an existence.

Verse 15. *Continual burnt offering* means the same as "perpetual ordinance."

Verse 16. The main point in this verse is that a gift of real estate from a prince to his son was to be permanent. That is, no circumstance was to alter that gift so as to turn it back to the prince.

Verse 17. The year of *liberty* was the same as the jibile described in Leviticus 25. In that year certain readjustments were made in the relations of property and also of servants, and that is what is meant by this verse.

Verse 18. The *prince* did not have the right to use his position in a special favor to even his own sons. He could not cut off even them from the enjoyment of their inheritance no matter how much reason he would think he had so to do. Being restricted from such an act as to his sons, the temptation would be to defraud the people not related to him of their possessions so as to give them to his sons, and this verse is a law against such an injustice. *That my people be not scattered* states one of the Lord's motives for the regulations just described. If the people were assured of the uninterrupted possession of their property, they would not be induced to scatter out to find houses and lands.

Verse 19. Having revealed to Ezekiel the foregoing laws and ordinances for observance by Israel in the future, the man brought him through the entry of the side gate. The purpose of this movement was to show the prophet the spot where some of the ordinances that he had been hearing were to be carried out.

Verse 20. Some of the sacrificial offerings were boiled and others were baked or roasted in an oven. The parts that were to be consumed by fire were offered on the altar. Hence there were different places used in the preparation and use of the materials furnished by the people and turned over to the prince or priest. It will give the reader some light on this subject if he will examine carefully the first 5 chapters of Leviticus, also some verses in the 6th and 7th chapters of that book.

Verse 21. *Court* is a rather indefinite word whose general meaning is any space enclosed by a fence or wall or otherwise marked off from the surrounding area, hence in this verse we read of courts within a court. Moffatt renders this, "at the four corners of the court there were four small courts."

Verse 22. This verse refers to the same smaller courts referred to in the preceding verse and adds some information about their size and other arrangement. Each of the courts was 40 by 30 cubits in size. *Joined* is rendered "bound to" by Young which is a reasonable translation, as we know they were near the main wall of the larger court.

Verse 23. There is no separate original word for *building*, but *row* is from TUWR which Strong defines, "to arrange in a regular manner." *Made with boiling places under the rows* means the arrangement in the definition of *row* had provision made at the bottom for boiling the flesh of the sacrificial offerings.

Verse 24. By way of explanation the "man" told Ezekiel the above-named "rows" were the places (fireplaces) where the *ministers* ("attendants") were to boil the sacrificial offerings that were brought by the people.

EZEKIEL 47

Verses 1, 2. The entire book of Ezekiel was written after he was taken to Babylon at the time of Jehoiachin's captivity. The first half of the book consists to a great extent of chastisement of Israel for the many corruptions committed by the nation. The next half is an extended prediction of the release of Israel from Babylonian captivity and the rebuilding and restitution of the ordinances of the Lord that will have gone down in national ruins. The whole document is a mingling of literal and figurative passages and intended to encourage the unfortunate people not to lose heart because of their sad state of affairs. Many popular commentators think that the last chapters are a prediction of things to come in the age after the judgment day. Evidently this is because of the similarity of the figures used to the ones in Revelation 21 and 22. There is a striking resemblance between the figures but that is because all of the grand provisions of God for the children of men require the finest of pictures to represent them to the human understanding. As to how far the following portions of this book should be regarded in the light of the present or the eternal ages, I now insist that the reader again consult the KEY at the beginning of chapter 40. The present verse begins the ideal picture with the waters that issued from the house of the Lord. I do not understand that any special significance is to be attached to the directions of the flow of these waters, because so many directions and places are mentioned. It would indicate the general greatness of the favor of God whatever that is.

Verse 3. The preceding verses indicate the widespread extent of these waters; this one begins to tell how deep they were. It reveals that for every thousand cubits or 1500 feet at the start the water was ankle deep.

Verse 4. The good things produced

by man often diminish, while those from God never fail but rather do they increase. These waters were ankle deep at the start, and with each 1500 feet a great increase in depth was shown until they were waist deep.

Verse 5. This last 1500 feet brought the water to the depth that could not he waded, for it amounted to the volume of a river.

Verse 6. This paragraph is a pause in the procedure to call special attention of the prophet to the scene, also to conduct him to the bank of the river just described.

Verse 7. This verse begins the language that was referred to in comments on verse 1; that of the similarity of figures used to those in Revelation. Be sure to consult verse 1 again, and also the other notes referred to in that place. Nobody thinks the river and trees and other objects named in Revelation are literal in their meaning, neither should he think that of the ones used here. Both documents intend to picture some of the glorious blessings in store for those who become the objects of God's favor, whether they be the saved of earth after the day of judgment (as in Revelation), or the restored people of Israel after the return as in the present passage.

Verse 8. *Sea* and *waters* refers to people generally speaking, but the second word is used in a rather complex sense in this place. Both the people and the stream that flows around or before them are indicated by the waters. *Shall be healed* is one of the places where the similarity of figures is evident. In Revelation 22: 2 we read of a tree that is for the *healing of the nations*, and in our present text the waters that issue from the house of God have healing in them.

Verse 9. Whenever a writer adopts a certain imagery for his figurative description of a subject, he usually sticks to the terms that properly belong to the subject. Hence this verse, though really considering human beings, speaks about a *great multitude of fish* because they are the creatures that live in water.

Verse 10. The same imagery is continued and in the favors intended for God's people are compared to those that would be connected with a good body of water and the advantages connected with it. One favorable thing that would be expected of a desirable body of water would be a successful experience for a fisherman; accordingly, we are told that the bank of this river will be occupied by *fishers* from *En-gedi* and *En-eglaim*. These were towns near the Dead Sea where no fisherman could have any success at his trade. But now even they will find plenty of opportunity for their business because the healing waters from the headquarters of the Lord will heal the *sea* upon flowing into it, thereby encouraging the men to use their nets. Not only will the waters supply good fish for the fishermen, but the banks will provide a suitable place to *spread forth nets* for drying which would be necessary after a successful catch.

Verse 11. In spite of all the goodness of God in providing a remedy for the ills of mankind, there are some people who will not accept it. Such folks are here called *miry places* and *marshes* which will not be healed. *They shall be given to salt.* According to Deuteronomy 29: 23; Zephaniah 2: 9 and some other passages, salt is sometimes used to represent a condition of barrenness. Such was to be the lot of those who rejected the favors offered by the Lord.

Verse 12. This verse is almost identical in its terms with Revelation 22: 1, 2 and they are highly of the character belonging to ideal or figurative speech. For further comments on this subject see those on verse 1 of this chapter, and also the KEY at the beginning of chapter 40.

Verse 13. In "general remarks" at the beginning of chapter 40 a statement is made regarding the last 9 chapters as a group, classifying them among the highly figurative writings of inspired prophets. Such a view has been maintained and the comments have been made accordingly. The place has been reached, however, where an exception should be made to that classification. From here on to the end of the book the ideal or figurative form of speech will be dropped, except perhaps some statements that are unusually strong numerically for the purpose of emphasis, and the language will be a literal description of the redistribution of the land after the return from captivity. But while the nature of the language is literal, I do not know that every detail of the allotment was to be carried out. Having no specific history of the procedure as to the land after the return, I shall take up the verses in their order and offer such comments on any technical statements that seem necessary. *Joseph . . . two portions*. This is according to a prediction that was made by Jacob in Genesis 48: 5, 22. This was because the two sons of Joseph, Manasseh and Ephraim, were each to become a full tribe as indicated in the passage in Genesis just cited.

Verse 14. An inheritance is something that comes to a person by reason of his relationship (either by blood or law) to another. God had promised the fathers of the nation of Israel that the land of Canaan would be theirs for a possession.

Verse 15. The *great sea* is the Mediterranean forming one boundary.

Verse 16. The towns named were for the purpose of tracing the boundary.

Verse 17. Damascus belonged to the nation of Syria but it was just outside of Canaan. It is named here as another aid in establishing the boundary of the land.

Verse 18. The eastern boundary according to this description started from a point near Damascus, running through the territory called Gilead and following downward near the Jordan until it reached the Dead Sea.

Verse 19. This verse gives a general description of the south border, beginning at Tamar for the southeastern corner, and extending through a place called *waters of strife* (Numbers 20: 12), thence to the stream called "river of Egypt" (Numbers 34: 5), and on to the *grea sea* which means the Mediterranean.

Verse 20. The west line was to extend from this junction of the south line with the *great sea* to the place of beginning.

Verse 21. Verse 13 said *twelve* tribes and this says *tribes* without stating any number. That is because two and a half tribes had taken their possessions on the east side of the Jordan, and the outline described in this chapter is all west of it.

Verse 22. One word in Strong's definition of the original for *inheritance* is "occupancy," which is evidently its meaning with regard to the *strangers* among the tribes. The actual possession of land was restricted to the people of Israel, but the Lord was always mindful of the sojourner among His people and instructed them as to how they should be treated (Exodus 22: 21; 23: 9; Leviticus 19: 10).

Verse 23. The word *sojourner* means one who is a temporary dweller in a place. Hence the word *inheritance* would have the sense of "occupancy" only as defined in the preceding verse.

EZEKIEL 48

Verses 1-7. I have grouped these verses into one paragraph because no special explanation for them separately would serve any necessary purpose. The comment that seems most appropriate is that by assigning the land specifically to the separate tribes, the Lord gives us a lesson on the subject of individual rights amidst a community of people all of whom had rights that should be respected.

Verse 8. This *offering* is called an "oblation" in chapter 45: 1 which was to consist of certain portions of the land; a *sanctuary* is a holy place.

Verse 9. This verse merely states the specific size of the offering.

Verse 10. This special *oblation* was for the specific use of the priests. They were from the tribe of Levi and did not have any general possession of land as others.

Verse 11. Not all of the tribe of Levi were permitted to act in the priesthood, only the descendants of Zadok (chapter 40: 46). The reason for this special favor to them is given; they had remained faithful to the Lord previous to the captivity.

Verse 12. This priestly group was to have this assignment (or offering) of the land, and it was to be near the border of the other Levites.

Verse 13. The Levites as a tribe were to have this assignment, even though most of them would not be eligible for the priesthood.

Verse 14. This land must not be disposed of either by sale or trade, and neither should the products be *alienated* which means transported into another vicinity.

Verse 15. *Profane* is not a word with any special moral meaning, but is the opposite of sacred or is temporal; the space was for the people in general.

Verse 16. This area was 4500 cubits or about a mile square.

Verse 17. These *suburbs* consisted of open border that was about 400 feet wide, and it extended all round the other district described in the preceding verse.

Verse 18. The strip of land described in this verse was to be cultivated, and the food raised was for the support of those living in the space described above.

Verse 19. *Out of all the tribes* means that the entire nation was to contribute to the support of those who rendered service for the common good.

Verse 20. The entire reservation described in the foregoing verses was several miles square if measured by modern standards or terms.

Verse 21. Near this reserved territory was a strip that was for the use of the prince, which means some person in a position of leadership or other outstanding relationship to the rest of the nation. This area was to be regarded as an *oblation* or offering for the sacred service of God.

Verse 22. This part that was assigned to the prince is described as having come out of the sacred possession of the Levites. That was proper since it was to serve a specific use in the service rendered to the Lord.

Verse 23. Special consideration is given to Benjamin in that this particular group of assignments begins with the mention of that tribe. There might have been some remembrance of the fact that Benjamin was one of the tribes of the kingdom of Judah, and hence a part of the people who went into Babylonian captivity.

Verses 24-28. For comments on this manner of grouping verses see those at verses 1-7.

Verse 29. *Divide by lot.* In ancient times the lot was used to decide certain questions, and when resorted to by uninspired men it amounted to a "game of chance" only. Sometimes, however, the Lord authorized its use, and when that was done (as in the case here) He would see that the proper decision was reached (Proverbs 16: 33).

Verse 30. *Goings* is from TOTSAAH which Strong defines, "Exit, i.e., (geographical boundary." The verse means to designate the outer extent of the territory to be named.

Verse 31. The second chapter of Numbers gives the order of encampment for the children of Israel when they paused in their journey through the wilderness. There is a similarity between that arrangement and that described in this verse in that three tribes were to be grouped together in the four units.

Verse 32. It was not always the same three tribes as are named in Numbers, but the "goings out" in our case were the same in each of the sides. The tribe of *Joseph* is named in this place but Ephraim and Manasseh will not be given here. That is because they were the sons of Joseph and each was at the head of a whole tribe. Hence if Joseph is counted there would not be any point in mentioning his sons in this report.

Verse 33. *Measures* is given an indefinite meaning in the lexicon. It would denote that whatever rule or standard was used on any given occasion, the thing being "checked for dimensions" would count up to the number given.

Verse 34. This verse brings the measurements round to the place of beginning. There being three gates on each of the four sides of the city reminds us of the description which John gives of the Eternal City in Revelation 21: 13.

Verse 35. *Round about* means the circumference which was 18,000 measures. *The Lord is there.* What an appropriate and important phrase by which to close up a great book! The greatest thing that could be said of any institution or place is that the presence of the Lord will bless it which would assure it of everything needed for joy and prosperity. If the Lord is not in the place nothing else will count for good. All through the ages God has provided something by which His presence could be realized and enjoyed by those who loved Him. In the Patriarchal Dispensation it was at the family altar; in the Mosaic era the Lord was present in the temple and tabernacle and it is promised in the present verse that the same Presence would be there to bless the people after returning from the captivity.

DANIEL 1

General remarks. The scope of time covered by this book begins 606 B.C., and extends to the beginning years of the Persians in Babylon. It is an interesting coincidence that this period is the same as that of the 70-year captivity of Judah, also of the entire period of the Babylonian Empire as a world power. Many commentators and other writers divide the book of Daniel into two equal divisions as to chapters namely, history and prophecy. That is probably correct from a general viewpoint, but both history and prophecy will be in evidence more or less in the comments all through the book, and in many instances the two will be seen to blend together. Of course many of the prophecies will look far beyond the scope of years mentioned in the beginning of this introduction for their fulfillment. One more remark that should be made before taking up the several verses is that the various chapters and events of the book are not always chronological as to the years of their occurrence. Attention will be called to any such variation as each case comes up wherever it is thought necessary for clearness.

Verse 1. *Third year* should be considered in connection with 2 Kings 24: 1. It seems that Jehoiakim had formed some kind of mutual agreement with Babylon but that he broke that relationship after three years. That brought Nebuchadnezzar against Jerusalem with an army and that was the beginning of the "first captivity" which means the first stage of the noted 70-year exile. In Jeremiah 25: 1 this event is said to have occurred in the fourth year of Jehoiakim, which might be confusing at first thought. However, if a thing takes place at the end of a man's third year, it could be thought of as as happening in his fourth year since the term third and fourth are just that indefinite in their force.

Verse 2. *The Lord gave* shows that Nebuchadnezzar's advance against Jerusalem was by the decree of God. The account in 2 Kings 24: 3, 4 goes farther than this verse and tells why it was done, that it was because of the sins that the nation had committed. This event was not intended to cause the complete ruin of Jerusalem, for it says that the king of Babylon took *part* of the vessels of the Lord's house with him.

Verse 3. The first *king* means Nebuchadnezzar and the next is Jehoiakim. *Ashpenaz* was an important servant under the king of Babylon, whose specific duty was to oversee the other servants or any others who might become subject to the king. This man was told by his master to bring from Jerusalem to Babylon some of the *king's seed*. That does not mean exclusively his bodily offspring, for we shall see that others were taken. But it includes men near the king within the royal family, and also some of his *princes* which means outstanding men in his service.

Verse 4. The terms Chaldeans and Babylonians may be used interchangeably for all practical purposes, although the latter is nowhere used in the book of Daniel. For the information of the readers I shall quote from three works of reference: "The Chaldeans were a Semitic [descended from Shem] people who passed into Babylonia from the south, and occupied the whole seacoast region of South Babylonia." — Funk and Wagnalls, New Standard Bible Dictionary, article Chaldea. "In the Old Testament, from the time of Jeremiah and the establishment of the new Babylonian Empire under Nabopolassar and Nebuchadnezzar, the terms Chaldeans and Chaldees denote the inhabitants of Babylonia, or the subjects of the Babylonian Empire." — Schaff-Herzog Encyclopaedia, article Chaldeans. "It appears that the Chaldeans were in the earliest times merely one out of the many Cushite tribes inhabiting the great alluvial plain known afterwards as Chaldea or Babylonia. Their special seat was probably that southern portion of the country which is found to have so late retained the name of Chaldea. In process of time, as the *Kaldi* grew in power, their name gradually prevailed over those of other tribes inhabiting the country; and by the era of the Jewish captivity it had begun to be used generally for all the inhabitants of Babylonia. It appears that while, both in Assyria and in later Babylonia, the Shemitic type of speech prevailed for civil purposes, the ancient Cushite dialect was retained, as a learned language for scientific and religious literature. This is no doubt the 'learning' and the 'tongue' to which reference is made in the book of Daniel, 1: 4. The Chaldeans were really the learned class; they were priests, magicians or astronomers, and in the last of the three capacities they probably effected [accomplished] discoveries of great importance. In later times they seem to have degenerated into mere fortune-tellers." — Smith's Bible Dictionary, article, Chaldeans. When considering the subject from a political or national standpoint the two terms are used interchangeably and I trust the reader will keep that truth in mind. When some special personal characteristics are under consideration, the Chaldeans will be spoken of as a distinct group of people. Hence in this verse we see the reference to these special subjects which Nebuchadnezzar wished to develop in the lives of the Jews who had been selected out from the general population in Jerusalem. The mental qualifications were not the only points the king wished these Jews to have. Their bodies were to be without blemish and they were to be well *favored*.

The last word is from MAREH which Strong defines, "A view (the act of seeing); also an appearance (the thing seen), whether (real) a shape (especially if handsome, comeliness; often plural the looks), or (mental) a vision." The Babylonian king instructed his chief servant to select some Jews who already possessed these traits of mind and body, then he purposed to develop them further by a schedule of special diet.

Verse 5. The schedule as to their bodies consisted of a special provision of food and drink taken out of the store that was brought in for the king's personal use. Having been selected for the special use of the monarch, these articles of diet were supposed to possess unusual qualities for the developing of bodily strength and appearance. This schedule was to be followed for three years after which the men were to be presented to the king for his approval.

Verse 6. This verse tells us that Daniel was taken to Babylon at the "first captivity," that means the first stage of the noted 70-year exile.

Verse 7. This *prince of the eunuchs* must have been allowed a considerable amount of authority, for he took the liberty of changing the names of Daniel and his three companions, or at least of giving them names in addition to the ones they had. These companions of Daniel are the familiar "Three Hebrew Children" who are so often referred to in the stories of heroes of the Bible.

Verse 8. Daniel knew that Nebuchadnezzar was an idolater and that a portion of the royal provisions was given over to consecrate the idol in connection with the feasts. For this reason his conscience would not consent for him to take part in the false religion by accepting the food. He requested the prince to be excused from partaking.

Verse 9. The prince of the eunuchs was responsible for the development of these specially-chosen men, and he would naturally be unwilling to grant to Daniel the exemption requested. But God took a hand in the matter and caused him to have a tender love for Daniel which led him at least to be personally disposed to favor him.

Verse 10. *Sort* means age, and the prince was fearful lest Daniel should not look as well as the others of his age if he were permitted to abstain from the diet provided for him. Of course that would endanger the life of the man who was made responsible for the welfare of the prisoners allotted to him. He made this protest to Daniel who was reasonable enough to see the position the prince was in, and he seems to have said nothing more to him on that matter.

Verse 11. But the prince of the eunuchs had placed the actual work of providing the food in charge of a steward named Melzar. As far as the record informs us, the prince of the eunuchs saw no more of Daniel and his companions until the time for their appearance before the king. He left the task of serving the food to this steward Melzar.

Verse 12. Daniel's proposition was fair to all parties concerned, for, regardless of the success or failure of the diet he requested, it could not have any ill effect that would show up after three years. On the other hand, his faith in his God was so strong he was certain that such a period would be sufficient to bring about the desired effect. It might be asked if the Lord could not have accomplished the same result in one day. True, he could have done so, but had the transformation been made in one day, the steward would have known that it was not the effect of the diet, and that would have caused an investigation which might have interfered with Daniel's plans. And yet a period of ten days would be enough to expect some results from the schedule of diet used. *Pulse* is sometimes defined as seeds of any kind of vegetables, and in some lexicons it is defined simply as a vegetable food. Since the heathen always used animals in their sacrifices, Daniel knew he would be safe if his diet was restricted to vegetables.

Verse 13. Daniel was willing to leave the decision to the steward. At the end of the ten-day period he was to compare the *countenances* (from same word as "favoured" in verse 4) of him and his three companions with those who ate of the king's food.

Verse 14. The steward agreed to the test proposed by Daniel.

Verse 15. As it was doubtless expected by the reader, the test came out as Daniel wished. One word in the definition for *fatter* is "plump," and *fairer* means "beautiful." I am sure the reader will give the Lord full credit for this favorable experience of the four faithful Hebrews. It was an instance of the assurance God had given, that while all citizens of Judah had to share in the national calamity of the captivity, the individuals who were righteous would be given special favors from God even though they were in a strange land. The apparent disagreement of some statements on this subject is explained in a long note given with comments on 2 Kings 22: 17, in volue 2 of this Commentary.

Verse 16. Seeing the results of the test, Melzar removed the food that had been taken from the king's supplies, and permitted Daniel to continue with his vegetable diet throughout the period of three years that was appointed by the king for the test.

Verse 17. In acquiring the physical developments desired the *four children* could co-operate with God since it included the partaking of food. In the mental advancement they had no opportunity for their own activity because they were being put through the trial to test out their appearance in body. But God wished them to be as well qualified in mind as in body when the time of their appearance before the king arrived, hence He gave them all those talents as a direct gift.

Verse 18. *End of the days* means after three years (verse 5). It was then time for the prince of the eunuchs to act since he was next to the king with regard to his rank as a servant. Accordingly he brought Daniel and his three companions before Nebuchadnezzar for his official "review."

Verse 19. *The king communed with them* indicates that Nebuchadnezzar was not interested only in the bodily appearance of his captives, for that could have been observed without any conversation. T h i s communication proved to the king that Daniel and his companions excelled all the others who appeared before him.

Verse 20. There is very little difference between the meaning of *wisdom* and *understanding*. The latter could be regarded as knowledge and the former as the ability to use the knowledge rightly. Like the two words italicized above, the words *magicians* and *astrologers* differ very little in their meaning. They both refer to persons who pretend to acquire knowledge of the past, present and future by the relative position of the stars either to each other, or to men and things on the earth. The wisdom manifested by Daniel and his tree companions was ten times better than that possessed by all the so-called wise men of Babylon.

Verse 21. *Continued* is from HAYAH which Strong defines, "To exist, i.e. be or become, come to pass." The verse means that Daniel lived to see the end of the Babylonian captivity, not that he did not live any longer. It is significant that the man who was among the first to be taken to Babylon, and who gave prophecies that they would finally be released, should live to see the fulfillment of that prediction. It was in the *first year of king Cyrus* that the Jews were released (Ezra 1: 1-4).

DANIEL 2

Verse 1. Paul says that God spoke in times past to the fathers by the prophets (Hebrews 1: 1) and that He did it at sundry times and in diverse manners. And we also know that He delivered messages to heathen men by dreams and visions and various signs. Thus we now have an instance of it in this chapter, and the king of Babylon is the person who was caused to have a dream. This date is definitely given, the second year of the king's reign which was also the second year of the Jewish captivity. A dream comes to a man in his sleep, but this verse says that Nebuchadnezzar's sleep *brake from him*. The situation is understandable, for the dream caused him to awaken, and its mystifying character so worked him up that he was unable to go to sleep again. What added to his worries was the fact that he could not even recall the dream, much less understand its meaning.

Verse 2. As was usual in such cases, the king called for his so-called wise men to help him out of his confusion. Among them the Chaldeans are named in a way that indicates they were a special class of men. See the comments on chapter 1: 4 for information concerning them. The first object in calling for these wise men was that they might *shew the king his dreams* because he had forgotten them.

Verse 3. With the preceding verse in view we understand that *know the dreams* here means to be told what he dreamed. This is indicated also by a statement in verse 5.

Verse 4. *Syriac* was similar to the language spoken by the Jews, and was the common tongue of the court of Babylon. This explains why the wise men used it when speaking to Nebuchadnezzar. They made what they doubtless thought was a reasonable statement, that if the king would tell them his dream they could give the interpretation of it.

Verse 5. But the wise men were not to get off so easily, for they were demanded to tell the king both the dream and its interpretation. The word *dunghill* occurs 6 times in the Old Testament, and when used figuratively means a foul or corrupt condition.

Verse 6. These *gifts* and *rewards* are not to be regarded in the light of bribes, but as legitimate returns for services rendered. These men were subjects of the king and any assistance they could give towards clearing up the confusion their master was undergoing would be proper and would entitle them to some reward.

Verse 7. The men could only repeat their statement of verse 4.

Verse 8. *Gain* is from ZEBAN, which Strong defines, "To acquire by purchase." These men had nothing of purchasing power or value by which literally to obtain more time, so we know the word is used figuratively. The explanation is in the closing words of the verse, *because ye see the thing is gone from me*. In the hope that the king's memory would finally return and he could recall the dream, they kept repeating their suggestion as a means of gaining more time.

Verse 9. *Tell me the dream, and I shall know*. The logic of Nebuchadnezzar was correct, for if these men possessed the superhuman knowledge they professed to have, it would have been as easy to recall the dream as to interpret it. If there was any difference it would have been easier, since the dream was something that had already occurred while the interpretation was in the future. This consideration led the king to doubt the sincerity of all their pretensions of being wise men in the sense that term was used, and it showed him their reason for seeking more time, which is the meaning of *till the time be changed*. But *one decree* means that no change would be made in the decree that was threatened in verse 5.

Verse 10. The statements the wise men made to the king were true, but they disproved their claims to being possessed with superhuman knowledge. It is true that no mere normal man can reveal that which is unknown or hid from humanity, but the Chaldeans professed to be superhuman beings as to their knowledge.

Verse 11. The statements of these Chaldeans shows they believed in the existence of invisible, supernatural beings who did not live among men. It indicates also that these gods possessed knowledge that was never transmitted to men, for they claimed to have knowledge that ordinary men did not have. The gist of the verse is that the king was asking something that was impossible even of men possessing superhuman talents.

Verse 12. However, such a conclusion rested only on the assertion of these men, for no authority was cited for limiting the extent to which these gods could transmit their knowledge to men if they saw fit to do so, hence there was no valid excuse for the failure of these Chaldeans. The king evidently saw this point and concluded that the so-called wise men were frauds as a class and decided to destroy them all.

Verse 13. *Wise men* was a term that designated all men who were looked upon as belonging in the group possessing special talents pertaining to the mind. That is why the executioner of the king's decree *sought Daniel and his fellows*, knowing they had been pronounced even by the king himself as belonging in such a class (chapter 1: 19, 20).

Verse 14. The executioner found Daniel and informed him of the king's decree. Daniel would have been helpless had he tried to resist the actions of the officer, and it would also have been helpless had he tried to resist the actions of the officer, and it would also have been foolish to use any rash language to him, especially since the executioner had no choice in the matter. Instead of such a course, Daniel spoke with *counsel* and *wisdom*, which is defined in the lexicon as "prudence" and "judgment."

Verse 15. So far the executioner had only announced to Daniel the decree of death with which he was provided as he contacted him and his three companions. *Hasty* is from CHATSAPH and Strong defines it, "A primitive root; properly to shear or cut close; figuratively to be severe." This is what shows Daniel's good judgment in his speech to the captain. He did not raise any question as to the authority of the king, nor as to whether none of the so-called wise men were guilty of death. He only asked why the decree was so severe or sweeping in its decision to slay *all* the wise men. This question induced the executioner to tell Daniel the particulars of the situation that ended with the wholesale death sentence from the king.

Verse 16. Having learned that disappointment at failure to obtain the interpretation of his dream was the real cause of the king's action, Daniel requested him to give him the opportunity and he would get the desired information for him. This request of Daniel produced a "stay of execution" for a while.

Verse 17. *Went to his house, and made the thing known.* This indicates that Daniel and his three companions lived together, or at least were together much of the time. That would be a fair conclusion since they were such close companions in tribulation as we shall see in later chapters of this book.

Verse 18. The purpose of telling his companions of the situation was that they unite with him in prayer to God. It is good to observe that his personal safety was not the first consideration as a motive for the prayer, but that God would give him information concerning the secret of the king's dream to relieve the tension holding him. Their escape from the threatened destruction was the next purpose of their prayer.

Verse 19. After this prayer service Daniel retired for the night, and God answered the prayer in a vision. (See Hebrews 1: 1.) The prophet was grateful and blessed the God of Heaven for the vision. This is another instance discussed in the note cited at chapter 1: 15.

Verse 20. This verse continues Daniel's prayer of thanksgiving for the favor of God in giving him the information asked for. He attributes all *wisdom* and *might* to God, and that is more significant than might be realized at first thought. Wisdom would qualify Him to formulate decrees and might would furnish the ability to do them.

Verse 21. *Times* is from IDDAN which Strong defines, "A set time," and *seasons* is from ZEMAN which is defined, "An appointed occasion." It indicates control over periods and arrangements that are supposed to be fixed. The right and ability to replace one king with another was shown in the histories of the books of Samuel and Kings. *Wisdom to the wise* means that God will favor those who show their appreciation for and the judgment to use more wisdom; the same thought is in the words *knowledge* and *understanding* as to God's dispensing of them to men.

Verse 22. The gist of this verse is that there is nothing that is hid from the knowledge of God, hence he is able to expose all secrets.

Verse 23. This verse sums up the powers and favors of God, in giving to Daniel the revelation of the matter that was troubling the king.

Verse 24. Daniel was now ready to make good his word to the king. He got in contact with Arioch who was the king's captain and who was the one to execute the death sentence on the wise men. The unselfishness of Daniel is shown by his desire to save all the wise men of Babylon. He requested a hearing before the king which he expected to be arranged through the services of the captain.

Verse 25. The meeting was arranged without delay and the captain brought Daniel into the presence of the king. He was introduced as one of the Judean captives who had the ability to interpret the king's dream.

Verse 26. In chapter 1: 20 is a statement that might seem to have made the inquiry of the present verse unnecessary. However, that other occasion only pertained to matters supposed to be within the mental qualifications of magicians or astrologers and Chaldeans, and the king had been told that they were not able to solve such a problem as the present situation presented. Now comes this Daniel who, though found in the first interview with him to exceed the other wise men, was yet in their classification. Hence it was consistent to ask him the questions of the present verse.

Verse 27. In his answer to the king, Daniel confirmed the statements of the Chaldeans related in verses 10 and 11, but which did not explain the inconsistency in the pretensions of the wise men to high abilities regarding mysterious subjects.

Verse 28. Daniel is about to fulfill his promise to the king that he would give him the answer to his problem. But before doing so he makes it clear that it will not be through his ability as a soothsayer. It is to be through the wisdom of *God in heaven* that the vision is to be recalled and explained.

Verse 29. *Thy thoughts came upon thy bed* signifies that Nebuchadnezzar had not seen some image or statue somewhere among the works of men. It was all a mental picture that came to him while asleep and hence was not a material one.

Verse 30. When God revealed this

great secret to Daniel it was not in recognition of any special talents he already possessed; in truth, it was not for any personal consideration of Daniel at all. The word *their* is not authorized by the original and it is in the way of the proper rendering of the passage. The American Standard Version translates the passage, "But to the intent that the interpretation may be made known to the king," and Moffatt's translation and others agree with this rendering.

Verse 31. Daniel will first recall the vision to the king then tell him the interpretation. *Image* is from TSELEM which Strong defines, "An idolatrous figure." It was appropriate for the Lord to use such an object for the present purpose since Nebuchadnezzar was a worshiper of idols. *Brightness* has been rendered also by "countenance," and *excellent* is defined in the lexicon by "preeminent." It means that the image had an imposing appearance. *Form* is from a word that means "appearance," and *terrible* means to be dangerous or threatening. This image with its various parts represented the four world empires described or figurized by the "four living creatures" in Ezekiel 1 namely, Babylonian, Medo-Persian, Macedonian and Roman. In our present chapter the Lord saw fit to represent the four governments by a giant of mixed materials in his bodily composition.

Verse 32. Three of the world empires are represented in this verse, using the image down as far as the thighs, which will be shown when Daniel comes with his interpretation of the whole vision.

Verse 33. This verse is very brief, making only a short mention of the materials composing the remainder of the image, which we shall learn represents the fourth and last of the world empires to which reference has been made in verse 31.

Verse 34. The speech of Daniel is still about his recalling what the king saw in his dream. After the image stood before Nebuchadnezzar until its impression of terrible greatness was fastened upon him, another subject mysteriously appeared on the scene. *A stone was cut out*, and verse 45 supplies the word *mountain* which will be explained at that place. This stone was cut out *without hands* which also will be commented upon when we come to studying the interpretation of the vision by Daniel. We will observe only at present that the stone smote the image on his feet and broke them; more will be said on that later.

Verse 35. The immediate effect of the smiting on the feet by this stone was the crushing of the entire image into powder. It was not only crushed to pieces, but the fragments were blown out of sight as chaff is blown away. *Summer threshingfloors* has reference to an ancient method of threshing grain. The whole straw was piled on the floor in the path of the wind. It was beaten with a flail or trodden by oxen until the grain was forced out of the hull and the whole mass was a mixture of grain and chaff. Then it was scooped up and tossed into the air by an instrument called a winnowing shovel (called "fan" in Matthew 3: 12). The passing breeze blew the chaff away because it was light, and the grain, being heavier, fell back to the ground to be recovered for use or to be stored. It should be noted that *after* this attack was made by the stone, it enlarged until it filled the whole earth.

Verse 36. *Interpretation* is from an original word which Strong defines with the simple phrase, "An interpretation," and neither is it rendered by any other word in the King James version of the Bible.

Verse 37. The description which Daniel gives of Nebuchadnezzar is for the purpose of showing why he should be represented by the most valuable of the materials. *King of kings* means not only that he is king over other rulers, but the phrase has the force of an adjective to describe the greatness of his power. *God of heaven hath given thee* means that the greater power of Nebuchadnezzar was not solely by his personal achievements, but that it was the divine will that he be a great ruler. Neither should we conclude that it was in reward for his personal merit, for this king was an idolater and a wicked man who had to be humbled severely later. But the Almighty had a great scheme of the ages that called for the existence of such a monarch.

Verse 38. *Wheresoever . . . men dwell* is what justifies the term "world power" that has been ascribed to Nebuchadnezzar and his dominions. *Beasts . . . fowls . . . into thine hand*. It helps to arrive at the meaning of a statement to learn first what it does not mean, especially if some explanation has previously been offered that may be incorrect. A popular theory is that when man sinned, God deprived him of his dominion over the beasts of the field that was given him in Genesis 1: 28, and that it was renewed on behalf of this king. But such a theory is disproved by Genesis 9: 2 where the same dominion is given to man which was after the "fall of man." Also, James 3: 7 declares that "every kind of beasts . . . and serpents . . . *is tamed* of mankind," and that was in the days of the writer, many centuries after the sin of Adam. So by the process of elimination, the theory mentioned must be rejected which will require us to look for another explanation. The reasonable conclusion is that while God gave man the right to rule over the beasts and birds, the *extent* of that power was not specified. Hence our verse means that Nebuchadnezzar was given that dominion to a complete degree. It is an indication of the complete co-operation that this heathen king enjoyed with the many units of his vast domain. *Thou art this head of gold* includes Nebuchadnezzar and his kingdom, for when Daniel goes on to the next division of the image he says "another kingdom," which shows that an absolute monarch and his dominions are one unit.

Verse 39. This verse introduces briefly the two world powers that succeeded Nebuchadnezzar. The first is mentioned simply as one *inferior to thee* [Nebuchadnezzar], and the next the prophet calls a *kingdom of brass*, and he says it was to *bear rule over all the earth* which is the reason it is designated as a "world empire" in history. By referring to comments on verse 31 the reader will see that this *kingdom of brass* was the Macedonian, otherwise called the Greek. We have seen in a number of instances the advantage of citing secular history by way of explaining and corroborating the statements of the scriptures, and I shall do that here on the statement that the third kingdom was one of *brass*. "After Psammetichus [an Egyptian ruler] had passed some years there, waiting a favorable opportunity to revenge himself for the affront which had been put upon him, a courier brought his advice, that brazen men had landed in Egypt. These were Grecian soldiers, Carians and Ionians, who had been cast upon the coast of Egypt by a storm, and were completely covered with helmets, cuirasses, and other arms of brass." — Rollin's Ancient History, volume 1, page 223. "Knowing, then, that he [Psammetichus] had been exceedingly injured by them, he entertained the design of avenging himself on his persecutors; and when he sent to the city of Buto to consult the oracle of Latona, where is the truest oracle that the Egyptians have, an answer came, 'that vengeance would come from the sea, when men of brass should appear.' He, however, was very incredulous that men of brass would come to assist him. But when no long time had elapsed, stress of weather compelled some Ionians and Carians [Greek soldiers], who had sailed out for the purpose of piracy, to bear away to Egypt; and when they had disembarked and were clad in brazen armour, went to the marshes to Psammetichus, and told him that men of brass, having arrived from the sea, were ravaging the plains. He perceiving that the oracle was accomplished, treated these Ionians and Carians in a friendly manner, and having promised them great things, persuaded them to join with him."—Herodotus, Book 2, section 151.

Verse 40. The fourth and last one of the world kingdoms was the Roman Empire which Daniel describes as being *strong as iron*. This does not refer to the extent of territorial position, for all four of the kingdoms in the general prediction were to be known as world powers. The characteristic of iron attributed to the fourth one pertains to its power. On this point I shall quote a paragraph from an authentic work of reference: "The last of the Old World empires was the one having its capital on the seven hills of Rome. Like most of the others, it was the dominion of a single city; but, unlike others, it represented the conquests, not of a single conquering king, as Nebuchadnezzar or Cyrus, but of a SELF-GOVERNING AND CONQUERING PEOPLE; and, unlike its predecessors, it was not a loose aggregation of states, ready to fall apart as soon as the hand that fettered them was removed, but an empire, carefully welded together, building up in every land its own civilization, and developing a national unity which held its possessions together for a thousand years."—Rand-McNally Bible Atlas. Edward Gibbon, author of The Decline and Fall of the Roman Empire says of it, "The frontiers of that extensive monarchy were guarded by ancient renown and disciplined valor. The gentle but POWERFUL influence of laws and manners had gradually cemented the union of the provinces."—Chapter 1. The above estimates by the authentic writers fully justify the prediction of Daniel that the fourth kingdom was to be *strong as iron*, and that it would be able to *break in pieces* the elements of resistance which might be encountered by it in the world.

Verse 41. The Lord selected the form of a giant man for the imagery of this prediction in the vision of Nebuchadnezzar because it would serve certain features of the subject better. In proceeding along that line we observe a being with ten toes which represents something that was a part of the Roman Empire. It refers to ten of the prominent governmental units that were incorporated within the Empire and that formed a great part of its strength. I shall reserve the more detailed comments on these ten governments until we reach the 7th chapter of this book. *Shall be divided* does not mean organic or bodily division, but was to be composed of two elements.

Verse 42. This verse is much the same as the preceding one, but it adds the statement that the mixture of clay with the iron will cause the kingdom to be partly *broken*. That is from TEBAR and Strong's definition is, "To be fragile." That justifies the rendering of "brittle" that is in the margin of some Bibles, and Moffatt's version renders it by the same word. The thought is that, while the presence of iron will make the kingdom strong, the mixture of clay will force it to have within itself the elements of weakness that will eventually cause it to fall.

Verse 43. *Mixed* and *mingle* both are derived from a word that Strong defines, "A primitive root; to braid, i.e., intermix; technically to traffic (as if by barter); also to give or be security (as a kind of exchange; to commingle." *Cleave* is from DEBAQ which the same lexicon defines, "To stick to." *Seed of men* is from an original that means human posterity, indicating that the "mingling" predicted was to be some human relationship, whether by business and political association, or by intermarriage. The above predictions are fully carried out in the vast historical field pertaining to the Roman Empire. It can be seen that the Roman government and institutional life was infiltrated through the civilized world even in cases where the people did not surrender their personal traits. On the other hand, the Romans were also averse to losing their patriotic identity although they were striving to enlarge the power of Rome through the means of colonization. Hence we read in Acts 16: 21 a complaint against the Jews because they "Teach customs, which are not lawful for us to receive, neither to observe, being Romans." In other words, the Roman Empire was eager to enlarge its borders by any means that would accomplish that purpose. That included war, colonization, political and commercial traffic, and marriage. But so particular was the empire to retain its own inherent character that the above relationships did not result in a genuine fusion or merging together of all the personalities that professed to embrace the Roman cause. This created an element of weakness that was destined finally to result in the decay of the empire.

Verse 44. A question that is susceptible of two answers calls for the consideration of both. *These kings* could mean those represented by the ten toes, or the entire four kingdoms represented by the giant man considered as a whole. Both would be correct, but the first is more specific since it was literally in course of the ten smaller divisions of the Roman Empire that the event occurred just here being predicted. One very important item which must not be overlooked is that the mentioned event was to take place while the Roman Empire was in its full power, not after it ceased to be. The great event consisted of the setting up of another kingdom, and its character is indicated by the fact that the *God of heaven* was to set it up, whereas the four world powers of the image had been set up by man. It would seem scarcely necessary to state that this institution that was to be set up is the church or kingdom of Christ, set up by the God of heaven and delivered to His well beloved Son. *Not left to other people* was said in contrast with these kingdoms of the image, concerning which it was said that one was to come after the other, and history shows that was accomplished by the one in power being given over to another. The kingdom of Christ will have no successor and hence it will *stand forever. Break in pieces and consume all these kingdoms.* Note that it was to destroy all THESE kingdoms, not just destroy kingdoms. True that is a distinction of only one word, but there is a vast amount of meaning in the distinction, for without it the prediction would be that all temporal governments were to be overthrown by the kingdom of Christ. That not only is not the prediction here, but it would contradict the teaching of the New Testament. Without taking space by quoting the many lines that are in point, I shall cite references that prove beyond any doubt that Christ endorses and expects man to have his own governments and that His servants are to be in subjection thereto. (See Romans 13: 1-6; 1 Timothy 2: 1-3.) It is an unavoidable conclusion that God would not ask His servants to pray for an institution if the very one of which those servants are members was divinely intended to destroy the one to be prayed for. But the key thought in the noted passage is that the kingdom that God was to set up would destroy *these* kingdoms, which means it would bring about the end of world-wide empires such as the four represented by the giant man. Neither does it mean that the church would destroy such empires by a direct and arbitrary attack on the very existence of such governments but it was to accomplish that end through the principles of individual responsibility, and the inherent right of all human beings to have a part in their own government, that were to be taught by this kingdom of God and Christ. In proportion as men received this teaching thus offered to them through the kingdom which the *God of heaven* set up, they were to see that world-powers with their stifling of individual rights were improper and they would rebel against them, which would result in their overthrow. Such was the prediction which Daniel made and it was fulfilled according to history and other authentic sources to which the attention of the reader is next invited. I shall first make a quotation from Myers' Ancient History (page 495) to show the influence that Christianity had on the Roman Empire. "It was in the midst of the reign of Tiberius that, in a remote province of the Roman Empire, the Saviour was crucified. Animated by an unparalleled missionary spirit, his followers traversed the length and breadth of the empire, preaching everywhere the 'glad tidings.' Men's faith in the gods of the old mythologies, the softening and liberalizing influence of Greek culture, the unification of the whole civilized world under a single government, the widespread suffering and the inexpressible weariness of the oppressed and servile classes,—all these things had prepared the soil for the seed of the new doctrines. In less than three centuries the pagan empire had become Christian not only in name but also very largely in fact. This conversion of Rome is one of the most important events in all history. A new element is here introduced into civilization, an element which has given color and character to the history of all succeeding centuries." The next historical information will be from Edward Gibbon, author of the famous Decline and Fall of the Roman Empire. Gibbon was an infidel and would not write anything with the motive of corroborating the scriptures. But he was an authentic historian, and any testimony that comes from him that is favorable to the claims of the Bible will be valuable. In the first paragraph of his great history is the following statement: "During a happy period of more than fourscore years, the public administration was conducted by the virtue and abilities of N rva, Trajan, Hadrian, and the t o Antonines. It is the design of this, and of the t o succeeding chapters, to describe the pros erous condition of their empire; and afterwards, from the death of Ma cus Antonius, *to deduce the most important circumstances of its decline and fall;* a revolution which will ever be remembered, and is still felt by the nations of the earth." (Emphasis mine, E.M.Z.) My purpose in this quotation is to show that the succeeding chapters of Gibbon's work are histories of facts that he regarded as causes of the fall of the Roman Empire, the event that Daniel said was foreshown by the dream of Nebuchadnezzar. Among the causes of that "decline and fall," Gibbon devotes two lengthy chapters (15 and 16) to the "Progress of the Christian Religion," and "The Conduct of the Roman Government Towards the Christians." The mere fact of his devoting these t o chapters to an end which he declares is to show the causes of the fall of the Roman Empire is very significant, and impresses us with the truth of Daniel's prediction. However, I deem it helpful to quote from the first paragraph of the 15th chapter: "A candid but rational inquiry into the progress and establishment of Christianity may be considered as a very essential part of the history of the Roman empire. While that great body was invaded by open violence, or undermined by slow decay, a pure and humble religion gently insinuated itself into the minds of men, grew up in silence and obscurity, derived new vigor from opposition, and finally erected the triumphant banner of the Cross on the ruins of the Capitol." In the third paragraph of this 15th chapter is the following: "Our curiosity is naturally prompted to inquire by what means the Christian faith obtained so remarkable a victory over the established religions of the earth. To this inquiry an obvious but satisfactory answer may be returned; that it was owing to the convincing evidence of the doctrine itself, and to the ruling providence of its great Author." The foregoing citations to history are sufficient to show that the principles brought to the world through the church or kingdom of Christ resulted in the downfall of the Roman Empire as predicted by Daniel. That was the fourth of the world-wide empires and it was to be the last. Not that no one would ever desire and try to set up another; Napoleon, the German Kaiser and Hitler thought they could accomplish a universal rule, but all of them failed. And any other man or group of men who attempt to accomplish such a world-wide government are doomed to failure.

Verse 45. *Mountain* is from TAWR and defined in the lexicon, "A rock or hill." Stones are often cut out from a bed of rock by some quarry instrument in the hands of a workman, but this one was seen to be extracted out of a hill of rock and no human worker was visible. The thought is intended to be a contrast with the kingdoms represented by the giant man, which were the productions of man. The stone and the kingdom that the God of heaven was to set up are the same inasmuch as it was said of both that they were to smite and destroy the giant image. Of course the church or kingdom of Christ is not a production of man, hence it was said to have been cut out *without* [human] *hands. As thou sawest* was to recall to Nebuchadnezzar the dream that he had, and since Daniel was able to do this, it was evidence to the king that the prophet knew what he was talking about. That constituted the assurance that both dream and interpretation were decreed by the Lord and would prove to be sure.

Verse 46. It was natural for the king to act as the account shows for gratitude alone would prompt it. And there would not be anything strained about his views of propriety seeing he had never known any kind of religious activities other than those belonging to idolatry which usually involved some priest or other attendant to represent the deity being worshiped. Nebuchadnezzar had forgotten his dream, but there was nothing to prevent him from remembering it after Daniel recalled it for him. He could not know that the prediction would be fulfilled, but he could know whether the recalling of the dream was correct. He then employed the reasoning he had made with the Chaldeans in verse 9, and concluded that Daniel was a true magician and worthy of devotions. But the record does not say that he accepted them, and we are sure he did not judging from his conduct at other times. Instead, he informed the king that it was not through any superior wisdom that he possessed that he could explain the situation, but that it was by the help of his God. This is indicated by the word *answered* in the following verse which is properly translated.

Verse 47. The king then acknowledged that Daniel's God was greater than all other gods or rulers. That meant that He had honored Daniel by enabling him to reveal this secret to the king.

Verse 48. Offering *gifts* to Daniel was on the same principle as those promised to the wise men in verse 6 and was proper. The king was eager to do something to show his appreciation for the favor that Daniel had shown him. Making him *ruler* over the province of Babylon means he was to manage the affairs, even having seniority over other managers, but of course it would be under the jurisdiction of the king. There was a logical reason for offering such a position to him. The monarchs all had need of such subordinates in their dominions, and Daniel had shown that he possessed great wisdom and was qualified and worthy of such a trust.

Verse 49. Daniel's unselfishness manifested itself again, and through his request the king gave the honor to the prophet's three companions while he was content to remain at the court of the palace, ready to perform any service that might be desired. In thus passing the honor on to his friends Daniel gave a good example of the performance that Paul teaches in Romans 12:10.

DANIEL 3

Verse 1. We know the events of this chapter came after those in the preceding one for verse 12 mentions the promotion of the three companions of Daniel, which is recorded in the close of that chapter. King Nebuchadnezzar was an idolater and continued to be one as long as he lived, as far as our information goes. However, he was made to know and acknowledge the superiority of the God of heaven more than once, although he never became a worshiper of Him in the complete sense. It seems that God wished to use him as an instrument by which to demonstrate to the world that there is one only true God, and that men are blessed in proportion as they serve Him. That was done in the preceding 2 chapters, it will be done in the present one, and will be done again in later chapters. *Image* is from TSELEM which Strong defines, "An idolatrous figure." This statement in the lexicon is all the information we have as to the form or appearance of this image outside of what the text says of its size and some of its dimensions. We may get some useful suggestions, though, from historians and ancient writers, both heathen and believers in God. Such writers as Herodotus, Augustine and Dean Prideaux suggest that the 60 cubits includes the base and pedestal of the image; also that the *breadth* means the distance from front to back of the image, and not that from side to side, and that would describe a more likely proportion. The image was set up at a place called *plain of Dura*, a place not far from Babylon.

Verse 2. The persons referred to were the officers of various ranks in the service of Nebuchadnezzar, and their specific work does not need to be inquired into here. It was to be expected that such individuals would be present on such an important occasion as the dedication of the huge idol.

Verse 3. The men summoned came to the dedication of the image except the three companions of Daniel. Nothing is said about their absence, but even had they been present there would not have been anything to call for a complaint against them, for no one was asked to perform any act of worship that would have been recognized by the idolaters. It says these officers *stood before* the image and that would not have amounted to an act of worship in the eyes either of the king or the officers. When the worship was to be done it would require the citizens to *fall down*. However, the three Hebrews could not conscientiously give even their presence at the dedication of something they would not endorse.

Verse 4. Smith's Bible Dictionary says the following of *herald:* "One who makes public proclamation. The only notice of this officer in the Old Testament occurs in Daniel 3: 4." The Babylonian Empire embraced virtually all the *people, nations*, and *languages*, hence the herald addressed these units of the government.

Verse 5. *Hear . . . cornet . . . all kinds of music.* The Babylonian Empire was a vast domain composed of many kinds of people. They could not be expected to leave their homes and all go to Babylon to appear before the image, but were to do this worshiping wherever they might be. They would not all be acquainted with each instrument named, but all would be expected to know some of them and to recognize instrumental music by some one or more of these instruments. *Worship* is from CAGAD and Strong defines it, "A primitive root; to prostrate oneself (in homage)." Hence the kind of worship demanded did not call for any removal of the people from their places, neither did it stipulate any formal schedule in the service; it required only that the people prostrate themselves when they heard the music.

Verse 6. It is a principle that is recognized universally that a law that has no penalty is useless. Hence the decree of Nebuchadnezzar gave the penalty of being cast into a fiery furnace. Jeremiah 29: 22 tells of two men whom the king of Babylon roasted in the fire, so we see this was not to be something new for the Hebrews to be cast therein. Also, verse 19 of our chapter shows the furnace was *wont* to be used.

Verse 7. In obedience to the decree, when the people heard the sound of this music, they prostrated themselves in respect for the image which the king had set up. There is no evidence that either the people or the king were aware that any objection would be made by anyone to the kind of action called for, since there would be no outward feature of it that would prevent any man from believing in some other god.

Verse 8. But the three Hebrews would not prostrate themselves, for to do so would have violated Exodus 20: 5 which not only forbade them to serve false gods, but also prohibited them from *bowing down to them*. This conduct was not overlooked by *certain Chaldeans* who doubtless were the officers mentioned in Chapter 2: 48 called "governors." They came near the king to make accusations against the Jews.

Verse 9. *Live for ever* was a phrase used in old times to denote a feeling of good will. It was sometimes said in a spirit of flattery when the speaker did not really want the one to live endlessly. As an instance, in 1 Kings 1:31 the mother of Solomon used the expression to the frail king David just after he had made her the promise that her son should reign after him. Had David lived for ever, Solomon never could have been king, hence we know she was using the term as a compliment. The Chaldeans used it as a bid for the favorable attention of the king.

Verse 10. They reminded the king of the decree he made that required all people to fall prostrate to the image upon hearing the musical instruments.

Verse 11. They reminded him also of the penalty he had attached to the decree. This was all in a pretense of concern for the dignity of the king's decree, but that was not the real point of their interest as we shall see.

Verse 12. *There are certain Jews whom thou hast set over the affairs of the province of Babylon.* I have quoted this part of the verse just as it is in the text because it reveals the actual motive of these Chaldeans in reporting the case of disobedience to the king. They made no accusation against Daniel although we are sure he also refused to worship the image. And they certainly knew about it, for the four Hebrews were very close friends and spent much of their time together. (See the comments at chapter 2:17, 18.) But the three named here were the ones who had been placed in a position of honor over even the other governors (chapter 2:48, 49), and that filled these subordinate governors with envy. But they used their pretended interest in the dignity of the decree to instigate a persecution of the envied Hebrews. Hence they reported to the king that the men of the Jews named had refused to worship the image.

Verese 13. It is probable that Nebuchadnezzar was actually surprised at the report of disobedience on the part of these Hebrews. He had not realized that his decree would be objectionable to them. But the bare possibility that the report was true caused him to fly into a rage and proceed to investigate for himself.

Verse 14. In spite of his intense feeling Nebuchadnezzar was disposed to question the correctness of the report, or, if it was found to be true, to give the accused parties another chance. Hence he put the question directly to them and specified the charge that he had heard against them.

Verse 15. Before receiving their reply the king repeated the degree they were accused of disobeying, and informed them of their chance still to avoid the penalty attached to the decree. *Who is that god that shall deliver you?* I have not capitalized the word *god* because this heathen king used the word in the same sense as applied to the gods of the heathen world. It was a challenge to them to test their respective gods.

Verse 16. *Careful* is the key word in this verse, but it is rendered somewhat indefinitely. It is from CHAS-HACH and Strong defines it, "To be necessary," and Young's definition is, "To be or think necessary." We thus can see that it was not a flippant expression of the three men as if the situation did not merit any serious consideration. It means they did not consider that their fate depended on any speech of defense they could make, and they proceeded to tell the king why they thought so.

Verse 17. *If it be so* means the same as the phrase "if God will." These men did not know what would be the Lord's will in the case. They had the s me thought as Paul expressed in 2 Corinthians 1:9, 10. He did not know whether God was ready to permit his faithful apostle to be put to death yet, or would prolong his life for further service, but whichever it was he was resigned to his lot. And the Hebrews did not know whether their God was ready to give them miraculous deliverance although they believed He was able to do so. They also believed that if it were His will to deliver them, it would be done without any speech of defense from them.

Verse 18. They then gave to the king their ultimatum, that regardless of the will of their God (as to miraculous deliverance), they would not serve the gods of Nebuchadnezzar nor worship the golden image.

Verse 19. Upon learning that the report was true, the rage of Nebuchadnezzar returned with increased fury. *Visage* means face and *changed* means distorted. The king was so enraged that his face was twisted out of its normal shape as he looked at the three Hebrews who were brave enough to defy his decree. *Wont* means accustomed and it shows that the furnace had been in use for some time. (See comments at verse 6.) *Seven* is derived from a word that Strong defines, "A primitive root; properly to be complete." If a furnace had been accustomed to being heated enough that it would roast a man to death (Jeremiah 29:22), then it would be impossible for a human being to make it literally seven times that hot. The statement therefore means they were to make it as hot as possible. The king allowed his anger to blind him to the inconsistency of his order. He evidently wished to slay these men, yet also intended that they should be tortured first. A furnace "seven times" as hot as usual would cut off their lives all the sooner and hence cause less torture.

Verse 20. There was no occasion for Nebuchadnezzar to employ the *most mighty men* for this execution, for the Hebrews had given no indication that they would resist. But the king was being driven on by a blinding fury and was inclined to exhibit the worst possible spirit of vengeance.

Verse 21. *Hosen* is from PATTIYSH which Strong defines, "A gown (as if hammered out wide)." Many versions render the word "mantle" or cloak. It was a loose-fitting garment worn over the regular articles of clothing for a man, even including the hat in the present case. All of these articles were tied fast around the men and then they were cast into the burning fiery furnace.

Verse 22. *Exceeding hot* is a good definition of "seven times" in verse 19. It was not only the intensity of the heat that slew the executioners, but the extent of the fire. *Flame* is from a word which Strong defines, "Flame (as split into tongues)." I do not know by what means the furnace was heated, but whatever was the fuel generally used, it was increased because of the king's urgent order. The result was that the flame shot out from the furnace or its heat reached to a radius that included the soldiers and slew them.

Verse 23. *Fell down bound* denotes that whatever was done on behalf of the three men was after they were on the inside of the furnace; no act of trickery was performed by some friend on the outside to free them from their shackles.

Verse 24. Nebuchadnezzar must have been near when the men were cast into the furnace, for it was immediately following the act that the text says *then* the king was astonished at what he saw in the furnace. As if he did not believe the testimony of his eyes, he asked whether they did not cast *three* men *bound* into the furnace, and his servants gave him an affirmative answer.

Verse 25. There are three words of special importance in this verse as regards the miraculous character of the situation, and they are *four, loose* and *walking.* There was one more man in sight than were cast into the furnace. They were loose whereas they had been bound by strong men. The fire might have dissolved the fetters that bound them, but the men were walking around in the furnace which showed they were alive and unhurt. *Like the son of god.* Again I have changed the capitalization because the principles that would make such marking proper were unknown to this heathen king. In verse 28 he is commenting on the circumstance and calls this same person an angel. What the king meant was that the extra person was different in appearance from that of ordinary men, hence he must have been related to the gods.

Verse 26. We are sure that God took a part in the whole proceeding else the king could not have come near enough to the furnace to speak to the men without being injured by the heat. The men inside were not harmed, yet they were prisoners of Nebuchadnezzar and would not be guilty of "breaking jail" until authorized to come forth by him. The king said nothing to the "fourth man," but spoke only to the three Hebrews; the angel evidently had disappeared. Besides, Nebuchadnezzar would not have felt at liberty or considered it necessary to give instructions to him.

Verse 27. Such an event as this would naturally attract the attention of the leading men in the empire, and they were present when Shadrach and his companions came forth. *Nor . . . hair . . . singed* indicates the complete control that was had over the fire. To a believer in the infinite God this miracle is no greater than any other. There are no great and small miracles as far as ability is concerned, for there is nothing too hard for Him (Jeremiah 32:17, 27). The same God who created fire is the author of all its laws, and it would be no greater task to control those laws than to create them. These men were members of a nation that had to be sent into captivity, and in that sense they had to suffer along with their fellow citizens. But they were personally righteous and hence were entitled to the special favors that God had promised to such servants. It is important that the reader now consult the note given at 2 Kings 22: 17 in volume 2 of this Commentary.

Verse 28. We have no evidence that Nebuchadnezzar ever ceased to be an idolater, but he was led to believe that the one god whom the Hebrews worshiped was superior to others. And he understood that the deliverance of the three Hebrews was in reward for their refusal to worship any god but their own.

Verse 29. We note that Nebuchadnezzar made no decree that required any person to worship the god of Shadrach and his fellows, only that it would be unlawful to say anything against him. The reason he assigned for the decree was that *no other god can deliver after this sort*, not that he deserved to be given exclusive worship.

Verse 30. To *promote* is from a word that merely means "to advance," whether in matters of temporal success and prosperity or otherwise. All that we can understand from it is that the king bestowed some additional favors upon them besides the position of trust they already had.

DANIEL 4

Verse 1. Chronologically, the first 3 verses of this chapter should be the last 3, yet it was proper to place them where they are as an explanation of why the king is going to tell his story. The message is addressed to all the people of the earth, and is accompanied with his best wishes for their peace.

Verse 2. *I thought it good* gives the purpose of Nebuchadnezzar in sending the proclamation to the nations of the world. The subject of the message is the great things the high God had done toward him.

Verse 3. This verse expresses the opinion the king had of God after the events that are recorded in the rest of the chapter. He was convinced that the wonders of Him were great, and that His kingdom was destined to be an everlasting one.

Verse 4. With this verse begins the report of Nebuchadnezzar's experience that is referred to in the preceding verses. The king was at *rest* which is defined in the lexicon, "to be secure," and *flourishing* means to be prosperous. He seems to have been lulled into a feeling of assurance that nothing could ever happen to endanger his independence as a monarch over the whole civilized world.

Verse 5. It was the appearance of the things Nebuchadnezzar saw in his dream that frightened him, not what it meant, for he did not know what that was.

Verse 6. We do not know why the king did not call Daniel at first, since he had previously shown his superiority over the wise men. Perhaps the force of habit, or his natural attachment to his own kind had its influence with him. At any rate the usual result followed the call of the Chaldeans, for they could not interpret the dream.

Verses 7, 8. It could be that the king did not specify by his decree just who of the wise men should be called in, and that Daniel might have responded to the call to "bring in all the wise men," since he was thus classified by the men of the empire according to chapter 2: 13. But whatever was the situation, we are not to think of it as being on the principle of "the last resort" for the king to call Daniel. Nothing is said about any specific call for him at all, only that *at the last Daniel came. Spirit of the holy gods* was Nebuchadnezzar's way of describing Daniel to the people of his dominions. He had formed that opinion of him at the time he explained the problem of the giant man recorded in the 2nd chapter.

Verse 9. The king remembered this dream, not because it was any more impressive, for it could not have been more important than the one of the giant man. But in that case the Lord wished to convince him that Daniel had superhuman knowledge, which would not have been done merely by offering an interpretation of a dream, for any man might do that and nobody could know whether it was correct. But when he recalled the king's dream it proved his divine standing. That evidence was not needed in the present case, hence the Lord enabled Nebuchadnezzar to relate his dream.

Verse 10. *See* and *behold* is thought of as being the same, but the idea is that Nebuchadnezzar directed his attention to something that seemed to call for it, and what he beheld was as follows. *A tree in the midst of the earth.* Being situated in that way would indicate that the tree was the center of attraction amidst a vast territory.

Verse 11. *Tree grew* denotes that it became larger and therefore stronger,

Daniel 4:12-19

until it was so high that it *reached into heaven*, meaning it reached up into the sky or higher air zone. The height of the tree was so great that its top was visible to all the people of the civilized world. That denotes that the curvature of the earth was overcome and it could have harmonized with some scientific discoveries of our day.

Verse 12. This verse gives a description of a fruit tree which, if taken literally, would present one that is beautiful to the sight, affords shelter from the heat by its shadow, a resting place in its boughs for the birds, a gathering place for the beasts, and food for all living creatures. We shall learn, however, that it is a figurative description of something else.

Verse 13. *Watcher* and an *holy one* does not mean there were two persons. The first word is from IYR which Strong defines, "A watcher, i.e., an angel (as guardian)." *Holy one* is added as an adjective for *watcher*. Moffatt's version renders this place, "One of the angel-guard," and this also agrees with the singular pronoun with which the next verse begins.

Verse 14. The king heard the watcher shout with a loud voice that the tree must be shorn of its leaves (its beauty), its branches (place of resting) cut off, its fruit (food) be scattered, be forsaken by the beasts and birds, and the body of the tree be cut down. This would seem to be the end of the tree, but we shall see that the condition was not to be permanent.

Verse 15. As a rule if a tree is cut down it means the death of the plant, but that is chiefly because the stump is exposed as a flat surface to the sun which will cause it to crack open, admitting the rain and other weather conditions to penetrate further until it reaches the roots. But this stump was to be bound with a ring of brass and iron which would hold it from opening. *In the tender grass* indicates this stump was in a field that had plenty of moisture, and that would be favorable for the roots of the tree and tend to sustain the life until they could sprout up into new growth. This very thought is expressed in Job 14: 7-9 and Isaiah 11: 1. Then the spokesman switches from the stump to the person represented by the tree that had grown on it and uses a personal pronoun. This person is destined to have his portion with the beasts that feed upon this "grass of the field."

Verse 16. The *heart* or mind of this unfortunate person was to be changed or deranged so that he would have an intellect no better than a beast. And being thus he will eat grass as they do (verse 25). This condition was to continue until *seven times pass over him*. *Times* is from IDDAN which Strong defines, "a set time; technically a year." Moffatt renders the place "seven years," so the meaning is clear that a period of 7 years (complete number; see definition at chapter 3: 19) was to pass with above conditions.

Verse 17. *Watchers* is plural because it refers to the "angel-guard" mentioned in verse 13, of which the one was a member and a representative when he *came down from heaven* (verse 13) to deliver the decree. *Demand* is from SHELA which Strong's lexicon defines, "Properly a question (at law), i.e., judicial decision or mandate." The passage gives us an interesting and beautiful thought. Everything and all creatures in existence are subject to the will of God, but it is wonderful when that subjection is conducted in the spirit of willing cooperation. As long as the angels are permitted to reside in heaven they will be thus in harmony with the wishes of their Commander-in-Chief. Knowing that He willed to demonstrate a certain great truth, this "angel-guard" (the *watchers*) agreed on a *demand* ("judicial decision") that one of their number (the one in verse 13) should go down to earth and carry out the decree upon the king of Babylon. That decree is so fundamental that I shall here copy it in full in order to make the connection the more impressive: "To the intent that the living may know that the Most High ruleth in the kingdoms of men, and giveth it to whomsoever he will, and setteth up over it the basest of men."

Verse 18. With the preceding verse the king completed the telling of his dream, and now he requests Daniel to give him the interpretation of it. He expresses his confidence in Daniel's ability to do what *all the wise men* could not do. The grounds of that confidence are that *the spirit of the holy gods is in thee.*

Verse 19. *Troubled* is from BAHAL which Strong defines, "To tremble inwardly (or palpitate), i.e. (figuratively) be alarmed or agitated; by implication to hasten anxiously." *Astonied* is from SHAMEM and Strong defines it, "To stun (or intransitively grow numb), i.e., devastate or (figuratively) stupefy." *Hour* is from SHAAH and the same lexicon defines it,

"Properly to look, i.e., a moment." With these definitions of key words the meaning of the passage is clear. The story of Nebuchadnezzar's dream was so unusual that for a moment Daniel was stunned with amazement. However, he soon recovered himself and spoke to the king. *Let not . . . trouble thee* was said to reassure the king, since Daniel had recovered from his own surprise. *Dream be to them that hate thee*. The enemies of Nebuchadnezzar were the ones to worry, for the dream will reveal that the king will yet be victorious over his foes.

Verses 20, 21. This paragraph merely repeats the description of the tree as the king gave it to Daniel, and does not call for any additional comments.

Verse 22. *It is thou, O king*, is a similar expression to the one Daniel made to this same king in connection with the dream of the giant man (chapter 2:38). But the application is somewhat different, for that included the king and his kingdom, while this pertains to the king personally. That is, his connection with the kingdom was to be affected by the events indicated in the dream.

Verse 23. This verse repeats the statements in verses 13-15, and *watchers* and *holy one* is explained with the comments on verse 17.

Verse 24. The description of the dream having been repeated, Daniel will next give the interpretation, which he says will be by the decree of the Most High.

Verse 25. *They shall drive thee* means the same as if it said "thou shalt be driven," for it is worded *he was driven* in verse 33. This also corresponds with *mine understanding returned* in verse 34 which indicates that the driving was done by some condition within the king's own being. The conclusion is clear, that Nebuchadnezzar was driven from his throne by the strange mental affliction that God sent upon him. That was what the angel meant in verse 16 when he said, "let a beast's heart be given unto him." The rest of the verse has been explained at verse 16.

Verse 26. *They commanded* has the meaning of "it was commanded." *Thy kingdom shall be sure unto thee* is explained by the comments at verse 22.

Verse 27. Having interpreted the dream of Nebuchadnezzar, Daniel concluded his speech with some advice regarding his conduct. *Break off thy sins by righteousness* is like the advice that Isaiah gave Judah in his book, chapter 1:16, 17, "Cease to do evil; learn to do well." Both phrases of the passage must work together, for it is certain that nobody will learn to do well while continuing in his evil doing. *Tranquility* is from a word that means security and prosperity. It also has about the same sense as "rest" in verse 4. At the time Daniel stood before Nebuchadnezzar the king was in the midst of great power and peace and royal success. The prophet suggested that if he would make the reformation in his life as just advised, it might mean the prolonging of his *tranquility*.

Verse 28. This verse merely introduces the sequel of the story.

Verse 29. God was very lenient and gave Nebuchadnezzar a year to change his ways but to no avail. Therefore it was time to bring the fulfillment of the dream upon the king, and the Lord chose a time that was especially appropriate. Nebuchadnezzar gave a demonstration of his chief fault (pride) as he was walking around the palace.

Verse 30. The greatness of Babylon was not to be questioned, for the prophet had already declared it to be so. If the king had expressed his appreciation for the good fortune that was his and given proper credit for it, there would have been no objction to his admiration. The fault lay in his pride and claiming that *he* had accomplished the great work, and that it was done in honor of *his* majesty.

Verse 31. *While the word was in the king's mouth* is very significant. It is a recognized principle of discipline, both as to human beings and dumb creatures, that an act of punishment is the more effective if administered as near as possible to the evil for which it is a chastisement. Hence, just as the king was uttering his boastful sentence, he was interrupted by *a voice from heaven* with the announcement, *The kingdom is departed from thee*.

Verse 32. Beginning with verse 28 the language has been in the third person, because the king is composing the account of his own experiences according to the announcement in the beginning of the chapter. *They shall drive thee* means "thou shalt be driven," and the announcement was repeated that was shown in the dream.

Verse 33. Without further delay the Lord smote Nebuchadnezzar with the strange mental derangement with the result that *he was driven* from men, which means that he forsook his throne and fled out into the field. He was exposed to the outdoor conditions of the weather. In course of this period and in such a state of mind, all care of the body would naturally be neglected. This resulted in a sort of wild development which made his nails and hair become coarse.

Verse 34. *End of the days . . . lifted up mine eyes . . . understanding returned.* These phrases are written in reverse of the order in which the events occurred. It is certain that Nebuchadnezzar would not look toward heaven while the mental derangement still possessed him. And it is equally certain that God would not end the days of the punishment of the king if he were in his right mind but refused to recognize heaven; hence the order of events is as follows. When the Lord considered that Nebuchadnezzar had been punished enough He replaced the beast's heart with the normal one. Then the king was convinced of the truth by his condition of body and his remembrance of the past. Being thus convinced, he was penitent and looked respectfully toward heaven, when the Lord ended the period of exile from the throne. It is not necessary for the text to state that the Lord also changed the debased condition of the king's body; that is taken for granted here, but will be implied in the 36th verse.

Verse 35. Continuing his praise of the *Most High*, Nebuchadnezzar declared that He doeth whatsoever is according to His will, and that the inhabitants of the earth are as nothing.

Verse 36. *Reason* is from the same original word as understanding in verse 34, so this is merely a repetition of that statement. However, another thought is added which is that his *honor and brightness returned*, and the reason for it is stated namely, *for the glory of my kingdom.* Verses 15 and 26 had assured the king that his throne would be reserved for him after he had learned that "the heavens do rule." God would not return a man to the throne of such a glorious kingdom as Babylon who was not worthy of it. Therefore Nebuchadnezzar was placed back on his throne a changed man, both in body and mind and one fitted to rule over his former dominions.

Verse 37. The king concluded the proclamation that was made to "all people, nations, and languages" (verse 1), and in this verse expresses the final impression that his experience left on his mind. It caused him to praise the King of heaven and to acknowledge that He is able to abase every man who is guilty of *pride.* This is all we will hear of the actual reign and life of Nebuchadnezzar in this book, except what will be said of him historically, referring to his reign as a thing of the past.

DANIEL 5

Verse 1. Between the close of the preceding chapter and the beginning of this is an interval of 25 years. We are down at the last year of the Babylonian Empire and Belshazzar is on the throne in the capital city. The Biblical account overlooks a few comparatively unimportant rulers between Nebuchadnezzar and Belshazzar. This man is called *the king* in this verse, but that title must be understood as meaning he was only "acting king," because his father Nabonadius was the actual king, but had left his son on the throne in Babylon while he was conducting a war in another part of the country. This fact accounts for other statements occurring in the record, and it is of such great importance that I shall quote a paragraph from ancient history. "But out of all this confusion and uncertainty a very small and simple discovery made a few years since has educed order and harmony in a very remarkable way. It is found that Nabonadius, the last king of the Canon [royal blood line], associated with him on the throne during the later years of his reign his son, Bilshar-uzar [Belshazzar], and allowed him the royal title. There can be little doubt that it was this prince who conducted the defense of Babylon, and was slain in the massacre which followed the capture; while his father, who was at the time in Borsippa, surrendered, and experienced the clemency which was generally shown to fallen kings by the Persians. . . . My attention has been further drawn to a very remarkable illustration which the discovery of Belshazzar's position as joint ruler with his father furnishes to an expression twice repeated in Daniel, fifth chapter. The promise made and performed to Daniel is, that he shall be the third ruler in the kingdom. Formerly it was impossible to explain this, or to understand why he was not the second ruler, as he seems to have been under Nebuchadnezzar, and as Joseph in Egypt, and Mordecai in Persia. It now appears that, as there were two kings at the same time, Belshazzar, a subject, could only make him the third personage in the Empire." — Rawlinson, Historical Evidences, pages 139, 442. This information will be referred to again and I urge the reader to make careful note of its location. The simple word *feast* means a good meal of food for the fleshly body, but the context shows this was a banquet for they drank wine in connection with it. Moreover, it was a royal or state affair for it was attended by a thousand of his *lords*, which is defined "a magnate" in Strong's lexicon. These men were princes or outstanding persons in the Babylonian Empire and hence were special guests at this great feast. The king participated in the drinking and did so in a cooperative attitude, for it says he *drank wine before the thousand*. That was unusual for the rule was that kings indulged themselves with wine and royal gratifications in their own private apartments.

Verse 2. *Whiles he tasted the wine.* Belshazzar was an idolater in general life, but nothing indicates that this feast was at first intended to be anything but a royal banquet. But intoxication will cause a man to do things he would not do when sober. This drunken king commanded to bring the golden and silver vessels that had been taken from the temple at Jerusalem. We have no account of their having been used before this after being brought to Babylon. The text says the vessels had been taken by his *father* Nebuchadnezzar, because that word is used very generally in the Bible and other literature. It sometimes means any forefather; in this case it means his grandfather. Perhaps it will be well to verify the last statement by a quotation from ancient history. "LINE OF KINGS—(of Babylon) Nabapolassar, Nebuchadnezzar, Evil-merodach, Neriglissar, Laborosoarchod or Labossoracus, and Nabonadius the last king. He, not being of royal birth, married a daughter of Nebuchadnezzar (probably Neriglissar's widow), and as soon as his son by this marriage, Belshazzar (Bel-shar-uzur), is of sufficient age, associated him on the throne."— Rawlinson, Ancient History, page 49. For the difference between *wives* and *concubines* see the comments on Genesis 22: 24, Volume 1.

Verse 3. The order of Belshazzar was obeyed and the king and his company drank wine from the sacred vessels that had been taken from the Lord's service at Jerusalem.

Verse 4. The writer must have been greatly affected by the conduct of the king and his party. In one unbroken statement he says they *drank wine and praised the gods of gold*, etc. Thus an occasion that started out as a royal banquet was turned into a drunken, religious service to dumb idols that were made by human hands.

Verse 5. The familiar expression "handwriting on the wall" is not technically correct, for this verse begins and ends with a distinction between the hand and its fingers. A well known commentator thinks that when the king saw the writing but could not see Him to whom the *hand* belonged, the invisibility of that One would heighten the "awful impressiveness of the scene." I will agree with that opinion, but will add that the "impressiveness" of the scene would be even more awful to see only the fingers that held the writing instrument. Such a scene would eliminate every hint of any mechanical trick of some objector to the merrymaking.

Verse 6. *Countenance* is from ZIYV which Strong defines, "cheerfulness." The statement means that the merrymaking spirit that had been showing itself in the king's face was altered and he looked pale. Strong defines the original for *loins*, "vigor; the loin (as the seat of strength)." Webster defines the English word, "The seat of generation or procreation." *Joints* is from a word that means something that binds or holds together, and in this place it refers to the muscles. So the clause *the joints of his loins were loosed* means that the abdominal region of his body had a feeling as if it were falling apart. The same thought is expressed in Psalms 22: 14 by the words, "My heart is like wax; it is melted in the midst of my bowels." This is a prophecy of Christ on the cross and the moral nature of the case is different, but it describes the mental and physical feeling that was being experienced. *Smote* is derived from NAQAPH and Strong says it means "to knock together." Thus we can get a mental picture of the king as he looked upon the weird performance going on over on the wall of his palace. His face turned ashy pale, the abdominal portion of his body seemed to be all in a quiver, and his knees pounded each other.

Verse 7. *Aloud* means more than merely being audible; it is from an original that means "with might." In addition to the physical feelings the king had by reason of the strange sight, he was perplexed because he could not even read the writing, much less understand what it meant. His common sense told him that such a demonstration had a great significance and that it concerned him since it occurred within his palace. In his fright and perplexity he shouted his orders to summon the Chaldeans and other so-called wise men. Those heathen rulers were so accustomed to relying on their soothsayers and their kind for special information that Belshazzar never thought about calling for Daniel. It was natural for him to expect his own Babylonian wise men to solve the problem that confronted him. See the comments on chapter 2: 6 on the subject of offering gifts to these men. They were asked to perform a double feat; read the writing and tell its meaning. (See quotation at verse 1 on "third ruler.")

Verse 8. *All the king's wise men* means those ordinarily employed by him and who were supposed to be "standing by" for service whenever needed; that is why Daniel was not present at this call. As we would expect, these men could not do the king any good in his great confusion.

Verse 9. The failure of the king's wise men to read the writing affected his countenance in the same way that writing did in verse 6, but it did not seem to have the same effect on his body. Doubtless he had consulted these wise men many times and had been satisfied with their work. However, there was never a situation like the one before them now. It was similar to that of Nebuchadnezzar in some respects. The failure to recall to that monarch his dream indicated that they could not have interpreted it either. So with the wise men before Belshazzar, for if they could not even read the writing, something that was present before them and needed no future knowledge to do, it was evident they could not give the interpretation after it was read. It is no wonder, then, that the king was worried and his lords astonished.

Verse 10. A *queen* was not the king's wife as a rule but instead she was his mother, and the word is so rendered by various versions. See an example of this subject in 1 Kings 15: 13, and it is further explained by the following from Smith's Bible Dictionary. "This title is properly applied to the queen-mother, since in an Oriental household it is not the wife but the mother of the master who exercises the highest authority. Strange as such an arrangement at first sight appears, it is one of the inevitable results of polygamy." This helps to explain, also, why the *queen* was so well acquainted with the events in the life of Nebuchadnezzar. Being older, and also associated near the throne for many years, she would have some personal recollection of those events, and she also had access to the records of the empire. (See comments on chapter 4: 1, 2.) Learning of Belshazzar's difficulty in solving the mystery about the writing, she came into his presence to console him with her information.

Verse 11. The queen related to the king the story of a certain man in whom was *the spirit of the holy gods.* For information on "thy father" see the comments on verse 2. *Master of the magicians* means he was given a rank of "chief magician," not that he had any authority over them. The point the queen was making was the superior wisdom this particular "magician" must have possessed for the king to give him the rank.

Verse 12. The most of this verse is the same description of Daniel's talents we have had before, but the word *doubts* adds an interesting feature. It is from QETAR and Strong defines it, "A knot (as tied up), i.e. (figuratively) a riddle." It means that Daniel was able to untie all "hard knots."

Verse 13. When Daniel was brought in, the king first asked him a question for the purpose of identification. The text does not state whether Daniel made any direct reply, but its silence indicates that the king understood the prophet's affirmative attitude toward the question.

Verse 14. As a reason for calling him into the situation, Belshazzar told the prophet of the favorable reputation that he had concerning his knowledge.

Verse 15. *Wise men, the astrologers* is very significant. All of the astrologers were considered wise men, but there were wise men who were not astrologers. Hence the king made the distinction as to which class of wise men had been brought in; it was the astrologers. He did this in respect for Daniel, who, though classed as a wise man (chapter 2: 13), was a higher rank than astrologers; he was one in whom was *the spirit of the gods.* Daniel was informed of the failure of the astrologers.

Verse 16. The king repeated a part of the report he had heard of Daniel, then made him a proposition. If he could read the writing AND make known its interpretation, he would receive personal gifts and other rewards. (See the comments at verse 1 for the meaning of *third ruler*.)

Verse 17. *Let thy gifts be to thyself*, etc. This is not to be taken to mean that Daniel thought it would be wrong to accept the gifts, for verse 29 shows he did accept them afterwards. *Rewards* is rendered "fee" in the margin which helps to describe the situation. (See comments at chapter 2: 6.) The meaning is that Daniel wanted the king to know he would tell the answer desired without regard for the reward.

Verse 18. Before going into the subject of the writing, Daniel related to Belshazzar the background that led up to the present crisis. The meaning of "father" for Nebuchadnezzar is explained by a quotation from history given at verse 2. It should be noted that Daniel says God gave to Nebuchadnezzar his kingdom and his glory.

Verse 19. *For the majesty* means in view of or because of that majesty, the nations *trembled* and *feared*. The first is from ZUWA which Strong defines, "To shake (with fear); the second is from DECHAL and the same lexicon defines it, "To slink, i.e. (by implication) to fear, or (causatively) be formidable." We see these words are used in their worst or most unfavorable sense which agrees with the very next phrase, *whom he would he slew*. It is still to be understood that God gave to Nebuchadnezzar his great might and glory, but that does not mean that He approved of the abuses that the king made of the favors thus bestowed upon him.

Verse 20. The abuses were manifested by the things described in this verse. The pride of the king over his greatness was so displeasing to God that he caused the cruel monarch to be taken from his throne and he was shorn of his glory.

Verse 21. This verse repeats in detail what happened to Nebuchadnezzar, and it was what Daniel had prophesied should occur (chapter 4: 25). The only way that Daniel could know of its fulfillment was either by inspiration or from the word of the king himself (chapter 4: 2, 3), for it came upon him while away from *the sons of men*. However it was, all acounts agree and hence we know that they are true.

Verse 22. The general sense of the terms *son* and *father* is explained at verse 2. *Though thou knewest all this*. The kings of great empires kept records of their transactions and the people, especially men in high positions, had access to those records. Daniel knew that Belshazzar had seen the account of Nebuchadnezzar's experience. The example should have taught him a lesson but it seems to have failed.

Verse 23. In conducting the kind of feast that was being done on this night, Belshazzar was in rebellion against *the Lord of heaven*. The king did not need to be informed of what was actually done on that night, but Daniel enumerated the items so as to make the contrast stand out. He and his family and royal group had given praise to gods that have no intellect of any kind, but had no glory to give to Him from whom even his breath was derived.

Verse 24. *Then*, because of and at the time of this abominable conduct, God sent the *part* of the *hand*. (See the comments in verse 5 about the fingers only being seen.)

Verse 25. We should remember that the wise men not only were unable to interpret the writing, but they could not read it (verses 8, 15), so the first thing done was to pronounce the words. In this paragraph I shall copy the words and give Strong's definition from the standpoint of a lexicon. *Mene*. "(Chaldee), past participle of *mena*, numbered." *Tekel*. "(Chaldee), to balance." *Upharsin*. "(Chaldee), to split up."

Verse 26. The lexicon definitions of the writing were given in the preceding verse. I shall now comment on Daniel's explanation of their significance. *Numbered* is derived from a word that is defined, "To weigh out; by implication to allot or constitute officially; also to enumerate or enroll." According to Daniel's interpretation it meant that the days of the Babylonian Empire had reached the number allotted to it by the Lord and the kingdom was to be declared ended.

Verse 27. A balance is a weighing device with a beam poised with its center on a neutral pivot. An article to be weighed is placed at one end of the beam, and a weight supposed to be equal to the article is placed at the other end. If the article is correct the beam will remain level or perfectly horizontal. The balance was a familiar instrument in Biblical times (1 Samuel 2: 3; Job 31: 6; Psalms 62: 9). When a balance is used figuratively it means that a man is weighed or compared with what is required of him and if he stands the test the "beam" will be level, and if not the balance will sink on the heavier end which will condemn the other. Belshazzar was weighed in the balances of God's character requirements but was "found wanting," or was unable to hold the beam level.

Verse 28. *Peres* and *upharsin* are from the same original word. The word means to split and was a fitting one here because the Babylonian kingdom was doomed to be taken over by another kingdom that was composed of two parts, the Medes and Persians.

Verse 29. Belshazzar fulfilled his promise in rewarding Daniel for solving the problem. See the comments at verse 17 on the matter of Daniel's accepting these rewards. The quotation cited at verse 1 explains the meaning of *third ruler*.

Verse 30. The history above explains in what sense Belshazzar was king.

Verse 31. *Darius the Median*. As was stated at verse 28, the empire that succeeded the Babylonian was composed of the Medes and Persians, thus forming a dual monarchy. This kingdom is referred to in various ways; sometimes by its full title and at others as the Persian. It is occasionally mentioned by the single branch Median, which it is in this verse. I shall copy a statement from ancient history on this subject as follows: "After the death of Belshazzar, Darius the Mede is said in scripture to have taken the kingdom; for Cyrus, as long as his uncle lived, allowed him a joint title with him in the empire, although it was all gained by his own valour, and out of deference to him yielded him the first place of honor in it. But the whole power of the army, and the chief conduct of all affairs being still in his hands, he only was looked on as the supreme governor of the empire, which he had erected; and therefore there is no notice at all taken of Darius in the Canon of Ptolemy, but immediately after the death of Belshazzar (who is there called Nabonadius), Cyrus is placed as the next successor, as in truth and reality he was; the other having no more than the name and the shadow of the sovereignty, excepting only in Media, which was his own proper dominion."—Prideaux's Connexion, Book 1, Part 2, Year 538. Verse 30 merely states that Belshazzar was slain on the night of this feast, but nothing is said about what was going on near and inside the city. The lengthy quotation from history on that interesting subject may be found in connection with Isaiah 13: 7, 8 in Volume 3 of this Commentary.

DANIEL 6

Verse 1. We should bear in mind that historically speaking the 70-year captivity ended at the same time the Babylonian Empire fell, which event was effected by the death of Belshazzar recorded in the close of the preceding chapter. That means the present chapter is at the beginning of the Medo-Persian reign in Babylon. We also should distinguish between the Darius named here and the men of the same name who will be referred to later on who were Persian rulers. The present one is Darius the Median (uncle of Cyrus), named in the last verse of chapter 5. It will be very helpful for the reader if he will make frequent reference to the passages of history quoted from time to time in my comments. When Cyrus slew Belshazzar and took possession of Babylon, he seems to have turned the political affairs over to his uncle Darius, and the appointment of the 120 princes was one of his first acts.

Verse 2. These *princes* were more official than the word generally means. It is derived from a word that Strong defines, "Of Persian derivation; a satrap or governor of a main province of Persia." These men were to manage the affairs as they pertained to the business matters, on behalf of the king, and over them were placed three men called presidents to whom they were to report their work. This was all done as an organization to see that the king would not suffer any *damage* or loss of any kind. Daniel was one of the three presidents and the statement is that he was *first*, which will prove to be very significant later on in our story.

Verse 3. *Was preferred* means that Daniel distinguished himself by his superior talents, and the writer of the text accounts for it by saying that *an excellent spirit was in him*. This was naturally brought to the attention of Darius and it made a favorable impression on him. The king had already delegated most of the business cares to the 120 princes, and now he was thinking of setting Daniel *over the whole realm* which means to give him a ruling authority that would have made him superior to the other presidents as well as to the princes.

Verse 4. Envy is a terrible spirit and will lead men to commit great crimes. The favorable position which Daniel acquired filled the other presidents and princes with this evil spirit and they began to plot against him. They wished to get him into trouble by some kind of disagreement or rebellion against the government. But Daniel was a law-abiding subject so that no statute could be found that he was violating.

Verse 5. These envious men admitted among themselves that no charge could be cited in connection with any of the existing laws. The only chance was to do something that would bring him into conflict through his religion. To do so it was necessary to have some specific statute which they knew would interfere with his religious practice; something that could be reported as an actual performance. To do this they took notice that one of his regular religious performances was to open the windows of his room that faced in the direction of Jerusalem, and there upon his knees three times daily to pray to God. That furnished them the subject for their wicked plot.

Verse 6. With their envious motive in their wicked hearts they came before the king. They introduced themselves with the familiar salutation, *King Darius, live for ever.* Such a salutation was sometimes uttered out of genuine respect for a dignitary without any selfish motive prompting it. In the present case, however, we know it was for the purpose of getting the king into a favorable attitude toward them and hence it was said in flattery.

Verse 7. There would not seem to be anything wrong with the proposition on first hearing it, only an overture for the purpose of showing honor to the king. Yet a little thought should have at least raised the suspicion of Darius. Why limit the decree to thirty days? If there was any good reason for limiting all petitions, that they should be addressed to the king only, that reason would continue after the period named. Another thing, the proposed decree made no specification as to whether the petitions involved pertained to religion or temporal matters. Had any such distinction been made it might have at least aroused the curiosity of the king and the plot been exposed, so they chose to word it with this indefinite form so as to give it the impression of a movement just for his honor. Daniel was accustomed to praying daily and hence thirty days may seem to be longer than necessary. But sickness or some other unavoidable circumstance could interrupt his devotions for a few days. Also, something might intervene in their own personal affairs that would make it uncertain to specify a shorter period. So the time allotted would be enough to cover all of these possible emergencies. These men evidently understood the principle of government that requires a law to have a penalty in order to be effective, hence they suggested that one be attached and even named the penalty they wished to be used.

Verse 8. *Sign the writing, THAT it be not changed.* The Persians had the foolish notion that when their king signed a decree it made it so sacred that it could not be repealed or changed even by the king himself. Had the king merely authorized the decree, there might have been some flaw discovered and it could have been set aside. That is why these abominable men induced him to put his signature to the document. The later conduct of Darius proves that he would have repealed the decree had he not signed it, which act took the law out of his hands for ever.

Verse 9. The *writing* pertained to the body of the document which stipulated what the people were prohibited from doing, and the *decree* was the paragraph that was to place it in the class of enactments that could never be repealed, and Darius signed all.

Verse 10. *When Daniel knew* might be taken to mean that Daniel went to his house to pray just because he learned of the edict, and that he did it for spite. His whole life and character would forbid such a conclusion. Besides that, the verse concludes with the words *as he did aforetime.* This shows that he did not make any change in his practices just because of this edict. In truth, it was evidently their witnessing that practice that caused the men to bring about that particular kind of degree. But the phrase means as if it said, "though Daniel knew," or "notwithstanding that Daniel knew." The point is that Daniel was not intimidated out of his regular service to God by hearing the persecuting edict of the king.

Verse 11. The men would naturally be expected to spy on Daniel to be able to report as witnesses of his conduct to the king.

Verse 12. Their speech to the king was that of a group of hypocrites. They pretended to be shocked and surprised at what they had discovered. But it might be well to remind Darius in the form of a question of the decree he had made and signed. It might have a more active effect upon him to have the edict brought fresh to his mind, and to have him verify it verbally before them.

Verse 13. Every statement these men made in this verse was true, but was uttered with a vicious motive and without regard for the context. It was true that Daniel ignored the decree of the king, but it was not because he did not respect temporal and royal government as they wished to imply. Instead, it was because the decree would hinder his religious service to God, and it has always been taught in the scripture that if a human law conflicts with the law of God. the servants of righteousness should "obey God rather than man" (Acts 5: 29).

Verse 14. The king realized he had been entrapped into something he would not have done had he known what these men were plotting. He had no ill feeling against Daniel but was displeased *with himself. Labored . . . to deliver him.* We are not told what the king did in his "labor," whether he was acting the part of an unscrupulous lawyer and trying to find some technical loophole, or thought perhaps that if he would not be in too much of a hurry in putting the edict into execution, something, somehow, might turn up that would release Daniel.

Verse 15. Unlike the decree concerning the image set up by Nebuchadnezzar (chapter 3: 6, 15), nothing was said in this one about the hour at which its violation was to be punished. The delay of Darius in executing it seemed to cause the men to become uneasy lest he fail for some reason. Therefore they assembled before him and reminded him of the unchangeableness of the decree which he had signed.

Verse 16. Being thus goaded by these men, the king was impelled, against his personal inclination, into carrying out the wicked decree. As the prophet was being thrust into the den the king commended him to his *God whom thou servest continually.* Whether "the wish was father of the thought," or he was making a challenge of the issue I do not know. However, whatever the expectations of the king were, we may truly consider it a test, both of Daniel's faith and of the might of his God.

Verse 17. A stone was brought and laid *upon* the mouth, not at the mouth or door. That language is appropriate because the den was a pit dug out in the ground. The stone was sealed with the king's own signet, which was a ring equipped with an engraving for making a stamp such as a notary uses today. That sealing had nothing to do with the confinement of Daniel, but protected the place against outside interference.

Verse 18. The whole circumstance was grievous to Darius, for he thought well of Daniel, and had realized that he was the victim of a plot caused by the envy of the lords and princes. The king passed a very restless night. *Musick* has no separate word in the original, but the phrase *instruments of musick* is from DACHAVAH and the most that Strong says of it by way of definition is, "probably a musical instrument (as being struck)," and he says it is equivalent to another original word that he defines, "a primitive root; to push down." Young says the word is of "uncertain meaning." Moffatt renders the word for *instruments of musick* by "dancing girls," and a footnote in the American Standard Version gives the same rendering. Another work of reference renders it "concubines." From the foregoing information we can get a reasonably clear picture of the situation. Darius was an idolater, also was a weak, pleasure-loving king. Under less serious circumstances a man unable to sleep would pass the time in the indulgence of his appetites and passions. But the wakefulness of Darius was caused by a grief so profound that he had no desire for "wine and women."

Verse 19. After a sleepless night the king arose and went to the den. When one is forced to go through a night without sleep from physical causes, the morning usually finds him in a very disturbed frame of mind; how much more so when it has been caused by a feeling of guilt. The entire nervous system of Darius was shattered with remorse.

Verse 20. He approached the den with mingled feelings, torn between hope and despair. The record of Daniel's life was evidently known somewhat to the king, which would tend to give him hope that he would be miraculously protected. And yet he was not certain that Daniel's God would see fit in this case to intervene. *Lamentable* is from ATSAB and Strong's definition is, "to afflict." The meaning of the passage is that Darious cried with a voice that expressed his affliction in both mind and body. We may condense the heart-rending cry to "O Daniel, has thy God seen fit to preserve thee?"

Verse 21. I have no words fully to describe the suspense in which the king must have hung after uttering the foregoing, wailing cry. He could scarcely wait long enough for Daniel to respond should he be still alive, for seconds would seem like minutes or hours. And yet, even a seemingly long silence would not be quite enough time; perhaps when a reasonable pause has passed the prisoner will speak. And again my words fail me in trying to describe the joyous relief the king must have felt when he heard the brief but respectful salutation, *O king live for ever*. No tinge of bitterness or resentment, but the same attitude of respect for his earthly master he had always shown.

Verse 22. In a candid but respectful manner Daniel explained to his king that his God had preserved him. He then accounted for the miraculous escape from the lions' mouths. He had been innocent in the sight of his God, and also had done no *hurt* to his king. That word is defined as "crime" in Strong's lexicon, which proves to us that Daniel was justified in his use of the word. It is true that he had disobeyed the decree of the king, but it was one that he had signed without any knowledge of the circumstances. Since Darius would not have signed the edict had he known the facts, the act of Daniel in continuing what had been his practice all along without any disapproval of the king, constituted no deed that injured the dignity of his sovereign.

Verse 23. We are sure that whatever show of gladness the king made because of Daniel's preservation was sincere. Not only was he preserved but he was not injured in any way. The word *hurt* in this verse means bodily damage. It is the writer who says that Daniel escaped all damage *because he believed in his God*.

Verse 24. In the ordinary sense of *accuse* it means to charge one with something wrong. It is a stronger word in the present case and means "to eat or consume." The thought is that the men desired to have Daniel destroyed by being eaten by the lions. Instead of such a fate happening to the prophet it came upon the accusers. *Their children and their wives* were thrown into the den with them. The reason for casting these people into the den is clarified by a statement of Josephus, Antiquities, Book 10, Chapter 11, Section 6, as follows: "Now when his enemies saw that Daniel had suffered nothing which was terrible, they would not own that he was preserved by God and by his providence; but they said, that the lions had been filled full with food, and on that account it was, as they supposed, that the lions would not touch Daniel, nor come to him, and this they alleged to the king; but the king, out of an abhorrence of their wickedness, gave order that they should throw in a great deal of flesh to the lions; and when they had filled themselves, he gave further order that Daniel's enemies should be cast into the den that he might learn whether the lions, now they were full, would touch them or not; and it appeared plain to Darius, after the princes had been cast to the wild beasts, that it was God who preserved Daniel, for the lions spared none of them, but tore them all to pieces, as if they had been very hungry, and wanted food. I suppose, therefore, it was not their hunger, which had been a little before satisfied with abundance of flesh, but the wickedness of these men that provoked them to destroy the princes. For if it so pleased God, that wickedness might by even those irrational creatures, be esteemed a plain foundation for their punishment." No doubt these wicked enemies of Daniel thought they had a sufficient explanation of his preservation in claiming that the beasts had been previously fed to their full. Whether Darius seriously considered their suggestion we have no way of knowing. But it was a fair test for these accusers to have the lions fed under the king's orders before offering them these human bodies. If being filled before caused them to ignore the body of Daniel (as these men had claimed), then the same condition should work that way again. *Or ever* means "before ever" they reached the bottom of the cave or den. The beasts were so vicious towards these people, even though they had their stomachs filled with fresh meat, that they lunged up and seized them before they had a chance to alight.

Verse 25. The world empires were made up *of all people, nations, and languages* of the civilized world, hence a proclamation such as the king wished to be made would be so addressed in order to reach and affect all the subjects of his realm.

Verse 26. *Every dominion of my kingdom* is explained by the comments on the preceding verse. Religion was a state affair with the ancient empires, hence it was in line with the rule for Darius to make the requirement set forth in this decree, though the Lord did not depend on the worldly governments to stipulate the form of worship that was to be offered to Him. The king made a specific mention of his reasons for issuing the decree which were true and very respectful.

Verse 27. The king continued his general remarks about the greatness of "the God of Daniel," but he did not stop with generalities; he cited the case of Daniel's deliverance from the power of the lions.

Verse 28. Strong defines *prospered* as, "A primitive root; to push forward, in various senses (literally or figuratively, transitively or intransitively)." Cyrus is called *the Persian* because the Darius named in the same connection was a Mede. The Persians also had kings with that name but they will come into the history of the empire after the events of this book. This verse is intended as a general statement covering the span of time that Daniel and his work as a prophet had recognition before the rulers of the world.

DANIEL 7

Verse 1. With this chapter the book takes on a different characteristic and will be made up almost entirely of prophecies. However, since the chapters are not chronological as to dates, it will be necessary for the author to make reference to some of the visions of Daniel in connection with their historical settings. Some of them occurred while the Babylonian Empire was yet in power, while others came to him after the Persians took over. The vision of this chapter came to Daniel in the first year of Belshazzar king of Babylon. That takes us back a number of years prior to the fall of Babylon. God has used various methods in making revelations of his purposes to the world (Hebrews 1: 1). Sometimes He will cause a heathen to become the instrument for service and give him a vision or dream. Sometimes the prophet will be given the dream and be enabled to explain it to the proper persons. Such was done in this and other chapters of this book.

Verse 2. Prophecies are frequently made in symbols and the interpretation consists in determining what the symbols stand for. It is not so difficult to do that if we may find the history of such prophecies as have been fulfilled. *Four winds* signifies the whole world is to be involved because there are four directions on the compass. Strove is from *giyach* and Strong defines it, "To push forth," which means to cause some commotion or movement. Since the outcome of this rushing will result in something pertaining to human beings, we know *the great sea* means the inhabitants of the civilized world that were to become subjects of this empire.

Verse 3. When this great sea of humanity was stirred up by the four winds it brought forth *four great beasts*. They correspond to the four world kingdoms of chapter 2: 36-40. These kingdoms were *diverse one from another*, which means that although the four governments were alike in that they were world powers in their scope, yet each had characteristics peculiar to itself.

Verse 4. The first beast (Babylon) was like a *lion* which indicates strength. (See chapter 2: 37.) It had *eagle's wings* which indicates the ability to soar and cover the whole area of mankind. (See chapter 2: 38.) *Man's heart given to it* signifies the beast referred to something composed of intelligent, human beings, which was true of the Babylonian Empire.

Verse 5. The second beast (Medo-Persia) was like to a *bear*. That animal is cruel and vicious (2 Kings 2: 24), and likewise the Persians were a cruel people. See the comments on chapter 6: 24, and note that women and children were cast together into the lions' den. The *three ribs* denotes a devouring disposition, and it was told to *devour much flesh*, which means this kingdom would conquer many people. The beast raised itself up *on one side*. It was composed of the Medes and Persians (two sides), and one side (the Persians) rose higher as a political institution than the Medes. To verify this I shall quote some history. "Although the Persians were destined to become the *dominant tribe* (emphasis mine, E.M.Z.) of all the Iranian Aryans, still the Medes were at first the leading people."—Myers' Ancient History, page 88. This statement is verified also by Herodotus, Part 1, section 130.

Verse 6. A *leopard* is of the same family of beasts as the lion (the cat), but is smaller and apparently with less prospect of accomplishing much in the world. But it is a swift animal (Habakkuk 1: 8) and can make up in speed what it lacks the size of body to perform. This feature of the beast will be described soon. The kingdom represented by the leopard was the Greek or Macedonian (two names applied interchangeably to the same government). This empire was started by Philip of Macedon, but its world-wide proportions were accomplished by his son, known in history as Alexander the Great. In 12 years he covered the territory of the Medo-Persian Empire and brought it under the control of the Grecian, and by such swift military accomplishments justified the comparison to the leopard made by the prophet Habakkuk. *Four wings* and *four heads* refers to the four divisions into which the conquests of Alexander fell upon his untimely death. This great event is well described by the historian from whom I shall quote. "There was no one who could wield the sword that fell from the hand of Alexander. It is said that, when dying, being asked to whom the kingdom should belong, he replied 'to the strongest,' and handed his signet ring to his general Perdiccas. But Perdiccas was not strong enough to master the difficulties of the situation. Indeed, who is strong enough to rule the world? Consequently the vast empire created by Alexander's unparalleled conquests was distracted by the wranglings and wars of his successors, and before the close of the fourth century B.C. had become broken into many fragments. Besides minor states, four monarchies rose out of the ruins."—Myers' Ancient History, pages 286, 287.

Verse 7. The *fourth beast* (Roman) is described as *dreadful* and *terrible*. The first word is from an original that means to look dangerous; the second is defined in the lexicon as "mighty," and both of these characteristics were true of the Roman Empire as history abundantly shows. *Iron teeth* is explained by the comments and history quoted at chapter 2: 40, and also are *devoured* and *brake*. I trust the reader will see that place before going further with the study of this verse. The *ten horns* corresponds to the ten toes in the 2nd chapter that belonged to the giant man in Nebuchadnezzar's dream. They refer to ten European governments that were within the Roman Empire and whose kings or other heads ruled their dominions in subjection to the great head in the city of Rome. It does not mean that just that number was all of such governments that existed, but they were representative of the group of local powers that made up the fourth and last world empire. The reason for selecting the number of ten is that the initial symbol for the subject was a human form which would call for ten since that is the proper number for the toes. The ten governments are, England, Germany, Italy, France, Holland, Belgium, Austria, Switzerland, Portugal, and Spain.

Verse 8. Religion was a state affair in the world empires, and the success or failure of any conflict between church and state depends on which was the stronger at any given time. The ten horns of the fourth beast were the temporal powers named in the preceding verse, and each of them had some jurisdiction over the religious lives of its subjects. As a rule that jurisdiction was exercised in harmony with the will of the beast to which the horn belonged. But in time a *little horn* sprang up among these temporal powers, and it also had a religious theory, and there was some kind of conflict between it and the temporal powers and the result was that three of them were subdued or *plucked up*. The *little horn* was the papacy that started with small proportions but expanded as the years went by. There is some uncertainty as to which temporal powers were the *three* and I shall not attempt to determine it. But the purposes of this commentary do not require any definite conclusion here. The characteristics of *eyes of a man* and *mouth speaking great things* identify the horn as the papacy.

Verse 9. Not only was religion a state affair in the world empires, but that religion was forced upon the subjects without regard for their personal convictions. As long as that condition existed, such institutions as world empires could exist also. But God purpossed to introduce an institution into the midst of "these kings" (chapter 2: 44) that was to change things and teach the principle of individual responsibility that would result in the downfall of these world powers. That is the prediction in the words *till the thrones were cast down* in this verse. The *Ancient of days* is the same being as is called the *God of heaven* in chapter 2: 44.

Verse 10. *Fiery stream* is a symbol of the forceful discharge of truth that proceeds from God. The many *thousands* refers to the extent of God's dominion over the lives of mankind. *Judgment set; books opened* indicates that God is about to put into execution His determination to overthrow the reign of the world empires. The words italicized are used for this great revolution because such is the usual procedure when anyone or any group is to be brought to a test. In its fulfillment it refers to the predictions made by both Ezekiel and Daniel previously that the dominating world powers were to be overthrown by the influence of God's teaching on individual responsibility.

Verse 11. Two creatures or institutions are referred to in this verse, and they seem to be in collusion for the one purpose of depriving men of their personal liberty of thought and action. Those two creatures are the *horn* and *beast.* The first is the papacy and the second is the world empire of Rome. We do not usually think of these as being in the same class, for one is political and the other is religious; yet they both were opposed to the personal liberty mentioned a few lines above. It is true that the papacy was formed many years after the kingdom was to be set up. And it is true also that the beast (Rome) continued many years after it was started. But it received the "death stroke" when that heavenly kingdom was *set up* and some time was required for it to succumb to the stroke. But knowing that it would do so, God directed a vision that is to be dated according to the time of the "stroke," some more particulars of the same which will be seen in the following verses. *Beast was slain* is the event resulting from the "death stroke" stated above, and the *burning flame* is the *fiery stream* of verse 10.

Verse 12. *Rest of the beasts* refers to the same as the ten horns. When the world empires were made to be a thing of the past, the kings of those governments lost the position they once held (*had their dominion taken away*) as part of such an empire. Yet *their lives prolonged* is a figurative way of saying they would not be entirely blotted out. When the next great event occurs, soon to be predicted, these governments will find that their existence as temporal institutions, independent of the world monarchies, will be recognized and encouraged.

Verse 13. The *Son of man* is Christ and the *Ancient of days* is God his Father. *Near before him* denotes the close association of these two divine Beings in bringing into the world the principles destined to accomplish the things just predicted.

Verse 14. This verse predicts the same things as chapter 2: 44, slightly different terms being used. *Given him* means that God was to work through his Son in "setting up" the kingdom that was never to be destroyed. *All people* were to serve Him even as all nations of them had been under the sway of the world empires. But those empires dominated the people by their political control to such an extent that they perverted even their religious conduct. The kingdom of the God of heaven (the church) was to rule all who became its subjects with the rod of divine truth, which would give to each man the liberty of conscience and conduct that is in harmony with individual responsibility under the principles of that divine truth.

Verse 15. Up to this verse the chapter is describing the dream or vision that Daniel had. The interpretations and comments that I have been giving on the verses are not those of the prophet, for he had not known them himself as yet, but is soon to learn them through another. My comments are based partly on some of the statements of *one of them that stood by* (verse 16), and partly on the facts and truths of history as quoted. We may note here that Daniel was not given the interpretation of his dream along with the vision itself, as was done in other cases, but he must obtain that information from another. So it is another instance of the "divers manners" spoken of in Hebrews 1: 1. After having this vision, the prophet was *grieved* and *troubled* because he did not know what it meant. However, upon awaking he recalled it and made a record of it, "wrote the dream," and also "told the sum" of it (verse 1).

Verse 16. This verse tells us to whom Daniel told his dream; it was to *one of them that stood by.* This was evidently some person sent by the Lord to explain to Daniel the interpretation of his dream. It is true that God could have inspired the prophet with the interpretation also even as he did in other instances, but He has not always done his work after the same manner (Hebrews 1:1). After the one that *stood* by had given to Daniel the interpretation of the dream he disappeared from the scene and the rest of the chapter will be the direct words of Daniel, repeated, of course, after the interpretation as he received it. We may be sure that the Lord will give the prophet whatever help is necessary to assure a correct report of that given him.

Verse 17. I shall avoid lengthy or unnecessary repetition of interpretations that have been given in the forepart of the chapter. The *four kings* are the same as the *four great beasts* in verse 3, and the four kingdoms of chapter 2: 38-40.

Verse 18. *Saints of the Most High* are members of the kingdom that the God of heaven was to set up. *Take the kingdom* is equivalent to "break in pieces and consume these kingdoms" in chapter 2: 44. *Possess . . . for ever and ever* means the overthrow of world empires by the influence of the church, and this influence was to last always.

Verses 19, 20. The one that *stood by* at first gave Daniel a brief interpretation of the *four great beasts*, that they represented four kings who were to arise, and then he added that the saints of the Most High would take *the* kingdom, indicating that this particular prediction pertained to only one of them, and naturally it would be the fourth and last one. Just then he recalled that in his dream he saw much more concerning it than of any of the others. That caused him to ask for the interpretation of those events, and to make sure that his inquiry was appreciated he repeated the description and doings of the fourth beast; such is the subject matter of these verses.

Verse 21. It is not an unusual thing for a prophecy in the Bible to have a twofold application, or for it to have its original application extended so as to include other things farther in the future, and that was done in this prediction. But to get the background that leads up to this extended application I must take the reader back to a word in the beginning of verse 19 which is the word *truth*. We know Daniel was not in any doubt as to whether anything the one standing by said would be true, hence we must look for a special meaning of the word. It is derived from YATSAB which Strong defines, "A primitive root; to place (any thing so as to stay); reflexively to station, offer, continue." The last word in the definition is the one for our use here. It signifies that Daniel wanted to know the application of the prophecy so that it "continued" until it included the horn (the papacy). Continuing his inquiry of the man, he saw some additional symbols, and they are the things of the present verse and others to follow. The *war* this horn made against the saints was the persecution of Christians by the church of Rome, that received such strong support from the empire of Rome (the fourth beast) before that beast was overthrown.

Verse 22. The war mentioned in the preceding verse was to continue until God gave his saints some relief from the persecutions they were enduring. This general prediction will become more specific a little farther down.

Verse 23. For some reason the prophet goes back to an earlier time and repeats some things about the fourth beast, describing it as a world power and devouring men.

Verse 24. The story continues on with the inclusion of the ten horns, which have been previously explained to be the ten European governments that were a part of the Roman Empire. Perhaps we can see the logical connection between this and what is soon to come before the chapter is concluded. It was among or out of "these kings," including the ten horns, that *another* "little horn" was to arise which was the papacy. It was necessary to refer anew to this institution in order to connect the story up with the important revolutionary events yet to be foretold.

Verse 25. The pronoun *he* stands for the "little horn" which is the papacy or church of Rome, and the passage is a description of the character and conduct of that institution through a long period of years. *Wear out the saints* is a repetition of the "war with the saints" in verse 21. *Think to change times and laws* is still a prediction of the church of Rome which was to be in cooperation with the fourth beast, the Roman Empire; as long as that government existed, and the two thus united composed what is known in history and prophecy as Babylon the Great, otherwise described as the union of church and state. The words italicized means the church of Rome boastfully will claim authority to regulate public matters the same as if it were God. (See a like prediction of this institution in 2 Thessalonians 2: 4.) *Shall be given into his hand* means they will be persecuted and suppressed during the period soon to be described. That period is known in the language and literature of Christian teachers as the Dark Ages, and its length is acknowledged to have been 1260 years. But the period here is stated in symbols, and we know that all inspired symbols must be interpreted in harmony with the known facts of history. So the symbols denote the following: A *time* (the original for which Strong defines, "a set time; technically a year"), *times* (which would require at least 2 years), and the *dividing of time* (which would be half a year.) Altogether there would be three and a half symbolical years. In prophecy or symbols a day stands for a year. There are 360 days in a prophetical year; multiply 360 by three and a half and we get 1260, the number of years of the Dark Ages. This is not simply an arbitrary conclusion of a devoted advocate of the Bible, but even the historian Edward Gibbon, who was an infidel as regards the Bible, gives us in round numbers the same period for the reign of the church of Rome, and I shall quote a paragraph from his Decline and Fall of the Roman Empire, chapter 28, as follows: "In the long period of twelve hundred years, which elapsed between the reign of Constantine and the reformation of Luther [which are the beginning and ending dates of the Dark Ages according to Christian scholars], the worship of saints and relics corrupted the pure and perfect simplicity of the Christian model; and some symptoms of degeneracy may be observed even in the first generations [See 2 Thessalonians 2: 7] which adopted and cherished this pernicious innovation."

Verse 26. This verse is a prediction of the period in history known as the Reformation, started by Martin Luther and conducted in cooperation with others of that time. *Take away his dominion* means the union of church and state was to be dissolved as a result of the Reformation, for that event overthrew the despotic rule of the church of Rome over the lives of men in both public and private life.

Verse 27. The language of this verse is similar to that of chapter 2: 44, and it is fitting that it should be. Each passage had to do with the perpetuity of the church or kingdom of Christ. In the first place the teaching of that church resulted in the overthrow of the world empires, and in the second it resulted in the downfall of Babylon the Great, and in spite of all the tests its enemies forced upon it, the kingdom of Christ stood and is still standing.

Verse 28. *Hitherto is the end* means that Daniel has related the whole story of this dream. *Cogitations* is defined by Strong as, "a mental conception." The prophet repeats what he said in verse 15, that what he saw in the vision troubled him. Yet he was able to *keep the matter in his heart* and relate it to the one who *stood by*.

DANIEL 8

Verse 1. Again the Lord gave to Daniel a prophecy, but this time it was in the form of a vision instead of a dream. It was shown to him two years after the dream of the preceding chapter. Another difference in this chapter is that, whereas the other considered the four world empires, this will be about the Medo-Persian and Grecian.

Verse 2. At the time Daniel saw this vision he was on the banks of a river in the province of Elam. Shushan (sometimes spelled Susa) was one of the capitals of the Medo-Persian Empire. The reason for saying one of its capitals is that after the ascendency of this world power, its rulers resided sometimes in this place and sometimes in Babylon. However, at the time of this chapter the Babylonian Empire was still in power, and the reference to the *palace* was because the province had once been a prominent territory and had its own local rulers who had their mansion here. Since Daniel had this vision while the first of the four world powers was in force, it would make the events shown in the vision truly prophetical.

Verse 3. The *ram* in this vision was the Medo-Persian Empire, the two parts of the empire corresponding to the two horns of the beast. In symbols an event may occur that is different from the natural procedure, yet one which truly represents the actual transaction in the application. Thus we here have two circumstances that differ from the natural course of events. The horns of this ram did not grow up together, nor did they maintain the same greatness or height. That was fulfilled in the history of the two parts of the empire, the Medes and the Persians. The Medes were the older of the two groups but never did attain to the proportions of the Persians. The historical evidence of this may be seen in the comments on chapter 7: 5.

Verse 4. The three directions mentioned are significant. A glance at the map will show the original headquarters of the Medes and Persians were in the east-central portion of the then civilized world. If the empire was to expand it would have to do so in these directions. It continued to do so until it grew into the proportions of a world empire. This was the second one of the four kingdoms that had been predicted by both Ezekiel and Daniel. And both of these prophets predicted that it would be subdued and replaced by another, which brings the story up to the next event of the vision seen by Daniel.

Verse 5. Daniel was interested in the event he had just seen and was thinking over it when another sight came before him. A *he goat* was selected by the Lord, that animal being rougher and stronger and better adapted to the action about to take place. The goat represented the Greek or Macedonian Empire which was the third of the world empires we have been reading about. Like the Babylonian Empire, its first king was not its greatest. The first of the Babylonian rulers was Nabopolassar, but its greatest one was Nebuchadnezzar. The first ruler of the Macedonian Empire was Philip of Macedon, but by far its greatest one was his son Alexander, represented by *a notable horn*. In symbolic literature a horn represents power and authority, and Alexander surely possessed both. *Touched not the ground* is figurative and refers to the swiftness of Alexander's march across the Persian dominions. He covered that vast territory in twelve years with very little resistance.

Verse 6. This verse refers to the furious advance of Alexander upon Persia.

Verse 7. In this one verse the complete subjugation of Persia by Alexander was indicated by the vision. *Choler* means bitterness according to Strong's lexicon, but it does not necessarily refer to the personal character of Alexander only. The idea is that the defeat that was inflicted upon the Persians was a bitter experience.

Verse 8. *When he was strong* denotes that Alexander was at the height of his success when he died, and that event also fulfilled the rest of the prediction, *the great horn was broken*. I shall quote a passage from one of the "church fathers," otherwise called the Nicene Library. "Again, the sons of Greece celebrate Alexander the Macedonian as the conqueror of many and diverse nations; yet we find that he was removed by an early death, before he had reached maturity, being carried off by the effects of revelry and drunkenness. His whole life embraced but the space of thirty-two years, and his reign extended to no more than a third part of that period. Unsparing as the thunderbolt, he advanced through streams of blood and reduced entire nations and cities, young and old, to utter slavery. But when he had scarcely arrived at the maturity of life, and was lamenting the loss of youthful pleasure, death fell upon him with terrible stroke, and, that he might not longer outrage the human race, cut him off in a foreign and hostile land, childless, without successor, and homeless. His kingdom, too, was instantly dismembered, each of his officers taking away and appropriating a portion for himself. And yet this man is extolled for such deeds as these."—Eusebius, Life of Constantine, Book 1, Chapter 7. The *four notable ones* refers to the four divisions into which Alexander's conquests fell upon his death, predicted by the four wings and four heads in chapter 7: 6.

Verse 9. In the comments at verse 1 it is stated that this chapter would be concerned with only two of the world powers. That is, all of the chapter would be about those two or some part of them. However, to avoid confusion, I think it should be explained that the four divisions into which Alexander's conquests fell at his death, while still a part of the third world empire, will receive some special attention. It was not long until two of these divisions were absorbed by the others, leaving only two which occupy the prophecy and history until they, too, were absorbed by the growing power of the fourth world empire, the Roman. The two remaining divisions will be referred to as Syria and Egypt. The former embraced the country formerly called Syria, and most of the countries as far eastward as the Indus River, and it included Palestine also, which will account for much of the important prophecy yet to come. The latter embraced the country of Egypt and the territory immediately surrounding it. These two kingdoms are also referred to in history and prophecy as the "northern" and the "southern" kingdoms, and the two were almost constantly in a state of hostility against each other. The present verse has to do with the kingdom of Syria, and especially with one of its kings who was one of the most vile and wicked men in history. Much of this chapter has to do with this man whose name was Antiochus Epiphanes, sometimes referred to by either one of the names only. He is the *little horn* of this verse, and is represented as becoming eager for more and more power. Hence he pushed outward to other territories and included the *pleasant land* which means Palestine.

Verse 10. *Stars* is from KOWKAB which Strong defines, "figuratively a prince." The words *host of heaven*, therefore, means the citizens of this "pleasant land," and the *stars* has reference to the outstanding men among them. This wicked king had a bitter feeling against the Jews, and was disposed to do them all the harm he could.

Verse 11. The *daily sacrifice* was presided over by the priest, hence we know that in this passage the *prince of the host* refers to the priest. The meaning of the prediction is that Epiphanes would stop the offering of the daily sacrifice. *Place of the sanctuary cast down.* Not only was the sacrifice to be stopped, but the altar and temple were to be desecrated. The fulfillment of prophecy is to be seen in the events of history, hence it will be appropriate for me to quote some now: "At the same time that Antiochus, who was called Epiphanes, had a quarrel with the sixth Ptolemy [one of the kings of Egypt] about his right to the whole country of Syria, a great sedition fell among the men of power in Judea, and they had a contention about obtaining the government; while each of those that were of dignity could not endure to be subject to their equals. However, Onias, one of the high-priests, got the better, and cast the sons of Tobias out of the city; who fled to Antiochus, and besought him to make use of them for his leaders, and to make an expedition into Judea. The king being thereto disposed beforehand, complied with them, and came upon the Jews with a great army, and took their city by force, and slew a great multitude of those that favored Ptolemy and sent out his soldiers to plunder them, without mercy. He also spoiled the temple, and put a stop to the constant practice of offering a daily sacrifice of expiation for three years and six months. But Onias, the high-priest, fled to Ptolemy, and received a place for him in the Nomus of Heliopolis, where he built a city resembling Jerusalem, and a temple that was like its temple; concerning which we shall speak more in its proper place hereafter.

"Now Antiochus was not satisfied either with his unexpected taking of the city, or with pillage, or with the great slaughter he had made there; but being overcome with his violent passions, and remembering what he had suffered during the siege, he compelled the Jews to dissolve the laws of the country, and to keep their infants uncircumcised, and to sacrifice swine's flesh upon the altar; against which they all opposed themselves, and the most approved among them were put to death. Bacchides also, who was sent to keep the fortresses, having these wicked commands, joined to his own natural barbarity, indulged all sorts of the extremest wickedness, and tormented the worthiest of the inhabitants, man by man, and threatened their city every day with open destruction; till at length he provoked the poor sufferers, by the extremity of his wicked doings, to avenge themselves." —Josephus, Wars, Book 1, Chapter 1, Sections 1, 2.

Verse 12. We might wonder why God would suffer as wicked a man as Antiochus to be so successful against His people. It was not the first time He had used evil characters as instruments by which to chastise the Jews. The last great instance was that of the king of Babylon who was empowered to take them off into captivity to punish them for their idolatry. But after that experience the Lord assured his people that they would never again be sent as a nation out of their own land. However, He did not tell them they never would be punished at all if they disobeyed the divine laws. And when they again became corrupt in other ways (not idolatry), He determined to punish them. This time it was by suffering the wicked king Antiochus to interrupt their sacred practice of the daily sacrifice, and the present verse has to do with that sad affair. *Host* is from TSEBAAH which Strong defines. "A mass of persons (or figuratively things), especially regularly organized for war (an army); by implication a campaign, literal or figurative)." The prediction means that Antiochus would be given an army to be used in a campaign against the practice of the daily sacrifice. The passage further tells why he was given this service against the Jews; it was *by reason of transgressions*. This point is verified by ancient history, and I shall quote an interesting paragraph on the subject. "Epiphanes ridiculed all religions. He plundered the temples of Greece, and wanted to rob that of Elymais. He exercised his impious fury chiefly against Jerusalem and the Jews, and almost without resistance. The Almighty seemed to wink for a time at all the abominations which were committed in His temple, till his wrath against his people was satisfied." — Rollin's Ancient History, Volume 4, Page 242. But however faithfully an instrumentality of man is used to carry out the divine will, the Lord never tolerates the wicked motive with which that service is rendered, but will eventually bring the proper punishment upon that person or persons. We shall learn before this chapter is finished that Antiochus received the full reward for his wicked treatment of the Jews who were the people of the God of heaven.

Verse 13. The disgraceful condition produced about the temple and altar aroused the anxious inquiry of the *saint* who beheld it. The verse may well be abbreviated by the words, "How long will it be until this condition will be corrected, and the daily sacrifice be resumed according to the law?"

Verse 14. The answer was addressed to Daniel instead of the saint who had asked the question, because it had been asked in the hearing of the prophet who was to be the reporter of the scene. The number of days, 2300, is nearly six and a half years. This includes the time the altar lay desecrated and idle, and also the period required for the war for the repossession of the holy institution. The war was conducted by Judas Maccabeus, a faithful and zealous Jew. The history of that war is too extensive to copy here, but the reader may see the information in Josephus, Antiquities, 12-7-1-6.

Verse 15. As in the vision of the preceding chapter, after the prophet had seen this one just related, he wished to know its interpretation. We do not know the identity of the person who will speak first, but he evidently was a messenger acting under divine orders, for his directions were obeyed.

Verse 16. That spokesman used the voice of a man, and Daniel heard him speak to the one who *stood before* the prophet, who had the *appearance of a man*, and bade him explain to Daniel the vision, at the same time addressing him by the name of Gabriel.

Verse 17. The appearance of this messenger from heaven filled Daniel with surprise and terror, and in reverence he fell face downward upon the ground. Then Gabriel made an introductory remark as to the time when the vision would be fulfilled. The *time of the end* could not be the end of the world, for the events predicted do not agree with that period. Neither could it mean the end of the four world empires, for there was still one more of them to come which was to exist for centuries. Hence, on the basis of elimination, the conclusion is that it refers to the end of the second one of the world powers that are pictured in the vision. That is in harmony with the facts of history, for Antiochus Epiphanes, with whom the vision concludes, appears in the historical records about 150 years B.C., and the reign of the Macedonian Empire was tapering off toward its end, to be supplanted by the Roman Empire, which was then beginning to cast its shadow ahead.

Verse 18. The prophet was still under the effect of his prostrating surprise which had thrown him into a deep sleep. That not being the desirable condition in which to receive such an important communication, Gabriel restored him to full consciousness.

Verse 19. *Last end* means the same as *time of the end*, explained by the comments on verse 17. However, there is a more specific item added to the prediction as to the date and that is, *end of the indignation*. The vision ended at the final downfall and death of Antiochus, whose wicked conduct provoked the *indignation* of God.

Verse 20. This is fully explained at verse 3.

Verse 21. *King* of Grecia means the royalty in general, for a particular one of the kings will be alluded to at the end of the verse. *First king* is explained at verse 5.

Verse 22. The *four kingdoms* is explained at verse 8. *Not in his power* means that the four divisions into which the conquests of Alexander fell at his death were none of them as strong as he. This prediction and conclusion may be verified by secular history, and I shall again quote from Myers' Ancient History, page 286: "There was no one who could wield the sword that fell from the hands of Alexander. It is said that, when dying, being asked to whom the kingdom should belong, he replied, 'to the strongest,' and handed his signet ring to his general Perdiccas. But Perdiccas was not strong enough to master the difficulties of the situation. Indeed, who is strong enough to rule the world?"

Verse 23. *Their* kingdom has special reference to the four divisions of Alexander's empire, of which Syria was the most important. Near the close of that period (see the comments on "last end" in verse 19) a condition was to exist described by *transgressors are come to the full*. This subject of transgression is treated at length by comments and quotation from history at verse 12, which includes the name and some of the traits of the *king* referred to in this verse. *Fierce countenance* is defined by Strong as meaning "harsh of face." *Dark sentences* is from one original word which is CHIYDAH, and Strong defines it, "A puzzle; hence a trick, conundrum, sententious [brief or pithy] maxim." *Shall stand up* means to appear and become very prominent. Hence we understand that Antiochus Epiphanes was a man with a hard looking face and a character equally harsh. He was an expert in matters of trickery, and would not hesitate to use it to his own advantage when the opportunity came before him.

Verse 24. *Not by his own power* is explained at length at verse 12. *Prosper and practice* refers to the success of Antiochus in his wicked transactions. *Destroy the mighty and holy people.* Antiochus was to overthrow those with whom he came in contact, whether they be the strong people of the world or the good people of God.

Verse 25. *Cause craft to prosper* is explained under *dark sentences* in verse 23. *Magnify himself* denotes he will be puffed up with a feeling of his own importance, and will plot and scheme various kinds of wickedness to gratify his egotism. *Peace* is from SHALVAH which Strong defines, "security (genuine or false)." Antiochus would win the confidence of men by his false promises and then would destroy them. *Against the Prince of princes* refers to his attack upon the institutions of God as we saw in verse 11. *Be broken without hand.* One word in the definition of the original for *hand* is "means," and the thought is that no apparent or human means would be used to cause the ruin of Antiochus. This violent and supernatural death of the wicked man is so outstanding in the annals of the times that I shall quote from history as follows: "When this concern about these affairs was added to the former, he [Antiochus] was confounded, and, by the anxiety he was in, fell into a distemper, which, as it lasted a great while, and his pains increased upon him, so he at length perceived he should die in a little time; so he called his friends to him, and told them that his distemper was sore upon him and confessed withal, that this calamity was sent upon him for the miseries he had brought upon the Jewish nation, while he plundered their temple and condemned their God; and when he had said this he gave up the ghost."—Josephus, Antiquities, 12-9-1.

"On his arrival thither [Antiochus Epiphanes at Ecbatana in Media], greatly grieved for this baffle and disappointment at Elymais, news came to him of what happened to Nicanor and Timotheus in Judea; at which being exceedingly enraged, he hastened back, with all the speed he was able, to execute the utmost of his wrath upon the people of the Jews, breathing nothing else but threats of utter destruction and utter extirpation against them all the way as he went. As he was thus hastening toward the country of Babylonia, through which he was to pass in his return, he met on the road other messengers, which brought him an account how the Jews had defeated Lysias, recovered the temple at Jerusalem, pulled down the images and altars which he had erected, and restored that place to its former worship; at which being enraged to the utmost fury, he commanded his charioteer to double his speed, that he might be the sooner on the place to execute his revenge upon the people, threatening, as he went, that he would make Jerusalem a place of sepulchre [burying place] for the Jews, wherein he would bury the whole nation, destroying them all to a man. But while these proud words were in his mouth, the judgment of God overtook him; for he had no sooner spoken them, but he was smitten with an incurable plague, a great pain seizing his bowels, and a grievous torment following thereupon in his inward parts, which no remedy could abate. However, he would not slacken his speed; but still continuing in the same wrath, he drove on the same haste to execute it, till at length, his chariot overthrowing, he was cast to the ground with such violence, that he was sorely bruised and hurt in all the members of his body; whereon he was put into a litter; but not being able to bear that, he was forced to put in at a town called Tabae, lying in the mountains of Paraetacene, in the confines of Persia and Babylonia, and there betake himself to his bed, where he suffered horrid torments both in mind and body. For in his body a filthy ulcer broke out in his secret parts, wherein were bred an innumerable quantity of vermin continually flowing from it; and such a stench proceeding from the same, as neither those that attended him nor he himself could well bear; and in this condition he lay languishing and rotting till he died. And all this while the torments of his mind were as great as the torments of his body, caused by the reflections which he made on his former actions. Polybius [a heathen historian] tells us of this, as well as Josephus, and the authors of the first and second books of Maccabees; and adds hereto, that it grew so far upon him as to come to a constant delirium, or state of madness, by reason of several spectres and apparitions of evil spirits, which he imagined were continually about him, reproaching and stinging his conscience with accusations of his past evil deeds which he had been guilty of. Polybius saith, this was for the sacrilegious attempt which he made upon the temple of Diana in Elymais, overlooking that which he had actually executed upon the temple at Jerusalem. Josephus reproves him [Polybius] for this, and with much more reason and justice, lays the whole cause of his suffering in this sickness, as did Antiochus himself, to what he did at Jerusalem, and the temple of God in that place, and the horrid persecution which he thereon raised against all that worshiped him there." —Prideaux's Connexion, year 164. God used Antiochus to chastise his own people "by reason of transgression," (verse 12), yet He was not willing that they should have charge of the last part of the just punishment upon the wicked king, but instead He struck him with a terrible affliction that tormented him in mind and body.

Verse 26. *Evening; morning* is in reference to the number of days mentioned in verse 14. The marginal rendering there is "evening, morning." That agrees with the expression "evening and morning" which occurs six times in Genesis 1 in enumerating the days of creation. The things predicted in the vision were some time in the future, hence Daniel was told to *shut it up* or keep it a secret for the time being.

Verse 27. Daniel obeyed the instructions about keeping the vision as a secret so well that *none understood it*. But the tension of the whole circumstance was so great that it affected him physically for some days. He finally recovered and resumed his duties under the king which is the meaning of *did the king's business*.

DANIEL 9

Verse 1. Another jump is made in the chronology of dates and the prophet comes down to the year following the taking of Babylon. This is the same Darius named in chapter 5: 31, who was explained to be the uncle of Cyrus the Persian. Although Cyrus was the one who actually made the successful attack upon Belshazzar and took over the city, he permitted his uncle to ascend the throne as the ruler as stated in this verse. It was in the first year of the reign of Darius that Daniel was reading the records.

Verse 2. The prophet read in the book of Jeremiah (chapter 25: 12) that the *desolations of Jerusalem* (the Babylonian captivity) was to last seventy years. That period was just ended when his attention was called to the prophecy. Of course he did not stop with the mere item of the length of the captivity, but read the history of the facts that caused God to send that calamity upon the nation.

Verse 3. Daniel was shocked by the history of his people, because their conduct was so rebellious that all this humiliation had to be imposed upon them. He was not personally responsible for the situation, but had to share in the sad debasement of the nation because he was one of its citizens. He *set his face* or made a firm resolution that he would approach God in prayer and supplication on behalf of his countrymen. He accompanied that prayer with fasting and wearing of sackcloth, a practice of devout people in olden times when under the weight of distress or anxiety.

Verse 4. *Made my confession*. This is in the first person because Daniel is speaking on behalf of the nation as a whole of which he was a member at the time of the great iniquity. *Great and dreadful God* is used in the sense of the supreme reverence and awe that should be accorded to Him. *Them that love him* is the condition on which

God will fulfill the promises made to mankind.

Verse 5. *We have sinned* is to be understood in the same light as "confession" in the preceding verse. *Have sinned* is made more specific by the words *departing from thy precepts;* forsaking a law is the same as disobeying it.

Verse 6. Daniel recognizes the prophets to have been the *servants* of God, and that they *spake in thy name* which gave their words the weight of divine authority.

Verse 7. The switching back and forth between the first and third persons, and between the plural and singular pronouns, is because of the relationship of Daniel to the nation as a whole. We have no evidence that he ever had an opportunity even to protest against the corruptions of the nation before his prophetic call, which came to him after being taken to Babylon.

Verse 8. *Confusion of face* refers to the state of humiliation that was felt by the people of Israel after being exiled into a foreign land.

Verse 9. The justice of God had been poured out upon the rebellious nation in the 70-year captivity that was just ended. Now the prophet is praying for the *mercy and forgiveness* that can come only from the same God.

Verse 10. It is not enough to profess faith in the Lord, but we must show our faith by *walking in his laws* that had been set out by the prophets.

Verse 11. One outstanding place where Moses gave the threat of God's course upon a disobedient nation is Deuteronomy 28. That passage was plainly written in the book of the law, and the people had no excuse for their disregard of it.

Verse 12. The *evil* that God brought upon the nation means a punishment, not in the sense of something wrong. By imposing this distress upon the nation God *confirmed his words* that were spoken against it.

Verse 13. This verse indicates the thought expressed at verse 11, that the people had been given plenty of opportunity for knowing the law of God, but they had turned from it unto their own wicked ways.

Verse 14. *Watched upon the evil* denotes that God sees all that is done by His servants. Daniel acknowledges that everything that God does is righteous, which includes the chastisement He had brought against the nation.

Verse 15. The gratitude of the prophet is so great that he goes back to the very beginning of Israel's history as a nation. He recalls the deliverance from Egyptian bondage which was many centuries before; now the same people are just emerging from another bondage. However, there is a wide difference between the two cases. The former was imposed upon God's people for no wrong on their part, while the latter was decreed by the same God as a punishment for sin.

Verse 16. Daniel continues his prayer on behalf of his people, and acknowledges that all of their suffering is because of their sins. The most disheartening feature of it is that the nation has become a reproach in the eyes of the other nations.

Verse 17. *Sanctuary that is desolate* is in reference to the condition of the temple in Jerusalem. The captivity had just been ended, but the Jews had not yet rebuilt it which they will later on. *For the Lord's sake* means that he prays for the holy place to be restored for His sake, not that the people deserved the favor.

Verse 18. *Open thine eyes.* The first word is from PAQACH which Strong defines, "to be observant." God never literally closes his eyes, but Daniel means for Him to take favorable notice of them in their sad condition. The closing statement of the verse is very humble and respectful towards God. Daniel does not claim that his people deserved the favor of God on the ground of their righteousness; he is relying solely on the mercy of the Lord.

Verse 19. This verse is an excellent example of a supplication made to God. That word is a stronger one than merely praying or asking for a favor. It consists in expressions of deep and earnest entreaty, made impressive by repetitions of terms that indicate great humility and a profound sense of helplessness. And again the prophet portrays more concern for the dignity of the name of God than for any personal favor for himself or his people.

Verse 20. *My sin and the sin of my people* is explained at verse 4. *Holy mountain of my God* is a figurative reference to the nation of God whose capital city was Jerusalem which was in ruins at the time the prophet was offering this prayer.

Verse 21. Daniel is about to receive an answer to his prayer, and the thing to be promised will be far greater or include more than he is asking. The favor the prophet is seeking pertains to the restoration of the capital city of Jerusalem. That is going to be granted, and it also will be the dating place for an event concerning his people that will be without a parallel in all history. He is not going to be held waiting very long for the answer to his prayer, for even while he was praying the angel Gabriel came and contacted him. *Time of the evening oblation* means the daily sacrifice that the Jews' religion included when they were in their own land. The sacrifice was conducted twice daily, at 9 and 3 o'clock respectively. Daniel only refers to it by way of designating the hour when Gabriel contacted him, not that such an offering was being made, for the Jews were not permitted, even by the Lord, to perform their altar services in the strange land (Deuteronomy 28: 36; Isaiah 43: 24).

Verse 22. *Skill and understanding* means mental skill, that which comes from special understanding. Gabriel informs Daniel he was sent to him for the purpose of giving him this favor. God could have inspired the prophet directly with the information as had been done previously, but He saw fit to do it in a different manner this time by sending an angel to him. In this circumstance we have an instance that is spoken of in two passages of the New Testament; Hebrews 1: 1 and 14.

Verse 23. As soon as Daniel had begun his prayer, the Lord gave the order to Gabriel to go unto the earth and deliver the message. We do not know when the angel began his flight to the land of Persia, for he did not interrupt the prophet until he was near the conclusion of his prayer. When it was the proper instant to make the contact, Daniel saw him in a "forced march" or flight as he approached him. As a personal merit on the part of Daniel for his receiving the favor just promised, the angel tells him he is *greatly beloved*. The severe tests of faith which Daniel had undergone and withstood, endeared him to the God of heaven and determined Him to bestow upon the prophet this honor.

Verse 24. This verse introduces the most important time prophecy in the Bible; important because it concerns the last act in God's provision for the salvation of mankind. The reason the subject should be considered as an answer to Daniel's prayer for his people, is the fact that it was to be accomplished through the instrumentality of those people and while their dispensation was still in force. The verse is a general statement that covers the entire period of the great transaction, after which the prophet starts with the details of the prophecy. *Seventy weeks* is figurative as to "weeks," and means 70 times 7 years. In other words, the period to be covered by the great prophecy will be 490 years. The grand purpose to be accomplished, and with which it will complete the fulfillment of the prophecy, will include the items referred to in general terms in this verse. *Make an end of sins* means to perform the final act of God for the salvation of mankind from their sins. *Bring in everlasting righteousness* refers to the same fact that was predicted before Nebuchadnezzar about the kingdom that would "stand forever" (Daniel 2: 44). *Seal up the vision and prophecy* means to ratify the prophecy about to be made through the prophet. *Anoint the most Holy* refers to the crowning of Jesus as "'King of kings" for the whole earth, both Jew and Gentile.

Verse 25. This verse includes 69 of the 70 weeks, which brings us to the beginning of the public ministry of Christ, here expressed by the words *unto the Messiah the Prince*. This 69-week space is subdivided into smaller periods of 7 and 62 weeks. The first period (and hence the whole 70-week period) begins with *the commandment to restore and to build Jerusalem*. When we learn the date of that commandment, we will know when the famous 70-week time prophecy began. It is thought by some that the work of Nehemiah could not figure in the question of the beginning time, but the reference to the rebuilding of the streets undoubtedly connects the work of that great reformer with it. And since the work of Ezra and others had to do with the temple and the services so vitally connected with Jerusalem, we may well include that also in the subject. But there is a difference of 13 years between the work of Ezra and that of Nehemiah. If each of the men is used as a beginning point, will they both come out at the one time, that of the beginning of the public work of Christ? Yes, the apparent difficulty is clarified by remembering that in those times both the lunar and solar years were used. The solar year contains some 11 or 12 more days than the lunar, hence if the beginning point of Ezra be taken, using solar years, there will be enough extra days to make up for the 13 years between that and the work of Nehemiah, using the lunar year from his date. The work of Ezra began in the year 457 B.C. which is to be regarded as the beginning of the 70-week time prophecy now under consideration. There is a good reason for marking off the first *seven weeks* into a period to itself, for that was about the time covered by the commotions set up by the enemies of the Jews at the work and reforms of Ezra, Nehemiah and other zealous Jews, referred to here by *troublous times*. After that the prophet ignores all the events of the intervening years down to the beginning of the public ministry of Christ, merely mentioning the period as *threescore and two weeks*.

Verse 26. *After threescore and two weeks* means 62 weeks after the first 7 (69 weeks in all) *shall Messiah be cut off*, but it does not say how long after. We shall see that it was to be three and a half years after, for it was that many years after Jesus began his public ministry that he was *cut off* by the crucifixion. *Not for himself*. The last word has no separate term in the original and it must be understood in the light of the context. Moffatt's translation renders the phrase, "leaving no successor," and the American Standard Version says, "shall have nothing." These renderings agree with Isaiah 53: 8 on the same subject which says, "who shall declare his generation?" The statement is in question form but it is actually an affirmative prediction. The meaning is that when Jesus died he left no successor, and the thought is most significant and beautiful. Daniel 2: 44 and many other passages predict that the kingdom of Christ was to "stand forever." In that case He would have no need for a successor, and God would see to it that even death should not prevent his Son from ascending the throne of the everlasting kingdom to be set up soon after his death and resurrection. *People of the prince*. The last word is from NAGID which Strong defines, "A commander (as occupying the front), civil, military, or religious." The *prince* in this passage is Titus, who commanded the Roman forces at the siege and destruction of Jerusalem. The reader should secure the history of Josephus and read the third volume if possible, for the matter is too lengthy to copy here. He will find that the stubbornness of the Jews forced Titus to press the siege with unspeakable suffering being imposed upon them, "ending in desolations" as this verse states. That event occurred 40 years after the death of Christ, and we may wonder why it is injected at this place, when the passage as a whole is not through with the public ministry and death of Christ. It was appropriate to interrupt the prophecy because of the direct relationship between the death of Christ and the destruction of Jerusalem. When Jesus was before Pilate (Matthew 27: 25) and that governor was hesitating about what to do with his prisoner, the Jews cried out, "His blood be on us, and on our children." God sometimes takes people at their word, as he did in this case. Forty years after that terrible sentence the city of Jerusalem was destroyed with all the afflictions referred to above, and it was a punishment upon them for their murder of Jesus. The death of the Son of God was necessary for the salvation of the world, and it was to be accomplished by the wicked Jews as predicted. But the Lord never did tolerate a wrong attitude shown by any of His agencies, even when they were carrying out the divine decrees. Hence we have the crucifixion of Christ and the destruction of Jerusalem (40 years apart) predicted in one connection, after which the prophet resumes predictions of the Messiah.

Verse 27. The *one week* is the last one of the 70-week period, being the seven years from the beginning of Christ's public ministry to the conversation of Cornelius. The *covenant* is the one made with Abraham in Genesis 12: 3 that "In thee shall all families of the earth be blessed." In other passages the same covenant includes the words "and in thy seed," which we know refers to Christ (Galatians 3: 16). The Mosaic covenant was for the Jews only but the one in this passage was for Jews and Gentiles alike, which is signified by the words *with many*. The reason it required a week (of years) for Jesus to confirm or fulfill the covenant, is the truth that His office required him to continue the good work until both Jews and Gentiles had been accepted. The *covenant* demanded that, because it was to bless "all the families of the earth." Jesus accomplished the work for the Jews in person while in his personal ministry of three and a half years; but this was for the Jews only (Matthew 15: 24). The part for the Gentiles was performed by the apostles in the course of the three and a half years after the crucifixion, which culminated with the conversion of the household of Cornelius. Twice three and a half years gives us a week (of years), designated in this verse as *one week*. *In the midst of the week* denotes the time of the crucifixion, which came three and a half years after Jesus began his public ministry, and the same length of time before Cornelius. Before proceeding with the verse, I shall sum up the dates to show how this time prophecy was literally fulfilled in 70 weeks of years or 490 years. The work of Ezra began in the year 457 B.C., the public ministry of Christ began in the year 26 A.D., the conversion of Cornelius was in 33 A.D.; 457 plus 33 is 490, the number of years required by the time prophecy. *Shall cause the sacrifice and oblation to cease* means that the death of Christ put an end to all other sacrifices for sin (Romans 10: 4; Hebrews 10: 8, 9, 14). *For the overspreading of abominations, etc.*, was commented upon in the preceding verse. The crucifixion of Christ and destruction of Jerusalem are very properly mentioned here in direct connection; for while the crucifixion had to be, yet the motive of the Jews in destroying Him brought upon them the destruction of their city.

DANIEL 10

Verse 1. When giving a date for any event, a reference to either Darius or Cyrus is the same. This is because the Medo-Persian Empire was ruled jointly by the two men, hence they may be used interchangeably for dates since they took possession of Babylon together as far as chronology was concerned. The preceding chapter began with the first year while the present one comes down to the third year of the same reign. This verse is composed in the third person and Daniel writes it only as a historian. *True, but . . . long* signifies that an inspired prophecy is not weakened any as to its reliability just because it looks far into the future. God knows as much about the future as he does of the past, hence an inspired prediction cannot fail.

Verses 2, 3. Fasting or making of vows was not required as a general practice under the law of Moses. However, such devotions were approved when entered into by servants of God, and they were generally done in times of great anxiety or sorrow. Daniel put on a three-week fast because of his concern for the Jews, who, though formerly released from the Babylonian captivity, were yet in an unsettled state due to the desolated condition of their city of Jerusalem. Ate no *pleasant* bread means he abstained from the food of his choice and ate only what was necessary to support an existence. The people among whom Daniel then dwelt used aromatic ointments upon their bodies for the purpose of its pleasant odor and sensation, but he abstained from the use of that costly delicacy during the period of his fast.

Verse 4. Apparently the fast that Daniel observed was to bring no results, for it was three days before he heard any word of encouragement. The reason for the delay will be explained later. The prophet was on the bank of one of the rivers of Babylon; Hiddekel, later known as the Tigris.

Verse 5. *Uphaz* is another word for "Ophir," a place that produced an unusually fine quality of gold. The fine clothing this *certain man* was wearing indicated the dignity of his mission and the glory of the authority behind it.

Verse 6. All of these descriptive words were used for the same purpose that was stated in the preceding verse. Whether the person was directly from heaven, sent to the earth in the form of a man, or was a being of the earth and especially adorned and qualified to serve the present purpose, I do not know. In either case we may regard him as a person being used by the Lord to accomplish certain ends with conditions on earth.

Verse 7. Daniel had some men with him, but upon the approach of this unusual person they became frightened and ran away, and as a result Daniel was the only one who saw the vision and heard the words spoken.

Verse 8. The prophet did not flee, yet he was greatly affected by the circumstance so that he had a prostrated feeling or a loss of bodily strength. However, this prostration did not interfere with his hearing and activity of mind.

Verse 9. Daniel heard the voice of the man, which, in addition to the state of his mind and body already produced by the appearance of such an unusual person, caused him to fall upon his face to the ground.

Verse 10. Before continuing the communication, the man caused Daniel to have a bodily posture of resting on his hands and knees.

Verse 11. While in this position the prophet received assurance that no harm was intended against him for he was greatly beloved. But before any further part of the message would be delivered he was told to stand up. He obeyed the instructions to arise, but his full strength had not returned and he trembled as he stood in the presence of this awe-inspiring personage.

Verse 12. In this verse the man again encourages Daniel and acknowledges the three-week fast that he had observed. He assures him that his words of prayer were heard from the beginning, and that it was *for his words* or because of them he had come.

Verse 13. In this verse the "man" (or angel) will explain to Daniel why his prayer was not acknowledged sooner, although it was observed favorably from the start. To use a familiar form of speech, the man was engaged in other business which detained him. Some commentators think that Daniel was contending with this *prince of the kingdom of Persia* to persuade him to permit the Jews to return to Jerusalem. I do not understand how that would be, for according to Ezra 1: 1-4 that privilege had been granted them two years before. If this controversy had anything to do with that subject, it must have been with some outstanding men of Persia who were not in full accord with the edict of Cyrus. Whatever it was, it pertained to the interests of the Jews, and this man or angel could not go to the relief of Daniel for a while. He finally had "reinforcements" in the person of Michael, and together they got matters in shape so that the latter could "hold the fort" for a time, which released the "man" to go and comfort Daniel.

Verse 14. The situation is similar to that described in chapter 9: 23, in that Daniel is to have his prayer answered favorably, but is also to be given more information than he had expected. In the present instance, if the prophet was asking for some reassurances of the return of his people to Jerusalem he was granted that consolation. But this inspired messenger was to tell him of some events in the centuries ahead that would involve these same people of the Jews. Since that *vision is for many days*, however, the specific predictions will not be given him until the next chapter. But in recognition of his devotion and concern for the people of God, the messenger was sent to give him the encouragement.

Verse 15. Daniel was again overcome by the presence and communication of the man, but nothing is said about his being frightened as before. He was rendered *dumb* or speechless but it did not affect his body otherwise, and he could only bend his head toward the ground.

Verse 16. I do not understand that more than one man or angel came to Daniel, though the language seems to indicate that there was. The general subject has been the same all through these verses and hence there would be no occasion for another messenger. The person was in the form of a man whoever he was, but he was endowed with supernatural power and knowledge for he was yet to make many predictions for us to examine. This angel recovered Daniel from his dumbness, and also renewed his bodily strength after a few moments. After regaining his power of speech, Daniel told the angel of his sorrow and its effect upon his bodily feeling.

Verse 17. Daniel felt humiliated and inferior in the presence of the person whom he called *my lord. Neither is there breath left in me* is figurative as to its extent, and means that the prophet was virtually exhausted by the vision.

Verse 18. *Then came again* means the same man or angel again contacted Daniel for the purpose of further strengthening him and making him feel assured.

Verse 19. Being comforted and strengthened by the angel, Daniel requested him to speak, which indicated that he felt prepared in body and mind to give attention.

Verse 20. The angel asked Daniel if he knew or understood why he had come to him. There is no recorded answer to the question that is available to us, but the absence of everything to the contrary implies that he understood. Thus the subject or occasion of the present meeting between Daniel and the angel was dropped, and the latter informed the prophet that he was going back to Persia to resume the controversy that is mentioned in verse 13. He added a general reference to another great event that was to occur between Persia and Greece after this angel has conducted his "fight" with the former. But this item is out of place chronologically and it will be treated in its proper place in the next chapter.

Verse 21. Chronologically speaking, the first part of verse 20 has been fulfilled and the last part of it is due; that is, it is the proper place to go more into detail as to the meaning of the words *prince of Grecia shall come.* Before doing so, the angel assures Daniel that what he is going to reveal to him will be in harmony with what the scriptures had previously foretold. On the present matter of predictions, Michael was the only one of the angels who was taken into the same confidential service as the one now talking to Daniel.

DANIEL 11

Verse 1. The pronoun *I* means the person described in chapter 10: 18 and other verses in that chapter. The reader should "keep his bearings" as to the chronological place we have reached in this most wonderful prophecy. In chapter 10: 20 it was shown that Persia was to be contacted by the king of Grecia. But that was a long jump into the future and other events were to happen first. This angel is still in the presence of Daniel, and even before returning *to fight with the king of Persia,* he is going to reveal to the prophet the things that are to happen to Persia and Greece and the Jews who will be involved in the whole affair. Remember, this conversation or visit of the angel with Daniel is taking place in the third year of Cyrus (chapter 10: 1), but in this meeting the angel inserts the present verse to tell the prophet of his work in the *first* year of that reign, that it consisted in *confirming and strengthening* the kingdom of the Medes and Persians. That confirmation was done because the change from the Babylonian Empire to the Medo-Persian was according to God's decree. And now after two or three years have gone by, this angel is in the presence of Daniel and ready to reveal to him the events referred to in the forepart of this paragraph.

Verse 2. We now come to the grand drama of the nations that was referred to by the angel after he had made the necessary preliminary explanations to Daniel, and while he was still in the presence of the prophet on the bank of the Tigris River. *The truth* refers to that mentioned as "scripture of truth" in the last verse of the preceding chapter. No other scripture goes into as many details as does the present chapter, but the prophecy as a whole was seen by inspired eyes, and made known by the prophets in various places and under diverse figures. *Stand up yet three kings in Persia.* At the time this speech by the angel was made, Cyrus and Darius were the joint rulers of the empire. The three to follow were unimportant and are passed over with the brief numerical statement italicized, to bring the prophecy down to the *fourth* king in this enumeration, who was to be a very important king. The pronoun *thee* refers to Daniel to whom the angel was delivering this prophecy. The prediction is that this *fourth* king was to be rich and strong and finally would cause such a stir among the nations of the world that he would bring the powerful kingdom of Greece (destined to be the third world power) into a hostile attitude because of the encroachments of Persia upon that realm. In this chapter there are no less than 20 characters referred to, either directly or otherwise, and it will be helpful if not necessary for the understanding of the great passage to have the history that confirms the predictions. Hence I shall make numerous quotations from time to time from authentic sources for the information of the reader. The *fourth* king of this verse was XERXES I, and history has this to say of him: "For eight years all Asia was astir with the work of preparation [for the expedition against Greece]. Levies were made upon all the provinces that acknowledged the authority of the Great King [Xerxes I], from India to Macedonia, from the regions of the Oxus to those of the Upper Nile. From all the maritime states upon the Mediterranean were demanded vast contingents of war galleys, transport ships, and naval stores. While these land and sea forces were being gathered and equipped, gigantic works were in progress on the Thracian coast and on the Hellespont to insure the safety and facilitate the march of the coming hosts."—MYERS' Ancient History, page 191.

"Xerxes thus levied his army searching out every region of the continent. For from the reduction of Egypt, he was employed four whole years in assembling his forces, and providing things necessary for the expedition. In the course of the fifth year he began his march with a vast multitude of men. For of the expeditions with which we are acquainted, this was by far the greatest, so that that of Darius against the Scythians appears nothing in comparison with this."— HERODOTUS, Book 7, Sections 19, 20.

"Xerxes, in the four years which followed on the reduction of Egypt, continued incessantly to make the most gigantic preparations for his intended attack upon Greece, and among them included all the precautions which a wise foresight could devise in order to ward off every conceivable peril. A general order was issued to all satraps throughout the Empire, calling on them to levy the utmost force of their province for the new war; while, as the equipment of Oriental troops depends greatly on the purchase and distribution of arms by their commander, a rich reward was promised to the satrap whose contingent should appear at the appointed place in the most gallant array. . . . His army is said to have accompanied him; but more probably it joined him in the spring, flocking in, contingent after contingent, from the various provinces of his vast Empire. Forty-nine nations, according to Herodotus, served under his standard." — Rawlinson, Five Great Monarchies, Volume 3, Chapter 7, pages 448, 452.

"All these expeditions, and any others, if there have been any besides them, are not to be compared with this one. For what nation did not Xerxes lead out of Asia against Greece? What stream, being drunk, did not fail him, except that of great rivers. Some supplied ships; others were ordered to furnish men for the infantry, from others cavalry were required, from others transports for horses, together with men to serve in the army; others to furnish long ships for the bridges, and others provisions and vessels."— Herodotus, Book 7, Section 21.

"The Decline and Fall of the Persian Empire.—The power and supremacy of the Persian monarchy passed away with the reign of Xerxes. The last one hundred and forty years of the existence of the empire was a time of weakness and anarchy, and presents nothing that needs claim our attention in this place. In the year 334 B.C., Alexander the Great, king of Macedonia, led a small army of Greeks and Macedonians across the Hellespont intent upon the conquest of Asia. His succeeding movements and the establishment of the short-lived Macedonian monarchy upon the ruins of the Persian Empire are matters that properly belong to Grecian history, and will be related at a later stage of our story." —MYERS' Ancient History, page 94.

"From Xerxes we have to date at once the decline of the Empire in respect to territorial greatness and military strength, and likewise its deterioration in regard to administrative vigor and national spirit."—Rawlinson, Five Great Monarchies, Volume 3, Chapter 7, Page 471. There were some other rulers in Persia, but they were inferior to the one just seen in these quotations and will not claim our attention at this time.

Verse 3. This *mighty king* was Alexander the Great of Macedonia, the same who was referred to in chapter 8: 5. The angel passes immediately from Xerxes to Alexander, thus ignoring all the intervening history. This was evidently because of its unimportance; also because Alexander's work was the next important event for prophecy after Xerxes. I shall quote some more history in confirmation of the predictions of this verse: "Alexander was now free to carry out his father's scheme in regard to the Asiatic expedition. In the spring of 334 B.C., with all his plans matured, he set out at the head of an army numbering about 35,000 men for the conquest of the Persian Empire. Crossing the Hellespont, Alexander first proceeded to the plain of ancient Troy, in order to place a garland upon the supposed tomb at that place of his mythical ancestor Achilles. Proceeding on his march, Alexander met a Persian army on the banks of the Granicus, over which he gained a decisive victory. Three hundred suits of armor, selected from the spoils of the field, were sent as a votive offering to the temple of Athena at Athens. The victory at the Granicus laid all Asia Minor open to the invader, and soon practically all of its cities and tribes were brought to acknowledge the authority of the Macedonian."— Myers, Ancient History, pages 274, 275.

Verse 4. *When he shall stand up* means that just as Alexander reaches the height of his glory he will come to his end, and his conquests will be divided into four parts. See the comments and quotation from history at chapter 8: 8. *Not to his posterity* refers to the fact that Alexander died without any descendants to receive his kingdom, as may be seen in the historical quotation referred to. *Nor according to his dominion* means that no man lived in Greece who was strong enough to handle the dominion left by Alexander, since no one was as strong as he. I shall quote again from history as follows: "And when he [Alexander] shall stand up, his kingdom shall be broken, and shall be divided towards the four winds of heaven and not to his posterity, nor according to his dominion which he ruled; for his kingdom shall be plucked up, even for others namely, besides the four greater princes. We have already seen the vast empire of Alexander parcelled out into four great kingdoms; without including those foreign princes who founded other kingdoms in Cappadocia, Armenia. Bithynia, Heraclea. and on the Bosphorus. All this was present to Daniel."—Rollin, Ancient History, Volume 3, Page 597. From the various citations to history that have been offered the reader, he may understand that the pronoun *those* with which the verse closes, refers to *the four winds* or the four divisions into which Alexander's conquests fell at his death. *Others besides* means the forces in the world that finally swallowed up the realms of the four princes of Alexander, since they were not strong enough to retain them. As the statement has already been made by the historian elsewhere, "No one was strong enough to handle the sword that fell from the hand of Alexander."

Verse 5. We have seen that when Alexander died his dominions were divided into four parts and taken over by his generals. Two of these divisions were short-lived and were absorbed by the other forces about them. The two that remained were ruled by Seleucus Nicator, and Ptolemy. The dominions of the former are referred to in this chapter as *king of the north*, the latter as *king of the south*. They may occasionally be referred to simply by a pronoun, in which case an explanation will be given. These two divisions of Alexander's conquests were ruled at first by the two men named, but their realms were ruled successively by different persons as long as they existed as governments, until all was finally absorbed by the Roman Empire. This *northern* and *southern* kingdom were constantly hostile toward each other, in spite of a few occasions of pretended friendliness, and the entire chapter from here on is a series of predictions of their dealings with their respective conditions. I shall now take up the comments on the verses in their order. The *king of the south* was Ptolemy Soter who ruled over Egypt. *One of his* (Alexander's) *princes* was Seleucus Nicator who ruled over Syria. *Strong above him* means the king of the north was stronger or had more extensive dominions than those possessed by the king of the south. The history and geography of the times will verify this prediction. Syria embraced "Syria and the countries eastward to the Indus," while "Ptolemy held sway over Egypt," according to the history of Myers. It can thus be seen why the prediction is that the king of the north was to be *strong above him* (the king of the south).

Verse 6. The rulers of these two dominions were succeeded by others as the years went by, but the scripture does not make mention of the new kings by name. The two governments are merely referred to as the north and the south, and if a change in kings in either has taken place, we will have to learn it and find the name of the king by history. For this reason it will be necessary to make quotations from the historical sources. In order that the reader may the more readily detect the particular word or words concerned in the prediction, I shall add my own emphasis to them. It will be the rule to make the quotation first, then interpret the verse or verses in the light of the history, hence it is very important that the reader give careful attention to the quotations. The history to be used for the present verse is as follows: "The commotions and revolts which happened in the east, making Antiochus (Theos) weary of his war with King Ptolemy (Philadelphus), *peace* was made between them on the terms, that Antiochus, divorcing Laodice, his former wife, should marry Bernice, daughter of Ptolemy, and make her his queen instead of the other, and entail his crown upon the male issue of that marriage. And this agreement being *ratified by both sides*, for the full performance of it, Antiochus put away Laodice, though she were his sister by the same father, and he had two sons born to him by her; and Ptolemy carrying his daughter to Pelusium, there put her on board his fleet, and sailed with her to Selucia, a seaport town near the mouth of the River Orontes in Syria; where having met Antiochus, he delivered his daughter to him, and the marriage was celebrated with great solemnity. And thus 'the king's daughter of the south came, and was married to the king of the north'; and, by virtue of that marriage, 'an agreement was made between those two kings,' according to the prophecy of the prophet Daniel, 11: 5, 6. For in that place, by the king of the south, is meant the king of Egypt, and by the king of the north, the king of Syria; and both are there so called in respect of Judea, which lying between these two countries, hath Egypt on the south, and Syria on the north. For the fuller understanding of this prophecy, it is to be observed, that the holy prophet, after having spoken of Alexander the Great (verse 3) and of the four kings among whom his empire was divided (verse 4) confines the rest of his prophecy in that chapter to two of them only, that is to the king of Egypt, and the king of Syria, and first he begins with that king of Egypt who *first* reigned in that country after Alexander, that is, Ptolemy Soter, whom he calls the king of the south, and saith of him that he should be strong. And that he was so, all that write of him do sufficiently testify; for he had under him Egypt, Libya Cyrene, Arabia, Palestine, Coele-Syria, most of the maritime provinces of Lesser Asia, the island of Cyprus, several of the isles of the Aegean Sea, now called the Archipelago, and some cities also in Greece, as Sicyon, Corinth, and others. And then the prophet proceedeth to speak of the four successors (or princes, as he calls them) of Alexander, and he was Seleucus Nicator king of the north; of whom he saith 'should be strong above the king of the south, and have great dominion'; that is, greater than the king of the south. And that he had so, appears from the large territories he was possessed of; for he had under him all the countries of the east, from Mount Taurus to the river Indus, and several of the provinces of Lesser Asia, also from Mount Taurus to the Aegean Sea; and he had moreover added to them, before his death, Thrace and Macedon. And then, in the next place (verse 6) he tells us 'the coming of the king's daughter of the south, after the end of several years, to the king of the north, and the agreement, or treaty of peace, which should thereon be made between these two kings.' Which plainly points out unto us this marriage of Bernice, daughter of Ptolemy Philadelphus king of Egypt, with Antiochus Theus king of Syria, and the peace which was thereon made between them; for all this was exactly transacted according to what was predicted by the holy prophet in his prophecy. After this the holy prophet proceeds, through the rest of the chapter, to foreshadow all the other most remarkable events that were brought to pass in the transactions of the succeeding times of those two races of kings, till the death of Antiochus Epiphanes, the great persecutor of the Jewish nation; all which I shall take notice of in the following series of this history, and apply them to the prophecy for the explication of it, as they come in my way.—PRIDEAUX'S CONNEXION, year 249.

"Details of this reign. [That of Antiochus Theos]—Marriage of Antiochus with Laodice, daughter of Achaeus. Her influence, and that of his sister Apame, wife of Matas, engaged him in war with Ptolemy Philadelphus, B.C. 260, which is terminated, B.C. 252, by marriage between Antiochus and Berenice, Ptolemy's daughter. Soon after the close of this war, B.C. 255, Parthia and Bactria revolt and establish their independence. On the death of Philadelphus, B.C. 247, Antiochus *repudiates Berenice* and takes back his former wife Laodice, who however, doubtful of his constancy, murders him to secure the throne for her son, Seleucus, B.C. 246."— Rawlinson, Ancient History, page 251.

"As soon as Antiochus Theos had received intelligence of the death of Ptolemy Philadelphus, his father-in-law, he divorced Berenice, and recalled Laodice and her children. This lady, who knew the variable disposition and inconstancy of Antiochus, and was apprehensive that the same levity of mind would induce him to supplant her, by receiving Berenice again, resolved to improve the present opportunity to secure the crown for her son. Her own children were disinherited by the treaty made with Ptolemy; by which it was also stipulated that the issue Berenice might have by Antiochus should succeed to the throne, and she then had a son. Laodice, therefore, caused Antiochus to be poisoned. . . . Laodice, not believing herself safe as long as Berenice and her son lived, concerted measures with Seleucus to destroy them also; but that princess, being informed of their design, escaped the danger for some time by retiring, with her son, to Daphne, where she shut herself up in the asylum built by Seleucus Nicator; but being at last betrayed by the perfidy [treachery] of those who besieged her there, by the order of Laodice, first her son, and then herself, with all the Egyptians who had accompanied her to that retreat were murdered in the basest and most inhuman manner."—Rollin, Ancient History, Volume 3, Book 16, Chapter 3, Section 1.

In view of the foregoing information from history we may be able to comment, briefly, on the leading terms of this verse. The first pronoun *they* means the kingdoms of the north and the south. *King's daughter* is Berenice, daughter of Ptolemy Philadelphus, whom her father gave in marriage to the king of the north in hopes of bringing about a peace. But the plan did not have the effect that was expected, which is the meaning of the words *not retain the power of the arm. Shall be given up*, etc. All who were involved in this "love triangle" were brought to disappointment.

Verse 7. The preceding paragraph informs us that the ones involved in the affair of Berenice were disappointed and that she was slain. But her death did not end the matter, for at the time she was being held there were certain forces at work to avenge her misfortune. I shall quote from history again as follows: "While Berenice [daughter of Philadelphus and former wife of Antiochus Theos] continued shut up and besieged in Daphne, the cities of Lesser Asia [or Asia Minor], hearing of her distress, commiserated [sympathized] her case, and immediately, by a joint association, sent an *army* toward Antioch for her relief; and Ptolemy Euergetes, her brother, hastened thither with a greater force out of Egypt for the *same purpose*. But both Berenice and her son were cut off before either of them could arrive for their help; whereupon both armies turning their desire of saving the queen and her son into a rage for the revenging of their death, the Asian forces joined the Egyptians for the effecting of it, and Ptolemy, at the head of both, *carried all before him;* for he not only slew Laodice, but also made himself *master* of *all* Syria and Cilicia, and then passing the Euphrates, brought all under him as far as Babylon, and the River Tigris, and would have subjugated to him all the other provinces of the Syrian Empire, but that a sedition arising in Egypt during his absence called him back to suppress it." — Prideaux's Connexion, year 246.

Verse 8. The very things predicted in this verse took place, therefore the best and only comments necessary will be offered in another historical quotation which is as follows: "Ptolemy III, Euergetes, ("well-wisher"), B.C. 247-222; alluded to in Daniel 11: 7-9; invaded Syria in 246, to avenge the repudiation and murder of his sister, Berenice (See Antiochus II, page 95), and had conquered it as far north as Antioch, and was moving eastward towards Babylon, when he was recalled by troubles at home. His policy towards the Jews in Egypt was generous; while, in token of his victories, he sacrificed in the temple at Jerusalem 'after the custom of the law' (Josephus: C. Ap., 11: 5). He brought *back* to *Memphis* the *gods* taken from Egypt by Cambyses. It was for this he received the epithet, 'well-doer.'"— Schaff-Herzog, Article, Ptolemy III.

"And therefore, having appointed Antiochus and Xantippus, two of his generals, the former of them to command the provinces he had taken on the west side of Mount Taurus, and the other to command the provinces he had taken on the east side of it, he marched back into Egypt, carrying with him *vast treasures*, which he had gotten together, in the plunder of the conquered provinces; for he brought from thence with him *forty thousand talents of silver*, a vast number of precious vessels of silver and gold, and *images also to the number of two thousand five hundred*, among which were many of the *Egyptian idols*, which Cambyses, on his conquering Egypt, had carried thence into Persia. These *Ptolemy* (son of Philadelphus and brother of Berenice) having restored to their former temples, on his return from this expedition, he thereby much endeared himself to his people,"—Prideaux's Connexion, year 246.

Verse 9. *King of the south* was Ptolemy Euergetes of whom we read in the preceding verse and historical comments. The reader should see that paragraph for the explanation of this verse. We note that in verse 8 the statement is made that the king of the south was to continue more years than the king of the north.

Verse 10. This is one of the verses where we have only the pronouns for the kings, and their names must be learned from history. Since the events of the preceding verse another king has arisen over the north by the name of Seleucus Callinicus, and the pronoun *his*, second word of this verse, refers to him. But he was to be opposed by another man in his kingdom referred to in the words *one shall certainly come;* that "one" was Antiochus the Great, sometimes titled Antiochus III. He not only opposed Callinicus, but carried his operations even to the border of Egypt. The last *his* refers to the Egyptian king Ptolemy Philopator who had succeeded Ptolemy Philadelphus. That is what is meant by the words *he stirred up even to his* (Philopator's) *fortress.* In confirmation of the predictions of this verse I shall quote some more history: "The weakness of Philopator, and the mis-

Daniel 11: 11, 12

management of the State by Sosibius, who was at once incapable and wicked, laid the empire open to attack; and it was not long before the young king of Syria, Antiochus III, took advantage of the condition of affairs to advance his own pretensions to the possessions of the long-disputed tract between Syria Proper and Egypt. . . . Details of the war. Antiochus commenced B.C. 219, by besieging Seleuceia, the port of Antioch, which had remained in the hands of the Egyptian governor of Coele-Syria. He invaded that country, took Tyre and Ptolemais (Acre), and *advanced* to the frontiers of Egypt." — Rawlinson, Ancient History, Page 275.

Verse 11. It may be a surprise and yet a help to the reader to know that, beginning with the second verse of this chapter and including the rest of the chapter, a space of over 300 years is covered. It is natural to think that since the rulers and other outstanding characters in the chapter, about 20 in all, belonged to the two governments, there would be both long and short reigns among them. In some instances the ruler in one of the kingdoms would reign as long as two or more kings in the other. Hence we may pass from one verse to another without a change of kings in one or the other. Before making further comments on this verse I shall quote from history:

"Ptolemy Philopator, was an indolent, effeminate prince. It was necessary to excite and drag him, in a manner, out of his lethargy, in order to prevail with him to take up arms, and repulse the enemy, who were preparing to march into his country. At last he put himself at the head of his troops; by the valor and good conduct of his generals, obtained a signal victory over Antiochus (the Great) at Raphia." — Rollin's Ancient History, Volume 4, Page 143.

"It might have been expected that, under the circumstances, he (Antiochus the Great) would have been successful. But the Egyptian forces, relaxed though their discipline had been by Sosibius, were still superior to the Syrians; the battle of Raphia (B.C. 217) was a repetition of the lessons taught at Pelusium and Gaza. The invader was once more defeated upon the borders, and by the peace which followed, the losses of the two preceding years were, with one exception, recovered (by Philopator). . . . In the third year of the war, B.C. 217, Philopator marched out from Alexandria in person, with 70,000 foot, 5,000 horse and 73 elephants. Antiochus advanced to give him battle, and the two armies met at Raphia, on the eastern edge of the desert. After a vain attempt on the part of Theodotus to assassinate Philopator in his camp, an engagement took place, and Antiochus was completely defeated. He then made peace, relinquishing all his conquests but Seleuceia." — Rawlinson, Ancient History, Page 275.

The *king* of the *south* is Ptolemy Philopator who was a weakling in character, but others insisted and agitated him until he finally bestirred himself. He gathered a large army and came with *choler* (bitterness) against *him*, king of the *north* who is the Antiochus the Great of verse 10. *Multitude shall be given into his* (Philopator's) *hand.*

Verse 12. *He* is Ptolemy Philopator, king of Egypt. His success against Antiochus the Great filled him with pride and *his heart shall be lifted up. Shall not be strengthened by it* means that his kingdom did not profit by the success against Antiochus, although he personally had the arrogant satisfaction of looking upon his victory. We shall learn in the next verse that defeat finally came to his kingdom from the very man whom he had beaten. But for the present verse, let the reader keep the foregoing comments in mind as he reads the following quotations from history:

"Antiochus III lost upwards of ten thousand foot and three hundred horse, and four thousand of his men were taken prisoners. Philopator, having marched, after his victory, to Jerusalem, was so audacious as to attempt to enter the sanctuary, ("his heart shall be lifted up"); and being returned to his kingdom, he behaved with the utmost pride toward the Jews, and treated them very cruelly. He might have dispossessed Antiochus of his dominions had he taken a proper advantage of his glorious victory; but he contented himself with recovering Coele-Syria and Phoenicia, and again plunged into his former excesses; 'but he shall not be strengthened by it.' "— Rollin's Ancient History, Volume 4, Page 143.

"Ptolemy (Philopator) having thus regained these provinces, made a progress through them; and, among other cities which he visited in his perambulation, Jerusalem was one that had this favor from him. On his arrival thither, he took a view of the temple, and there offered up many sacrifices to the God of Israel, and made many oblations to the temple, and gave several valuable donatives to it. But, not being content to view it only from the outer court, beyond which it was not lawful for any gentile to pass, he would have pressed into the sanctuary itself, and into the holy of holies in the temple, where *none* but the *high priest only, once a year,* on the great day of expiation, was to enter. This made a great uproar all over the city. The high-priest informed him of the sacredness of the place, and the law of God which forbade his entrance thither. And the priests and Levites gathered together to hinder it, and all the people to deprecate it; and great lamentation was made everywhere among them on the apprehension of the great profanation which would hereby be offered to their holy temple, and all hands were lifted up unto God in prayer to avert it. But the king, the more he was opposed, growing the more intent to have his will in this matter, pressed into the inner court; but, as he was passing farther to go into the temple itself, he was smitten from God with such a terror and confusion of mind, that he was carried out of the place in a manner half dead, On this he departed from Jerusalem, filled with great wrath against the whole nation of the Jews, for that which happened to him in that place, and venting many threatenings against them for it."—Prideaux, year 217.

"Ptolemy IV, Philopator ("father-loving"), B.C. 222-205; alluded to in Daniel 11: 10-12, defeated Antiochus the Great at Raphia, near Gaza (B.C. 217); sacrificed in the temple, and attempted to enter the sacred precincts, when a shock of paralysis stopped him. He was indolent, effeminate, and licentious, but capable, on occasion, of splendid and vigorous deeds."—Schaff-Herzog, Article, Ptolemy IV.

Verse 13. This verse begins with the word *for* which indicates a continuation of some of the thoughts in the preceding verse. Those thoughts were regarding the success of Ptolemy Philopator against Antiochus the Great. It is stated as verse 12 concludes, that those thousands of men would not strengthen the kingdom of Philopator, and the present verse proceeds to tell us why it would not. And since that subject consists in the further activities and success of Antiochus the great, my comments on the verse further will be some historical quotations:

"Antiochus, after he had ended the war beyond the Euphrates, raised a great army in those provinces. Finding, fourteen years after the conclusion of the first war, that Ptolemy Epiphanes, who was then but five or six years of age, had succeeded Philopator his father, he united with Philip of Macedon, in order to deprive the infant king of his throne. Having defeated Scopas [a general conducting the war on behalf of the infant king] at Panium, near the source of the river Jordan, he subjected the whole country which Philopator had conquered, by the victory he gained at Raphia."—Rollin's Ancient History, Volume 4, page 144.

"He (Antiochus III) then turned towards the eastern frontiers of his realm, against Parthia and Bactria; penetrated into Northern India and organized a *formidable army,* including a hundred and fifty Indian elephants. In 204 Philopator died; and the Egyptian crown devolved on his son, Ptolemy V, (Epiphanes) a boy of five years. This circumstance Antiochus meant to utilize. He conquered Coele-Syria, Phoenicia, and Palestine, and gained a decisive victory in 198 at Paneas in Coele-Syria. Peace was then concluded." — Schaff-Herzog. Article, Antiochus III.

"Antiochus, king of Syria, and Philip, king of Macedon, thinking to serve themselves of the advantage they had by the death of Philopator, and the succession of an infant king after him, entered into a league to divide his dominion between them, agreeing that Philip should have Caria, Libya, Cyrene, and Egypt, and Antiochus all the rest. And accordingly Antiochus forthwith marched into Coele-Syria and Palestine, and partly this year, and partly in the next, made himself master of these provinces, and all the several districts and cities in them."—Prideaux's Connexion, year 203.

"Return of Antiochus from the East, B.C. 205 and resumption of his Egyptian projects. A treaty is made with Philip of Macedon for the partition of the kingdom of Ptolemies between the two powers. War in Coele-Syria, Phoenicia, and Palestine with varied success, terminated by a great victory over Scopas near Panias, B.C. 198. Marriage of Cleopatra, daughter of Antiochus, with Ptolemy V. Coele-Syria and Palestine promised as a dowery, but not delivered."—Rawlinson, Ancient History, page 254.

Verse 14. The first half of this verse

is virtually a repetition of the prediction in the foregoing, but I shall insert a brief quotation again from history as an explanation: "Antiochus, king of Syria, and Philip, king of Macedon, thinking to serve themselves of the advantage they had by the death of Philopator, and the succession of an infant king after him, *enetred into a league* to divide his dominions between them." Prideaux's Connexion, year 203.

The second half of this verse introduces a new item into the prediction. *They* is a pronoun referring to Daniel, against whose *people* the *robbers* were to *exalt themselves*. But the prediction is that they were to fail which the history shows did happen. I have departed somewhat from the rule suggested a short while ago to quote the history for each verse first and then make my own comments upon it. Whichever may seem to be the better plan in given cases will be followed. I now shall insert the history that confirms the prediction favorable to the Jews in the last of this verse.

"At this time [reign of Ptolemy Epiphanes] Antiochus having passed into Lesser Asia, and there engaged himself in a war with Attalus, king of Pergamus, the minister of Alexandria took advantage hereof to send Scopas with an army into Palestine and Coele-Syria, for the recovery of those provinces; where he managed the war with such success that he took several cities, and reduced all Judea by force, and put a garrison into the castle at Jerusalem; and, on the approach of winter, returned to Alexandria with full honor for the victories he had obtained, and with as great *riches*, which he had *gathered from the plunder of the country*. . . . The Jews were at this time very much alienated in their affections from the Egyptian king; whether it were by reason of the former ill treatment of their nation by his father, or for some fresher ill treatment they had received, is not said. It is most likely it was because of the ravages and *robberies* of Scopas, in his taking *Jerusalem* the former year; for he was a very *covetous* and *rapacious* man, *laying his hands everywhere on all that he could get;* and therefore, on Antiochus' marching that way, they willingly *rendered all places unto him*, and on his coming to Jerusalem, the priests and elders went out in a solemn procession to meet him, and received him with gladness, and entertained him and all his army in their city, provided for his horses and elephants, and assisted him with their arms for the *reducing* of the *castle* where *Scopas* had left a garrison."—Prideaux's Connexion, year 198.

"Now it happened that in the reign of Antiochus the Great, who ruled over all Asia, that the Jews, as well as the inhabitants of Coele-Syria, suffered greatly, and their land was sorely harassed; for while he was at war with Ptolemy Philopator, and with his son, who was called Epiphanes, it fell out that these nations were equally sufferers, both when he was beaten and when he beat the others; so that they were very like a ship in a storm, which is tossed by the waves on both sides; and just thus were they in their situation in the middle between Antiochus' prosperity and its change to adversity. But at length, when Antiochus had beaten Ptolemy, he seized upon Judea; and when Philopator was dead, his son sent out a great army under *Scopas* the general of his forces, against the inhabitants of Coele-Syria, who *took many of their cities* and in *particular our nation;* which, when he fell upon them, went over to him. Yet was it not long afterward when Antiochus *overcame Scopas*, in a battle fought at the fountains of Jordan, and destroyed a *great part of his army*."—Josephus, 12-3-3.

Verses 15-17. The persons and facts of this series of verses are so interwoven that I think it will the better be explained by grouping them into one paragraph. I shall quote some lines from history, then explain the events in their relation to the persons involved in the light of the history. Let the reader give close attention to the following: "Antiochus, besieged and took, first Sidon, then Gaza, and afterwards all the cities of those provinces, notwithstanding the opposition made by the chosen troops which the king of Egypt had sent against him. 'He did according to his own will,' in Coele-Syria and Palestine, and nothing was able to make the least resistance against him. Pursuing his conquests in Palestine, he entered Judea, 'the glorious,' or, according to the Hebrew, 'that desirable land.' He there established his authority and strengthened it, by repulsing from the castle of Jerusalem, the garrison which Scopas had thrown into it. This garrison being so well defended that Antiochus was obliged to send for all the troops in order to force it, and the siege continuing a long time, the country was ruined and consumed by the stay the army was obliged to make in it. . . .

Antiochus, seeing that the Romans undertook the defence of young Ptolemy Epiphanes, thought it would best suit his interest to lull the king asleep, by giving him his daughter in marriage, in order to 'corrupt her,' and excite her to betray her husband; but he was not successful in his design; for as soon as she was married to Ptolemy, she renounced her father's interests, and embraced those of her husband. It was on this account that we see her join with him in the embassy which was sent from Egypt to Rome, to congratulate the Romans on the victory which Acilius had gained over her father at Thermopylae."—Rollin's Ancient History, Volume 4, pages 144, 145.

It should be remembered that a reference to the *north* always means Syria in this chapter, and the king who is ruling there at the time, and the *south* means Egypt. *Cast up a mount* means that Antiochus III would prepare to attack the cities of the *south*, which would not be able to withstand the attack. *He that cometh against him* means that Antiochus was to come against Ptolemy Epiphanes and the latter would not succeed. To make his gains further sure, the king of the north was to give his daughter (whose name was Cleopatra as supplied by history) in marriage to the king of the south, thinking that she would place her love for her father above that for her husband, and thus really act as a spy for her father in the household of her husband. But she was true to her husband; *not stand on his* (her father's) *side, neither be for him.*

Verse 18. Antiochus III was a noted man and accomplished many exploits among the nations. However, we have just seen that he had some reverses, and we shall see some more of the same in the present verse. Before making further comments on it, I shall make some historical quotations:

"Antiochus, having put an end to the war of Coele-Syria and Palestine, sent his two sons, at the end of the land-army, to Sardis, while he embarked on board the fleet, and sailed to the Aegean Sea, where he took several islands, and extended his empire exceedingly on that side. However, the prince of the people, whom he had insulted by making this invasion, that is L. Scipio, the Roman consul, caused the reproach to turn upon him, by defeating him at Mount Sipilus, and repulsing him from every part of Asia Minor."—Rollin, Volume 4, page 145.

"He (Antiochus III) then invaded Asia Minor, and in 195 he crossed the Hellespont, and advanced into Europe. Here he encountered the Romans; but in 190 he was totally defeated at Magnesia by Scipio Asiaticus, and he obtained peace from Rome only on very severe conditions."—Schaff-Herzog. Article, Antiochus III.

"The conquests of Antiochus in Asia Minor and Europe, B.C. 197 to 196. bring him into contact with the Romans, who require him to evacuate the Chersonese and restore the Greek cities in Asia Minor to freedom. He indignantly rejects their demands, and prepares for war. Flight of Hannibal to his court. B.C. 195. Antiochus makes alliance with the Aetolians. and in B.C. 192 crosses into Greece, lands at Demetrias, takes Chalcis. Great battle at Thermopylae between the Romans, under Acilius Glabrio, and the allied forces of Antiochus and the Aetolians. Antiochus, completely defeated, quits Europe and returns to Asia B.C. 191. His fleet has orders to protect the shores and prevent the Romans from landing. But the battle of Corycus ruins these hopes. The Romans obtain the mastery of the sea; and their army, having crossed the Hellespont without opposition, gains under the two Scipios the great victory of Magnesia, which places Antiochus at their mercy, B.C. 190. He purchases peace by ceding all Asia Minor except Cilicia, and by consenting to pay a contribution of 12,000 talents. The ceded provinces are added by the Romans to the kingdom of Pergamus, which is thus raised into a rival to Syria."—Rawlinson, Ancient History, page 254.

With the facts of history before us, we can understand the present verse and properly assign the pronouns. *Isles* means inhabited spots, and that is the meaning of the places where *he* (Antiochus III) turned his face. That called the Romans into action and they sent their military leader, Scipio, into the field. When Antiochus invaded the territories in which the Romans were interested it was considered a *reproach* upon them. But Scipio was successful in repulsing Antiochus, so that he caused it to rebound upon *him* (Antiochus) without having any reproach of *his* (Scipio's) *own*.

Verse 19. Antiochus, completely defeated, turned his steps towards his own country. *Stumble and fall* refers to his failure in another matter of his obligations, and the explanation of the predictions is best shown in the historical quotations which will be quoted before making further comments.

"Antiochus, after his defeat, returned to Antioch, the capital of his kingdom, and the strongest fortress in it. He went soon after into the provinces of the east, in order to levy money to pay the Romans; but having plundered the temple of Elymais, he there lost his life in a miserable manner."—Rollin's Ancient History, Volume 4, page 146.

"The defeat of Magnesia is followed by the revolt of Armenia, B.C. 189, which henceforth becomes independent. It leads also to the death of Antiochus, who, in order to pay the war contribution imposed upon him by the Romans, is driven to the plunder of the Oriental temples. Hence a tumult in Elymais, wherein the king is killed, B.C. 187."—Rawlinson, Ancient History, page 254.

"Retiring to his eastern provinces in order to raise money for the tribute he (Antiochus III) owed Rome, he was slain in 187, while plundering the temples of Belus in Elymais." — Schaff-Herzog, Article, Antiochus III.

Verse 20. *His estate* means in the place of Antiochus III whose death was predicted in the preceding verse. The prediction *raiser of taxes* means he will be an extortioner and will lay heavy tax burdens on the people. He was to be destroyed, *neither in anger nor in battle* denotes he would not die in open warfare nor by voluntary bodily contest with another, but will die unresistingly by the hand of another. I shall give the reader the history which confirms the predictions of this verse.

"These few words (Daniel 11: 20) denote, evidently, the short and obscure reign of Seleucus, and the kind of death he was to die. The Hebrew text points him out still more clearly. 'There shall arise up in his place, (of Antiochus) a man who, as an extortioner, a collector of taxes, shall cause to pass away, and shall destroy, the glory of the kingdom.' And, indeed, this was the sole employment of his reign. He was obliged to furnish the Romans, by the articles of peace concluded between them, a thousand talents annually; and the twelve years of this tribute exactly ended with his life. He reigned but eleven years."—Rollin's Ancient History, Volume 4, page 203.

"Antiochus was succeeded by his son, Seleucus IV, who took the name of Philopator, and reigned eleven years, B.C. 187 to 176. This period was wholly *uneventful*. The fear of Rome, and the weakness produced by exhaustion, forced Seleucus to remain quiet, even when Eumenes of Pergamus seemed about to absorb Pontus. . . . Seleucus was murdered by Heliodorus, his treasurer (B.C. 176), who hoped to succeed to his dominions."—Rawlinson, Ancient History, page 255.

"After the death of Antiochus the Great, Seleucus Philopator, his eldest son, whom he left at Antioch on his departure thence into the east, succeeded him in the kingdom, but made a very poor figure of it, by reason of the low estate which the Romans had reduced the Syrian Empire to, and the heavy tribute of one thousand talents a year, which, through the whole time of his reign he was obliged to pay them; by the treaty of peace lately granted by them to his father. The whole of this king's reign is expressed by Daniel 11: 20. For in that text it is foretold, that after Antiochus the Great, who is spoken of in the foregoing verses, 'there should stand up in his estate a raiser of taxes.' And Seleucus was no more than such all the time, for the whole business of his reign was to raise the thousand talents every year, which, by the treaty of peace that his father had made with the Romans, he was obliged for twelve years together, annually to pay that people; and the last of these years was the last of his life. For, as the text saith, 'within a few years after he should be destroyed, and that neither in anger, nor in battle'; so accordingly it happened. For he reigned only eleven years, and his death was neither in battle nor in anger; that is, neither in war abroad, nor in sedition or rebellion at home, but by the secret treachery of one of his own friends. His successor was Antiochus Epiphanes his brother, of whom we shall treat in the next book."—Prideaux's Connexion, years 186, 176.

Verse 21. The pronoun *his* refers to Seleucus IV, also called Philopator, and is referred to in the preceding verse as a "raiser of taxes." *Shall stand up* means he shall get the place occupied by the preceding king. The man who was to take this place is named Antiochus Epiphanes, brother of the murdered Philopator. The predictions indicate that he was to obtain the throne in an irregular manner, not in an honorable way. The details of that event are described in the following historical quotation:

"On the death of Seleucus Philopator, Heliodorus, who had been the treacherous author of his death, endeavored to seize the crown of Syria. Antiochus, the brother of Seleucus, was then on his return from Rome. While at Athens in his journey, he there heard of the death of his brother, and the attempt of Heliodorus to usurp the throne; and finding that the usurper had a great party with him to support him in his pretensions, and that there was another party also forming for Ptolemy, (who made some claim to the succession in right of his mother, she being sister to the deceased king) and that both of them were agreed 'not to give unto him (though the next heir in the absence of Demetrius) the honor of the kingdom,' as the holy prophet Daniel foretold, he applied himself to Eumenes, king of Perhamus, and Attalus his brother, and (by flattering speeches and great promises of friendship) prevailed with them to help him against Heliodorus. And by their means that usurper being suppressed, he was quietly placed on the throne, and all submitted to him, and permitted him, without any further opposition, peaceably to obtain the kingdom, as had been predicted of him in the same prophecy. Eumenes and Attalus, at this time having some suspicions of the Romans, were desirous of having the king of Syria on their side, in case a war should break out between them, and Antiochus' promises to stick by them, whenever such a war should happen, were the inducements that prevailed with them to do him this kindness." — Prideaux's Connexion, year 175. See also, Rawlinson, Ancient History, page 255.

This Antiochus Epiphanes is described here as a *vile person*, which refers to his character as a man as well as to his conduct in public affairs. In view of his prominence in the prophecies and history of things pertaining to God's people, I believe it will be helpful to quote at length from the historical sources. As this quotation may be referred to again, the reader is urged to give it careful attention, particularly the parts which I shall emphasize.

"On his being thus settled on the throne, he took the name of Epiphanes, that is, The Illustrious; but nothing could be more alien to his true character than this title. The prophet Daniel foretold of him that he would be 'a vile person,' so our English version has it; but the word NIBZEH in the original rather signified despicable than vile. He was truly both in all that both these words can express, which will fully appear from the character given him by Polybius, II, Philarchus, 12, Livy, 13, and Diodorus, 14, who were all heathen writers, and the two first of them his contemporaries. For they tell us, that he would get often out of the palace and ramble about the streets of Antioch, with two or three servants only accompanying him; that he would be often conversing with those that graved in silver, and cast vessels of gold, and be frequently found with them in their shops, talking and nicely arguing with them about the mysteries of their trades, that he would very commonly debase himself to the meanest company, and on his going abroad would join in with such as he happened to find them met together, although of the lowest of the people, and enter into discourse with any of them whom he should first light on; that he would, in his rambles, frequently drink with strangers and foreigners, and even with the meanest and vilest of them; that, when he heard of any young company met together to feast, drink, or any otherwise to make merry together, he would, without giving any notice of his own coming, intrude himself among them, and revel away the time with them in their cups and songs, and other frolics, without any regard to common decency, or his own royal character, so that several, being surprised with the strangeness of the thing, would, on his coming, get up and run away out of the company. And he would sometimes, as the freak took him, lay aside his royal habit, and putting on a Roman gown, go round the city, as he had seen done in the election of the magistrates of Rome, and ask the votes of the citizens, in the same manner as used to be there practiced, now taking one man by the hand, and, then embracing another, and would thus set himself up, sometimes for the office of aedile, and sometimes for that of tribune; and, having thus voted into office he sued for, he would take the chair, and sitting down in it, hear petty causes of contracts, bargains, and sales, made in the market, and give judgment in them with that serious attention and earnestness, as if they had been matters of the highest concern and importance. It is said also of him, that he was much given to drunkenness; and that he spent a great part of his revenues in revelling and drunken carousals; and would often go out into the streets while in these frolics, and there scatter his money by handfuls among the rabble, crying out, 'Let him take to whom fortune give it.' Sometimes he would go abroad with a crown of roses upon his head, and wearing a Roman gown, would walk the streets alone, and carrying stones under his arms, would throw them at those who followed after him. And he would often wash himself in the public baths among the common people, and there expose himself by many absurd and ridiculous actions. Which odd and extravagant sort of conduct made many doubt how the matter stood with him; some thinking him a fool, and some a madman; the latter of these, most thought to be his truest character; and therefore, instead of Epiphanes, or the Illustrious, they called him Epimanes, the Madman. Jerome tells us also of him that he was exceedingly given to lasciviousness, and often by the *vilest* acts of it debased the honor of his royal dignity; that he was frequently found in the company of mimics [clowns], *pathics* [boys kept for unnatural purposes], and *common prostitutes*, and that with the latter he would commit acts of lasciviousness, and gratify his *lust* on them *publicly* in *sight* of the *people*. And it is further related of him, that having for his *catamites* [same as pathics] two vile persons, called Timarchus and Heraclides, who were brothers, he made the first of them governor of Babylonia, and the other his treasurer in that province, and gave himself up to be governed and conducted by them in most that he did. And having, on a very whimsical occasion, exhibited games and shows at Daphne, near Antioch, with vast expense, and called thither a great multitude of people of foreign parts, as well as from his own dominion, to be present at the solemnity; he there behaved himself to that degree of folly and absurdity, as to become the ridicule and scorn of all that were present; which actions of his are sufficiently abundant to demonstrate him both despicable and vile, though he had not added to them that most unreasonably and wicked persecution of God's people in Judea and Jerusalem which will be hereafter related."—Prideaux, year 175.

Verse 22. This is still making predictions about Epiphanes; in fact, this wicked character will figure in most of the affairs throughout the rest of this chapter. *Arms of a flood* refers to the military forces that Epiphanes brought against the Egyptian king. The pronoun *him* refers to Epiphanes, and the *prince* is Heliodorus who had seized the throne. The fulfillment of this verse will be seen in the following history.

"Heliodorus, the murderer of Seleucus, and his adherents, as also those of the Egyptian king, who had formed designs against Syria, were defeated by the forces of Attalus and Eumenes, dispersed by the arrival of Epiphanes, whose presence disconcerted all their projects. By the 'prince of the covenant,' we may suppose to be meant, either Heliodorus, the chief of the conspirators, who had killed Seleucus; or rather Ptolemy Epiphanes king of Egypt, who lost his life by a conspiracy of his own subjects, when he was mediating a war against Syria. Thus Providence removed this powerful adversary, to make way for Antiochus Epiphanes, and raised him to the throne." — Rollin's Ancient History, Volume 4, page 236.

"On the death of Seleucus, the throne was seized by Heliodorus; but it was not long before Antiochus Epiphanes, the brother of the late king, with the help of Pergamene monarch, Eumenes, recovered it. This prince, who is known in history as Antiochus IV, or (more commonly) as Antiochus Epiphanes, was a man of courage and energy." — Rawlinson's Ancient History, page 255.

Verse 23. Another king is in power in Egypt by the name of Ptolemy Philometor, and the pronoun *him* stands for this man. The pronoun *he* is Epiphanes who is to come against this new king in Egypt. He will have a *small people* which means he will have a smaller army than usual, but yet by certain tactics he will win the contest. The fulfillment of the verse may be seen in the following history.

"Antiochus Epiphanes, though he was already determined on the war, 'yet shall he assume a specious [deceptive] appearance of friendship for the king of Egypt.' He even sent Apollonius to Memphis, to be present at the banquet given on occasion of that prince's coronation, as a proof that it was agreeable to him. But soon after, on pretence of defending his nephew, he marched into Egypt, with a *small army*, in comparison of those which he levied afterwards. The battle was fought near Pelusium. Antiochus was strongest, that is, victorious, and afterwards returned to Tyre. Such was the end of his first expedition."—Rollin, Volume 4, pages 236, 237.

"Antiochus, having, ever since the return of Apollonius from the Egyptian court, been preparing for the war which he found he must necessarily have with Ptolemy about the provinces of Coele-Syria and Palestine, and being now ready for it, resolved to defer it no l o n g e r — and then forthwith marched his army toward the frontiers of Egypt, where, being met by the forces of Ptolemy (Philometor) between Mount Casius and Pelusium, it there came to battle between them, in which Antiochus having gotten the victory . . . without attempting anything further this year, returned to Tyre; and there, and in the neighboring cities, put his army into winter quarters."—Prideaux, year 171.

Verses 24-26. We have another series of verses that can better be considered as a group. The predictions are still about Epiphanes and his dealings with the king of the *south* which means Egypt. Epiphanes is still pictured as an insincere person, making plausible offers of friendship that he did not mean. Another expedition is here predicted and the history showing his fulfillment will now be quoted:

"In these three verses (Daniel 11: 24-26) appear the principal characters of the second expedition of Antiochus into Egypt. His mighty armies, his rapid conquests, the rich spoils he carried from thence, and the dissimulation [hypocrisy] and treachery he began to practice with regard to Ptolemy. Antiochus, after employing the whole winter in making preparations for a second expedition into Egypt, invaded it both by sea and land, as soon as the season would permit. 'Wherefore, he entered into Egypt with a great multitude, with chariots, and elephants, and horsemen, and a great navy. And made war against Ptolemy king of Egypt; but Ptolemy was afraid of him, and fled; and many were wounded to death. Thus they got the strong cities in the land of Egypt, and he took the spoils thereof. I Maccabees, 1: 17, 18, 19.' Diodorus relates, that Antiochus, after this victory, conquered all Egypt, or at least the greatest part of it; for all the cities, Alexandria excepted, opened their gates to the conqueror. He subdued Egypt with an astonishing rapidity, and did that 'which his forefathers had not done, nor his father's fathers.' Ptolemy either surrendered himself, or fell into the hands of Antiochus, who at first treated him with kindness; had but one table with him; seemed to be greatly concerned for his welfare, and left him the peaceable possession of his kingdom, reserving to himself Pelusium, which was the key to it. For Antiochus *assumed* this *appearance* of *friendship*, with no other view than to have the better opportunity of ruining him. 'They that feed of the portion of his meat shall destroy.' Antiochus did not make a long stay in Egypt at that time, the news which was brought of the general revolt of the Jews obliging him to march against them. In the mean time, the inhabitants of Alexandria, offended at Philometor for having concluded an alliance with Antiochus, raised Euergetes, his youngest brother, to the throne in his stead. Antiochus, who had advice of what had passed in Alexandria, took the opportunity to return into Egypt, upon pretext of restoring the dethroned monarch, but in reality to make himself absolute master of the kingdom."—Rollin, Volume 4, pages 237, 238.

"Antiochus, having been making preparations during all the winter for a second expedition into Egypt, as soon as the season of the year would permit, again invaded that country both by sea and land. . . . While Antiochus carried on his vast invasion, Philometor came into his hands; whether he were taken prisoner by him, or else voluntarily came in unto him, is not said; the latter seems most likely. For Antiochus took not from him his library, but they *did eat at the same table*, and conversed together as friends; and for some time Antiochus pretended to take care of the interest of this young king his nephew, and to manage the affairs of the kingdom as tutor and guardian to him. But when he had, under this pretence, made himself master of the country, he seized all to himself; and, having miserably pillaged all parts where he came, vastly enriched himself and his army with the spoils of them."—Prideaux's Connexion, year 171.

Verse 27. The first sentence of verse 28 should be included in this paragraph, for the historical quotation that will be made includes it. *Both these kings* means Philometor and Epiphanes. They both put on a show of friendliness, even eating at the same table which was one of the strongest indications of friendship in ancient times. But all the time they were thus

Daniel 11: 28, 29

chatting in a good-natured manner at the table, Epiphanes was plotting the ruin of Philometor. The latter actually suspected the treachery of Epiphanes, but pretended not to see anything wrong; thus they did *speak lies at one table.* Nothing decisive was accomplished and Epiphanes returned to his own land, having only the consolation of obtaining some great possessions of personal property. I shall give the reader some history, showing the fulfillment of this prophecy.

"The third expedition of Antiochus could scarcely be pointed out more clearly (in Daniel 11: 27, 28). That prince, hearing that the Alexandrians had raised Euergetes to the throne, returned to Egypt upon the specious pretence of restoring Philometor. After having overcome the Alexandrians in a sea fight at Pelusium, he laid siege to Alexandria. But, finding the inhabitants made a strong opposition, he was contented with making himself master of Egypt again, in the name of his nephew, in whose defence he pretended to have drawn the sword. They were then at Memphis, ate at the same table, and behaved towards one another with all the outward marks of a sincere friendship. The uncle seemed to have the nephew's interest at heart, and the nephew to repose the highest confidence in his uncle; but all this was mere show, both dissembling [acting hypocritically] their real sentiments. The uncle endeavored to crush his nephew, and the nephew, who saw through his design, strove immediately to be reconciled to his brother. Thus neither succeeded in deceiving the other; nothing was yet determined, and Antiochus returned into Syria."—Rollin, Volume 4, page 239.

"Antiochus, on hearing of this [the raising of Euergetes to the throne of Egypt] laid hold of the occasion for his making a third expedition into Egypt, under pretence of restoring the deposed king, but in reality to subject the whole kingdom to himself. Ptolemy Euergetes and Cleopatra his sister, who were then shut up in the town, being hereby much distressed, sent ambassadors to the Romans to represent their case, and pray relief. And, a little after there came ambassadors from the Rhodians, to endeavor to make peace between the two kings. But while they were proceeding in long harangues on these topics, Antiochus interrupted them, and in a few words told them that there was no need of long orations as to this matter; that the kingdom belonged to Philometor the elder brother, *with whom he had some time since made peace,* and was now in *perfect friendship with him;* that, if they would recall him from banishment, and again restore him to his crown, the war would be at an end. This said he, not that he intended any such thing, but only out of craft farther to embroil the kingdom, for the better obtaining of his own ends upon it. . . . And, with this view having withdrawn from Alexandria, he marched to Memphis, and there seemingly again restored the whole kingdom to Philometor, excepting only Pelusium, which he retained in his hands, that, having the key of Egypt still in his keeping, he might thereby again enter Egypt, when matters should there, according to the scheme which he had laid, be ripe for it, and so seize the whole kingdom; and, having thus disposed matters, he returned again to Antioch."—Prideaux, 169.

Verse 28. The latter part of this verse predicts the wicked conduct of Epiphanes toward the Lord's institutions in Jerusalem. That subject comes up again in this chapter, and I shall defer any further comments together with historical quotations till later.

Verse 29. This paragraph must include half of verse 30 to get the predictions. It is a prophecy of the fourth expedition of Epiphanes into Egypt. *Not be as the former or as the latter.* Some indefiniteness is seen in the historians as to which expeditions are meant since he had made three of them before. But it is clear that the fourth one would not be as successful as the others had been. The reason for it is given in the statement about the *ships of Chittim* that were to come against him. I shall quote the history for this paragraph:

"Fourth expedition of Antiochus into Egypt—Advice being brought to Antiochus, that the two brothers were reconciled, he threw off the mask, and declared publicly that he intended to conquer Egypt for himself. And, to support his pretensions, 'he returned toward the south,' that is, into Egypt, but was *not so successful* in this expedition as before. As he was advancing to besiege Alexandria, Popilius and the other Roman ambassadors, who were on board a fleet composed of Macedonian or Greek ships, for this the Hebrew word Chittim signifies, which they found at Delos, obliged him to lay down his arms, and leave Egypt. He obeyed, but 'with the utmost reluctance, and made the city and temple of Jerusalem feel the dire effects of his indignation,' as will be presently seen."—Rollin's Ancient History, Volume 4, pages 239, 240.

Verse 30. The conduct of Epiphanes as it pertained to the Jews was so vicious, and it occupies so much of the prophecy and in so many places, that I think it will be proper to copy at length from history before making any more of my own comments on that subject. After doing this shall resume my interpretation of the various statements in the verses, relying on the history quoted for the basis of my comments, and adding other historical quotations from time to time as the subject matter may require. I again insist that the reader give the most possible attention to these quotations as they will be needed in the understanding of the predictions.

"At the same time that Antiochus, who is called Epiphanes, had a quarrel with the sixth Ptolemy about his right to the whole country of Syria, a great sedition fell among the men of power *in Judea*, and they had a contention about obtaining the government; while each of those that were of dignity could not endure to be subject to their equals. However, Onias, one of the high-priests, got the better, and cast the sons of Tobias out of the city; who fled to Antiochus, and besought him to make an expedition into Judea. The king being thereto disposed beforehand, complied with them, and came upon the Jews with a great army, and took their city by force, and slew a great multitude of those that favored Ptolemy, and sent out his soldiers to plunder them, without mercy. He also spoiled the temple, *and put a stop to the constant practice of offering a daily sacrifice of expiation for three years and six months*. . . . Now Antiochus was not satisfied either with his unexpected taking the city, or with its pillage, or with the great slaughter he had made there; but being overcome with his violent passions, and remembering what he had suffered during the siege, he compelled the Jews to dissolve the laws of their country, and to keep their infants uncircumcised, *and to sacrifice swines flesh upon the altar;* against which they all opposed themselves, and the most approved among them were put to death."—Josephus, Wars, Book 1, Chapter 1, Sections 1, 2.

"And when the king [Epiphanes] had built an idol altar upon God's altar, he slew swine upon it, and so offered a sacrifice neither according to the law, nor the Jewish religious worship in that country. He also, compelled them to forsake the worship which they paid their own God, and to adore those whom he took to be gods; and made them build temples, and raise idol altars in every city and village, and offer swine upon them every day. He also commanded them not to circumcise their sons, and threatened to punish any that should be found to have transgressed his injunction. He also appointed overseers, who should compel them to do what he commanded. And indeed many Jews there were who complied with the king's commands, either voluntarily, or out of fear of the penalty that was denounced; but the best men, and those of the noblest souls, did not regard him, but did pay a greater respect to the customs of their country than concern as to the punishment which he threatened to the disobedient; on which account they every day underwent great miseries and bitter torments; for they were whipped with rods and their bodies were torn to pieces, and they were crucified while they were still alive and breathed; they also strangled those women and their sons whom they had circumcised, as the king had appointed, hanging their sons about their necks as they were upon the crosses. And if there were any sacred book of the law found, it was destroyed; and those with whom they were found, miserably perished also." Josephus, Antiquities, Book 12, Chapter 5, Section 4.

"After this, having spoiled the city of all its riches, they [forces of Epiphanes] set it on fire in several places, demolished the houses, and pulled down the walls round about it; and then, with the ruins of the demolished city, built a strong fortress on the top of an eminence in the city of David, which was over against the temple; and overlooked and commanded the same, and there placed a strong garrison; and making it a place of *arms* against the whole nation of the Jews, *stored* it with all manner of *provisions of war*, and there also they laid up the spoils which they had taken in the sacking of the city. And this fortress, by the advantage of its situation, being thus higher than the mountain of the temple, and commanding the same, from thence the garrison soldiers fell on all those that went up thither to worship, and shed blood on every side of the *sanctuary, and defiled it with all manner of pollutions;* so that from this time the temple became deserted, and the *daily sacrifices omitted;* and none of the true servants of God durst any more go up thither to worship, till *Judas,* after *three years and a half,* having recovered it out of the hands of the heathens, purged the place of its pollutions, and, by a new *dedication,* restored it again to its pristine use."—Prideaux's Connexion, year 168.

Before leaving this verse I shall make a few comments. This *indignation* was caused by the trouble the Jews gave Epiphanes by not all submitting to him. But some of them did submit and furnished him with "inside" information concerning the confidential interests of the holy service. We notice this information or *intelligence* was furnished by *them that forsake the holy covenant.* It is true that the worst enemies the work of the Lord has are those in the ranks of His professed servants who turn spies.

Verse 31. The *arms* were seen in the historical quotation, which Epiphanes used to further his opposition to the Jews. *Abomination that maketh desolate* is a descriptive phrase that might be used at different times. In general it means any condition where some abominable character or group of characters threaten the decency and dignity of the service of God. That is why Jesus applies the saying to the presence of the Roman army near the holy city of Jerusalem (Matthew 24: 15). In the present case it means the corrupt condition created by Epiphanes about the temple and altar of sacrifice.

Verse 32. *Shall he corrupt by flatteries* refers to the persons who gave Epiphanes "intelligence" in verse 30, who were the real enemies of the Jewish nation although they professed to love it. *The people that do know their God shall be strong, and do exploits* refers to a family known in history as the Maccabees. This family performed the service of rescuing the altar from the corrupt servants of Epiphanes and restoring it to its lawful use. I shall quote some history on this subject.

"Mattathias and Judas Maccabeus supported the distressed nation, and the almost universally abandoned religion, with so *small a number of forces,* that we can consider the success which the Almighty gave their arms no otherwise than a miracle. The troops grew more numerous by degrees, and afterwards formed a very considerable body." — Rollin's Ancient History, Volume 4, page 242.

"At this time Judas Maccabeus, with some others that accompanied him, fled into the wilderness, and there lived in great hardship, subsisting themselves upon herbs, and what else the mountains and woods could afford them, till they gained an opportunity of taking up arms for themselves and their country, in a manner as will be hereafter related." — Prideaux's Connexion, year 168.

"These measures [of Epiphanes] induced an open revolt, whose leader was the priest and patriot Mattathias of Modin. His bold deed of the public murder of a royal official was the sign for the beginning of the revolt. Fleeing to the mountains, he, with the co-operation of five heroic sons, organized war on a *small* scale. He died in 166 B.C."—Schaff-Herzog. Article, Maccabees.

Verse 33. "Judas, one of the younger sons, who had taken the most prominent part in the plans of his father, was appointed his successor. For six years he led the party with almost superhuman effort and varrying success. Decisive battles he had to avoid. But in innumerable skirmishes he defeated the hated foreigners; and his enthusiastic followers called him 'Maccabi,' or the 'Hammerer,' from which his family has received the appellation 'Maccabees.' It is apparent that this conflict had more of a religious than of a national character."—Schaff-Herzog, Article, Maccabees.

This verse predicts the hardships endured by the Maccabees in their struggles against the vicious Epiphanes. They had an army finally that fought under them, and its men suffered the hard treatment here named, including the sword, fire and prison.

Verse 34. The chief item predicted in this verse is the fact that the forces with which the conflict for the altar was waged were a *little help,* which means that the number was small, as we have seen in the history quoted.

Verse 35. There is not much new in this verse as it is still speaking of the hardships that the Maccabees endured in their struggles for the restoration of the worship in Jerusalem. *Make them white* refers to the purification that results to the righteous when they are "persecuted for righteousness' sake."

Verse 36. This *king* is still Epiphanes whose wicked doings we have been observing through many of the verses. *Do according to his will.* This king was selfish and headstrong and acted according as his own will dictated, regardless of others' rights and whether the thing he wished to do was right or wrong. The predictions of the verse are general but the main thought is the same as that in verse 31. *Till the indignation be accomplished.* This means the indignation of God against his own people because of their sins at this time. Epiphanes was suffered to oppress the Jews in order to punish them, and as soon as the wrath of the Lord was satisfied, the wicked king was to be brought to his own punishment. This prediction is the same as that made in chapter 8: 12. There is an extended comment with a quotation from history at that place and the reader is asked to see it again.

Verse 37. *Nor the desire of women.* Epiphanes was a very immoral man, and most of his immoral actions were unnatural. The prediction does not mean he never was intimate with women for he was, but that was not the chief object of his carnal desires. Another lengthy paragraph is devoted to the vile character of this king at verse 21 which the reader should see. The rest of the items of this verse have been explained.

Verses 38, 39. Epiphanes had no regard for the true God, neither for the rights of good men. The only god he served was that of military and financial *forces.* Such is the gist of this paragraph, and the many historical quotations that have been given clearly prove the predictions to be true.

Verses 40-43. No advantage would be gained by separating these verses into paragraphs for each, for all of them are on the same subject and have been virtually explained previously. The paragraph is a summing up of the activities of Epiphanes in his mad hostilities against Egypt and other peoples.

Verses 44, 45. The historical quotation that belongs with this paragraph is quoted at chapter 8: 24, 25. Briefly summing up, Epiphanes was madly pursuing his attacks in the south when he learned of the disturbances going on in another part of his dominions. In his *fury* he started thither, determined to wreak severe vengeance upon the Jews whom he blamed for most of the disturbances. But he was not suffered to carry out his wicked designs. In the midst of his mad performances he was smitten by the Lord and finally died in a most shameful and loathsome manner. In this way he fulfilled the prediction, *yet he shall come to his end, and none shall help him.*

DANIEL 12

Verse 1. *That* is a demonstrative pronoun but does not necessarily refer to any definite *time* as to exact date. It means that a certain time is referred to and is designated by this pronoun because of the importance of the events to be predicted. The closing events of the preceding chapter bring the date down to a century and a half before Christ. Since those events were directly connected with the bitter experiences of the Jews, it was appropriate to speak of the good things about to be predicted as being for the sake of *thy* (Daniel's) *people.* However, there were to be some more hardships imposed upon God's people, only they will be His people belonging to all nations and not the Jews alone. Altogether, the things predicted in this chapter will pertain to the greater part of the Christian Dispensation, even including the general resurrection at the last day. No doubt the prophecy in this verse is still remembering the persecutions of the Jews because of Epiphanes' wicked treatment of them, and that Michael was an instrument in God's hands to help them according to Hebrews 1: 13, 14. But the passage is not restricted to that subject for the vision passes immediately in the next verse to the events of the resurrection day.

Verse 2. Beyond any question, this verse predicts the general resurrection since it includes the two classes of mankind, the good and the evil. In John 5: 28, 29 the Lord Jesus makes the same prediction in virtually the same language. As further evidence that this is a prediction of the general resurrection we have Paul in Acts 24: 15 mentioning the general resurrection, and says of it that *they* (the Jews) *themselves also allow,* or admit. Yet the Jews could not have known of this doctrine but from the prophecy of Daniel. *Many of them* does not signify that not all will arise. The word *many* is defined by Strong as "abundant," and the phrase merely means that a vast number of people will have lived and died by the time of the resurrection day.

Verse 3. This verse has been perverted to teach that the saved will have stars in their crowns. That theory is wrong from every standpoint, and entirely misses the things predicted. The saved are said to shine *as the stars* but that has nothing to do with their possessing any stars in their crown, for there is not even any mention of crowns.

Verse 4. *Shut up the words, and seal the book* indicates that the fulfillment of the predictions would be far in the future. Before they are fulfilled *knowledge shall be increased.* This refers to the general diffusion of the light of truth to be sent out through the kingdom of Christ, and predicted also in Isaiah 11: 9.

Verse 5. The prophet next sees a vision of things to take place in the Gospel age, or at least things that will be a part of its blessings. The Lord often uses rivers and other streams figuratively to represent His blessings upon the righteous. However, at the present time Daniel is still by the river where he received his last message from heaven. Now there is a person on each side of the river prepared to give some information in the hearing of the prophet.

Verse 6. One of the men spoke to the man *clothed in linen* (chapter 10: 5) and asked how long it would be to the end of *these wonders.* The answer that will be given indicates the question pertained to a period in the far-off future that would be similar in principle to that previously predicted to come in the nearer future on the Jews.

Verse 7. The answer came in figurative language, that it was to be after a *time, times* and *a half.* This is the same symbolic prediction that is made in chapter 7: 25 and means the "dark ages" of 1260 years. The figure is explained at that place which the reader should see. *Scatter the power of the holy people* refers to the persecutions of Christians by Rome during the dark ages.

Verse 8. Daniel saw the men and heard them speak, but he was concerned because he did not understand the answer to the question.

Verse 9. The spokesman rather put Daniel off with an indefinite reply for the same reason as expressed in verse 4 where he was told to *seal the book* because the fulfillment was to be in the long future.

Verse 10. While the man or angel would not go into all the details of the things predicted, yet Daniel was given some further information as to what would happen in the course of the "dark ages." *Many shall be purified, and made white, and tried* by the persecutions of the dark ages. *None of the wicked shall understand* refers to the blindness of the Roman clergy, and the same is predicted by Paul in 2 Thessalonians 2: 11.

Verse 11. *Daily sacrifices* and *abomination that maketh desolate* are used figuratively or comparatively. The terms are those used of the corruption of the sacrifice by Epiphanes, but they are used to denote the time when the dark ages would start, because at that time the pure worship would be polluted by Rome. The prophet was told it would be 1290 days, while the period of the dark ages was 1260 (years). But it took some time before the work got a good start, so the addition of 30 (years) is allowed in this figurative prophecy.

Verse 12. When the work of Luther and his co-laborers got well underway, the clergy of Rome and leaders of the temporal dominions of the State that formed the union known as Babylon the Great, began to see what it was all about and began to persecute the reformers. For some time they were subjected to bitter experiences, comparable with the ones suffered by the Maccabees, and the distress was so great that some yielded and gave up the struggle. There were others, though, who *waited* and *came* through until the battle of the Reformation was won, which the passage sets at the end of 1335 days (years), and a blessing is promised to those who endured to that time. Of course the number of years indicated is only approximate, but it gives the general idea of the great epoch.

Verse 13. The vision is ended and Daniel is dismissed to go on his way. He has faithfully and patiently given attention to the address of man or angel. *Thou shalt rest* is a blessing pronounced upon him in view of his righteous life. He has been an exile from the land of his fathers since the beginning of the great captivity and it is now the third year since that period ended. *Stand* in *thy lot.* The first word means to be established and the last means fortune or destiny. The promise means that when the last great day comes *(end of the days)*, Daniel will be among those who will be able to join with the faithful of all ages in sharing the blessings of Him whose faithful servant he has been while living on the earth.

HOSEA 1

Verse 1. According to the compilation of the books of the Bible, Hosea is the first of the "Minor Prophets." The term is a little misleading as it implies a difference of importance between them and the others. The Schaff-Herzog Encyclopaedia says this on the subject: "The Minor Prophets ("brief in words, mighty in meaning"), are twelve in number; viz., Hosea, Joel, Amos, Obadiah, Jonah, Micah, Nahum, Habakkuk, Zephaniah, Haggai, Zechariah and Malachi. In the Hebrew canon [books accepted as being inspired] they constitute only one book. They are called the 'Lesser, or Minor Prophets' because their prophecies were brief, not because they were less important, than those of the four Greater Prophets (Isaiah, Jeremiah, Ezekiel and Daniel.) All these writings together do not equal in length those of Isaiah. Yet Hosea exercised the prophetic office longer than any other prophet." This verse gives the period covered by the vision of Hosea, which agrees with the statement just quoted from the reference book. The first four kings named were rulers of the 2-tribe kingdom of Judah, and the last one was a king of the 10-tribe kingdom of Israel. The captivity of the kingdom of Israel took place in the days of Hezekiah, king of Judah, and Hosea's work extended over that period, hence he lived to see the fulfillment of some of the predictions that he made concerning that kingdom.

Verse 2. It has been seen in numerous instances that prophets have been required to do some "acting" in connection with their prophetic office, and Hosea is another in that class. The case is so strange that I consider it advisable to copy most of my comments on the subject given on 1 Kings 20: 35: "At various times inspired men have been called upon to go through certain physical performances as a form of prediction. Some of such instances will be cited. The torn garment, 1 Kings 11: 29-31; the wounding of the prophet, 1 Kings 20: 35; the cohabiting with the wife, Isaiah 8: 3; wearing a girdle, Jeremiah 13: 1-7; eating of filth, Ezekiel 5: 1-4; moving of household goods, Ezekiel 12: 3-7; eating a book, Revelation 10: 8-11. We are not told specifically why all this was done; but it was in line with the statement of Paul in Hebrews 1: 1. It might be suggested that visible exhibitions of divine predictions are sometimes impressive where the simple wording is not." Harlotry is compared to idolatry and other forms of unfaithfulness all through the Bible. The Jews were so generally guilty of this spiritual adultery that the Lord wished them to be impressed with its seriousness through seeing this kind of performance by the prophet. We know that such was His purpose in the instructions, for they are immediately followed by the words, *for the land hath committed great whoredom, departing from the Lord.*

Verse 3. There was a specific woman and her specific name is given whom Hosea married, so that no basis exists for building up some fanciful theory about the transaction. The people of Israel were grossly guilty of idolatry and some shocking demonstration was needed to impress them with the gravity of the abomination, hence the prophet was commanded to be the instrument of God for the performance. There is no occasion for us to make more out of the case than the facts set forth. No personal immorality can be charged against Hosea in this situation. He was not a priest and hence the restrictions of the law against marriage to such a character would not apply to him. In Leviticus 21 the Lord forbade the priests to "take a wife that is a whore, or profane." This very law indicates that at least it might be expected that other men would marry such a character if they so desired. Another thing to be remembered, is that no intimation is in evidence that the wife of Hosea was required to continue in her former practice. There are numerous instances on record where women of immoral "pasts" have married, settled down and made good wives and mothers. Whether Gomer proved to be that kind remains to be seen; but whatever it may turn out to be, the Lord will know how to use the situation with good effect in His infinite wisdom. Hence, let the reader keep his attention focused on this most unusual and interesting life drama.

Verse 4. In Biblical times many proper names had significant meanings and they were applied to persons and places frequently to express some lesson, either of prophecy or history. The name Hosea's son was given by the Lord, which was Jezreel. The word is defined in the lexicon as, "God will sow or scatter." It was also the name of a place where Jehu, king of Israel, committed some of his most horrible outrages, and God intended this name of Hosea's son to be an omen of what

He would do to the house of this wicked king. The prediction was even made that the kingdom of the house of Israel would be caused to cease. And since the name assigned to this son means to sow (as seed strewn abroad) or scatter, it was a fitting symbol of the time when the kingdom would be scattered over the land of Assyria.

Verse 5. *Break the bow* is figurative and means that the men of the 10-tribe kingdom would not be able to withstand the attacks of the invading forces. The fulfillment of this prophecy is recorded in 2 Kings 17th chapter.

Verse 6. A daughter was born to the house of Hosea and the Lord named her also with a word with an appropriate meaning. The lexicon of Strong defines Loruhamah as "not pitied." The meaning is that Israel continued in her idolatry, even after the birth and naming of the first child, so the Lord would not change His mind concerning what was determined to be done to the nation.

Verse 7. *Will have mercy upon the house of Judah.* This may sound strange to the reader who will remember that the kingdom of Judah also became corrupt and was finally exiled from her native country as well as Israel. That is true, but that was not the same time when the Lord meant he would have mercy upon Judah, but it was at the same period that the ten tribes were taken captive by the Assyrians. At that time the same heathen country threatened Judah and God here promises that He will have mercy upon her then. *Not save by sword nor bow* means that Judah would not have to go to war to drive off the Assyrians. 2 Kings 19: 35, 36 shows how the nation was saved by a miracle.

Verse 8. *When she had weaned,* etc. This is merely an incidental allusion to the rule as to the liability of conception after the bearing of a child. It has no particular connection with the story but is stated for the sake of coherence.

Verse 9. Here a fact about literal Israel is used as a symbol of a spiritual fact. The name which God gave to be used for this son means "not my people." When the nation of the Jews became corrupt, God suffered it to be taken off into a strange land. By such an event it could be said that He no longer considered the Jews as His people since they ceased to exist as a free political people. That circumstance is used as a symbolic prediction of the time when a Jew could not claim to belong to God merely on the ground of his being a Jew. That agrees with the statement of Paul in Galatians 3: 28 on what it means to be in Christ. In that relationship he says, "There is neither Jew nor Greek [Gentile], . . . for ye are all one in Christ Jesus."

Verse 10. This verse continues the thought that was introduced in the preceding one. *Israel* is used spiritually, and refers to the Gentiles who were to become God's people in the future after the kingdom of Christ was established. Apparently the Gentiles had no prospect of being a people of God at all, much less becoming a numerous one. But after the middle wall of partition between the Jews and Gentile was broken down, the latter showed more readiness of mind to accept the Gospel than the former, and consequently they produced more Christians than the Jews. And there was also a numerical fact that helped to account for the difference. The Gentiles constitute by far a larger per cent of the earth's population than the Jews. Hence, when the door was opened to them, it brought in a greater number of converts to Christ, and that would have been true even had the comparative willingness of the two been the same.

Verse 11. The prediction of this verse was fulfilled literally and spiritually. The former was fulfilled by the return of all the Jews from the Babylonian captivity. Israel, the 10-tribe kingdom, went into exile under the Assyrian Empire, and Judah, the 2-tribe kingdom, went into exile under the Babylonian Empire. The two events were a century apart, in the course of which time the Babylonians had taken over the Assyrian Empire with all its "holdings," and that virtually threw all of the Jews together. When the Persians overthrew the Babylonians, they released all of the Jews which permitted them to return to Palestine as one nation. The prediction was fulfilled spiritually when the distinction between Jew and Gentile was removed, and both were brought together under *one head.* Jesus is that head and His fold or kingdom is the place where God's people are together as under one shepherd (John 10: 16).

HOSEA 2

Verse 1. There were always some individuals in the Jewish nation who were righteous, and they are the *ye* of this verse. The exhortation means for *ye* (as individuals who were the righteous) to speak to their *brethren* and *sisters*, which means the nation as a whole and which formed the group spoken of in terms of family relationship.

Verse 2. These righteous individuals were to plead with their *mother* (the nation as a whole). *She is not my wife* is a prediction in the form of a warning, referring to the captivity that was to come upon Israel, which would be like a man putting his wife away because of her unfaithfulness. Israel (as a whole) was totally corrupted with idolatry, which is compared to adultery in the Bible. These righteous individuals were to plead with the leaders of the nation, exhorting them to abolish idolatry.

Verse 3. A wronged husband would be disposed to treat an unfaithful wife in the manner described here. Its application refers to the national rejection by the Lord of Israel, and her shameful exposure by the Assyrians.

Verse 4. *Her children* means the members of the nation. Even the individuals who were righteous had to suffer nationally with the unfaithful ones in that all had to be exiled together. This is the sense in which it is predicted that the Lord would *not have mercy upon her children*.

Verse 5. The complaint the Lord has against his people is because of their unfaithfulness in connection with the false gods. And as the comparison is made with spiritual adultery, the language is in the form of that pertaining to fleshly harlotry. A literal harlot might profess to have turned away from her corrupt associations, and become the companion of a good man. This wife had done that very thing when she became the partner in life with Hosea. If this woman actually returned to her former life of looseness, it would be a specific illustration of what Israel as a nation did. In that case, the treatment of Hosea towards her would be like that of God towards Israel. Or, if she is only supposed to do that, it is still intended for the same lesson. I will not attempt to decide which theory is correct (both having been advanced by commentators), for either serves the same purpose of portraying the record of Israel's conduct toward God! And in the following verses and chapters, I shall make my comments on the basis of spiritual adultery, because we know that such was the actual condition of affairs for centuries. However, that will not need to shut out all references to fleshly unfaithfulness when the occasion arises for the purpose of illustration.

Verses 6-8. An unfaithful wife may use provisions given her by her husband, to contribute to the uses of her guilty paramours (Ezekiel 16: 31-34). Thus Israel bestowed her spiritual instructions and provisions upon the heathen around her.

Verse 9. But even a lenient and patient husband will finally turn and put his unfaithful wife to shame and take from her the good things he had bestowed upon her. Likewise, God gave his people up to exile and thus deprived them of the good things they enjoyed while in their own land and were a nation under the Lord.

Verse 10. If a woman deserts the men who have been paying her for her gratification of their lust, they may look upon her as a traitor and will have only a feeling of contempt for her. Hence we may understand the thought in this verse of exposing this woman's impure body to the loathing eyes of her former partners. This figurative prediction was fulfilled when the people of Israel were sent into a heathen land and there compelled to continue in the spiritual adultery.

Verse 11. The mental or emotional feature of this prediction was especially fulfilled upon Judah, as described in Psalms 137. But it was all true of the Jews generally while in the land of their exile. God would not permit them to attempt carrying out His services while there; and He even caused them to continue in their practices of idolatry while in that heathen country (Deuteronomy 4: 28; 28: 36, 64).

Verse 12. This destruction was to be literal and to be accomplished by the very people with whom Israel had committed spiritual adultery. The land of Palestine was to be left deserted, untilled and unkept, and the beasts were to be allowed to overrun the whole country.

Verse 13. Baalim is the plural form of Baal, the invisible god of many of the idolaters in ancient times, and Israel took up with that abominable practice. *Visit upon her the days of Baalim* means to punish her for the days she spent in serving the idols of Baal. The *lovers* were the people of the idolatrous nations with whom Israel associated in her false worship.

Verse 14. From this verse and through verse 20 is a prophecy of the return from captivity. That great event is compared to a wronged husband receiving back his wayward wife after he had abandoned her for a while to the company of her guilty partners in sin. God is more compassionate than an earthly husband and hence predicted that His unfaithful wife would be given a chance to return to Him.

Verse 15. *Give her her vineyards.* The husband drove his unfaithful wife from the possession that had been given her in the beginning of their marriage, but they were to be kept for her if and when she reformed and showed a desire to come back to her first love. *Achor* is used figuratively, and the events connected with it are compared with the experiences of Israel in the times being predicted by Hosea. The word means "trouble," and it was given to the place and circumstance when Achan sinned at Jericho and brought so much "trouble" upon the congregation. But the next encounter they had with the enemy proved successful. Likewise, Israel in the days predicted by Hosea was destined to get into trouble because of sins. However, the release from captivity was to be as joyful as the exile was troublous. That will be similar to the success at Ai following the trouble about the valley of Achor. *Day . . . Egypt* is another event used for the same purpose of illustration. Israel had much trouble in that land, but the deliverance from the bondage brought much joy.

Verse 16. Strong says that *Baali* is from BAALIS, an Ammonite king, and *Ishi* is from IYSH, which he defines, "A man as an individual or a male person." Since the whole figurative setup along here is based on the marriage relationship, we can understand why the first of the words is preferable. A wayward wife who is eager for an agreeable home life would prize a *man* (husband) above all other relationships. Hence the term is used to indicate the joy to be experienced by Israel when she is again taken into the bosom of her loving and faithful Husband.

Verse 17. The one great thing to be accomplished by the captivity was the cure of idolatry. This verse predicts that accomplishment, for it does not merely state that Israel will cease the practice of that abomination, but the very terms of the institution *shall no more be remembered by their name.* This indicates a complete purge of the whole system. The historical quotation that shows the fulfillment of this prediction may be seen in comments on Isaiah 1: 25, volume 3 of this COMMENTARY.

Verse 18. During the absence of the Jews from their country, the beasts were given free range over the land and they ravaged it at will. But after the return to it of its proper inhabitants, God was going to protect the country from such damaging conditions. That is what is meant by a covenant *for them* (for Israel) *with the beasts of the field. Break the bow and the sword* means they will not have to go to war in order to reclaim the land after the captivity.

Verse 19. *Betroth thee unto me for ever* is a phrase that belongs to the marriage relation, and that is the comparison that has been used all along concerning God and his people. *For ever* indicates that the marriage will never be broken again, and that has specific reference to the truth that the Jewish nation was never again to be sent away bodily into exile as it was in this case.

Verse 20. *Betroth . . . in faithfulness* means that God will always be a constant and faithful husband to His people.

Verse 21. See the comments on Daniel 12: 1 on the significance of the pronoun "that," and learn how indefinite it is as to exact dates. In the present instance it refers to the day when the Gentiles were to hear the Gospel and accept it, thus presenting to God a group of people from a new source. *I will hear, heavens shall hear.* This unusual language indicates the unity of interest and general cooperation of all forces in the final dispensation that God will give to the world for spiritual salvation.

Verse 22. The same idea of cooperation is continued in this verse. The mention of *corn and wine* is for figurative purposes. It is true that such temporal blessings were predicted for ancient Israel after they returned from captivity, but the fact is used as a type of the spiritual prosperity that was to come through the Gospel.

Verse 23. This is again a prediction of the call of the Gentiles, for they had never been called a people of the Lord before the Gospel period. They had the provision of the Patriarchal Dispensation for their spiritual salvation, but that was a family religion and did not constitute them a "people" in the sense of that term in the Bible.

HOSEA 3

Verse 1. See the comments on chapter 2: 5 as to whether this situation was literal or figurative regarding the wife of Hosea. We know the wife of the Lord had acted in the way that is spoken of about Hosea's wife. Israel had proved unfaithful to the Lord and committed spiritual adultery. He had put her away and abandoned her to her lovers (the idolatrous heathen). But the prediction is that the wife was to be taken back, although she had been living with the enemies of her rightful Husband.

Verse 2. *Bought her to me.* The Persians were not given any ransom for the release of the people of God, but in this "buying" the Jews themselves were the other parties to the bargaining. They were encouraged to return to their former estate by the promise of good things in the home land.

Verse 3. The prediction we are now considering was made before Israel had even gone into exile, although as far as the Lord was concerned, the separation was a surety since with Him all things of the future are as certain as if a present fact. This makes it logical to use the idea of this verse. The wife, though taken back (in the Lord's foresight), was not to be received into her former intimacy with her husband until she had been tried, to see if she could be weaned away from the unfaithful life that she had been following before. The trial will be described in the next verse.

Verse 4. The trial mentioned in the preceding verse was the captivity, in which the people of Israel were left no choice between serving idols or not. They were compelled to serve them, and hence were made to continue in the manner of life which they had followed when they did have the opportunity of making a choice. It might be asked how this could be a test if they had no voice in the situation. The test will be in evidence after the trial is over, for if they went on through the practice of idolatry even by force, yet if they were not being taught the lesson intended, then they would not have made the complaint that we know they did. While they were in captivity, all of their national activities were discontinued, including the work of a king and a priest. The *image* and other articles named refer to the ornamented garments worn by the priests during the altar services.

Verse 5. This verse is a prediction with both Jewish and Christian application. The Jews returned from the captivity and resumed the national life as it pertained to their religious activities. Also, in the time of Christ the Jews looked to the Lord through the system that was set up by Christ. *David their king* is expressed because he was the first king of the tribe of Judah under the Jewish Dispensation, and he was the ancestor of the King in the Christian Dispensation.

HOSEA 4

Verse 1. When people depart from the proper rule of life on any one fundamental point, there is no logical reason why they will not take up with other evils. The people of Israel had forsaken the first commandment in the law and had become a nation of idolaters. They did not stop at their corrupting the true religion, but they disregarded the law as to their personal conduct. They carried such abominable ways to such an extent that all respect for the truth was lost. The original word for *controversy* is defined in Strong's lexicon as, "A contest," and it means the same as the trial described in the comments at chapter 3: 3.

Verse 2. This verse is a literal description of the corrupt way of life into which the people of Israel had fallen in Hosea's day. *Blood toucheth blood* means one act of bloodshed would no sooner be committed than another would be done.

Verse 3. God sometimes punishes his people by sending some curses upon the land, and this verse is a warning that something of that kind would come upon the nation.

Verse 4. A glance at some verses ahead will help to grasp the meaning of this one. With that in view, I consider this to mean the common people are all guilty of unfaithfulness. And if the priest, with the advantage that he has, is so hardened in error that he cannot be affected by *striving* or reasoning with him, there is no use for any man to strive with the common people.

Verse 5. The *mother* is said of the nation as a whole, and the threat is that the whole group is destined to fall or be cut off from the land.

Verse 6. Ignorance is never any excuse for wrong doing, especially if the party has the opportunity of knowing what is right. The simple statement that God's people were to be destroyed or severely punished because of their lack of knowledge might seem harsh or unjust. But the explanation that follows makes the justness of the condemnation evident. This lack of knowledge was due to the fact that they *had rejected knowledge*. It is the same truth expressed in Isaiah 1: 3, where God's people are charged with ignorance of their Master, and then follows the explanation of why it is so; "my people doth not consider." There is an old and true saying which is as follows: "No one is as blind as he who will not see, nor deaf as he who will not hear." Because God's people had rejected divine knowledge, they were to be rejected by Him.

Verse 7. The more numerous the people of God became the more they increased their unrighteousness. They had become vain because of their numerical strength and were glorying in it. But the Lord decreed that the condition was to be reversed, and in place of glory would come shame.

Verse 8. *They* evidently refers to the priests who were supposed to be teachers and lead the people in the ways of righteousness. Instead of doing that, it is said they *eat up the sin of my people*. The meaning is that they found satisfaction in the sin of the people, and that is as objectionable to God as to be the direct doers of the wrong. This principle of responsibility is taught by Paul in Romans 1: 32.

Verse 9. *There shall be* is an expression looking forward to something to come, though the condition of which the Lord complained was present when the statement was made. The meaning is that when God brings the threatened punishment on the people, He will treat both the people and priest alike, and that is because they were both to blame. Jeremiah gives a brief but clear view of the mutuality of the corruptness of the nation as it pertained to the various classes, in chapter 5: 31. That statement is so fundamental in its bearings that I shall quote it for the convenience and information of the reader: "The prophets prophesy falsely, and the priests bear rule by their means; and the people love to have it so."

Verse 10. This verse specifies some of the things that God threatened to impose as a punishment upon the unfaithful nation. The people were to be unsatisfied even after partaking of food. *Commit whoredom, and not increase*. There are two motives back of the natural law that attracts the sexes to each other. One is the experience of pleasure and the other is for the perpetuation of the human race. Both are right if practiced under proper regulations. The people of Israel practiced the first without regard for law and order, hence God was going to punish them by denying them the increase of their population. Such a penalty would mean much to a nation that wished to boast of its numerical strength.

Verse 11. The word *wine* occurs twice and is from altogether different Hebrew originals. The first means the fermented kind and the second is the juice of the grape newly pressed out. The first would intoxicate and the second would tend to satiate or glut. *Heart* means the mind or intellectual part of man. The whole verse is a picture of the corrupt practices of the people, especially in their disorderly assemblages where they gave themselves up to revelry and lust and drunkenness.

Verse 12. *Stocks* and *staff* refers to the wooden idols which they had made. They had become so confused by their debased manner of life that their judgment was deranged. This *whoredom* was both fleshly and spiritual, for when the people became merged with the heathen in their worship of idols, they also took up with the immoral practices that was a part of their religion.

Verse 13. Fleshly and spiritual adultery seem to have been closely associated in Biblical times. The forepart of this verse describes the latter form of the abomination, for the hills were used as desirable spots for idolatrous practices, and trees of all kinds were brought into it because the idolaters like the attractiveness of the large plants for such performances. The last part of the verse refers to fleshly adultery, and it is a prediction with a suggestion of threat. Since fleshly unfaithfulness is no worse than spiritual (if as bad), and these leading men of the nation were guilty of the latter, it will serve them justly if their own wives prove unfaithful to them by committing the former.

Verse 14. It is true that "two wrongs do not make one right," but God sometimes suffers certain things that are wrong in order to teach a lesson. In the present instance the Lord declared he would not punish the women folks of the men of Israel for their immorality. *Themselves* is a pronoun that stands for these men, and they also were guilty of a like sin. *Separated with whores* means they were associated with them, not only in their immorality, but also in their idolatrous worship. *Doth not understand* refers to the men and women in general, and reminds us of the statement in verse 6, also the statement of Isaiah in chapter 1: 3.

Verse 15. The Lord has been directing the prophet to write against Israel most of the time. In this verse a warning is slipped in for the benefit of Judah, for her to learn a lesson from the example of the 10-tribe kingdom. *Gilgal* and *Beth-aven* were once places of respect for the true God, but had been desecrated by the idolaters. Therefore Judah was warned to stay away from such places when they wished to offer their vows to the Lord.

Verse 16. The original for *backsliding* is defined in the lexicon, "To be refractory," and that means to resist. In the case of a heifer it would mean she would throw off the yoke and refuse to pull her share of the load. *Feed* . . . (or pasture) *them in a large place.* A lamb turned out into a large field would not have much chance in case of attack from wild beasts. God did not intend to let his people become entirely destroyed, but he did decree to "turn them out" into the wide field of exile in the Assyrian Empire.

Verse 17. *Ephraim* refers to the 10-tribe kingdom, which was so closely attached to idolatry that it was useless to hope for improvement while in his own country. For this reason the prophet was told to *let him alone* or not to try reforming him. Jeremiah was given similar instruction in chapter 7: 16 of his book.

Verse 18. *Drink is sour* is an unusual figure of speech meaning "utter abandonment." Rulers love *give ye* means the leaders of the nation were coveteous and wanted to be paid for doing their duty.

Verse 19. *Wind hath bound her up.* When the lightness of something is to be compared or described, it is often done by likening it to "chaff which the wind driveth away" (Psalms 1: 4), and Israel is so pictured in this passage. *Ashamed because of their sacrifices* refers to the complete cure of idolatry that resulted from exile.

HOSEA 5

Verse 1. *Mizpah* and *Tabor* were prominent places in Palestine, and the complaint of the Lord was that the priests had taken advantage of them to mislead the people of the congregation. It was expected that the priests would be teachers of the people (Leviticus 10: 11; Deuteronomy 17: 9; Malachi 2: 7). But instead of leading them aright, they laid snares for them and got them caught in the meshes of idolatry.

Verse 2. A revolter is one who resists authority, and the leaders of Israel had done that very thing. In pursuing their abominable practices they did not shrink from murder when their plots called for that crime.

Verse 3. *Ephraim* and *Israel* are named separately as if they were not the same people. The former has specific reference to one of the tribes, but the capital of the 10-tribe kingdom was located in his possessions, hence Ephraim is often used as a name for the kingdom. In the matter of guilt, since the capital was in that possession, it is understandable that much of the evil influence would issue from it.

Verse 4. *Frame their doings* indicates the planning for the activities, including the teaching that would affect others. These leaders would not plan to turn unto the Lord themselves, nor to lead the people back to Him from their life of unfaithfulness. *Spirit of whoredom.* This indicates that they not only had given way to a sinful life, but their controlling principle of life was one of harlotry, to such an extent that they had forgotten the Lord.

Verse 5. *Pride . . . testify . . . face.* The folly of Israel in being influenced by the dominating pride is in evidence as the prophet writes his message. *Israel* and *Ephraim* are referring to the same people virtually; see comments at verse 3. With prophetic eyes the prophet beholds the future of Judah, although at present the main complaint of the Lord is against Israel. Many of the complaints and predictions being made were true of both divisions of the Jewish people, Israel and Judah.

Verse 6. The thought intended by this verse may be realized some better by making it read, "Although they go with their flocks" etc., they shall not find him. The Lord had called for these articles of service by the law, therefore it might seem strange to have Him withdraw so that the people could not find him. This apparent contradiction is explained in a comprehensive note at Isaiah 1: 10 in volume 3 of this COMMENTARY.

Verse 7. The treachery of which they were guilty consisted in mingling their blood with the people of other nations. The Lord wished to maintain a pure blood down through the ages, and to do so it was necessary for His people to marry within the Jewish families. The children born of these unlawful unions were considered *strange* because that word means "outside." *Month* is used indefinitely, meaning their ruin would be accomplished in a short time after it began.

Verse 8. Trumpets were used to sound any alarm of danger that might come or threaten to come on the nation (Numbers 10: 1-5; 31: 6). The language is used here by way of prediction that the country would be attacked by an enemy force.

Verse 9. *Ephraim* is used to mean the 10-tribe kingdom, otherwise called Israel. *Day of rebuke* refers to the time when the country was to be invaded and the people carried off into exile.

Verse 10. Judah is brought into the prediction because she also was destined to be punished for her departures from the Lord. When the pouring of water is used figuratively, it denotes an overflowing of some kind of misfortune. The people of God were destined to be invaded by the heathen nations.

Verse 11. The *commandment* could not mean that of the Lord, for that would not have been condemned. We know, therefore, that it refers to some idolatrous ordinance. It is the one in 1 Kings 12: 28-30, where Jereboam made the idols and told the people to worship them, which they did.

Verse 12. Again the two divisions of the Jewish people, *Ephraim* (Israel) and *Judah*, are named in the predictions of God's wrath. A *moth* consumes the material which it attacks, and the Lord decreed to attack his unfaithful people in time to come.

Verse 13. *Ephraim saw his sickness* means he was confronted with a dangerous situation, which was the presence of a foreign king (2 Kings 15: 19). Judah sent to *Jareb* which Strong defines, "A symbolical name for Assyria." The name seems to be used figuratively and means that Judah sought help from an outside source instead of God.

Verse 14. God is always displeased when his people look to strangers for help; it is an indication that they have lost faith in Him. Hence, when these kings of the Jews appealed to the heathen for help, they not only failed to obtain any, but brought down upon them the wrath of the Lord.

Verse 15. *Return to my place* denotes that God would abandon his people to their fate; leave them in the hands of the heathen to whom they had appealed. This was not to be in the spirit of spite or resentment, for God is incapable of such a principle, but it was in order to make them see their folly, and repent. *In their affliction they will seek me early* is forcefully described in Psalms 137 and the fulfillment may be seen in Ezekiel 37: 11, which was written in Babylon at the time it was happening.

HOSEA 6

Verse 1. This verse may be considered both as an exhortation and a predction. The Lord through his prophet exhorts the people to come to themselves and the prophet sees them doing so. See the comments on the last clause of chapter 5: 15.

Verse 2. The numerals are used figuratively, meaning that he (the Lord) would punish them for a while, then receive them back again. This is one form of prediction that indicates the captivity and the return.

Verse 3. *If we follow on to know the Lord* is a fundamental principle of the Bible. Following the Lord effectively always includes the interest sufficient to learn about Him. It was taught by Jesus in Matthew 11: 29 where he says for men to "learn of him." But no one can truly learn what he should of the Lord unless he is a faithful follower of Him. *Latter and former* ["early"] *rain*. The significance of this expression will be better appreciated by remembering that the rainfall in Palestine was periodical. Also, that the *latter* rain came before the *former* or "early" rain with reference to the production of crops. I shall quote from Smith's Bible Dictionary on this subject: "RAIN. In the Bible 'early rain' signifies the rain of the autumn, Deuteronomy 11: 14, and 'latter rain' the rain of spring. Proverbs 16: 15. For six months in the year, from May to October, no rain falls, the whole land becomes dry, parched and brown. The autumnal rains are eagerly looked for, to prepare the earth for the reception of the seed. These, the early rains, commence about the latter end of October, continuing through November and December. January and February are the coldest months, and snow falls, sometimes to the depth of a foot or more, at Jerusalem, but it does not lie long; it is very seldom seen along the coast and in the low plains. Rain continues to fall more or less during the month of March; it is very rare in April." Since the falling of these rains in their proper seasons meant much to the production of crops, the phrase is used to signify the blessings in general coming from the Lord.

Verse 4. The Lord frequently uses expressions that are common to man (Romans 6: 19), in order to convey the thought to the ones involved. A human parent who was "at the end of his efforts" with his wayward children would likely speak in the manner of the first half of this verse. The reference to the dew or early cloud is to compare the instability or lack of permanence in the character of God's children.

Verse 5. *Hewed them by the prophets* is figurative and means that when God decreed to punish his people he would warn them about it by the voice of the prophets. See Jeremiah 1: 10 and Ezekiel 43: 3 for similar statements, and note the marginal reading at the latter place. *Thy* is a pronoun that stands for the wayward people of God, and their judgments are described to be as fickle as their *goodness* is in verse 4.

Verse 6. This verse is quoted by Jesus in Matthew 12: 7, and applied to the cruel and hypocritical Jews of His time. The statement has been perverted by false teachers who wish to avoid a strict adherence to the New Testament teaching. They make it mean that Jesus is not as particular in having the "doctrinal" points observed as he is in "practical" religion. But that use of the passage does violence to the authority of Christ. The remark was made concerning the self-righteous and grasping leaders among the Jews, who would oppress the poor to obtain gain, then think to come to the altar with a part of the possessions they had extorted from the poor, and try to make it right before the Lord by making a sacrifice. Under those circumstances the Lord would not want their sacrifices, but rather that they show mercy to the people whom they had defrauded. It will again be appropriate for the reader to see the note offered at Isaiah 1: 10, in volume 3 of this COMMENTARY.

Verse 7. The lexicon of Strong defines *men* as follows: "Ruddy, i. e., a human being (an individual, or the species, mankind, etc.)" In most Bibles the marginal reading gives the rendering "like Adam." In Job 31: 33 the text says, "as Adam," and the margin at that place says, "after the manner of men." The thought in the verse is that Israel had followed the trend of mankind in general instead of conducting themselves as the servants of God. *There* means, with reference to the *covenant;* there is where they had dealt treacherously against Him.

Verse 8. *Gilead* is a word of various significance in the Bible, usually referring to an extensive region of the land of the Jews. But it sometimes refers to a city and it is so used in this verse. The inhabitants of that city were sinners to a special degree and hence are mentioned in this specific manner. The particular evil of which they were guilty was murder.

Verse 9. Single or individual acts of lawlessness are bad enough, but when men conspire to commit sin as a group it is much worse. That is what these Jews were doing, and they are likened to *troops of robbers*. Even the priests acted "in a body" or as *the company of priests*, and they did so *by consent* which means a conspiracy. *Lewdness* is an indefinite translation of the original in this place. The Hebrew is ZAMMAH and Strong defines it, "A plan, especially a bad one." Hence the word is meant as an additional expression showing the spirit of conspiracy in which the priests acted. Lewdness, in its usual sense, is bad, and these people were guilty of that; but it was not the particular evil in the mind of the Lord here.

Verse 10. Both fleshly and spiritual whoredom were practiced in the Jewish nation, but the latter is evidently what the Lord has especially in mind here. *Ephraim* and *Israel* are named separately, because the capital of the latter was located in the possessions of the former.

Verse 11. A passing notice is given frequently to Judah (the 2-tribe kingdom), but the main subject of this book is the affairs of Israel (the 10-tribe kingdom). In the present verse a wide space of time is covered. The prophet sees into the future when Judah, like Israel, will be sent into captivity for idolatry, but afterwards be returned to the home land.

HOSEA 7

Verse 1. *Iniquity of Ephraim* was *discovered*. God does not have to *discover* a fact as we commonly use that word, in order to learn of it. He knows all about everything even before it happens. The word is from GALAH, which Strong defines, "A primitive root; to denude (especially in a disgraceful sense); by implication to exile (captives being usually stripped); figuratively to reveal." The term as used in this passage means that God would have been inclined to heal or approve Israel as being acceptable, but the iniquity of the nation was so evident or bare that He could only condemn her. *Ephraim* was one of the tribes, and *Samaria*, the capital city, was situated in the possession of that tribe.

Verse 2. In spite of all the experiences that Israel had known directly, and the record of God's dealing with unrighteous persons in the past, they seemed to feel as if He did not know what was going on. And even if the Lord had been unable to see the future or to know about facts that were invisible, He would have known all about the iniquity of Israel for it was *before his face*.

Verse 3. The pronoun *they* refers to the people in general, and their conduct was agreeable to the king and princes, because all classes had conspired to corrupt the law of the Lord. (See Jeremiah 5: 31.)

Verse 4. This is an unusual and highly figurative passage, intended to illustrate the intensity of Israel's lusts. While the baker is mixing the dough, he is also applying the fuel to the oven. After the mixing is done it will not require very long for it to rise or become *leavened*. And it is only during that short space that he does not apply any more fuel to the oven, which indicates that it is hot enough to bake the dough, and hence a fitting comparison for the heat to their corruptions.

Verse 5. The people of Israel were corrupt both fleshly and morally. They were guilty of unfaithfulness both literally and figuratively, and all classes conspired together in the iniquity. (Jeremiah 5: 31.) *Day of our king* probably refers to one of his birthday anniversaries. It was celebrated in drunkenness and association with evil characters like the heathen nations around them.

Verse 6. The prophet continues the figure of a baker and his oven, and the thought is the same that was contained in the illustration before. While the people were waiting for the opportunity to practice their wickedness, they were stirring up the fierce anger in their hearts. *Baker sleepeth all the night* is a figure of speech, referring to the periods of inactivity during which the people were awaiting an opportunity of doing some mischief, at the same time working up their wicked hearts to the point of a blaze. *In the morning* (the moment at the end of the period of waiting) the pent up heat bursts out into a *flaming fire*.

Verse 7. They had not literally devoured their judges, but the conspiracy was so strong that it engulfed even the rulers and other leading men. This is evidently the meaning, for the result of the *heat* is directly expressed by the closing words *none among them that calleth unto me*.

Verse 8. Mixing with the (heathen) people agrees with the figure that follows, *a cake not turned*. Such a mixture would bring in some ingredients that would render a cake unsuitable for food. Likewise, a cake not turned would be raw on one side and burnt on the other, hence unfit to eat. The two figures in the verse are unrelated except at the point common to each, namely, both are unfit to be eaten.

Verse 9. *Strangers* means people of outside nations who had brought in their heathenish practices. A man cannot see the hairs of gray sprinkled here and there upon his head, neither did these Jews realize the evil that had crept into their national life.

Verse 10. *Pride of Israel testifieth*, etc., is explained at chapter 5: 5. The folly of their conduct was made clear by this "testimony," yet they were not induced thereby to seek the Lord for help.

Verse 11. *Without heart* means without a good mind or judgment. A silly dove would flit about from one place to another without any fixed purpose. The people of Israel looked to such unworthy sources as Egypt and Assyria for help instead of relying wholly upon the Lord who had always done them good.

Verse 12. Continuing the figure of a bird in flight, the Lord threatens to capture the silly dove with a net. The instrument to be used as a net was to be the Assyrians, the very people to whom the bird was seeking to fly. *Congregation hath heard* refers to the warnings that had been given the nation in such passages as Leviticus 26: 14-39; Deuteronomy 28: 15-68.

Verse 13. We note that the *woe* and *destruction* were decreed upon the people after or *because* they had fled from the Lord and transgressed his law. God never causes a good man to become a bad one, but if he chooses the life of sin, then the Lord will treat him as an evil person. *Have redeemed them* refers to past favors that God had bestowed upon the nation of the Jews, such as the deliverance from Egypt, and the many rescues that are recorded in the book of Judges. But all of these favors had been forgotten and they became guilty of one of the greatest faults, that of ingratitude.

Verse 14. The people *howled upon their beds* because they were suffering from the evil effects of their sinful deeds. They did not cry to the Lord with a pure heart, but only out of a selfish desire for their own indulgencies. They would clique together to obtain the luxuries of life, at the same time rebelling against divine law.

Verse 15. The Lord had bestowed upon his people an abundance of good things. He had strengthened them when they were weak, and had defended them when they were unjustly attacked. In turn for these great favors, the people would *imagine* mischief against the Lord. That word is from CHASHAB and Strong defines it, "To plait or interpenetrate, i. e. (literally) to weave or (generally) to fabricate; figuratively to plot or contrive (usually in a malicious sense); to think, regard, value, compute." Thus the word the Lord had the prophet to write is a stronger one than we ordinarily think it to be. It has the meaning of a malicious scheming against the good Lord who had done so much for them since their beginning as a nation.

Verse 16. *The land of Egypt* is used figuratively to indicate the evil character of their plans. Not all bows are *deceitful* but some are, and such a bow will fail to cast the dart in the direction indicated by its position. The people of Israel professed to be looking or be aiming toward the Lord, but they swerved and became interested in idols and their service with the heathen nations.

HOSEA 8

Verse 1. The pronouns in this verse represent three different nouns; they are the people of Israel, the Assyrians and the Lord. A trumpet was used as an alarm of war (Numbers 10: 9), and the statement is used figuratively as a prediction. *He shall come* means the Assyrian army shall come against the land. This will be according to the decree of the Lord to punish Israel because *they have transgressed my covenant, and trespassed against my* (the Lord's) *law.*

Verse 2. This short verse predicts the distress of Israel when he realizes the results of disobeying the Lord.

Verse 3. The thing that Israel had cast off was the covenant of the Lord. *The enemy* will be the Assyrian, and the prediction was fulfilled in 2 Kings 17.

Verse 4. This verse has special reference to the events of 1 Kings 12. The nation of the Jews divided because of the unwise actions and announcements of Rehoboam. Ten tribes revolted and set up a line of kings, starting with Jeroboam, that was in opposition to the God of Israel. It is true that Rehoboam tried to interfere with the division, and that God rebuked him for it, saying *this thing is from me.* But that was because the conditions were such that He saw the need for the revolution to chastise the nation. But originally such an arrangement of the kings was *not by me,* saith the Lord. *Princes, and I knew it not* means that the Lord did not approve of the appointment of princes that was made by Jeroboam. The word *prince* means any leading person in a community, official or unofficial. After the division of the tribes, Jeroboam made priests of the lowest of the people (1 Kings 12: 31). *Made them idols* is recorded in 1 Kings 12: 28-32.

Verse 5. *Samaria* is named because that city became the permanent capital of the 10-tribe kingdom (1 Kings 16: 24). *Thy calf* means the idols that are referred to in the preceding verse. *Hath cast thee off* is a prediction with a twofold meaning. The idolatry of the nation was to bring upon it the wrath of God, and when that came, the idols were to be powerless to save it or prevent the invasion by the enemy.

Verse 6. The idol came from Israel, originated there, because their *workman made it.* The true God is the maker of all things and is the only One who should be worshiped. But these people of Israel were worshiping a god that was the work of their own hands. *Calf of Samaria shall be broken* predicts that idolatry was to be uprooted and excluded from the practices of the nation. The fulfillment of this is shown in the quotation from history at Isaiah 1: 25, volume 3 of this COMMENTARY.

Verse 7. *Sown wind . . . reap whirlwind* agrees perfectly with Galatians 6: 7. The only difference in principle between a wind and a whirlwind is in degree or quantity, for both are wind. A whirlwind is a greater and stronger thing than a wind but is in the same class as a substance. It is likewise in the case of sowing and reaping. If a man sows wheat he expects to reap wheat; but he should get more wheat at the harvest than he sowed. A whirlwind would destroy all the other growth virtually, and if any remained standing after the storm passed by, strangers would get it.

Verse 8. This is a figurative prediction of the overthrow of the kingdom of Israel. Gentiles is a word for the heathen nations. Israel was destined to live in the midst of such people, but that was not to be regarded by these heathens as any great advantage; they would look upon this captured group as a *vessel of no pleasure.*

Verse 9. *Are gone up* is present tense in form, but it is a prediction of the captivity of the 10-tribe kingdom by the Assyrian Empire. *Ephraim hath hired lovers.* Idolatry is likened to adultery in the Bible, and the practice of that abomination by the people of God is compared to the unfaithfulness of a wife in her marriage relationship. An ordinary lewd woman practices adultery for the money she receives for it, but Israel was worse than such a woman. She is compared to an unfaithful wife who pays men to come in to her; and she pays them with money that her faithful husband had given her. (See Ezekiel 16: 17, 31-34.)

Verse 10. *Sorrow a little* means that the nation was to be exiled for a *little while* (comparatively speaking), during which time it would not engage in appointing unworthy kings and princes, such as the accusation in verse 4. *Gather* usually has a meaning opposite of scatter, yet this verse predicts the exile of Israel into a foreign land. The idea is that God would scatter his people from their own land, but they would be gathered into the net of the heathen country. The original for gather is defined in Strong's lexicon, "to grasp, i. e., collect."

Verse 11. Another wording of this verse would be to say that Ephraim (the 10-tribe kingdom) had sinned by making many idols or altars for the false worship. Therefore, the nation was destined to continue that abominable practice while suffering the punishment of exile in the country from which the abomination was learned.

Verse 12. Israel was not to be excused on the ground of ignorance, for God had *written to him the great things of my law.* However, that law was ignored and treated as if it were something from the outside.

Verse 13. The corruptions of the nation as a whole became so great that God would not accept the things they did that would have been approved otherwise. *Return to Egypt* could refer to the frequent instances when the people of Israel looked to Egypt for help in time of their trouble with Assyria and Babylonia. The phrase has also a figurative application, referring to their enslavement under the Assyrians that was as distressing as the original bondage in Egypt.

Verse 14. In a summing up of the Lord's complaint against Israel, the kingdom of Judah received a notice because that kingdom also was becoming corrupt. Both houses of Jews were destined to be overthrown by the foreign forces to be brought against them.

HOSEA 9

Verse 1. *Rejoice not* is a prediction in the form of an announcement that Israel was headed for a fall, and it would be on account of the unfaithfulness of the nation. *Gone a whoring* refers to the lusting after the gods of the heathen, and also the reliance that Israel placed in the heathen themselves. *Reward upon every cornfloor.* The cornfloor means the grain that was threshed out at such a place. The Israelites thought they would have their temporal prosperity assured by the support of the heathen nations.

Verse 2. This verse is a simple prediction of the industrial provisions of the country, that they would be cut off by the invasion of a strange force.

Verse 3. This verse gives the reason for prediction of the preceding one; that Israel was to be deprived of dwelling in the *Lord's land,* which means Palestine. *Ephraim* means the 10-tribe kingdom, and so named because its capital city was located in the possession of that tribe. *Return to Egypt;* not literally, but into a bondage as bad as the Egyptian enslavement was. *Eat unclean things in Assyria* is literal, referring to the exile of the ten tribes into the land of Assyria.

Verse 4. The general meaning of this verse is the dissatisfaction which God felt for the entire conduct of His people. They professed to be consecrated to the true God, and to take delight in the ordinances of the law, but all their performances were tinctured with the poison of idolatry. Because of all this abominable way of life, God's people were destined to be taken away into the land of Assyria. When they got there the practices described in this verse which they professed to be doing because of their devotion to God (but not with sincerity), will not be attempted at all in the strange land. *Bread for their soul.* When the people of Israel were performing these sacrifices in a lawful manner, and in connection with a life devoted to the true God, it benefited their *soul;* was for their spiritual as well as legal upbuilding. In the foreign land there would be no bringing of such articles into the house of the Lord.

Verse 5. *What will ye do,* etc. This is a reminder that when the period of exile comes upon Israel, the nation can have nothing to do with the solemn feast days that they once practiced in the home land.

Verse 6. Most of this verse is figurative and refers to the shameful interest that Israel had shown for the heathen countries. That very interest will prove to be the undoing of the nation, as much so as if it had been taken bodily to Egypt.

Verse 7. *Day of visitation* denotes the day when God's threatened judgments would be heaped upon them. *Prophet . . . spiritual man mad . . . fool.* According to Lamentations 2: 14; Ezekiel 13: 3; Micah 3: 11 and Zephaniah 3: 4, this prophet and spiritual man means the false prophet who had made predictions about the safety of the nation. When the exile comes upon the people they will realize that their prophets were fools.

Verse 8. The *watchman* means the man who was faithful to his God. (See Ezekiel 3: 17.) Such a servant gave true warnings of danger whether the people gave him heed or not. The (false) prophet is a *snare of a fowler* (a hidden trap such as those used by a hunter for fowls), that gets the people into trouble because they are not giving heed to the warnings of the watchman.

Verse 9. The comparison to Gibea is because of the gross immorality that was committed at that place (Judges 19). The people of Israel were guilty of both physical and spiritual pollutions. *Will visit their sins* means that God will punish his people for their sins by a visitation of some unpleasant experience.

Verse 10. *Grapes in the wilderness* would indicate something that was unattended and unpossessed by any particular person. Israel is likened to such an article because the Lord made the nation to become great out of an insignificant beginning. *Firstripe fig* is used in the same sense concerning the early existence of the nation. The illustration supposes a man finding a fruit thus growing wild, uncultivated and producing inferior fruit. He takes charge of the plant, cultivating it and making it possible to produce better fruit. But instead of doing that, it produced worse crops than it had done in the beginning. Likewise, after God took Israel under his care, the nation was cultivated and given the opportunity to produce the desirable kind of fruit, namely, true religious devotion to the Lord. But instead of doing so, the nation began to bear the fruit of idolatry, Baal-peor being one of the false gods. *Abominations according as they loved* indicates that they became as abominable as the false god that they loved. That conclusion is logical, for it is well known that a person tends to become like his ideal. This is true whether the ideal is a good or an evil character or principle. Paul taught this great truth in 2 Corinthians 3: 18. How important, then, that we select the proper ideal for our life model.

Verse 11. *Ephraim* is a brief name for the 10-tribe kingdom of Israel, against whom the prophet Hosea directed most of his book. *Birth, womb, conception* is a condensed tracing of human existence, going back to the very beginning of the individual. The first is the conception, then the womb retains the conceived germ until time for it to be ushered forth by birth into the outside life. The picture means to show the complete degeneration of the nation from the glory of true devotion to the true God, down to the low estate of an idolatrous worshiper.

Verse 12. A common desire in ancient times was to have a generation of descendants to take the place of the present race. This was especially true in view of the need for sons to defend the homes and country against foreign foes. But the unfaithfulness of the nation brought from God the prediction that though the children would be produced they would be taken away. This was accomplished partly by misfortunes and judgments imposed upon them while living in the home land, and partly by the exile.

Verse 13. The original prosperity of Ephraim (Israel) is compared to that of Tyrus that was once a flourishing city. But all of this was reversed against the unworthy nation, and its children were to be murdered by the enemy.

Verse 14. The man power of the nation was to be reduced in another way. Either the mothers would not be able to carry their infants through to mature birth, or, if they did so, they would not be able to nourish them because of failing breasts.

Verse 15. The reference to Gilgal pertains to the sin of Saul who was the first king of the Israelites. From that time the people had been more or less guilty of disobedience (See 1 Samuel 13: 8, 12). *There I hated them.* We generally shrink from using the word "hate" because we think of it as being always wrong; especially when used with reference to God. But since God cannot do anything wrong, it follows that the word is not always an objectionable one. The English definition is given by Webster as follows: "1. To feel an intense aversion to; detest; abhor. 2. To dislike exceedingly." Such a sentiment would not necessarily lead to unjust treatment of a person hated. The true application of the word is to think of hating the things a man does and not the man individually. But it is often impossible to deal with the wicked things that are hated without doing so with the persons who are guilty. Hence the nation of Israel was destined to feel the sting of God's hatred for sin. *Will love them no more* is to be understood from the same basis as the word "hate," just explained. God's evidence of ceasing to love the nation was to be seen in the event when He would *drive them out of his house,* which was to be accomplished by the exile into a foreign land.

Verse 16. This verse is virtually the same as verse 13.

Verse 17. This verse is a direct prediction of the exile of the ten tribes into the land of Assyria, the record of which is in 2 Kings 17.

HOSEA 10

Verse 1. The thought of this verse may well be expressed by the one word, "selfishness." It is illustrated by supposing a vine to retain the substance of its fruit within itself instead of depositing it on the outside in clusters where the owner could make use of it. The situation is made worse by the wrong use the vine makes of this substance that is retained. It would be bad enough were the vine to convert the substance into grapes and then consume the fruit selfishly. But this vine diverted it into unlawful uses, literally referring to idolatrous altars in the application of the parable. *According to the goodness,* etc. The more prosperous Israel became, the more corrupt he became with idolatry.

Verse 2. *Heart is divided* denotes that Israel mixed his devotions, giving most of them to the idols but professing to be serving the true God. Continuing the illustration of a vine, this nation produced *faulty* or objectionable fruit. An owner of a vineyard would reject such a plant and remove it from his soil. Likewise the Lord threatened to *break down* the altars of the idolaters.

Verse 3. This verse is a prediction that Israel was to be deprived of a king. It was fulfilled when the Assyrians took the ten tribes into captivity as recorded in 2 Kings 17. *What then should a king do to us?* The words are put into the mouths of the Jews by the Lord, signifying that it would do them no good to have a king as long as they had no fear for the Lord.

Verse 4. The people of Israel were not sincere when they made their vows. They would swear to serve the Lord, then break that oath at the first opportunity for worshiping at an altar. As a punishment for this impure manner of life, the Lord predicted that He would bring judgment upon the people that would be likened to poisonous weeds in their fields.

Verse 5. The gist of this verse is a prediction that Israel will come to regret the whole practice of idolatry. The calves of Beth-aven is an indirect reference to the idol calves that Jeroboam reared up in Bethel and Dan (1 Kings 12: 29), which became a signal for a national corruption that finally resulted in the exile of the ten tribes into the land of the Assyrian Empire.

Verse 6. The antecedent of *it* is "glory" in the preceding verse, and it was to be carried into Assyria as a present. Strong's lexicon says that Jareb was a symbolical name for Assyria. That country will be the victor in the conflict with the people of *Israel* whose capital city was Samaria.

Verse 7. *Foam* is a figure to illustrate the lightness and lack of importance of the kingdom of Israel. Foam is also something that denotes a frothy discharge, making more of a threatening show than possessing real strength or merit.

Verse 8. *Aven* is an abbreviation of Beth-aven, and that name refers to the idolatrous practices at Bethel. It is predicted here that the sin was to be destroyed, and that was fulfilled by the exile. The land was to be deserted by its idolatrous inhabitants so that the *thorn and thistle* could grow up over the spots where the false worship had been conducted. *Say to the mountains . . . fall on us* is figurative and refers to the dejected state of mind that Israel was to have as a result of the national corruption of idolatry.

Verse 9. *Israel* is used in the sense of a nation, and this institution had Saul for its first king. But he committed a grievous sin and set the example of disobedience for the generations following. Gibeah was an important city connected with the public life of Saul, hence the reference to the place in connection with the evils carried on by the nation over which he was the first king.

Verse 10. The purpose of the distress that God was going to bring upon his people is expressed in the words *that I should chastise them*. The people who were to be *gathered against them* were the Assyrians. *Two* means twofold and *furrows* means misconduct or transgressions. Their iniquity was twofold in the sense of being great or more than ordinary. It also was literal in that the chief national evil (idolatry) was begun with the two idols which Jeroboam reared up when he led away the ten tribes and formed the kingdom of Israel (1 Kings 12: 29).

Verse 11. Cattle were used for two purposes in Biblical times; to tread out corn and to pull the plow. The former was much easier and any heifer would prefer that work. Ephraim (Israel) is likened to a heifer that desired to be left at that work because she was *taught* or accustomed to it. But her owner was going to make her get into the yoke and help pull the plow. This is the meaning of *passed over upon her fair* (arched or proud) *neck*. *Ride* means to go forward into the work of pulling the plow. Of course this is all figurative and means that Israel had been blessed with the comparatively easy task of serving God in their home land (likened to the treading out of the grain), but now she is going to be forced into exile (likened to the heavier task of pulling the plow). And while in the figure, a few words are used to include Judah (the 2-tribe kingdom) in the prediction, since that kingdom also was destined to go into captivity as a punishment for its idolatry.

Verse 12. This verse is an exhortation based on the familiar illustration of sowing and reaping, that "whatsoever a man soweth, that shall he also reap" (Galatians 6: 7). *Righteousness* (the thing sown) will bring the reaping of *mercy*. *Break up your fallow ground* means to make use of the ground that is capable of producing good crops but which has been allowed to lie uncultivated. The writer offers his own explanation of this figure in the words *time to seek the Lord*. The figure is then resumed in the words *rain righteousness*, since it is necessary to have rain to produce a crop.

Verse 13. Plowing and reaping is again used figuratively, and this time it pertains to the evil kind of products. The things sowed (plowed) is *wickedness* and the harvest is *iniquity*, and the particular kind of iniquity is *lies*. Israel was deceived by the leading men in the nation, who were selfish and unscrupulous in their teaching.

Verse 14. The *tumult* threatened was to be the result of the Assyrian invasion. *Shalman* is another form for Shalmaneser the Assyrian king who came against Israel in a hostile manner and finally overcame the nation (2 Kings 17: 3).

Verse 15. The reference to Bethel is because of the idol that was set up there by Jeroboam (1 Kings 12: 29), which started the 10-tribe kingdom on its national record of idolatry. *Bethel do unto you* denotes that the ruin of the nation was to be as a chastisement for its constant worship of idols, beginning with the one placed at Bethel. *Morning* is used figuratively, meaning that the king of Israel would be overthrown in a short time after his country was invaded.

HOSEA 11

Verse 1. This verse is both history and prophecy. Its first meaning is history, for in chapter 2: 15, the time when Israel literally came out of Egypt is called *the days of her youth*. That is virtually the same language as our present verse. And we know it is prophecy also, for Matthew 2: 15 quotes it and says that the calling of Jesus out of Egypt was a fulfillment of the words of the prophet. The moral of the statement is that God cared for His people when they were the most helpless, bringing them out of a condition from which they could not have escaped by their own strength.

Verse 2. God sent the call to Israel, but it was done through representatives, and the pronoun *they* refers to them. The entire history of Israel is a record of rebellion against the true prophets and other leaders sent by the Lord to warn them against the evil nations around them. *Baalim* was the name of the invisible or imaginary gods, and the graven images were the ones carved out of wood, stone and metal.

Verse 3. The Lord offered his teaching to *Ephraim* (Israel), but he did not profit thereby. *Taking them by their arms* denotes the tender care and assistance that God extended to them. *Knew not that I healed them* means that the people of Israel did not realize the benefit that would have been enjoyed by them if they had accepted the offers of mercy from God.

Verse 4. *Cords of a man* and *bands of love* denote the same thing. God was kind and tender with his people and did not use harsh cords with which he might draw a beast along. *Take off the yoke* is stated with the same significance, meaning that He would relieve his people of the hardships that an enemy would have imposed upon them. He not only lifted the load from their bodies, but offered food for their nourishment.

Verse 5. The backsliding ways of Israel would have entitled him to be sent back into the bondage in Egypt, but the Lord would not use that form of punishment this time. However, he must have some form of chastisement, hence the decree to suffer the Assyrian king to invade the land and take its people away into exile.

Verse 6. There was not much actual warfare between Assyria and Israel, but the sword of the invader was present as a threat, and hence made the invasion effective.

Verse 7. *People are bent* means they are inclined to backsliding. *They* is explained at verse 2. The people were so interested in their idols that they paid very little attention to the call for worship of the true God.

Verse 8. The gist of this verse is a lamentation of the Lord over the unfaithfulness of His people. He regrets that he will need to give them up and deliver them into the hands of a foreign nation for punishment. *Admah* and *Zeboim* were two of the cities that were destroyed in the days of Lot (Genesis 14: 2; 19: 25). It does not mean that Israel was to be literally destroyed as were those cities, but the rejection was to be as certain. *Turned* means changed or reversed; *repentings* means compassion or leniency; *kindled* means to contract or be reduced. The sentence denotes that God's attitude is changed toward the people of Israel because of their unfaithfulness.

Verse 9. *Not execute the fierceness of mine anger* denotes that if they were treated as they deserved they would be destroyed. But God is more long-suffering than man, hence He will chastise his people and give them another chance. *Not enter into the city* as a destroying enemy, but He will suffer their cities to be taken over by the foreign army in order to have them chastised.

Verse 10. When the people have been chastised *they will walk after the Lord*. *He* (the Lord) *shall roar* refers to the expressive threatenings that will be heard by the sinful nation, and *tremble* is from a word that virtually means the same as response. The one subject is continued through the verse, which is the good effect the chastisement will have on the people. *Tremble* means to respond to the treatment received from God. *The West* is somewhat indefinite, but as it is used here the indication is that a general response will be given to the Lord's call for repentance.

Verse 11. The bulk of the citizens of the 10-tribe kingdom was to be carried into Assyria, but some of them were scattered here and there in other countries. Hence this "trembling" (response) will be in evidence in Egypt as well as in Assyria. *Place them in their houses* is a prediction of the return from the captivity. The historical fulfillment of this prediction is quoted with the comments on Isaiah 14: 1 in volume 3 of this COMMENTARY. The Biblical fulfillment may be seen in Ezra and Nehemiah.

Verse 12. *Ephraim* and *house of Israel* means the same people. The *lies* and *deceit* refers to the false prophecies of the unfaithful teachers in the country. *Judah yet ruleth* means that at present the 2-tribe kingdom was in a fairly favorable relation with God, not having gone so far into idolatry.

HOSEA 12

Verse 1. *Ephraim* (Israel) *feedeth on wind* denotes that he is interested in that which is without substance.

East wind is an allusion to the wind that blows off of the desert of Arabia called a simoon. Webster defines this word, "A hot, dry, violent wind laden with dust, that blows occasionally in Arabia, Syria, etc." This wind would hence be of no value, but would be injurious. It is used figuratively, to denote the evil nature of the manner of life that the people of God were following. The literal instance of this sinful conduct was the traffic which was carried on by Israel with Assyria and Egypt.

Verse 2. It has been stated that most of this book is about the affairs of the 10-tribe kingdom (Israel), but some verses are written concerning Judah, the 2-tribe kingdom. So here it is stated that the Lord had a *controversy* (accusation) with Judah. *Jacob* is a more general term and applies to the descendants of that patriarch. In spite of the advantage of observation on the conduct of Israel, these descendants of Jacob who formed the 2-tribe kingdom of Judah finally were wrong also.

Verse 3. This verse specifies some of the indications of Jacob's special favors. The action of the infant while in the mother's womb was necessarily a miraculous one, and was caused by the Lord, in keeping with His prediction in Genesis 25: 23. The assertion is made that it was by the power of God, and that power will be further explained in the next verse.

Verse 4. The *power* referred to in the preceding verse is recorded in Genesis 32: 25. As long as the angel conducted his wrestling as "a man," he was unable to prevail against Jacob; and only when he employed his supernatural talent as an angel, did he succeed in the contest. The events of this verse are not chronological, for the wrestling with the angel took place many years after the night at Bethel. At that time the people of Judah were in existence only in the loins of Jacob, but the things said and done were regarded as pertaining to the interests of said people, hence the word *us* with which the verse closes.

Verse 5. *Hosts* means an army, especially the army of heaven. *Lord is his memorial* denotes that the holy name is that by which He is to be remembered.

Verse 6. The exhortation given had special application to the leaders or princes of the nation who were cruel to the common people, and who denied them their just rights in matters of controversy.

Verse 7. *Merchant* is from KENAAN and Strong defines it, "Kenaan, a son of Ham; also the country inhabited by him." The thought of the verse is an accusation that the people of the land had become deceitful, especially their leaders.

Verse 8. *Ephraim* (Israel) had become prosperous, and it caused him to be vain and rebellious. (See Deuteronomy 32: 15.) It was bad enough for Israel to become disobedient in his prosperity, but he even used his condition as a basis for denying that he had any guilt.

Verse 9. *From the land of Egypt.* God has always existed, but Israel as a people first knew Him at the time they left Egypt. At the time they left that country they had to begin living in tents, and the fact was commemorated by a special feast designated by the name. *Yet make thee to dwell in tabernacles* is a prediction of the return from the captivity, at which time they were to resume their festivities of services towards the Lord. (See Nehemiah 8: 17.)

Verse 10. These various methods of communicating with His people are referred to in Hebrews 1: 1. The present purpose of mentioning this is for a reminder that the people of the land of Canaan were without excuse in their unlawful conduct. Also, when the calamity of exile comes against them, they will have no ground of complaint as if they had been taken unawares.

Verse 11. This verse is a general statement of the national corruptions of the people of God. *Gilead* was a large area in the vicinity of Palestine that was supposed to produce healing articles; but it had become tinctured with the germs of a false religion. *They are vanity* means that all of the devotions to false gods would prove to be empty of any value. The emptiness of the idol worship is likened to the demolished condition of an altar whose stones have been scattered over the ground.

Verse 12. We know that Jacob went into the country far beyond what is commonly understood as Syria. The subject will be clarified by a quotation from a reference work as follows: "Aramaic Languages are so called from *ARAM*, a geographical term which in old Semitic usage designates nearly the same district as the Greek word, Syria. Aram, however, does not include Palestine, while it comprehends

Mesopotamia (Hebrew, Aram of two rivers), a region which the Greeks frequently distinguish from Syria proper. Thus the Aramaic languages may be geographically defined as the Semitic dialects originally current in Mesopotamia and the regions extending S. W. from the Euphrates to Palestine,"—Britannica, Volume 2, page 307. He is called *Israel* at the time he was serving Laban, although that name was not given to him until he returned to his home land (Genesis 32: 28); but it had become history at the time that Hosea wrote his book. The significance of mentioning this was to remind the people of the humble estate of the man from whom they received their name.

Verse 13. The dependence of the people upon the Lord is still the thought in the passage. The *prophet* referred to was Moses, who was given divine power in his leadership of the people, else they never could have escaped from the land of Egypt, and been preserved after escaping and going through the wilderness with all its perils.

Verse 14. Ephraim (Israel) provoked *him* (the Lord) with his many acts of rebellion. *Therefore shall he* (the Lord) *leave his* (Ephraim's) *blood upon him*, meaning that the people of Israel were to be chastised for their iniquity.

HOSEA 13

Verse 1. As long as the people of Israel *trembled* or had reverence for the Lord, they were exalted in the divine favors. But they did not remain thus faithful; instead, they committed the offence of sacrificing to the false god called Baal. When that took place the Lord decreed that the nation should die. That means it was to die nationally, and it was fulfilled when it was dethroned and taken away into the captivity (Isaiah 22: 14, 18).

Verse 2. Baal was one of the invisible gods that the idolaters worshiped which was foolish enough, but God accused them of sinning *more and more*. That was because they were not content to serve a god that was invisible, and in that respect was like the true God, but went further and served the gods of their own making. A little reasoning should have shown them the folly of depending upon a god of human origin, for such a thing could not possibly possess any more power than a human being.

Verse 3. A *morning cloud* and *early dew* soon disappear, and the comparison is made to the shortness and uncertainty of all false gods and the success of those who worship them. All of the illustrations in this verse are for the same purpose, and they predict the overthrow of the rule of corruption which the men of Israel had maintained to the disadvantage of the common people.

Verse 4. *From the land of Egypt* is explained at chapter 12: 9. *Shalt know no god but me* has a twofold bearing. It denotes the commandment of the Lord and is the first of the ten commandments (Exodus 20: 3). It is also a prediction of the state of Israel to be manifested after the captivity. The history quoted in connection with Isaiah 1: 25 shows that Israel was completely cured of idolatry after the captivity.

Verse 5. *I did know thee* denotes the attention the Lord gave to Israel in the wilderness. There were many times that the nation would have perished for the necessities of life had God not been good enough to provide food and water for them.

Verse 6. *According to their pasture.* The Lord provided abundant pasturage for his flock, but the sheep devoured it to excess and then forgot the Shepherd who had done so much for them. *Heart was exalted* refers to the pride that took possession of the people as a result of their prosperity.

Verse 7. The Lord was a tender shepherd over his people while they respected the divine law. However, they were unappreciative of the many favors that were shown them, and then God changed his attitude toward them and threatened to act as a harsh beast. The figure has reference to the exile into a strange land that was destined to come upon the unfaithful nation.

Verse 8. This verse continues the figures that indicate the fierceness of God's wrath against the wicked nation. *Caul* is from CEGOWR, which Strong defines, "Shut up, i. e., the breast (as inclosing the heart)." The clause means that God will rend the protecting covering of their heart, and expose it to the rigors of the chastising wrath of Him whom they so ungratefully disobey.

Verse 9. Self-destruction in the physical sense is called suicide, and is classed with the most wicked of deeds. It should be regarded with equal or greater horror when it pertains to moral or spiritual matters; the Lord accused his people of this very evil thing. By plunging into a life of idolatry, Israel incurred the wrath of the true God which was to be satisfied only by the national death (Isaiah 22: 14). Since this calamity was to be the result of their own rash deeds, it should be regarded as nothing short of national suicide.

Verse 10. The first sentence of this verse is rendered, "Where is thy king" in the margin of the Bible. Moffatt's translation renders it likewise and 2 Kings 17: 4 gives the reason for the humiliating question. That passage states that the king of Israel had been shut up and bound in prison by the king of Assyria. The Lord further asks them the accusing question about their having anyone else to take the place of this king who was then in prison.

Verse 11. The subject of the "state of the nation" was brought up to the point where it was appropriate to make the statement of this verse. The overthrow of the last king this part of Israel ever had was not to be regarded as an unexpected or unavoidable event, for the very first king they ever had was the victim of God's wrath. The first clause of the verse refers to the fact that God was displeased when the people called for a king, although he suffered them to have one (1 Samuel 8: 7). The second clause was fulfilled when the Lord declared that Saul was to be removed from the throne because of his rebellion (1 Samuel 15: 23).

Verse 12. *Bound up* and *hid* are said in the sense of being held under consideration by the Lord, to be dealt with as the sin deserves when the proper time comes.

Verse 13. The thought of the preceding verse is continued in this, but it is represented in a figure. The pains of approaching childbirth are used to compare those soon to come upon Israel when the time arrives for him to go through the ordeal of invasion and overthrow. The figure is continued and is worded to fit the facts as they were to occur. The pains of the birth were not to be continuous or lasting as is sometimes the case, which is indicated by the words *not stay long in the place of the breaking forth of children*. The fulfillment of this was to be when the captivity (the event illustrated by the pains of childbirth) would be ended. This passage lays the foundation for a wonderful twofold prediction of the rescue of Israel from the national grave, and that of mankind from the literal grave at the resurrection.

Verse 14. This verse gives the twofold prediction mentioned in the preceding paragraph. Its first fulfillment was to be when Israel was released from the captivity in Babylon, predicted in so many places. And we are certain the second fulfillment is to be at the general resurrection of mankind, for Paul uses virtually the same language in 1 Corinthians 15: 55, where we know he is writing upon that subject. *Repentance shall be hid* means the Lord has his mind made up on the matters predicted and it will not be changed.

Verse 15. *Though he be fruitful* denotes that the apparent success of the unfaithful leaders of Israel will be reversed. As the east wind (see the comments at chapter 12: 1) would destroy all vegetation, so the wrath of God will put an end to the unrighteous rule of these proud leaders. It is significant that the figurative *east wind* was to be accomplished by a nation (Assyria) that was literally east of Palestine.

Verse 16. *Samaria shall become desolate* is a prediction that was to be fulfilled literally, for that city was the capital of the 10-tribe kingdom, and it was destined to be overthrown by the Assyrians. The reason for such a fate against the people of Israel is stated in the words *for she hath rebelled against her Lord*.

HOSEA 14

Verse 1. The general subject of this chapter is a prediction of the return from the captivity. One of the objects to be accomplished by that terrible experience was the reformation of the nation. In keeping with that object, this verse is an exhortation to the people to *return unto the Lord*.

Verse 2. They are exhorted to make the proper supplication to God on account of their departures from the true worship. *Render the calves of our lips* is a very comprehensive phrase. It is formed in view of the idolatrous worship of the calves set up by Jeroboam (1 Kings 12: 28). Instead of such religious exercises, the people were exhorted to offer proper prayers to God, which is the meaning of the italicized words above. Paul makes the same figurative use of the subject in Hebrews 13: 15.

Verse 3. The attitude of penitence toward God is still indicated by the prayer proposed for Israel. Asshur (Assyria) was the nation that took the 10-tribe kingdom out of its home land, and now the people are to realize that no dependence can be placed upon that idolatrous country. To *ride upon horses* would indicate a favor granted under the protection of a ruling power. There was a time when Israel might have expected to receive such favors from Assyria, but that will have been shown to be a vain thing. *Work of our hands* refers to the idols the people had made out of wood, stone or metal. They were to be convinced that such gods are vain and unable to bestow any blessings upon their worshipers. Instead, *in thee* (the Lord) the poor and helpless find mercy.

Verse 4. *Will heal their backsliding* is a prediction of the effect the captivity was to have upon the practice of idolatry. The anger of God is always caused by the unrighteous conduct of man, and when that is changed for the better the anger also will be reversed and the mercy of God will be shown.

Verse 5. The laws of vegetation under the conditions of nature are used for comparison. After a sultry day has caused the plants to droop, the dew of the night appearing in the morning will cause them to revive and lift up their heads. Likewise, after the scorching effect of the captivity, the dew of the release will rekindle hope again in the hearts of the people of Israel.

Verse 6. This is more on the same thoughts as the preceding verse.

Verse 7. The laws and procedure of vegetation are continued to be used to compare the favorable experiences of Israel. *His shadow* means the Lord's shadow or protection from the scorching heat of enemy fire. Under the soothing effect of the shade and the enlivening help of the renewed seasons of the "early and latter rain," the plant of God (Israel) was to take on new life.

Verse 8. This verse is a direct prediction of the cure of idolatry that was to be accomplished by the captivity. The historical quotation that shows the fulfillment of this prediction is shown in connection with Isaiah 1: 25, volume 3 of this COMMENTARY.

Verse 9. This verse is a general statement that would be appropriate at any time and place. A wise man will understand the ways of the Lord because such will "consider" what has been said. Israel had not done so previously and hence this great trouble came upon the nation (Isaiah 1: 3).

JOEL 1

Verse 1. There were a great many men bearing the name of Joel in the Old Testament time, hence it was proper for the writer of our book to designate which one was meant. The statement that the word of the Lord came to Joel is equivalent to saying that the book is inspired of the Lord.

Verse 2. The idea of this verse is that the condition about to be described was without a likeness, either in the present or the following days.

Verse 3. *Tell ye your children* is a general instruction to spread the information to all generations both present and future.

Verse 4. The subject that is referred to in the foregoing verses is now introduced in this. I have consulted various books on the subject of these pests as to whether they were literal or figurative, and there is left still the uncertainty among them as to the true answer. However, the purposes of the lesson to be derived will be the same, whether the literal or figurative view be taken. We know from Deuteronomy 28: 38, 39; 1 Kings 8: 37; Leviticus 26: 16 and such other passages, that the Lord did afflict the land with literal pests at times as a chastisement of the people. And we also know that the country was short of being as true to God as it should have been when Joel lived, and was deserving of some kind of judgment from the Lord for the same. It was also true that God intended to punish his people by the hand of a foreign army, and the pests could have reference to that. Or, the locusts and other insects could have been literal, and then used by the Lord as a type of the invading army that was to be let loose upon the land to take away all its wealth. I shall leave this question to the consideration of the reader, and proceed to comment on the several chapters and verses in their order, explaining the various terms as they are used.

Verse 5. The leaders of the nation were selfish and indulged themselves in the luxuries of the land to the detriment of the people. *Weep . . . because of the new wine* means for them to weep because it was to be *cut off from their mouth*. This would have been true whether literal pests were to destroy the products of the land, or they were to be cut off by an invading army.

Verse 6. The language of this verse is a strong indication that the Lord means an army from a heathen country, for the descriptive terms certainly apply to such.

Verse 7. The grammatical form of this verse is in the past or present tense, but that is a common thing to find among prophetic writings. As the fruit-bearing plants would be rendered barren by being treated as it is here described, so the invasion by a foreign army would destroy the products of the land as far as their moral and political usefulness was concerned.

Verse 8. The nation of Israel has always been compared to a companion in the marriage relation. The word *virgin* might seem to be contradictory of a woman who is supposed to be a wife. The word is from BETHUWLAH, which Strong defines, "Feminine past participle of an unused root meaning to separate; a virgin (from her privacy); sometimes (by continuation) a bride." The idea is to compare Israel to a woman who was put away from her husband in their early married life, and compelled to live alone as if she were a virgin. The fulfillment of it was to be when Israel was sent away from the husband's home (Palestine) and made to live among strangers. A young woman in such a situation would follow the custom of the day and clothe herself with this coarse material which we know as common sacking.

Verse 9. It was true that the services of the altar had been literally neglected and abused, but as a prophecy the time was coming when such practices would be stopped altogether, for God would not permit his people to attempt them in a heathen country.

Verse 10. This verse is a prediction of the condition to come upon the land after the invasion of the Babylonian army.

Verse 11. The leaders of the nation are likened to *husbandmen* and *vinedressers*. But they had abused their position in the Lord's vineyard and hence were destined to be deprived of all their privileges. *Be ye ashamed* is a prediction of the humiliation that was to be imposed upon them by the power of a foreign army.

Verse 12. There is nothing new in this verse, but it is a repetition of the devastation awaiting the unfaithful nation to be effected by the hand of Babylon.

Verse 13. *Gird yourselves* means for them to be prepared in mind for what was to come. It could not indicate that they were to prepare a defence against the enemy, for it had been declared many times that the invasion was bound to come, and that it would be according to the Lord's decree. The rest of the verse is the same as several of the preceding ones as to the general devastation to come on the land.

Verse 14. The law of Moses did not require fasting as a regular practice, but on special occasions the Lord called for it, and the present is one of them. Most of the gatherings had been turned into mere formalities that left no beneficial results upon the minds of the people. Now the Lord calls for them to *sanctify* a fast, which means to put on a season of fasting that is holy because it is sincere and observed from respect for God. The leaders were to assemble the people in the temple because that was the lawful place for public worship and prayers to God. They were to cry unto the Lord because of the great iniquity of the land, and the distress that it was going to bring upon it as a punishment.

Verse 15. *Day of the Lord* denotes that the calamity about to be inflicted upon the nation would be by the decree of Him.

Verse 16. The word for *meat* is defined in the lexicon as "food" because it refers to anything that may be eaten. The prediction is that there was to be a shortage of necessary supplies. Such a condition would render the exercises of God that were in His house a time of solemnity instead of *joy and gladness*.

Verse 17. These conditions are to be understood in the same light as such verses as 9-12. Whether it was all to come literally or figuratively, the cause of it was the evil conduct of the nation.

Verse 18. This is more along the same line as the preceding verse.

Verse 19. *Hath* ordinarily would denote a condition already present, but whether it was all history or part prophecy, the point is that God was angry because of the iniquity of His people and determined to punish them.

Verse 20. The beasts could not intelligently cry unto God, but their cry would be caused by His visitation of judgment upon the land as a chastisement for the unfaithfulness of its inhabitants.

JOEL 2

Verse 1. The blowing of the trumpet is figurative and expressed in view of the calamity that was to come upon the country. (See Numbers 10: 1-10 for the significance of trumpets.) In actual practice the people of Israel were to blow the trumpet in alarm when they were to go into battle against another nation. It does not have that meaning in this case because the passage is a prediction of the invasion of the Babylonian army. That event was to occur by the Lord's decree, and the people of Israel were not to resist that attack. Instead, they were advised to submit peacefully to the king of Babylon and thereby lessen their suffering. (See Jeremiah 38: 17, 18.) The thought in the passage here is that the alarm should be to summon the people to a sense of their undone condition, so that they will make what restitution they can for their own personal benefit.

Verse 2. The gloomy picture that is painted is to be the result of the invasion of the foreign nation. *A great people and a strong* refers to the Babylonians who were to be brought against Jerusalem and the people of Israel.

Verse 3. *Garden of Eden before . . . behind a wilderness.* This is a picture of the sad changes that were destined to come into the land of Palestine after the inroads made by the Babylonian army. It was to be a complete overthrow of the great country of Israel, inflicted upon it as a punishment for the evil conduct of the inhabitants in taking up with the idolatrous ways of the heathen.

Verse 4. *Appearance of horses* is literal, for the army of Babylon used that noble animal in its triumphant march through the country.

Verse 5. The horses were used to carry riders in battle array, and they were likewise used to draw the chariots of war which are mentioned in this verse.

Verse 6. *Faces be pained* will be on account of the dreadful appearance of the military forces of the Babylonian Empire. It was one of the most formidable armies ever sent against the Israelites, and well might their faces be drawn in alarm at the approach of such a foe.

Verse 7. *Not break their ranks* denotes the orderly conduct of the soldiers of the king of Bablyon. *Shall climb the wall* refers to the ability of the soldiers to mount over the walls that were erected as a barrier against an attacking foe. These barricades were to be no effective hindrance to the success of the invading army.

Verse 8. Sometimes the soldiers of an army became confused and attacked each other, and at other times they would interfere with each other's position in the battle formation; the Babylonians were not to do this. And even when they came in contact with a sword it would not injure them seriously, because the Lord will be using them as His agents to chastise the people of Israel.

Verse 9. The prevalence and success of the Babylonians is meant here.

Verse 10. This is a figurative description of the depression that will settle down upon Jerusalem and the inhabitants of Judah when the army of Nebuchadnezzar takes up the siege. The king of Israel and his leading men will be debased, which is likened to the dimming of the sun and other heavenly bodies.

Verse 11. The army of Babylon is called the Lord's because He will use it to carry out the purposes against the unfaithful people of Israel. *He is strong that executeth his word.* Since the king of Babylon will be executing the decree of the Lord, He will make that king strong enough to accomplish the task set before him. Without the Lord's support the Babylonian army could never have succeeded as it did; for later, when it was God's will that the same nation should be overthrown, it was accomplished by the Persians who were said to be "inferior to thee" (Daniel 2: 39).

Verse 12. In view of the coming disaster, the people of Israel were exhorted to repent and manifest a proper attitude toward God. We are again reminded of an apparent disagreement in the declarations of the Lord as to the fate of his people. At one time they are exhorted to repent and seek the favor of the Lord, and at another they are told that nothing could be done to prevent the downfall of the kingdom and the captivity of its people. The reader should see the long note on this subject in the comments for 2 Kings 22: 17, volume 2 of this COMMENTARY.

Verse 13. *Rend your heart and not your garments.* It was a customary action in times of great distress or anxiety for a person to grasp his garment and tear it. This performance was acceptable to God when it was done with sincerity of heart. But since it was purely a physical or mechanical movement, a man could perform it as successfully while his heart was corrupt, as he could when he was pure in heart. Hence the exhortation of the words italicized, which means to correct the heart before going through the outward motion of rending the garment.

Verse 14. This verse is explained at verse 12 and the note cited there.

Verse 15. This verse is virtually the same as verse 1.

Verse 16. For comments on this verse, see those on chapter 1: 14, also the note cited at verse 12 of the present chapter.

Verse 17. The outstanding corruption of the nation of Israel was idolatry. In Ezekiel 8: 16 the sun worshipers are shown as standing "between the porch and the altar," and thus were showing disrespect for the true God. Now the prophet Joel bids them go to that place to lament over the situation that their iniquity had created. And instead of serving a false god, they were to appeal to the true God on behalf of the people whom their corrupt leadership had betrayed. Of course we understand this to be a prophetic picture of the state of mind that would be experienced after they got down in the land of captivity. This is described in strong terms in Psalms 137 where it is prophecy, and in Ezekiel 37: 11 where it is history.

Verse 18. From this verse through 27 the passage is a prediction of the return from Babylonian captivity. The sending of Israel into a foreign country was not from an outburst of ill feeling for His people, but because their own good as well as the honor of the holy name of God demanded the chastisement. That is why it is said that He will be jealous for the land, because the Babylonians took too much personal satisfaction out of the distress of the people whom they had brought under their domination.

Verse 19. The Lord was to make these provisions for his people by returning them from the captivity so they could reap the products of the home land. It was a great reproach upon the nation of Israel to be held captive in a heathen land, but that was to be reversed and never again be repeated.

Verse 20. The *northern army* was the Babylonian army that had taken the people of Israel into captivity. At the time the captivity was to be ended, the Babylonian army would be in their own country. But it had come down from the north in order to take its inhabitants into captivity; and reversing the condition of bondage would be equivalent to removing the northern army from the land. And in making such a forced retreat toward his own country, the Babylonian king would be heading toward the desert of Arabia, and his back would be toward the *utmost sea* which means the Mediterranean.

Verse 21. Such inanimate things as *land* cannot literally rejoice, yet the language is directly addressed to it. In that respect it is like the passage in Ezekiel 36: 6-15. The thought is to be transferred to the people who are to inhabit and enjoy the land, and who will be able to rejoice because of the benefits that the Lord promises to bestow upon it.

Verse 22. The *beasts of the field* are animate creatures, yet they cannot intelligently respond to the Lord's promise of blessings upon the fields. However, they can enjoy those blessings and thrive upon them, which would enable them to yield benefits for the enjoyment of their owners.

Verse 23. The foregoing comments are verified by the first sentence of this verse; it is the *children of Zion* who are actually to rejoice. And the reasoning is made still clearer by the rest of the verse, for it specifies the favors that were promised to be shed upon the land that would enable it to produce the things necessary for man's enjoyment. *Moderately* is an unusual word as it is used in this place, and it is derived from an original that Strong defines as "righteous." The simple meaning is that God was to bestow the right seasons upon the land so that it could produce the crops for its citizens.

Verse 24. *Floors* refers to the places where the grain was beaten out of the husk and the chaff separated from the kernel by the wind. The *fats* means the vats or large tubs into which grapes were placed so that the juice could be pressed out.

Verse 25. I have commented at length on the subject of this verse, in chapter 1: 4, which the reader should see now before going further in the study of this passage. With those comments in mind, he may think of this verse as a part of the prediction of the return from the Babylonian captivity. We know that when that event occurred, the effects of former misfortunes (whether literal armies of locusts or that of the Babylonians), were to be reversed by the returning productiveness of the land.

Verse 26. This is more along the

line of the blessings promised to come to the people after being brought back to their own land. *My people shall never be ashamed* applies only to the idea of a national and bodily removal into a foreign country; it was never to happen again.

Verse 27. *Shall know . . . Lord your God, and none else.* This is very significant, for the main iniquity of Israel was their worship of false gods. But the captivity was destined to cure them permanently of that spiritual disease as predicted here. The historical quotation that shows the fulfillment of this prediction is given at Isaiah 1: 25 in volume 3 of this COMMENTARY.

Verse 28. This verse begins a noted prophecy which includes the rest of the chapter. It was quoted by the apostle Peter as recorded in Acts 2: 17-21, where he replies to the false statements of the Jews in his audience. *Afterward* is a somewhat indefinite term as to time, merely meaning "at some time later." Peter makes it more definite by saying "in the last days," meaning the last days of the Jewish Dispensation. It is not uncommon for an Old Testament prophet to pass immediately from some good event concerning fleshly Israel to one pertaining to spiritual Israel. So in the present case, Joel goes from the return from captivity to the starting of the church that was to embrace all nations in spiritual Israel. The meaning of *all flesh* is that the spirit of God was to bring blessings upon all, whether they were Jew or Gentile. These blessings would need to be introduced into the world in a miraculous manner, and it was to be accomplished by the gifts of the Holy Spirit, using various ranks of society for instruments, hence the mention of *sons* and *daughters*, *old* and *young* men upon whom the outpouring was to come.

Verse 29. *Servants* and *handmaids* are named to show that the blessings of the Gospel will be for all classes of mankind, whether high or low, rich or poor.

Verse 30. *Blood, fire,* etc., is figurative and refers to the disturbances that were to occur in close connection (as to time) with the outpouring of the Spirit.

Verse 31. This verse is still figurative but is more specific than the preceding one. It was fulfilled when Jesus was on the cross and the sun was prevented from showing its light for three hours (Matthew 27: 45). This was only 50 days before the giving of the Holy Spirit upon the apostles, which would give to the language here the meaning as if it said the event would occur "just before" the day of the Lord. *Terrible* is from the Hebrew word YARE, one of whose meanings is "to be reverenced"; and certainly it can truly be said of the day when the Lord gave to the world the kingdom that was to "stand for ever."

Verse 32. *Shall be delivered* is expressed by "shall be saved" in Acts 2: 21, which shows that the two expressions mean the same. To *call on the name of the Lord* means to look to Him for the means of salvation. (See Acts 22: 16; Romans 10: 13.) *Mount Zion* and *Jerusalem* are named together because the former was a special spot in the latter city. *Deliverance* means the same as "be saved" in Acts 2: 21. *Remnant* is from SARIYD, which Strong defines "a survivor." It is said with reference to the Jews who were to be still serving God at the time the Spirit was to be given. It is true that the benefits of the Gospel were for all nations, but the Jews were given the first opportunity of receiving them. (See Acts 13: 46; Romans 1: 16; 2: 10.)

JOEL 3

Verse 1. The prophet drops back to fleshly Israel and again refers to the return from captivity. *Judah and Jerusalem* are named because the former was the 2-tribe kingdom that had Jerusalem for its capital, and it was the part of the Jewish nation that went last into the captivity.

Verse 2. *Valley of Jehoshaphat* is a figure of speech intended to mean the judgment of God upon the nations that had oppressed His people. Moffatt renders the term *valley of Jehoshaphat* by "Judgment Valley," and that agrees with the figurative sense of the term attributed to it above.

Verse 3. This verse pertains to the disrespect that the heathen nations had imposed on the people of God. They treated them as if they were mere items of personal property which could be handled solely for their value in a business transaction.

Verse 4. *Tyre* and *Zidon* were among the lesser cities that had mistreated the people of Israel. *Will ye render me a recompense* is a way of saying that the wicked cities could never fully repay the Lord for the injustices they had heaped upon His people. *If ye recompense me* means that even if these cities thought they could make things right by some temporal offer, it would not meet the just demands of the case. Were they to attempt any such offer their worthless articles would be rejected.

Verse 5. It is bad enough to take from another his personal possessions unlawfully, but it is much worse when it is done with the intention of making an evil use of them. These heathen cities had stolen the precious metals out of the land of Israel and used them in their idolatrous worship.

Verse 6. Almost all countries dealt in slaves in ancient times. These cities had kidnapped the young people of Jerusalem and sold them for service to the Greeks who were located near the coast of the Mediterranean Sea.

Verse 7. All of God's people who had been enslaved were promised their freedom. *Return your recompense* denotes some kind of judgment that would be sent upon these wicked cities for their mistreatment of the Lord's people.

Verse 8. Again we see that slavery was a traffic in those times, and these wicked cities are threatened with being "paid with their own coin" by having their children sold as slaves. The Sabeans were a people living a great distance south of Asia, hence the prediction means to warn these cities that when their own children were taken from them, they would be sold and transported far away.

Verse 9. The preceding chapter followed a prediction of the return of fleshly Israel from captivity, by one of the introduction of the Gospel. The present chapter does about the same thing, for the verse of this paragraph begins a highly figurative prophecy of the Gospel Era, and it is the subject through verse 18. *Prepare* is rendered "sanctify" in the margin, and Strong's lexicon agrees with it. The thought is that a holy war was to be proclaimed, not one to be waged with literal steel weapons.

Verse 10. This verse might seem to disagree with the foregoing comments, but it will be seen that it is a figurative description of the conflict. Men who had been interested only in temporal pursuits such as agriculture or carnal warfare, were to turn their energies into another direction. *Let the weak say I am strong*. This is the very thing that Paul tells Christians to be as we read in Ephesians 6: 10. Under the Gospel administration, those who might be regarded as weaklings in temporal activities, may be able to feel strong by the spiritual help from the Lord.

Verse 11. *All ye heathen* is an invitation for all nations to come and partake of the blessings offered by the Lord of heaven and earth. *Cause thy mighty one* is rendered "the Lord shall bring down" in the margin, which agrees with the thought in the general context of the passage.

Verse 12. *Valley of Jehoshaphat* is explained at verse 2. The *heathen* or nations in general were to be brought under the rule of the Lord, put forth through the Gospel that is intended for both Jew and Gentile.

Verse 13. A *sickle* and *wine press* are instruments used to gather and make use of the products of the land. When used figuratively it denotes that an important ingathering is going to take place, and in the present case it means the harvest of souls gathered by the reapers for the Gospel system. These souls were to be rescued from a life of wickedness which was great, and that can be reversed only by divine truth.

Verse 14. *Valley of decision* is virtually the same as "Jehoshaphat" in verse 2. Sinners of all nations were to be called upon to submit to the decision or judgment of God against all doers of unrighteousness.

Verse 15. This appearance among the heavenly bodies identifies the whole passage as a prediction of the church (chapter 2: 31 and Acts 2: 20).

Verse 16. A roaring voice usually impresses us with being something fierce or savage; but it also means a voice that is strong and reassuring. Such was to be the kind of voice the Lord would utter from *Jerusalem*. This place is a contrast with that from which the Jewish law was given which was Mt. Sinai. Zion was a particular spot in Jerusalem that was the seat of the government and where David had his headquarters. *Heavens and earth shake* refers to the general shake-up among the nations that was to be caused by the introduction of the Gospel. This shaking was to cease and leave behind it a *kingdom which cannot be moved* (Hebrews 12: 28), and it was to be the hope of the people of God.

Verse 17. *Mountain* in symbolic language means a government, and in the present passage it means the government of Christ. *No strangers pass through* means literally that the nation would not be bodily taken over by a foreign army as it was done by Babylon. Spiritually it denotes that no stranger (one of the outside world) would enter this kingdom until he renounced his past relationship and became a fellow citizen (Ephesians 2: 19).

Verse 18. All of these figures of speech refer to the spiritual blessings to be given through the kingdom of Christ. They were to be as water in a thirsty land, and their fountain will reach even to the valley of *Shittim*. Funk and Wagnalls Standard Bible Dictionary says the following of this place: "Some dry, thirsty valley where acacias (a desert plant) were known to flourish is meant." The point is that the fountain of the water of life will be so full that it will flow and reach even to the regions formerly very dry.

Verse 19. The passage resumes briefly the subject of ancient Israel and the countries that mistreated them. These persecuting groups were destined to feel the weight of God's wrath for their mistreatment of His people.

Verse 20. *Judah* has the meaning of spiritual Israel, and it is a repetition of the prediction that the new kingdom was to "stand for ever" (Daniel 2: 44).

Verse 21. *Cleanse their blood* means the cure of idolatry if applied to fleshly Israel, and to the remission of sins when applied to spiritual Israel.

AMOS 1

Verse 1. Amos was not a prophet "professionally" (chapter 7: 14); that is, he was not devoting his life among the group of men classed as prophets, but was a shepherd by occupation. But the Lord can call upon a man from any walk of life to receive instruction and directions to whatever work is needed. For instance, the Lord called Moses from this very same occupation to take upon him the great work that was to engage him all the rest of his life (Exodus 3: 1, 2). Likewise, Amos was called upon to receive a prophetic message and write it down to become a part of the Bible. *Israel* and *Judah* mean the 10-tribe and 2-tribe kingdoms which were in power when Amos was called. The time of his call is specifically indicated by naming the kings who were reigning over the Jews, and the date is made still more definite by its relation to an earthquake that is recorded in history. I shall give the reader the information of this very unusual circumstance: "While Uzziah was in this state [condition of prosperity and power], and making preparations for futurity, he was corrupted in his mind by pride, and became insolent, and this on account of that abundance which he had of things that will soon perish, and despised that power which is of eternal duration (which consisted in piety toward God, and in the observation of his laws); accordingly, when a remarkable day was come, and a general festival was to be celebrated, he put on the holy garment, and went into the temple to offer incense to God upon the golden altar, which he was prohibited to do by Azariah the high priest. In the meantime, a great earthquake shook the ground, and a rent was made in the temple, and the bright rays of the sun shone through it, and fell upon the king's face, insomuch that the leprosy seized upon him immediately; and before the city, at a place called Erpge, half the mountain broke off from the rest of the west, and rolled itself four furloughs, and stood still at the east mountain, till the roads, as well as the king's gardens, were spoiled by the obstruction." — Josephus, Antiquities, Book 9, Chapter 10, Section 4. This was not the first and only time where God expressed his attitude toward a situation by some interference with the established order of things in creation. He caused the sun to stand still for Joshua (Joshua 10: 13), and the shadow to go backward for Isaiah (2 Kings 20: 11). The difference in the cases being that the two mentioned last were to show His approval of what was being done, while the one of our verse was to demonstrate His disapproval. It is all in keeping with the thought in Hebrews 1: 1.

Verse 2. See the comments on Joel 3: 16 for the various meanings of "roar." In the present case it signifies the intensity of the Lord's feelings against the wrongs of the heathen nations, as well as those of some of His own people. Jerusalem is named as the place from which the voice of the Lord will sound, because that was the capital of his kingdom on earth. *Carmel shall wither* implies that it would be a remarkable event for such a place to fail. I shall quote what Funk and Wagnalls Standard Bible Dictionary says: "It [Carmel] was also famed in literary composition for natural beauty. Together with Sharon, Lebanon, and Bashan it is one of the points of Palestine which especially show God's favor to Israel in bestowing such a country upon it. Its devastation is, therefore, a sign of the decided displeasure of Jehovah."

Verse 3. The prophet now takes up the Lord's denunciations against certain cities and nations. *Damascus* was the capital of Syria that lay just north of Palestine. *Threshed Gilead* is a figurative description of the cruel treatment that Damascus accorded that district. *For three transgressions, and for four.* This form of speech is used a number of times, and means that the ones accused had not been guilty just once or even twice, but they had done so three or four times; had been guilty repeatedly.

Verse 4. Hazael and Ben-hadad were father and son who reigned successively over Syria (2 Kings 13: 24). God threatens to destroy the buildings of these men because of the "three or four" transgressions.

Verse 5. A *bar* is used to defend a house or other place against an unfriendly intruder. To break the bar of Damascus would therefore mean to overcome the defence of the city and expose it to an enemy. *Him that holdeth the scepter* means the king, and he was to be cut off from the *house of Eden.* Smith's Bible Dictionary renders this phrase "Beth-Eden," and says it means "house of pleasure," and that it was probably a country residence of the kings of Damascus. The *captivity unto Kir* was fulfilled and the account of it is in 2 Kings 16: 9.

Verse 6. *Gaza* was an important town of the Philistines, and 2 Chronicles 28: 18 records an instance of the greediness of those people for conquest. *Carried captive the whole captivity* means that the Philistines were not satisfied with taking some of the people, but wished to remove the entire population and sell them as slaves to the Edomites.

Verse 7. The Philistines were punished for their cruelty, and 2 Kings 18: 8 gives an account of one instance of it.

Verse 8. All of the towns named were in the land of the Philistines, and were to share in the chastisement that God threatened to bring against that land.

Verse 9. *Tyrus* (or Tyre) was the principal city of the Phoenicians, a country lying along the east coast of the Mediterranean Sea. The complaint against this city was that it had taken some of God's people and turned them over to the Edomites who had long been bitter foes of Israel. *Brotherly covenant* means that fraternal understanding that should exist between nations located near each other. This friendship had been indicated previously in the dealing with David and Solomon (2 Samuel 5: 11).

Verse 10. *Devour the palaces* means to destroy the houses of the kings of Tyre.

Verse 11. The Edomites were always bitter enemies of Israel. They were descended from Esau and seemed to have harbored a resentment for the people of Israel who were descendants of Esau's twin brother Jacob. *Did pursue his brother with the sword* had been predicted in Genesis 27: 40, yet God was always jealous of his own people and would not tolerate any improper motive that any nation showed against them.

Verse 12. *Teman* and *Bozrah* were cities of the Edomites, and they were destined to feel the wrath of God for their injustices against Israel.

Verse 13. The Ammonites were descendants of Lot (Genesis 19: 38), and sometimes were given favorable regard by the Lord because of their relation to Israel, but He always condemned even his own children when they did wrong. These Ammonites were so greedy for territory that they committed the brutal acts in order to destroy the population of the territory they wished to seize.

Verse 14. Smith's Bible Dictionary says that Rabbah was the chief city of the Ammonites, hence the most valuable of their buildings would be there. But the city was threatened with invasion from an enemy army that would *devour* (destroy) those houses.

Verse 15. To go into captivity merely means to be taken captive by the attacking army and be taken from his seat of authority.

AMOS 2

Verse 1. The Moabites had the same origin as the Ammonites (Genesis 19: 37). The historians and commentaries offer various suggestions about this strange act of the king of Moab. It is questioned whether he actually burned the bones of the reigning king of Edom, or that he dug up the bones of the son who (had he lived) would have reigned over Edom. But the main point in the passage is not affected either way it may be understood. God would not endorse such an inhuman performance that could have been prompted only by the spirit of wicked vengeance.

Verse 2. *Kirioth* was an important city of the Moabites and it was destined to be destroyed by fire from an attacking army. The success of the invader was to be accompanied with shouts and the instruments commonly used in warfare.

Verse 3. *Judge* and *princes* means any of the leading men of the nation. In all military operations it is regarded as of special importance to remove the most outstanding men of the city or nation attacked.

Verse 4. While the Lord was giving these threatening messages through the prophet, He did not overlook his own people in their misconduct. To *despise the law* means to belittle it and hence treat it as if it had very little or no important purpose with them. *Their lies* refers to the false predictions of peace that the unfaithful prophets were issuing to the nation. The effect of these false messages was to cause them to err in following in the steps of their unfaithful ancestors.

Verse 5. This verse was literally fulfilled as recorded in 2 Kings 25: 9.

Verse 6. Judah was named in verse 4, therefore we should understand *Israel* to be the 10-tribe kingdom. This agrees with chapter 1: 1 that states that Amos "saw" some things concerning Israel. Both the kingdoms of the Jews were yet in power when he began his writing. *Sold the righteous for silver, poor for a pair of shoes.* No proper money value can be placed upon a human being, but to sell one for such a paltry price denotes a most contemptible estimate of him.

Verse 7. All the terms of any passage should be interpreted in view of the general thought of the whole writing in the connection. We know the prophet is writing about the mistreatment the leaders of Israel were imposing upon the poor and otherwise dependent common people. They had very little regard for even the humble customs and religious practices of their brethren. It was a custom in ancient times to put dust upon the head in times of grief and anxiety, or at such occasions when devout servants of the Lord wished to emphasize their feeling of reverence for God. These wicked leaders were so bitter against the common poor people that they panted or selfishly sought to cast this dust of devotion from the heads and dash it to the ground. They were also very loose in their conduct of the intimate affairs of life. All the laws of decency forbade a man and his son being intimate with the same woman, but these corrupt men did not stop short of that kind of iniquity.

Verse 8. The law of Moses permitted a man to take a garment as security for a financial obligation, but he was not allowed to keep it overnight (Exodus 22: 26; Deuteronomy 24: 12). But these evil men made personal use of garments that had been taken temporarily, and intensified their guilt by lounging around in them in the temples of idolatrous worship. *Condensed* is from ANASH, which Strong defines, "A primitive root; properly to urge; by implication to inflict a penalty, specifically to fine." The law authorized fines to be levied on certain conditions (Deuteronomy 22: 19), but it must not be done unjustly. These men abused their authority by fining the poor without cause, then spending that money for wine which they drank in the idolaters' house.

Verse 9. There was a distinct tribe of early inhabitants in Palestine that went by the name of Amorite. They were so outstanding in iniquity that the name came to be used sometimes as a designation for all the heathen. (See Genesis 15: 16.)

Verse 10. Ingratitude is a very bad principle and is condemned in both sacred and profane literature. The Lord had done so much for Israel that it made their evil conduct all the more to be condemned, and they are being reminded of the subject in a number of verses. The one event of rescuing them from the Egyptians after four centuries of bondage should have bound them to God in a firm spirit of unmixed devotion. And their release from that country put them in a situation that would have been distressing from the unsettled state of the wilderness, yet the Lord took care of them miraculously for the entire journey of 40 years, so that they could come into possession of the land being held by these Amorites.

Verse 11. After settling the people of Israel in the land promised to the fathers, the Lord honored them with national distinction and gave their children an honorable part in the conduct of public affairs. Prophets were given the important work of standing between God and the people in delivering inspired messages of instruction and consolation, and the Nazarites were permitted to form a special class of servants for God, with the provision that they would have distinctive favors from Him.

Verse 12. One of the conditions of a Nazarite's vow was that he abstain from the use of wine or any other part of the grape during the term of his vow (Numbers 6: 2-4). *Gave the Nazarites wine to drink.* Two wrongs never make one right, and no one is justified in doing evil just because some one places the temptation before him. But it is also true that if one furnishes the occasion that causes another to go wrong, he will be held accountable for that wrong (Romans 14: 15, 16; 1 Corinthians 8: 11, 12). There were devout persons in the congregation who took upon themselves the obligations of the Nazarite vow in order to obtain some special favor, and to satisfy their desire for a distinctive service to the Lord. And there are people in the world who are so selfish that they do not want anyone else to have some blessing that they do not have. They seem to be acting under the idea that says, "if I cannot have certain favors, I do not want others to have them either." These persons did not want to make the sacrifice required to obtain the blessings coming upon a Nazarite, hence they induced them to drink wine so they would not receive them either, having violated their vow. They also obstructed the work of the prophets because they did not like the warnings and exhortations to duty that were spoken by them.

Verse 13. We cannot think of God as being pressed in the sense of being burdened by a load that would feel heavy to Him. The marginal reading is, "I will press your place as a cart full of sheaves presseth," and also the American Standard Version words the passage in the same way. Such a rendering also is in keeping with the general thought, for the Lord is threatening to bear down upon these leaders of Israel so heavily that they will not be able to travel.

Verse 14. The reasoning in this verse justifies the conclusion expressed as to the proper rendering of the preceding one. Because of the pressure the Lord was to put on the shoulders of the unfaithful men of Israel, they would not be able to make any progress in traveling. Being unable to travel as satisfactorily as desired, they would not be able to *deliver them*selves from the condition that He had in mind to bring upon Israel, namely, the Assyrian captivity.

Verse 15. The *bow* and the *horse* were used in warfare, either offensive or defensive. Hence when the Assyrians make their invasion into the realm of Israel they will overcome them because of their insufficient ability either for fighting or fleeing.

Verse 16. *Naked* is defined by Strong as "Naked, either partially or totally." The idea is that they would strip themselves of part of their wearing articles so that they might be the more able to flee.

AMOS 3

Verse 1. The chief part of the nation to which this book is directed is the 10-tribe kingdom, but a part of it is so composed that it may be properly addressed to the *whole family of Israel.*

Verse 2. *You only have I known* means that God had not recognized or accepted any other family. It is forcefully expressed in Deuteronomy 7: 6 as follows: "The Lord thy God hath chosen thee to be a special people unto himself, above all people upon the face of the earth." This favor placed them under greater obligation to conduct themselves in a manner pleasing to Him. They did not do so, therefore it was divinely decreed to *punish you for all your iniquities.*

Verse 3. Two men might unexpectedly come together while each is out walking and that would not require any previous understanding, but they would not continue their walk together without it. *Together* is from YACHAD, which Strong defines, "Properly a unit, i. e. (adverbially) unitedly." This means not only that the two might happen to walk in the same general direction, but that they were doing so as a unit of action. The statement (in question form) is that the men will not do so except they be *agreed.* That word is the key to the whole passage. It is from YAAD and Strong's definition is, "A primitive root; to fix upon (by agreement or appointment); by implication to meet (at a stated time), to summon (to trial), to direct (in a certain quarter or position), to engage (for marriage)." Moffatt renders the word "have planned it." I have gone into much detail here because of the fundamental importance of the subject being considered. The principle is clearly set forth that in matters of right and wrong it is not enough that the parties be "all striving for the same place," but that they be a UNIT in their activities. Not only so, but that unity must have been agreed upon by the parties proposing to walk together. Since the actual case at hand is that of "walking with God," it is a foregone conclusion that He is the one to do all the planning, and that man is expected and should be glad to agree to the plan.

Verses 4-6. I have grouped these verses into one paragraph because they are all written for one purpose, and that may well be expressed by the phrase, "no effect without a cause." For instance, a lion does not roar if there is no prey; a bird cannot be entrapped unless there is a trap; a snare cannot be taken up if there is no snare to take; a trumpet would not be blown unless there was some danger to be announced. *Evil* is used in the sense of some chastisement, and its presence is proof that there is some cause for it in the mind of the Lord.

Verse 7. God will not cause any false alarm, and when He instructs the prophets to sound a warning, there is a cause for it.

Verse 8. In view of the foregoing logical conclusions, how foolish it would be were the people not to fear since the lion (God) has roared; and what neglect of duty it would be for the prophets not to utter the predictions of warning since the Lord has spoken of them through the channel of inspiration.

Verse 9. This and the next two verses are a prediction of the Assyrian siege. Ashdod was a city of the Philistines and Egypt was another of the heathen countries. In a figurative manner these foreign people were invited to come and witness what was going to happen to Samaria, the capital of the 10-tribe kingdom of the Jews. The *tumults* and *oppression* would be the natural result of a siege.

Verse 10. *They* refers to the people of the kingdom of Samaria. *Know not to do right* is said in the same sense as Isaiah 1:3; they knew not because they did not consider what the Lord had told them in his word. Instead of dealing justly with their brethren, they increased their own store of wealth by means of violence and robbery.

Verse 11. *An adversary even round about the land* is a direct prediction of the Assyrian siege, and the fulfillment is recorded in 2 Kings 17:5. *Spoiled* is from BAZAZ, which Strong defines, "A primitive root; to plunder." While the Assyrians were conducting the siege of Samaria, they entered the houses of the city and took possession of their valuables.

Verse 12. From this verse through the close of the chapter the passage is a prediction of the Assyrian captivity of Israel. If the shepherd could rescue only the legs and piece of an ear of his sheep from the mouth of the lion, it would be because the sheep was almost wholly devoured. The figure is used to indicate the "close call" that Israel was to make to being entirely destroyed. But the great Shepherd would not let his flock (the 10-tribe kingdom) be entirely ruined, and so He will *take out* a part of it even though at the time the members of the flock will be lounging on beds and couches. *Damascus* is from DEMESHEQ, which Strong defines, "Damask (as a fabric of Damascus)." The idea is that the people of Israel (especially the leaders in the capital city of Samaria) will be taking it easy, lolling their time away on beds and couches adorned with the luxurious fabrics of Damascus.

Verse 13. The Lord bids the prophet call upon the house of Jacob (from whom came the name Israel) to hear what the God of hosts has to say.

Verse 14. *Visit the transgressions* means to bring judgment upon them for their transgressions. Those sins consisted in their sacrifices to idol gods, and Bethel is named because one of the idol calves was erected there (1 Kings 12:29). *Horns of the altar shall be cut off* is a prediction of the destruction of idolatrous worship, which was to be accomplished by the captivity.

Verse 15. *Winter house and summer house.* The luxury-loving leaders had the two separate houses erected in such a manner and in such places as to give them comfort at the various seasons. *Houses of ivory* were a part of the extravagancies indulged in by the pleasure-mad princes of Israel. Smith's Bible Dictionary says the following about this subject: "The ivory house of Ahab, 1 Kings 22:39, was probably a palace, the walls of which were panelled with ivory, like the palace of Menelaus, described by Homer's Odyssey 4, 73. Beds inlaid or veneered with ivory were in use by the Hebrews."

AMOS 4

Verse 1. According to Moffatt's translation these kine were the wives of the nation's men who practiced oppression and injustice against the poor for their own selfishness. Their *masters* were their husbands who were bidden to join with them in providing luxuries of wine at the expense of the poor.

Verse 2. There is virtually no difference in the meaning of *hook* and *fishhook*. Each of them may mean a hook in the ordinary sense of the word, or it may refer to a thorn from a tree; again they may have specific reference to a metal ring that was originally made for the control of a vicious animal by running it through his nose. This is the origin of the expression "leading one around by the nose" when speaking of someone who humbly does what a domineering person demands. In view of the indefinite uses and meanings of the word, we should take our verse to denote that the evil characters of Israel were to be treated with the cruelty and humiliation they deserved.

Verse 3. *Go out at the breaches* refers to the protecting wall around the capital city that was to be pierced, and the inhabitants forced to leave the city by way of these *breaches* or gaps. *Cast them into the palace* is explained in the margin to mean that the inhabitants of the palace will be forced to discard the things belonging to it.

Verse 4. *Bethel* was one of the cities where an idol god was erected. (1 Kings 12: 29) by the first king of Israel, and *Gilgal* was the place where the first king of Judah committed his serious offence (1 Samuel 10: 8; 13: 8-10). Both parts of the people of the Jewish nation had been guilty of much transgression. *Come to Bethel*, etc., sounds as if the Lord was bidding the people to continue in their sin. We know that is not the case, but it has the force of saying, "You have gone so far in your corrupt practices that you will not change them now until you are given the deserved chastisement."

Verse 5. The last part of the preceding verse and beginning of this describes some of the rites authorized by the law of Moses. The prophet is condemning these people indirectly, which raises the question of why it is so if the law provided for such services. The explanation is in the first part of the preceding verse, where the practice of idolatry is included with the things set out by the law. Such a mixture was always displeasing to God and he rejected their entire religious life because of such an impure combination. The reader should see the long note offered with the comments on Isaiah 1: 10 in volume 3 of this COMMENTARY. *For this liketh you* is an accusation that the people not only practiced the things named, but they did it because they liked to do so; their heart was in it.

Verse 6. *Have given you* is present and past tense in form, but it is one of the styles of prophetic speech. However, there was also such a condition referred to as a matter of the past, for God had before punished his people with some of these temporal shortages. *Cleanness of teeth* is a figurative designation for the results of famine. The phrase is followed immediately with the words *want of bread*, which would be a cause for the cleanness of teeth; no food to cause them to be unclean.

Verse 7. This verse gives some more of the punishment that God imposed on the land because of the iniquity of the people. He is the creator of the rain and the seasons, and therefore would have the ability to control them as He sees fit.

Verse 8. The scarcity of drinking water is indicated by the fact that the citizens of several cities would consume all the supply in one of the more favored ones, and even then their thirst was not satisfied. What made the condition more deplorable was the fact that none of these chastisements brought the rebellious people to repentance.

Verse 9. The reader may still be wondering why the Lord brought all these misfortunes upon the land of Israel. It was just what he had warned them of in more than one place. It may help some to quote a statement written by Moses as follows: "But it shall come to pass, if thou wilt not hearken unto the voice of the Lord thy God, to observe to do all his commandments and his statutes which I command thee this day; that all these curses shall come upon thee, and overtake thee. Cursed shalt thou be in the city, and cursed shalt thou be in the field. Cursed shall be thy basket and thy store" (Deuteronomy 28: 15-17). With all these threatenings recorded in the Sacred Text, the people of Israel should have been induced to observe the divine laws. They were not, for the passage complains, *yet have ye not returned unto me, saith the Lord.*

Verse 10. *Pestilence of Egypt* means a pestilence like that sent upon the land of Egypt. (See Exodus 9: 3, 8; 12; 29.) The losses cited in this verse would be suffered when a foreign force came against the land, which God would cause to happen for a punishment upon them. The *stink of your camps* would be a natural result of the death of so many living creatures, both human and brute.

Verse 11. They were not destroyed literally in the same manner as was Sodom, but their destruction was just as sure. *Firebrand plucked out of the burning* denotes the near complete ruin that the Lord suffered to come upon His unfaithful people. But God still loved the nation and saw to it that the enemy could not put the nation entirely out of existence as a distinct people.

Verse 12. *Prepare to meet thy God.* Many impassioned speeches have been made on this statement by public speakers, exhorting men to get ready for "the great judgment day." The exhortations are important in themselves, but they are a farfetched application of this passage. The last words, *O Israel*, are generally omitted in the exhortations, and hence the correct meaning of the statement is lost. The admonition is addressed to the 10-tribe kingdom of Israel, and it is said in view of the things about to happen to the nation. A key word to the verse is *thus*, referring the reader back to verses 2, 3, where the Lord is predicting the siege and captivity of the kingdom. Verses 4-11 recounts the various instances of their misbehaviour in the past, and of the temporal misfortunes that God brought upon the people for their sins. But those chastisements had failed to bring them to repentance, therefore God determined to *do unto them* according to the prediction in verses 2 and 3. In view of that great event to come upon the nation, it is exhorted to *prepare* (get ready) for the time. The word *meet* is from QIRAB, which Strong defines, "An encountering." It is called an encountering with God because He is the one bringing the Assyrians against them.

Verse 13. As proof that God is able to bring this great encounter upon the nation, mention is made of the other vast works that He has already done in creation.

AMOS 5

Verse 1. The severe denunciations which the Lord expresses against the people from time to time should not be interpreted as an indication of bitterness. He is grieved at the wrongs of the nation that has always been favored with divine assistance, and these strong declarations are prompted by the spirit of sorrow, hence are said to be in the form of a lamentation.

Verse 2. The word *virgin* is often applied to God's people because the first definition of the original is, "to separate." Israel had been separated from the other nations of the world to be the Lord's own special people (Deuteronomy 7: 6; 14: 2), hence the term *virgin* is an appropriate one. *Shall no more rise* denotes that Israel had sunk so low as a nation that it would not be able to rise above the fate of the siege and captivity threatened.

Verse 3. The nation was destined to be greatly reduced by the exile as indicated by the contrasting terms *thousand* and *hundred*. It is a prediction of the remnant that was salvaged from the captivity, and the fulfillment is in Ezra 2: 1, 64.

Verse 4. *Seek ye me and ye shall live* presents the same apparent contradiction that has been mentioned several times. The explanation lies in the distinction between the nation as a whole, and certain individuals in it. See the long note on the subject, offered with comments on 2 Kings 22: 17, volume 2 of this COMMENTARY.

Verse 5. The significance of *Bethel* is in the fact that it was one of the places where the first king of the 10-tribe kingdom of Israel erected an idol calf, and the nation had practiced idolatry ever since. *Gilgal* is the place where the first king of Judah committed his first great sin after entering upon the throne (1 Samuel 10: 8; 13: 8-14). Beer-sheba was once a stronghold of idolatry and hence not a proper place to receive a favorable impression on the subject of service to God.

Verse 6. *Seek the Lord and ye shall live* is commented on in verse 4.

Verse 7. *Wormwood* was a very bitter substance and is used much as a figurative likeness of any unpleasant experience. The leaders in Israel were selfish and regulated the lives of others in view of their own personal interests. Instead of dealing justly with those who looked to them for advice and decisions in times of difficulty, they deprived them of their rights and thus turned their case into bitterness.

Verse 8. *Seven stars* is the same as Pleiades in Job 9: 9, the cluster of stars that is popularly called "the seven sisters," and *Orion* is defined by Strong, "Any notable constellation." Instead of being interested in the gods of the heathen, Israel is exhorted to seek the Maker of these heavenly bodies. He is the one who can rule day and night and turn one into the other at will; who can control the mighty waters of the sea and use them in whatsoever manner He pleases.

Verse 9. *Strengtheneth the spoiled* means to support the man who has been overcome by a stronger force, and enable him to turn against his oppressor successfully.

Verse 10. This verse describes a kind of character that has existed ever since there has been man on the earth. It is not always manifested in the same way, but the principle is the same. The reason a man is hated who rebukes sin is that the person rebuked realizes he is guilty and does not want to be reminded of it. The rebuke does not always have to be done directly or in words. It may be done by the righteous life of one in contrast with the wicked life of the other, the good life being a silent rebuke to the other. It is thus we read about the first family where Cain and Abel had their experience. There is nothing said about Abel's rebuking Cain verbally, but his righteous life was a stinging rebuke of Cain's evil one. So John says that Cain slew Abel "because his own works were evil, and his brother's righteous (1 John 3: 12)." The people of Israel did not like to be told of their sins, so they insisted that the teachers give them messages that suited them (Jeremiah 5: 31; Isaiah 30: 10). Since the people wanted the teachers to give this false instruction, they catered to them and hence brought upon them the wrath of God. Another bad thing that resulted from the practice of false teaching was the chance it gave them of making improper rules of conduct, and that also opened the way for them to impose upon the poor.

Verse 11. We should remember that the rebuking running through most of these verses is addressed chiefly to the leaders of the nation who took advantage of their standing to oppress the poor. They forced them to furnish unjust portions of their crops so that they could live in luxury. They had also indulged themselves with costly houses and had planted vineyards to suit their own extravagant desires. But God now warns them that it will all be taken from them and their luxurious provisions will be in vain.

Verse 12. Everything that is done is open before the eyes of the Lord. The leaders took advantage of their position to oppress the poor so that they could enlarge their own possessions. Not only so, but if some one of the poor had the misfortune of being treated with fraud in a deal, it would not avail him anything to appeal to these leaders who were the rulers, for they could be bribed by the fraudulent dealers to render a verdict against the victim.

Verse 13. A prudent man is one who does not "speak out of turn," and in the present case it means not to speak any word of protest against what the Lord is threatening to do. The times are so evil that all wise men should endorse the Lord's judgments.

Verse 14. This verse takes the same comments and note as verse 4.

Verse 15. There is no uncertainty in the promises of God. *It may be* has the force of saying "it will be," on condition that the people will hate evil and love the good. *Remnant of Joseph.* The 10-tribe kingdom, to which most of these messages are addressed, was also called "Ephraim," and since he was a son of Joseph, the name is used as a designation of the whole group, the *remnant* meaning those who survive the captivity.

Verse 16. When the people see the presence of the Assyrian forces, they will make the wailing here stated. They will even call for a public demonstration of regret over the sad condition of their country.

Verse 17. There were two outstanding occupations in Palestine, the production of sheep and the growing of vineyards. It would therefore be a special cause of regret to be deprived of their vineyards.

Verse 18. *Woe . . . desire the day of the Lord.* In times of distress men will often call upon the Lord, even though they have been disrespecting Him in the past. These inconsistent leaders will pretend that they would like for the Lord to "show his hand" when the clouds of trouble seem to be gathering. But that is just what He will be doing when those clouds begin to hover, and they will bring national darkness and not light.

Verse 19. The comparisons in this verse are similar to a familiar one, "jumping out of the frying pan into the fire," and the prophet is using them in connection with his statements in verse 18. When a man rebels against the Lord as these wicked leaders had done, it is inconsistent to expect Him to furnish relief; instead, He is the very one whose wrath will be felt if the guilty person turns in that direction.

Verse 20. This verse repeats the thought of the **preceding** ones.

Verse 21. Before taking up the comments of each verse, I request the reader to indicate, either in his Bible if he is marking it, or in whatever place he is making notes, that all of the verses from the present one through the end of the chapter, and through the first 6 verses of the next chapter, are to be regarded as one paragraph with one general subject. That has to do with one of the outstanding apparent contradictions in God's threatenings and predictions against His people. In more than one place they have seemed to be condemned for doing some of the very things that the Mosaic system required. We cannot believe that God would tell a man to do something, and then condemn him for doing it. When it seems to be so, there is an explanation in the premises and we should examine them for it. I have composed at length a note, based on the truths and facts of history, both sacred and profane, that fully clarifies this seeming difficulty, and the reader is urged to consult that note again with extreme care, before proceeding with the study of these comments. That note is offered in the comments on Isaiah 1: 10, volume 3 of this COMMENTARY. I shall now take up the comments on the verse of this paragraph, followed with the others in their order, explaining them in the light of the general subject of the suggested general paragraph. The note referred to will explain why God hated their feast days. In their solemn assemblies they used sweet incense under the law, and the only use that could be made of it would be to smell it. God refused to smell the odor of their incense for the same reason that he hated their feast days.

Verse 22. The sacrifices and offerings mentioned were required by the law of Moses, but God was rejecting them for the same reason mentioned above.

Verse 23. Instrumental music was not introduced by the law of Moses, but it was later instituted by David and the Lord sanctioned it by giving it His glory (2 Chronicles 29: 25; 5: 14). But although the Lord had blessed the use of the musical instruments with his glory, after the leaders became so corrupt, that service was rejected on the same ground as were the others mentioned above.

Verse 24. *Judgment* is from MISHPAT, which Strong defines, "Properly a verdict (favorable or unfavorable) pronounced judicially." Since the term is connected with *righteousness as a mighty stream*, we know the word means a favorable verdict. The leaders had imposed upon the poor and decided matters unjustly against them. This verse is an exhortation for them to reverse that practice and render decisions that are just.

Verse 25. God never asks a question for the sake of his own information, so this one is a reminder for the people of Israel, calling their attention to the practices that they followed all through the wilderness.

Verse 26. The Lord admits that Israel had performed the services stated in the preceding verse, but they were offset by their practices of idolatry. Moloch was one of the invisible gods of the heathen, and the Israelties took up the worship of that false deity. Chiun was an image that they made, a *star* or chief article they made in honor of the heathen god that they worshiped.

Verse 27. *Therefore* means that God concluded to punish his people because of these idolatrous practices which they thought they could add to the ordinances of the divine law. *Captivity beyond Damascus*. That city was the capital of ancient Syria and it was located just north of Palestine. But the Jewish nation was destined to go into captivity under both the Assyrian and Babylonian Empires, which were located far away in the territory of the Euphrates, and that was literally *beyond Damascus*. The two empires were in control in succession from one another, but they were virtually in the same part of the world, hence the Jewish people all came finally to be held in captivity in the same general location according to the various prophecies.

AMOS 6

Verse 1. *Woe* is pronounced just once in the present connection and it applies to all the leading men in Israel who are described in the first 6 verses of the chapter. It is from HOWY and Strong defines it with the single word "oh!" It has been rendered by ah, alas, ho, O, and woe in the A. V. It signifies that something very distressing is going to come upon those of whom it is spoken. *At ease* means to be feeling secure and contented, and unconcerned about the comfort of others. And that, too, even when the feeling of security might be at the expense of the poor and be causing them much distress. *Zion* is used figuratively to denote the people of Israel as a nation. Samaria was the capital of the 10-tribe kingdom, and that portion of the Jews trusted in the power of their headquarters to stand between them and all trouble. *Named chief of the nations*. These leaders of the Israelites had obtained a high standing even among the heathen nations because of their partaking with them in idolatrous practices. *House of Israel came*. These princes had so much power that the common people looked to them for leadership, notwithstanding the unjust treatment they had received concerning their own rights.

Verse 2. *Calneh, Hamath* and *Gath* were communities of the heathen which were once powerful. But what was their condition now as Amos was writing? It was one of humiliation brought about by the same people who were predicted to come against Israel. Since the people of the Lord were no stronger than the mentioned ones who were subdued, they should not loll around with a feeling of "security" as if nothing evil could come upon them.

Verse 3. The false teachers denied that the nation was in any danger, or at least for the time being. Such assurances of security misled the people because they believed their prophets. The result of it was to encourage further acts of injustice. This is along the same line as a statement of Solomon in Ecclesiastes 8: 11: "Because sentence against an evil work is not executed speedily, therefore the heart of the sons of men is fully set in them to do evil."

Verse 4. The simple meaning of this verse is that the princes and other leaders of the nation were living in the height of luxury. That fact alone would have been bad enough, but by picking out the choicest food only, they deprived the common people of their share of the good things that were intended for all of the citizens.

Verse 5. With all of the facts and truths before him that have been so clearly set forth, surely the reader is prepared to avoid a fundamental error that has been made in commenting on this verse. It is a common thing for certain teachers to use this verse in showing that God condemned instrumental music even in Old Testament times. In such teaching they miss entirely the point the prophet is making. The verse is but another item of the practice I have already explained, that of mixing some things that would have been endorsed previously, with their idolatrous and other evil things, thinking that God would accept the whole program.

Verse 6. In the preceding chapter we saw how these selfish leaders had sandwiched their evil doings with some of the original ordinances of the law, and the same thing is done in this. Verse 5 is the "filling" composed of instrumental music, something introduced and endorsed by David with the Lord's blessing. Then around that are the things that were prompted by their own evil desires. *Drink wine in bowls*. The last word is from MIZRAQ, which Strong defines, "A bowl (as if for sprinkling)," and the word has also been rendered by "basin." It indicates the extravagance and selfishness of these men. They were not satisfied with what a regular drinking cup would supply, but drank so much wine that it required these large vessels to serve them. The ointments were all precious and costly, but these men appropriated to their personal use the chief or choice ones. After his description of the general program of these leaders, the prophet states his concluding charge against them in the words, *but they are not grieved for the affliction of Joseph*. For some reason the name of Joseph is occasionally used to designate the nation as a whole, especially when the writer is dealing with the sorrows and injustices of its common people. This is doubtless because he was such an unusual example of patience and virtue even under the most trying circumstances. But the hardships of the poor did not mean anything to these leaders among the Israelites, for they persisted in gratifying their own selfish desires at the expense of their poor brethren.

Verse 7. When an army invades a city or territory, it is considered good strategy to capture its leading men first if possible (for example see 1 Kings 22: 31). That idea seems to have been followed in this case, for the men who were "out in front" in their selfish domination over the common people, were destined to be first to go when the enemy came against the land. That will put an end to their *banquets* and other indulgencies. The reader should again consult the long note in connection with the comments on Isaiah 1: 10, volume 3 of this COMMENTARY.

Verse 8. *Excellency* is from a Hebrew word that means arrogance or pride. *Jacob* is used as a designation for the nation as a whole, but especially the leading men who dominated the common people. These men exalted themselves in their pride of power, and did many evil things under the pretense of their position. It was all this that God said he abhorred, and caused Him to decree the complete destruction of their city.

Verse 9. The destruction threatened was to be so complete that if a house contained 10 men, they would all die and would need to be disposed of by someone outside the building who was supposed to be interested in their cases.

Verse 10. It was customary in ancient times for the nearest relative living to bury the dead (see Genesis 25: 9; 35: 29; Judges 16: 31), which is the reason that the uncle is mentioned here. *Burneth* is rendered "burial" in Moffatt's translation. I shall quote from Funk and Wagnalls Standard Bible Dictionary on the subject of "Mode of Burial." "Cremation was not practiced in Israel; the usage was rather to bury the dead, while cremation, of criminals for example (Leviticus 20: 14; 21: 9; Joshua 7: 25), appears as a disgrace added to the penalty of death." The burning of incense in connection with burial ceremonials sometimes might be mistaken for the burning of the bones of the dead (1 Samuel 31: 12; 2 Chronicles 16: 14; Jeremiah 34: 5). *By the sides of the house* means someone near the house where those 10 men were just found dead. *Is there yet any with thee;* is there one that I have overlooked? *Hold thy tongue,* etc. The destruction decreed for the place was to be so complete that it would be of no use at that late hour to make any appeal to the Lord.

Verse 11. This verse explains why the remark was made in the close of the preceding one. The Lord had commanded that just such a complete destruction was to come upon the people and houses of Israel as is described.

Verse 12. The two questions in the beginning of this verse should be answered in the negative. The wickedness of the nation had turned good *judgment* into gall (bitterness), and *righteousness* had been supplanted by *hemlock* (poison). Therefore the Lord determined to strip the land of its fertility, and render it useless to work their beasts.

Verse 13. Strong says the figurative meaning of the original for *horn* is "power." These exacting leaders of Israel were boasting that they had power by reason of their own merit. The truth of the matter was that they beat down all who asked for their own rights, and usurped a position of almost absolute power.

Verse 14. *Hemath* was a place at the northern extremity of Palestine, and *the wilderness* refers to the valley at the south near the Dead Sea. The prediction is that a nation was to come against Israel and subdue the whole territory between the points.

AMOS 7

Verse 1. We see Amos in the role of an intercessor for Irsael, and by his plea to God causes the divine wrath to be turned back. The subject is presented figuratively and begins with the idea of insects being created to destroy the young vegetation. After the main crop is harvested, called the *king's mowings,* a tender growth of grass comes up in the same field, here called the *latter growth.* This is what the insects destroyed according to the figurative prediction.

Verse 2. After this destruction by the insects, Amos made his plea on behalf of Jacob (Israel), suggesting that the nation was too small to withstand such a loss.

Verse 3. *Lord repented* means the Lord changed his mind and removed the insects.

Verse 4. But the people were not truly penitent and did not make the proper reformation even though the Lord had relieved their distress. Then He brought a more severe chastisement upon the land. This time it was in the form of fire that dried up the *great deep* which means the water supply in the veins of the earth.

Verse 5. Again the prophet pleads on behalf of the people.

Verse 6. The Lord was again entreated to relent and withdraw His wrath, to give the nation a chance to reform or change the way of life from bad to good.

Verse 7. The repeated acts of mercy that God showed toward Israel were not appreciated, but they always slipped back into their former way of sin, if they even ceased it at all. The patience of the Lord finally was exhausted and He determined to use more severe measures against the unfaithful nation. It is indicated by the use of the plumbline which will be explained with the comments on the next verse.

Verse 8. *Plumbline* is from ANAK, which Strong defines, "To be narrow,"

In symbolic language it indicates something strict and exacting, and was an appropriate article for the decree that God was about to make. He had been lenient with the unfaithful people until they no longer deserved mercy as a nation. *Not pass by* means that the Lord would not overlook their iniquity again but would bring severe punishment on them.

Verse 9. We have seen the names of Joseph and Jacob used to signify the nation of Israel, now it is Isaac that is used in the same way. In all of the cases it is because of the important relation the men sustained to the race. The predictions and rebuke of the book frequently apply with equal force to all of the Jewish nation, but the writings of Amos generally are made with reference to the 10-tribe kingdom. That is why this verse mentions *Jeroboam*, he being the man who led the revolt resulting in the establishment of that kingdom (1 Kings 12).

Verse 10. This is not the Jeroboam mentioned in the preceding verse, but the one named in chapter 1: 1, and who is often referred to as Jereboam II. Bethel was one of the places where the first Jeroboam erected altars for idolatrous worship (1 Kings 12: 29), and of course such a place would call for the services of a priest; hence the statement that Amaziah was the *priest of Bethel*. That will also explain why he objected to the work of Amos. In all ages, men have opposed those who offered them unpleasant truth, especially if it condemned their conduct. The predictions by Amos that the nation was to be overthrown were made in view of the corruptions of which the services of Amaziah were an important part. He realized that truth and hence was aroused against the prophet and sent the message to the king of Israel. He doubtless thought he was acting the part of a loyal citizen in giving this information to his master. *Not able to bear* means they could not endure or be reconciled to the predictions of the prophet.

Verse 11. There is no evidence that Amos predicted the death of Jeroboam in the manner accused by Amaziah. 2 Kings 14: 26-29 shows the death of that king not to have been caused by the sword. But the other statement of Amaziah was true, for Amos was authorized to predict the exile of the kingdom of Israel. It is a common trick of evil men to mix some truth with their error so as to deceive their hearers and cause them to accept the entire story.

Verse 12. A seer is the same as a prophet; it means literally one who *sees* into the future. Amaziah thought he could get rid of the unpleasant predictions of Amos by having him move into some other locality. He suggested that he go and deliver his messages in the land of Judah, which was the 2-tribe kingdom. Such a suggestion had the appearance of being fair and that he recognized him as a prophet of God who was qualified to contact His people wherever they might be.

Verse 13. Amaziah spoke on behalf of Jeroboam who was the king and whose *chapel* (religious headquarters) was at Bethel, one of the seats of idolatry. He seems to think that by the removal of the one who was giving the unpleasant predictions, he could be rid of the fulfillment of them. It was as foolish as it would be to discharge a doctor who discovered a dreadful disease in one's body.

Verse 14. The speech of Amaziah implied that he considered Amos as one of the regular prophets who had no other occupation. In that case it would not matter very much where he worked, just so he did the work of a prophet. He would then not be idle from his life's work were he to go into the land of Judah and continue his regular occupation. But Amos enlightened him on the subject and told him that he was not that kind of prophet, but was a shepherd by occupation. He had been called as a special servant of the Lord for the mission of delivering the predictions intended for the 10-tribe kingdom, and only incidentally to include some things pertaining to Judah. *Prophet's son* means one of the young men who were being trained by the regular prophets, not a son in the usual sense of that word.

Verse 15. While Amos was engaged about his work with the flock, the Lord appeared to him by inspiration and told him to go and prophesy unto *Israel*, which here means the 10-tribe kingdom, not Judah as Amaziah wanted him to do.

Verse 16. Amos wants Amaziah to know that he is not speaking his own ideas, but that it is the *word of the Lord*. House of Isaac has the same meaning as house of Israel since he was one of the important men in the blood line from Abraham.

Verse 17. Amos was not intimidated by the criticism of Amaziah but gave him the final paragraph of his predictions. Not only was the nation to suffer the captivity but his own family was to be disgraced. *Divided by line* means the land would be measured off into lots and taken possession of by the enemy.

AMOS 8

Verse 1. *Summer fruit* is used figuratively to indicate the end of the season. The original is a word that means the product of any kind that has come to full growth, and in its application to the predictions of the nation it means that the season is over.

Verse 2. In answer to the Lord's question Amos acknowledged the vision of the basket of fruit. The meaning of it was then stated, that *the end is come upon my people of Israel*. The "season" that was ended was the period of God's leniency toward the unfaithful nation. *Not pass by* means the Lord would not overlook their iniquity any more, but would bring an enemy force against them.

Verse 3. *Songs of the temple* refers to the religious performances that the people of Israel had so inconsistently carried out, even while their minds were polluted with the belief in false gods. But instead of those songs, the people were to be made to howl by the attack of the foes. *Cast forth with silence* denotes that these hypocritical songsters would be silenced by their death, caused by the might of a hostile army that the Lord would suffer to come against His people.

Verse 4. The main complaint all along has been against the head men of the nation, who imposed upon the poor and common people to advance their own interests. This is the meaning of the expression *swallow up the needy*.

Verse 5. The days of new moons were holy days with the Jews (1 Samuel 20: 24-27; 1 Chronicles 23: 31), and on such days they were not to work or transact any secular business. These covetous men could not dismiss from their minds the worldly subject in order to give "undivided attention" to their religious duties, but even while the holy day was being (outwardly) observed, they were thinking of the deals they intended to perform. Their worldly-minded interests were made worse by the unjust means they intended to take for profit. *Ephah small, shekel great*. They tampered with the scales by causing the balancing weights to show more than they actually contained, then cheated their customers in another way which was to increase the price unjustly.

Verse 6. *Poor for silver, needy for shoes*. See the comments on chapter 2: 6 for this subject. *Sell the refuse of wheat* means they sold the worthless part of their grain as if it had full value.

Verse 7. *Excellency* is also rendered by "pride" and "arrogance," so we may rightly conclude that it is used in an unfavorable sense. The Lord would not have something favorable as a basis for an oath, hence the sense of the verse is that God made an oath in view of the pride of Jacob, or the people of Israel. *Their works* refers to the unrighteous practices of the leaders in Israel, and the Lord was *never to forget* or never to overlook it. Because of such an oath it meant that something very serious was going to come upon the unfaithful nation.

Verse 8. The antecedent of *this* is the chastisement threatened in the preceding verse. Well might the land (its people) tremble at thought of the wrath of God that was prophesied to come upon it. *Floods* and waters are used figuratively in the Bible to signify some overwhelming condition, and the particular application in this case is to the national calamity to come by the agency of the Assyrians or Babylonians. The specific reason for connecting Egypt with the figure is that the original word for *flood* means any large body of water, and the Nile River in Egypt is such a body.

Verse 9. *Sun to go down at noon* is a figure of speech and indicates that the national sun (power) was to cease to shine prematurely. Had Israel been faithful to God the nation would have remained in power through the entire Jewish dispensation. Instead, that power was cut off many centuries before that age ceased. *Darken the earth in the clear day* has the same meaning as the preceding figure.

Verse 10. The thought running through this verse is that all conditions were to be reversed, changing from favorable to unfavorable. On occasions of feasts there was usually great enjoyment, but it was to be turned into mourning. Songs were expressions of cheer, but they were to be changed into those of lamentation. In their prosperity they wore gay clothing, but it was to be replaced with the coarse material called sacking. Smith's Bible Dictionary says that artificial baldness was a sign of mourning, and so it is predicted that the distress to come upon them would cause them to shave off the hair in their mourning. The comparison as to that for an only son is to indicate how profound will be the grief when the nation has been humiliated by invaders.

Verse 11. *Famine of . . . words of the Lord.* The people will have resisted the teaching of those who would have given them the truth (such as Amaziah against Amos, verses 12, 13) until God will cease to offer them such teachers.

Verse 12. They will realize when it is too late what they have done, and will seek frantically to find some of the true teachers. However, it will be in vain because of the famine just predicted in which no spiritual food will be available.

Verse 13. Virgins and young men are usually possessed of more reserve vitality than others, but the famine was to be so severe that even they would faint.

Verse 14. The reference to Samaria and Beer-sheba is because of the idolatry that was set up and practiced in those places. Dan was one of the 10 tribes that formed this kingdom, and it had trusted in this false religion started in Samaria.

AMOS 9

Verse 1. As a general comment on this and several verses following, it should be stated that *them* and kindred pronouns stand for the people of Israel who have been so unfaithful to God, and who were destined to be punished with exile into a foreign land. Idolatry was the predominating corruption of the nation, hence the *altar* spoken of pertained to that used in the idolatrous worship. The *lintel* and *door* were parts of the idols' temple and they were to be smitten by the prophet at the commandment of the Lord. *Posts may shake* signifies that the temple of idolatry was to be overthrown and its worshipers to be scattered. *That fleeth . . . not flee away* means that although the unfaithful idolators attempt to get away from the wrath of God they will not succeed. *That escapeth . . . not be delivered* denotes virtually the same as the preceding statement. Some may escape the immediate capture by the enemy but they will not succeed in the end, for they will be taken into the territory of the foreign foes.

Verse 2. The impossibility of escaping the wrath of God is the thought of this verse. *Hell* and *heaven* are used figuratively because they are opposite terms, and denote the complete presence of God no matter where a man might flee. David used the same figure in Psalms 139: 8 where he was considering the subject being discussed by Amos.

Verse 3. In seeking to escape the wrath of God it would be natural to hunt out places that were considered as a good place of seclusion. Carmel was thought of as such a spot because it was a high point and was situated at the top of a long range that was separated from the country in general. Nothing is actually hidden from the vision of the Lord, hence the phrase *hid from my sight* means to become invisible to the general view. Even though the victim of God's wrath might seek refuge in such an apparently secret place, the Lord would find some kind of means to take him. Ordinary serpents do not live in the bottom of the sea, hence the statement means that some agency would be called upon to carry out the vengeance of God upon the evil servant of Him who was so displeased at the corruption of the divine law.

Verse 4. Even after the Lord's people have been moved into the territory of a foreign land, the wrath of an offended God will not be satisfied, for the severity of their captors will reduce their numbers. *Evil* is not something wrong morally for God does not use such means to punish his people. The term refers to something in the nature of a chastisement that would cause great humiliation.

Verse 5. God of *hosts* means he is the God of armies and all other forces that could be used in proper causes. The *touch* of His hand when administered in wrath will result in the overthrow of that land or other object that might be touched; will cause it to *melt. Flood of Egypt* is explained at chapter 8: 8.

Verse 6. The leading term in the lexicon definition of *stories* is, "superiority of station," and the statement of the verse means that God is the high and exalted One. *Troop* is a strained rendering of the original which simply means to bind together as a man would a group of articles that he wanted to handle. The entire first sentence of this verse means that God is as exalted as the highest heaven, and also is strong enough to take possession of all things on the earth. As a specific example of this power, mention is made of the *waters of the sea* which have been made subject to Him more than once (Exodus 14: 16-31; Jonah 1: 4, 15; Matthew 8: 26, 27).

Verse 7. The children of Israel are named in a group with a number of heathen nations. That is for the purpose of showing the vast power of the Almighty, and to indicate the dependence of the whole world upon the independent God.

Verse 8. The comparisons and figures of speech are dropped and the literal prediction of the fate of the nation of Israel is stated. *Saving*, etc., refers to the remnant that was to be left after the captivity was ended (Ezra 2: 64).

Verse 9. This verse has the same subject matter as the preceding one, only it is expressed in figurative language. The heathen nations are the sieve and God was going to use that means of separating many of the people of Israel. In literal actions a sieve retains the good grain, while the dwarfed and otherwise objectionable particles will drop through and fall to the ground. The prediction of the verse is that none of the *grain* among the people of Israel would fall.

Verse 10. The context will justify the insertion of a word between this and the preceding verse, making the present one read: But, *all the sinners of my people*, etc. The particular *sinners* referred to were the false prophets who belittled the idea that any danger was threatening the nation, and who were all the time preaching "peace, peace; when there is no peace" (Jeremiah 6: 14).

Verse 11. *That day* denotes the time when the nation of Israel will have reecived its chastisement at the hands of the heathen. God promised to restore the service that had been interrupted by the exile. *Tabernacles of David* is a phrase used in the sense of the regime that started with that great patriarch, the first ruler of Judah.

Verse 12. Israel had previously been troubled by these peoples, but the promise is that it will be favored by the Lord and the downtrodden people will rejoice.

Verse 13. The prosperity that was to return to Israel was to be prompt and great. The strong expressions of this verse are rather figurative, yet they are a true picture of the speed with which the blessings of God would come to the land.

Verse 14. *Bring again the captivity* means that the captivity will be reversed, and the Lord's people were to be brought out of it. They also were to be restored to their own land to produce and enjoy the crops of the soil.

Verse 15. *No more be pulled up* applies to them as a nation, for Israel was never moved bodily out of Palestine after the return from captivity. The nation was finally subjugated by another government and the power of the same was taken from it, but it took place while living in its original territory.

OBADIAH

Verse 1. The book of Obadiah is the shortest one in the Old Testament and is one of the minor prophets. There are two main subjects treated in the book; the denunciations against Edom and the return of Israel from the captivity. According to verse 11 the book is to be dated about the time of the destruction of Jerusalem by Nebuchadnezzar. *Vision of Obadiah* means that he was shown a picture of the doom of Edom. *Rumour* means an authentic message from the Lord, not merely some floating speculation as the word usually denotes. An *ambassador* is a herald or messenger who is sent out from an authoritative source to deliver a decree. Such a messenger had been sent out among the nations concerning the land of Edom and Obadiah had heard about it. The gist of the *rumour* or message was that the nations were to rise up and be arrayed against the doomed people.

Verse 2. *Among the heathen* might imply that Edom was not one of the heathen as he is said to be *among* them. However, the word is also rendered "nation" in many places and it is so used in this one. The original word means any group or nation of people regardless of what religion they profess. This verse means that the Edomites were doomed by the Lord to become one of the smaller nations and to be looked down upon.

Verse 3. I shall make a quotation from an authentic work of reference concerning Edom: "Edom is emphatically a land of mountains. On the west, along the side of Arabah, is a line of low limestone hills. Back of these rise higher, igneous ROCKS [emphasis mine, E. M. Z.], surmounted by variegated sandstone, of peculiar color,

2,000 feet high. The eastern side of the mountain slopes gently away into the Arabian Desert. But, though rough, the land is rich, and the terraced hillsides have in all ages been bright with vegetation, and its people have been prosperous . . . Mount Seir was first settled by the Horites, or Horim, like the inhabitants of Palestine a people of unknown origin. During the later patriarchal age it was conquered and possessed by Esau, the brother of Jacob, and ever after occupied by his descendants, the Edomites . . . They joined the Chaldeans under Nebuchadnezzar in the destruction of Jerusalem, for which the later prophecies and Psalms gave them bitter denunciations . . . The Edomites, or Idumeans, south of Palestine, were conquered by the Maccabean princes and incorporated with the Jews, B. C. 130, and the Nabathean kingdom was annexed to the Roman Empire, A. D. 105."—Rand-McNally Bible Atlas, page 45. This quotation will explain the phrase *clefts of the rock* in this verse, and it also will show the fulfillment of predictions in the other verses about the downfall of the Edomites. The reader will therefore do well to take notice of its contents, for it will be referred to again.

Verse 4. The pride and self-exaltation of Edom is the subject of this verse. The Lord has no objection to a nation's desire to be strong and self-supporting, but He will not tolerate pride in either nations or individuals.

Verse 5. Moffatt's translation renders the words in parenthesis by, "What a downfall is yours!" The thought is that the ruin predicted to be coming on Edom will be so great and complete that even the Lord is caused to make an exclamation. It will be even more complete than the work of thieves in looting a place. They would at least have stopped when they had what they wanted for themselves, and hence there would have been *some* [margin says "gleaning."] grapes left. But when the Lord gets through with the chastisement of Edom there will be nothing left.

Verse 6. This verse is another prediction in the form of an exclamation, and corresponds with the thought of the preceding paragraph.

Verse 7. *Men of thy confederacy* has reference to the allies of Edom. When the test comes they will turn against him and drive him *to the border*, which means that Edom will be driven to the last extremity. It frequently happens that the professed friends of a man will reverse themselves and become his enemies. The last two words of the verse are rendered "of it" in the margin, and both Moffatt and the American Revised version agree with it. The idea is that Edom's professed friends were weaving a web around him and he did not have the good sense to realize it.

Verse 8. *That day* refers to the time when the overthrow of Edom was to take place. The nation as a whole was to be ruined, but also its wise men were to be shown to be unable to preserve the country by their leadership.

Verse 9. *Teman* was a district located by or adjoining the land of Edom if not a part of it. *Mount of Esau* is equivalent to "Mount Seir" (Genesis 14:6). The *mighty men* means the leaders upon whom the inhabitants of the country of Edom relied for guidance. Their apparent wisdom will be exposed and they will be left overwhelmed with dismay.

Verse 10. The relation of *brother* to *Jacob* was a bodily one (Genesis 25:25, 26), and their descendants are referred to in history and prophecy as if they were meant personally. The two groups were always regarded as being in a state of hostility against each other; especially the Edomites against Israel.

Verse 11. The various works of reference differ as to whether this verse is history or prophecy. I do not believe it makes any difference as far as its truthfulness is concerned, for Obadiah was writing by inspiration (verse 1) of God, and with Him all is an absolute "now" as to its surety. The truth of the matter is that Edom took pleasure from the misfortunes of his brother Jacob, and also participated to some extent in connection with those misfortunes. An important principle is expressed in this verse by the first and last groups of words: *In the day that thou stoodest on* the other side . . . *even thou wast as one of them*. Even had Edom taken no physical part in the misfortunes of Israel, the fact of his standing on the side opposite him, *the other side*, would have included him among the enemies of his brother; this principle is taught by Jesus in Matthew 6:24; 12:30. There is no "neutral" ground in questions of right and wrong, but every man is either for or against that which is right.

Verse 12. The date referred to in this verse is evidently the time recorded in 2 Kings 25, for then it was that the kingdom of Judah was destroyed. *Became a stranger* means the inhabitants of Judah were carried away into a strange land (Babylonia). *Looked* is from RAAH and among the many words with which it is rendered in the King James version are approve, enjoy, gaze, regard, respect and think. These translations together with the preceding verse, suggest that Edom *looked* with delight upon the miseries of his brother. That alone would have him the object of God's wrath, but we shall see that he did not stop with the pleasure of his eyes at gazing at the misfortune of Israel.

Verse 13. *Not entered . . . day of calamity.* It is proper to show a friendly spirit for one in distress, but his home should not be invaded at such a time by morbid curiosity seekers. The context indicates that Edom entered and *looked on* the affliction of Israel with eyes of satisfaction. But he did not stop at that; instead, he took advantage of the distressed state of affairs to seize upon some of the valuables present.

Verse 14. Edom further opposed Israel by blocking the road by which he might have escaped from the invader. And there were some who were remaining in the home land, whom Edom helped in some way to be taken over by the enemy forces.

Verse 15. *All the heathen* implies that other people besides the Edomites were to feel the wrath of God. That was true in more than one sense, for in overthrowing that one nation, others were given an indication and warning of what was to be the fate of all kingdoms of the world that followed practices displeasing to God.

Verse 16. Drinking a cup figuratively means to partake of some experiences, either pleasant or unpleasant (Psalms 23:5; 116:13; Jeremiah 25:15; Matthew 20:23; 26:39). Edom was destined to drink the cup of God's wrath because of his assaults upon His *holy mountain*, and also the other nations were to feel the wrath of the Lord.

Verse 17. This verse introduces the second of the main subjects mentioned with the comments on verse 1, the return of the people of Israel from captivity. Other verses following will continue to predict some of the returning fortunes of the nation, including its retaking of certain lost territory.

Verse 18. *Fire* and *flame* are used figuratively of the glowing recovery of the people of God from their depressed state, and of the downfall of their old enemy, the *house of Esau* which means the Edomites. This nation was to be utterly overthrown as a separate ruling power as already predicted in this book.

Verse 19. The mention of *the south, mount of Esau, plain, the Philistines*, etc., is to indicate the various settlements that were to be observed when the Jews repossessed the land of Palestine after the return from exile.

Verse 20. This verse continues the subject started in the preceding one.

Verse 21. It is not a rare thing for the prophets to pass from a prediction of favor to come to fleshly Israel, and prophesy some good fortune to come upon spiritual Israel. (See Isaiah 1:29 with 2:1-4; 4:2, 4; 40:1-4; Ezekiel 21:24-27.) This is very understandable, for even the New Testament system of religion was introduced into the world through the Jewish nation, and they were the first to accept the Gospel. So this verse is a prediction of the kingdom that was to be the Lord's and "stand for ever."

JONAH 1

Verse 1. The book of Jonah is composed almost wholly of history. The only prophecy it contains is that of the threatened destruction of Nineveh (chapter 3:4), which was to be only forty days in the future. But he is called a prophet in 2 Kings 14:25 and Matthew 12:39, hence we know that his work entitled him to that classification. We have no details of his work outside of this book except what is briefly mentioned in the first reference above and the allusion to his preaching by Jesus. And the Old Testament reference gives us the information as to the general date of his life and work, for he gave instructions to Jeroboam II who reigned in the 10-tribe kingdom of Israel about 800 B. C., which was a century before the Assyrian captivity of Israel. This verse says the word of the Lord came to Jonah, so we see that his work was by inspiration of God as far as his writing and teaching was concerned.

Verse 2. Nineveh was the capital of the Assyrian Empire, the power that God intended to use in the chastisement of the kingdom of Israel at a future date. This capital city was located on the east bank of the Tigris River. It had become so wicked that the Lord wished to have it improved before using its forces in His campaign against the people of Israel. Jonah was therefore given the command to go and *cry against it*. The details of that "cry" are not stated here but they are given more attention later.

Verse 3. This is the only place in the Bible that says anything about the attempt of Jonah to flee from his duty, hence we see him as a faithful scribe since he makes no effort to "whitewash" his action, either in this particular verse or in his explanation to the mariners. Tarshish was a city on the coast of Spain and hence was about as far away in the opposite direction from Nineveh as Jonah could think of. He was merely showing a common weakness and foolishness of mankind in thinking he could escape *from the presence of the Lord*. He certainly believed that God is everywhere and that it is impossible to get out of His sight, but in his panicky frame of mind he gave way to the impulse of evading an unpleasant task. Joppa was a coast town of Palestine and a shipping port. Jonah learned of a boat that was scheduled for Tarshish and bought passage on the same.

Verse 4. Jonah was to learn "the hard way" that it is impossible to evade the hand of God by fleeing. Yet the Lord did not wish to injure him since He expected to use him after the present lesson had been taught and appreciated. Neither did God intend that any damage should come to the owners of the ship as we shall see. So He sent forth a wind that threatened to rend the vessel by the violence of the waves.

Verse 5. These mariners were idolaters and showed their faith in their gods by praying to them. But they did not depend wholly on them for help but co-operated by lightening the load for the ship, an example that could well be observed by Christians who seem to think that "God will take care of us" whether we do anything or not. The *sides of the ship* means the recesses or nooks of the vessel that were more or less secluded and suitable for repose. Jonah was sound asleep in one of these and unaware of the storm that was raging outside.

Verse 6. Up to now the mariners knew nothing of Jonah's connection with the situation, so the *shipmaster* or captain was surprised that he could be so unconcerned about it. *Sleeper* is from RADAM which Strong defines, "A primitive root; to stun, i.e. stupefy (with sleep or death)." Nothing indicates that they had been at sea very long, and there was no apparent reason why anyone would be needing sleep hence the captain thought that Jonah was stunned by some cause unkown to him. So he aroused the "sleeper" and told him to join in the general petition to their respective gods for help in their time of distress. The name of *God* is capitalized which is the work of the translator or editor of the A. V., but it should not be so for this heathen captain knew nothing of the God of Jonah. All he meant was that he was to do as all the rest had been doing, call upon his god for help, and perhaps the god would come to their aid.

Verse 7. Nothing is said in the text about whether Jonah made any response to the request of the captain or not, but the indication is that he did not. He knew that the very God to whom he would have "called" was the One from whom he was fleeing, and that it would be inconsistent for him to make such a call. The mariners were still ignorant of the true situation, but they concluded that some special reason must exist for the storm since it came up so unexpectedly and out of season. In their extremity they felt that some person present must be responsible for the disturbance. Had they been the people of Israel they might have expressed it by saying there was "sin in the camp" as it is usually said in the case of Achan in Joshua 7. Being heathen they did not have that view of the case, yet they were religiously inclined and thought that something was wrong. The casting of lots would ordinarily be only a chance decision, but Proverbs 16:33 shows that the Lord sometimes takes a hand in it and "disposes" the decision according to His will. Such will be done in the present case because God really wants these innocent mariners to know on whose account the distressful situation has come upon them. Accordingly, when they cast their lots the "lucky number" was drawn by Jonah because God directed the operation.

Verse 8. The captain was surprised when he found Jonah in profound sleep while a violent storm was raging, and now that feeling was doubtless increased by the outcome of the lot. It prompted him to make the inquiries stated in this verse, for Jonah must have belonged to a mysterious clan to have had such a significant part to play in the affair that was overwhelming the whole crew with fear.

Verse 9. Jonah gave the captain and other mariners a brief but clear explanation of the case. All of the men on board professed to be religious and to be worshipers of some god, but Jonah claimed devotion to the God who had made the very sea that was threatening to destroy their ship with all its passengers and men. He told them further (as we may learn from the next verse) that he was fleeing from his own God when he went on board their ship.

Verse 10. *Then were the men exceedingly afraid.* This was the most logical result that could have come after the explanation of Jonah, for it harmonized with all the facts as they had seen them. Only the creator of the sea could throw it into the condition it then manifested as he willed, and hence such a being should be feared.

Verse 11. It was logical and fair for them to appeal to Jonah for instructions about the proper course to pursue. He would be the only person to know the spirit of the deity from whom he was fleeing, and what it would take to appease him.

Verse 12. Jonah was still the beloved servant of God, and He did not intend to let him be destroyed. God could have calmed the sea as completely just by speaking to it as Jesus did (Matthew 8: 23-27), but there was another object to be gained for future generations. I believe the Lord intended to use this occasion to establish a type of the great event when Jesus was to spend three days and three nights in the bowels of the earth (Matthew 12: 38-40). for He plainly declares in that passage that the event of Jonah was to be a sign. Hence, by casting the would-be escaper overboard the Lord would accomplish two purposes at the same time. The truth that it was *for his sake* the great tempest had come upon them did not make it necessary for him to be cast over as shown above, therefore the conclusion is unavoidable that God inspired him to give those instructions to the alarmed boatmen.

Verse 13. The men did not wish to use such severe means to save themselves as Jonah directed, but tried to avoid it by returning the boat to the shore. Had they been acquainted with the character of the Lord, they would have known better than try to overcome His work by their physical strength. However, the fact of their attempt to avoid so drastic a treatment of Jonah showed they were humane in their disposition. They could not have known what was to be the actual outcome, but had every reason to think that it would mean the death of Jonah for them to do as he said. No wonder, then, that they *rowed hard* to bring the vessel to land.

Verse 14. All that these men knew of the Lord was what Jonah had just told them, for they were worshipers of false gods. However, the prayers they uttered came from the heart and all they said was the truth. In casting Jonah overboard they would be doing exactly what they were told to do by him, and now they were praying to whatever being it was who gave him the inspiration for such an order.

Verse 15. In casting Jonah into the sea the mariners unconsciously carried out the plan of the Lord. (See the comments on this point at verse 12.)

Verse 16. It was a part of the religious practice of all devoted men, whether worshipers of the true God or of the false, to offer sacrifices and make vows of reverence for the god to be honored. No doubt these men were sincerely sorry for having done what they believed would cause the death of Jonah. It was a very fitting time for deep humility and seriousness of mind. We have no information whether they ever afterward heard of the rescue of their supposed victim.

Verse 17. I almost hesitated at giving any serious attention to the foolishms that carping infidels make on this verse. There is either a Supreme Being or there is not; and if there is, He would be able to do what he willed with the things of creation. If God is able to take a camel through the eye of a needle (Matthew 19: 26), He could confine a man in the body of a minnow if he so desired. But for the sake of some who might think the criticism is unanswerable, I will state that I have personally seen the skeleton of a fish whose throat was large enough to permit a very big man to creep through easily. And it should be remembered that what I saw was the dead bone, while the fish in the case of Jonah was alive and the framework of the throat would be capable of expanding to a much larger opening than the dead bony structure that was on exhibition. This is all I care to say on this phase of the subject at this time. But we should observe that Jonah was in the fish *three days and three nights.*

JONAH 2

Verse 1. Nothing that is right is impossible with God (Matthew 19: 26), therefore He could preserve Jonah alive and conscious in the bowels of the fish. Being a worshiper of the true God, it was not strange that he would engage in prayer in his unusual surroundings. Aside from being cut off from the normal kind and amount of air, he was unharmed by the act of the fish, and of course the Lord could take care of that situation by His great power.

Verse 2. *And said, I cried.* We know that Jonah did not do any writing while in the body of the fish, but wrote his account of the affair afterward as he was composing his book. He was being preserved miraculously but that did not prevent him from feeling the unpleasantness of the surroundings. That experience together with the remembrance of his error in trying to flee from the Lord, placed him in a frame of mind to offer a humble petition to God. The word *hell* is from SHEOL and Strong's definition of it is, "Hades or the world of the dead (as if a subterranean retreat) including its accessories and inmates." In the King James version the word is rendered grave 31 times, hell 31 and pit 3; it is the only word for "hell" in the Old Testament. It is evident that Jonah used the word only in the sense of its being a "subterranean retreat," since he was alive and in good health. The happy fact is stated that the Lord heard the prayer and took a favorable attitude toward Jonah (though we do not have all of his prayer).

Verse 3. Jonah had told the men to cast him into the sea, but here he says the Lord did it. This is a reason for the remarks on chapter 1: 12, showing that Jonah gave his instructions to the men on the authority of God.

Verse 4. Nothing is ever invisible to the eyes of God, so *out of thy sight* refers to Jonah's side of the matter. He was hidden from all the scenes of the earth, yet he had faith in the existence of God and now turned to Him in his distress.

Verse 5. The original word for *soul* generally means any living and breathing creature. Jonah means he felt that his entire being was overwhelmed by the water. He not only was a prisoner on the inside of the fish, but that was a water creature and it was in its natural element which was not a suitable place for man. *Weeds* is from CUWPH which Strong defines, "A reed, especially the papyrus." It is the word for "flags" in Exodus 2: 3, and hence refers to the reedy plants growing in the water. Doubtless when Jonah was cast overboard he first felt these reeds about him as he sank beneath the water and the impression was still with him for a time.

Verse 6. Jonah is describing the way he felt when he was cast out of the boat, not that it is an inspired literal report of what actually happened. *Bottoms of the mountains.* The hilly land of the vicinity would extend on down into the water and Jonah felt as if he had sunk down to the bases of them. *Earth . . . bars . . . for ever.* Again Jonah is describing the way it seemed to him as he was shut off from the entire world. This conclusion is justified by his words immediately following that the Lord brought him out of the corruption that threatened his life.

Verse 7. This verse suggests an old and true saying, "Man's extremity is God's opportunity." When the conditions here described overcame Jonah, he was induced to look to God for help. Then he *prayed unto the Lord his God out of the fish's belly.*

Verse 8. The prayer of Jonah not only contained his appeal for help, but also was a recognition of some of the great principles which God has ever held out before mankind. *Lying vanities* evidently has reference to the devotion to idols which is constantly regarded as vain in the Bible. Whoever depends on such helpless objects are working against their own best interests.

Verse 9. The mention of *Sacrifice* and *vows* is a promise of continued devotion to God upon his deliverance from the helpless condition surrounding him; in other words, it is an indication of a truly penitent heart. Jonah is certain that if he is ever enabled to resume a life of religious services it will have to be through the help of God, for *Salvation is of the Lord.*

Verse 10. Strong says the original for *spake* is "used with great latitude." A fish is not an intelligent creature, but God could induce it to perform any act suitable to His will. *Dry* does not necessarily mean absolutely without moisture, but ground not covered or saturated with water on which a man could stand with sure footing. The fish could float out to the brink of the sea and spue Jonah from his mouth onto the place where the ground was not covered with water.

JONAH 3

Verse 1. Having "learned his lesson" and been restored to the land, Jonah was ready to receive renewed instructions from the Lord; accordingly the divine word came to him the second time. There is no mention in the text of the event just closed, and as far as the record is concerned the Lord delivered his command just as if nothing had happened to the prophet.

Verse 2. We are given the added detail that Jonah was to say whatever was stated to him when he arrived in the city of Nineveh. The report does not show any objections to his preaching hence we must conclude that the declaration Jonah made was what the Lord had bidden him to deliver.

Verse 3. This time Jonah went in the direction of his duty *according to the word of the Lord. Three days' journey* might have referred to the distance round the city or across it either, as far as the expression of the text goes. But the rule of consistency indicates that the latter is meant, for the same *days' journey* is used in the next verse in connection with Jonah's entry into the city and across it. As to what a day's journey is would depend upon the means of journeying that is being used at a given time. *Journey* is from MAHALAK which Strong defines, "A walk, i.e. a passage or a distance." It is the word for "walk" in Ezekiel 42: 4 where we know it was a place in which men traveled on foot. So the conclusion is that a man would walk across the city of Nineveh in three days at the ordinary speed of such a mode of travel.

Verse 4. Jonah waited until he got to the more thickly populated portion of the city before he began his preaching. The only thing he said according to the text was the announcement that the city would be destroyed in forty days. Verse 2 says he was to preach what the Lord told him and all the reports of the event indicate that he was faithful to his commission. Nothing said about why it was to be destroyed, and we know that no specific proviso such as repentance was stated by which the city could avoid destruction. We get this from the announcement of the king who had commanded his people to perform acts of penitence, and then expressed the hope that God would be thereby induced to change the decree of destruction. Had the condition of reformation been stated in connection with the threat made by Jonah, there would have been no occasion for the "wishful thinking" of the king.

Verse 5. Voluntary fasting and wearing of sackcloth was a custom in ancient times on occasions of grief or anxiety. The only reason this verse assigns for the acts of these people is that they *believed God*. This justifies us if we "read between the lines," for the preceding verse says nothing about God or of any reason why the city was to be overthrown; but some following verses report the acknowledgement of the *evil way* of the citizens. A mere prediction of some calamity to come upon a place would not have to mean that it was to be a punishment for sin, hence there was something said or done that informed these Ninevites what it was about.

Verse 6. This verse tells us that the foregoing actions of the people had been by the direction of the king. He also set the example of penitence by temporarily deposing himself and putting on the customary sackcloth and sitting in the ashes.

Verse 7. The king even went so far as to include their service beasts in the fasting. They were dumb creatures and could not be morally responsible for any wrong-doing, so why penalize them? It was not for that purpose, but as a further restriction upon the people. If the beasts were deprived of food it would render them unable for work, and hence the condition would actually be a sacrifice for the owners.

Verse 8. This verse is a direct confession that the people of Nineveh, *from the greatest of them even to the least of them* (including the king), were guilty of wrong-doing. Moreover, they were told what they had been doing that was wrong, else they could not know what "evil way" it was from which they were to turn.

Verse 9. See the comments on verse 4 for the explanation of this.

Verse 10. *God repented* means he

changed his mind or plan as at first threatened. However, even that was no change in His established principles of dealing with mankind. He has always given man the opportunity of repenting and "making his wrongs right," with the promise that if it was done, the punishment threatened would be remitted. The reader should see Jeremiah 18: 7-10 on this important subject.

JONAH 4

Verse 1. Anger is not necessarily a sin (Ephesians 4: 26) unless one lets his feeling lead him into doing something that is wrong. Jonah did not do or say anything that was sinful in his anger, but was vexed over the turn of affairs. He seemed to think that the Ninevites should have been punished since he had gone through so much inconvenience and humiliation on their account.

Verse 2. We do not know to whom Jonah addressed this *saying*, for it is not recorded elsewhere. It really means that he thought the Lord would be too merciful to bring such a severe correction upon the city when it came to the actual test. Perhaps we should not conclude that he was angry at any particular person, but was displeased in a general way with the whole situation.

Verse 3. This verse expresses the frantic wail of a man in despair. The whole situation is so disappointing and confusing to Jonah that he lacks the courage to face the future. However, he does not manifest any of the spirit of a man who "threatens suicide," for he is not that kind of man. When a man in his right mind takes his own life, he is no less a murderer than the one who slays another. But Jonah was so willing to be released from the worries of the case that he turned to the Lord for relief. Since God is the giver of all life, if He should see fit to relieve the prophet of the distress of living it would be right in his sight, hence his fervent prayer to the Lord to be separated from life in this world.

Verse 4. When the Lord asks a question it is never for the purpose of obtaining information for himself. This one means as if He said, "Do you think you have reason to be angry?" The statement implies that Jonah was not justified in giving way thus to his feelings, and the implication is that the Lord gave him to understand that his prayer would not be granted.

Verse 5. Having been denied his request, and being given to understand that the Lord was determined to go through with His plan, Jonah wondered what the fate of Nineveh would be now that it had exhibited the signs of penitence and God had reversed his threat. So he went outside the city and took a position under a temporary shelter from the sun, there to maintain a season of "watchful waiting."

Verse 6. *Gourd* is from QIYQAYOWN which Strong defines, "The gourd (as nauseous)." He also says it is derived from another Hebrew word that means "To vomit." I shall quote from Smith's Bible Dictionary on the subject. "The plant which is intended by this word, and which afforded shade to the prophet Jonah before Nineveh, is the *Ricinus communis*, or castor-oil plant, which, a native of Asia, is now naturalized in America, Africa and the south of Europe. This plant varies considerably in size, being in India a tree, but in England seldom attaining a greater height than three or four feet. The leaves are large and palmate [shaped like a palm leaf], with serrated [notched] lobes, and would form an excellent shelter for the sun-stricken prophet. The seeds contain the oil so well known under the name of 'castor oil,' which has for ages been in high repute as a medicine. It is now thought by many that the plant meant is a vine of the cucumber family, a genuine gourd, which is much used for shade in the East." I have quoted the entire paragraph which presents the two opinions as to the plant meant by the gourd, in order to give the reader "the benefit of the doubt." The marginal rendering in the common Bible favors the first of the two descriptions, likewise the definition of Strong which refers to the feeling of nausea or act of vomiting, which would agree with one effect of the castor bean. However, in either case the plant would furnish additional protection from the strong rays of the sun which could penetrate through the booth that Jonah was enabled to make for the moment. The double arrangement for shade would provide the advantage of insulation between the booth and the plant, somewhat like a tent under a tree. The situation accomplished the Lord's purpose, for it is stated that Jonah was exceeding glad of [because of] the gourd.

Verse 7. Physical experience is often

the most effective way of impressing a lesson on the mind of a man. It is the same principle as corporal punishment inflicted on the body of a child. He may not be capable of seeing the lesson with his reason alone, hence it is necessary to reach his mind through his body. It is the same in the case of an adult, except that a form of physical punishment may be used of such a character that the victim can understand as well as feel the force of the chastisement. In the present case God started the punishment by using a worm that destroyed the gourd.

Verse 8. After destroying the gourd the Lord left conditions as they had been by the normal heat of the sun. Next some additional distress was to be inflicted upon him by another miracle upon the elements. *Vehement* is from CHARIYSHIY and Strong defines it, "In the sense of silence; quiet, i. e. sultry (as noun feminine, the sirocco or hot east wind)." The idea is that it was not a rushing current of air, for that motion itself would have somewhat counteracted the desired effect. Instead, it was a quiet but intensely hot and sultry wave of air that was terribly depressing. Jonah's request to die was from a different cause described in verse 3, but his attitude toward death should have the same comments as are offered in that verse.

Verse 9. The Lord's question calls for the same comments as the ones on verse 4. Jonah will be shown the reasons for which he had no valid cause for wishing death just because the gourd had withered and died.

Verse 10. The comparative unimportance of the gourd when considered with the importance of a city of people is the thought in this verse. *Pity on the gourd* means that Jonah would have spared it because of its usefulness to him. And all this in spite of the truth that he had put no time or effort into it to bring it into existence, while God was the maker of the city and all things therein. If the personal interest of Jonah in the plant would justify his regret at seeing it destroyed, he should have praised God for sparing a city that was destined in the near future to co-operate with Him in one of the great events concerning Israel.

Verse 11. The gourd was small even from the standpoint of material volume, while the city contained 120,000 human beings. *Cannot discern between their right hand and their left hand* is a figure of speech used to describe the ignorance of the people as to what is right and wrong. This does not contradict the comments on chapter 3: 8 as to the people's knowledge of right and wrong, for it is shown there that they knew it only after the Lord had informed them through the prophet.

MICAH 1

Verse 1. *The word of the Lord that came to Micah* shows that he was inspired to write his book. Moreover, in Jeremiah 26: 17, 18 we have his writing referred to favorably by some elders of the land and there is no indication that his predictions were called in question by anyone. His predictions pertained to the 10-tribe and the 2-tribe kingdom of the Jews, for Samaria was the capital of the first and Jerusalem that of the second. The date of his writing is identified with the reigns of some of the kings of the 2-tribe kingdom. A glance at the history of those times will show that Micah began writing about 40 years before the captivity of the 10-tribe kingdom and some 150 years before that of the 2-tribe kingdom. Since those revolutionary events were so near, we may expect the prophet to have a great deal to say on the subject. He will also say many things relative to the corruption that was the cause of God's wrath toward his people, namely, their worship of idols.

Verse 2. The Lord God was about to be a witness against the people. The significance of that is that since God knows everything, there could be no question as to the truth of the testimony about to be uttered. *From his holy temple* refers to the throne of the universe, which indicates the supreme headquarters from which the testimony was to be issued.

Verse 3. The holy temple in heaven is the Lord's personal dwelling place, but He is everywhere at all times in a spiritual sense. And He is spoken of as being in or coming to specific spots on the earth when some definite work is to be accomplished, such as inflicting a chastisement on His people for their sins.

Verse 4. The power of God is illustrated by the figurative melting of mountains and cleaving of the alleys. All of the material events mentioned in this verse are for the same purpose, to indicate that God can do as he wills with kingdoms of men.

Verse 5. This verse gives the key to the figures of the preceding one. The two kingdoms of the Jews are meant by Jacob (or Israel) and Judah. The same is meant by Samaria and Jerusalem because they were the capitals of those kingdoms. They are named in direct connection with sins and transgressions because the kings and other leaders of nations are located in their capitals. *High places* identifies the particular corruption of these kingdoms to have been idolatry.

Verse 6. For the present the predictions are against the 10-tribe kingdom whose capital was Samaria. *Heap* is from a Hebrew word that Strong defines as "a ruin (as if overturned)." When the Assyrian army subjugated the kingdom of Israel it left the country in ruins, at least as far as its government was concerned. The history of this event is recorded in 2 Kings 17.

Verse 7. God's complaint against his people was about their idolatry, and he was determined to abolish it through the agency of the Assyrians. *The hires thereof* refers to the possessions of the people of Israel which they claimed they had obtained by the help of their gods. *Hire of an harlot.* Idolatry was compared to adultery in ancient times, and the gains that were claimed to have been acquired through the favor of the gods is here likened to the money that a harlot would receive in payment for her service to immoral men. *Shall return to the hire of an harlot.* Israel claimed to have received these material possessions through the favor of the gods. The italicized clause means that the heathen nations from whom the people of Israel learned the corrupt practice of idolatry would come upon the country and take possession of these very goods that were claimed to have been received through the favor of the gods.

Verse 8. The first person of pronouns is used in the prophetic writings somewhat interchangeably as referring to either God or the prophet. That is because the writing is inspired of God although the prophet is doing the writing. But when language describes such actions as the ones in this verse we should understand the pronoun to refer to the prophet. We have seen instances where the prophets were induced to do some "acting" on account of the affairs of God's people. In the present verse the prophet goes through some of the ancient customary acts of mourning over the deplorable condition of the nation.

Verse 9. Israel had become so corrupt in devotion to idols that God saw no cure for it except by the services of a foreign nation which was to be the Assyrians. *Wound . . . come unto Judah.* The Assyrians did not rest content after having taken the kingdom of Israel into captivity, but came on and threw Jerusalem into a panic of fear. The history of this is recorded in 2 Kings 18 and 19.

Verse 10. *Gath* and *Aphrah* were places in the land of the Philistines bordering on the country of Israel. The verse means that Israel should not make too much ado over the unfortunate situation, or these heathen communities would hear about it and take pleasure from it. Instead, in their distress let them quietly sit down or roll in the dust as a silent token of their humiliation.

Verse 11. The revolutionary events that were to come upon the country involved various cities and communities in one way or another. Some cities had encouraged Israel in wrongdoing, and others had taken the opposite trend and refused even to sympathize with the people of the Lord in their many misfortunes. The places and persons alluded to in this verse were among the descriptions given and all were destined to fall.

Verse 12. Maroth was another town in Palestine that was destined to feel the sting of the Lord's wrath. *Waited carefully . . . evil came.* The gist of this verse is virtually the same as the preceding one, and predicts that this was another city that was to be disappointed of its expectations regarding the continuance of its prosperity.

Verse 13. *The swift beast* refers to the horse which is a swift animal and can draw a chariot with speed. The purpose of binding the chariot to this beast was to try to escape from the foe. This does not mean that any city's inhabitants could actually escape the foe, for God had decreed that all were to become captives. The statement is a prediction that when the invasion came the unhappy citizens would wish to flee away for safety. *She is the beginning of the sin to the daughter of Zion.* The pronoun *she* stands for the city of Lachish, a place of importance south of Jerusalem. According to 2 Kings 18: 14, 17 and 2 Chronicles 11: 5, 9, Lachish was among the first cities to take up with the corruptions of Jeroboam, leader of the revolt of the ten tribes from the government in Jerusalem. Such is the meaning of the italicized clause, and it also explains the statement, *the transgressions of Israel were found in thee.*

Verse 14. *Give presents to* ["for" in the margin] *Moresheth-gath. Give presents* is a term of military and political significance, meaning to make a formal surrender to another, or at least to acknowledge his superiority. This was another idolatrous place and the people of God were destined to *give presents* to the Assyrians for or because of their corrupt practices in this and other cities. *Achzib shall be a lie.* The last word is from AKZAB which Strong defines, "falsehood; by implication treachery." The kings of Israel had counted on this city and others like it for support in times of national need. The prediction means that when the test comes they will fail the kings and will prove to be traitors.

Verse 15. *An heir* means one who will become the possessor of the place and that was to be the Assyrians. They were destined soon to invade this territory and take possession of the cities and put the inhabitants under subjection.

Verse 16. *Make thee bald* is an allusion to a custom of shaving the head as a symbol of distress. This is a prediction that the places mentioned would mourn over their children (citizens) because they would be taken away into captivity.

MICAH 2

Verse 1. *Work evil upon their beds.* In the first Psalm David pronounces a blessing on the man whose delight is in the law of the Lord and who meditates in that law day and night. The phrase cited from this verse gives an indication of the force of David's statement as to the advantage of meditation. In the hours of night when the activities of life are subsided for the time being, these workers of iniquity were planning some kind of mischief for the next day. Then when the night was over they went forth to carry out their wicked plot. *Because it is in the power of their hand.* Having thought upon their evil work and figured out the details, these wicked men had only to perform the physical execution of it since the "head work" had been done.

Verse 2. Some details of the wicked schemes of these men are stated. A man would be lying in his bed thinking about increasing his possessions. He would think of some field that impressed him as being very desirable, but it might not be for sale so he would plan some way to get it by violence if necessary. There is a notable instance of this kind of wickedness performed by Ahab, recorded in 1 Kings 21: 1-16.

Verse 3. *This family* means such as the preceding verse describes. The *evil* the Lord devised against such a family was not something wrong, but it was to be the chastisement imposed through a foreign nation for the purpose of correction. The *evil* at the end of the verse is the same that is explained above, and it was so sure to come that Israel need not become *haughty* over it, for their necks would not be released from it until the Lord's plan was accomplished.

Verse 4. *That day* means the time when the prediction against Israel would be fulfilled. When that time arrives someone will express the situation with a *doleful lamentation.* The form of that lamentation is like that predicted by David in Psalms 137.

Verse 5. The one who will express such a depressing sentiment will not be popular in the minds of the people. *Cord* is from a word that means a group of people bound together by some common opinion. The meaning is that the man making the above lamentation will not have any group of sympathizers for his gloom *in the congregation of the Lord.*

Verse 6. The people did not like to hear predictions of such unpleasant experiences indicated by this doleful lamentation and they cried for the prophet to stop it. Isaiah had the same objectors to contend with in his book, chapter 30: 10 and they were like certain characters predicted by Paul in 2 Timothy 4: 3, 4.

Verse 7. This verse is a rebuke to the people for questioning the word of the Lord. *Not straitened* means the Lord's word is not cramped or short of the truth, and hence the predictions expressed by the prophet are true for they are according to divine inspiration. I will caution the reader again not to be confused by the question form of the language. It is the Lord's manner of making positive declarations through Micah.

Verse 8. *Of late* denotes that the

accusation is a consideration of something very recent, showing that God was not complaining of something the people had done long ago and that should have been dealt with then or not at all. *Robe with the garment.* The last word is the article worn next to the body and was a close fitting piece, while the *robe* was like a mantle or loose piece that was worn over the other as an extra protection. These cruel thieves took both of the articles from their victims even as they were passing by. *As men averse from war.* Had these men been in uniform and serving in the enemy's army it would not have been so bad to strip them of their clothing; but they were civilians quietly going about their own business.

Verse 9. The outrages against the helpless women was similar to that charged against the hypocrites by Jesus (Matthew 23:14). It is one of the traits of men who are greedy of material gain to take advantage of those who cannot protect themselves.

Verse 10. *Arise and depart* is a prediction that they will depart from their home land and be lodged in the land of their exile. *This is not your rest.* They will not be permitted to rest or remain in possession of their ill-gotten property. *It is polluted.* The very place where these gains were made was polluted with the corruptions of idolatry and for that reason the nation was doomed to be overthrown.

Verse 11. True prophets were required to make predictions about the false ones or otherwise describe them. In this verse Micah describes the kind of prophet that the people of Israel were willing to accept. Jeremiah 5:31 also records a description of this conspiracy between the people and the false prophets.

Verse 12. The subject changes and the prediction pertains to the restoration of Israel to the home land. *Gather the remnant* refers to the comparatively small number of the Jews that survived the ravages of the captivity (Ezra 2:64). *Put them together as sheep* denotes they will be gathered from their scattered condition and grouped together as a flock in their own fold. *Make a noise* refers to the lively expressions that the people will make on being released.

Verse 13. *Breaker* is said with reference to the Lord because he will use his agency (the Persians) to break through the gates of the city to release His people. *Their king* means Cyrus who will be the instrument in God's hands for the delivering of Israel.

MICAH 3

Verse 1. The bulk of this chapter is against the head men of the nation. *Heads of Jacob* would be the outstanding men whether they were prophets or men in high social rank. The class of men had for many years taken advantage of their position to impose on the poor and otherwise unfortunate people. The last clause means that the princes were expected to know how to act with good judgment.

Verse 2. Instead of being examples of righteousness, these leaders reversed the proper attitude toward good and evil as to which they loved and hated. The pronouns *their* and *them* stand for the common people who were the victims of the cruelty of the leaders. *Pluck off their skin,* etc., is said figuratively and refers to the severe treatment they imposed on the people, similar to that mentioned in chapter 2:8.

Verse 3. This is more along the same line as the preceding verse.

Verse 4. The pronouns change now and stand for the heads and princes of Israel who are mentioned in verse 1. *Then* applies to the time when God would bring judgment upon the wicked men. When that time arrives it will be in vain for them to cry to God for mercy. He will turn his face away because *they have behaved ill in their doings.*

Verse 5. *Bite with their teeth, and cry, peace.* The selfishness of the leaders is still the topic in the mind of the inspired prophet. As long as they had food to bite they were peaceable and satisfied and not disposed to be unpleasant even in their teaching. They would even gratify their ear-itching and servile brethren with visions of *peace*, though such predictions were false. But when those downtrodden people refused to contribute to their selfishness; when they *putteth not into their mouths,* then they became spiteful and *prepared* [predicted] *war against them.*

Verse 6. The thought in this verse is against the prophets personally. They made a selfish use of their ability to issue predictions, so the Lord was going to deprive them of that information. *Night ... not vision* means that instead of giving them further visions as prophets, God would leave them in the dark as far as the future was concerned which would constitute the "night" of this phrase. *Shall not divine* denotes they will not be permitted to make predictions. The last clause of the verse means the same as the first part just explained.

Verse 7. *Seers* and *diviners* are names for the prophets who were supposed to be inspired of God for making their predictions. But when they abused their position by using it for their selfish enjoyment. He determined to deprive them of all information and that was to make them ashamed and confused. They would *cover their lips* which means their lips would be closed because they had nothing to say. The reason for that will be that when they sought for divine instruction *there was no answer from God*.

Verse 8. The first personal pronoun is again to stand for Micah who was a faithful prophet, and the *power of the spirit of the Lord* was guiding him. *Jacob* and *Israel* are used in the same sense, having special reference to the 10-tribe kingdom, but in a general sense the writing of the prophet applies to all the Jewish nation. *Declare* is from NAGAD, and the word in Strong's definition that especially applies in this case is "expose." It was the work of the faithful prophet to expose and denounce the corruptions of Israel.

Verse 9. The leading men in the nation are still the ones especially in the mind of the prophet. *Abhor judgment* refers to the right judgment which they should have manifested instead of abhorring it. A result of such an attitude was to *pervert* or corrupt all *equity* (fairness in dealing).

Verse 10. Since *Zion* and *Jerusalem* were names of the capital of the 2-tribe kingdom, this indicates that the prophet was considering the whole nation somewhat in his book. See the comments on this subject in verse 8 and also at chapter 1: 1.

Verse 11. This verse describes the same condition as Jeremiah 5: 31, but it goes further and states the motive for the corrupt conduct of the leaders. It verifies the statement of Paul in 1 Timothy 6: 10 that the love of money is a root of all kinds of evil. After all this wicked procedure these hypocrites had the boldness to *lean upon the Lord* or pretend to rely upon Him. They even pretended to believe that the Lord would preserve them from all harm in spite of their inconsistent lives.

Verse 12. *Zion* was an important spot in *Jerusalem* which was the capital of the 2-tribe kingdom. *Heaps* means ruins either material or political, and this prediction refers to the ruin of Jerusalem (2 Kings 15: 9, 10).

MICAH 4

Verse 1. The first five verses of this chapter as a group predict the kingdom of Christ, but I shall comment on the several verses in their order. *In the last days* corresponds with "afterward" in Joel 2: 28, and "last days" in Acts 2: 17. It means the last days of the Jewish dispensation, for that system was still in force when the Holy Spirit came upon the apostles to set up the kingdom of Christ. *Mountain* in symbolic language means a government, so the government of the Lord was to be established above all others, which was predicted also in Daniel 2: 44.

Verse 2. *Many nations* means people from many nations, not that any government as a body would attach itself to the kingdom of Christ. This prediction of the many nations was begun to be fulfilled in Acts 2: 5. *Shall say, come let us go up* refers to the generous response that was made to the call of the apostles recorded in Acts 2: 41. 47; 4: 4 and other passages. *The law* means the law to govern the kingdom of Christ, not the Jewish government, for that had been given many centuries before by Moses (John 1: 17) It was the law or government predicted by the patriarch Jacob in Genesis 49: 10, which makes the wording of this verse very appropriate.

Verse 3. In the midst of a group of verses most of which consist of figures and symbols, it would be unreasonable to give the present one a literal interpretation. It does not predict that carnal warfare will cease after the kingdom of Christ is established. It is true that the tendencies of the Gospel are in the opposite direction from violence of any kind in the conduct of the true followers of Christ. But it is also true that as long as the world stands the scriptures teach us that the great majority of mankind will reject the Gospel, hence this verse could not be a prediction of the end of carnal warfare. The explanation lies in the difference between the Jewish and Christian dispensations. The former was a combination of religious and political government, hence it was right to use the support of carnal warfare. That is why Jesus said that if his kingdom were of this world his servants would fight in his defence (John 18:36). But the Christian dispensation is strictly religious and its citizens will not resort to the material sword for its propaganda and support. Hence the members of the Lord's kingdom will use their metal for instruments of peaceful industry, and depend upon the "sword of the Spirit, which is the word of God" for the defence of the kingdom of Christ. Let the reader understand that this paragraph has nothing to do with the subject of Christians engaging in carnal warfare as a citizen of the temporal government. When he does that he is acting as a citizen of the temporal government and in its defence, and not for the defence of the kingdom of Christ, for they are two separate and distinct institutions and a Christion is a member of each just as Paul was a Christian and a Roman at the same time (Acts 22:25).

Verse 4. Like the preceding verse, this one uses terms figuratively to express the thought in the mind of the prophet. If a country was sure there would be no hostile army invade it, the inhabitants would feel no need of secluding themselves within protective buildings but would feel safe in the great outdoors. The vine and fig tree were prominent sources of nourishment and good cheer, and a land that was permanently free from danger could offer these comforts to its inhabitants without fear. I have gone into these details to explain the significance of the illustrations used by the prophet. However, the reader should remember that they are illustrations only and that they represent the spiritual safety and feeling of security that a citizen of the Kingdom of Christ was to enjoy. This prospect was guaranteed by the Lord who gave the vision to the prophet Micah to be delivered to the people of the nation.

Verse 5. *All people* means the people of the world in general. It was not expected that the kingdom of Christ would be able to enlist the majority of the race of mankind, but instead it was even predicted in literal language that the many would be in the service of sin. That would include the idolatrous practices of walking *in the name of his god*. *We* is prospective and means the inhabitants of the kingdom of Christ who would honor the true God only.

Verse 6. In a number of places we have seen the prophet pass from the release of Israel from captivity to the establishing of the kingdom of Christ. In the present chapter the order is reversed, for the rest of it beginning with this verse is a group prediction of the return from the captivity. *That day* is a familiar term in the Bible and the context usually has to be considered in determining the day meant; it here stands for the day of Israel's release. *That halteth* means the national halting or lameness brought about by the captivity. *Driven out* refers to the exile of Israel from her native land which was yet in the future when the prophet wrote this. *I have afflicted* is said because the Lord used the heathen nations as instruments in His hands to inflict the chastisement on the disobedient people.

Verse 7. We usually think of a *remnant* as something rather inferior, a "scrap" of material left after the best has been taken. However, it has the opposite meaning in the present case, and indicates a superiority of strength in that it was able to survive after the bulk of the nation had succumbed to the ravages of the captivity. Thus this verse uses the word in the same connection with *strong nation*. God promises to use the remnant as a nucleus of a nation with Zion (Jerusalem) as its headquarters.

Verse 8. *Tower* is also rendered "castle" and is here used to designate Jerusalem as a watchtower for the kingdom the Lord promised to make out of the "remnant." *First dominion* denotes that God had a dominion over the same people and at this same place long before. *Daughter of Zion* and *daughter of Jerusalem* are terms of endearment used frequently to represent God's people whose headquarters were in Jerusalem.

Verse 9. The verse is predicting a condition of sorrow to be felt by the nation in captivity, but with the understanding that the sorrow will be turned into joy by the deliverance from bondage. *Is there no king* is a prediction in question form that Israel will have the services of a king when the important day arrives.

Verse 10. The pains preceding childbirth are used to compare the distress of the captivity, but with the added thought that, as the pains are an indication of the approaching joy of parenthood, so the captivity must precede the return and establishment of the "strong nation" predicted above.

Verse 11. In a group of verses predicting the restoration of Israel from bondage, it was fitting to insert a few lines regarding the opinions of the nation's enemies and such is the present verse. Many nations were ill disposed toward the people of God and took pleasure in their misfortunes, but they were going to learn that the Lord would come to the rescue of his own nation after the necessary chastisement was given.

Verse 12. *They know not the thoughts of the Lord.* The heathen nations misunderstood the Lord's dealings with his people and thought it was because He had turned against them. Because of this misunderstanding they regarded the victories which they had experienced over Israel as a sign of God's personal favor for them, whereas the Lord was using them as instruments for the necessary chastisement of a disobedient and ungrateful people. *Gather them as sheaves into the floor.* The *floor* means the place where grain was piled for threshing by beating the whole straw until the grain was separated from the chaff. Since only the good sheaves would be taken to such a place, the fact is used to represent the profitable use which God proposed to make of the nation that had gained so much at the expense of His people.

Verse 13. *Daughter of Zion* is an endearing term frequently used to designate the people of God whose headquarters were in Zion, a special spot in Jerusalem. God accomplished much of his plan against the unfaithful Jews through the agency of the heathen nations. Now the order is reversed and He will use the Jews as instruments in bringing the heathen nations into the service of their restoration to the home land; such is the meaning of the figures used in this verse. Since the figure of "sheaves" was used for the heathen in the preceding verse, it was consistent for the prophet to use *thresh* in this. In figurative language *horn* means power, and God here promises to give his people the power to contend with the heathen through their influence and superior wisdom, not necessarily through military action. Sometimes the ox was used in treading out the grain that had been piled upon the floor (Deuteronomy 25: 4; 1 Corinthians 9: 9; 1 Timothy 5: 18), so the promise of brasen hoofs is appropriate in this connection. *Consecrate their gain unto the Lord* was to be fulfilled literally and morally. The heathen nation was constrained to contribute material help for the rebuilding of Jerusalem (Ezra 1: 2-4; 6: 8-10), and also the same nation was brought to respect the God of Israel.

MICAH 5

Verse 1. This verse is a continuation of the thought started in the last verse of the preceding chapter, namely, the triumph of Israel over all her misfortunes. *Troops* literally means soldiers and indicates military conflicts, but it is used figuratively only, for Israel did not have to fight for the release from captivity. The pronouns should be carefully distinguished in order to avoid confusion. *Thyself* and *us* means Israel, while *he* and *they* are the enemies of God's people. *Laid siege* and *smite* refer to the siege and capture of the nation of Israel, which was to be reversed when the "return" was accomplished by the Lord's decree.

Verse 2. This verse is another of the numerous instances of the passing from some favorable event for ancient Israel to one of spiritual Israel. It is understandable why the inspired prophets would do so; while the spiritual advantages pertaining to the New Testament times are for both Jews and Gentiles yet the system was given to the world through the Jews (Romans 3: 2). We know this verse is a prediction of the times of Christ, for the New Testament makes such an application of it (Matthew 2: 6). *Whose going forth . . . from everlasting.* Jesus was not personally connected with the affairs of the Old Testament, but He was recognized by his Father throughout all of the dealings intended for the benefit of mankind (Matthew 25: 34).

Verse 3. After a brief interruption to make a prediction concerning Christ, the prophet returns to the original subject of ancient Israel. *Give them up* means that God would suffer the foreign nation to have possession of His people. *Until . . . travaileth . . . brought forth* means when the captivity and its ravages will be ended and the nation of Israel will be given a "new birth of freedom" in its own native land. *Remnant shall return* refers to the surviving number stated in Ezra 2: 64.

Verse 4. The antecedent of *he* is the *remnant* of the preceding verse, meaning the part of Israel that was to survive the captivity. One meaning of the original for *feed* is "to rule," which the remnant of Israel was to do after returning from the captivity. *In the strength of the Lord* denotes that the leaders in Israel were to rule the flock under and with the help of the Lord. They were to do this in the name of the Lord and because of the majesty of the God of Israel. *And they shall abide.* The Jewish nation was never again to be removed bodily from its home land as it had been in the captivity.

Verse 5. The specific exile generally meant in this book is that of the 10-tribe kingdom under the Assyrian Empire recorded in 2 Kings 17. Of course when the final "return" was accomplished (Ezra and Nehemiah), that included the 10 tribes also since the territory formerly controlled by the Assyrians was later taken over by the Babylonians. This verse is a figurative prediction that Israel would not be retained in exile by the Assyrians. *Seven shepherds* means that complete triumph would be enjoyed by Israel over all foes.

Verse 6. The predictions of this verse are virtually the same as those in the preceding one. *Nimrod* is mentioned in connection with *Assyria* because the founder of the Assyrian Empire *went forth* out of the land under the domain of Nimrod (Genesis 10: 9-11), and the two names are frequently linked together in prophecy and history.

Verse 7. Small things are sometimes very effective in their influence. The dew is light and small compared with the vegetable kingdom, yet it can enliven an entire field of dry and parched grass. Likewise, the influence of the remnant of Israel was to be great when it was settled down upon the (politically) dry land of Palestine.

Verse 8. This verse continues the thought of the preceding one but with a different figure. Now the remnant is likened to a lion among other beasts, with the added specific thought that Israel was to be like a lion in a flock of sheep. Not that the people of Israel were actually to exercise any violence against the surroundings, but the illustration is to show the power of God's nation.

Verse 9. The greatest enemies the people of Israel ever had were those who led them into idolatry. All of that was to be reversed by the revolutionary effects of the captivity. This is the sense in which the enemies were to *be cut off*.

Verse 10. The general subject of the verses from 8 to the close of the chapter is the return from captivity, including the things that were to be accomplished by that sad experience. Chief among these was the cure of idolatry and the worldly interests the people of Israel had manifested. This verse cites one of those as being the horse and chariot. Such things should not have led them into wrong-doing, but it seems they did. The Lord knew the tendencies of them and had forbidden their use as early as in Deuteronomy 17: 16 which Solomon disobeyed after he became king (1 Kings 10: 28).

Verse 11. The mere fact of being a city was not objectionable to God, but some of them had been devoted to the service of idolatry, and He proposed to deprive the land of such.

Verse 12. The belief in *witchcraft* and *soothsaying* was based largely on that of the supposed power of the invisible false gods of the heathen. As an item in removing the indications of such false service, the presence and use of such evil characters as witches and soothsayers had to be removed.

Verse 13. Idolaters were not content to offer service to the invisible gods, but made images of them out of metal and other materials. All of this was to be discontinued as a result of the captivity, and the reader should keep his memory informed about this important subject. See the historical note that records the fulfillment of the prediction at Isaiah 1: 25, volume 3 of this Commentary. A very foolish fact in connection with the worship of graven images is that they were the *work of their hands*. The idea of serving a thing as a god that was the work of that same servant is the height of folly and inconsistency.

Verse 14. Not all groves were objectionable to God, for he is the creator of all vegetable life. But the heathen nations turned many groves into places of idolatrous worship, and in some cases they even singled out individual trees and consecrated them to the worship of false gods. It was these abominable groves that were meant by the prediction of this verse and others on the same line of denunciation. The very presence of all such growing objects might remind the people of Israel of their former practices and rekindle in them a desire to return to the abomination. As a precautionary movement the Lord decreed that such groves should be destroyed. The cities that had been used for the same purpose were to share in the same fate as these groves.

Verse 15. The people of God learned of the practice of idolatry through the heathen nations, hence He was incensed against them and determined to take vengeance on them.

MICAH 6

Verse 1. The writers of the Bible do not always adhere strictly to chronology in their treatment of subjects. The preceding chapter closes with a prediction of the return from the captivity; the present one comes back and resumes the complaints against Israel for her unfaithfulness to God. Israel is called upon to contend or defend herself if such a thing can be done truthfully. *Before the mountains.* If you have a just defence for your conduct let the whole world hear it.

Verse 2. But while the universe is to hear the defence of Israel (if she can produce any), the Lord will also make His complaints just as public. He has a *controversy* or accusation to make against the ungrateful nation.

Verse 3. The Lord challenges his people to point out any fact that they can justly call mistreatment from Him.

Verse 4. We know (and Israel knew) that no truthful complaint could be made against God in his treatment of his people. On the other hand, God had done much for Israel that should have induced her to cling faithfully to a life of true devotion. After being in bondage under the Egyptians for four centuries, the Lord brought them out a free people and started them on their way toward the land that had been promised to their fathers. And they were not left to wander in uncertainty as they journeyed toward their goal, but had the helpful presence of the three members of one family; Moses to give them law, Aaron to assist him in the addresses to kings, and Miriam to strengthen their morale with her songs and music.

Verse 5. God reminds his people of some things that were done in their defence against the enemies. After they had about completed their journey through the wilderness they were opposed by the Moabite king Balak. His iniquity was made worse in that he *consulted* with another wicked person who was a degenerate prophet. The Bible always regards sins that are done as a conspiracy in a worse light than done independently of others, and this sort of conspiracy was committed between Balak and Balaam.

Verse 6. This and the following verse sound like a penitent and complete confession on the part of Israel for the sins of the nation. It doubtless might have been the sincere sentiments of some individuals in the nation, but it certainly was not an expression of the nation as a whole. I understand the passage to be the prophet's way of showing what should have been the attitude manifested, and my comments will be made on that basis. The nation as a whole had become so corrupt that it was inconsistent to come with the outward rituals of animal sacrifices. Such formalities had been ordained by the law of Moses and were right in themselves, but whem they were performed in connection with so much abomination as these leaders practiced, the whole service was displeasing to God and he rejected it all. See the long note offered with the comments on Isaiah 1: 10 in volume 3 of this Commentary.

Verse 7. The suggested appropriate confession is continued through this verse, but with stronger terms as to the offerings made to God. The great number of animals would not avail anywise if the corruptions in their general lives were continued. Olive oil in small amounts was prescribed by the law and the Lord blessed the service when it was accompanied by a consistent life; but if not, even thousands of rivers of it would count for nothing. God never authorized human sacrifice although some heathen people practiced it. The performance furnished an appropriate illustration to be used as a most significant kind of emphasis. For a sinful Jew to sacrifice his child in atonement for his spiritual iniquity, would in reality be offering a part of his flesh to atone for the corruption of his soul.

Verse 8. As if the preceding two verses were the actual inquiry of a penitent man of Israel, the prophet makes an almost verbatim quotation from the writing of Moses in Deuteronomy 10: 12. The requirements were general in their statement, but had they been honestly respected it would have prevented the leaders from committing their cruelties against the poor, and then their sacrifices of animals would have been acceptable to God as a discharge of a duty enjoined by the divine law.

Verse 9. The declaration in the preceding verse is by the voice of the Lord, and a wise man will recognize the name of Jehovah in it. *Hear ye the rod* means to take heed to the chastening rod of the Almighty, and realize that it was He who appointed it.

Verse 10. The question form of accusation is again used in this verse. *Treasures of wickedness* refers to the gain the leaders held which they obtained unjustly from the poor. *Scant measure* signifies one of the means by which the poor were defrauded out of their possessions. It was by tampering with the legal scales and weights to be used in business transactions. (See Amos 8: 5.)

Verse 11. *Shall I count them pure* is rendered "shall I be pure" in the margin, and the American Standard Version also gives us that rendering. Moffatt translates it "Can I condone wrong balances?" The thought is that if God were to tolerate or accept the dishonest dealings of the people, then He would not be pure from such evils either.

Verse 12. This verse is a direct charge against the rich men in the nation. That was not because they were rich but because they had obtained their wealth by violence against the poor and helpless. The people were not entirely free from guilt, for they did not make the protest they should but seemed to defend the unrighteous deeds of the very ones who were robbing them, even doing it with speeches of falsehood. The explanation of the strange attitude is indicated by Jeremiah 5: 31 and chapter 3: 5 of this book. In order to avoid any unpleasant predictions and other teaching from the prophets, the people were willing to be defrauded and would even lie about it. This was their "bribe" to induce the wicked leaders to keep their unpleasant and unwanted predictions to themselves.

Verse 13. The common people were destined also to feel the wrath of God because of their falsehood in behalf of the wicked leaders. They were to be made "sick" in that many disappointments would come to them in their experiences of life.

Verse 14. This verse is an indefinite list of the reverses that were to be inflicted upon the people even while they were occupying their own land. These details could have occurred in so many forms that I do not have any specific history upon it.

Verse 15. Regardless of any disappointments that might come upon them in a general way as indicated in the preceding verse, we are sure that the present one was fulfilled literally when the nation was taken into exile and the foreign people reaped the benefit of the labors of their captives.

Verse 16. *Statutes of Omri*. He was not the only wicked king in Israel and I know of no special reason for citing him in this connection. It might be suggested, however, that he was the one who founded the city of Samaria as the final and permanent capital of the 10-tribe kingdom (1 Kings 16: 16), and a reference to that city in connection with the national policy was afterward a suggestion of evil. As a punishment for the keeping of the wicked statutes of Omri which he had adopted from Ahab, another wicked king, the Lord threatened to overthrow his people with desolation. That fact would be pleasing in the eyes of the heathen and cause them to hiss and reproach God's people.

MICAH 7

Verse 1. The prophet uses the first person in describing the undone condition of the nation, not that he is personally involved in the misdeeds so generally being committed. He describes the situation by likening the nation to a vineyard from which the main crop has been gathered. In such a stage one would not even find a single whole bunch of grapes that had matured, much less a piece of fruit among the *firstripe*.

Verse 2. Dropping the figures, the prophet uses literal language and explains that there is scarcely a good man. Most of them have taken to murder and treachery and to the defrauding of the righteous out of their rightful possessions.

Verse 3. The main subject of this verse is conspiracy to do wrong, which we have learned is especially displeasing to God. There were three classes who formed the conspiracy; the *prince*, the *judge*, and the *great* or "older." The thing which the three conspirators wished to obtain was a *reward* which is used in the sense of bribe. *Wrap* is from ABATH, and Strong's definition is, "A primitive root; to interlace, i.e. (figuratively) to pervert."

The first part of the definition is especially applicable in this place, because to conspire together is the same as being interlaced in a transaction.

Verse 4. A brier and a thorn are very undesirable objects, and the prophet uses them to illustrate the best that Israel as a whole could produce. *Day of thy watchmen* means the day that had been seen coming by the watchmen on the walls of the cities. It was the duty of a watchman to be on the alert and to warn his fellow citizens when he saw an enemy approaching. Of course only an inspired watchman could see the enemy in the present case, which was the army of the Assyrian Empire, and a true prophet constituted such a watchman. (See Ezekied 3: 17.) *Visitation* means the arrival and application of the perplexing chastisement of siege and capture.

Verse 5. This verse certainly paints a dark picture of society, for the advice given seems to be a contradiction of all the well established rules of friendship. It is a clear example of the incompleteness of many passages in the Bible if we stop with any particular verse, for such divisions are the arbitrary work of man and are done for convenience, and often cause a thought to be divided in the wrong place. We should always be watchful for this condition and not form a conclusion until we know we have considered all that is being offered on the subject.

Verse 6. The apparent difficulty in the preceding verse is accounted for in this. When people are normal in their attitude toward others such advice as the foregoing is uncalled-for. But all the usual influences between the various relations of members of families had become so corrupted that nobody could be trusted. Jesus predicted a similar condition would come after He had done his work on the earth (Matthew 10: 34-36). In his case the situation was to be caused by the teaching which was to be delivered to mankind, because many would reject it and hence would become enemies of those who accepted it. Doubtless some such motives figured in the case as Micah saw it.

Verse 7. A companion verse for this one is Psalms 27: 10 which I shall quote in its entirety: "When my father and my mother forsake me, then the Lord will take me up." Micah advised his people to be distrustful of even their nearest relatives, hence it was appropriate for him to say, *Therefore I will look unto the Lord.* This would be a good plan for general use at all times. Our flesh and blood relatives cannot be relied upon as infallible supports, especially when the matters of the soul are at stake.

Verse 8. God has frequently used the heathen nations to chastise His wayward people, but never would tolerate their selfish motive in the performance of it. Such is the thought in this verse, and the enemy is given to understand that the depression of Israel was not to be permanent. The people of God cannot fall so low but that He can raise them up again and show the divine love for the nation.

Verse 9. This verse represents the attitude that the people of Israel should show with reference to the Lord's punishment of them. They should be willing to *bear the indignation* because it is just and proper since they *have sinned against Him.* When the proper time comes God will *plead their cause* and *execute judgment* against the enemies who have been instruments in the Lord's hands in administering chastisement upon the disobedient nation. When that time arrives the people of Israel will realize that all of the Lord's dealings have been in righteousness.

Verse 10. Not only would Israel see the justice in the punishment she had suffered, but the nation that had been used as the instrument of God for such a purpose will be brought to *see it, and shame shall cover her which said, Where is the Lord thy God?* The fulfillment of this prediction may be seen in Daniel 5.

Verse 11. This is a prediction of the restoration of Israel to her own land and to the rebuilding of her city. The fulfillment of this is recorded in Ezra and Nehemiah.

Verse 12. The general return of God's people from all places of exile is predicted in this verse. Assyria is named because the first deportation out of Palestine was to be at the hand of that people, but before the final return to the home land they will have been taken over by another great empire, the Babylonians. *The river* refers to the Euphrates River which was the easternmost boundary of the territory promised to Abraham (Genesis 15: 18).

Verse 13. But before the happy event

can happen, the land must go through the experience of desolation. This is to be charged up against *them that dwell therein* (the people of Israel) because of *the fruit of their doings.* The exile or captivity of both kingdoms of the Jews was to be a chastisement upon them for their unfaithfulness to God regarding the law that had been enjoined upon them at Mt. Sinai.

Verse 14. *Feed* (or rule or guide) *thy people* is Micah's way of predicting that God would again care for His people after they have gone through their desolation period.

Verse 15. The reference to the day of Egypt is for comparison. Israel was brought out of bondage in that country, and she will also be released from Babylonian captivity.

Verse 16. In view of the comparatively small number in Israel at the time of the release, it will be a surprise to see their accomplishments. *Lay their hand upon their mouth* indicates that the circumstance will be so marvelous in the eyes of the heathen that they will not be able to say anything.

Verse 17. *Lick the dust* is a figurative prediction of the humiliation of the heathen nations when they see the triumph of Israel. *Be afraid of the Lord our God* means they will be stunned with awe and forced to respect the might of the God of Israel.

Verse 18. The most wonderful feature of God's treatment of his unfaithful people is his willingness to forgive them. Their many abominations would seem to justify their utter extinction, yet His great love preserved them and restored them again to their home land after the necessary punishment had been administered.

Verse 19. *Subdue our iniquities* has special reference to the complete cure of idolatry that the captivity effected upon Israel. See the historical note on this subject with the comments on Isaiah 1: 25 in volume 3 of this Commentary.

Verse 20. *Perform the truth* means that God will prove the truth of all His promises to Jacob or Israel, which had first been made to Abraham the founder of the race.

NAHUM 1

Verse 1. Nahum was one of the minor prophets who wrote about 6 or 7 centuries before Christ. *Burden* is from an original that means "an utterance," and is used here to mean that the prophet has something to say about Nineveh. That was the capital of the Assyrian Empire that was still in power as Nahum wrote. But the Lord gave him a vision of the fate of that nation and he wrote about it in his book. Assyria was the empire that had carried the people of the 10-tribe kingdom of Israel off into exile. It was God's decree that such an event should take place, yet He was incensed at the personal satisfaction that heathen nation got out of Israel's downfall, and of the unnecessary cruelty that was imposed in connection with the case. As a consequence, it was decreed that Assyria in turn should be made to suffer some reverses. The nation finally fell before the Babylonian power.

Verse 2. Jealousy is what causes a person to cling to that which he possesses and to resent any attempt of another to take it from him. Assyria had taken possession of a portion of God's people. He was determined to take vengeance because of it. *Reserveth* is defined "to cherish" in the lexicon, and the clause means that God holds a store of wrath for his enemies.

Verse 3. *Slow to anger.* This phrase is in keeping wtih the last sentence of the preceding verse. If God reserves wrath for certain characters, then He can take as much time as his wisdom suggests in executing it upon His wayward people. But he will not entirely overlook even their wrong-doing, which is the meaning of the words *not at all acquit the wicked.* That is why He suffered the Assyrians to take the people of Israel into exile. *Hath his way* means that God does as he wills with all the elements of the universe. If He wishes to use these agencies to carry out some of the decrees of chastisement upon a nation it will be done.

Verse 4. This is further specification of the power of God over the parts of the universe, and it denotes that if He wills to control them as agencies against men and nations it will be accomplished. *Bashan* was in a heathen territory and *Carmel* with *Lebanon* was in the possession of Israel. However, wherever the place might be that incurs the divine wrath, it will have to suffer whatever form of chastisement that He deems proper.

Verse 5. All of these statements are made as a description of the power of

God. This verse is quite inclusive, for it begins with the inanimate things in creation, and ends with the living in the words *world, and all that dwell therein*. God is able not only to control the material things that have no intelligent power of resistance, but He can rule all living creatures in the world which includes men and nations.

Verse 6. It is logical to ask the question with which this verse begins, for if God has such universal power it is folly for anyone to think of resisting Him. His fury is compared to fire because of its effect upon corruption to which it is applied. Paul makes the same figurative comparison of God in Hebrews 12: 29 which is also a quotation from Deuteronomy 4: 24.

Verse 7. *The Lord is good* denotes that God's wrath is not to be regarded in the light of a destructive fire that ruins everything before it whether good or bad. It should rather be thought of as a purifying flame that affects only such combustible matter as refuse, leaving unhurt and purified all elements that are useful.

Verse 8. The same might is now compared to a flood that sweeps everything before it that is not firmly attached. *Darkness* is used figuratively, and among the words of the lexicon definition of the original are "misery, destruction, death, ignorance, sorrow." These conditions come upon those who are enemies of the God of Israel.

Verse 9. *What do ye imagine against the Lord?* This is a challenge especially intended for Assyria. *Affliction . . . not . . . second time*. When God moves to accomplish a certain result He makes a success of it and does not have to "try, try again."

Verse 10. *Folden* is from CABAK and is defined in the lexicon by "to entwine." *Drunken* and *drunkards* are from COBE, which means "carousal." The thought in both clauses is that of being in a conspiracy. But though the Assyrians form such an opposition against the people of Israel, they will *be devoured as stubble fully dry*, which means that the resistance will be no more effective than dry stubble would be against a fire.

Verse 11. The pronoun *thee* stands for Assyria as a nation that was hostile toward the kingdom of Israel. But a whole empire would not march against a foe; instead it would go in the person of a chief representative. This is the significance of *one come out of thee* who is described as *a wicked counsellor*. The wicked counsellor could be understood to be the man representing the Assyrian Empire in its rage against God's people, whether we consider the 10-tribe kingdom (2 Kings 17), or the vicious but unsuccessful tirade against the 2-tribe kingdom (2 Kings 18 and 19).

Verse 12. *Quiet* means to be calm and having a feeling of security. The verse means that though the enemy have that feeling, encouragd perhaps by the fact that they were *many*, yet they (the enemy) shall be cut down. The passage now is addressed to Israel for consolation or encouragement. God afflicted his people by suffering the heathen nations to subdue them, but He promises that it will not be repeated.

Verse 13. This is a prophecy of the release from captivity. *His* means the Assyrians and/or Babylonians, depending on whether the reader applies it to the 10-tribe or the 2-tribe kingdom, for either could be considered properly.

Verse 14. The language is still addressed to God's people. Idolatry was the national evil for which it was to be sent into captivity. Idols were to be *cut off* or abolished by the effects of the period of exile in a foreign and heathen land. *I will make thy grave* is figurative. The land of Babylon was to be the grave and the nation of Israel was the corpse, for it underwent national death when Jerusalem was destroyed. (See another statement of this in Isaiah 22: 14, 18.)

Verse 15. Once more the prophet leaps from some experience of fleshly Israel to predict a great favor as spiritual Israel. The terms used are those of the rituals used by fleshly Israel but are figuratively used in this case, and refer to the spiritual practices under Christ. The prediction is cited by Paul in Romans 10: 15.

NAHUM 2

Verse 1. The prophet is still making predictions against Nineveh, the capital of the Assyrian Empire. *He that dasheth in pieces* means the military force that was to come against the city and country. *Before thy face* denotes that the hostile army was to come into the immediate presence of the city. *Keep the munition* (military equipment) and the other phrases of the verse are said by way of warning that the city would need all of its reserves in the conflict coming upon it.

Verse 2. A natural question would be, why did the Lord have such a severe lot in store for the city? The answer is that it was to be in return for her cruelty against His people. It is true that God decreed the downfall of the nation of Israel, which is meant by the statement *the Lord hath turned away the excellency of Jacob*, and it was to be done through the agency of Assyria. But He never did approve of the motives of these heathen servants nor of the unnecessary cruelties which they used. The last clause is still a statement of the harsh treatment the Assyrians imposed upon Israel. This verse is inserted by the prophet to explain why the Lord is predicting such a complete overthrow of the capital city of Nineveh.

Verse 3. *His mighty men* refers to the great men in the Babylonian army that will be invading Assyria. The *red* and *scarlet* has reference to the appearance of the equipment, caused either by the artificial coloring or by the reflection of the sun. It would make it imposing in the sight of the intended victims and thus would tend to weaken their morale. *Chariots with flaming torches* has about the same meaning as the coloring appearance of the *red* above. The rapidity with which the wheels would revolve would cause them to reflect a glittering appearance as they sparkled in the sun. *Fir trees* comes from BEROWSH and Strong defines it, "A cypress (?) tree; hence a lance or a musical instrument (as made of that wood)." *Terribly shaken* are both from the one word RAAL and defined, "To reel, i.e. (figuratively) to brandish." The whole clause means that in the operation against Nineveh the lances of the Babylonians will be brandished in a threatening manner.

Verse 4. The *chariots* in ancient times were used either for purposes of transportation or as a war implement, more generally the latter. This verse is a prediction of the great numbers of the vehicles to be used in the attack upon Nineveh's streets and the *broad ways* or open country. They were to be so numerous they would *justle* (jostle) *one against another*. *Seem like torches* and *run like the lightnings* is to be understood in about the same sense as the conditions for the sake of appearance in the preceding verse. Most of the war chariots had swords or large scythes attached to them in order to mow down the men of the enemy. These were made of bright metal and would give off the appearance of torches as they revolved on the wheels in the sunlight.

Verse 5. When the watchmen of Nineveh see the enemy approaching they will announce it to the king (or queen as the case may be), then he shall make preparations to defend the city. *Recount his worthies*. The king of Nineveh will investigate the conditions of his forces and will count up to learn the military strength he has in the way of good soldiers. But they will *stumble* (or falter) in the excitement of the hour as they prepare to defend the wall of the city. *Defence* is rendered "covering" or "coverer" in the margin, and the definition in the lexicon agrees with it. The context also justifies the rendering, for the inside attempts at defence are already dealt with in the beginning of the verse and the defenders have had their failure. After this is when they find that the *defence shall be prepared*. It means that after the citizens of Nineveh have made their excited attempt to protect the city and march out to the wall, they will find that the invading forces maintaining the siege will have provided themselves with this protecting "covering."

Verse 6. As a result of the conditions described in the preceding paragraph, the gates of the city were forced open by the besiegers and the soldiers entered the place. With a reversal of the expectations of the citizens, we are not surprised that *the palace was dissolved*.

Verse 7. Huzzab is capitalized as if it were a proper name, but Strong says it is not. His definition of the original is, "A primitive root; to station, in various applications (literal or figurative)." It means that the station or spot where the palace stood will be taken and the chief inhabitant of it will be led away captive. Also, the attendants of the palace will accompany said person in a procession of mourning, *tabering* or drumming, beating upon their breasts in their despair.

Verse 8. The lexicon definition for *pool* uses a stronger word and calls it a reservoir which denotes a larger body. It represents Nineveh as a place containing many people which the history and geography of the city will bear out. *Yet they*, etc., means they of this reservoir of people will flee when they see the invading army coming. *Stand, stand,* is the cry of the more resolute inhabitants, trying to stop the fleeing citizens, but they will not be able to stop the fleeing which will have become what is virtually a panic of fear and desperation.

Verse 9. *Take ye the spoil* is a form of prediction that the invader will take the valuables of the city as a spoil of war. *None end of the store* denotes that there was much wealth in the city of Nineveh. *Pleasant furniture* means the vessels in which these precious metals were kept, including the gold or silver contained therein.

Verse 10. *Empty* and *void* and *waste* is a prediction of the utter ruin that was to come upon the city. The rest of the verse is a description of the agitated state of mind that the citizens in the city will experience at the destruction of their city. *Faces gather blackness* is a somewhat unusual rendering with regard to the last word. Moffatt renders it "black fear," while the American Standard Version gives us "waxed pale." Strong defines the original, "Illuminated, i.e. a glow; as noun, a flush (of anxiety)." Whatever particular translation we adopt, it is clear that the terrible disturbance within the city was to have its effect upon the facial expression of the citizens. It will be helpful to quote a paragraph from history that shows the fulfillment of this eventful revolution as follows: "Saracus, who came to the throne towards the end of the 7th century B.C., was the last of the long line of Assyrian kings. For nearly or quite six centuries the Ninevite kings had now lorded it over the East. There was scarcely a state in all Western Asia that during this time had not, in the language of the royal inscriptions, 'borne the heavy yoke of their lordship,' scarcely a people that had not suffered their cruel punishments, or tasted the bitterness of enforced exile. But now swift misfortunes were bearing down upon the oppressor from every quarter. Egypt revolted and tore Syria away from the empire; from the mountain defiles on the east issued the armies of the recent-grown empire of the Aryan Medes, led by the renowned Cyaxares; from the southern lowlands, anxious to aid in the overthrow of the hated oppressor, the Babylonians joined the Medes as allies, and together they laid close siege to Nineveh. The city was finally taken and sacked [plundered], and dominion passed away forever from the proud capital. Two hundred years later, when Xenophon with his Ten Thousand Greeks, in his memorable retreat passed the spot, the once great city was a crumbling mass of ruins of which he could not even learn the name."—Myers, Ancient History, page 66.

Verses 11-13. These verses are grouped into one paragraph because they all are on the same subject. The terms are generally all used figuratively, especially the lions and their breed. The heroes and leaders of the Assyrian nation are likened to the lions because of their savage treatment of men and women who fell into their hands. They showed no mercy toward others and now the Lord will bring a nation against them that will burn their chariots and slay their strong men. (See historical quotation.)

NAHUM 3

Verse 1. The leading men in Nineveh would not hesitate at bloodshed if it would help their plots to overcome the other citizens. *Prey departeth not* denotes that the practice of preying upon the helpless citizens never ceased. Thirst for power was merciless.

Verse 2. This verse begins describing the details of the "woe" with which the chapter begins. *Noise of a whip.* Military operations were carried on largely with chariots drawn by horses, and this phase predicts the lashing of the animals in urging them on through the city. Streets had rough and rocky surfaces and the chariot wheels were equipped with hard tires, hence the *rattling* noise they would make. *Jumping* is from RAQAD which Strong defines, "A primitive root; properly to stamp, i.e. to spring about (wildly or for joy)." The word has been rendered by dance, jump, leap and skip. The *prancing horses* would naturally produce such movements in the chariots.

Verse 3. *The horseman* means the man driving the horses drawing the chariots of the preceding verse, for the charioteers did not restrict their activities to their driving. They would leap from the rear of the vehicle (which was open at that end) and make close attack upon any person of the enemy nearby. Or they would cast the spear from the chariot at those farther away. The great number of the slain is indicated by the words *stumble upon their corpses.*

Verse 4. This verse sets forth the evils for which the Lord decreed this awful fate for Nineveh and the nation. Literal whoredom was doubtless practiced there, but the term is also used to mean the abominable evils of idolatry. This would include various kinds of traffic such as witchcraft, by which outside people were defrauded out of their belongings and other rights.

Verse 5. Idolatry is compared with adultery in the Bible, and a harlot is likened unto a city or nation that practices the false religion, hence the accusations were m a d e against Nineveh recorded in this passage. *Discover thy skirts upon thy face.* The harlot's skirt was lifted up as far as her face to make sure that her nakedness was exposed. A harlot would not have any sense of shame as far as modesty is concerned, but to have her body exposed by someone who did not intend to patronize her would be humiliating. This is a prediction that Nineveh was literally to be exposed to the gaze of the world.

Verse 6. The *filth* is figurative and refers to the insults and shame that would be cast upon Nineveh by the nations. *Make thee vile* means to expose the city so that her true condition could be seen and she would be known to be vile.

Verse 7. This verse means the same as verse 10 of the preceding chapter.

Verse 8. *No* is another name for Thebes, an important city in Egypt. In connection with the description of the city given here, I shall quote from Smith's Bible Dictionary which will verify it: "The description of No as 'situate among the rivers, the waters round about it' (Nahum 3: 8), remarkably characterizes Thebes. It lay on both sides of the Nile, and was celebrated for its hundred gates, for its temples, obelisks, statues, etc. It was emphatically the city of temples, in the ruins of which many monuments of ancient Egypt are preserved. The plan of the city was a parallelogram, two miles from north to south and four from east to west, but none suppose that in its glory it really extended 33 miles along both sides of the Nile. T h e b e s was destroyed by Ptolemy, B. C. 81, and since then its population has dwelt in villages only." The argument of the prophet in this verse is that if such a stronghold as Thebes could be overthrown, then Nineveh should not feel so confident of resisting the invader.

Verse 9. The fall of No (Thebes) cannot be explained on the ground that the city had insufficient support. She had the backing of two countries, Egypt and Ethiopia, and of the groups known as Put and Lubim.

Verse 10. In spite of the greatness of this Egyptian city, her inhabitants were *carried away*, the *captivity* meaning the humiliation that they suffered at the hands of other forces among the nations. *Cast lots for the honorable men* means the various nations that came against No divided these important men among themselves by casting lots.

Verse 11. *Thou* means *Nineveh* and she is hereby warned that as surely as the city of No was overthrown so she will be ruined also. *Shalt be drunken* means she will be dealt such a blow that she will be stunned and caused to stagger. *Shalt be hid* denotes that the city would become obscure and *seek strength* or help (but in vain).

Verse 12. The firstripe fruit of the fig tree would be very desirable, and the *strong holds* or fortified places in the city would be the spots most to be desired by an enemy. If the mere shaking of a tree would place the fruit into the mouth of the eater, it would illustrate the ease and surety with which the invading army will obtain these coveted spots in Nineveh.

Verse 13. *People* is from AM and a part of Strong's definition is, "Collectively troops or attendants." The thought of the prediction is that the military forces in the city will be no stronger than if they were women, and they are not considered qualified for military service. As a consequence, the gates will be early thrown open as was illustrated by the mere shaking of the tree in the preceding verse. *Bars* is defined "a bolt" in the lexicon and it denotes that the fasteners on the gates will be easily destroyed by the fire of the enemy.

Verse 14. The actions detailed are those of a city preparing to resist a siege, and the verse is a prediction that Nineveh will need all the preparation she can make.

Verse 15. Notwithstanding all the preparations suggested in the preceding verse, the fire of the besiegers will devour the fortifications. The *cankerworm* and *locust* were destructive insects and consumed that which they attacked. Though the people of Nineveh should make themselves as numerous as these insects were, yet they were to be attacked and destroyed by the invading forces which will be still more numerous.

Verse 16. Nineveh had grown in her business and political interests until it was compared with the stars of the heaven. But in spite of all this apparent strength, the *cankerworm* (invading enemy) will present great numbers to attack the city and *flee away* or make a success in the operation.

Verses 17-19. There is nothing new in these verses that has not been set forth in other verses of the book. The subject is the utter defeat of Nineveh, the capital of Assyria, with not a possibility of a "come-back." (See the historical quotation at chapter 2: 10.)

HABAKKUK 1

Verse 1. See Nahum 1: 1 for comments on the word *burden*. Habakkuk was given something to say and it was to be written in this book.

Verse 2. The prophet laments the corruption and violence that were being practiced by the people of Judah. Habakkuk was not responsible for the wickedness of his people but he felt a personal interest in their fate. *Thou wilt not save* means that Judah had gone too far in her abominable course to be spared the judgment of God.

Verse 3. *Why dost thou show me iniquity* is a continuation of the prophet's lament at the low ebb of spirituality among his people. He specifies some of the evils that the nation was committing; violence and strife and contention.

Verse 4. *The law is slacked* means that the people had become careless or even positively disobedient regarding its requirements. *The wicked doth compass about the righteous* was true in more than one sense. The wicked leaders hindered those who would have been righteously carrying out the law. Also the leaders' wicked conduct in general was so bad that it covered up or counteracted what things they did that would have otherwise been acceptable. (See the long note in connection with Isaiah 1: 10, volume 3 of this Commentary.)

Verse 5. Some prophecies in the Bible had a twofold bearing, or were destined to be fulfilled twice, and the present verse is one of them. It first refers to the marvelous work of the Lord in which the heathen were to behold the judgment of God against his nation. *Not believe, though told.* They would rush heedlessly on in their evil course although they had been plainly and authoritatively told about it. The same kind of experience was threatening in Paul's day as he cites it in Acts 13: 41.

Verse 6. The Chaldeans were a special race of people who got in the lead in the land of Babylon, hence the terms Chaldeans and Babylonians are used in the same sense. From this verse through 11 is a prediction of the great captivity that God was going to bring upon Judah. *Hasty* is from a word that is defined "prompt" in the lexicon. The Chaldeans were prompt in their movements, especially when they were induced thereto by *bitterness* as they were against Judah. They were to come through the land of God's people and take possession of the whole country.

Verse 7. *Dreadful* is from the same original word as "reverend" in Psalms 111: 9 where it is applied to the name of God. It shows us therefore that many words in the Bible are to be interpreted according to the connection in which they are used. *Shall proceed of themselves* means the Chaldeans were independent in disposition and followed their own inclination regardless of all others.

Verse 8. The horse was a prominent means of warfare in ancient times, both for the drawing of chariots and carrying of cavalrymen. The Chaldeans possessed some of the finest specimens of that noble creature. *Evening wolves* is a figure denoting the viciousness with which they would lunge into battle. A wolf that had been fasting through the day would be hungry and ravenous by evening. The fact is used to illustrate the activities of the Chaldeans when their cavalry operated in the battle. *Fly as the eagle* is another figure of speech that means the same as the above comments.

Verse 9. The pronouns "they" and "their" stand for the Chaldeans (or Babylonians) who will be using the horses in the action. *Shall come for violence* means that when these forces come against Judah it will be with the intention of getting what they want even if they have to use violence in getting it. *Sup up* is from one word and it is explained in the lexicon to mean "to accumulate by impulse."

Gather as the sand indicates that the Chaldean army will sweep all before it as the east wind would drive the sand ahead of it and pile it up in great heaps.

Verse 10. The gist of this verse is that the Chaldean army will have no fear of kings or other men in official position. They will be treated as if they were only a heap of sand that had been drifted by the east wind.

Verse 11. *Change* means to be active and move promptly toward the objective. *Offend* is from ASHAM and defined by Strong, "To be guilty." The thought is that, though the Chaldean army was to be the instrument in God's hand in this great event, yet they will make a serious mistake in giving the credit for their achievement to their god.

Verse 12. Dropping the predictions of the captivity and the characteristics of the Babylonians, the prophet addresses the Lord on behalf of the people of Israel. He draws a contrast between Him and the Babylonian army. The latter was a mighty force but was destined to be overthrown. But the Lord is *from everlasting* and will be able to care for His people even though they are suffered to go into captivity. *We shall not die* means that Judah will not cease to be although she must be severely punished. It was *ordained* that they have the experience of *judgment* for the purpose of *correction*.

Verse 13. *Behold evil* is said in the sense of approving it, and *looking on* iniquity is used in the same sense. God actually sees everything that is going on but He does not favor the evil. The latter part of the verse represents the anxiety of the prophet over the situation. He is more impatient than the Lord, and seems to think that He should deal more harshly with the wicked and treacherous enemy.

Verse 14. This verse is a further description of the kind of enemy that the Lord's people had to endure. *Makest men as the fishes of the sea* means that the Babylonians had no more regard for men than they did for the dumb creatures.

Verse 15. Continuing his figure of the fishes, the prophet represents the Babylonians as dealing with the people of God in the same way they would the fishes which they caught in a net to be consumed upon their own appetites.

Verse 16. The *net* is now used to represent the idolatrous god of the heathen. Since the *net* had contributed gain to its owners, they concluded that it was a god and worthy to have worship paid to it.

Verse 17. The prophet asks in a deploring attitude, if the Lord will suffer these heartless fishermen to continue their cruel business. A fisherman empties his net so that he may use it to take more fish. The complaint of the prophet really is a prediction that the enemy (Babylon) will not be permitted to continue the wicked dealing with God's people.

HABAKKUK 2

Verse 1. The preceding chapter closes with the plea of the prophet to put a stop to the wicked business of the enemy. This verse represents him as waiting at his post of duty and listening to hear what the Lord will say to him in response. *Watch* is a short term for watchtower, because prophets were regarded as watchmen on the walls of Zion and looking out for the welfare of the people (Ezekiel 3: 17). The prophet is watching and sees the enemy approaching (with his prophetic eye) and has reported it to his great Commander-in-chief and wants to know what is to be done about it.

Verse 2. This verse begins the Lord's answer to the prophet's inquiry. He is instructed to *make it plain* which is from BAAR, defined in the lexicon, "A primitive root; to dig; by analogy to engrave." *Tables* is from LUACH which Strong defines, "To glisten; a tablet (as polished), of stone, wood or metal." The means of advertisement were not very plentiful in ancient times, and public notices were supposed to be so arranged that all could know about it. The verse means that Habakkuk was to select a writing tablet or plate and engrave the announcement upon it. He was to engrave the words on this plate and display it in a conspicuous place. Then a man running by could read it as he was passing very much as a traveler today can read the road signs as he is driving along.

Verse 3. The gist of this verse is that some time will pass by before the prediction is fulfilled, but it is sure to come and the people should be expecting it.

Verse 4. *Lifted up* is said in the sense of pride, something that the

Lord abhors as not being the proper spirit of an *upright* man. Such a principle will not direct anyone in the way pleasing to Him. Instead, the man who will live or be in the favor of God is one who *shall live by faith* and who is not prompted in conduct by pride.

Verse 5. This and a number of verses following describe some characteristics of the Chaldeans who were destined finally to come against Judah. *Neither keepeth at home* indicates the practice of that heathen nation in seeking further territory to subdue. In the pursuit of such a desire it *gathers unto him all nations.* This explains the motive that Babylon had in subduing Judah although it was the decree of God that his people be taken into that captivity. But since the motive was wrong, the Lord was determined to punish that heathen nation, which accounts for these verses against it.

Verse 6. After the Babylonians have been overthrown the nations that were mistreated by them will rejoice in their downfall. They will refer to the covetous practices of which they had been victims and consider them as reasons why the dreaded nation was itself conquered. *Thick clay* in the original is ABTIYT which Strong defines, "Something pledged, i.e. (collectively) pawned goods." Moffatt renders it "what he must repay." The passage means that when the Babylonian king seized the property of all these nations he was taking on a load that he would not always be able to carry. It is likened to a man who obligated himself by pawning something that he would not be able to redeem. That was because God was going to bring the King of Babylon to account and he would not be able to meet it.

Verse 7. This verse is in question form, but it is a prediction that the nations that Babylon had depressed would rebound and take vengeance on it.

Verse 8. *Spoiled many nations* refers to the plunder that the Babylonians took from the helpless countries.

Verse 9. The prophet now turns his writing into a general discussion of certain principles pertaining to the conduct of man and of God's attitude toward the same. *Coveteth an evil covetousness* means to desire that which would be wrong to have. That which would make it wrong is his evil motive, namely, that he might *set his nest on high* which means the act of self-exaltation or pride.

Verse 10. Concerning such a person described in the preceding verse, the prophet charges him to have *consulted shame* which means that his conduct will bring on his house the shame of defeat. He has really sinned against his own soul or life because in the end he will be the loser.

Verse 11. *Stone* and *beam* are inanimate objects and are used figuratively to represent the miraculous judgment that will come upon the man guilty of these wrongs.

Verse 12. It is right to build towns for habitations of needy people, but it is wrong to do so by violence against other helpless men.

Verse 13. The Lord has decreed that all who pursue such wicked courses for gain shall find themselves laboring in vain. Their own practices will turn out to be as a fire about them that will destroy all their evil labors.

Verse 14. The general knowledge of God's glory was to come to the nations when He brought the mighty Chaldean power into subjection. But we can see a greater fulfillment of the prediction in the universal distribution of the Gospel (Matthew 28: 19; Mark 16: 15; Romans 10: 18; Colossians 1: 23).

Verse 15. The Bible teaches that a drunkard will not inherit the kingdom of God (1 Corinthians 6: 10), so that such a character will be condemned for his own act. And our present verse condemns those who encourage or induce others to drink. It is especially to be condemned when the motive is as low as indicated in this verse. The statement gives us an additional thought, namely, that when a man is drunk his mentality is depressed and he is rendered unreliable in his actions and judgment.

Verse 16. As a degrading suggestion befitting the character of such a tempter, he is told to drink with his intended victim and thus be induced to expose his own nakedness. *Shame for glory* is rendered "more with shame than with glory" in the margin which is evidently correct. The tempter intended to get glory from the shame of his victim, but instead he was destined to bring shame upon himself. The *cup* is figurative and means the cup of God's wrath against such an evil character. He was to be forced to drink of it and be thereby induced to vomit out his own filth instead of glorying over the debauched condition of his victim.

Verse 17. *Violence of Lebanon.* The violence of Lebanon or the city of Jerusalem means that which was intended against the holy territory. But such violence was to rebound and cover the wicked nation or king who designed such drastic actions.

Verses 18, 19. The weakness and foolishness of idolatry is the subject of this paragraph. *Teacher of lies.* Every expectation that an idol seems to offer its maker is a lie. Man made the idol and therefore it could not possess any wisdom or power that man does not already have and so it could contribute nothing to him.

Verse 20. *Silence* is defined as "hush" in the lexicon. The servants of God are everywhere encouraged to sing and speak their praises of Him which would not seem like silence. The thought is to show a contrast with the foolishness of idolatry and the wisdom of an intelligent Deity. An idol is only a *teacher of lies* and should not be listened to. The Lord is in his rightful place, the temple, and on the throne of the universe. Therefore when He speaks it is the truth and all the earth should be hushed and with reverent ears receive the divine words.

HABAKKUK 3

Verse 1. *Shigionoth* is the name of a certain poetic metre, and this prayer of Habakkuk was composed in accordance with that.

Verse 2. Habakkuk acknowledges the threatening predictions of the Lord and declares that he is dreading them. *Revive thy work* is rendered "preserve alive" in the margin which expresses the thought in the original. It means that while the Lord must execute vengeance upon the wicked yet He is implored to temper justice with mercy.

Verse 3. *God came from Teman.* This place was near enough to Sinai to be associated with the giving of the law. It was through this document that God came to the people of Israel. *Selah* is a musical and poetic term and means a pause in the composition. It is not to be pronounced but only observed as a punctuation mark in literature.

Verse 4. *Horns* is a figurative symbol of power and glory and it is ascribed to God.

Verse 5. God controls pestilences and all the elements of the earth. If such forces are needed to carry out His plans they will be used.

Verse 6. *Measured* is defined "to shake" in the lexicon. That agrees with the verse in general which describes the Lord as having complete control of the earth.

Verse 7. *Cushan* or Cush refers to Ethiopia, a country near Egypt, and the prophet saw the Lord in control of that territory. *Curtains* is defined "A hanging (as tremulous)." The sentence denotes that the Midianites were caused to tremble by the might of the Lord as they beheld its manifestations against their weakness.

Verse 8. The questions asked in this verse should have a negative answer. God has controlled these parts of the earth and many times has disrupted their usual functions, but it was for the purpose of showing His wrath against the evil inhabitants. *Horses* and *chariots* signify the forces of war and the Lord is always at war with evil influences that He might effect salvation for the righteous.

Verse 9. The power and greatness of God, whether in war or peace, is the subject of this verse. *Bow made naked.* A bow was an instrument of war and to be made naked denotes that it is uncovered and ready for action. *Oaths of the tribes.* God had sworn that he would protect the tribes of Israel against their many foes. *Selah* is explained at verse 3. *Cleave the earth with rivers.* One of the most wonderful and artistic works of God is the river system of the earth. These streams of water ever flowing on and on, century after century, through rich or infertile countries, until they reach at last the sea, demonstrates the unchanging law of gravitation. And it all adds up to the conclusion that the God of the universe is all-wise and all-powerful.

Verse 10. The inanimate things of creation are said to praise the Lord because he controls them by the dictates of His will.

Verse 11. This refers specifically to the event recorded in Joshua 10. *Arrows* and *spears* are instruments of war, and when mentioned figuratively indicate God's power to overcome all conditions that might be a hindrance to the divine will.

Verse 12. *Didst* is past tense in form but means that God is always able to overcome the heathen nations in whatever land they may be dwelling.

Verse 13. The events of rescue mentioned here are both history and prophecy. God redeemed his people from Egypt and promised to rescue them from Babylon.

Verse 14. This verse has special reference to the events in Egypt when the children of Israel were about to be delivered. The pronouns are used in a rather indefinite manner; they stand for Egypt or the Lord or for his people. The thought is that God overthrew all forces of Egypt that had been arrayed against Israel.

Verse 15. This event is recorded in Exodus 14.

Verse 16. *When I heard* is said for the general report that was heard of the marvelous passage through the Red Sea which followed the judgments upon the Egyptians. The *trembling* and *quivering* denotes the impression that was made upon the nations when they heard about the dreadful occurrence. (See Joshua 2: 8-11.)

Verse 17. The misfortunes described in this verse were sometimes brought upon a country as a punishment for the sins of its people. He even sometimes visited his own people with like chastisements.

Verse 18. These judgments did not weaken the faith of the prophet in his God.

Verse 19. Habakkuk gives honor to God as being the source of all strength and success. The chapter ends with a reference to rhythmic measures similar to the term used in its beginning.

ZEPHANIAH 1

Verse 1. *Word of the Lord came unto Zephaniah* denotes that the prophet wrote by inspiration of God. *Days of Josiah* definitely gives us the date of the book which was near the end of the kingdom of Judah.

Verse 2. *Utterly consume* means to remove the things from the land.

Verse 3. *Consume* still means to remove, although it is used somewhat figuratively with reference to dumb creatures, for we know from history that there was no actual disturbance of such things. But by removing the people from the land it removed them from all use of them. The idols were the chief stumblingblocks of God's people so that is what is meant that would be removed. History shows that Israel never committed idolatry after the return from captivity.

Verse 4. Jerusalem was the capital of Judah and it was doomed to be taken into captivity. *Cut off the remnant of Baal* refers directly to the idols and they were to be cut off even before the people were removed. (See 2 Kings 23: 4, 5.)

Verse 5. *Host of heaven upon the housetops* refers to the worship of the stars, and the people went to their housetops for that practice. *Swear by the Lord* and by *Malcham* (national idol of the Ammonites) means they tried to mix the idolatrous worship with that of the true God of Israel.

Verse 6. *Cut off* is still the verb that tells what is to happen to certain evil characters. *Turned back from the Lord* means those who proved unfaithful to Him and directed their attention to idols. These persons did not seek information from the Lord nor even make any inquiry after Him.

Verse 7. *Hold thy peace* has about the same force as the bid for "silence" in Habakkuk 2: 20. *Day of the Lord* means the day of judgment against Judah when she was to be taken into captivity. *Prepared a sacrifice* is figurative and refers to the turning over of Judah to the Babylonians. *Bid his guests.* When a man makes a feast he invites a number of guests, and in like manner the Lord bids the whole world to behold the judgments about to be sent upon a disobedient people.

Verse 8. The leaders in Jerusalem were chiefly responsible for the corruptions of the nation and they are given special notice here.

Verse 9. *Leap on the threshold* means those who enter the houses of their abominable masters and thus endorse them in their evil way of life.

Verse 10. The gates and hills are mentioned which indicates that the tumult to be caused by the invasion would be general.

Verse 11. *Maktesh* was a spot in Jerusalem that was evidently a commercial center. The traffic had become questionable and the merchants were to be punished for it which is the reason they are told to howl.

Verse 12. *Candles* should not convey the thought of a weak light because such articles in ancient times were not made as they are today. The original word means something that would furnish a searching light. *Lees* are the settlings of wine that has become fixed and undisturbed. It is used figuratively to indicate the feeling of satisfaction that the leading men in Jerusalem had in spite of the warning predictions of the prophets that a calamity was soon coming upon the city. *Not do good or evil* means that they did not believe that the Lord was really going to do anything about the situation. They had lulled the people into a state of indifference as to their conduct by the false prophecies of peace made to them by the corrupt teachers.

Verse 13. This verse is a prediction of the invasion from the Babylonian army that was to take possession of the property of the inhabitants of Jerusalem.

Verse 14. *The great day of the Lord is near.* Zephaniah wrote this in the days of Josiah which was less than a quarter of a century before the captivity.

Verse 15. This verse describes the terrible conditions that came upon the land at the siege and capture of Judah by the Babylonion army. The fulfillment of the prediction is recorded in 2 Kings 24 and 25.

Verse 16. The *trumpet* was sounded in a time of war and this is a prediction of such an occasion. *Fenced cities* were those that were walled and fortified, but all such means of protection or defence were destined to prove insufficient.

Verse 17. This verse is a description of the humiliation to come upon the men of Judah when the Babylonians came against the land. The reason for all this terrible judgment is expressed by the words *because they have sinned against the Lord.*

Verse 18. Sometimes a victorious army can be induced to make peace by the offer of money. But the Babylonians were not wanting that, instead they were bent on the subjugation of the city of Jerusalem and its surrounding territory.

ZEPHANIAH 2

Verse 1. *Gather together* is an exhortation for them to concentrate their attention upon the situation. *Nation not desired* means that their present state and conduct failed to meet the approval of the Lord.

Verse 2. *Before the decree bring forth.* If anything is to be done to avert the impending doom it must be done soon for the time of the invasion is near. *As the chaff* denotes that the nation was to be threshed and the worthless parts blown away.

Verse 3. Here is another instance of the apparent disagreement between the different announcements made to the people of Israel. The subject is explained by the long note offered in the comments on 2 Kings 22: 17 volume 2 of this Commentary.

Verses 4, 5. The towns and places named in this paragraph were those of the Philistines and adjoining territory. Those people had been enemies to God's nation and He decreed that they should be punished. And when the Lord's own people have received their just chastisement and have come back to their native land, these other spots will serve for the use of the returning nation.

Verse 6. Some of the uses that will be made of these territories are specified in this verse. One of the chief industries in the land of Palestine was that of the production and raising of sheep. The area under consideration was to furnish shelter for the shepherds and their flocks.

Verse 7. This verse specifically looks beyond the captivity about to come upon Judah and includes the return to Palestine. The captivity was to serve as a chastisement for the people of Judah and was not intended to be continued any longer than was necessary to accomplish the Lord's purposes.

Verse 8. These heathen nations had spoken lightly of the Lord's people and he was aroused in his jealousy over it, so that He was determined to make them feel the sting of divine wrath.

Verse 9. *Sodom* and *Gomorrah* were destroyed by fire from heaven (Genesis 19), and these Moabites and Ammonites were to be destroyed; not literally by fire, but with a destruction as decisive. *Residue of my people* means the remnant that was to return from the captivity (Ezra 2: 64).

Verse 10. A feeling of self-importance is often attributed to pride, and such was the case of the nations that arrayed themselves against Judah.

Verse 11. The heathen nations all depended upon their false gods and the Lord proposed to expose their weakness. *Men shall worship him* when they see His power to be superior to that of the idols. This does not mean they will become true servants of God in all of the requirements of divine law, but they will recognize Him as the superior deity over all beings claiming the adoration of mankind,

Verse 12. Ethiopia was another heathen nation that had made light of God's people and hence was threatened with divine vengeance.

Verse 13. The rest of the chapter is against the Assyrians and especially against the city of Nineveh which was their capital. That empire had invaded the land of Palestine in the days of the 10-tribe kingdom and had taken it into exile. As a punishment its territory was destined to become a wilderness.

Verse 14. After the Assyrians lost control of their territory, the same was to be used by their successors as a pasturage for their stock. Not only so, but wild creatures were to infest the desirable spots and enjoy themselves in the doleful place. *Uncover the cedar work.* The important buildings of ancient countries were lined with this beautiful wood, and the Lord predicted that they were to be ransacked and the ornamental cedar finishing be exposed to decay.

Verse 15. The disgrace of Nineveh is the subject of this verse. This was one of the proudest cities of the ancient world, but her pride was doomed to be brought down so low that all people passing by would cast reproachful glances and sneers at her.

ZEPHANIAH 3

Verse 1. The prophet now resumes his accusations against Jerusalem. The *filth* and *pollution* refers chiefly to her conduct towards false gods and her unjust treatment of her unfortunate citizens in private stations of life.

Verse 2. There were four things that Jerusalem should have done that she did NOT do, namely, *obeyed*, *received*, *trusted* and *drew* not near to her God. This combination of failures resulted in the anger of the Lord till he determined to bring swift judgment upon the city and its surrounding territory.

Verse 3. The leading men in Jerusalem were so cruel toward their brethren that they were compared to roaring lions. *Evening wolves.* A beast that had been without food all day would be especially ravenous. Moffatt renders the last clause, "leave not a bone till the morning," which agrees with the context that describes a greedy beast.

Verse 4. *Light and treacherous* means they are frivolous and unreliable. Such a prophet would refuse to be serious concerning the danger overhanging the nation. The priests made a mere formality of the services and violated the law whenever it would interfere with their plots against the common people.

Verse 5. The *just* Lord is a significant term in view of the conditions. It denotes that a severe chastisement is to be meted out against these wicked princes. God's disapproval of the corruptions is made known every day, yet the unjust leaders are not impressed thereby but continue in their wickedness.

Verse 6. *Have cut off* is past tense in form but is a prediction of the doom about to come from the Lord. The watchtowers of the cities were destined to be thrown down and the streets exposed to the passing enemy.

Verse 7. *I said*, etc., denotes that God expected the people to be impressed with the importance of His judgments, yet they continued on in their evil course. Their keenness to do evil is indicated by the words *they rose early and corrupted their doings.*

Verse 8. This long verse is only a prediction of the captivity of the nation that was just due. God had warned and exhorted his people by the faithful prophets, but they would not give heed thereto and hence He was determined to bring complete and prompt judgment upon the nation. *All the earth* is a figure of speech and denotes that the whole territory of Judah was to be devastated by the invading forces.

Verse 9. From this verse through the rest of the chapter the prophet deals with the effects the captivity was to have on the people and then of their return from the exile. *A pure language* means the people will speak in proper words concerning the true God of their nation and of the world. They will praise Him as being the just and holy One instead of the idols they had served in their home land before the captivity.

Verse 10. The main captivity was in the land of Babylon, but God had some people scattered in various other parts of the world, even in Ethiopia beyond Egypt. These dispersed people were to learn of the restoration of the service in Jerusalem and come forth to that place with their offerings for the divine service.

Verse 11. *In that day not be ashamed* might seem to disagree with other statements upon that subject, but the explanation is in the words later in the verse. The proud leaders will have been taken away and the ones remaining will have a feeling of satisfaction toward God because of their renewal of freedom in their own country.

Verse 12. The *afflicted and poor people* were the ones who had been mistreated by the princes and false prophets. These were to be restored to their native land so that they could resume the holy service.

Verse 13. *The remnant* are the ones designated in Ezra 2: 64. *Shall not do iniquity* is the prediction that idolatry will have been eradicated from the practices of the people by the effects of the captivity. The other good things mentioned in the verse were to result also from the purifying effects of the captivity.

Verse 14. *Daughter of Zion* is an endearing term for Jerusalem and her people. She is bidden to sing and rejoice and that is because her people were to be released from the Babylonian captivity.

Verse 15. *Taken away thy judgments* refers to the reversal of the state of servitude that had been imposed upon the nation for its sins. The enemy (Babylon) was overthrown and God's people were relieved from the oppression.

Verse 16. Zion was a special spot in Jerusalem that was used as the headquarters for the kings. The return from captivity was to bring joy again to the place.

Verse 17. The success of Zion was to be assured by the presence of the Lord who had never ceased to love His people. He is mighty and will enable the nation to express its joy by singing the Lord's praises.

Verse 18. *Solemn assembly* pertains to the national gathering in the name of the Lord. All such meetings had been discontinued during the captivity.

Verse 19. *Undo all that afflict thee* denotes the overthrow of the heathen who had oppressed Israel. *Her that halteth* refers to the nation of God that had been held back by the chastisement from proceeding in the regular services of Jerusalem.

Verse 20. The gist of this verse is in the words *when I turn back your captivity*. The exile in Babylon was decreed by the Lord as a punishment upon his people for their sin of idolatry. When that event had accomplished the Lord's purpose it was decreed and predicted that the nation would return home.

HAGGAI 1

Verse 1. The reader should consult the book of Ezra, especially the last part of the 4th and first part of the 5th chapter; that will throw much light on the book we are studying. The Jews had been given authority by the king of Persia to rebuild the house of God in Jerusalem but they had let the work cease for various reasons. Then the prophets were used by the Lord to stir up the people and shame them for their selfishness in being more concerned with their own affairs than they were with those of the Lord. After the prodding by these prophets the workers upon the building resumed their task. The reference in Ezra is very brief but our present book will give us a fuller view of the situation. The date of the book is given as the second year of Darius who was king in the Medo-Persian Empire at that time.

Verse 2. This verse reveals the excuse that was given by the people why they were not going on with the work of the temple. It was the age-old attempt at defence by saying it was not the right time yet, or that "there is plenty of time yet."

Verse 3. This was the word of the Lord although the people received it at the mouth of the prophet who was His inspired spokesman.

Verse 4. Haggai chides them with their inconsistency because they were interested in their own personal affairs instead of the Lord's. They were building homes for their personal use and allowing the Lord's house to lie waste.

Verse 5. As a means of arousing them to a sense of their real position before God, the prophet calls their attention to some circumstances in their affairs that should have indicated to them that something was wrong.

Verse 6. The general subject of this verse is that almost everything in their personal occupations was having very little success. Those were the years when God sometimes punished his people with temporal reverses of various kinds, and their experiences were along that line.

Verse 7. Calling attention to their unrighteous ways, the prophet proceeds to tell his people what they should do to regain the good will of the Lord.

Verse 8. The temple was constructed of various materials such as stone, metal and wood. The wood was to be obtained from the mountains because the valleys did not produce it. They were told that by taking this interest in the work of the Lord they would glorify Him and their conduct would be pleasing in the divine sight.

Verse 9. The prophet backs up the exhortation of the preceding verse by resuming the thought expressed in verse 6. The key to the subject is in the words *because of mine house that is waste*. They could not make the plea of inability for work, for they were at that very time running *every man unto his own house*.

Verse 10. Moisture from above and fertility from the earth had been withheld from their crops as a punishment for their neglect of duty.

Verse 11. This verse sums up the general shortages they had suffered in about all the departments of their industrial and agricultural life. Of course they knew they had been thus restricted but they acted as if they thought it had been by accident. Hence the Lord informs them that He had called for all of their afflictions.

Verse 12. The exhortation of the prophet had the desired effect. It is interesting to note that in their obedience it includes the words of the prophet with those of God. It was as it should be, for when God inspires a man to deliver an order to the people it comes with as much authority as if He spoke directly to them.

Verse 13. When the people showed a willingness to obey the Lord, the prophet encouraged them by assuring them that the Lord was with them.

Verse 14. *The Lord stirred up the spirit of Zerubbabel*. The context shows what means the Lord used to do this stirring, for it was through the mouth of the prophet. When God does anything through the words of an inspired spokesman it is equivalent to doing it direct and will have the same result as if done in such a manner.

Verse 15. The date of the events of this chapter is made more specific than it was in the first verse by giving the particular day of the month; the 24th.

HAGGAI 2

Verse 1. This chapter begins about a month later than the close of the preceding one. In that time the work on the temple has gone forward to the point of getting the foundation laid. That made it possible to see something of the appearance of the completed building when that time came.

Verse 2. The Lord then gave the prophet instructions to call the attention of the builders and the people to the work as it then appeared.

Verse 3. There were pople living who had seen the temple that was destroyed by the Babylonians. They were asked to make the comparison, and it was suggested that they would conclude the present building to be inferior to the first one. This event of comparison is given more detailed notice in Ezra 3: 12.

Verse 4. This verse begins with the word *yet* which indicates that God did not profess to regard the present building as actually as good as the other. However, He encourages them to be of good cheer and promises them to be with them in the work.

Verse 5. The same God who brought Israel out of Egypt and sustained them with His spirit, is the one who has led them through the trials just now going on and will continue to lead them if they will obey.

Verse 6. Following a practice we have before seen with the prophets, the Lord has Haggai to leap from a fortunate event in the history of fleshly Israel to one of spiritual Israel or the church. This and the following three verses deal with that subject, and the imagery is drawn from the literal shaking of Mt. Sinai when the Mosaic system was given to the people of Israel. After that shaking had subsided it left remaining the organized institution that was to serve the people through that dispensation. Now the Lord predicts that one more great shaking will occur that will affect *the heavens and the earth*.

Verse 7. Desire of *all nations* was to be fulfilled when the Gentile as well as the Jew would be offered the same benefits. *This house* refers to the house of the Lord composed of Christians (Hebrews 3: 6).

Verse 8. These material substances used to make the literal temple all belonged to God. Likewise the materials composing the spiritual temple all belong to him according to 1 Corinthians 6: 19, 20.

Verse 9. *Glory of the latter house greater than the former*. This was predicted of the church which is the greatest organization that God ever placed on the earth. We need not be uncertain about the above application of this noted prophecy, for Paul makes that use of it in Hebrews 12:26-28.

Verse 10. About two months later than the preceding verse the Lord gave another message to the prophet. Inspiration is not a condition that is settled upon a man as if it were a part of his natural faculty. When God wished to have any revelation made known He would call the spokesman into the service and inform him just what he was to say. That is why we are told that "holy men of God spake as they were moved by the Holy Ghost" (2 Peter 1:21).

Verse 11. The priests were the men who had supervision of the altar services and hence were acquainted with the requirements of the law. The prophet was given the present message to them for the purpose of explaining why the Lord was making his severe complaints against the nation.

Verse 12. *Holy flesh* means that kind that had been selected and prepared for the altar according to the demands of the law. But while holding that flesh in his skirt before reaching the altar he comes in contact with these other articles that had not been consecrated. The priests admitted that it would render that flesh unholy.

Verse 13. The ceremonial law regarded a dead body as unclean and everything that touched it was so. Even the people in general knew or had known that such was the stipulation in their instructions that came from the Lord through Moses.

Verse 14. Having reminded them of the provisions concerning cleanness as they pertained to individual items of the service, Haggai makes comparison to the state of the nation. The services that were being attempted might have been legal in themselves, but the nation had come in contact with that which was unclean which rendered the whole procedure unholy. (See note offered at Isaiah 1:10, volume 3 of this Commentary.)

Verse 15. This verse asks them to take a view of their history going back to the time before any work had ever been done on the temple.

Verse 16. The points he wishes to have them recall are those pertaining to their temporal disappointments. This subject was treated previous to this chapter as may be noticed in the comments on some earlier verse.

Verse 17. They are reminded of the stubbornness that the nation manifested in spite of these chastisements from the Lord, which was the reason they had been doomed to spend a period in captivity under a foreign power.

Verse 18. The prophet brings the review down to the present date.

Verse 19. He reminds them that not only did the corruption of the past years cause them to be sent into captivity, but since that event their neglect of duty had brought about these shortages in their crops down to that very date. Notwithstanding all this, if they will begin *NOW* to serve the Lord faithfully they will be blessed.

Verse 20. On the same date as the foregoing message the Lord gave the prophet one to deliver unto another important person in the congregation.

Verse 21. Zerubbabel was *governor* in the sense of being captain or leader in the work of the temple (Ezra 1:1-4; 3:8; Nehemiah 12:1). This message was a repetition of the prediction shown in verses 6-9 concerning the "shaking" that God was going to do.

Verse 22. The comments on that passage shows the prediction to have reference to the church or kingdom of Christ. The present verse adds the specific prediction that God would *overthrow the throne of the kingdoms*. This is the same prediction that is meant in Daniel 2:44 concerning the perpetuity of the kingdom of Christ.

Verse 23. *In that day ... make thee as a signet.* The last word is defined in the lexicon as, "a signature-ring." It has been rendered also by "seal" elsewhere in the A.V. The thought is that when Zerubbabel performs his full duty of completing the work of the temple, he will be accepted by the Lord and his work will have the divine approval. And as a prediction in the nature of a type, when the Lord does the "shaking" predicted, those who carry out the work of the new kingdom will have the approval of "the God of heaven" who had set up the kingdom according to Daniel 2:44.

ZECHARIAH 1

Verse 1. This book begins two months later than the beginning of the preceding one. It takes up the same subject, however, that of the negligence of the Jews in the work of the temple. The reader should consult my comments on the first few verses of that book to avoid taking up space at this time. Zechariah, like Haggai, was a true prophet of God and was inspired to write this book we are studying.

Verse 2. *Fathers* is used as referring to the ancestors or other near relatives. The relationship first mentioned is that between the prophet and his older brethren with whom he was then associated.

Verse 3. When a man departs from serving the Lord, he is the one who must make the first move in being reunited. Hence God here promises to return to his people if they will return to Him which means they are to become faithful in their lives.

Verse 4. The present *fathers* are exhorted not to repeat the mistakes that their ancestors had made. The prophets had warned them to turn from their evil ways but the warning was unheeded and even spurned in many instances.

Verse 5. These fathers are reminded that the former ones had passed away, and the implication is they had gone down in disfavor in the eyes of the Lord.

Verse 6. *Take hold of your fathers* means that the warnings that God made to them came to pass; that their experiences were according to the threatenings that God had made to them. Indeed, so exactly did they come to be fulfilled that the people realized it and acknowledged it to be as a punishment for their evil ways. Such is the meaning of the latter part of this verse.

Verse 7. Zechariah received another message and it was in the form of a vision. It came in the same year as the first one but in the eleventh month of that year.

Verse 8. This vision (which will take up several verses) had to do chiefly with conditions in general in the political world following the Babylonian captivity. For a time the nations were undisturbed and even unconcerned about the dejected morale of the people of Israel. God wished to inform his people of what was in store and concluded to do so in connection with the vision. It starts with a group of red horses and a man riding on one of them who will finally be a spokesman for the Lord.

Verse 9. This verse reveals one form in which God sometimes appeared to the men who were to be inspired, namely, that of an angel. There is a number of cases recorded in the Bible where He appeared in that way. Zechariah asked the angel the meaning of the vision and was promised an answer.

Verse 10. The "man" spoken of in verse 8 gave the prophet the information that was promised by the angel. These horses were used as messengers of the Lord to go to and fro through the earth.

Verse 11. Having previously made one of their journeys over the earth, they now report in the hearing of Zechariah what they found out in their tour of inspection. The chief fact they learned was that all the earth was *at rest*. This is explained in verse 15 to mean that the people of the earth were *at ease*, meaning that they were unconcerned about the interests of God's people who had been through so much trouble and still were in a state of anxiety as to what they might expect next.

Verse 12. *These threescore and ten years* identifies the whole passage as a complaint or plea addressed to God because of conditions after the Babylonian captivity. Not that the enemy was still trying to hold them in bondage, for the Persians had control of the country previously held by the Babylonians and they had given the Jews their freedom. But there were some of the heathen in Palestine and that was making some trouble locally. The people of Israel were anxious about conditions and longed for the former settlement of their own services.

Verse 13. The Lord was sympathetic toward the nation and gave the angel a comfortable message of assurance, which he was to give over to the prophet who was in turn to deliver it to his people for their benefit and encouragement of mind.

Verse 14. God never lost his love for the nation notwithstanding its waywardness but was jealous over them. He had used the heathen nations as a means of chastisement in the same way that a loving father would administer severe but necessary punishment upon a child for whom he had the sincere parental love.

Verse 15. God's feeling against his people is contrasted with that of the heathen by the words *little displeased*. But He was *sore displeased* with the heathen because of their unconcern over the afflictions of Judah. The chastisements that the Lord imposed upon Israel were for their own good, but now the heathen were adding to those afflictions by being "at ease" or indifferent about it.

Verse 16. For the encouragement of the dejected people, the Lord gave the assurance that the holy house would be built in Jerusalem. *Line shall be stretched forth upon Jerusalem.* The first word is from QAV which Strong defines, "A cord (as connecting), especially for measuring; figuratively a rule." The passage shows not only that the city would be rebuilt, but that it would be done accurately and scientifically.

Verse 17. This verse adds the promise that other cities throughout the country would prosper and grow in number. Also that the original capital city of Jerusalem with its particular spot of Zion would be comforted.

Verse 18. Horns in symbolic language means governments or other powers. The four that are mentioned here are the same as the four living creatures of Ezekiel 1: 5, 6, meaning the four world empires beginning with the Babylonian.

Verse 19. The angel explained that the four governments were the ones that had scattered the Lord's people. That does not mean that all four of them had a hand in the affair, for two of them were yet in the future when Zechariah was writing. But the four were considered as a unit because they represented the powers that were to be permanently removed from among mankind. And all of them had one characteristic in common, that of absolute domination over people who had a right to be free. It was this phase of them that prompted Babylon to oppress Israel, but the entire regime was destined to be overthrown by the means to be described shortly.

Verse 20. *Carpenters* is from CHARASH which Strong defines, "A fabricator of any material." The word has a wide range of meaning and this place is used in reference to some forces that were to erect something in the place of these four horns that had scattered Judah, for they were to be destroyed and replaced by the carpenters' work.

Verse 21. The pronoun *these* is used three times but for different nouns. The first and third refer to the carpenters of the preceding verse, while the second means the *four horns* that had *scattered Judah.* The carpenters had come to *fray* (subdue and destroy) the four horns. In other words, the four world empires were to come to an end, and within their territory and upon their ruins these new builders were to erect another kind of structure. The whole passage including verse 18 through 21 is a prediction with the same meaning as Daniel 2: 44. That prophecy assures the world that the four world empires were to come to an end, and at the same time the God of Heaven would set up a kingdom that was to stand forever. The work of setting up that kingdom was to be accomplished through the agency of these *carpenters,* which would be fulfilled by the labors of the apostles of Christ.

ZECHARIAH 2

Verse 1. The direct meaning of this whole chapter is a prediction of the return from the captivity. In a figurative and spiritual sense it portrays many of the truths of the Gospel age, but that application should not be stressed too much.

Verses 2, 3. Upon inquiry, the man with the measuring line told Zechariah he was going to measure Jerusalem. This is the same thing that is stated in chapter 1: 16. It pertains to the reconstruction period when the building of Jerusalem and vicinity was to be restored after the return from exile.

Verse 4. *This young man* means Zechariah who was expected to put his information in a book for the benefit of the people in future generations. *Towns without walls* might convey the idea of places unprotected and in danger from exposure to possible enemies. Part of the explanation is in the fact of the crowded condition of the city, and further information about it will be shown in the next verse.

Verse 5. No material wall is needed for a town that is protected by the presence of the Lord. This truth may be said also of the New Testament age under Christ.

Verse 6. *Land of the north* means Babylon in which the people of Judah were soon to be inclosed with the captivity. (See the note with comments on Isaiah 14: 31 in volume 3 of this Commentary.) The verse is a prediction of the return from that land of the *north,* expressed in the words *flee from.*

Verse 7. *Deliver itself* means the same as the preceding verse.

Verse 8. The prophet was sent as a messenger to the people of Judah to assure them of their return from the *nations which spoiled* them which means the Babylonians. *Apple of his eye* is a figure of speech that means the most cherished part of His being.

Verse 9. *Shake mine hand* was to be fulfilled when God sent another nation (the Persians) against Babylon. *Spoil to their servants* was accomplished when the very people whom Babylon had held in servitude were able to obtain benefits from them.

Verse 10. *Sing and rejoice* was fulfilled in Nehemiah 8: 10-12.

Verse 11. *Many nations shall be joined to the Lord* was fulfilled first according to Esther 8: 17, and fulfilled spiritually according to Acts 2: 5.

Verse 12. Judah means the 2-tribe kingdom because it was the legal portion of the nation as to the original headquarters in Jerusalem. The prediction is that the capital was to be restored after the captivity.

Verse 13. *Be silent* is a call for all to hear the word of God.

ZECHARIAH 3

Verse 1. *He* means the angel who has been talking with Zechariah (chapter 2: 3; 4: 1). This angel continues the vision for the information of the prophet, in which he sees a scene that pertains to the service of the Mosaic system, and in this scene is another angel of the Lord. *Satan* is from the Hebrew word SATAN and Strong defines it, "An opponent; especially (with the article prefixed) Satan, the arch-enemy of Good." The first term of the definition is its general meaning, for the original word is used in a number of other places where it cannot mean the devil as that word is commonly used. The thought of this verse, however, regardless of the personal identity of the *Satan* mentioned, is that some being stood there to oppose the services of the high priest. The vision represents conditions as they were to be just after the return from the captivity. The entire altar and other services of the Jewish church had been corrupted by the mixture with heathenism, and it could have been truly said that the priesthood was unfit to participate in that profession.

Verse 2. Even though the situation was as described in the preceding paragraph, it was not appropriate for this adversary to be criticizing it, for it was none of his business. Notwithstanding, the Lord (in the person of the angel Michael, Jude 9) did not rail out against him. He merely appealed to a "higher court" by saying, *The Lord* [in heaven] *rebuke thee. A brand plucked out of the fire.* The people of God had been salvaged from the captivity as a brand of a body that was burning but was snatched out before it was completely destroyed. This brand is the remnant that is revealed in Ezra 2: 64 that came back from the captivity.

Verse 3. It was true that the service had been corrupted by the mixture with heathenism, and the priests had been guilty of the abomination.

Verse 4. The captivity, however, had cured the nation of idolatry and now the people are to be permitted to resume the former services. Hence this verse shows that the filthy garments of the priest were to be replaced with a *change of raiment.*

Verse 5. The *mitre* and *garments* represent the attire that was worn by the priests under the Mosaic system (Exodus 28). These were to be used again after the body of the service had been reconsecrated.

Verse 6. *Protested unto Joshua* means he admonished him.

Verse 7. The admonition was for the priest to walk in the ways of the Lord. On this condition he was given the promise that he would have the divine favor. *Give thee places* denotes that if the priest would walk consistently with his high office, then he would have a good standing among the people of the city and nation.

Verse 8. This and the following two verses evidently have a twofold bearing, first on the restored condition of fleshly Israel, then on the established system under Christ. *Branch* is from the same Hebrew word so rendered in chapter 6: 12; Jeremiah 23: 5 and 33: 15, where the context shows beyond any doubt that it means Christ.

Verse 9. The rebuilding of the temple required the use of literal stones, likewise the temple of Christ used "lively stones" built upon the chief Stone who was Christ. (See Ephesians 2: 20; 1 Peter 2: 5.) *Seven eyes* were *upon one stone.* Seven is a complete number in figurative language and this denotes that the complete, all-seeing eyes of the Lord would be on the new building (1 Peter 3: 12). *Remove the iniquity in one day* was fulfilled first by causing Israel to be cured of idolatry in one period of captivity. It was fulfilled next by giving the Gospel on the day of Pentecost which is recorded in Acts 2.

Verse 10. *Under the vine and under the fig tree* is explained by the comments on Micah 4:4 and needs not be repeated here.

ZECHARIAH 4

Verse 1. Strong says the word for *waked* has both a literal and figurative meaning, which accounts for the way it is used in this place. It means that the attention of Zechariah was aroused as he had been musing like being in a day dream over the profound revelations of the preceding chapter.

Verse 2. The revelations of the angel were continued in the form of a vision. The things Zechariah saw pertained to the service of the tabernacle under the Mosaic institution of government and religion (Exodus 25: 31-40).

Verse 3. The oil that was used in the lamps was olive oil, hence the need for the olive trees which were literal in the first application.

Verse 4. Zechariah asked for an interpretation of the olive trees.

Verse 5. These questions might seem to be unnecessary, but they evidently were asked by way of focusing the attention of the prophet, and also to indicate an assurance that he would be given the desired information.

Verse 6. The trees are explained to represent the spirit of the Lord. That was because spiritual light comes from that source, even as oil furnishes temporal light.

Verse 7. *Mountain* is used figuratively to represent a supposed great difficulty. Such a condition was apparent when the Jews got back from the captivity, and the local enemies tried to make that mountain still higher. But that condition of apparent distress was to be overcome, which is symbolized by the act of converting a mountain into a plain. Zerubbabel is the one who is meant that would accomplish the feat because he was the man who was chosen to lead in the work of reconstruction (Ezra 2:2; 3:2).

Verse 8. Such language as this short verse is used frequently in order to keep the impression before the reader that the whole book is inspired of God.

Verse 9. After the work on the temple was started it was hindered and finally stopped by the enemies (Ezra 4:1, 24). But the Lord assured the people that it would yet be completed which was fulfilled according to Ezra 6:15.

Verse 10. The work of rebuilding the temple had a comparatively small beginning. It was so much so that some of the older citizens wept when they viewed it and rememberd the original temple (Ezra 3:12; Haggai 2:3). However, they should not have allowed it to discourage them. They should not have *despised* (belittled) the small beginning of the work because they had the assurance of the Lord that it would go unto complete restoration of their service. *Seven eyes* is explained at chapter 3:9.

Verse 11. Zechariah repeats the inquiry that was made in verse 4, but the repetition of the inquiry is prompted by something more that he sees which will be stated in the next verse.

Verse 12. The additional detail the prophet saw was the pair of branches through which the oil was poured into the bowls of the lamps. It indicates the idea of the Lord's doing things by various agencies.

Verse 13. The prophet still is unaware of the meaning of the vision.

Verse 14. *Two anointed ones* is rendered "sons of oil" in the margin. All along through the vision we have seen oil used to typify spiritual light. We have likewise observed in more than one instance that the writer would pass from fleshly to spiritual Israel. God has given the world just two organized religions, the Mosaic and the Christian, each of which has furnished light to the people of the earth. Accordingly, each of these religions has had its own law guidance, its own means of furnishing spiritual light for mankind. Since that light has been figurized in this vision by olive trees and their fruit, the conclusion is plain that the *two anointed ones* are the Old and the New Testament.

ZECHARIAH 5

Verse 1. The next item in the vision was a *flying roll*.

Verse 2. In ancient times all documents were written on strips of the material selected and then rolled up. *Flying roll* indicates that the roll was to be sent out through the land. Zechariah stated the dimensions of this roll to be 15 x 30 feet. The great size of the document would indicate the vast importance of it.

Verse 3. The angel explained the roll to be the *curse* or judgment of God against evildoers. Before the captivity the leaders were guilty of much injustice against the poor. Now the Lord is going to head off any recurrence of such dealing. By announcing a curse upon all guilty ones they would be given a solemn warning to beware of conducting themselves as they previously did. *This side* and *that side* means to threaten a complete judgment against whoever thinks to resume the old fraudulent transactions. *One that sweareth* means the one who deals dishonestly and then tries to cover up the deeds by false oaths.

Verse 4. *It shall enter into the house of the thief* means the curse of God that is pronounced in this flying roll. The course was to remain in the house of this dishonest dealer until it was consumed and the stones destroyed or removed.

Verse 5. The angel called the attention of Zedekiah to something else before him.

Verse 6. The prophet is usually induced to inquire for the meaning of all the visions. He is told in the present case that what he sees is an *ephah* which means a measuring device. *Their resemblance* means the evils that had been committed by the false dealers were as great as this measuring unit of the ephah.

Verse 7. A condensed comment on the rest of the chapter would be that it represents the sin of idolatry that the people of God learned from the heathen. But the captivity in the land of Shinar (which represents Babylon) cured them and the abomination was left in that land when God's people came away. I shall comment on this and the other verses in their order. Woman is the one who gives birth to living beings, and she is used in symbolic language to represent the propagation of sin as it was practiced by the people of Judah. That is why she is shown as sitting in the ephah, which we have previously learned represents the vast sins of the nation. But she was destined to be sealed up in this ephah and shipped off to a country that normally uses such a product. Strong defines the original word for *talent* as, "a round loaf; also a talent (or large round coin)." This was used as a cover for the ephah or measuring vessel that had the form of a large cask or barrel.

Verse 8. This woman who represented *wickedness* was pushed down into the vessel and the *talent* or "round coin" was clamped on to seal her in. The package was then ready to be transferred to its proper destination.

Verse 9. Of course someone must convey this package to its destination and hence two women who were interested in the same sins as the other came to make the transference. Since Israel and Judah had gone, respectively, into Assyria and Babylonia, that would call for the two women. The wind would help any creature that flies, hence these women were given wings and a wind was raised so they could make their transit with all surety and speed.

Verse 10. The prophet saw the women leave and inquired about their destiny.

Verse 11. They were going to the land of Shinar which represents Babylonia according to Genesis 10: 10. *Be established . . . upon its own base.* This signifies that such abomination as idolatry belongs in a country like Babylonia, and the history shows that when Judah left that country she left her idolatry of all forms there for ever. This testimony is presented in a long note in connection with the comments on Isaiah 1: 25, volume 3 of this Commetary.

ZECHARIAH 6

Verse 1. The first 8 verses of this chapter have virtually the same meaning as the closing ones of the preceding chapter. *Four chariots* represents the four corners of the earth unto which the power of God reaches, and this power was sent forth from Jerusalem that is situated in the midst of various mountains.

Verse 2. Red symbolizes bloodshed and black brings famine. Both of these conditions had to come before the revolution predicted could be accomplished.

Verse 3. These horses merely signify some of the various effects that would result from the events of the invasion by a heathen power.

Verse 4. Again the prophet is left to make inquiry on the subject, evidently to get the matter in the focus of his attention and also to direct the thoughts of the reader.

Verse 5. *Four spirits* are the same as "four corners" in verse 1.

Verse 6. As the *north* country denotes Babylon (see the comments on Isaiah 14:31), so the *south* would mean Judah that was taken to Babylon.

Verse 7. These horses represent the activity in general that took place as all this revolution was going on that was to chastise and reform God's people.

Verse 8. *Quieted my spirit in the north country.* This is a reference to the fact that the people of God were cured of idolatry by their stay in that country. When they came out of the captivity in that land they left their idolatry in it and that "quieted" the spirit of God; it satisfied Him with their reformation.

Verse 9. This verse is another assurance of the inspiration of Zechariah.

Verse 10. The men named were among them who came back from Babylon. Zechariah was told to take these men and enter the house of Josiah who was then living in Judea.

Verse 11. The men named who had come from Babylon had brought along some silver and gold. They did this by the direction of the reigning king in Babylon according to Ezra 1:4. Zechariah was to use some of that metal in making a crown to be placed on the head of the high priest. This was to indicate that the service of the altar was to be resumed.

Verse 12. This is another instance where the prophet advances his prediction of favor for God's people from fleshly to spiritual Israel. This and the following verses of the chapter predict the work of Christ and his kingdom upon the earth. He is called The Branch by way of importance and because His work was destined to *grow up out of his place*. The temple that he was to build is the church which is recognized by that name in 1 Corinthians 3:16 and 2 Corinthians 6:16.

Verse 13. *Priest upon his throne.* Christ was to unite in himself the two offices of priest and king. That was never permitted in the Mosaic system; the two were not even from the same tribe. The kings were from the tribe of Judah and the priests were from the tribe of Levi. In 2 Chronicles 26:16 is an account of a king who tried to assume the office of priest but got into serious trouble with the Lord over it. Not only was Christ to be both king and priest, but his followers are said to be, likewise. (See 1 Corinthians 4:8; 1 Peter 2:9; Revelation 5:10; 19:16.) However, we should understand that Christians rank second in these positions compared with Christ. *Counsel of peace shall be between them both.* The first word is defined by "advice" and "plan" in the lexicon, and it has been rendered "purpose" in the A.V. The thought is that the two functions will cooperate in complete harmony.

Verse 14. The men named were outstanding Jews who came back from the captivity. The crowns (mentioned in verse 11) were to serve to them, or in their sight, as memorials or reminders of the prediction made in verse 13.

Verse 15. The term *far off* identifies the prediction as applying to the Gentiles who were to be included in the service under this Priest-King. (See Acts 2:39 and Ephesians 2:13-19.) This great twofold office of Christ was to be for the benefit of all mankind regardless of race or nationality.

ZECHARIAH 7

Verse 1. This chapter begins two years later than the beginning of the book. Darius in this verse was the first man of that name to reign who was a Persian. It was in the second year of his reign that the work on the temple was resumed after having been stopped for a number of years (Ezra 4:24), and it was in his sixth year that it was completed (Ezra 6:15). Hence the present chapter starts midway of the great work that was performed after the prophets Haggai and Zechariah aroused the builders with their exhortations and warnings.

Verse 2. According to Ezra 3:2, 6 the altar of sacrifices was built some time before the temple was completed. The interest in the service of the Lord was indicated by sending these men to Jerusalem to pray on behalf of the work.

Verse 3. These men seem to have been either confused about the whole situation, notwithstanding they were sent to pray for the work, or they were acting without sincerity after arriving there. Now they protest to the priests and prophets that there is no use that *I* (meaning the people) should offer these services now, when the same had been done through many years and they had been rejected.

Verses 4, 5. Then the word of the Lord was revealed to Zechariah in order to explain why the service should be performed now even though it was rejected before, meaning their attempts at such services during the *seventy years* of the captivity. God had previously predicted that if his people so conducted themselves that they would need to be sent into captivity, they would not be permitted to render service to Him in the strange land, but would be compelled to continue their idolatrous practices while in the heathen country. (See Deuteronomy 28: 35, 64; Jeremiah 16: 13; Hosea 5: 6; Psalms 137). But now since that program has been carried out, the worshipers of God need not hesitate to resume the lawful services.

Verse 6. Even had the Jews attempted to perform the services while in the strange land, their own personal enjoyments of the body would have been all they would have received from them, for the Lord would not have received them. It would have been a situation very much like that described by a familiar saying concerning an unlawful prayer that does not "rise any higher than the head" of the one offering it.

Verse 7. This verse is a reminder of the past conduct of the people when the prophets spoke to them the word of the Lord. The prosperity of the country seemed to be overlooked and the warnings of the prophets were ignored. The force of the present verse is that they should now profit by the mistakes of the ancestors.

Verse 8. The word comes from the Lord but it was to be delivered to the people as a warning and exhortation to deal gently and justly with each other.

Verse 9. *Lord of hosts* means He is Lord of armies or other multitudes. The fathers had suffered through the unjust dealing of the princes and God wished his people to be spared such hardships now that they were back safely in their own land.

Verse 10. It is not only wrong to engage in the actual cruel dealings against the helpless, but also to be only thinking about it.

Verse 11. *They* means the former princes and they *pulled away the shoulder*. That means they backslid from the work or service of the Lord and refused to do their share. The figure is based on a common means of service from the ox in those days, when the beast was required to press his shoulder against the yoke.

Verse 12. An *adamant stone* is one of the hardest kind of stones and is used to illustrate the stubbornness of the people against the law of the Lord. When the prophets spoke the words of the Lord it was equivalent to His voice as to authority, hence the rejection of them brought down His wrath.

Verse 13. The refusal of the people to hear the call of the Lord resulted in His refusal to hear when they cried out for mercy.

Verse 14. A whirlwind not only overthrows what is in its path, but picks up and carries it away. The fact is used to illustrate the work of God's wrath in gathering up the unfaithful nation and carrying it into a strange land.

ZECHARIAH 8

Verse 1. *Lord of hosts* means he is Lord of armies or great numbers of people. Such a Being could properly demand attention to His word.

Verse 2. Exodus 20: 5 tells us that the Lord is jealous and gives the reason. He will not divide his love with false gods and when they receive or attempt to obtain (through their worshipers) a part of that devotion it provokes the divine wrath. The people of Israel *(Zion)* had gone off after these gods and then the jealousy of their true God was aroused. It is the logical thing for a jealous husband to chastise an unfaithful wife, hence God did so with his wife by sending her into captivity.

Verse 3. But a husband does not thus punish his wife because he has ceased to love her, but rather because he still loves her in spite of her unfaithfulness. Hence this verse says that He will *return unto Zion* which means that He will show his unbroken love for his wife by living with her again; *will dwell in the midst of Jerusalem.*

Verse 4. This prediction is literal and denotes the perfect safety that will be enjoyed in the city of Jerusalem. Even the man so old that he has to walk with a cane will be living on the streets as a peaceful citizen which indicates not only the safety of the place, but that it has been that way for a long time.

Verse 5. There are at least two points of significance in this verse.

One is the assurance of a numerous young population, which was something much desired by the Jews. Another is that Jerusalem will be so secure after its recovery from the effects of the invasion that came before the captivity that the children will be safe while playing in the streets and open places of the city.

Verse 6. *If it be marvelous* or difficult means that, although it seems "too good to be true" in the eyes of the people, it will not be so with the Lord who is powerful.

Verse 7. *East country* and *west country* signifies that God will gather up his people from all places where they have been scattered. The bulk of the nation was in Babylon, but some were scattered in various other places.

Verse 8. *Be my people* does not mean they will have to become Jews, for they have always been that. It means they will be a part of a people as an organized nation with Jerusalem as its capital.

Verse 9. The Lord offers these words for the encouragement of His people. *Which were . . . days . . . foundation was laid.* The work on the temple was started almost a score of years prior to this verse but was stopped until the second year of the present king of Persia. It is now the fourth year of this king (chapter 7: 1) and the work on the temple is in good progress. The people are exhorted to be as cheerful over the prospects as they were at the very beginning. They now have the same prophets and they are speaking by the same divine authority that they did in the start of the reconstruction period, hence there is much reason for feeling reassured.

Verse 10. An observation that should encourage the people now is that previously the times were hard. There was internal strife and incomes were small and scarce.

Verse 11. It has all been changed by the Lord and there is no enemy to fear as there was in the days just gone.

Verse 12. This verse promises a state of general prosperity for the land. This will be through the fertility of the seed and soil, also by the help of the seasons in which an abundance of moisture will be dropped from the sky.

Verse 13. *Judah* and *Israel* are named separately which shows us that all 12 tribes of the Jews came back from the captivity and that proves that the doctrine of "the lost ten tribes" is a false one and at variance with the facts of history and truth of prophecy.

Verse 14. The former generations were punished severely by the Lord. That was not because of the mere fact that they sinned, but because they ignored all the admonitions and refused to repent when they could have done so. Then it was too late for them to avert the doom decreed for them, for the Lord had declared what was to be the fate to come and He *repented not;* would not change it.

Verse 15. The Lord promised to be as firm in his forecast of blessings for His people as he was in the predictions of the chastisement.

Verse 16. The promise of favor from God was made on condition of the proper conduct of the people. Whereas they had formerly been cruel and unjust toward each other, they were now expected to deal in truth or true security for a neighbor.

Verse 17. *False oaths* were forbidden in Old Testament times even, while all oaths of every kind are prohibited in the New (Matthew 5: 33-37; James 5: 12).

Verse 18. The inspiration of Zechariah is the thought in this verse.

Verse 19. The feasts were seasons of celebrations for the blessings of God. They were done on various occasions, and the ushering in of the months was one of the chief times for such activities. The numerical references to the months is for emphasis only, because each of the 12 months had its holy day signified by the new moon.

Verses 20-23. Contrary to my usual procedure, I have made one paragraph of these verses because the comments will apply to them as a whole. It is another instance where the prophet jumps from fleshly to spiritual Israel. It is a prediction of the setting up of the church and the reign of Christ in his kingdom starting at Jerusalem. The same prediction is in Isaiah 2: 1-4 and Micah 4: 1-5, and the fulfillment is recorded in the book of Acts, beginning in the second chapter. It is the kingdom the prophet Daniel saw in his prediction of the kingdom to "stand for ever" (Daniel 2: 44).

ZECHARIAH 9

Verse 1. *Burden* means that the Lord has something to say about certain places and it is recorded here. *Hadrach* refers to Assyria and *Damas-*

cus was the capital of ancient Syria. The prediction pertains to the fact that the eyes of mankind will be toward the Lord. This situation will be the result of God's triumph for his people over all other nations.

Verse 2. *Hamath* was an important city of Syria and *Tyrus* and *Zidon* were cities of the Phoenicians. All these places were destined to see and recognize the greatness of God's people after he has rescued them from the effects of the captivity.

Verse 3. *Tyrus* (Tyre) was a strong commercial city which is signified by the words *heaped up silver as the dust*. But this proud city felt the sting of defeat.

Verse 4. *Power in the sea* refers to the traffic carried on by Tyre on the Mediterranean Sea because the city was situated on the coast of that body of water, and that gave her good shipping accommodations in connection with the principal ports of the world in which to exchange her manufactured products for raw materials.

Verse 5. All of the towns named in this verse were in the land of the Philistines. They were destined to witness the defeat of heathen nations and the success of Israel.

Verse 6. *Bastard* is from MAMZER which Strong defines, "From an unused root meaning to alienate; a mongrel, i.e., born of a Jewish father and a heathen mother." The verse means that the proud heathen city of Ashdod would have to tolerate the presence of a half-breed, one with Jewish blood in his veins which would be humiliating to the high minded heathen people.

Verse 7. Even this half-breed will be reformed from his practice of bloodshed. He will not talk about such acts but will imitate the principles of the rulers in Judah. The people of Ekron (a Philistine city) will act as if they were citizens of Jerusalem which is meant by a *Jebusite*.

Verse 8. The gist of this verse is that God would be a sure protection against any passing group that might seek to disturb His people.

Verse 9. This prediction was cited and fulfilled in Matthew 21: 1-11. The significant phase of the event was to be that the King would ride on both mother and colt. There would have been nothing unusual in the mere act of riding on one beast as that was a common means of transportation in those days.

Verse 10. *Ephraim* stands for the 10-tribe kingdom or Israel, and Jerusalem is for the 2-tribe kingdom or Judah. *Chariot* and *battle-bow* signifies war and the prediction is that it was to be cut off. The verse is a prediction that temporal warfare will not be used in defence of the spiritual kingdom of Christ. The prophecy also includes the spreading of the new kingdom among the Gentiles.

Verse 11. The pronoun *thee* stands for *Zion* in verse 9. *Blood of thy covenant* is rendered "whose covenant is by blood" in the margin which is correct. God had made a covenant with Abraham that his seed (blood descendants) were to be His people and that he would never entirely cast them off. That is why God caused them to be released from captivity. *Pit . . . no water*. A pit with water in it would have destroyed those cast therein, but a dry pit could serve as a prison but permit the victims to live. That is why God sent his people into Babylon, so they would be in bondage but not destroyed.

Verse 12. *The strong hold* means the city of Jerusalem and its country, for God was throwing great defences about that place and the people were encouraged to trust them.

Verse 13. The bow and arrow are used figuratively to represent *Judah* and *Ephraim*. Judah (the 2 tribes) and Ephraim (the 10 tribes) are illustrated by a bow and arrow. This is another proof that the 12 tribes all returned from the captivity and God was using them to overthrow all opposition from the heathen.

Verse 14. *Be seen over them* denotes that the Lord will be in evidence in sight of the heathen who have been against His people.

Verse 15. *Subdue with sling stones* does not necessarily mean literally, but when God fights for his people it is as victorious as if it had been done with carnal weapons.

Verse 16. *Stones of a crown* refers to the ornaments on the head piece that denotes victory. God's people were given assurance that they would surmount all difficulties that the enemies raised in their path.

Verse 17. *Corn* and *wine* were products of a fertile field that has been left undisturbed while the owners were cultivating it. During the captivity the land could not be cultivated by the people of Isarel and hence it lay idle through that period.

ZECHARIAH 10

Verse 1. The Lord is continuing his promise of temporal blessings. The land was given a rest for 70 years to compensate for the ones of which it was defrauded for years.

Verse 2. The false prophets had given the people assurances of peace which they said their idols would provide for them. Notwithstanding, all such promises had failed and the people had to go away into captivity. Now the chastisement is over and the true God is assuring them of prosperity.

Verse 3. God's people have always been likened to sheep and the leaders to shepherds. But both shepherd and the flock had gone astray, so the Lord regarded the shepherds as worthy of condemnation and the sheep likened to goats. But the program has been changed and the people are now likened to the noble horse in battle against His enemies.

Verse 4. *Corner* is defined in the lexicon as a chieftain and *nail* is a figurative term for a support or fastener. *Oppressor* is from a word that means a ruler. The verse means that God produced men of stability to uphold His nation who knew how to govern.

Verse 5. The terms are those still belonging to warfare and signify that God will assist his people in their contests with the enemy.

Verse 6. The captivity proper had been ended when Zechariah was writing, but much of the reconstruction work was still to come or was just under way. The verse is a promise of the continued support of God.

Verse 7. *Ephraim* means the 10-tribe kingdom when not mentioned as a single tribe. (Isaiah 7: 2, 9, 17; Ezekiel 37: 15-22.) That group is here promised God's favor now.

Verse 8. *Hiss* means to whistle or call loudly and the clause means that God will call for the 10 tribes to be gathered at Jerusalem. *I have redeemed them* applies to the 10 tribes having been redeemed from the captivity. This all upsets the doctrine so popular in some groups about the "lost ten tribes."

Verse 9. Jews of the 10 tribes as well as those of the 2 tribes were scattered out through various countries, although the bulk of the nation had been in Babylon. All of these were assured of a return to the home land after the restoration.

Verse 10. This verse names some of the countries in which these displaced Jews had been living. *Gilead* and *Lebanon* were districts in Palestine or near it and forming parts of the home country. *Place shall not be found* means that the restoration of these scattered Jews will be so successful that they will fill all the space in these territories.

Verse 11. This verse promises that Ephraim will overcome all his afflictions among the countries where he had been scattered. The heathen people who have oppressed them were doomed to feel the wrath of God because of their cruelties.

Verse 12. The strength of Ephraim was to come from the Lord.

ZECHARIAH 11

Verse 1. This chapter as a whole is a prediction of the overthrow of Judaism as the religion of God's people. The self-righteous Jews had become proud and scornful by the time Christ came into the world and they were destined to be brought down by the institution of the new covenant under Him. The cedar is a lofty tree and is used in figurative language to represent that which is proud and self-exalted. Lebanon was the territory where this tree grew in greatest abundance, hence its mention in the present connection. *Open thy doors,* etc. is a prediction that the haughty Jews (here figurized as the cedars of Lebanon) were to be subdued and humiliated by the king of the new regime.

Verse 2. The *fir* and *oak* trees were more common than the cedar, but they are represented as howling over the falling of the lofty tree. If such an important plant as the cedar was doomed to humiliation, there was no prospect of the survival of these ordinary ones, hence they were induced to howl in dismay.

Verse 3. This verse predicts that the leaders among the Jews were to be humiliated and they were to complain of their lot. All of this was fulfilled when Jesus came into the world and introduced the Gospel.

Verse 4. This verse is a prediction that the Lord would feed the flock that had been *slaughtered* (mistreated) by the cruel and self-righteous princes among the Jews.

Verse 5. The *possessors* and *shepherds* of this verse means the wicked rulers and princes among the Jewish people who imposed on the common population.

Verse 6. This verse predicts that God would plunge the entire Jewish nation into confusion and revolution. The common people were to suffer along with the leaders because they did not resist the corrupt prophets and priests. (See Jeremiah 5: 31.)

Verse 7. God decided to take over the feeding of the flock that had been so neglected by the shepherds. And in order to make the proper progress it was necessary to make a change in the whole system of the feeding by disposing of the unfaithful feeders, or at least by taking charge of their work and directing it according to the new program (the system under Christ). The things the Lord was going to dispose of are termed *Beauty* and *Bands*. The first means "agreeableness" and the second is defined "a district or inheritance." The first stands for the Sinaite covenant as a document or constitution as a basis for some form of government. The second stands for the religious nationalism that resulted from the aforesaid constitution.

Verses 8, 9. This paragraph should be regarded as a parenthetic statement inserted to indicate God's abhorrence of his unfaithful feeders. Some of them were so objectionable that He disposed of three of them in one month. The prophet will then resume the general prophecy to show what the new Shepherd was going to do about it.

Verse 10. The first thing he did was to break the staff called Beauty which means that the Sinaite covenant was to be canceled.

Verse 11. After the old law was canceled, the common Jews finally learned that they would no longer be dependent on the self-righteous leaders for spiritual guidance.

Verses 12, 13. In order for the old law (here called Beauty) to be broken, it was necessary for Christ to nail it to the cross. And in order for that to happen it was necessary for Him to be betrayed and sold for silver. Hence the prophet interrupts his story long enough to go back a few hours before the crucifixion to show how it was done, even as it had been predicted according to Matthew 27: 9, 10. Hence this paragraph should be regarded as another parenthetic passage on that particular item of the whole transaction, to connect up all the vital parts of God's great plan.

Verse 14. Having nailed the old law to the cross. Christ put an end to the Jewish covenant as a religious rule for the Jews. In other words, the religious *brotherhood* for the whole 12 tribes (Judah and Israel) was broken up by the crucifixion which cleared the way for a new religion. (See Romans 10: 4.)

Verse 15. Having annulled the Jewish religious law, the Lord was ready to give the world a new one. This was to be the Gospel of Christ, and it was to be taken to the people of the world by preachers. In 1 Corinthians 1: 21 this Gospel is termed "the foolishness of preaching," and that is the meaning of our present verse that predicts it with the words *instruments of a foolish shepherd*.

Verse 16. The terms of this verse are those that would describe the treatment of an unfaithful shepherd by his displeased master. The meaning is a prediction that Christ would not seek to restore Judaism, but would condemn the corrupt Jewish leaders. Matthew 23 gives an extended treatment of this attitude of Christ toward them.

Verse 17. This verse is a summing up of the entire chapter. The unfaithful Jewish leaders are condemned to complete rejection.

ZECHARIAH 12

Verse 1. God never forgot the treatment the Babylonians and other heathen people accorded His nation in the past, and now he has a burden or weighty prediction to make concerning it. His ability and right to do so is assured by the truth that He is the same One who created the heavens and the earth. He not only could create inanimate things like that, but was able to bring into being the living creatures like man. His eternal power was not limited to the creation of a being with life to be called *man*, but within that creature already endowed with a living soul (Genesis 2: 7), He was able to form a spirit thus elevating him above the rank of a living creature and causing him to be a human living creature possessing three parts according to 1 Thessalonians 5: 23. Surely, then, such a Creator can do what His will dictates on behalf of His own nation that had been formed for His glory among the people of the earth.

Verse 2. *Trembling* is from RAAL and Strong's definition is, "A reeling from intoxication." *When they shall be in the siege* is said reflectively. The verse means that the Lord remembered how they treated Judah and Jerusalem and was determined to avenge them. It was going to be done by enabling His people to force the heathen to drink from a cup that would send them forth staggering like a drunken man.

Verse 3. This is a general repetition of the preceding verse.

Verse 4. The reference to the horse pertains to the siege because the cavalry was used to support the movement. God was going to smite them of the heathen because of what they had done to Jerusalem.

Verse 5. The demonstration of God's power will produce encouragement in the heart of the inhabitants of Jerusalem.

Verse 6. *That day* all through these verses refers to the time when the promised favors should be accomplished for Judah and Jerusalem. All of the things predicted throughout this chapter and onward have a twofold bearing. The first applies to ancient Jerusalem and her triumph over her heathen foes. Then, following a practice so often observed in the prophetic writings, the verses look far beyond and after the ancient experiences of fleshly Israel to the time of Christ and the New Testament age.

Verse 7. An evil condition so common was for the people to be imposed on by the leaders in Jerusalem. The Lord's influence will be to *save the tents of Judah* (the common people), so that the glory and advantage of the inhabitants of Jerusalem shall not impose on them. In the government of Christ there will not be any partiality as to true greatness. This was taught by Him while on earth in Matthew 20: 25-28.

Verse 8. This is virtually the same as the preceding verse in meaning.

Verse 9. This was true temporally, and it was true figuratively, for the government to be founded at Jerusalem was destined to conquer the sinners by bringing them under the power of Christ through the teaching of the Gospel.

Verse 10. This spirit of *supplication* was to be caused by the awful treatment accorded the Son of God in the city of Jerusalem. We are sure this is the meaning of this passage, for it is quoted and so applied in John 19: 37. The remainder of the verse applies to others who were to be grieved over the cruel treatment given to Jesus. For the proof of this see John 16: 20.

Verses 11-14. This whole passage is a description of the great state of sorrow that was to be caused by the condemnation and crucifixion of Christ.

ZECHARIAH 13

Verse 1. *That day* means the day designated in chapter 12: 10 when "they shall look upon me whom they have pierced." This is one of the most precious prophecies in the Bible because it predicts the "Fountain, filled with blood, drawn from Emanuel's veins." It refers to the flow of blood that came from the pierced side of Christ, and poured down upon the ground to satisfy the wrath of God against sin, and made it possible for Him to save mankind from sin and its consequences.

Verse 2. Idolatry will have been banished from ancient Israel by the captivity. Then, passing on to the first part of the age under Christ, the prophet makes another weighty prediction. When the new and final religious system has been fully established, all special and miraculous means will no longer be necessary and hence they will all cease to be used. That is why the prediction is that *the* (inspired) *prophet and the unclean spirits shall pass out of the land.* Casting devils out of men required miraculous power, but when the need for miracles ceased to exist there was no longer any occasion for the people to be afflicted with devils.

Verse 3. After the age of miracles has passed it will be false for anyone to claim to have the power of supernatural prophesying. If some person does so he will be regarded as an impostor and will be opposed even by his parents who have learned better.

Verse 4. *Not wear a rough garment to deceive.* Prophets of the miraculous times wore a special garb, and this means that those who would impose upon others will be forced to shed these garments.

Verse 5. This verse is virtually the same as the preceding one.

Verse 6. The subject becomes more specific and pertains to Christ personally. The *wounds* are those made in His hands and feet. *In the house of my friends* refers to Judas who was one of the apostles and who caused Jesus to be betrayed.

Verse 7. *Smite the shepherd*, etc. refers to Jesus who was to be attacked and leave his disciples in a discouraged and scattered condition. He cited this saying and so applied it to himself in Matthew 26: 31.

Verses 8, 9. The numerical terms are used figuratively, and the meaning is that more people will reject Christ than will accept him and conform to the Gospel.

ZECHARIAH 14

Verse 1. The general subject of this whole chapter should be considered before trying to conclude on the meaning of any particular verse. The subject is the triumph of the Gospel over all the enemies of the Lord. The mention of unusual events of a material nature is only for the purpose of illustration and emphasis, and I shall comment on them from that standpoint. *Spoil be divided in the midst of thee*. The good things available will not be given into the hands of the enemy but will be retained by the Lord's people.

Verse 2. The events described here are the kind that would be done in a literal siege around Jerusalem. It will be accomplished figuratively in that much opposition will be attempted against the new system of the Lord to be set up in Jerusalem.

Verse 3. This fight will be with the "sword of the Spirit" (Ephesians 6: 17).

Verse 4. The mount of Olives was a small but very important spot in Biblical times, especially in the days of Christ. It was from that place that He ascended to heaven in sight of some of the disciples. He will come back at the last day in person but in spiritual form. He will not come literally in the meantime, but will come spiritually when he sends the Holy Spirit to set up the church. In that sense he will *stand upon the mount of Olives*. Of course the reader should bear in mind that the future tense of this language is used because at the time of this writing the church was in the future. A valley can be formed by the two halves of a mountain and such a valley would provide a place of security for a mansion.

Verse 5. This verse is figurative and refers to the same commotions indicated in the first part of the chapter. The reason for referring to the earthquake in the days of Uzziah is only as an illustration. The history of this earthquake is quoted in connection with the comments on Amos 1: 1. The upheaval that was caused by the introduction of the Gospel was likened to the material one described in this note.

Verses 6, 7. On the basis of reasoning from the simple to the complex, or from the known to the unknown, I will conclude this paragraph is an indefinite prediction of the general diffusion of Gospel light that was to be shed from Jerusalem at the beginning of the kingdom of Christ. We may be certain that is the chief subject of the chapter as a whole, and hence these peculiar expressions should be interpreted in that light. *Not clear nor dark* means there will not be extremes either way. *One day known to the Lord.* It will not be done exactly as man might have suggested, but it will be according to the Lord's wisdom. *Not day nor night* has about the same meaning as the phrase "not clear nor dark" above. *Evening it shall be light.* So consistent will the spiritual day be that when it would normally be expected to dim toward the night it will still continue to be light.

Verse 8. *Former sea . . . hinder sea* is a figure meaning from east to west. These *living waters* of God's truth will not be confined to one spot but will flow out to all parts of the earth. *Summer and winter* is another figure of speech which means the living waters of truth will flow continuously.

Verse 9. This verse justifies the comments on the foregoing ones. It is a prediction of the universal dominion of the Gospel of Christ as differing from that of the Mosaic law that was for the Jews only. *One Lord and his name one* corresponds with "one fold and one shepherd" in John 10: 16.

Verse 10. The places and objects named are used figuratively. The meaning is the same as the general subject of the chapter, namely, general spreading of the truth.

Verse 11. This verse was fulfilled materially and spiritually. Jerusalem became settled after the captivity and was a safe place for the people of Israel to inhabit. It also was the headquarters of the kingdom of Christ that was to be a safe place for the spiritual citizens of the household of faith.

Verse 12. These afflictions are figurative terms for the humiliation and defeat of the enemies of the Gospel of

Christ. It is similar in thought to the statements in the beginning of the chapter relative to the victory of truth over error.

Verse 13. General confusion was to overwhelm those who tried to resist the new institution set up in Jerusalem. So great was that confusion to be that the enemies would be turned against each other as if they were strangers.

Verse 14. *Judah shall fight at Jerusalem.* The margin renders it "against Jerusalem" which denotes that the people of God will oppose the wealth of the heathen that will accumulate around the city.

Verse 15. These beasts of service that are used by the heathen will not enable them to prevent the great work of the Lord, but will be defeated according to verses 1-3.

Verse 16. Many who had opposed the Lord will be converted and will *go up to worship.* They will look to Jerusalem for the divine model of true worship. This great truth is predicted in Isaiah 2: 1-4 and Micah 4: 1-5.

Verse 17. *Shall be no rain* is a figurative prediction that all who refuse the Gospel will be denied the spiritual favors of the Lord.

Verse 18. This is the same in meaning as the preceding verse. The heathen (or Gentiles) will all be given a chance to enjoy the blessings issued from Jerusalem, but if they refuse it they will be rejected by the Lord.

Verse 19. *Keep the feast* is a figure drawn from the literal practices of the Jews in Jerusalem under the Mosaic system. It here refers to the spiritual system or institution set up in Jerusalem to supplant the former one.

Verse 20. Horses were used in temporal warfare by the people of Israel. They are used figuratively for the spiritual war under Christ against sin in all its forms. The objective in all the great warfare will be plainly announced to all the opposing forces. It will be done by a banner-like engraving upon the equipment of the horses, and it will read *HOLINESS UNTO THE LORD.*

Verse 21. These vessels refer to those used in the Jewish service, but denote the spiritual ones under Christ. *No more the Canaanite* means that no one of the heathen shall be admitted until he has submitted to the rule of heaven under Christ.

MALACHI 1

Verse 1. *Burden* means an important message or saying, and the Lord had something of that character to say to the people of Israel. Malachi was the last of the Old Testament prophets and wrote about four centuries before Christ. This would place him not long after the work of reconstruction following the return from the captivity. The people of Israel never worshiped idols after the return, but they often were careless about their duty to God and became selfish in their desires.

Verse 2. When the Lord censured them for their worldliness they complained that He did not love them. The Lord's reasoning that he still loved his people is couched in the question *was not Esau Jacob's brother?* The fact that while these men were brothers, the Lord chose Jacob or Israel instead of Esau was proof that He loved him.

Verse 3. *Hated Esau* means the Lord denied him any special favors, also He chastised him severely for wrong doings.

Verse 4. Esau was the founder of the Edomites who thought they could resist the work of God that was meant for their punishment. Yet they failed for the Lord was determined to *throw down* their work. All of this was evidence that Israel had fared better than his brother and hence was beloved by the Lord.

Verse 5. The objective of the Lord in thus punishing Esau or Edom was that He might be magnified. Israel was supposed to see all this and acknowledge God's greatness.

Verse 6. The usual treatment of a son for his father or a servant for his master is cited as an example of proper respect. God's people were not that respectful to Him, but at the same time they were denying their guilt of neglect.

Verse 7. The services of the Jews were beneath their abilities and short of the requirements of the law. Their neglect of duty was rendered more objectionable by their attitude. They would ask what was wrong in a way that implied that they could see nothing for the Lord to complain about.

Verse 8. The animals to be used in the services were required to be those in the best condition. These Jews were bringing the blind and otherwise defective ones and seemed to think the

Lord would accept them notwithstanding their poor qualities. He challenged them to try it out with their earthly ruler and see if he would accept it.

Verse 9. The prophet implies that it will be in vain for them to seek mercy of God while they are conducting such inferior services. *Been by your means* denotes that the corrupt situation was brought about by their own greed.

Verse 10. These Jews had become so selfish that they wanted to be paid for all of their services. They would not even close a door unless they were promised a reward for it. With such motives behind their activities the Lord was displeased with them.

Verse 11. God had intended from the start that the services of the law were to be temporary (Galatians 3: 19), but when these people became so insincere in their sacrifices it caused Him to be all the more displeased with them. This will shed some light on the language of Hebrews 10: 5-8 as to the *displeasure* of God with the animal sacrifices. *Among the Gentiles* is a prediction that another law and service will be instituted that will be offered to all people, not to Jews only.

Verse 12. To profane a thing means to cause it to become merely a temporal something instead of a sacred one. These Jews were pronouncing the services of the Lord to be only common activities and thus they profaned them.

Verse 13. This verse means the same as most of the preceding ones.

Verse 14. The Jews were required to offer the best of their animals for sacrifice on the altar. *A male* means just such a beast with all the special requirements as to qualities directed under the law. God never asks more of a man than he is able to give, but He will not accept any service that is less than one is capable of performing.

MALACHI 2

Verse 1. The priests were the men who supervised the services at the altar and who were responsible for their proper performances. That is why this passage is addressed to them as stated in the beginning of the verse.

Verse 2. *Not lay it to heart* signifies that the priests were tolerating this inferior service of the people. They had been guilty of such corruption even before the years of the captivity (Jeremiah 5: 31). The present generations of priests were drifting into the same unfaithfulness and the Lord was pronouncing a curse upon them.

Verse 3. *Dung of your solemn feasts.* In preparing an animal for the altar it was required that the internal parts be washed and that would include the removal of the dung. This verse threatened to take that matter and spread it on their faces.

Verse 4. Such shameful treatment as described would emphasize guilt. It would also impress them with God's respect for the service that had started with Levi which means the tribe from which the priesthood came.

Verse 5. Levi as a tribe showed his fear or reverence for God when he responded to the call to take a stand on the Lord's side (Exodus 32: 26).

Verse 6. This description of Levi (or that tribe) applies to the time when he came over to the Lord's side and showed his sincerity by fighting against the rebels.

Verse 7. The Lord then honored that tribe with being the custodian of the law. (See Leviticus 10: 11; Deuteronomy 17: 9.) With such a charge the priests were expected to be informed about the law and see that it was followed. Instead of doing so they had become indifferent and were encouraging the people in their formalities.

Verse 8. The indifference of these priests was causing the common members of the congregation to stumble or become corrupt in their practices.

Verse 9. The priesthood was an important and dignified office and should have been respected by the people. But the corruptions that were allowed to creep into the service had lowered the priests in the eyes of all people.

Verse 10. The common brotherhood of the Jews under one Father should have induced the leaders to treat the others respectfully. They did not do so but used their office to take advantage of the poor and common people.

Verse 11. The tribe of Judah had nothing to do officially with the altar services, but those men became guilty with the priests by offering these inferior articles to be used as sacrifices. They also showed their greed for gain in all of their conduct as was seen in verse 10 of the preceding chapter. *Married the daughter of a strange god.* The last word is defined in the lexicon as meaning "any deity." The Jews never worshiped idols as that word is used after the captivity, but there are other kinds of gods whom one might worship. Paul says that covetousness is idolatry (Colossians 3:5), and the Jews were certainly covetous. And Jesus compared mammon (a word meaning riches) to a god (Matthew 6:24). Hence the *god* these Jews had married was doubtless the god of mammon or riches as we have seen by their attachment to their wealth.

Verse 12. *Master* means the man who originates these unlawful practices and *scholar* means the one who cooperates by using them and both classes were to be condemned.

Verse 13. This verse describes the hypocritical performances of the covetous priests about the altar. All their tears and weeping were for the purpose of making a show. Because of their insincere devotions the Lord refused to accept their offerings.

Verse 14. They said *wherefore*, meaning to ask why God was rejecting their service. The answer was in the form of an accusation of their unfaithfulness to their marriage relation. The priests had behaved treacherously against the women whom they had taken into covenant relation to be their life companions.

Verse 15. *Did not he make one?* This refers to the original plan of the Lord that one man and one woman should constitute the number composing the marriage unit. These corrupt priests had disregarded that law and were paying attention to other women besides their lawful wives to whom they had promised their exclusive love.

Verse 16. *Garment* is used figuratively and means something for a covering over another person or object. These priests were guilty of *violence* (unfaithfulness) against their wives, but were hiding behind the leniency of Moses on the subject of tolerating plurality in marriage. (See Mathew 19:8.)

Verse 17. God never tires in the sense of becoming weak bodily as man does, but His patience can be exhausted. These priests were charged with having *wearied* the Lord with their words of falsehood. Those words were in the form of confusing good with evil and then implying that God was not just in condemning them.

MALACHI 3

Verse 1. The book of Malachi is the last of the inspired writings until we come to the New Testament, and there is a space of about 4 centuries to intervene. The prophets have frequently gone from fleshly to spiritual Israel in their predictions and exhortations, either drawing parallels or showing contrasts as the nature of the occasion suggested. This book so far has consisted mostly of condemnation and admonition for fleshly Israel because of the worldliness and selfishness of their officials especially. It was appropriate, therefore, to jump across the chasm of four hundred years to the time when the Lord expected to give the world a new religious system that would be far superior and more exacting than the old one. This and the following chapter is taken up with alternating between fleshly and spiritual Israel, speaking first of one and then the other, going back and forth from one of them to the other. Our present verse goes to the time of spiritual Israel and predicts that the importance of that system is so great that a preparatory work will need to be done before the Author of that system begins His work. Hence God said he would send his *messenger* ahead, and according to Matthew 11:10, 11; Mark 1:2-4 he was John the Baptist. *Come to his temple* means his kingdom or church, for that institution is so called in 2 Corinthians 6:16. *Messenger of the covenant*. The most important covenant that God made with Abraham is recorded in Genesis 12:3 and 22:18, which is a promise of Christ. That would identify Christ as "the messenger of the covenant."

Verse 2. *Abide the day of his coming* means to face it or feel equal to the awfulness of that day. It is because it will be very thorough in its treatment of sinners in the process of cleansing or purifying them.

Verse 3. A refiner's fire is used to separate the dross from precious metal, and the fact has been used throughout the Bible to illustrate the work of purifying men from their sins. *Sons of Levi* is said figuratively because they were the ones who were the priests under the Mosaic system. They had become corrupt in their office and the prediction means that the priests of this new covenant will be purified by the refining influence of the Gospel.

Verse 4. *Judah* and *Jerusalem* are used spiritually to refer to the services under Christ, in about the same sense that Levi is mentioned in the preceding verse to signify the spiritual priesthood in the system under Christ.

Verse 5. The evils named in this verse had been committed by the Jews in Malachi's time, and the words of condemnation were meant as a severe rebuke of them. And they were also a prediction of the exacting regulations regarding such practices to be instituted in the time of Christ.

Verse 6. God has never dealt with man as his conduct deserved or he would have been long since consumed. It has always been thus with God for he *changes not;* that is why the sons of Jacob had not been consumed.

Verse 7. As proof that God has always been the same lenient One he is at the present time, they are reminded of the wayward conduct of the fathers in spite of the pleadings which He made with them, in which they were urged to *Return unto me, and I will return unto you.*

Verse 8. *Will a man rob God?* was doubtless answered with an emphatic "no" by these people. But they recognized the question actually to be an accusation that they had robbed Him, and then they asked in what way they had done so. The Lord's reply was that it was done in tithes and offerings. When the Jews held back a part of their tithes, or brought some inferior products to the service, they were thereby robbing God.

Verse 9. The whole nation could justly be charged with the evils complained of because all the people upheld the corrupt priests and prophets (Jeremiah 5: 31).

Verse 10. There never was or will be a time when it pays to defraud the Lord out of His deserts. On the other hand, it is always profitable in the end to be liberal and cheerful in the service to God. Hence these people are challenged to cast their trust on the Lord and cease holding back what they were obligated to give into the service of Him because it will be to their advantage to do so in reality.

Verse 11. The Lord even promised to protect their increasing products from the ravages of those who would devour them. The plants for fruit and other articles of food were guaranteed to bring their yield to maturity.

Verse 12. Besides the general favors indicated in this verse that fleshly Israel could have acquired, the greater one pertained to them as spiritual Israel. The words *all nations* were fulfilled when the Gospel was offered to Jew and Gentile alike.

Verse 13. The Lord again takes up his complaint against fleshly Israel. One of their chief faults was to deny that what they were doing was wrong. In so speaking they virtually charged God with making a false accusation against them.

Verse 14. The Lord specifies some of the things they were saying unjustly. Perhaps the most serious was to deny that it was worth while to obey the law.

Verse 15. Here is another serious charge that reflects against the justice of God. They said that the proud and wicked persons were the ones who were accorded the most happiness by the Lord, which was the very opposite of the truth. It is no wonder that the Lord said he was "wearied" with them.

Verse 16. Going back to the subject in verse 12 and others, the prophet looks forward to some of the glorious features of the Gospel age. *Then* is an adverb of time, referring to things that were to be done in the Gospel system under Christ. The past tense is a grammatical form often used in prophetic writings, but it was several centuries in the future when Malachi wrote it. *Spake often* are from one word which is DABAR and Strong defines it, "A primitive root; perhaps properly to arrange; but used figuratively (of words) to speak." Young defines it, "To speak (consult) together." Among the many words by which it has been rendered in the King James Version are answer, communication, counsel, language, message, promise, question, reason, report, request, saying, speech, talk, and word; the last one is used 770 times. With all this critical information at hand it would indicate that the wording in our common version is justified. It undoubtedly means that the citizens in the kingdom of Christ were to be in close touch with each other, which would require that they assemble whenever they can. This all agrees with the admonition of Paul in Hebrews that the disciples of Christ should not forsake the assembling together of themselves (Hebrews 10: 25). *Book of remembrance* does not mean that God needs any mechanical plan to keep Him from forgetting anything. The expression is used figuratively and means that the names of God's children are carefully inscribed in the heavenly record, and the fact is spoken of as being recorded in a book. (See Luke 10: 20; Hebrews 12: 23; Revelation 3: 5; 21: 27.)

Verse 17. *They shall be mine.* If I were to buy and pay for something it certainly would be mine. Jesus purchased the church with his own blood and it is said to be His. (See Acts 20: 28; 1 Peter 1: 19; 2: 9.) *Jewels* is from CEGULLAH which Strong defines, "wealth." It is the word for "peculiar treasure" in Psalms 135: 4. The Lord regards the members of his church as jewels since they are so valuable, He having paid such a great price (his blood) for them. *That day* means the Gospel dispensation in which time He was to *make up* or gather these jewels into the fold or church. *I will spare them,* etc., is equivalent in thought to that in Hebrews 8: 11.

Verse 18. The gist of this verse is that the members of the new kingdom will have superior knowledge of what is right and wrong. That is because they will have the "perfect law of liberty" for their guidance. But this is not all, for the leaders of the Jewish kingdom, especially in the days of Malachi's writing, had mixed together the good and the evil and had refused to make any difference between them. (See chapter 2: 17.) The Gospel was to be clear and exacting and those who believe it will be trained to "have no fellowship with the unfruitful works of darkness, but rather reprove them" (Ephesians 5: 11).

MALACHI 4

Verse 1. The preposition *for* is used to connect the present passage with the one immediately preceding it in chapter 3: 18. The strictness of the Gospel in its requirements as to the citizens of the new kingdom is the subject. (See Acts 17: 30 and 1 Peter 4: 17, 18.) We also recall the many instances where Christ showed the contrast between the old and the new. He would refer to certain liberties that had been tolerated in "old time" and then say "but I say unto you," etc. This strictness of the new law is figuratively referred to as an oven for burning refuse. *Leave them neither root nor branch* refers to the complete condemnation and rejection of the ways of sin that was to be manifested by Christians.

Verse 2. The healthful effects of the Gospel of Christ is likened to the warm and healing rays of the sun. *Go forth* is from PUWSH which Strong defines, "To spread; figuratively act proudly." Moffatt renders it to "leap." The verse as a whole means that the citizens in the kingdom of Christ were to be blessed with great spiritual strength and activity.

Verse 3. We know that Christians are not permitted to use any kind of literal violence against sinners, hence this treading of them is explained by the comments on verse 1. And we know this "burning" and "treading" did not refer to the time after the judgment day, for it was to occur *in the day that I shall do this,* referring to the time of the Gospel age.

Verse 4. A last exhortation is given to the Jews of the time of Malachi, that they should remember the law of Moses. There was never to be another law of government given to them until that one so forceably predicted in this book of the prophet.

Verse 5. But while no other written law was to be given before that new age is ushered into the world, there was to be a man sent just before that time to speak orally to the Jews by way of preparation for the new law. That man was to have the power and spiritual strength of Elijah. *Dreadful* day means that the kingdom of Christ would be severe against sinners (see comments on verses 1 and 3), but would be respected by the righteous.

Verse 6. The phrases of this verse refer to the reformative work that was to be accomplished by this Elijah (or John the Baptist). Without the effects of this forerunner and the new kingdom to follow, the whole world would have suffered the wrath of an outraged God.

www.ingramcontent.com/pod-product-compliance
Lightning Source LLC
Chambersburg PA
CBHW050512170426
43201CB00013B/1933